Tobacco and Slaves

Tobacco and Slaves
The Development of Southern Cultures in the Chesapeake, 1680–1800

ALLAN KULIKOFF

Published for the Institute of Early American History and Culture
Williamsburg, Virginia
By the University of North Carolina Press
Chapel Hill and London

The Institute of Early American History and Culture
is sponsored jointly by The College of William and Mary
and The Colonial Williamsburg Foundation.

98 97 96 95 94   9 8 7 6 5

Library of Congress Cataloging in Publication Data

Kulikoff, Allan.
  Tobacco and slaves.

  Includes index.
  1. Chesapeake Bay Region (Md. and Va.)—Economic
conditions. 2. Chesapeake Bay Region (Md. and Va.)—
Social conditions. 3. Agriculture—Economic aspects—
Chesapeake Bay Region (Md. and Va.)—History.
4. Tobacco industry—Chesapeake Bay Region (Md. and
Va.)—History. 5. Plantation life—Chesapeake Bay
Region (Md. and Va.)—History. 6. Slavery—Chesapeake
Bay Region (Md. and Va.)—History. I. Institute of
Early American History and Culture (Williamsburg, Va.)
II. Title.
HC107.A12K85   1985   306'.09755'18   85-8452
ISBN 0-8078-1671-X
ISBN 0-8078-4224-9 (pbk.)

Design by Laura Dunne.

An earlier version of chapter 8 appeared as "The Origins of Afro-American Society in Tide-water Maryland and Virginia, 1700 to 1790," *William and Mary Quarterly*, 3d Ser., XXXV (1978), 226–259.

An earlier version of chapter 9 appeared as "The Beginnings of the Afro-American Family in Maryland," in Aubrey C. Land *et al.*, eds., *Law, Society, and Politics in Early Maryland* (Baltimore, 1977), 171–196, and is reprinted here by permission of The Maryland State Archives.

Artwork by Hannah Gibbs.

Title page: "An overseer doing his duty. Sketched from life near Fredericsburg," 13 March 1798. By Benjamin Henry Latrobe, from Sketchbook III, 33. Reprinted by permission of The Papers of Benjamin Henry Latrobe, Maryland Historical Society.

The publication of this work was made possible in part through grants from the National Endowment for the Humanities, a federal agency whose mission is to award grants to support education, scholarship, media programming, libraries, and museums, in order to bring the results of cultural activities to a broad, general public.

The cost of editorial work on this volume was assisted by a grant from the Commonwealth of Virginia Fund for Excellence.

To my mother and to the memory of my father

Acknowledgments

I began research on this project in the spring of 1972. Dissatisfied with the then current emphasis on New England and the neglect of every other part of early America, I visited Darrett and Anita Rutman, already embarked on their major study of Middlesex County, Virginia, for advice on studying the southern colonies. They encouraged my interest, explained the data they were examining, and urged me to visit southern archives.

The first archive was the Maryland Hall of Records (now the Maryland State Archives), at Annapolis, and I stayed there more than three years completing research on a dissertation on Prince George's County. I owe that institution a debt difficult to repay. The Hall of Records is one of the best archives in the country: its staff is very helpful, its manuscripts are well preserved and magnificently indexed, and its leadership encourages innovative research. Edward C. Papenfuse, the state archivist, has continued the tradition of scholarship and fine records management begun by his illustrious predecessor, the late Morris Leon Radoff. Papenfuse and his assistant, Gregory Stiverson, have welcomed historians to the Hall of Records, provided a home for the St. Mary's City Commission, and conducted major research projects themselves. Phebe R. Jacobsen and the late Frank White also were always helpful, shared data, and found many documents I would have overlooked.

At the St. Mary's City Commission, Lois Green Carr built the historical office into a superb research center almost single-handedly. She and her staff eagerly shared data, suggested what materials to consult and how to use them, and organized a program for data collection that benefited all who worked at the Hall of Records. Ever gracious to colleagues, she encouraged me to focus on Prince George's County, despite her own fine work thereon.

The library at the Research Department of the Colonial Williamsburg Foundation houses an outstanding microfilm collection of dissertations on Chesapeake history, manuscripts from other archives, and all the British records filmed by the Virginia Colonial Records project. I received prompt service and helpful advice from every staff member, but especially from Cary Carson, the director, and from Harold Gill, who placed his immense knowledge of Virginia at my disposal. Also very helpful were the staffs of the Maryland Historical Society, the Virginia State Library, the Virginia Historical Society, and the manuscript reading room of the Library of Congress and librarians at Brandeis University, the University of Maryland, the

College of William and Mary, the University of Virginia, the University of Illinois at Chicago, the Newberry Library, Harvard University, Bryn Mawr College, Haverford College, the University of Pennsylvania, and Princeton University.

The abundant financial aid I have received made completion of this work possible. Brandeis University provided initial support through its Irving and Rose Crown Fellowships, and the National Science Foundation provided a grant for dissertation research in the social sciences (GS-35781). The Institute of Early American History and Culture awarded me a two-year fellowship for 1975–1977, which permitted me to extend my research beyond the disseration to the entire Chesapeake region in a congenial atmosphere. I continued that work while with the Office of Social and Demographic History at the University of Illinois at Chicago, where a light teaching load and administrative support were especially helpful. I drafted most of the manuscript during the 1979–1980 academic year while a fellow at the Charles Warren Center of Harvard University. Both Bryn Mawr College and Princeton University provided administrative support that, with a summer stipend from the Department of History at Princeton, made completion of this work possible.

I particularly thank Patricia Denault of the Charles Warren Center for typing much of the first version of this work. Bryn Mawr College provided student assistants, and Isle Nehring and Megan Wallace completed work essential for several chapters. Teresa Holt and Thomas Beck, my research assistants at Princeton, checked footnotes. The University of Maryland, the College of William and Mary, the University of Illinois at Chicago, Harvard University, and Bryn Mawr College all contributed computer time and computer staff services. Frank Wann, Janice Reiff, Donald Parkerson, and Kenneth L. Sokoloff gave particularly useful programming advice, and Jay Anderson, the director of the Bryn Mawr Center, aided this work by teaching me computer graphics.

Other scholars sent me unpublished papers and allowed me to use data they had collected. The late Margaret Cook, a first-rate local historian, spent days with me poring over her voluminous files of materials on Prince George's County. The present and former staff of the St. Mary's City Commission—Lois Carr, Russell Menard, and Lorena S. Walsh—donated many statistical series from their data. In addition, Edward Ayres, Richard Beeman, Paul Clemens, Douglas Deal, Jeannie Dissette, Elizabeth Fox-Genovese, Lawrence Harper, John Hemphill, Sarah Hughes, Kevin Kelly, Ross Kimmell, John McCusker, Paula Martinac, Michael Nicholls, Philip Schwarz, David C. Skaggs, Kenneth L. Sokoloff, Gregory Stiverson, Donald Sweig, James Trussel, and Georgia Villaflor all broadened my study with data, unpublished papers, and other assistance.

Many colleagues and critics have gone over the arguments found here. My first intellectual debt is to David H. Fischer, who directed the original dissertation. His lengthy and forceful critique compelled me to define precisely the argument of the present work and to organize it coherently. He not only dissected several chapters but thoroughly read the penultimate draft. It was he that first suggested I attempt a grand thesis in the French style, and I hope he is pleased with the results as a book.

Three fellow students of the Chesapeake participated in a long seminar on the region's history. Lois Carr eagerly discussed every problem in my research and writing, always making cogent suggestions, and her critique of the first draft of the book saved me from many errors. Russell Menard, my colleague at Annapolis and Williamsburg, not only formulated some of the conceptions that lay at the interpretive core of the book but read over early chapter drafts. It was my great fortune to discuss my work at length with Thad W. Tate, the director of the Institute of Early American History and Culture, during my tenure there and after.

Five historians provided an essential outside view of the work. Stanley Engerman read every chapter of each draft of the manuscript and replied promptly with detail and insight. The late Herbert Gutman read early drafts of my slavery chapters and explained with great enthusiasm the cultural meaning of the data I had collected. Daniel Scott Smith read chapters on demography and family life and not only pointed out methodological errors but suggested new ways to interpret the material. Robert Fogel read several chapters, discussed them at length, and twice invited me to his Economic History Workshop at Harvard, where two chapters were scrutinized. Elizabeth Fox-Genovese wrote several perceptive and very helpful critiques of an early version of this work, stressing problems of argument and structure.

Seven other colleagues read the final draft of some or all chapters. Miriam L. King took time to edit superbly much of the book before I submitted it. Paul Clemens and Richard Beeman wrote valuable and contrasting reports that materially improved the text. John Murrin and Sean Wilentz, colleagues at Princeton, also read the manuscript. Murrin's detailed comments and Wilentz's theoretical understanding were both very useful. Rhys Isaac wrote a splendidly enthusiastic critique of my analysis of white community life, and Michael Zuckerman's jeremiad attacking my use of *patriarchy* forced me to rethink my position.

Various chapters were presented at colloquia, conferences, and conventions. Sessions at the Shelby Cullom Davis Center for Historical Studies, the Economic History Workshops at the University of Chicago and Harvard University, the Institute of Early American History and Culture, the Philadelphia Center for Early American Studies, and the University of Maryland were especially useful. At these seminars, and on other occasions,

I was aided by the comments of Linda Auwers, Ira Berlin, David Boh-mer, Fred Carstensen, Kathleen N. Conzen, Michael Conzen, John De-mos, Mary Maples Dunn, Richard Dunn, Carville Earle, Claudia Goldin, P. M. G. Harris, James Henretta, Sarah Hughes, Alice Bee Kasakoff, Au-brey C. Land, Michael McGiffert, Michael Mullin, Michael Nicholls, Mary Beth Norton, James Oakes, Elizabeth H. Pleck, Janice Reiff, Darrett Rut-man, David Souden, and Lorena Walsh, among others.

I enjoyed the great luxury of choosing as I saw fit from the collective, and often contradictory, advice of this army of critics. I accept full credit for the leaps of faith and strange interpretations that survive, and only my critics will know how I adapted and sometimes mangled their suggestions.

This book was edited at the Institute of Early American History and Culture, where a concern for vigorous prose and careful argument still prevails. Norman Fiering began working on the manuscript before he left the Institute and edited several chapters, finding logical inconsistencies wherever they dwelt and improving style and organization as he proceeded. Following him, David Ammerman expeditiously finished the job. Gil Kelly expertly edited the completed text.

My mother fully understands how all-consuming this book often be-came over the past years. Her understanding and that of my late father, who did not live to see its completion, are noted elsewhere.

Contents

Part III: Black Society

Illustrations

Maps

Figures

Tables

Tobacco and Slaves

Introduction
The Making of a Slave Society

In March 1798, Benjamin Henry Latrobe, the renowned engineer, architect, and artist, came upon "an overseer doing his duty . . . near Fredericsburg" in Virginia and "sketched [the scene] from life" (title page). Latrobe's drawing shows a white man standing on a stump and directing two slave women as they hoe the ground and burn tree stumps, preparing the soil for planting corn. The slaves, while decently clothed, wear no jackets in the chilly March weather; the cigar-smoking overseer, however, is elegantly dressed and holds a large walking stick (perhaps as a silent threat) as he watches the women work.[1]

This scene, a common one throughout the late eighteenth century in the Chesapeake region, vividly depicts relations between social classes, men and women, and masters and slaves at that time and suggests even more about the course of social change over the preceding 150 years. It is a young overseer (perhaps the son of a neighboring small planter), and not the plantation owner, who directs the slaves; the master himself is out of sight, pursuing the very different responsibilities and prerogatives of his class—planning the plantation work schedule, perhaps, or gathering with his fellow planters at a local tavern. Although the drawing does not show them all, slave men and women work in the fields together. White women remain aloof from this heavy labor, finishing their own household duties, directing the slave domestics, sewing, cooking, and keeping house. Had a similar scene been sketched in the 1670s, much would have been different: the master himself would have been in the fields, overseeing the hands; the field workers would have been white servants (including some white women) instead of black slaves; and these workers would have cultivated tobacco as well as grain. In all, Latrobe's 1798 drawing captures the outcome of a long-term economic, demographic, and political transformation that replaced the farmsteads of the first Chesapeake settlers with the kind of slave society described by numerous visitors to the early national South and interpreted in detail by modern historians of the antebellum South.

This study is an attempt to describe and explain this transformation—

1. The drawing is reproduced from the microfiche collection of the Latrobe papers; but see also Lee W. Fromwalt, "An English Immigrant Views American Society: Benjamin Henry Latrobe's Virginia Years, 1796–1798," *Virginia Magazine of History and Biography*, LXXXV (1977), 403–408.

and thus elucidate the origins of southern slave society. After a brief survey of the social structure of the region in the seventeenth century, this work analyzes economic and demographic change between 1680 and 1750 and describes how men and women—white and black—forged new social relations in the light of that experience. After the crystallization of new class relations in the mid-eighteenth century, substantial changes in the social structure occurred very slowly, as a new white ruling class turned all sorts of social and economic changes—including such disruptive events as the transition from tobacco monoculture to diversified farming and the massive out-migration of whites and their slaves at century's end—toward strengthening existing social relations, thereby enhancing its own power. In sum, this is an effort to relate the history of seemingly impersonal shifts in demography and economic life to the rise of new forms of power and understanding.[2]

The seventeenth-century Chesapeake was full of opportunities. Thousands of English men (but many fewer women) arrived in the region as indentured servants. Many of these immigrants fell ill and died before completing their term of service, and others lived only a few years as free men or women. Those who survived, however, would serve their term, work a few years for other planters, and then procure their own land and servants. Since the price of tobacco remained high, freedmen often became prosperous. These men on the rise refused to accept the permanent authority of any group of rulers, and those few established gentlemen who migrated to the Chesapeake region died off as rapidly as the servants.[3]

In the decades after 1680, an intertwined series of demographic, economic, and social changes transformed this social world and promoted increasingly hierarchical relations between men and women, masters and slaves, and gentlemen and yeomen. Rapidly falling tobacco prices discouraged white immigration and created conditions conducive to the beginnings of white natural population increase. Planters turned to African slaves to replace white servants, thereby elevating the status of poor whites. At the

2. The literature on the Chesapeake colonies is synthesized in Thad W. Tate, "The Seventeenth-Century Chesapeake and Its Modern Historians," in Tate and David L. Ammerman, eds., *The Chesapeake in the Seventeenth Century: Essays on Anglo-American Society* (Chapel Hill, N.C., 1979), 3–50; Allan Kulikoff, "The Colonial Chesapeake: Seedbed of Antebellum Culture?" *Journal of Southern History*, XLV (1979), 513–540; and Russell R. Menard, "Population, Economy, and Society in Seventeenth-Century Maryland," *Maryland Historical Magazine*, LXXIX (1984), 71–92.
3. The best summary of economic opportunity during the seventeenth century will be found in Lois G. Carr and Russell R. Menard, "Immigration and Opportunity: The Freedman in Early Colonial Maryland," in Tate and Ammerman, *Chesapeake in the Seventeenth Century*, 206–242.

same time, political dynasties appeared, composed of the descendants of officeholding families. Three structural changes—the decline of opportunity, the beginnings of natural increase, and the rise of chattel slavery—deserve special emphasis.

Although the price of tobacco declined continually from 1620 to 1680, productivity improved so much that tobacco cultivation remained profitable. Ex-servants bought both land and other servants with profits from tobacco sales. By 1680 tobacco prices had declined so much, however, that planters earned barely enough income to recover their costs of production, and tobacco prices sometimes dipped below that level. Prosperity returned when tobacco prices rose after 1740, but the tobacco boom of the seventeenth century did not reappear. As a result, opportunities for freed servants to buy land nearly disappeared, and immigrants soon avoided the Chesapeake. Sons of poor men rarely procured land or unfree labor; sons of men of substance usually replicated the status of their fathers.[4]

The timing of the transition from a naturally declining population (in which deaths outnumbered births) to a naturally increasing population (in which births exceeded deaths) varied by race and subregion, but the processes that led to high levels of natural population growth were the same throughout the region for both whites and blacks. Far more men than women immigrated. Immigrant women married in their middle or late twenties and gave birth to a few children, but their daughters married and began childbearing in their middle to late teens. These first-generation natives had large families, but there were so many male immigrants in the region that there were still more deaths than births in the population. Nonetheless, the size of the native-born population grew rapidly enough that the impact of immigration on the adult population diminished. At some point (the 1690s or 1700s for whites, the 1720s or 1730s for blacks) the number of native women grew large enough to ensure generational replacement. The declining opportunities for servants speeded the process for whites, and nearly as soon as planters realized that slaves could, demographically, reproduce themselves, the slave trade began to decline. Since roughly equal numbers of boys and girls were born, the surplus of men nearly disappeared. Women continued to marry early and bear many children. At the same time, adult life expectancy apparently rose. As a result, population grew rapidly by natural increase.[5]

4. The best analysis of the tobacco market is found in Russell R. Menard, "The Tobacco Industry in the Chesapeake Colonies, 1617–1730: An Interpretation," *Research in Economic History*, V (1980), 109–177.
5. Russell R. Menard, "Immigrants and Their Increase: The Process of Population Growth in Early Colonial Maryland," in Aubrey C. Land *et al.*, eds., *Law, Society, and Politics in Early*

The growth of the slave population revolutionized Chesapeake society. African immigrant slaves provided the material basis for the development of a gentry ruling class in the region: wealthy men invested heavily in slaves, and these men and women produced vast quantities of tobacco for their masters. At the same time, these new Negroes (as they were called) created problems for their masters and temporarily impeded progress toward the beginnings of a self-conscious gentry class. Planters had to use nearly all their spare capital to buy slaves because they could not rely upon Africans to reproduce themselves. Most of the slaves brought from Africa were male, and the women among them bore few children. In the masters' view, African-born slaves required unremitting discipline, understood little English, sometimes refused to obey orders, and often ran away. Masters found it difficult to weld their slaves into an efficient—or simply adequate—laboring class. Inescapably, the masters' difficulties with their slaves simultaneously resulted from and shaped their equal difficulty in welding themselves into a mature slaveholding class. They spent so much money for slaves and so much time running their plantations that they had little time to distinguish themselves from less wealthy planters by pursuing education or organizing clubs or societies with their peers. These two processes, making slaves efficient workers and devising a ruling class ideology, were inseparably intertwined and, together, constituted what is called *class formation*.

The achievement of natural increase among blacks and the resulting decline in the slave trade encouraged both class formation and racial unity among whites. Masters at once controlled the means of production (slaves) and had the ability to reproduce this capital stock without buying new slaves. Although Africans were far too strange ever to become members of households headed by whites, planters could (and did) perceive their native-born slaves as inferior members of their own "families" (a word the planters themselves used) with important roles within the natural order of the plantation. Masters could leave sons or overseers to direct their growing labor force, and invest the spare capital they now had to procure education and leisure. Finally, slaveholding spread remarkably rapidly through the white population; at least half of the householders in tidewater counties owned slaves by the 1750s, and many of the rest were children of slaveholders and could expect to inherit slaves. At the same time that the growth of large plantations accentuated differences between wealthy and poor planters, the spread of slavery, reinforced by the return of prosperity, muted

---

Maryland (Baltimore, 1977), 88–110; and Allan Kulikoff, "A 'Prolifick' People: Black Population Growth in the Chesapeake Colonies, 1700–1790," *Southern Studies*, XVI (1977), 391–428, summarize patterns of population growth for the white and black populations, respectively.

social conflict among whites, who, whatever their class differences, were consolidating their position as the master race.[6]

These structural changes had significant social and cultural consequences. This work analyzes six of the principal consequences, three each for whites and blacks. Among whites, patriarchal families replaced relatively egalitarian families; kin groups replaced neighborhoods as the primary focus of social interaction; and two new classes formed, a gentry ruling class and a class of yeoman planters. At the same time, black communities, often encompassing more than one plantation, developed. Slaves created extended families and kinship networks, and they (and their owners) mastered a new racial etiquette.

A functioning patriarchal family system developed slowly in the Chesapeake region because the paternal continuity necessary to sustain the father's authority was missing. Some English patriarchal family law made its way to the Chesapeake, but frequent paternal death and remarriage filled families with step-siblings and half-siblings, thereby confusing lines of authority within the household and emphasizing the power of orphans' courts over the family. A wife, always fearing the death of her husband, had to be ready to take over his responsibilities in addition to meeting her own. Married women primarily pursued domestic tasks, but sometimes also labored alongside their husbands in the tobacco fields, especially during the 1680s and 1690s, when tobacco prices were low and bound labor was in short supply.[7]

During the early eighteenth century, for the first time, white men and women in the Chesapeake colonies could devise a patriarchal form of family government. Three events made domestic patriarchy possible. First, the slave trade accelerated, thereby resolving the labor shortage and permitting wives of slaveholders to cease producing tobacco. Second, the decline of white immigration reduced the sex ratio and reduced the demand for teenage brides. Mothers could then keep daughters at home long enough to teach them housewifery. Third, increased adult life expectancy led to longer marriages because of less frequent parental death and so allowed clearer patterns of authority within the household.

Domestic patriarchies in the eighteenth-century Chesapeake region were productive units. Each member of the household had prescribed duties: men worked in the fields, directing slaves and sons in producing to-

6. Gerald W. Mullin analyzes differences between African and native-born slaves in *Flight and Rebellion: Slave Resistance in Eighteenth-Century Virginia* (New York, 1972), chaps. 1–3.
7. The classic article on white women in the early Chesapeake remains Lois Green Carr and Lorena S. Walsh, "The Planter's Wife: The Experience of White Women in Seventeenth-Century Maryland," *William and Mary Quarterly*, 3d Ser., XXXIV (1977), 542–571.

bacco and grain; women cultivated vegetables, made clothes and candles, kept house, and reared children. Fathers controlled the family property and retained the right to approve (or disapprove) their children's marital choices. This system contrasted greatly not only with the more egalitarian pattern found in the seventeenth-century Chesapeake, when men and women worked together, but with later forms of middle-class domestic family government. These last families, first found in the Northeast in the first decades of the nineteenth century, were units of consumption rather than production. Although men still dominated family government, they sought love matches and treated their wives as equals within the family. Husbands worked outside the home for a salary; wives dominated their new domestic sphere, rearing their children (a task given great ideological importance for the first time as "child nurture") and keeping their homes neat.[8]

Seventeenth-century white immigrants and their children lived such short lives that only infrequently did they form extensive kinship networks, spread over numerous plantations. Even though planters lived great distances from each other, they formed close attachments to neighbors, especially to those of the same sex. Men visited neighbors (sometimes with their wives), drank and hunted with them, and petitioned local authorities for public improvements with friends who lived nearby. The children of neighbors married one another and thereby helped to develop kinship networks. As the white population achieved natural increase and neighborhood children continued to marry into the same families, these networks strengthened.

Although gender-specific activities, church communions, and neighborhood gatherings became more intensive as population density increased, extensive networks of cousins structured social intercourse within social classes by the middle third of the eighteenth century (and even earlier in some old counties). Neighboring kinfolk regularly visited one another, cousins played together from infancy and married one another with great frequency, adult siblings and cousins shared church pews, and they all petitioned local justices for roads and bridges to connect their farms. One's family, as well as one's wealth, determined social position. Strong political dynasties formed by the early eighteenth century, and sons continued to

8. See Elizabeth Fox-Genovese, "Gender, Class, and Power: Some Theoretical Considerations," *History Teacher*, XV (1982), 255–276, for an analysis of the problems surrounding the use of the concept of *patriarchy*; her "Cavaliers and Ladies, Bucks and Mammies: Gender Conventions in the Antebellum South" (paper presented at the Smith College Conference on Conventions of Gender, Feb. 1984), compares northern and southern developments after the Revolution.

succeed their fathers as justices and legislators through the rest of the century.

Two new social classes, the gentry and the yeomanry, formed out of the social and cultural changes just described. It is important, however, to clarify what is here meant by *class*. Although members of distinct classes share similar levels of wealth, education, and power, classes are not merely collections of such people. Nor does the existence of relations of domination (found in all societies) prove the existence of classes. Rather, social classes form, disappear, and re-form as the processes of production change. Class relations might be understood as systems of domination and subservience within production and reproduction and in the political society created to support and perpetuate these economic relations. Classes are formed when discrete groups of people with similar levels of wealth and similar relations to the dominant means of production come to understand their place in the social order and develop coherent ideologies to legitimate or challenge that place. In this context, the ruling gentry class included the wealthiest planters, who dominated both polity and economy and who shared reciprocal patron-client and creditor-debtor relationships with a less wealthy group of freeholders and small slaveholders.[9]

The gentry and yeoman classes formed only after conflict and struggle between groups of white men that lasted more than a century. During the seventeenth century there was little class conflict; instead, social conflict took other forms, as groups of immigrants and a few natives competed for prestige and office. The social experiences of natives and immigrants were far different; eastern counties contained established plantations with strong families and slave labor, while some frontier areas were settled by immigrants and threatened by Indians. It therefore hardly seems surprising that Indian troubles and economic difficulties led to violent confrontations in the 1670s (Bacon's Rebellion), the 1680s (tobacco-cutting riots), the 1710s (tobacco regulation), and the 1710s and 1720s (slave conspiracies). Most of these conflicts began in frontier areas, but they often spread to more settled regions.

The process of class formation began during the mid-seventeenth century but was not completed for several generations. Political dynasties began even before natural increase. Sons of Maryland legislators first entered the assembly or council during the 1670s, but their numbers increased thereafter; and by the 1720s approximately half the fathers of all legislators had served in that body. Similar patterns, with somewhat different timing, oc-

9. Classic definitions of *class*, *class formation*, and *class consciousness* are found in E. P. Thompson, *The Making of the English Working Class* (New York, 1963), 9–12; and Raymond Williams, *Keywords: A Vocabulary of Culture and Society* (Glasgow, 1976), 51–59.

curred in the Virginia assembly and among justices of the peace. These men formed a new economic and political elite, but they did not yet constitute a ruling class. Even though they were much wealthier than other planters, these gentlemen often owned too few slaves to avoid field labor themselves or personal direction of their slaves, and they had not yet formed class-segregated institutions or a class ideology. Moreover, wealthy planters had not yet achieved political legitimacy. Endemic conflict between wealthy and poor men over tobacco regulation and cultivation (vital to the welfare of all planters) exploded in the 1710s from attempts to centralize the trade, and in the 1720s and 1730s, when new tobacco-cutting riots occurred and when poor Virginia planters burned four tobacco warehouses (part of the new inspection system that reduced poor men's crops). In the 1730s and 1740s wealthy planters finally imposed tobacco regulation on poorer men.

Thus the gentry and yeoman classes emerged from the gentry's victories in the conflicts of the 1720s and 1730s. Once gentlemen won political dominance, they could secure legitimacy only by establishing an intricate web of social and political relations with poorer yeoman planters. By supporting gentlemen, the yeomen secured protection of their property and assured themselves a role in politics. Gentlemen, moreover, now owned growing numbers of acculturated native slaves, whom they could leave under the direction of overseers. They used this newly acquired leisure to form class-segregated institutions like clubs, legislatures (which became societies exclusively of large planters in the 1720s), and the College of William and Mary, and they disseminated the new ruling-class ideology that they forged in these institutions in the newspapers they supported. In these media, gentlemen proclaimed themselves guardians of virture and insisted upon their right to govern.

Slaves experienced upheavals far more disruptive than did whites, but they too eventually formed communities and families. Africans forced into slavery in the Chesapeake colonies spoke a wide range of incompatible languages, lived on small plantations with only a few other slaves and often none of their tribesmen, formed families with great difficulty because so few women were enslaved, and were forced to submit to the almost incomprehensible labor demands of their new masters. Like white immigrants, they frequently died soon after arrival in the region and long before they found wives. These new slaves often refused to be integrated into plantation society, but instead sometimes ran away to escape their bondage.

The achievement of natural increase among slaves provided a demographic base for community formation. As increasing numbers of slave children were born and matured, the proportion of native Africans in the adult slave population diminshed. Since masters could for the first time maintain and even increase the size of their unfree labor force without buying newly enslaved Africans, the slave trade declined. An ever-increasing proportion of slaves lived on large units because masters usually kept all the children born to their slaves. The increase in the proportion of Chesapeake-born slaves and the decline of the slave trade led to nearly equal ratios of black men and women, since natural increase produced equal numbers of boys and girls.

During the middle and late eighteenth century, native slaves formed black communities that encompassed both their own and neighboring plantations. Large plantations, especially those villages of a hundred or more slaves owned by the wealthiest gentlemen, became community centers for neighborhood slaves. Plantation slaves worked together in the tobacco fields and cultivated their gardens, cooked, and talked with each other in the yards surrounding their cabins each evening. Even though slaves who lived on small plantations could not create viable communities at home, their isolation diminished when they participated in cross-plantation communities. Men from smaller plantations often visited wives owned by other masters and friends on large plantations after dark.

Slave families quickly became the most important element of slave communities. Native-born slaves built a family system from the demography of the plantation and vaguely remembered West African beliefs about appropriate family organization. Since both slave men and women performed similar tasks and had to accept the domination of their masters, slave families were probably more egalitarian than whites families. Numerous extended kinfolk lived in adjacent cabins on larger plantations, and a majority of children born on such units resided with both parents and other siblings. Kinfolk labored together, sometimes forming separate work crews, and slave artisans taught sons and nephews their special skills. Slave women on smaller plantations usually lived with their children, but their husbands often resided elsewhere in the neighborhood. Although their husbands visited them as often as they could, these women, like women in some West African societies, relied upon brothers and other male kindred to help rear their children.

Slave families and communities developed in part out of conflicts between slaves and masters. Masters tolerated extended slave families and cross-plantation marriages and visiting as ways to keep slaves relatively contented and productive. But in turn, native slaves had to accept, however unwillingly, their status as property. Two kinds of conflict were particularly common. Although masters often considered slaves to be inferior members of their own families, they frequently sold slaves to neighbors or bequeathed them to their children, thereby breaking up slave families, kin groups, and communities. Slaves had no choice but to suffer these separations. Slaves forced to move eventually recreated kin groups and communities; meanwhile, they maintained contact with family and friends left behind. Cross-plantation communities, then, were forged in part out of the dislocation of slave sales. Slaves frequently ran away to escape work or a particularly harsh master. Although nearly all these truants were soon recaptured and punished, masters could not stop them from running away. Whenever a slave needed to get away from his master for a few days, he could always find kindred or friends willing to hide and feed him.

By the middle of the eighteenth century, Chesapeake slaves had become both a racial caste and a laboring class. Black people were members of a caste because they could rarely escape chattel slavery, a status that defined them both as the means of production and as people. They were a laboring class because of their complex and changing relation to production processes their masters controlled. Masters did not trust African slaves; they watched them continually and set them to work on the simplest tasks of tobacco cultivation. White artisans monopolized most plantation carpentry, cooperage, and smithing until the mid-eighteenth century. But slaveowners did teach these skills to their native slaves, who soon dominated all aspects of both agricultural and craft labor on tobacco plantations. Social relations between masters and slaves became profoundly ambiguous. Although masters expropriated much of the product their slaves produced, they depended upon slaves for their wealth and learned to tolerate slave direction of the pace of labor. Slave laborers, and especially the artisans, worked for themselves as well as for their masters and took pride in their accomplishments. Whites reacted to the growing competence and demands of their slaves by creating racial myths of black inferiority and incompetence that would proliferate during the nineteenth century.

The cultural transformations just described—the development of domestic patriarchies, of a strong class system, and of a slave society— were neither inevitable nor completely determined by economic and demographic change. For example, Chesapeake planters did not *have* to choose to form domestic patriarchies. They could have maintained the relatively egalitarian family system of the seventeenth century. That planters chose to organize patriarchal families almost as soon as they could do so suggests strongly that they believed this was the proper way to organize domestic life, that they may have considered older forms of family life to be less than ideal. Nor did wealthy men *have* to form dynasties just because rising life expectancy gave them that option; they might have continued the policy of rotation in office that ensured that most unrelated men of wealth and a few poorer freeholders served as justices and assemblymen. Wealthy planters probably looked back to England and insisted that class control of politics was the best way to guarantee social peace in the very different slave society of the Chesapeake. And, despite severe constraints, even slaves made choices. They formed communities from among the extended kindred who lived on large plantations, and they adapted those African forms of child rearing that were compatible with chattel slavery. And while masters determined who would work in each slave gang, slaves themselves set the pace of work.

The social changes that led to the slave society of the eighteenth century took nearly a century to complete in the places first settled by white immigrants, and they were repeated in every new frontier of the Chesapeake region. Although frontier society appeared less stable and structured than older regions, the transition to a conservative social order was much more rapid on the piedmont frontier than in the oldest tidewater regions. New frontiers were settled by a youthful cross section of the populace of settled areas and grew by natural increase almost from the outset of settlement. Within a generation, patriarchal white families, white kin groups, gentry and yeoman classes, and slave communities had developed.

Once this social order developed, it proved remarkably impervious to fundamental change, but was constantly beset by its numerous internal tensions. Reciprocal political relations between gentlemen and yeomen weakened the authoritarian ideals of partiarchal families. Masters sought to make slaves into inferior members of their families, but bequeathed slaves to their children to ensure the continued prosperity of their own lineage. Slaveowners demanded sustained work from slaves, while slaves wanted to control the pace of labor. Endemic conflicts between husbands and wives, gentlemen and yeomen, and masters and slaves at times temporarily broke the bonds that tied social groups together. Serious conflicts broke out in the 1760s when Baptist yeomen challenged the authority of gentlemen and again during the Revolution when gentry leaders fought to contain agitation from slaves and loyalists.

The ordinary tensions embedded within Chesapeake society provided subservient groups like slaves and women with means to challenge domination without seeking to overthrow the system itself. Gentlemen and masters were so used to seeking accommodation with their perceived inferiors that they readily adapted to changing economic, demographic, and political conditions. Despite the development of republican political institutions, the disappearance of tobacco cultivation from much of the region, and the migration of thousands of people from the area, Chesapeake society became even more patriarchal, hierarchical, and racist than before. Gentlemen adopted republican rhetoric, but maintained their authority; planters devised ingenious systems of slave hire that made slave labor profitable in a system of diversified agriculture; and migration permitted those who remained to continue to own land and grow crops in the same ways as their ancestors. And out-migrants carried the Chesapeake social system to the

Southwest, where they adapted it to the cotton agriculture of the antebellum South.

This work begins with an analysis of structural transformations in the region and then examines the consequences of change for whites and blacks separately. The first chapter offers a short description of developments during the seventeenth century. Chapters 2, 3, and 4 carry the story through the eighteenth century. Chapter 2 details the relationship between population growth and land and explains how both white and black populations attained natural increase. Chapters 3 and 4 examine the intersection of economic activity and political change in the early and later eighteenth century. Part II analyzes white society, stressing the formation of patriarchal families in chapter 5, of kin-based communities in chapter 6, and of social classes in chapter 7. Part III examines slave society, stressing the origins of black communities in chapter 8, the development of black kinship networks in chapter 9, and race relations in chapter 10. The Conclusion argues that the slave society of the mid-eighteenth century persisted into the nineteenth century.

The interpretations here are consistent with the very rich literature on the Chesapeake colonies, but seek to extend it. There have been two tendencies among modern historians of the region. A number of talented social, economic, and demographic historians, including Darrett B. Rutman and Anita H. Rutman, Russell R. Menard, Lois Green Carr, Lorena S. Walsh, P. M. G. Harris, Paul G. E. Clemens, Gloria L. Main, and Carville V. Earle, have detailed patterns of economic development, population growth, and family organization. Most of their work stresses seventeenth-century developments and emphasizes the origins of the region's population and economy and the causes of the great transformation of the decades after 1680.[10] A second group of historians, including such leading scholars as Edmund S. Morgan, Rhys Isaac, Ronald Hoffman, Edward C. Papenfuse, Gerald Mullin, Richard Beeman, Daniel B. Smith, and T. H. Breen, stresses political and cultural developments, especially among gentlemen and their families. Most of their scholarship focuses on the eighteenth century and seeks to explain the origins or consequences of the American

---

10. Representative works in this vast literature include Darrett B. Rutman and Anita H. Rutman, *A Place in Time: Middlesex County, Virginia, 1650–1750* (New York, 1984); Tate and Ammerman, eds., *Chesapeake in the Seventeenth Century*; Carville V. Earle, *The Evolution of a Tidewater Settlement System: All Hallow's Parish, Maryland, 1650–1783*, University of Chicago Department of Geography Research Paper 170 (Chicago, 1975); Paul G. E. Clemens, *The Atlantic Economy and Colonial Maryland's Eastern Shore: From Tobacco to Grain* (Ithaca, N.Y., 1980); and Gloria L. Main, *Tobacco Colony: Life in Early Maryland, 1650–1720* (Princeton, N.J., 1982). The review essays cited in n. 2 above contain numerous other references.

Revolution.[11] This work seeks to synthesize the findings of these two groups and add to their achievements. Both groups of historians tend to slight the significance of the half-century before the Revolution; in contrast, this book insists that the kind of familial, class, and race relations found in the antebellum South first developed in the Chesapeake region between 1720 and 1770.

Since there has been, thus far, relatively little work on the eighteenth-century Chesapeake, many of the findings here must be seen as tentative. Three major arguments documented here challenge other work in the field. Several historians of the seventeenth-century Chesapeake see the transformation in family organization, political life, and economic development as complete by the late seventeenth century and insist that the timing of change varied from county to county.[12] Other scholars question the development and persistence of patriarchal family government among whites, insisting that gentry marriages became more companionate, that fathers rarely controlled the fortunes of sons, and that kinship came to play a diminished role in family life during the late eighteenth or early nineteenth century.[13] Finally, several scholars question the vitality of slave culture and insist that slave life was quite precarious and that slaves assimilated to norms of their white masters.[14]

Sources and Methods

This work is based heavily upon quantitative measures computed from contemporary materials like probate inventories and vital registers. Every work that uses quantitative data provokes methodological questions about the way data are used and the inherent biases of the data. All historical works contain within them systems of inference, either explicit or implicit. Readers

11. Representative works include Edmund S. Morgan, *American Slavery, American Freedom: The Ordeal of Colonial Virginia* (New York, 1975); Rhys Isaac, *The Transformation of Virginia, 1740–1790* (Chapel Hill, N.C., 1982); Ronald Hoffman, *A Spirit of Dissension: Economics, Politics, and the Revolution in Maryland* (Baltimore, 1973); Daniel Blake Smith, *Inside the Great House: Planter Family Life in Eighteenth-Century Chesapeake Society* (Ithaca, N.Y., 1980).

12. Research in progress by the St. Mary's City Commission (especially P.M.G. Harris) and by the York County Project (at the Research Department of Colonial Williamsburg), not yet published; but see P.M.G. Harris, "Integrating Interpretations of Local and Regionwide Change in the Study of Economic Development and Demographic Growth in the Colonial Chesapeake, 1630–1775," *Working Papers from the Regional Economic History Research Center*, I, No. 3 (1978), *Economic Change in the Chesapeake Colonies*, 35–71, for an example.

13. Smith, *Inside the Great House*; Jan Lewis, *The Pursuit of Happiness: Family and Values in Jefferson's Virginia* (Cambridge, 1983).

14. Mullin, *Flight and Rebellion*, makes the best case for assimilation.

need to understand how these inferences are made. This work is predicated upon a form of historical materialism that gives material conditions (demography and the economy, in particular) a privileged role in the formation of ideologies, classes, and cultures. Demographic and economic data, collected from eighteenth-century sources, therefore form the empirical base of this book. Both the system of inference and the biases of the data used to make the inferences require further elucidation.

The arguments of this book are organized around sequences of research, inference, and further research that began with data collection and ended with statements about ideology, culture, and social relations. Research on a problem usually began with collection of structural data, such as commodity prices, ages at first marriage, or acres and number of slaves per plantation. These structural data suggested possible patterns of behavior, such as agricultural diversification or specialization, marriage customs, or methods of plantation management. In turn, these patterns of behavior hinted at the texture of social relations, as between husbands and wives or masters and slaves. Finally, these social relations themselves seemed to generate and conform to a system of belief—what we might call ideology and culture.

After making these inferences from structural data, I then examined a wide range of literary materials—depositions in court records, letters and diaries, plays and satires, and travel accounts and legislative proceedings—to test my theories. Quantitative evidence often suggests what ideas and values groups might adopt but does not allow the scholar to choose among alternatives open to individuals. Literary evidence illuminates the choices people actually made. This massing of many kinds of evidence is especially valuable where surviving data are inadequate or ambiguous. It has been called a "wigwam argument," in which "there are several pieces of evidence, each insufficient or untrustworthy in itself, which seem collectively to confirm it." While "each pole [of the wigwam] would fall down by itself, . . . together the poles stand up, by leaning on each other; they point roughly in the same direction, and circumscribe 'truth.' "[15]

The arguments made in this book nonetheless stand or fall on the quality of the evidence collected. Three biases must be addressed. Most of the literary sources emanate from the wealthiest planters; most of the quantitative measures were calculated from potentially unrepresentative sources; and comparable data for most economic and demographic measures are limited to a few counties, rather than the region as a whole.

Nearly all surviving diaries, letters, and belles lettres were written by members of the fifty wealthiest gentry families. Travelers who left accounts

15. Keith Hopkins, *Conquerors and Slaves: Sociological Studies in Roman History*, I (Cambridge, 1978), 19–20.

tended to identify with these families. Legislative proceedings rarely included information on the interests of poorer folk, and newpapers almost never reported local news. Even court proceedings tended to be unrepresentative, especially records of county courts during the eighteenth century. The richest court proceedings I examined were found in Maryland's Chancery Court Records. Cases with hundreds of depositions can be found there, but nearly all of them concern wealthy men and women. Local court records reflect either the interests of merchants and magistrates or the needs of poor supplicants for pensions.

Literary sources, when used with care, do yield some information about ordinary planters, women, and slaves. Diarists, letter writers, and travelers all left impressions of these folk, but they were hardly unbiased and often recorded only the most sensational happenings. These comments can be used, however, to examine the texture of social relations in particular milieus. Landon Carter's massive diary, for instance, is filled with details of the conduct of his slaves and their reactions to him.[16] Probate wills, which cover a wide range of the freeholding population, often relate the values of the will writer and always indicate how property was transmitted between generations. Finally, petitions to both local courts and legislatures suggest local landholder opinion on selected public issues.

The major bodies of quantifiable sources used in this book—probate inventories and wills, customs records, vital registers, genealogies, tax lists, collections of tithables and censuses, and deeds—are all unrepresentative to one degree or another, for they all leave out substantial parts of the population. Unless the scholar finds ways to incorporate these missing individuals, both distributions and measures of central tendency will be biased in often unknowable ways. In technical terms, one must develop an appropriate *population at risk*, in which every individual (a wealthholder, a white male, for instance) has an equal chance of appearing. This problem is especially critical in aggregate measures such as per capita wealth or life expectancy. I have attempted to devise methods to estimate the size and characteristics of missing data when needed to compute reliable statistics. Most of these methods were ad hoc, and accurate standard deviations and even distributions often could not be calculated. Readers should understand that all averages reported in this book have distributions surrounding the mean, even if they are not reported.[17]

16. Jack P. Greene, ed., *The Diary of Colonel Landon Carter of Sabine Hall, 1752–1778*, 2 vols. (Charlottesville, Va., 1965); Isaac, *Transformation of Virginia*, 332–346, provides a detailed example using Carter's diary.

17. These methods are reported in the notes and tables. A number of more general discussions of methods I used or borrowed from other scholars will be found in several of my works, including "Tobacco and Slaves: Population, Economy, and Society in Eighteenth-Century

The problems of method raised by quantitative materials are compounded by subregional variations within the Chesapeake colonies—notably, time of settlement, geographic characteristics, and local government. An example of each of these differences will illustrate this problem. Frontiers had a different social structure at any given time than settled counties had, yet they eventually came to resemble the older regions. Counties with river frontage and bottomland tended to attract wealthier settlers than isolated backcountry areas. There were numerous tenants on both shores of the Potomac River, where proprietors owned thousands of acres, but few tenants in other, nonproprietary parts of Virginia. Only a few counties of Maryland and Virginia have been studied in detail. While a great deal is known about southern Maryland, the Eastern Shore, and Middlesex, York, and Elizabeth City counties in tidewater Virginia, Lunenburg County is the only piedmont county studied intensively to date. This scattered knowledge raises two fundamental questions: how to define the Chesapeake region in spatial terms, and how to deal with sometimes unknowable subregional differences.

This work analyzes changes in the Chesapeake region during the eighteenth century. A region can be defined as a group of similar, geographically contiguous places that proceed through similar stages of development. African and Afro-American slaves produced tobacco for the international market throughout the Chesapeake region, as defined here, from initial settlement to the American Revolution. This functional definition of the Chesapeake region excludes parts of Maryland and Virginia where slaves grew wheat or where few slaves toiled. The Chesapeake region was bounded by the Chesapeake Bay on the east, by the Blue Ridge Mountains on the west, by the Patapsco River on the north, and by the Nansemond River and North Carolina on the south (see map 1).

I have devised three strategies to deal with the problem of subregional differences. First, I have collected a number of series of aggregate data on population growth and diffusion, tobacco and grain prices and output, and land settlement and prices. These regional data provide a scaffolding for interpreting changes in families, communities, and classes, but the richness of social life can be captured only through local case studies. Al-

---

Prince George's County, Maryland" (Ph.D. diss., Brandeis University, 1976), chaps. 12 (demographic methods), 13 (economic methods), a source sometimes superseded by "A 'Prolifick' People," *So. Stud.*, XVI (1977), 415–428, and by "The Economic Growth of the Eighteenth-Century Chesapeake Colonies," *Journal of Economic History*, XXXIX (1979), 277–282. Other important discussions of methods used in this book will be found in Clemens, *Atlantic Economy*, 225–232; Main, *Tobacco Colony*, 267–292 (both for probate records); and Lorena Seebach Walsh and Russell R. Menard, "Death in the Chesapeake: Two Life Tables for Men in Early Colonial Maryland," *MHM*, LXIX (1974), 211–227.

Map 1. *The Subregions and Rivers of the Chesapeake Region*

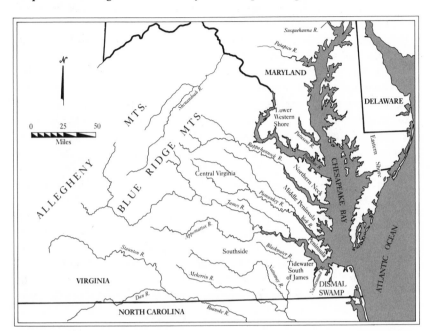

though I have collected data on such topics as the distribution of land and slaves from numerous counties, I have also used detailed case studies of Prince George's County in Maryland (from my own research) and Middlesex County (Darrett Rutman and Anita Rutman) and Lunenburg County (Richard Beeman) in Virginia.[18] While these three counties hardly exhaust variations in the Chesapeake region, they differed significantly: Middlesex, a small tidewater Virginia county, was first settled in the 1650s; Prince George's was a large upper tidewater county settled late in the seventeenth century; and Lunenburg, a large southside piedmont county, was not settled until the 1740s.

Data and examples from Prince George's County most frequently illustrate arguments made in the book. Though Prince George's was not the Chesapeake writ small, a study of that county does capture some of the

18. Rutman and Rutman, *A Place in Time*; Darrett B. Rutman and Anita H. Rutman, *A Place in Time: Explicatus* (New York, 1984); Richard R. Beeman, *Cavaliers and Frontiersmen: The Cultural Development of Lunenburg County, Virginia, 1746–1832* (Philadelphia, 1984). The Rutmans' volumes arrived too late for extensive use, but I benefited from a number of their earlier articles.

diversity of the region. This county, located between the Patuxent and Potomac rivers in southern Maryland (and including most of today's Washington, D.C.), was settled by British immigrants and by planters who moved from nearby counties, and included frontier and settled neighborhoods from the 1690s to the 1740s. From one-third to two-thirds of the people in its neighborhoods were slaves. In some places, nearly every planter owned slaves and land, but in others, most possessed neither. Anglicans, Presbyterians, and Roman Catholics all settled in the county in some numbers. Nearly every planter grew tobacco, but part of the county was served almost exclusively by Scottish merchants, and another part was dominated by London capital.

The eclectic strategies and inferential framework pursued here raise new questions about economic development, family structure, and class formation in the Chesapeake region during the eighteenth century. They suggest patterns of both the nature and timing of change and permit analysis both of broad regional patterns and of some subregional variations. Even more important, the inferences about gender, class, and race that form the interpretative core of this work link the history of the Chesapeake colonies in the eighteenth century to the later social history of the South and to more general patterns of American development.

I
The Political Economy of Tobacco

1
From Outpost to Slave Society, 1620–1700

Virginia and Maryland were founded as outposts of the English economy, and their initial settlement was financed by English merchants and speculators searching for quick returns on their investments. Royal officials supported these risky colonial ventures because they hoped that investors would lure many settlers to the area, find a staple crop England could not produce, and provide a market for the manufactures of the realm. Not only would colonization ultimately fill England's tax coffers, but it would also furnish a place to send the poor and dangerous men and women that wealthy Englishmen thought were overrunning the country.

For the better part of the seventeenth century, the Chesapeake region contained innumerable Indian villages that surrounded scattered outposts peopled by white planters and their indentured servants. The English learned how to survive from the Indians, made Indian corn their bread and Indian tobacco their staple, and then drove the Indians from lands they had always used. They slowly developed lands seized from the Indians, but even in 1700 only a few areas on the great rivers of the region were fully seated with plantations.

Once settlers discovered a market for tobacco in England, they dropped all other economic activities. Planters could take advantage of the tobacco market only if they commanded sufficient labor to increase their output. They therefore used the profits they made from the trade to bring over English servants to work in their tobacco fields. But the supply of indentured servants diminished at the end of the seventeenth century, and planters desperate for new laborers turned to African slaves. Slavery transformed the social relations of production in the region by creating a new class and racial-caste society. Black slaves became a permanent racial underclass without hope of emancipation, and planters who owned many slaves were far more affluent than their slaveless neighbors. Nonetheless, poor white families maintained a tenuous foothold in the region because tobacco cultivation—unlike sugar production—required only a small initial investment and could be farmed in small units.

From England to the Chesapeake

A tiny gentry class and a larger group of merchants, clerics, and substantial yeomen dominated English society during the early seventeenth century. Many of these men shared an integrated set of beliefs about the way a good society ought to be organized, and they attempted to instill these ideals in the rest of the English population. They believed that husbands ought to rule within the family, gentlemen ought to control the commonwealth, and communities ought to be free to follow local custom under the direction of the gentry. Though they taught these virtues to their children, they had to impose their ideas of good order upon domestic servants and the many poor folk who wandered through the countryside searching for employment.

Middling and gentry families were becoming increasingly patriarchal in seventeenth-century England. Husbands insisted that wives obey their dictates because women were members of the supposedly weaker and less intelligent sex; children were ordered to defer to their parents to learn to control their sinfulness. Fathers directed the family business, leaving the domestic organization of the household to their wives. Patriarchalism extended beyond the nuclear family. Children of poor laborers who became servants in yeoman or gentry households had to obey their master, or substitute father, or take direction from the lady of the house. Though few families attained this patriarchal ideal, some thinkers legitimated paternal authority by linking it to the political hierarchy: the fifth commandment, according to one catechism, ordered people to obey "Our naturall Parentes, the fathers of our Countrie, or of our house, the aged, and our fathers in Christ."[1]

English social life of the seventeenth century was organized into a hierarchy by status and wealth. Gentlemen idealized this hierarchy and insisted that it was established by God and therefore immutable. As John Winthrop asserted in his famous speech on the *Arbella*, "God Almightie . . . hath soe disposed of the Condicion of mankinde, as in all times some must be rich some poore, some highe and eminent in power and dignitie; others mean and in subieccion." Conservative social thinkers like Winthrop insisted that high and low social groups owed each other reciprocal obligations. The king ruled over his country with the same authority as a father dominated his family, but neither kings nor fathers were supposed to govern

---

1. Peter Laslett, *The World We Have Lost: England before the Industrial Age*, 2d ed. (New York, 1971), chap. 1; Lawrence Stone, *The Family, Sex, and Marriage in England, 1500–1800* (New York, 1977), chaps. 4, 5; Gordon J. Schochet, "Patriarchalism, Politics, and Mass Attitudes in Stuart England," *Historical Journal*, XII (1969), 413–441 (quote on 431).

arbitrarily. A gentleman was at the same time a father, husband, ruler of his subjects, and vassal of the king.[2]

English yeoman families owed loyalty to the clerical and gentry leadership of their local community rather than to any national unit. Villages were diverse and insular, and local custom regulated relationships between gentlemen and yeomen. Villagers rarely received news from other places even during the Revolution of the 1640s, and the information they learned from travelers, clergymen, or gentlemen was colored by the local attachments of both speakers and listeners. Of course, thousands of people did move from place to place, and many of them eventually reached London. Those who moved short distances probably retained local loyalties, while those who went to London might have begun to identify themselves as English.[3]

The values held by privileged and middling Englishmen implicitly assumed that England was a stable society of subsistence peasants, well fed and willing to defer to their betters. This vision hardly reflected social reality. England was organized into a series of integrated local markets, centered in market towns where husbandmen sold produce and bought consumer goods. Nor did most poor people practice the subservient roles gentlemen expected of them. Poor cottagers scratched out a living on a sliver of wasteland, and all members of the household—both men and women—supplemented their income from their tiny plots by agricultural and industrial labor. Laborers and even some cottagers tramped along the highways looking for seasonal labor or industrial employment.[4]

These poor folk may not have shared the patriarchal and hierarchical values of the gentry, but many may have wanted a more egalitarian social order where all worthy men held political rights, and a few might have wanted husbands and wives to share equally in family government. Poor people probably shared some of the radical ideologies that surfaced during the English Revolution of the 1640s. "Masterless Men" flocked to the New Model Army and listened to debates over political responsibilities and the franchise. Leveller leaders like Gerald Winstanley sought to "endeavour by our righteous acting not to leave the earth any longer entangled unto our

2. Laslett, *World We Have Lost*, chaps. 2, 8; John Winthrop, "A Modell of Christian Charity," in Perry Miller and Thomas H. Johnson, eds., *The Puritans*, rev. ed. (New York, 1963), I, 195.
3. Alan Everitt, *Change in the Provinces: The Seventeenth Century*, University of Leicester Department of English Local History Occasional Papers, 2d Ser., No. 1 (Leicester, 1969); E. A. Wrigley, "A Simple Model of London's Importance in Changing English Society and Economy, 1650–1750," *Past and Present*, No. 37 (July 1967), 44–70; Laslett, *World We Have Lost*, chap. 3.
4. Alan Everitt, "Farm Labourers," and "The Marketing of Agricultural Produce," in Joan Thirsk, ed., *The Agrarian History of England and Wales* (Cambridge, 1967), IV, chaps. 7, 8.

children by self-seeking proprietors; but to leave it a free store-house and common treasury to all, without respect of persons." Winstanley encouraged marriage across classes and insisted that men take responsibility for their sexual behavior; more radical sects approved of sexual freedom, easy divorce, and more nearly equal rights for women in marriage and society.[5]

English gentlemen feared poor folk and sought to regulate their behavior. Fewer than half the poor worked as servants in the homes of their masters. The rest, including vagrants and deserving poor widows and pensioners, could be controlled only by social coercion. The English poor laws of 1598 and 1601 defined vagabondage and permitted local authorities to whip anyone in that group, set up workhouses for idle men and women, and provided a stipend for the deserving poor.[6]

Neither discipline by masters nor the social control imposed by the English poor laws succeeded in making poor people subservient to their betters. English population rose greatly during the late sixteenth and early seventeenth centuries, and wages of agricultural laborers fell at the same time. The absolute and relative number of poor people, along with the problems they caused England's rulers, therefore rose greatly on the eve of American colonization. Some gentlemen considered new colonies ideal dumping ground for England's idle beggars and vagabonds. The Virginia Company expected to bring over shiploads of the unemployed to work as servants on its plantations, and James I ordered a large group of troublesome poor men kidnapped and sent there.[7]

During the initial decades of settlement of the Chesapeake colonies, the Virginia Company and the Calverts attempted to organize hierarchical societies that matched their vision of how England ought to be governed. In Virginia, the company's officers held all land and power and housed immigrants in barracks; their detailed rules sought to instill rigid discipline and obedience in the mostly poor adventurers who migrated to the colony. The

5. Christopher Hill, *The World Turned Upside Down: Radical Ideas during the English Revolution* (London, 1972), chaps. 3, 15; Christopher Hill, ed., *Winstanley: The Law of Freedom and Other Writings* (Harmondsworth, England, 1973), 99–108 (quote on 106), 388–389.

6. A good summary of the laws and some representative documents on the administration of poor law can be found in John Pound, *Poverty and Vagrancy in Tudor England* (Cambridge, 1971), esp. 53–58, and pt. 4.

7. Everitt, "Farm Labourers," in Thirsk, ed., *Agrarian History*, IV, 398–400; and Peter Bowen, "Agricultural Prices, Farm Profits, and Rents," *ibid.*, chap. 9, esp. 594–609, 617–633; E. A. Wrigley and R. S. Schofield, *The Population History of England, 1541–1871: A Reconstruction* (Cambridge, Mass., 1981), 166–191, 402–412; Karen O. Kupperman, *Settling with the Indians: The Meeting of English and Indian Cultures in America, 1580–1640* (Totowa, N.J., 1980), 135–140; and Edmund S. Morgan, *American Slavery, American Freedom: The Ordeal of Colonial Virginia* (New York, 1975), 32–33, 44–46, 65–68, document attitudes toward the poor in England or the desire of company officials to use them in Virginia.

Calvert proprietors of Maryland attempted to establish a manorial society modeled on their image of medieval Europe; they hoped that the strong judicial control and large plantations granted to each lord of the manor would encourage rapid development.[8]

How well the founders of Virginia and Maryland succeeded in creating their conservative utopias depended upon the kinds of people who migrated and how they adapted to the physical environment of the region. Migration by families, coupled with low adult death rates, would permit the creation of patriarchal families and provide a mechanism to control laborers and servants, but political control would be difficult if most immigrants were footloose young men. If migrants lived on farms and in villages similar to those of England and remained contented with lands granted them by the Virginia Company or manorial lords, the economy and social hierarchy the founders envisioned could develop. But if migrants insisted on farming land outside of settled communities, gentry social control might disappear soon after initial colonization.

The first English settlers found a vast land, thinly populated by European standards, with fertile soil, lush forests, and wide rivers. The Chesapeake Bay divided the country into two shores, but most early settlers stayed on the western side of the bay. Six great rivers—which the English named the James (near the southern entrance to the bay), York, Rappahannock, Potomac, Patuxent, and Susquehanna (near the northern edge of the bay)—drained into the Chesapeake. While parts of tidewater were nearly flat, much of that country was "not mountanous nor yet low, but such pleasant and plaine hils and fertle valleyes, one prettily crossing an other, and watered so conveniently with their sweet brookes and christall springs, as if art it selfe had devised them." Great waterfalls signaled the beginnings of the rolling hills of piedmont, and Indians told the English of vast mountains located far to the west (map 1).[9]

The early explorers of Virginia perceived the Indians as savages and thought the land they inhabited was a vast wilderness that contained a cornucopia of resources waiting to be used to turn the area into farms and villages. Even John Smith, who described the politics and culture of the

8. Morgan, *American Slavery, American Freedom*, chaps. 3–7; Sigmund Diamond, "From Organization to Society: Virginia in the Seventeenth Century," *American Journal of Sociology*, LXIII (1957–1958), 457–475; Russell R. Menard, "Maryland's 'Time of Troubles': Sources of Political Disorder in Early St. Mary's," *Maryland Historical Magazine*, LXXVI (1981), 124–140; Russell R. Menard, "Economy and Society in Early Colonial Maryland" (Ph.D. diss., University of Iowa, 1975), chaps. 1, 2.
9. John Smith, *A Map of Virginia* (1612), in Philip L. Barbour, ed., *The Jamestown Voyages under the First Charter, 1606–1609* (Hakluyt Society Publications, 2d Ser., CXXXVII [Cambridge, 1969]), II, 338.

Indians in great detail, shared this vision. Virginia, he contended, was a paradise: "The mildnesse of the aire, the fertilitie of the soile, and the situation of the rivers are so propitious to the nature and use of man as no place is more convenient for pleasure, profit, and mans sustenance." But it was a wild paradise. "All the Countrey is overgrowne with trees" and over-run with weeds, a situation that could "soone be amended by good hus-bandry," after the English took over the area from the Indians who had made "so smal a benefit of their land, be it never so fertill."[10]

Englishmen did not see that Indians exploited the lands of the Chesa-peake very efficiently. At least twenty-five thousand Indians lived within the eventual boundaries of the two colonies in 1600, and the population was probably much higher before untold numbers of Indians died from Euro-pean diseases after initial contact. They lived in small villages of two to fifty dwellings surrounded by fields of corn, beans, squash, and other vegetables. These crops, along with the fish and game Indian hunters caught, provided each village with sufficient food to feed its people and pay tribute to power-ful chieftains.[11]

Nor was Virginia a wilderness in 1607 when the first white settlers arrived. At least two hundred villages could be found in tidewater Virginia and Maryland, and wide Indian highways connected tidewater with pied-mont and the Potomac River with the James River, located eighty to one hundred miles to the south. Indians created hundreds of meadows out of the thick woodland that covered the area when they slashed trees and burned forests to prepare new fields for cultivation. Since Indians used a field only as long as yields stayed high and then let it lie fallow until fertility was restored, they steadily created new fields and yet more clearings from the forests.[12]

English settlers relied upon Indians for food and instruction in the use of the land during their first few years in the region. The first Virginians lusted for instant riches or a profitable staple and were too busy with these concerns to pay much attention to their own subsistence. They therefore

10. *Ibid.*, 353, 345, 354. For a general analysis of explorers' visions of the use of the environ-ment, see Louis B. Wright, *The Dream of Prosperity in Colonial America* (New York, 1965), esp. 32–34, 54–55; and Morgan, *American Slavery, American Freedom*, chap. 1.

11. Ben C. McCary, *Indians in Seventeenth-Century Virginia* (Williamsburg, Va., 1957), 1–10, 16–24; Raphael Semmes, "Aboriginal Maryland, 1608–1689," *MHM*, XXIV (1929), 157–171, 195–209, esp. 170–172, 208–209; G. Melvin Herndon, "Indian Agriculture in the Southern Colonies," *North Carolina Historical Review*, XLIV (1967), 283–297; Morgan, *American Slavery, American Freedom*, 51–57.

12. Edward G. Roberts, "The Roads of Virginia, 1607–1840" (Ph.D. diss., University of Vir-ginia, 1950), map facing 111, 122–127; Herndon, "Indian Agriculture," *N.C. Hist. Rev.*, XLIV (1967), 284–286; Morgan, *American Slavery, American Freedom*, 53–55.

turned to Indians for food, exhausting the Indian surpluses and cutting into their subsistence. Once the English started to grow their own food and tobacco, they adopted Indian methods of cultivation, including the system of field rotation the natives had perfected.[13]

Whites believed that Indians were savage heathens who held no real title to the lands they used, and therefore took up land near Indian settlements, disrupting their ability to hunt and collect wild fruit and herbs. Whenever a dispute erupted between the English and Indians, settlers resorted to violence and pillage of crops and villages. Finally, in 1622, the Indians revolted and killed 347 white settlers. English retribution for this attack, and for a similar uprising in 1644, was both swift and vicious. The English massacred many Indians and sent most of the rest into exile far beyond the limits of white settlement. By 1669, about two thousand Indians lived in tidewater Virginia, only a third the number found there in 1607.[14]

Though English settlers did not find a wilderness, they did create one. After they forced the Indians to leave tidewater, the old paths and villages filled with weeds and old pine forests. White families only slowly filled the lands Indians had left. Seventy years after the first Englishmen had arrived in Virginia, white settlement had progressed only about sixty miles west of the Chesapeake Bay, and even this area was thinly inhabited. Two English settlers and one Scottish settler commented in 1697 upon the natural riches of the province in words nearly identical to Smith's. They claimed that "not the hundredth Part of the Country is yet clear'd from the Woods, and not one Foot of the Marsh and Swamp drained," and the land appeared to them "like a wild Desart; the High-Lands overgrown with Trees, and the Low-Lands sunk with Water, Marsh, and Swamp." A quarter of a century later, Hugh Jones lamented that the "whole country is a perfect forest, except where the woods are cleared for plantations, and old fields, and where have been formerly Indian towns."[15]

13. Morgan, *American Slavery, American Freedom*, chaps. 2, 3; Herndon, "Indian Agriculture," *N.C. Hist. Rev.*, XLIV (1967), 286–288.
14. Morgan, *American Slavery, American Freedom*, 74–75, 97–101, 149. The debate over white images of Indians can be followed in Francis Jennings, *The Invasion of America: Indians, Colonialism, and the Cant of Conquest* (Chapel Hill, N.C., 1975), pt. 1; Kupperman, *Settling with the Indians*, esp. chap. 6; Bernard W. Sheehan, *Savagism and Civility: Indians and Englishmen in Colonial Virginia* (Cambridge, 1980), esp. chap. 6.
15. Henry Hartwell et al., *The Present State of Virginia and the College*, ed. Hunter Dickinson Farish (Williamsburg, Va., 1940 [orig. publ. London, 1727]), 3–4, 8; Hugh Jones, *The Present State of Virginia, from Whence Is Inferred a Short View of Maryland and North Carolina*, ed. Richard L. Morton (Chapel Hill, N.C., 1956 [orig. publ. London, 1724]), 74. Jennings, *Invasion of America*, chap. 2, deals imaginatively with white confiscation of Indian lands and shows how they became "widowed acres."

White planters replaced Indian villages with dispersed farmsteads; Virginians "seated themselves," the three observers complained in 1697, "without any Rule or Order in Country Plantations." Chesapeake planters, however, were not randomly scattered across the landscape, but farmed land along the banks of rivers and streams to be near trade routes and to take advantage of the best soil. Moreover, planters needed great quantities of land for timber, meadows, and fallow acres. Planters in Calvert County, Maryland, at the end of the seventeenth century feared that the population had grown too great, even though only about two or three families lived on each square mile of taxed land in the county. "Tho we are pretty closely seated," the county's minister wrote in 1699, "yett we cannot see our next neighbours house for trees," but he feared that "in a few years we may expect it otherwise, for the tobacco trade destroyes abundance of timber both for makeing of hogsheads and building of tobacco houses; besides cleareing of ground yearly for planting."[16]

Despite attempts of the two colonial assemblies to create towns during the last third of the seventeenth century, Marylanders and Virginians refused to move to them, fearing that "an hundred Families" would be "coop'd up within the Compass of half a Mile of Ground" to the disadvantage of everyone. The only towns of any importance in 1700 were Williamsburg and Annapolis, the two colonial capitals, and together they housed fewer than a thousand souls. A half-dozen inconsequential villages dotted the rivers, but most business was carried on at ship landings, large planters' homes, courthouses, inns, churches, and artisans' workshops scattered across the face of the land.[17]

The Age of the Small Planter

The utopian hopes of the Virginia Company and the Calverts for the development of stable, hierarchical societies in the Chesapeake region were

16. Hartwell *et al.*, *Present State of Virginia*, ed. Farish, 11; Michael G. Kammen, ed., "Maryland in 1699: A Letter from the Reverend Hugh Jones," *Journal of Southern History*, XXIX (1963), 367. Kevin P. Kelly, " 'In Dispers'd Country Plantations': Settlement Patterns in Seventeenth-Century Surry County, Virginia," in Thad W. Tate and David L. Ammerman, eds., *The Chesapeake in the Seventeenth Century: Essays on Anglo-American Society* (Chapel Hill, N.C., 1979), 183–205, provides a case study of the process of settlement; and Rhys Isaac, *The Transformation of Virginia, 1740–1790* (Chapel Hill, N.C., 1982), chap. 1, brilliantly evokes the Chesapeake landscape.

17. Hartwell *et al.*, *Present State of Virginia*, ed. Farish, 10–14 (quote on 14); Edward C. Papenfuse, *In Pursuit of Profit: The Annapolis Merchants in the Era of the American Revolution, 1763–1805* (Baltimore, 1975), 14, estimates the population of Annapolis in 1699 at 252 and 332 in

never fulfilled. Though many gentlemen emigrated with the first settlers, some died in the Indian attack of 1622, and others left when they discovered the difficulties of carving plantations out of the forests. Since other English gentlemen refused to migrate to either colony, hierarchical leadership was missing. Furthermore, planters lived scattered along the banks of rivers and streams, rather than in villages where the few remaining gentlemen could police their behavior. Ordinary small planters, who owned a freehold of several hundred acres and perhaps an indentured servant, filled the vacuum left by gentlemen and came to dominate the region's population and politics.[18]

The introduction of tobacco as the region's export staple in the 1620s ended any hopes the Virginia Company or the Calverts had of introducing their conservative plans for the region. All the settlers' effort went into producing tobacco for the market. Since tobacco production required labor, planters purchased large numbers of servants from among the poorer classes of England. When their term expired, these men started new households, built new plantations, and grew yet more tobacco. The social mobility that ex-servants enjoyed destroyed the hierarchical order English gentlemen desired, and led to a more egalitarian society than found in England.

The rapidly expanding market for Chesapeake tobacco in England created these substantial opportunities for freed servants and ordinary immigrants. Between 1620 and 1680 the price and production of tobacco followed a new product curve. Tobacco planters received a very high price for their product in the 1620s, and this price encouraged a search for new ways to increase productivity and enticed more men to grow tobacco. Annual output of tobacco per hand rose from about 710 pounds in the 1620s to about 1,600 pounds by the 1670s; at the same time, the costs of shipping a pound of tobacco diminished by half. Tobacco prices fell rapidly in the 1620s, from about sixteen to five pennies per pound, and then more slowly but steadily from the 1630s through the 1660s, reaching about a penny a pound by 1670. Nonetheless, planters were still able to make a profit from their tobacco because they produced more of the crop with the same input of labor. Lower tobacco prices led to greater consumption of Chesapeake tobacco in Europe; tobacco exports from the region exploded in the 1620s and 1630s and then increased less rapidly until the early 1680s. Virginians

---

1705; if the population of Williamsburg was double that of Annapolis (no estimate survives), then the population of the two places would range between 776 and 996.
18. Bernard Bailyn, "Politics and Social Structure in Virginia," in James Morton Smith, ed., *Seventeenth-Century America: Essays in Colonial History* (Chapel Hill, N.C., 1959), 90–115, esp. 92–96; Menard, "Economy and Society," chap. 5.

shipped an average of sixty-five thousand pounds of tobacco to England in the early 1620s, but more than a million pounds annually by the end of the 1630s; and Chesapeake planters exported an average of more than twenty million pounds a year by the late 1670s.[19]

Though the output of tobacco per hand rose over the middle half of the seventeenth century, planters soon discovered that the addition of new laborers to their fields increased production even more rapidly. Since Chesapeake population was still small, England provided the best source for labor, and planters enticed thousands of Englishmen to come to the region to escape depressed labor markets and low wages. About seventy-five thousand whites immigrated to the Chesapeake colonies from Britain between 1630 and 1680, and from half to three-quarters of them arrived as indentured servants. Emigrants tended to be poor, unskilled youths in their late teens or early twenties, a group that had disturbed the social peace of English gentlemen for half a century, and they were bound to be difficult to control once they arrived. Probably half of these young men were either unemployed or unskilled laborers, and only one servant in four came from a yeoman background.[20]

Planters particularly sought male workers they could put in their tobacco fields. They succeeded in this goal: more than six times as many men as women served terms during the 1630s, and more than three men migrated to the region for each woman between 1640 and 1680. This high

---

19. Russell R. Menard, "The Tobacco Industry in the Chesapeake Colonies, 1617–1730: An Interpretation," *Research in Economic History*, V (1980), 109–177, esp. 111, 145–147, 156–161. The figures are rounded means for half-decades. A more theoretical analysis of the tobacco industry will be found in David W. Galenson and Russell R. Menard, "Approaches to the Analysis of Economic Growth in Colonial British America," *Historical Methods*, XIII (1980), 6–10.

20. The estimate of white immigration adopted here will be found in Russell R. Menard, "British Migration to the Chesapeake Colonies in the Seventeenth Century" (paper presented at the Third Hall of Records Conference on Maryland History, "Maryland, a Product of Two Worlds," May 1984), esp. table 6; but see also Wesley Frank Craven, *White, Red, and Black: The Seventeenth-Century Virginian* (Charlottesville, Va., 1971), 15–16; Russell R. Menard, "Immigrants and Their Increase: The Process of Population Growth in Early Colonial Maryland," in Aubrey C. Land *et al.*, eds., *Law, Society, and Politics in Early Maryland* (Baltimore, 1977), 88–91; Henry A. Gemery, "Emigration from the British Isles to the New World, 1630–1700: Inferences from Colonial Populations," *Res. Econ. Hist.*, V (1980), 179–231, esp. 215; and David W. Galenson, *White Servitude in Colonial America: An Economic Analysis* (Cambridge, 1981), 212–219. Ages of servants are found in Galenson, 26–39, and James Horn, "Servant Emigration to the Chesapeake in the Seventeenth Century," in Tate and Ammerman, eds., *Chesapeake in the Seventeenth Century*, 62. Galenson's arguments (*White Servitude*, chap. 3) about the often low social origins of servants are more persuasive than arguments that most servants were yeomen made by Mildred Campbell, "Social Origins of Some Early Americans," in Smith, ed., *Seventeenth-Century America*, 70–74.

ratio of men to women in the servant population added countless footloose young men to the Chesapeake population, men who often died without heirs and thereby helped to perpetuate the need for immigrant labor.[21]

Planters had an insatiable demand for servants. Not only did they need to find replacements for men whose term had expired, but they had to get new laborers when servants died, as many did during their first year in the region, lacking both familiarity with the humid climate and immunity to the region's diseases. But even those men who lived through the seasoning of their first year suffered from chronic diseases like malaria that cut their productivity and put them at great risk of dying during periodic small pox and influenza epidemics.[22]

Tobacco planters had to turn to Britain to find new servants because immigrants did not replace themselves in the population. Late marriages, heavy mortality, and the high ratios of men to women among ex-servants all made family sizes small. Most women migrated as servants and were not available to marry until about age twenty-five. Former servant women who married and lived through their childbearing years would likely give birth to six children. But a large number of immigrant women died in their twenties and thirties and, accordingly, left fewer, if any, children. The typical immigrant woman in two Maryland counties gave birth to fewer than four children before she or her husband died, and one or two of them died before they reached adulthood. Since the ex-servant population counted three men for every woman, the offspring of immigrant women replaced only three-fifths of a given immigrant generation (see table 1).[23]

Even though the daughters of immigrants had larger families and more than replaced the mothers' generation (table 1), so many immigrants poured into the Chesapeake colonies that the greater fertility of this second

---

21. Menard, "Immigrants and Their Increase," in Land *et al.*, eds., *Law, Society, and Politics*, 95–97.

22. Lorena Seebach Walsh and Russell R. Menard, "Death in the Chesapeake: Two Life Tables for Men in Early Colonial Maryland," *MHM*, LXIX (1974), 214–219; Darrett B. Rutman and Anita H. Rutman, "Of Agues and Fevers: Malaria in the Early Chesapeake," *William and Mary Quarterly*, 3d Ser., XXXIII (1976), 31–60; Lorena S. Walsh, "Charles County, Maryland, 1658–1705: A Study of Chesapeake Social and Political Structure" (Ph.D. diss., Michigan State University, 1977), 39–52.

23. Menard, "Immigrants and Their Increase," in Land *et al.*, eds., *Law, Society, and Politics*, 96, 100–102; Lois Green Carr and Lorena S. Walsh, "The Planter's Wife: The Experience of White Women in Seventeenth-Century Maryland," *WMQ*, 3d Ser., XXIV (1977), 550–553; Walsh, "Charles County," 71; Daniel Blake Smith, "Mortality and Family in the Colonial Chesapeake," *Journal of Interdisciplinary History*, VIII (1977–1978), 412–414; Walsh and Menard, "Death in the Chesapeake," *MHM*, LXIX (1974), 220–223; Russell R. Menard and Lorena S. Walsh, "The Demography of Somerset County, Maryland: A Progress Report," *Newberry Papers in Family and Community History*, 81-2 (1981), 32–33, 36.

Table 1. *White Natural Increase and Decline in the Seventeenth-Century Chesapeake*

Component of Population Growth	Immigrants	Natives
(1) Female age at first marriage	24.9	16.8
(2) No. of children, all families	3.7	5.5
(3) Maximum proportion of children alive on 20th birthday[a]	60.8%	60.8%
(4) No. of children surviving to age 20 per couple[b]	2.2	3.3
(5) Adult sex ratio (men per 100 women)	300	100
(6) Index of generational replacement[c]	.6	1.7

Sources: Estimates calculated from data in Russell R. Menard, "Immigrants and Their Increase: The Process of Population Growth in Early Colonial Maryland," in Aubrey C. Land *et al.*, eds., *Law, Society, and Politics in Early Maryland* (Baltimore, 1977), 100–102; Lorena Seebach Walsh, "Charles County, Maryland, 1658–1705: A Study of Chesapeake Social and Political Structure" (Ph.D. diss., Michigan State University, 1977), 71; Daniel Blake Smith, "Mortality and Family in the Colonial Chesapeake," *Journal of Interdisciplinary History*, VIII (1978), 412–414; Walsh and Menard, "Death in the Chesapeake: Two Life Tables for Men in Early Colonial Maryland," *Maryland Historical Magazine*, LXIX (1974), 220–223; Menard and Walsh, "The Demography of Somerset County, Maryland: A Progress Report," *Newberry Papers in Family and Community History*, 81-2 (1981), 32–33, 36.

Notes: [a]Children of immigrants and of natives cannot be distinguished. [b](Item 2 × item 3) ÷ 100. [c](Item 4 ÷ 2), assuming sex ratios of item 5.

generation failed to generate a surplus of births over deaths in the whole white population. Only one of every eight free adult white men in Charles County, Maryland, in 1675 was native-born, and that proportion rose to only one in three by 1690. Similarly, the proportion of native-born people among *all* whites in Middlesex County, Virginia, rose from about one in five to nine in twenty between 1668 and 1687, and many of them were children.[24]

Seventeenth-century birthrates provided few workers for Chesapeake plantations. Only one son was born for every two planters in mid-seven-

24. For proportions native-born, see Darrett B. Rutman and Anita H. Rutman, " 'More True and Perfect Lists': The Reconstruction of Censuses for Middlesex County, Virginia, 1668–1704," *Virginia Magazine of History and Biography*, LXXXVIII (1980), 58–63; Lorena S. Walsh, "Mobility, Persistence, and Opportunity in Charles County, Maryland, 1650–1720" (paper presented at annual meeting of the Social Science History Association, Bloomington, Ind., Oct. 1982), table 1.

teenth-century Maryland, and even married immigrants could count on the service of just one adolescent son. Most first-generation native-born planters, in contrast, eventually employed two sons. Since these youths came of age to cultivate tobacco when their fathers were already in their forties, young married planters had to compete with bachelors for English servants if they wished to increase their output of tobacco. Once sons reached their twenties and left home, their fathers had to reenter the servant market.[25]

The servants and ex-servants who peopled the Chesapeake colonies during the seventeenth century molded unfavorable demographic conditions—the high ratio of men to women, heavy mortality, and late marriages—to their own advantage. Freedmen pursued two goals, the formation of a family and the purchase of their own land, with great vigor. These two objectives were linked: a man could not attract a wife, given the relative scarcity of women, unless he possessed land.

The goals of newly freed servants and already-established planters collided, and conflict between the two groups was inevitable. Since there was a constant shortage of labor throughout the Chesapeake, planters employed as many freed persons as they could find. Their goal, of course, was to increase their profits by hiring labor at low wages to grow tobacco, and freedmen who knew how to "work in the ground" and were willing to work for low wages could provide skilled help to achieve that goal. By hiring ex-servants, small freeholders could improve their land at little expense. Freedmen, on the other hand, wanted to save enough money to rent or purchase land and begin a household. Since freedmen, unlike servants, were not obligated to stay with a single employer, they traveled from place to place and worked for the planter who paid the highest wages. Planters feared that freedmen would rebel if their progress toward landownership was not rapid, and that fear was fulfilled when freed servants and tenants became the most vigorous supporters of Nathaniel Bacon's abortive rebellion against English authority in Virginia in 1676.

Most freedmen, however, eventually accumulated sufficient capital to begin a household and buy land, and their opportunities probably increased over the first two-thirds of the seventeenth century. During the tobacco boom of the 1620s, successful entrepreneurs amassed large fortunes by exploiting the labor of indentured servants, but servants often died before their term ended, and even those who survived gained freeholds with difficulty. Most servants after 1640 survived their seasoning, and at the same time, economic conditions for freedmen also improved. Though men could

25. Menard, "Immigrants and Their Increase," in Land *et al.*, eds., *Law, Society, and Politics*, 91–93. I divided the number of surviving children in table 1 in half to determine the number of adolescent sons a planter would have to help him.

no longer make great fortunes by growing tobacco, freed servants, on the average, amassed property worth two pounds sterling every year they were free. Between 1640 and 1670, ex-servants in several Maryland counties commonly remained in the Chesapeake region, worked as laborers for a few years, and then bought land and served in political office. Although the proportion of freedmen who left Maryland increased in the 1670s, nearly half of those who remained purchased land. As freedmen and poor farmers bought land and servants of their own, the economic distance between the wealthiest and poorest householders declined, while the percentage of owners of several hundred acres increased.[26]

Once a former servant gathered sufficient capital to rent or purchase land, he could begin to search for a wife. Freedmen must have felt some urgency, for life was still precarious, and a thirty-year-old man would probably die before his fiftieth birthday. Most ex-servants who lived through their early thirties set up households, married, and began a family, but marriages of immigrant couples were likely to last only nine to thirteen years before either husband or wife died. These parental deaths left children to be reared by a single parent, relatives, or unrelated members of the community.[27]

The social mobility of ex-servants, along with their short life span, led to a feverish search for profits that left little time for the imposition of social control upon servants, poor people, and women similar to that practiced by gentlemen and patriarchal husbands in England. Men competed with each other for power and profits and even refused to defer to men in positions of authority. Although local government, sustained by rudimentary social net-

26. These paragraphs on opportunity blend the view of Morgan, *American Slavery, American Freedom*, chap. 9 and 429–430, with the views of Russell R. Menard, Lois G. Carr, and Lorena S. Walsh found in Menard, "Economy and Society," chap. 5; Menard *et al.*, "Opportunity and Inequality: The Distribution of Wealth on the Lower Western Shore of Maryland, 1638–1705," *MHM*, LXIX (1974), 178–183; Menard, "From Servant to Freeholder: Status Mobility and Property Accumulation in Seventeenth-Century Maryland," *WMQ*, 3d Ser., XXX (1973), 37–64; Walsh, "Servitude and Opportunity in Charles County, Maryland, 1658–1705," in Land *et al.*, eds., *Law, Society, and Politics*, 111–133; and Carr and Menard, "Immigration and Opportunity: The Freedman in Early Colonial Maryland," in Tate and Ammerman, eds., *Chesapeake in the Seventeenth Century*, 206–242. A somewhat different view that stresses the economic interdependence of ex-servants and middling freeholders can be found in Darrett B. Rutman and Anita H. Rutman, *A Place in Time: Middlesex County, Virginia, 1650–1750* (New York, 1984), 72–75, 258–259.
27. Walsh and Menard, "Death in the Chesapeake," *MHM*, LXIX (1974), 214–217; Menard and Walsh, "Demography of Somerset County," *Newberry Papers*, 81-2 (1981), 30–32, 34; Walsh, "Charles County," 68; Darrett B. Rutman and Anita H. Rutman, " 'Now-Wives and Sons-in-Law': Parental Death in a Seventeenth-Century Virginia County," in Tate and Ammerman, eds., *Chesapeake in the Seventeenth Century*, 153–182; Lois G. Carr, "The Development of the Maryland Orphan's Court, 1654–1715," in Land *et al.*, eds., *Law, Society, and Politics*, 41–62.

works, usually held the contentious society of planters together, these institutions could not contain Bacon's Rebellion in 1676, a violent conflict over Indian policy and the control of Virginia's government that began along the frontier but spread to nearly the entire colony.[28]

The system of sex-role differentiation and family control over sexuality practiced in England also broke down. Since women were so scarce and laborsaving devices unavailable, women performed roughly the same tasks as men and sometimes worked in the fields with other servants or their husbands. Women possessed more sexual freedom than their English sisters, but they were also more likely to be pressured to submit to male sexual demands. Couples had to decide to have sexual relations outside marriage or to marry on their own; they often could not seek parental consent for marriage, because their parents were either in England or had already died. Freed from familial constraints in a society where many men sought sexual outlets, immigrant women sometimes submitted, willingly or unwillingly, to male blandishments. Close to a tenth of the births in Somerset County, Maryland, occurred out of wedlock, and nearly all women involved were still servants who could not marry. More than a third of immigrant women in that county, moreover, were pregnant when they wed. Sexual pressure on native-born women, who often married while in their mid-teens, must have been equally great. Even though these women wed at very young ages, a fifth of them were pregnant on the day they married.[29]

The Great Transformation: From Servants to Slaves

The dominance of small planters in Chesapeake society began to disintegrate in the 1680s because the economic base that had supported their ascendancy crumbled. Ordinary planters had relied upon the labor of servants and freedmen to increase their income, but fewer servants came to the region in the 1680s and 1690s, and the servant trade nearly disappeared after 1700. Ex-servants had accumulated capital to set up their own farms when tobacco prices were high, but planters often made no profit in the decades between 1680 and 1720, and the rate of social mobility therefore greatly diminished.

28. Morgan, *American Slavery, American Freedom*, chaps. 11–13; Bailyn, "Politics and Social Structure," in Smith, ed., *Seventeenth-Century America*, 93–99; Rutman and Rutman, *A Place in Time*, 79–93; Lois Green Carr, "Sources of Political Stability and Upheaval in Seventeenth-Century Maryland," *MHM*, LXXIX (1984), 44–70.
29. Carr and Walsh, "Planter's Wife," *WMQ*, 3d Ser., XXXIV (1977), 543–571; Menard and Walsh, "Demography of Somerset County," *Newberry Papers*, 81-2 (1981), 23–24, 34–35.

The decline of the servant trade transformed the labor system of the region in two ways. It forced planters to substitute African slaves for white servants, and it permitted the whole white population to reproduce itself. Planters sought to retain a white labor force, but they eventually replaced indentured servants with black slaves, and by 1700 slaves produced much of the region's tobacco. As the number of servants and other white immigrants declined and the children of earlier immigrants reached maturity, the proportion of native-born whites in the population rose. Native whites married at young ages and had enough children to ensure a naturally increasing population.

The transformation of the Chesapeake labor force from one dominated by immigrant planters and white servants to one operated by planters and their black slaves revolutionized the social relations of production. Political conflict between groups of whites diminished because there were fewer servants and ex-servants in the population, and even poor whites sought to become slaveholders and thereby exploit the labor of people they considered inferior. At the same time, however, the probability that poorer whites would advance economically decreased because they did not have sufficient capital to purchase a slave. By the early eighteenth century, an indigenous group of slaveholders who inherited wealth and place had replaced the relatively egalitarian social order of mid-seventeenth-century society with a hierarchical society.[30]

The adoption of slave labor resulted from a series of related economic and demographic events that stretched from the 1660s through the early decades of the eighteenth century. A decline in English birthrates during the second third of the seventeenth century, combined with rising real wages, had by the 1680s substantially reduced the number of men at risk to come to the New World. The new colonies of Pennsylvania and South Carolina, moreover, offered enticing opportunities. To attract their share of this diminished group of migrants, the Chesapeake colonies needed to offer opportunities for advancement that could compete with these new settlements.[31]

But severe depression in the tobacco economy at the end of the seventeenth century decreased relative opportunities in the Chesapeake colonies. Prices for the plant dipped below a penny a pound during the 1680s and

30. These themes are brilliantly evoked in Morgan, *American Slavery, American Freedom*, chaps. 14–17, but this section relies heavily upon the pioneering essay of Russell R. Menard, "From Servants to Slaves: The Transformation of the Chesapeake Labor System," *Southern Studies*, XVI (1977), 355–390.

31. Wrigley and Schofield, *Population History*, 179–187, 219–221, 402–412, 417–421, 531–532, 642–643; Menard, "British Migration," 14–18, table 6; Gemery, "Emigration from the British Isles," *Res. Econ. Hist.*, V (1980), 215.

stayed nearly that low during most years until 1715. Unable to absorb declining prices by increased output per hand, planters could not make a profit until markets improved. Since Europeans were unwilling to increase their consumption of tobacco even at these low prices and frequent wars raised the consumer's cost far above farm prices, exports did not rise. These conditions did not bode well for immigrants, who frequently decided they had better chances elsewhere. The proportion of British immigrants who came to the Chesapeake colonies, in fact, declined from a high of over two-fifths in the 1670s to just over a third by the 1690s.[32]

Chesapeake planters, however, still wanted servants, and some of them still had capital to purchase labor. The long depression hit some planters more severely than others. Farmers who grew tobacco on marginal land found they could no longer compete and substituted grains and livestock farming for tobacco. But planters who lived on more fertile lands, especially those who moved to new frontiers, often succeeded in improving their condition despite the general depression. These relatively prosperous families, unlike less fortunate farmers, could afford to buy servants.[33]

These Chesapeake planters failed to entice a sufficient number of Englishmen to meet their needs by coming to their depressed region. From 1680 to 1699 only about thirty thousand whites migrated to Maryland and Virginia, about four-fifths the rate of the previous three decades. Since the number of households had greatly increased, the number of white laborers that planters could command drastically declined. The number of servants and bachelors per household head in Middlesex County, Virginia, plummeted from five in 1668 to just one by 1687. There were two servants for each household in York County in the 1660s, fewer than two servants for every ten plantations by the 1690s, and during the same years the number of servants available to southern Maryland planters declined from six to fewer than two for every four households.[34]

Immigrant servants worked on tobacco plantations during their term,

32. Menard, "British Migration," table 6; Menard, "The Tobacco Industry," *Res. Econ. Hist.*, V (1980), 136–142, 114–115, 150–155, 159–161.

33. P.M.G. Harris, "Integrating Interpretations of Local and Regionwide Change in the Study of Economic Development and Demographic Growth in the Colonial Chesapeake, 1630–1775," *Working Papers from the Regional Economic History Center*, I, No. 3 (1978), *Economic Change in the Chesapeake Colonies*, 35–71. Harris insists that time of settlement, rather than the tobacco market, determined local economic behavior.

34. Migration estimates found in Menard, "British Migration," table 6; Craven, *White, Red, and Black*, 16–17; and Terry L. Anderson and Robert Paul Thomas, "The Growth of Population and Labor Force in the Seventeenth-Century Chesapeake," *Explorations in Economic History*, XV (1978), 296–298. For number of servants per household, see Rutman and Rutman, "'More True and Perfect Lists,'" *VMHB*, LXXXVIII (1980), 59; and Menard, "From Servants to Slaves," *So. Stud.*, XVI (1977), 368–369.

but many of them left the region after they were freed, and others estab-lished households and competed for scarce white labor themselves. About half the men who finished a term of service in Charles County, Maryland, during the 1690s left the county in search of employment, and more than three-quarters of those who stayed lived precariously as laborers or tenants. In total, only nine thousand migrants stayed in the Chesapeake colonies during the 1680s, and more people left the area than migrated to it during the 1690s.[35]

The decline of the servant trade transformed the labor force of the Chesapeake region. Planters preferred to employ English-speaking white servants rather than foreign whites or black slaves, but as the Chesapeake population rose and the number of men desiring white labor increased, they employed more and more alien workers. When the relative supply of ser-vants began to decline in the 1670s and 1680s and they could no longer procure white English men, they turned first to English women, and when the supply of English women ran low, they purchased Irish men.[36]

Once planters had exhausted the supply of white laborers, they turned reluctantly to African slaves. The slave trade to the Chesapeake colonies began slowly in the third quarter of the seventeenth century. In 1660 no more than seventeen hundred blacks lived in Maryland and Virginia, and by 1680 their numbers had increased to about four thousand. During the 1660s and 1670s most forced black migrants arrived in small groups from the West Indies, but about three thousand black people, including many Africans, were forced into slavery in the region between 1674 and 1695. Since the supply of servants had declined, these few blacks made up an ever-increasing proportion of unfree workers in the region in the late 1670s and 1680s. Only during the second half of the 1690s—two decades after the servant trade began to diminish—did planters buy substantial numbers of black slaves. They enslaved about three thousand Africans, as many as had arrived in the previous twenty years, between 1695 and 1700.[37]

The racial composition of the Chesapeake labor force changed gradu-ally during the last third of the seventeenth century, but by 1700 most unfree laborers were black. The transition occurred first in the wealthy sweet-scented tobacco counties along the York River and then spread northward on the western shore of the bay to areas that produced less

35. Walsh, "Mobility, Persistence, and Opportunity," 11 and tables 2–4 (modifies earlier work cited above, n. 26); Galenson, *White Servitude*, 217.

36. Menard, "From Servants to Slaves," *So. Stud.*, XVI (1977), 380; Menard, "Economy and Society," 414–417.

37. Menard, "Servants to Slaves," *So. Stud.*, XVI (1977), 363–375; Craven, *White, Red, and Black*, 85–86; Anderson and Thomas, "Growth of Population," *Explor. Econ. Hist.*, XV (1978), 300–305.

profitable oronoco tobaccos. Only a third of the unfree workers on plantations in York County were black during the 1670s, but the reduction in the number of servants available to county planters in the 1680s led them to procure nearly all the Africans who came into the region. As a result, four-fifths of the unfree workers on York plantations were black by the 1680s, and slaves accounted for nineteen of every twenty unfree laborers in the county during the 1690s. Planters who lived in Middlesex County, Virginia, which grew sweet-scented tobacco but was settled after York, and those who resided on Maryland's lower Western Shore, a poorer oronoco area, began to invest in slave labor a few years later. Only one in three unfree workers in these two areas was black in the 1680s, despite the declining number of servants available to planters. Nonetheless, from two-thirds to three-quarters of all unfree workers were slaves by the 1690s and early 1700s.[38]

Although planters clung to their preference for white servants over slaves for much of the late seventeenth century, they became reconciled, and even enthusiastic, about black labor by the early eighteenth century. When the supply of servants began to diminish during the 1670s and 1680s, the price of white men increased, both absolutely and relative to the price of full field hands. Planters in southern Maryland could buy three white men for the price of a single prime-age black male field hand in the early 1670s, but the same slave was worth only two servants by the end of the decade. This pattern strongly suggests that planters wanted servants more than slaves, for if they had believed that slaves were more profitable, the relative price of servants would have diminished. The ratio of servant to slave prices rose, however, over the 1690s and early 1700s and again reached nearly three servants per slave by the 1710s, despite the near-total disappearance of servants. By that time, planters had learned that slaves could be as productive as whites and sought them avidly every time a slave ship arrived.[39]

The decline of white servitude and the adoption of slavery transformed the family economy of white farmers. A short review of the argument suggests how slavery and family economy were linked. For most of the seven-

38. Menard, "Servants to Slaves," *So. Stud.*, XVI (1977), 368–369; Rutman and Rutman, " 'More True and Perfect Lists,' " *VMHB*, LXXXVIII (1980), 58. P.M.G. Harris argues for earlier timing of this transition in some older counties in "The Spread of Slavery in the Chesapeake, 1630–1775" (paper presented at the Third Hall of Records Conference on Maryland History, "Maryland, a Product of Two Worlds," May 1984).
39. Menard, "Servants to Slaves," *So. Stud.*, XVI (1977), 371–375. Harris's paper, "Spread of Slavery," argues that demographic forces, independent of economic change, led to this transformation.

teenth century, planters began their Chesapeake careers as servants and established households and bought land and their own servants after the completion of their term. As the number of immigrants declined, the proportion of native-born adults in the white population rose. These natives, unlike their immigrant parents, began adulthood unemcumbered by indentured service and often received inheritances from their parents. They therefore married at a young age and accumulated property more rapidly than did their immigrant forebears.

These changes in the economic prospects of white families could not occur until the white population *as a whole* had achieved natural increase, and natural increase could not begin until native-born men and women dominated the adult population of the region. The number of native-born adults apparently surpassed the number of immigrants sometime in the 1690s in most of the Chesapeake region. In Charles County, Maryland, the proportion of native-born white men rose from about a third in 1690 to three-fifths in 1705; and a similar pattern could be found in Middlesex County, where about three-quarters of the entire white population (adults and children) in 1699 had been born in the county.[40]

The increase in the proportion of native-born white adults accentuated the importance of the daughters of immigrants in determining the rate of population growth. These native women had larger families because they married, on average, before age twenty, or eight years younger than their mothers' generation. Despite these youthful marriages, native-born women were still likely to bear only two more children in their lifetime than immigrants did because only half of them lived through their childbearing years. Many of their children died before they reached adulthood. Still, the early marriages of first-generation women did lead to substantial natural increase, and rather than children replacing only three-fifths of the population, as had been the case with immigrants, the native-born women reproduced more than sufficiently to replace their parents (table 1).[41]

In the 1690s and 1700s, a large group of native-born women began bearing children, and these births (combined with the growing percentage of native adults) finally tipped the balance from natural decline to natural increase in much of the region. The earlier an area had been settled, the earlier this baby boom appeared: it began by the early 1690s in York County, Virginia, which had been settled in the 1620s; in southern Maryland, where settlement started in the 1640s, the boom began in the late

40. Walsh, "Mobility, Persistence, and Opportunity," table 1; Rutman and Rutman, " 'More True and Perfect Lists,' " *VMHB*, LXXXVIII (1980), 63, 66.
41. See studies cited in n. 23, above.

1690s; and on the Eastern Shore, settled after 1660, the boom began in the early 1700s. There was no surge of births in Middlesex County, where falciparum malaria, the most deadly form of the disease, hit with particular virulence in the 1680s and 1690s, but even there the number of births nearly equaled the number of deaths.[42]

Planter adoption of slave labor and white natural increase together created new social relations of production on Chesapeake tobacco farms. Even if seventeenth-century planters believed that the white servants and hired hands they employed were poor men who deserved little respect, they knew that many of them would eventually become independent tobacco farmers themselves and therefore kept discipline within tight bounds. Two kinds of plantations replaced these master-servant enterprises once slavery was established. The vast majority of planters owned family farms and commanded the labor of their children, a slave or two, and an occasional white hired hand. A minority of white men, who owned the preponderance of slaves, operated large enterprises with many slaves. They hired white youths from nearby smaller plantations to act as overseers and instructed them to discipline slaves harshly if they dared to overstep the bounds of white authority.

Although most white freedmen enjoyed similar opportunities for much of the seventeenth century, subject only to the vagaries of the economy, the great costs that slaves entailed placed a premium on inheritance as a means of wealth accumulation. Native-born children of substantial planters enjoyed a great advantage over all other whites, for they could count upon receiving numerous slaves on their marriage or on the death of their fathers. Poorer men, in contrast, had to build upon small investments and received little or no help from parents.

---

42. Menard, "Immigrants and Their Increase," in Land *et al.*, eds., *Law, Society, and Politics*, 88–110, but esp. 90–92, 100–103; Smith, "Mortality and Family," *Jour. Interdisc. Hist.*, VIII (1977–1978), 408; Menard, "Economy and Society," 408–413; Rutman and Rutman, "Of Agues and Fevers," *WMQ*, 3d Ser., XXXIII (1976), 31–60; Rutman and Rutman, " 'More True and Perfect Lists,' " *VMHB*, LXXXVIII (1980), 61–65; Anderson and Thomas, "Growth of Population," *Explor. Econ. Hist.*, XV (1978), 290–312; P.M.G. Harris, "Settling the Chesapeake: The Growth, Spread, and Stabilization of the European Population" (paper presented to the Philadelphia Center for Early American Studies, Nov. 1983), 15–26. The Rutmans see little improvement in the late seventeenth century; Anderson and Thomas argue for natural increase by the 1670s; Harris suggests that a similar rise of natural increase occurred everywhere, but at different times, starting in the mid-seventeenth century. Despite these challenges to Menard's model, I still find his general argument (but perhaps not his timing) persuasive. See Russell R. Menard, "The Growth of Population in the Chesapeake Colonies: A Comment," *Explor. Econ. Hist.*, XVIII (1981), 399–410; and Menard and Walsh, "Demography of Somerset," *Newberry Papers*, 81-2 (1981), n. 10.

The Legacy of the Seventeenth Century

The social order of the seventeenth century had a very ambiguous impact upon Chesapeake developments in the eighteenth century. The openness, opportunities, and freedom white men enjoyed during the middle decades of the century never returned, even in frontier areas, and the homogeneity of the population was forever severed after Africans poured into the region in the 1690s. Conflict among whites eventually diminished as most whites scrambled to procure as many slaves as they could and as they relied on one another to ensure the security of their property. Eighteenth-century social relations of production developed from the slave labor system: a class and caste society, where the ownership of slaves determined the standing of whites and where black people were a subservient class of slaves, replaced the conflict-ridden free white labor system.

Nonetheless, the social ideals of the founders of the colonies reappeared in the context of slavery. Planters adapted to their slaves the negative imagery English gentlemen used to describe poor whites, and they embellished that rhetoric with racist ideas. Chesapeake gentlemen, moreover, imposed patriarchal family structures upon their wives and children and demanded deference from yeomen and poor whites. The hierarchical social order the Virginia Company and the Calverts wanted to establish developed, ironically, within an alien system of slavery they could not have foreseen.

2
Land and Labor in the Household Economy, 1680–1800

English colonial authorities supported rapid population growth in the Chesapeake colonies, for they knew a growing population there would make more tobacco that could be charged royal tobacco duties. In 1730, the Board of Trade, which regulated colonial exports, asked Gov. William Gooch of Virginia how rapidly the colony's population was growing. He replied, "The number of the Inhabitants are greatly increased within these last ten years," and he connected that growth to the slave trade and to the colony's natural resources. "The great numbers of Negroes and white Servants imported since the year 1720," he commented, "together with the early Marriages of the Youth, prolifick Temperment of Women both White and Black, must necessarily Occasion a great Increase of People in a Country . . . where Nature has been bountifull as to furnish the conveniences of Life with less Labour and Anxiety than in many Places in the World."[1]

Both population growth and the rise of tobacco production rested upon the creation of new plantation households, a process increasingly tied to the availability of land. During most of the seventeenth century, the price of tobacco and English economic conditions determined the rate of household formation. Immigrants, who started most new households, tended to come to the region when times were good in the Chesapeake or depressed in England. The increase in the percentage of native white adults at the end of the seventeenth century reduced the direct impact of the tobacco trade and increased the significance of land availability for household formation. Native-born men formed households when they gained access to enough land to support themselves and their families. The quantity of land available for use rested upon the total number of laborers who "worked in the ground," because planters had to hold large quantities of land in reserve for each person they hired or owned. As long as vast amounts of land were open to settlement, land was cheap and household formation easily accomplished. Both the slave trade and the high rate of white natural increase, however, served to reduce the ratio of land to labor in older areas and thus make land more expensive and household formation more difficult.[2]

1. William Gooch to Board of Trade, 23 July 1730, C.O. 1322/5, 68–74/5, Public Record Office (P.R.O.), London (Colonial Williamsburg Research Department transcripts [CW]).
2. See chap. 1 for 17th-century developments.

The age of marriage of white women determined both the rate of natural increase and the ultimate rate of household formation. Each new household reduced the quantity of land open for exploitation, and this reduction in land availability in turn helped determine the typical age at marriage. As each new area was first peopled by white families and their slaves, a long demographic swing began. At first, men and women married at young ages to take advantage of abundant uncultivated acres. Pioneer women bore many children, and most of them reached adulthood and began their own households. But by this time much of the good tobacco land had already been cultivated, and this relative scarcity of land led men and women to postpone marriage, thereby cutting the size of families and reducing the number of new households in the third generation. At the same time, children from poor families—who were unable to gain access to land no matter how long they waited—moved to new frontier areas. On these new frontiers, the demographic swing repeated itself.[3]

The way tobacco was cultivated promoted land scarcity. All planters sought to employ slave workers to help produce more tobacco and thereby increase their income. But tobacco consumed land voraciously, and each additional laborer increased a planter's land requirements. Thus the more labor that a given household put on the land, the less was the acreage remaining open for cultivation. And to the same degree, the poorer folk postponed marriage and moved more rapidly to the frontier.

The quantity of labor available to householders depended upon the levels of growth of the working population. Both the white and black populations of the region grew vigorously by natural increase, but these similar population patterns had a markedly different impact upon household formation. Population pressure led whites to postpone marriage and, therefore, household formation, but masters encouraged slave women to bear as many children as they could. All of these slaves ultimately worked in the tobacco fields, thereby reducing the quantity of land available to new white households in settled areas and further raising marriage ages and slowing the rate of household formation.

This demographic regime characterized the Chesapeake region for most of the eighteenth century. Before mid-century, new land in much of tidewater disappeared, and the lack of land thus encouraged out-migration to the piedmont frontiers. By the 1790s or 1800s so much land had been taken up and so little remained, even in piedmont, that the entire system

---

3. Richard A. Easterlin developed this framework in "Population Change and Farm Settlement in the Northern United States," *Journal of Economic History*, XXXVI (1976), 45–75; but see also Darrett B. Rutman, "People in Process: The New Hampshire Towns of the Eighteenth Century," in Tamara K. Hareven, ed., *Family and Kin in Urban Communities, 1700–1930* (New York, 1977), 16–37.

collapsed. Not only did white youths universally postpone marriage, but when they did marry, large numbers of them left for frontier lands beyond the Allegheny mountains. Those who stayed behind on the tobacco coast relied upon inheritance to gain access to land or bought expensive acreage and cultivated less productive old fields rather than rich, new lands.

Tobacco, Land, and Household Formation

In 1775 the author of *American Husbandry* judiciously explained the reason Chesapeake tobacco planters needed vast quantities of land. "There is no plant in the world that requires richer land, or more manure than tobacco," he wrote. "It will grow on poorer fields," he added, "but not to yield crops that are sufficiently profitable to pay the expences of negroes." Planters therefore sought "fresh woodlands, where many ages have formed a stratum of rich black mould." "Such land will, after clearing, bear tobacco many years, without any change, prove more profitable to the planter than the power of dung can do on worse lands: this makes the tobacco planters more solicitous for new land than any other people in America, they wanting it much more."[4]

Tobacco planters systematically exploited thousands of square miles of land during the eighteenth century. They rotated fields rather than fertilizing their land or rotating crops on the same field. After they took up fresh land, they cleared a few acres of their holdings, planted tobacco on the parcel until the nutrients in the soil were exhausted, and then moved on to the next piece of land. Each old parcel lay fallow while new acres were cultivated, and eventually "old field pine" and new vegetation appeared on the land. This second growth told the planter that his land had recovered enough fertility to permit tobacco cultivation again. When planters had exhausted all their land in this manner, they either cleared and replanted old fields or moved to the frontier.[5]

Field rotation forced planters to hold large quantities of land in reserve. A white man or adult male slave could cultivate about three acres of tobacco, and the land could be planted with tobacco for three successive years. Then it had to lie undisturbed for twenty years. If a planter was to avoid exhausting his holdings, he had to own twenty acres for each worker he placed on the land. Planters needed additional land to grow corn, pas-

4. Harry J. Carman, ed., *American Husbandry* (1775), Columbia University Studies in the History of American Agriculture, No. 6 (New York, 1939), 164.
5. *Ibid.*, 163–166; Carville V. Earle, *The Evolution of a Tidewater Settlement System: All Hallow's Parish, Maryland, 1650–1783*, University of Chicago Department of Geography Research Paper 170 (Chicago, 1975), 24–30.

ture to graze livestock, and forests to construct and heat their homes, make fences, and build tobacco hogsheads. To meet these requirements, the writer of *American Husbandry* concluded, "a planter should have 50 acres of land for every working hand; with less than this they will find themselves distressed for want of room."[6]

Planters in tidewater ran out of good tobacco land during the first half of the eighteenth century. Much fertile acreage remained to be cultivated in tidewater Virginia in 1700, when there were about a hundred acres of land patented and taxed for each worker, double the current needs of planters. Between 1700 and 1770, the number of acres taxed in the region grew by half, but the working population more than doubled. As a result, there were only about sixty acres per worker in 1770, close to the minimum needed to continue the system of field rotation (see fig. 1). Population density reached even higher levels in southern Maryland, the prime tobacco-growing area of the colony, where there were only forty-nine acres for each worker to cultivate in 1782, less than the desirable minimum.[7]

Though field rotation prevented the total exhaustion of tidewater soil, the yield and quality of tobacco produced there declined over the eighteenth century. Old fields, despite the long period of lying fallow, did not regain their initial fertility and were less productive the second time they were cultivated. Furthermore, the most productive soil, found on bottomland located near rivers and streams, was in short supply; and after it had been fully exploited, planters had to turn to less productive acreage. All of these processes—the exhaustion of the soil, the recultivation of old fields, and the use of poor land—probably caused tobacco yields to decline by a sixth to a fourth in tidewater over the eighteenth century.[8]

6. Earle, *Tidewater Settlement System*, argues that 20 acres were needed per worker, but this figure includes only tobacco and does not consider other uses of land.

7. Maximum taxed acreage data from circa 1785 (proxy for total improvable acreage) adds land found in Land Tax Books, 1782–1785, Virginia State Library, Richmond (VSL), to 1770 acreages in Quitrent Returns, C.O. 1313–1353/5, and T. 90–503/1, P.R.O., collected by George Reese and on file at CW. Maryland data found in Allan Kulikoff, "Tobacco and Slaves: Population, Economy, and Society in Eighteenth-Century Prince George's County, Maryland" (Ph.D. diss., Brandeis University, 1976), 428–430, 469–471.

8. Earle, *Tidewater Settlement System*, 26–28, 97–99; Gregory A. Stiverson, "Landless Husbandmen: Tenants on the Maryland Proprietary Manors in the Eighteenth Century: An Economic Study" (Ph.D. diss., Johns Hopkins University, 1973), 94–98, 549–550, 555, 557; Peter J. Albert, "The Protean Institution: The Geography, Economy, and Ideology of Slavery in Post-Revolutionary Virginia" (Ph.D. diss., University of Maryland, 1976), 23–24; Darrett B. Rutman and Anita H. Rutman, *A Place in Time: Explicatus* (New York, 1984), 19–24. The question of "soil exhaustion" defies easy solution because so many variables (weather, soil quality, methods of cultivation) produce data on yields. The estimate of the impact of soil exhaustion here is a residual left after subtracting the influence of the Tobacco Inspection Act, considers evidence in early 19th-century gazetteers, and mediates between Earle's denial of

Fig. 1. *Population Density in Virginia South of the Rappahannock River,*
1702–1772

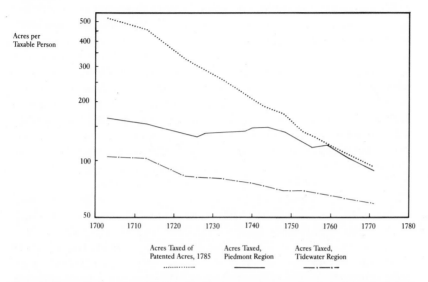

Acres Taxed of   Acres Taxed,   Acres Taxed,
Patented Acres, 1785   Piedmont Region   Tidewater Region

Sources: Evarts B. Greene and Virginia D. Harrington, *American Population before the Federal*
Census of 1790 (New York, 1932), 154–156; annual tithables collected from Virginia Court
Order Books, VSL; "A Statement of the Inspectors Accounts from Oct 1786 to Oct 1787,"
Auditor's Item No. 49, VSL; Quitrent Returns, C.O. 1313–1353/5, and T. 1/90–503, P.R.O.,
at CW.

Tidewater planters responded to the twin problems of falling relative
quantities of land and reduced yields on old fields by postponing marriage,
migrating to the frontier, or adopting more intensive farming techniques.
Although men in tidewater wed at very young ages when land was plentiful
early in the eighteenth century, they waited much longer by mid-century.
Some youths worked the same acres their ancestors had purchased, often
rejecting tobacco monoculture for a more diversified crop mix, but others,
when they had "exhausted their grounds," would "sell them to new settlers
for corn fields, and move backwards with their negroes, cattle, and tools, to
take up fresh land for tobacco."[9]
    In early modern societies, men married when they commanded the

---

soil exhaustion and Avery O. Craven's insistence on substantial exhaustion in *Soil Exhaustion as*
a Factor in the Agricultural History of Virginia and Maryland, 1606–1860 (Urbana, Ill., 1926),
chaps. 1, 2.
9. Carman, ed., *American Husbandry*, 164–165.

resources necessary to support a family.[10] Since men in tidewater rarely established households before they married and few married couples lived with their parents, the temporal pattern of male age at first marriage suggests how readily men could form households.[11] During the first half of the eighteenth century, when land was plentiful, men did not wait for an inheritance to marry, but received land from parents as a gift or purchased or rented cheap land almost as soon as they reached their majority. Young men born during the first quarter of the eighteenth century in tidewater married at remarkably young ages by European standards. Half of a sample of men born in Middlesex County, Virginia, between 1680 and 1719 married before age twenty-three or twenty-four. Young men born in Maryland during the same decades wed at even younger ages: three-quarters of a sample of men born in Prince George's and Anne Arundel counties married before age twenty-five, celebrating their nuptials at an average age of twenty-three. Men born in Stafford County, on the frontier of Virginia's Northern Neck, in the 1720s and 1730s married at ages as young as their neighbors across the Potomac River (see fig. 2).

As the ratio of land to labor declined in tidewater, fathers had less land to pass on to their sons, and men had to wait for an inheritance or travel great distances to buy unimproved acres. After frontier land in tidewater had disappeared, men postponed marriage to age twenty-seven or twenty-eight, on average, a pattern similar to that of thickly settled England. Only half the men born in southern Maryland in the 1720s and 1730s married before they reached twenty-five, and a sixth wed after their thirtieth birthday. These men, who took brides in the 1740s and 1750s, married at an average age of twenty-five. Similar rises in the age at first marriage occurred in Virginia. As population density rose, the male age at marriage continued to climb: a third of the men born in southern Maryland from 1740 to 1769 took wives after age thirty, and only a third married before twenty-five. While sons of middling planters married, on average, at twenty-seven, sons of poor tenants often waited another two years (fig. 2).[12]

10. J. Hajnal, "European Marriage Patterns in Perspective," in D. V. Glass and D.E.C. Eversley, *Population in History: Essays in Historical Demography* (London, 1965), 101–143; Charles Tilly, "The Historical Study of Vital Processes," in Tilly, ed., *Historical Studies of Changing Fertility* (Princeton, N.J., 1978), 3–55, esp. 35–38.

11. Only 4 of 660 nonhouseholders over age 16 lived in stem families in 1733 in Prince George's County. In 1776 in that county, 90% of all householders were married or widowed, 7% were unmarried, and 3% were sons who lived with their widowed mothers but were listed as heads ($N = 884$). At the same time, 80% of single men, age 20–29, did not head households, 7% headed households with their mothers, and 13% lived independently. Black Books, II, 109–114, Maryland Hall of Records, Annapolis (MHR); Gaius Marcus Brumbaugh, ed., *Maryland Records: Colonial, Revolutionary, County, and Church, from Original Sources*, I (Baltimore, 1915), 1–88; Kulikoff, "Tobacco and Slaves," 129–130.

12. Kulikoff, "Tobacco and Slaves," 35–36; E. A. Wrigley and R. S. Schofield, *The Population*

Fig. 2. *Male Age at First Marriage in Tidewater Maryland and Virginia,*
1680–1800

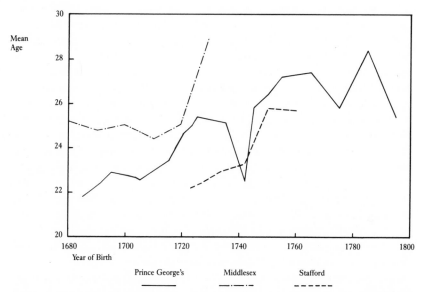

Sources: Maryland data calculated from vital registers and genealogies (see Allan Kuli-
koff, "Tobacco and Slaves: Population, Economy, and Society in Eighteenth-Century Prince
George's County, Maryland" [Ph.D. diss., Brandeis University, 1976], 35–36, 435–438);
Middlesex data from Darrett B. Rutman and Anita H. Rutman, *A Place in Time: Explicatus*
(New York, 1984), 65; Stafford data from Karla MacKesson, "Growth in a Frontier Society:
Population Increase in the Northern Neck of Virginia" (master's thesis, College of William and
Mary, 1976), 45. The Stafford series was changed from marriage to birth cohorts.

 The dowries or inheritances women received at marriage or their majority (usually defined as age sixteen) complemented property their grooms
accumulated. Assets inherited by the daughters of immigrants (who still
died young) early in the eighteenth century, in particular, encouraged men
as well as women to marry at young ages. As long as land remained plentiful, a girl often received a portion of her father's holdings, which the couple
might farm or sell, to add to the husband's estate. But once frontier land
disappeared and the number of acres a landowner held diminished, fathers
reserved all their land for sons. At the same time, male life expectancy rose,

History of England, 1541–1871: A Reconstruction (Cambridge, Mass., 1981), 255–257, 423–424.
Brumbaugh, ed., *Maryland Records*, I, 1–88, gives census data on age and marital status for men
in the poorer half of Prince George's in 1776. The singulate mean age at marriage of men
under 50, calculated from these data, was 28.6, 2.9 years higher than the birth cohorts from
1727 to 1756 in the linked marriage data.

and most daughters probably received only a few movables, like livestock and perhaps a slave, as dowry. Young men could no longer rely on their brides for land (or access to it), and that fact accelerated the trend toward later male marriages.[13]

Even though many tidewater youths migrated to the frontier and others postponed marriage, too little land remained in counties settled early in the seventeenth century for planters who stayed to grow tobacco on as their ancestors had done. Land scarcity was especially acute in six Virginia counties located between the York and the James rivers. There were only forty-five acres in the area for each taxable in 1770, and few additional laborers began to work the land in the 1770s and 1780s. Planters in this region dropped tobacco and took up grain farming and herding after the Revolution. Families in Elizabeth City County, a thickly settled area with only twenty-nine acres per worker in 1770, adopted grain and livestock farming to supply the West Indian provisioning trade before the Revolution, and most farmers in adjacent counties followed their lead after the war.[14]

Tidewater planters could, of course, avoid the consequences of diminished land supply by moving to the frontier. Thousands of planters left tidewater for piedmont with their families and slaves during the middle half of the eighteenth century. The peopling of the James River basin in piedmont Virginia suggests that the desire to produce tobacco motivated migration. In 1700 this 13,000-square-mile area was nearly uninhabited by Europeans and their slaves: about five thousand people lived on 550 square miles of taxed land located on the banks of the river. Between 1700 and 1770, the working population of the region multiplied twenty-nine times, and the number of taxed acres rose sixteen times. Planters came to the area to grow tobacco, and as soon as they had cleared land and built roads, they began exporting it. Tobacco exports from the Upper James Naval District (coterminous with the region defined here) rose from about five million pounds in the mid-1730s to about thirty million pounds in the early 1770s, a rate that approximated the growth of taxable population. Farmers did not rely on the export of corn and wheat, even though they exported more than families in other tobacco-growing areas. The export of grain fluctuated widely and did not sustain steady growth until the 1760s, when demand for that product in Europe skyrocketed (see fig. 3).

13. See below, chap. 5, and Lois Green Carr and Lorena S. Walsh, "Women's Role in the Eighteenth-Century Chesapeake" (paper presented at the Colonial Williamsburg Conference on Colonial Women, Oct. 1981), esp. table 3.
14. For sources of data, see n. 7; Sarah S. Hughes, "Elizabeth City County, Virginia, 1782–1810: The Economic and Social Structure of a Tidewater County in the Early National Years" (Ph.D. diss., College of William and Mary, 1975), chaps. 1, 6–8; Albert, "Protean Institution," chap. 1.

Fig. 3. *Settlement and Tobacco Output in the James River Basin*

Tobacco (lbs. × 1,000)	Taxable Population	Land (acres × 100)	Grain (bu. × 100)

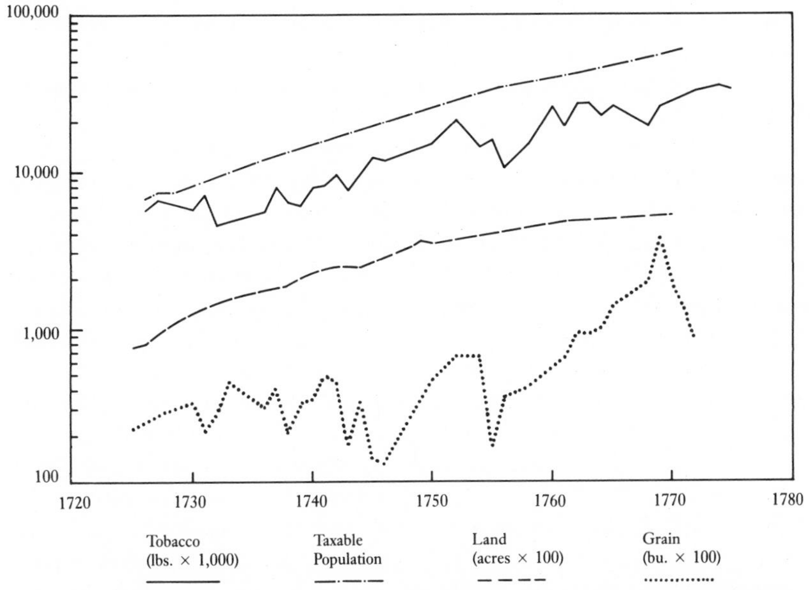

Sources: Tithable records (Evarts B. Greene and Virginia D. Harrington, *American Population before the Federal Census of 1790* [New York, 1932], 154–156; annual tithables collected from Virginia Court Order Books, VSL) for southside (Prince George and successor counties) and central Virginia (Henrico, Hanover, and successor counties); tobacco and grain exports from Upper James Naval District, C.O. 1442–1449/5, and Customs 16, 1, P.R.O. (CW), and James H. Soltow, *The Economic Role of Williamsburg* (Williamsburg, Va., 1965), table 3, following 122; and Quitrent Returns, C.O. 1313–1353/5 and T. 1/90–503, P.R.O.

During the second quarter of the eighteenth century, householders and speculators patented and paid taxes on sufficient acres in the James River basin to ensure homesteads for the current and the next generation: from 1720 to 1750, there were about 130 acres of land taxed for each adult working in the region. Nonetheless, even the vast reaches of piedmont Virginia were not limitless, and population density increased after 1750, with the number of taxed acres per worker declining to 100 in 1760 and 80 by the early 1780s. Counties settled before mid-century were nearly full by the Revolution. In Amelia and Lunenburg counties, first settled by planters in the 1730s and 1740s, the number of acres per worker declined from 87 in 1770 to 73 by 1787. Little space remained for new tobacco farms except in the hilly country at the western edge of piedmont, far from transportation. Half a million acres were patented in Pittsylvania County, located in the southwest corner of the region, in the 1770s and 1780s, and that county's population doubled during the same period. Migrants could create new plantations from the wilderness only in Pittsylvania, where there were still more than 150 acres for each worker in the county in 1787.[15]

Chesapeake planters searched for new land to grow tobacco on throughout the eighteenth century, and by the Revolution they had depleted much of the soil from the shores of the Chesapeake Bay to the mountains. The vast pool of nearly five hundred acres of land available to each worker south of the Rappahannock River in 1700 diminished rapidly over the century, becoming fewer than two hundred by 1740 and fewer than one hundred by 1770. As soon as the region's population doubled, an event that would take just a quarter of a century at the current rates of population growth, there would be fewer than the fifty acres each worker needed for growing tobacco using the method of field rotation, and planters would have to leave the area in large numbers or adopt more intensive agricultural techniques (fig. 1).

Demographic Determinants of Household Formation

Household formation, female fertility, and population growth were intimately connected in the Chesapeake region during the eighteenth century. Population grew almost exclusively from natural increase; only thirty-five thousand white immigrants landed in the region between 1718 and 1775, and they were lost in an ocean of native whites.[16] Since men habitually married women about five years younger than themselves, female age at first marriage followed a pattern similar to that of men.[17] As long as land remained plentiful, white women typically wed during their late teens and early twenties. These women bore many children, who in turn clamored for land when they matured. By mid-century, these high rates of natural increase were already creating population pressure on resources in tidewater. As a consequence of land scarcity, women began to postpone marriage until

15. Fig. 3. The increase in land taxed in Pittsylvania is estimated from incomplete 1770 Quit-rent Returns and 1782 Land Tax Books for Henry and Pittsylvania counties, VSL.

16. Abbot Emerson Smith, *Colonists in Bondage: White Servitude and Convict Labor in America, 1607–1776* (Chapel Hill, N.C., 1947), 117–120, 310, 324–332; C.O. 1442–1446/5, P.R.O.; David W. Galenson, *White Servitude in Colonial America: An Economic Analysis* (Cambridge, 1981), 220–227; Kulikoff, "Tobacco and Slaves," 92–93.

17. Age difference between spouses in southern Maryland calculated from age cohort data (Kulikoff, "Tobacco and Slaves," 437–438) shows a mean age difference of 4.6 years (standard deviation = 1.6 years), while the intercept of a regression of male on female ages was 4.5 years and the slope only .01 years.

their early and middle twenties. Later marriage reduced the rate of population growth in three ways: it reduced the number of years married women were at risk to have children, it concentrated childbearing in the less fertile years from thirty to forty, and it decreased the number of new households (and children) formed in the next generation.

During the late seventeenth and early eighteenth centuries, when land was plentiful, women throughout tidewater married in their late teens, but this age rose slowly to 20 when land supplies began to diminish. By the second half of the century, the age when women first married was 22; and at the time of the Revolution, it may have been as high as 23.5. The timing of this progression depended upon the first settlement of a place. Although the process was nearly complete by the early eighteenth century in Middlesex County, Virginia, a small county first populated in the 1650s, it took another half-century in southern Maryland, the Northern Neck, and the Eastern Shore, all larger areas with substantial frontiers during the first third of the eighteenth century (see fig. 4).[18]

A closer examination of the age of marriage in southern Maryland reveals more precisely the dimensions of the change. Three-quarters of the women born from 1680 to 1720 married in their teens, and the rest wed by their early twenties. As the frontier receded to the west during the 1730s and 1740s, women increasingly married between ages twenty and twenty-four: fewer than half the women born in the 1720s and 1730s wed before age twenty, a third wed between ages twenty and twenty-four, and the rest between twenty-five and thirty.[19]

The availability of land, rather than the ratio of men to women, determined when women first married in Maryland during the first half of the eighteenth century. Although marriages of girls under seventeen nearly disappeared when immigration declined and the number of women began to rise proportionately at the end of the seventeenth century, most women continued to marry before their twentieth birthday even after the adult sex ratio had declined from 157 men per hundred women in 1704 to 122 in 1712. The first cohort of women to marry mostly past age twenty was born in the 1730s, but by the time these women wed in the 1750s and 1760s, the number of free men and women had been nearly equal for several decades.[20]

---

18. See also, for the Eastern Shore, Russell R. Menard and Lorena S. Walsh, "The Demography of Somerset County, Maryland: A Progress Report," *Newberry Papers in Family and Community History*, 81-2 (1981), 33. The singulate mean age at marriage for women born in the poorest half of Prince George's in 1776 (age 15 to 43) was 23.6. See Brumbaugh, ed., *Maryland Records*, I, 1–88.

19. Kulikoff, "Tobacco and Slaves," 35, 436–437.

20. Russell R. Menard, "Economy and Society in Early Colonial Maryland" (Ph.D. diss.,

Fig. 4. *Female Age at First Marriage in Tidewater Maryland and Virginia,*
1680–1800

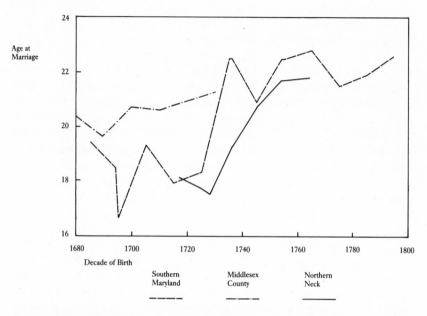

Sources: Allan Kulikoff, "Tobacco and Slaves: Population, Economy, and Society in Eigh-
teenth-Century Prince George's County, Maryland" (Ph.D. diss., Brandeis University, 1976),
35–36, 435–438, for Maryland; Darrett B. Rutman and Anita H. Rutman, *A Place in Time:*
Explicatus (New York, 1984), 65, for Middlesex; Karla MacKesson, "Growth in a Frontier
Society: Population Increase in the Northern Neck of Virginia" (master's thesis, College of
William and Mary, 1976), 45, for Stafford (changed from marriage to birth cohorts).

As frontier land disappeared from southern Maryland and adjacent
areas by the 1750s, the age at which women first married continued to rise.
More than three-quarters of the women born between 1740 and 1769 postponed marriage until at least their early twenties, and three-tenths of this
group wed after age twenty-five. Daughters of poor men, who had particular difficulty finding husbands, married two years later, on average, than
daughters of other planters. The dowries poorer women commanded attracted few suitors, and men of low economic status, who would be their
likely mates, tended to move to the frontier or required more years than
sons of wealthier men to amass enough capital to set up a household.[21]

University of Iowa, 1975), 402–409; "Number of Inhabitants in Maryland," *Gentleman's Maga-*
zine, and Historical Chronicle, XXXIV (1764), 261.
21. The low sex ratio for ages 20–29 (93) found in the 1776 Prince George's census (Brum-

Despite increasing population pressure on tidewater land during the second half of the eighteenth century, planters still sought young brides, and women married two or three years before their contemporaries in England. Tidewater women continued to marry in their early twenties for two major reasons. First, in the Chesapeake, families could still find some inexpensive frontier land. Nicholas Cresswell, a British visitor to the Chesapeake in the 1770s, argued that this abundance explained the early marriages of women in the region. Planters, he wrote, gained "a sufficiency to maintain and provide for a family" much sooner than Englishmen, and any white Virginian "with the least spark of industry . . . may support a family of young children." Second, a cultural norm of early marriage developed in the region that both reflected demographic conditions and perpetuated them. In 1728, William Byrd II half-facetiously called his twenty-year-old daughter Evelyn "one of the most antick virgins" he knew. Nearly half a century later an essayist in the *Virginia Gazette* contended that "the advantages of early marriage, both to the community and to particulars," were great, for early marriage allowed couples to spend more years in the happy state of matrimony with its mutual affection and obligation.[22]

Marital fertilty in tidewater remained high throughout the century, despite the diminished supply of land. Once women married, they gave birth about every thirty months during their twenties and early thirties and continued to bear children until menopause. Women who married in Prince George's in their late teens between 1680 and 1775 and lived through menopause with their first husband gave birth on average to ten or eleven children, roughly the same level of fertility achieved by women in Somerset County during the second half of the seventeenth century (see fig. 5). These levels of fertility were very high by historical standards, and more than a third above those recorded for eighteenth-century England.[23]

The female age at marriage was the most important mechanism in the

---

baugh, ed., *Maryland Records*, I, 1–88) suggests that more men than women migrated. I am indebted to John Modell for age distributions from these data.

22. *The Journal of Nicholas Cresswell, 1774–1777* (New York, 1924), 271; Byrd to Charles Boyle, Feb. 5, 1728, in Marion Tinling, ed., *The Correspondence of the Three William Byrds of Westover, Virginia, 1684–1776* (Charlottesville, Va., 1977), I, 370; Rind's *Virginia Gazette*, Feb. 4, 1773.

23. Wrigley and Schofield, *Population History*, 253–255; Ansley J. Coale, "Factors Associated with the Development of Low Fertility: An Historic Survey," in United Nations, Department of Economic and Social Affairs, *Proceedings of the World Population Conference: Belgrade . . .* (New York, 1967), II, 205–209, has devised an index of marital fertility (I_g) to compare the fertility of Hutterite women, who have the highest recorded fertility levels, to other populations. This scale, which runs from 0 to 1, was .77 for Somerset women, 1650–1695; .87 for Prince George's women, 1680–1720; and .81 for Prince George's, 1730–1775. All these rates indicate a regime of natural (noncontraceptive) fertility.

Fig. 5. *Age-Specific Fertility of White Women in Maryland, 1650–1775.* Data plotted at midpoint of cohorts. Hutterites represent maximum fertility in noncontraceptive populations.

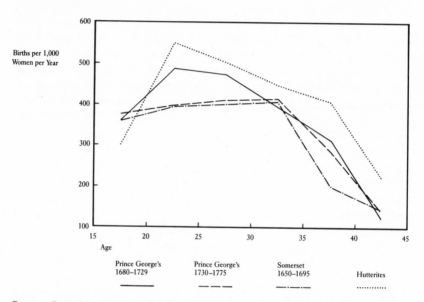

Prince George's 1680–1729	Prince George's 1730–1775	Somerset 1650–1695	Hutterites

Sources: Russell R. Menard and Lorena S. Walsh, "The Demography of Somerset County, Maryland: A Progress Report," *Newberry Papers in Family and Community History*, 81-2 (1981), 36; Louise J. Hienton, comp., "Index to Parish Register, 1689–1801, of Piscataway Parish, Prince George's County, Maryland," typescript (1961), MHR; and Helen W. Brown, comp., "Index to Register of Queen Anne Parish, 1686–1777," typescript, MHR; Harry Wright Newman, *Mareen Duvall of Middle Plantation* . . . (Washington, D.C., 1952); Gaius Marcus Brumbaugh, ed., *Maryland Records: Colonial, Revolutionary, County, and Church, from Original Sources,* I (Baltimore, 1915), 1–88.

determination of family size in tidewater. As the age at marriage rose, the size of families declined for women who completed their childbearing years married to their first husband. The decrease is particularly noticeable in Prince George's. Although the level of marital fertility declined 7 percent after 1750 because childbearing among women in their twenties apparently fell (fig. 5), the actual size of families of women who lived through their childbearing years fell 23 percent, from 9.0 to 6.9 children.[24]

24. This paragraph is based upon a comparison of completed family size (from table 2) in Maryland with the total fertility rate (number of children a woman would bear by age 45 who married at 15) in Prince George's, which fell from 10.8 (1680–1720) to 10.1 (1730–1775). See fig. 6 for sources for total fertility rate, and Kulikoff, "Tobacco and Slaves," 435–437, for sources for completed family size.

Though teenage marriages and high fertility diminished after 1750 in tidewater, women in frontier piedmont areas apparently married in their late teens and gave birth to numerous children. The ratio of children under ten for each woman between sixteen and forty-five in 1800, one measure of fertility, shows large differences between frontier and settled counties. The later a county was settled, the greater the number of children per woman. In counties organized before 1700, where women married in their early twenties, there were 140 children for each 100 women. In contrast, the ratio of children to women reached 195 in piedmont Virginia counties settled from 1740 to 1780. Women who lived in piedmont probably followed the pattern of early marriage and high marital fertility found in Prince George's earlier in the century.[25]

The combination of early marriage and high fertility led to a population explosion along the tobacco coast during the first half of the eighteenth century, when each adult in tidewater Maryland was replaced in the next generation by 2.5 offspring, an increase of nearly half from the late seventeenth century. The intensity of this growth was probably not anticipated by planter families, who were accustomed to high infant and childhood mortality and frequent death among parents before women completed their childbearing cycles.[26] High fertility, under these circumstances, would ensure perpetuation of the lineage. However, there were substantial increases in life expectancy during the early eighteenth century. In particular, women more often lived beyond age forty than in their mothers' generation and therefore bore more children than their predecessors. While the size of families of native white women who had completed their childbearing changed little from 1650 to 1750, the average number of children in all families rose by a third, from 5.5 to 7.4 (see table 2).

As population pressure on tidewater resources mounted after 1750, the rapid rates of natural increase of the first half of the century lessened.

25. This paragraph assumes a relatively constant rate of age-specific fertility in the region, and is calculated from U.S., Census Office, *Returns of the Whole Number of Persons within the Several Districts of the United States* . . . (Washington, D.C., 1802). The higher the 1800 Virginia fertility ratio, the later the mean year of county formation: counties with ratios under 140, formed, on average, in 1649; ratios 140–150, counties formed in 1672; ratios 150–170, counties formed in 1726; ratios 170–180, counties formed in 1751; ratios over 180, counties formed in 1765.

26. Lorena Seebach Walsh and Russell R. Menard, "Death in the Chesapeake: Two Life Tables for Men in Early Colonial Maryland," *Maryland Historical Magazine*, LXIX (1974), 211–227; Darrett B. Rutman and Anita H. Rutman, "'Now-Wives and Sons-in-Law': Parental Death in a Seventeenth-Century Virginia County," in Thad W. Tate and David L. Ammerman, eds., *The Chesapeake in the Seventeenth Century: Essays on Anglo-American Society* (Chapel Hill, N.C., 1979), 153–182; Daniel Blake Smith, "Mortality and Family in the Colonial Chesapeake," *Journal of Interdisciplinary History*, VIII (1977–1978), 408–415.

Table 2. *White Natural Increase in Tidewater Maryland*

Component of Population Growth	Marriage Cohorts of Native-Born Women		
	1650–1700	1700–1750	1750–1800
(1) Female age at first marriage[a]	16.8	18.6	22.2
(2) Completed family size[b]	9.4	9.0	6.9
(3) Size of all families[b]	5.5	7.4	5.5
(4) Maximum proportion of children surviving to age 20[c]	60.8%	66.9%	66.9%
(5) No. of children surviving to age 20 per couple[d]	3.3	5.0	3.7
(6) Index of generational replacement[e]	1.7	2.5	1.8

Sources: These estimates calculated from data in table 1 and figs. 2, 4, 5, 6, 7. See, especially, Allan Kulikoff, "Tobacco and Slaves: Population, Economy, and Society in Eighteenth-Century Prince George's County, Maryland" (Ph.D. diss., Brandeis University, 1976), chap. 12; Gaius Marcus Brumbaugh, ed., *Maryland Records: Colonial, Revolutionary, County, and Church, from Original Sources*, I (Baltimore, 1915), 1–88; Russell R. Menard and Lorena S. Walsh, "The Demography of Somerset County, Maryland: A Progress Report," *Newberry Papers in Family and Community History*, 81-2 (1981), 33; Walsh and Menard, "Death in the Chesapeake: Two Life Tables for Men in Early Colonial Maryland," *Maryland Historical Magazine*, LXIX (1974), 221–222; and Daniel Blake Smith, "Mortality and Family in the Colonial Chesapeake," *Journal of Interdisciplinary History*, VIII (1978), 412–414.

Notes: [a]1650–1700: see table 1; southern Maryland ages for birth cohorts 1680–1729 and 1730–1779. [b]1650–1700: see table 1; 1700–1800: Prince George's data, 1680–1720, 1730–1775. Completed family size is number of children born to women who survive to age 45. Total age-specific fertility was adjusted to calculate completed family size and size of all families by the distribution of ages at marriage and female deaths between age 15 and 45. [c]1650–1700: see table 1; 1700–1800: based on Prince George's data, 1690–1729. Whether survival rates changed cannot be determined. [d](Item 3 × item 4) ÷ 100. [e](Item 5 ÷ 2), assuming a sex ratio of 100.

Levels of mortality and fertility (fig. 5) stayed constant, but the age of women at first marriage rose by nearly four years. As a result of later marriages, the size of families declined by a quarter to 5.5, and each adult was replaced by 1.8 children, a decline of a third from earlier in the century. This rate of population growth was still high, however, and it equaled the growth achieved by the native white population during the second half of the seventeenth century, when marriages were earlier and adult mortality was higher.

The decline of mortality, then, played a key role in determining family size in the Chesapeake, where couples did not practice birth control. The life expectancy of white men gradually increased during the colonial period, and by the mid-eighteenth century nearly all lived until after their wives reached menopause. Judging from the evidence of four Maryland and Virginia counties during the seventeenth century, men born in the Chesapeake lived, on average, about 7 years longer than newly arrived Maryland immigrants. Once immigrants survived their seasoning, however, most of this difference disappeared. The introduction after 1650 of a new and deadly strain of malaria, falciparum, against which neither natives nor immigrants were immune, may well have equalized the mortality of both groups. The male death rate began to fall in the 1690s, a generation after falciparum arrived.[27] Second-generation natives of Charles County, Maryland, mostly born after 1690, lived 4.6 years longer on average than their first-generation native-born fathers. This improvement continued for several decades and then leveled off. Men born in Prince George's and Anne Arundel counties, Maryland, between 1690 and 1729 lived 9 years longer than men born in tidewater in the seventeenth century. But after about 1730 there were no further improvements in male life expectancy; men born in Prince George's and Anne Arundel between 1730 and 1769 lived no longer than their fathers (see fig. 6).

Life expectancy improved more slowly among women than men, perhaps because they lost their immunity to malaria during pregnancy.[28] Only about half the women born in Middlesex County, Virginia, and Somerset County, Maryland, during the seventeenth century lived until their fortieth birthday, but deaths of women between twenty and forty dramatically declined during the eighteenth century. Nearly three-quarters of women born in southern Maryland during the eighteenth century survived until age forty (see fig. 7). These declining death rates of young women inevitably resulted in higher birthrates, since the proportion of women who survived their most fertile years increased.

Even though adult mortality declined over the colonial period, the proportion of children who reached adulthood changed very little. Children under five were especially susceptible to endemic fevers like malaria that infested the entire region. Infant mortality rates were high, and large numbers of children between ages one and four died. About a fifth of all infants died before their first birthday in Charles, York, and Somerset counties during the seventeenth century, and nearly the same proportion died in Prince George's from 1690 to 1729. There may have been some improvement in childhood mortality, for the total mortality of children and youths, age zero to twenty, fell from 39 percent in the seventeenth century to 33

27. Darrett B. Rutman and Anita H. Rutman, "Of Agues and Fevers: Malaria in the Early Chesapeake," *William and Mary Quarterly*, 3d Ser., XXXIII (1976), 31–60, explore the relationship between malaria and mortality.
28. For the impact of malaria on pregnant women, see *ibid.*, 46–53.

Fig. 6. *Male Life Expectancy along the Tobacco Coast, 1650–1770*

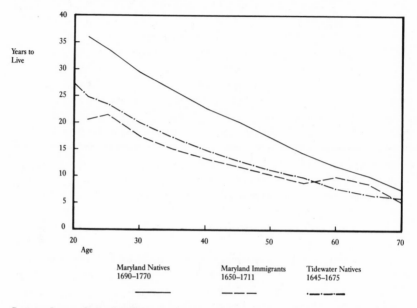

| | Maryland Natives 1690–1770 | Maryland Immigrants 1650–1711 | Tidewater Natives 1645–1675 |

Sources: Lorena Seebach Walsh and Russell R. Menard, "Death in the Chesapeake: Two Life Tables for Men in Early Colonial Maryland," *MHM*, LXIX (1974), 213–214 (immigrants, Charles County); Menard and Walsh, "The Demography of Somerset County, Maryland: A Progress Report," *Newberry Papers in Family and Community History*, 81-2, 36; Daniel Blake Smith, "Mortality and Family in the Colonial Chesapeake," *Journal of Interdisciplinary History*, VIII (1977–1978), 415 (York); Darrett B. Rutman and Anita H. Rutman, " 'Now-Wives and Sons-in-Law': Parental Death in a Seventeenth-Century Virginia County," in Thad W. Tate and David L. Ammerman, eds., *The Chesapeake in the Seventeenth Century: Essays on Anglo-American Society* (Chapel Hill, N.C., 1979), 177–182 (Middlesex); Allan Kulikoff, "Tobacco and Slaves: Population, Economy, and Society in Eighteenth-Century Prince George's County, Maryland" (Ph.D. diss., Brandeis University, 1976), 38–43, 435–436, 444–448 (southern Maryland, 1690–1729), and genealogies cited, 436, used to construct southern Maryland life table, 1730–1769.

percent during the early eighteenth century. This improvement, however, was much less than the decline in adult mortality and increased the number of surviving children by just 10 percent.[29]

In sum, the rate of household formation declined during the eigh-

29. Seventeenth-century data from Walsh and Menard, "Death in the Chesapeake," *MHM*, LXIX (1974), 221–222; Menard and Walsh, "Demography of Somerset County," *Newberry Papers*, 81-2 (1981), 32 (low mortality estimates); Smith, "Mortality and Family," *Jour. Interdisc. Hist.*, VIII (1977–1978), 412–414. Eighteenth-century data from Kulikoff, "Tobacco and Slaves," 443, 448–453.

Fig. 7. *Female Survival Rates in the Chesapeake, 1650–1775*

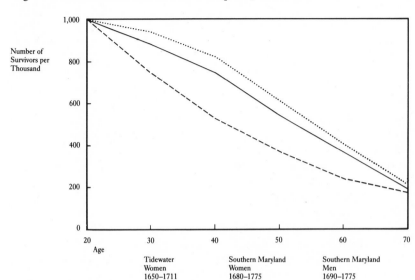

Sources: Seventeenth-century females: calculated from Russell R. Menard and Lorena S. Walsh, "The Demography of Somerset County, Maryland: A Progress Report," *Newberry Papers in Family and Community History,* 81-2 (1981), 36; and Darrett B. Rutman and Anita H. Rutman, "Of Agues and Fevers: Malaria in the Early Chesapeake," *WMQ,* 3d Ser., XXXIII (1976), 53. Eighteenth-century males: Allan Kulikoff, "Tobacco and Slaves: Population, Economy, and Society in Eighteenth-Century Prince George's County, Maryland" (Ph.D. diss., Brandeis University, 1976), 441, and fig. 6, above. Eighteenth-century females: calculated from Harry Wright Newman, *Anne Arundel Gentry: A Genealogical History of Twenty-two Pioneers of Anne Arundel County, Md., and Their Descendants* (Baltimore, 1933), and *Anne Arundel Gentry: A Genealogical History of Some Early Families of Anne Arundel County, Maryland,* rev. ed. (Annapolis, Md., 1970); Effie Gwynn Bowie, *Across the Years in Prince George's County . . .* (Richmond, Va., 1947).

teenth century in tidewater because the supply of inexpensive land diminished. Men responded to lower ratios of land to labor by postponing marriage, and since men took brides five years younger than themselves, women married at older ages as well. Women who married later had fewer children, and this diminished fertility—given relatively constant death rates for women and children over the century—reduced the number of people seeking to marry and form households in the next generation. This reduction, however, was insufficient to bring the quantity of available land and the number of potential householders into balance, and large numbers of men and women migrated to thinly settled parts of piedmont.

Land and Labor

As soon as tobacco planters established households, they sought laborers to help them produce more tobacco and thereby improve their standard of living. Planters, as we have seen, had to reserve about fifty acres for each worker they employed cultivating tobacco, and the more laborers they used, the more rapidly the supply of land would be depleted. The adoption of slavery at the end of the seventeenth century accelerated the depletion of tidewater lands and thereby reduced the level of household formation because proportionately more slaves than whites participated in tobacco production. Only white men cultivated tobacco and corn, but masters set slave men, women, and children as young as ten to work as agricultural laborers.[30]

The slave labor system encouraged frontier migration at the same time that it reduced opportunities for household formation in older areas. The ready availability of unimproved land, combined with land scarcity in older areas caused in part by the use of slave labor, propelled landless and slaveless planters to the frontier. Slaves, moreover, unlike land, constituted mobile capital and could therefore be used wherever a master thought they would be most productive. The movability of slaves greatly increased the propensity of slaveowners to migrate to new areas.[31]

The impact of slavery upon household formation and migration magnified over the eighteenth century. Most adults who worked in tobacco fields were white early in the century, but a large slave trade between 1700 and 1740 led to the dominance of slave labor in the region. At first most slaves were adult immigrants who died young, had few children, and failed to replace themselves, but by the 1730s there were sufficient native-born women in the slave population to permit the beginnings of natural increase. As long as planters had to replace their slaves with new imports, trade conditions limited their ability to buy slaves and thereby use more landed resources. But when slaves reproduced themselves, planters fortunate enough to own slave women saw their labor force increase over time and, with it, their need for land.[32]

Most tobacco cultivators in 1700 were still white householders, their sons, free white laborers, and a few white servants. Despite the decline of

30. See chap. 10 for slave work patterns.
31. Stanley L. Engerman, "Some Considerations Relating to Property Rights in Man," *Jour. Econ. Hist.*, XXXIII (1973), 43–65; Gavin Wright, *The Political Economy of the Cotton South: Households, Markets, and Wealth in the Nineteenth Century* (New York, 1978), 15–17, 116–119.
32. A more technical version of this part of the chapter was published as "A 'Prolifick' People: Black Population Growth in the Chesapeake Colonies, 1700–1790," *Southern Studies*, XVI (1977), 391–428.

the servant trade, only about a third of the laborers in tobacco-growing areas of Maryland and Virginia were slaves at the turn of the century.[33] Most homeowners relied on family labor and an occasional hired hand. Two examples illustrate this labor shortage on plantation households. Typical planters in Surry County, Virginia, could count upon only one other person, besides themselves, to help with field work. These laborers were evenly divided between whites and slaves, but only one household in four contained a white servant or freedman. Prince George's County, Maryland, in contrast, was one of the last places to attract many servants. In 1704, each household in that county included, on average, about one servant (or newly freed servant), one slave, and a male head of household (see table 3). The labor shortage soon hit Prince George's; by 1710, nearly all the servants in the county had completed their term and left the province, and they were not replaced by native-born white men.[34]

Pent-up demand for labor led planters to import 100,000 black people between 1690 and 1770, almost all from Africa. The slave trade, which had begun slowly in the third quarter of the seventeenth century, increased relentlessly from 1700 to 1740 and then leveled off and began to decline. From 1700 to 1739, when planter demand for slaves peaked, Chesapeake planters enslaved around 54,000 black immigrants. The size of the slave trade increased during each decade: the average annual number of black migrants rose from 1,300 in the early 1700s to 2,350 by the early 1740s. However, the slave trade subsequently slackened, because high rates of natural increase among native-born slaves reduced the need for new African imports. Only 42,000 blacks were enslaved in the region from 1740 to 1770, and the annual average declined to around 800 by the late 1760s and early 1770s, a level below that of the early eighteenth century (see fig. 8).[35]

33. Evarts B. Greene and Virginia D. Harrington, *American Population before the Federal Census of 1790* (New York, 1932), 128–129, 148–151; "Inhabitants in Maryland," *Gentleman's Magazine*, XXXIV (1764), 261. I estimated the slave share of Virginia's labor force circa 1700 by applying the growth rate of the slave share in Maryland, 1704–1755, to 1755 Virginia data.

34. Allan Kulikoff, "The Economic Growth of the Eighteenth-Century Chesapeake Colonies," *Jour. Econ. Hist.*, XXXIX (1979), 278; Kevin P. Kelly, "The Structure of Household Labor in Late Seventeenth-Century Virginia: Surry County, A Case Study" (paper presented at the Southern Historical Association annual meeting, Dallas, Nov. 1974), 19; Robert Wheeler, "Mobility of Labor in Surry County, Virginia, 1674–1703," MS, 4.

35. Details on the proportion of Africans in the trade are found in Kulikoff, " 'Prolifick' People," *So. Stud.*, XVI (1977), 392–393, 417–423. For Maryland, see Kulikoff, "Tobacco and Slaves," 72–76; U.S., Bureau of the Census, *Historical Statistics of the United States, Colonial Times to 1970* (Washington, D.C., 1975), II, 1172; and Darold D. Wax, "Black Immigrants: The Slave Trade in Colonial Maryland," *MHM*, LXXIII (1978), 33–40. Maryland imports were estimated for 1710–1750 when returns were scanty by assuming that Maryland's share of the trade in the 1710s equaled that of 1700–1708, and in 1720–1750 equaled that of 1750–

Table 3. *The Labor Force in Prince George's County*

	No. of Taxables per Household[a]			
Group	1704	1733	1755	1776
Whites				
Heads of families	1.0	.9	.9	.9
Sons	.2	.2	.2	.3
Free men[b]	.5	.2	.2	.2
Servants	.5	.2	.1	.1
Total	2.1	1.5	1.4	1.4
Slaves	1.1	1.8	1.9	2.3
Total taxables	3.1	3.3	3.3	3.8

Source: Allan Kulikoff, "The Economic Growth of the Eighteenth-Century Chesapeake Colonies," *Journal of Economic History*, XXXIX (1979), 278.

Notes: Discrepancies in totals in tables are due to rounding. [a]White males over 16 and blacks over 16. [b]Free laborers and all white nonheads not living with parents.

These long-term trends obscure shorter cyclical patterns in the slave trade. However desperately tobacco planters wanted to purchase slaves during depressions to overcome low prices by increasing their output, they could afford to buy large numbers of Africans only during prosperous times. Larger than usual numbers of slaves entered Virginia after the high tobacco prices of the late 1710s, mid-1720s, mid-1730s, early 1750s, and late 1750s. In fact, half the volume of the slave trade occurred during just twenty-one years. The slave trade nearly disappeared after the depressed tobacco prices of the early 1710s, late 1720s, mid-1740s, and early 1760s and during most of the Seven Years' War. Only a twelfth of Virginia's black immigrants came to the province during nineteen depression years (fig. 8).[36]

Slavers brought over predominantly male cargoes, for planters thought men would be most productive. Thomas Cable, a merchant on Virginia's Eastern Shore, suggested in 1725 that if he "could choose a Cargoe of Negroes as you propose 200—I would have 100 men able young Slaves, 60 women, 30 Boys and 10 Girls from 10 to 14 years of age. Such a Cargoe I could sell to great Advantage."[37] Slave ships that reached Virginia closely

1770. Annual averages in the text are Maryland estimates plus Virginia averages from a linear regression on imports to Virginia, 1744–1770.

36. Tobacco prices are discussed below, chap. 3.

37. Thomas Cable to John Walpole, July 16, 1725, Cable Letterbook, 1722–1757, Maryland Historical Society, Baltimore (MHS). I am indebted to John Hemphill for this source.

Fig. 8. *The Slave Trade in Virginia, 1700–1770.* Broken line indicates missing data that were linearly interpolated.

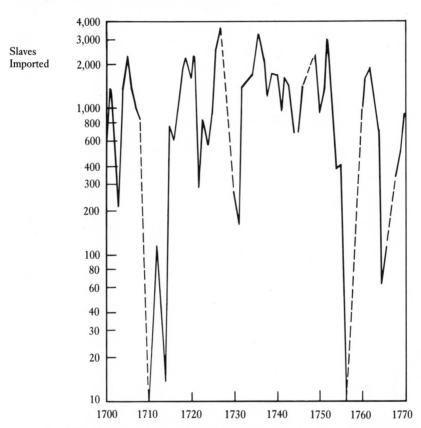

Sources: Elizabeth Donnan, ed., *Documents Illustrative of the History of the Slave Trade to America,* IV, *The Border Colonies and the Southern Colonies* (Washington, D.C., 1935), 17–18, 173–234; Herbert S. Klein, "Slaves and Shipping in Eighteenth-Century Virginia," *Journal of Interdisciplinary History,* V (1974–1975), 384–387; Allan Kulikoff, "A 'Prolifick' People: Black Population Growth in the Chesapeake Colonies, 1700–1790," *Southern Studies,* XVI (1977), 417–418.

followed this pattern. They typically contained two men for every woman, and fewer than a sixth of the migrants were children. Two-thirds of the older children were boys, but the younger children were more evenly divided by sex. Overall, however, far more males than females were imported (see fig. 9).

As long as most of the adult slaves in the region were forced African immigrants, black population in most of the region grew mainly by importa-

Fig. 9. *Composition of a Typical Slaver*

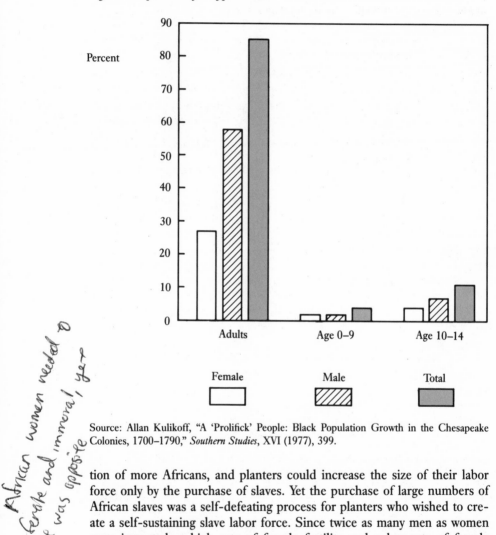

Source: Allan Kulikoff, "A 'Prolifick' People: Black Population Growth in the Chesapeake Colonies, 1700–1790," *Southern Studies*, XVI (1977), 399.

tion of more Africans, and planters could increase the size of their labor force only by the purchase of slaves. Yet the purchase of large numbers of African slaves was a self-defeating process for planters who wished to create a self-sustaining slave labor force. Since twice as many men as women were imported, a high rate of female fertility and a low rate of female mortality during childbearing years would have been required to achieve any natural increase. Unfortunately, high mortality and low fertility were endemic problems among African slaves.[38]

38. See P.M.G. Harris, in "The Spread of Slavery in the Chesapeake, 1630–1775" (paper presented at the Third Hall of Records Conference on Maryland History, "Maryland, a Product of Two Worlds," May 1984), who argues that demographic settlement patterns, rather than

When Africans came to the Americas, they left one disease environment and entered another. Since they lacked immunity to local diseases, many died soon after arrival. Between 1710 and 1718, more than 5 percent of African immigrants to Virginia died even before they could be sold. Many others died during the winter and spring of their first year in the region, mainly from respiratory diseases. The experience of thirty-two Africans bought by John Mercer of Stafford County, Virginia, between 1733 and 1742 suggests the extent of black immigrant mortality in Virginia. Eight of the thirty-two died by the end of their first year, and at least another seven died before they had lived ten years in the colony. If both the presale mortality and the deaths of Mercer's slaves were typical, then fewer than half the Africans who were forced to come to the Chesapeake lived even ten years.[39]

African women who were brought to the Chesapeake bore few children. Their health and social condition greatly mitigated against conception. Many of them were so severely undernourished after the middle passage that they could not conceive a child or, if they conceived, complete a pregnancy. The high rate of mortality during the first year suggests that considerable morbidity may have inhibited conception. Moreover, otherwise healthy women may have refused to have children, as a protest against their enslavement, for many women remained childless even after they had regained their health.[40] Edmond Jennings apparently purchased about twenty African women and placed them on his quarters in King William County, Virginia, by the time of his death in 1712. More than two-thirds of the twenty-two women on his quarters had no children early in 1713, and one-fifth had but one child. Some of them may have been purchased in 1712, but others had probably been purchased as early as 1705.[41]

Given the preponderance of men among black immigrants, one might

nativity of the slave population, triggered natural population growth, and that it began as early as the 1690s in places like York County.

39. Philip D. Curtin, "Epidemiology and the Slave Trade," *Political Science Quarterly*, LXXXIII (1968), 190–216; Elizabeth Donnan, ed., *Documents Illustrative of the History of the Slave Trade to America*, IV, *The Border Colonies and the Southern Colonies* (Washington, D.C., 1935), 175–181; John Mercer Ledger B, 12, Buck's County Historical Society, Doylestown, Penn. (copy at CW).

40. Russell R. Menard, "The Maryland Slave Population, 1658 to 1730: A Demographic Profile of Blacks in Four Counties," *WMQ*, 3d Ser., XXXII (1975), 41–42. Regular menstruation requires "a minimum weight for height, apparently relating to a critical fat storage." Rose E. Frisch, "Demographic Implications of the Biological Determinants of Female Fecundity," *Social Biology*, XXII (1975), 17–22.

41. Inventories of Negroes on the Estate of Edmond Jennings, 1712–1713, Francis Porteus Corbin Papers, Duke University, Durham, N.C. (CW film). The years mentioned were peak years for imports.

expect women to be pressured into sexual unions almost immediately, yet many women postponed marriage for years. On Jennings's plantation, 9 of 15 childless women lived on quarters where men outnumbered women. A similar situation prevailed on the many quarters of Robert "King" Carter. Carter owned some native-born women but bought numerous Africans in the 1720s. The adult sex ratio on his plantations in 1733, shortly before his death, was 142. Nearly a fifth (32 of 173) of the women over twenty were unmarried, and these women were probably Africans. Although Carter encouraged marriage among his slaves and allowed husbands and wives to live together, his African slaves ordinarily did not begin to have children immediately. In all, 41 percent of the women over fifteen on Carter's quarters were childless in 1733. The experience of these slaves suggests that many African women did not marry until their second year in the region and probably did not bear a child until their fifth or even sixth year as a Chesapeake slave.[42]

In sum, immigrant slaves in the Chesapeake could not reproduce themselves. Most African women, like white immigrant women, came to the Chesapeake in their early twenties.[43] By the time they conceived, they were at least twenty-five and had only fifteen fertile years left. These African women gave birth, on average, to only three children, and no more than two of their offspring survived into adulthood.[44] Since there were twice as many men as women among African immigrants, these two survivors replaced three members of the preceding generation, and only additional immigration kept the slave population growing.

Nonetheless, the black population of the entire region began to grow naturally during the 1720s and 1730s, and in some areas even earlier. The key to understanding this change is the increase in the proportion of natives among the black women of the region. Native women, both black and white, married younger and bore more children than their immigrant mothers. The differences in the fertility of immigrant and native black women can be illustrated by comparing slaves owned by Edmond Jennings in 1712, Robert Carter in 1733, and Charles Carroll and Thomas Addison of Maryland in

42. *Ibid.*; Inventory of Robert Carter, 1733, Carter Papers, Virginia Historical Society, Richmond (VHS). Carter bought 80 slaves for his own use in 1727. Carter to William Dawkins, May 13, 1727, Carter Letterbooks, VHS; Carter to Dawkins, June 3, 1727, Carter Letterbooks, University of Virginia, Charlottesville.

43. Menard, "Maryland Slave Population," *WMQ*, 3d Ser., XXXII (1975), 45–46; Lois Green Carr and Lorena S. Walsh, "The Planter's Wife: The Experience of White Women in Seventeenth-Century Maryland," *ibid.*, XXXIV (1977), 550–553.

44. Fertility and survivorship calculated from age-specific fertility of white women in Somerset County (see fig. 6) and from Jack Ericson Eblen, "New Estimates of the Vital Rates of the United States Black Population during the Nineteenth Century," *Demography*, XI (1974), 307–308.

1773–1774. Jennings's farms contained mostly Africans; Carter's included both Africans and natives; and female slaves on Carroll and Addison's quarters were almost all natives. Only seven of the twenty-seven women on Jennings's farms had any children, and four of these seven had just one child. The proportion of childless families declined from a fifth on Carter's quarters to a twentieth on the Carroll and Addison plantations forty-one years later, and the numer of slave households with four or more children rose from a seventh on Carter's farms to a third on the two Maryland plantations.[45]

The rate of growth of the black population of the Chesapeake colonies depended mainly upon the age at marriage and the fertility of black women, but it was also affected by the sex ratio and the mortality of both adults and children. Native slaves were probably healthier than immigrants, and as the native population increased, there was a corresponding rise in the proportion of women who survived their childbearing years. Whereas two men immigrated for each woman, nearly equal numbers of boys and girls that survived were born to both African and native women. As these children matured, the ratio of men to women became more nearly equal and, with the rising proportion of women, led to a higher overall birth rate.

The transition from a naturally declining to a naturally increasing black population occurred during the 1730s. In 1728, at the end of a peak in the slave trade, three of every five black adults in the region had been born in Africa, but by 1740 fewer than half the region's black adults were Africans, despite large-scale imports of slaves at the end of the 1730s. During the decade, the proportion of native women in the black population became high enough to compensate for the low fertility of African immigrant women. There were nearly two children for each woman in both southern Maryland and York County, Virginia. Thirty slave women born in Prince George's from 1710 to 1730 conceived their first child at about age eighteen. A woman who began sexual activity in her teens in the 1720s and 1730s would give birth to between six and seven children if she lived to age forty-four, and each adult in the population would be replaced by another adult in the next generation, even given high sex ratios and childhood mortality.[46]

45. Jennings Inventory, Corbin Papers; Carter Inventory, Carter Papers, VHS; Charles Carroll Account Book, MHS; Prince George's Inventories, GS#2, 334–336, MHR. Only children who could be placed with a particular mother or father were counted; the mean number of children per household was two on Carter's quarters and three on the Maryland farms.

46. Prince George's Inventories, 1725–1775; York Wills, Inventories, 1720–1740, VSL. The age of mothers born in Prince George's, 1710–1739, at the conception of their first surviving child was 18.5; when adjusted for infant mortality, the number falls to 17.9. For a detailed discussion of this transition and adjustments made to Menard's data that account for the

After 1740 the rate of black natural increase rose. As a result of this natural increase, the impact of African immigration was sharply reduced: fewer than a third of all black adults in the Chesapeake colonies in 1750 were immigrants, and the proportion continued to decline. Black adult sex ratios decreased throughout tidewater from 150 men per hundred women in the 1720s and 1730s to about 110 in the 1750s. Each woman in the population had to give birth to only two surviving children to ensure that every adult was replaced by another adult in the next generation. In fact, however, black women bore enough children in the 1760s and 1770s to more than replace the preceding generation, and the population grew at a rapid pace.

Afro-American women married and began having children when in their late teens. Slave women born in Prince George's from 1730 to 1759 conceived their first child, on average, by age eighteen, and women born in the 1760s on Francis Jerdone's plantations near Virginia's frontier began childbearing even earlier. Of the Prince George's women, 70 percent had conceived a child before they reached twenty, and only 3 percent had their first pregnancy after age twenty-four. Nearly every girl who reached her late teens had a child to raise on the Carroll and Addison plantations in the 1770s. Only one of ten girls age fifteen to seventeen, but four of seven girls age eighteen and nineteen, had already given birth. Most of the others were probably pregnant, however, for eight of ten women age twenty and twenty-one had children.[47]

Early marriages were followed by high fertility. Women in their twenties and thirties in the 1760s and 1770s gave birth every twenty-seven to twenty-nine months. A slave woman who married in her late teens, and lived to forty-five, would have had 9 children.[48] Some women, of course, married later or died young. Afro-American women on five plantations scattered throughout tidewater and piedmont bore 6 children on average— 2.5 more than African women—and those who survived through their childbearing years gave birth to 8 children.[49]

---

difference between his timing (1720s) and mine, see Kulikoff, " 'Prolifick' People," *So. Stud.*, XVI (1977), 403–406.

47. Prince George's Inventories, 1725–1775; Brumbaugh, ed., *Maryland Records*, I, 1–88; and Carroll Account Book, MHS, show that the age of mothers born 1740–1759 was, at the conception of their first surviving child, 18.6 (N = 150) and 18.0 when adjusted for infant mortality; 14 slave women born in Hanover, Louisa, and Spotsylvania counties bore their first surviving child at an average age of 18.6 (see Philip David Morgan, "The Development of Slave Culture in Eighteenth Century Plantation America" [Ph.D. diss., University College, London, 1977], 305).

48. Francis Jerdone Slave Book, VSL.; Brumbaugh, ed., *Maryland Records*, I, 1–88; Kulikoff, " 'Prolifick' People," *So. Stud.*, XVI (1977), 408.

49. Carroll Account Book; Jerdone Slave Book; William Bolling Register, VHS; Mary Beth

Many of these children died long before they matured. Records from plantations owned by Robert Lloyd in the 1740s and 1750s and by Robert Carter in the 1790s suggest that a quarter of slave children died before they celebrated their first birthday and almost another quarter died by age fifteen.[50] This abysmal record, more than two-fifths higher than white infant and childhood mortality, is perhaps explained by difficulties the slave regime placed upon black mothers. Slave women had to return to work soon after giving birth, and poor health care continued after children were weaned, for they were left with only slightly older children or with old women while their parents worked.[51]

Even with mortality levels this high, a sufficient number of slaves survived childhood to ensure natural increase by the 1730s. The number of surviving children per woman hovered between 2 and 3 in Prince George's in the early 1740s, then rose to about 4 by the 1770s. However, because of continuing high sex ratios, the slave population barely replaced itself in the 1730s and 1740s. But beginning in the 1750s, when an average of 1.6 children under fifteen replaced each parent, there was substantial natural increase in the county.[52]

By the 1750s, despite high infant and childhood mortality, the growth rate of the native black population equaled that of native whites. Contemporary observers insisted that blacks were even more prolific than whites. In 1759 Andrew Burnaby, an English visitor, wrote, "The number of Negroes in the southern colonies is upon the whole nearly equal, if not superior, to that of the white men; and they propagate and increase even faster." Peter Fontaine, a planter in Charles City County, Virginia, in a 1756 letter feared that slaves would soon "overrun a dutiful colony" and also said that "the females are far more prolific than the white women."[53]

Everywhere in the region, the slave trade and high black birthrates combined to increase the slave share of the labor force. While the Chesa-

---

Norton, *Liberty's Daughters: The Revolutionary Experience of American Women, 1750–1800* (Boston, 1980), 76 (on Jefferson). Records cover years from 1740 to 1800.

50. Lloyd Farm Book, MHS; Robert Carter Deed of Manumission, 1791–1796, Carter Papers, Duke University, Durham, N.C. (CW film). Data adjusted for unrecorded births.

51. Samuel Stanhope Smith, *An Essay on the Causes of the Variety of Complexion and Figure in the Human Species* (1787), ed. Winthrop D. Jordan (Cambridge, Mass., 1965 [orig. publ. New Brunswick, N.J., 1810]), 35, 61–62, 156–157.

52. Total fertility rates, calculated from Prince George's Inventories, were multiplied by the estimated proportion of children ever born who survived, in order to determine the number of surviving children per woman, and then this number was divided by two and adjusted by the sex ratio to determine number of surviving children per adult.

53. Andrew Burnaby, *Travels Through the Middle Settlements in North-America in the Years 1759 and 1760* . . . , 2d ed. (London, 1775; reprint, Ithaca, N.Y., 1968), 111; Peter Fontaine to his brothers, Mar. 2, 1756, in Ann Maury, ed. and trans., *Memoirs of a Huguenot Family* (New York, 1853), 347–348.

peake slave trade exploded during the first third of the eighteenth century, the number of adult slaves per household in Prince George's nearly doubled, from one to almost two. These African slaves replaced white servants who disappeared as soon as their term expired (table 3). African slaves worked in piedmont as well. In Amelia County in southside Virginia, for example, half the laborers were black in 1736, a year after the county's formation, and each householder owned, on average, more than one adult slave (see table 4).

The slave share of the labor force continued to rise after the decline of the slave trade, despite similar rates of increase in the white and black populations, because planters employed both black men and women in agricultural labor. In 1755 nearly six of every ten workers in tobacco-growing areas of the Chesapeake were slaves, double the proportion in 1700. The proportion of blacks in the work force grew in every part of the two colonies and in 1755 ranged from about half on the southside frontier to nearly three-quarters in counties located between the York and James rivers and settled early in the seventeenth century.[54]

The importance of slave labor in tidewater increased during the 1760s and 1770s, despite land scarcity and rising ages of marriage for men that should have kept more white youths working at home or for neighbors. But sons migrated from tidewater rather than work as agricultural laborers, and as a result, white labor supplies in tidewater did not increase. In Prince George's, the number of slave workers per household rose about a fourth between 1755 and 1776, while the number of white workers stayed about the same. Even though the average age at marriage for men in the county rose from twenty-five to twenty-seven, few mature sons were permanently added to the work force of white households. The number of county families with mature sons present did increase from one in five to nearly one in three between 1755 and 1776, but most masters could not count on family labor. Fathers under forty did not have any sons of working age, and the sons of men over sixty had probably left home to form their own families, either in the county or, more likely, on the frontier. More than two-thirds of the whites in the county had to own slaves to increase their tobacco output (table 3).

Planters who migrated to frontier areas between 1740 and 1775 employed slave labor because poor youths refused to work for other planters and began their own households almost immediately after they arrived. There were fewer white servants and free white workers in frontier Amelia

54. Greene and Harrington, *American Population*, 128–129, 148–151; "Inhabitants in Maryland," *Gentleman's Magazine*, XXXIV (1764), 261. The black share of the labor force in 1755 was 59% in tobacco-growing regions, 53% on the lower Western Shore, 73% on the peninsula, 68% on the middle peninsula, 64% in central piedmont Virginia, and 50% in southside Virginia.

Table 4. *The Labor Force in Southside Virginia*

| | No. of Taxables per Household[a] | | | |
| | Amelia County | | Lunenburg County | |
Group	1736	1749	1750	1764
Whites				
Heads of household	1.0	1.0	1.0	1.0
Sons	.1	.2	.2	.2
Other whites[b]	.2	.2	.1	.2
Total	1.3	1.4	1.3	1.4
Slaves	1.3	1.8	.8	1.8
Total taxables	2.6	3.2	2.1	3.2

Sources: Michael Lee Nicholls, "Origins of the Virginia Southside, 1703–1753" (Ph.D. diss., College of William and Mary, 1972), 120–123; Landon C. Bell, ed., *Sunlight on the Southside: Lists of Tithes, Lunenburg County, Virginia, 1748–1783* (Richmond, Va., 1930), 213–269.

Notes: [a]White males over 16 and blacks 16 and over. [b]Includes servants and free white laborers.

and Lunenburg counties, formed in Virginia's southside in 1732 and 1746, respectively, than in contemporary Prince George's, and the youths who dominated the white population of these counties had few adolescent sons. Fewer than half the households in these two counties could command even a single white worker besides the head of the family two decades after initial settlement (table 4).

Frontier planters increased the size of their labor force only by purchasing or inheriting slaves. The presence of numerous native-born slaves in tidewater accelerated the adoption of slave labor in piedmont. As soon as trade routes were established, large planters from adjacent tidewater counties started quarters, and residents used their farms as collateral to purchase slaves from tidewater planters. Slave women among these forced migrants bore a sufficient number of children to ensure black natural increase from the outset of the settlement of piedmont. The growth of the slave labor force in Amelia and Lunenburg counties illustrates this process. In wealthy Amelia County the number of slaves per household rose by nearly two-fifths between 1736 and 1749. In Lunenburg County, a poor neighbor of Amelia, the number of slaves per household doubled in the fourteen years after 1750, and the slave share of the labor force rose from less than two-fifths to almost three-fifths (table 4). The distribution of slave laborers throughout southside in 1755 suggests that the diffusion of slave labor was related to the date of initial settlement. The more recently a county had been organized, the lower the proportion of slaves among all workers: the black share of the work force in this region ranged from nearly two-thirds in Prince George County, formed in 1703, to a fifth in Halifax County, formed in 1752.[55]

Expansion and Its Disruption

As we have seen, there was a relationship between land and labor in both tidewater and piedmont through most of the eighteenth century. Vast quantities of untilled land found on the frontier and beyond the limits of white habitation led planters to rotate fields rather than crops. Extensive cultivation of land, combined with the rapid growth of both the white and black populations, moreover, prompted continual out-migration to new areas. Frontier planters, knowing that new lands were still plentiful, practiced the kind of extensive cultivation characteristic of more settled areas.

This agrarian system cut across changing demand for tobacco in Europe. No matter how low or high tobacco prices might be, planters left older counties for new frontiers. The settling of each new region followed a similar progression of rapid in-migration and population growth, the development of tobacco monoculture, increasing dependence on slave labor, and—finally—out-migration to yet newer frontiers. At any one time, different parts of the region would vary in social structure and economic organization because they had reached different stages in this developmental cycle.

The progressive settling of new frontiers reduced the number of poor people in tidewater. Although white adolescents often worked for neighbors, poor whites unable to form households by their late twenties moved to a frontier rather than continuing to work as agricultural laborers, overseers, or domestic servants in tidewater. These jobs were too closely identified with the labor of slaves to appeal to even the most destitute whites. As a result, no white agricultural proletariat ever appeared in the colonial Chesapeake region.

Men who lived on frontiers, including those found in tidewater early in the eighteenth century, bought land with great ease. As land scarcity increased in tidewater, land prices increased so much that youths who stayed in the region found the purchase of land more and more difficult. The

55. Harris, "Spread of Slavery," table 4; Greene and Harrington, *American Population*, 148–151; Michael Lee Nicholls, "Origins of the Virginia Southside, 1750–1753: A Social and Economic Study" (Ph.D. diss., College of William and Mary, 1972), 120–123. The exact proportions were: Amelia, 50% in 1736 and 73% in 1790; in southside in 1755, Prince George, 62%, Brunswick (founded 1732) and Lunenburg (1746), both 43%; Halifax (1752), 18%, and Bedford (1754), 29%.

familial system of provisional gifts and inheritance therefore became far more important. Sons (and sometimes daughters) lived on parcels of land their parents had purchased when acreage was cheap, but waited until their fathers died before gaining title to any land of their own. This trend obviously increased the power of middling and large landowners over their sons.

Nonetheless, the market for tobacco and foodstuffs in Europe, as we shall see in the next two chapters, greatly influenced the wealth of Chesapeake planters, what crops they would produce, and how actively they worked to diversify their operations. When tobacco prices were low during the first half of the century, tobacco regulation was the most important political issue in both Chesapeake colonies; after prices began to rise and prosperity returned to the region, an increasing tide of debt replaced tobacco regulation as a political concern in the region.

These processes of settlement began to disappear from the Chesapeake region about the time of the Revolution. Planters were running out of land east of the Blue Ridge Mountains to grow tobacco on unless they replaced the system of rotating fields with one of rotating crops and manuring fields. By 1800 nearly all piedmont land had been planted at least once with tobacco, and bulky tobacco hogsheads could not be profitably transported through high mountain passes.

By the 1760s and 1770s, for the first time, white families had to leave the Chesapeake region completely to make a living. More than a fourth of the youths born in the region during the 1750s and 1760s left the area before the Revolution, but only a fourth of those leaving were replaced by migrants from other colonial regions. This migration accelerated after the war. Nearly a quarter of a million whites, mostly tenants and nonslaveholders, moved from Virginia and Maryland to Kentucky, backcountry Carolina, Georgia, Tennessee, Alabama, and the Northwest between 1790 and 1820. These migrants represented almost an eighth of all whites living in Virginia during the 1790s and a sixth of those who resided there in the 1800s and 1810s. Some slaveholders left the region as well, taking about 175,000 slaves with them during these decades. Other slaveholders discovered a new market for their excess slaves in the southwestern states after the United States closed its borders to African slavers in 1808, and they sold perhaps 45,000 black people to slave traders during the 1810s alone.[56]

56. Pre-Revolutionary migration estimates from Georgia C. Villaflor and Kenneth L. Sokoloff, "Migration in Colonial America: Evidence from the Militia Muster Rolls," *Social Science History*, VI (1982), 541–547. Post-Revolutionary white migration estimates are based upon federal census data and upon varying rates of inferred natural increase in regions of the two states between 1790 and 1820 (from 2.5% in southside to 1.3% in tidewater). For forced migration of slaves, see Allan Kulikoff, "Uprooted Peoples: Black Migrants in the Age of the American Revolution, 1790–1820," in Ira Berlin and Ronald Hoffman, eds., *Slavery and Freedom in the Age of the American Revolution* (Charlottesville, Va., 1983), 147–153.

3

The Troubles with Tobacco, 1700–1750

Planters and their families suffered greatly during much of the early eighteenth century because tobacco prices were low. When tobacco prices declined, not only was it difficult for planters to purchase cloth and tools, but merchants called in old and overdue debts. During depressions, the standard of living of the wealthiest men declined, and the ordinary planter lived on the edge of destitution not even "able to Cloath his Family."[1] Recurring depressions in the tobacco trade generated the most important economic problem and the major political issue in both Chesapeake colonies during the first half of the eighteenth century.

Continued high levels of tobacco output, combined with stagnating productivity and ever-increasing costs of labor, intensified the impact of the low tobacco prices of the first half of the eighteenth century. The wealth of the economy (measured per capita) actually declined over that period. The Chesapeake economy performed so poorly that even ambitious men found it difficult to acquire the wealth attained by their fathers, and only planters who owned many slaves and commanded access to scarce capital prospered.

Planters adopted several strategies to cope with recurring depression. Some families migrated to frontier areas to find cheap land, but since these areas lay far from eastern markets for tobacco and transportation of fragile tobacco over poor roads was hazardous, their crops commanded even lower prices than those of tidewater producers. Those planters who stayed in older areas tried to become more self-sufficient and to diversify the crops they grew, but found that self-sufficiency unattainable and crops other than tobacco able to command only poor prices.

Since even wealthy planters could not solve the problems created by depressed tobacco prices, men turned to government for relief, thus making the regulation of tobacco production a divisive political issue. Some planters harked back to old models of political economy, demanding that fair prices be guaranteed for their tobacco by the imposition of quality controls upon tobacco exports. Other producers, mostly poorer men who made low-quality tobacco, saw their very existence threatened by these proposed

1. Spotswood to Commissioners of Trade, June 2, 1713, in R. A. Brock, ed., *The Official Letters of Alexander Spotswood, Lieutenant-Governor of the Colony of Virginia, 1710–1722* (Virginia Historical Society, *Collections*, N.S., I–II [Richmond, 1882]), II, 27–28 (hereafter cited as *Spotswood Letters*).

regulations. Class conflict between men of standing and ordinary planters lasted nearly half a century, until gentlemen finally attained a complete victory.

The Tobacco Economy, 1700–1748

Depressions recurred with appalling regularity between 1680 and 1750. From 1680 to 1715, except for a short boom between 1697 and 1702, the real price level was almost always low or declining, and the quantity of tobacco exported stagnated. The wars of the League of Augsburg and of the Spanish Succession raised shipping costs and cut European consumption; prices did not begin to recover until 1710, when a short crop reached England. After the war ended, tobacco exports began a rise that continued, with interruptions, until the Revolution. An upswing in prices and European demand from 1714 to 1720 was followed by more than a decade of depressed prices, caused by overproduction and sagging demand. Tobacco prices rose again in the mid-1730s, then fell from 1743 to 1748. During the entire five decades after 1700, in sum, prices substantially exceeded the costs of production during just one of every five years (see fig. 10).[2]

Even though farm prices for tobacco stayed low after peace returned to Europe in 1713, a rapid decline of the wholesale price of tobacco on the Continent led to increased demand and rising exports from the Chesapeake. Between 1705 and 1733, Dutch wholesale prices decreased by nearly one-half, and these declines continued, at a lower rate, until the 1750s. Falling prices were probably attributable to a reduction in transaction costs once tobacco reached Britain, for shipping costs declined only intermittently until the 1730s and 1740s. European tobacco manufacturers passed these savings on to their customers, and these newly reduced retail prices led to a massive increase in French and European consumption of

2. Price fluctuations are examined in John Mickle Hemphill, "Virginia and the English Commercial System, 1689–1733: Studies in the Development and Fluctuations of a Colonial Economy under Imperial Control" (Ph.D. diss., Princeton University, 1964), chaps. 1, 2, 4; Russell R. Menard, "The Tobacco Industry in the Chesapeake Colonies, 1617–1730: An Interpretation," *Research in Economic History*, V (1980), 123–142, 159–161; Lewis Cecil Gray, *History of Agriculture in the Southern United States to 1860*, I (Washington, D.C., 1933), 267–276; and Carville V. Earle, *The Evolution of a Tidewater Settlement System: All Hallow's Parish, Maryland, 1650–1783*, University of Chicago Department of Geography Research Paper 170 (Chicago, 1975), 14–18, 157–160. Charles Wetherell, "'Boom and Bust' in the Colonial Chesapeake Economy," *Journal of Interdisciplinary History*, XV (1984), 185–210, criticizes Menard's arguments about economic cycles but does not deny long-term economic swings examined here and in chap. 4.

Fig. 10. *Tobacco Prices on the Tobacco Coast, 1700–1775*

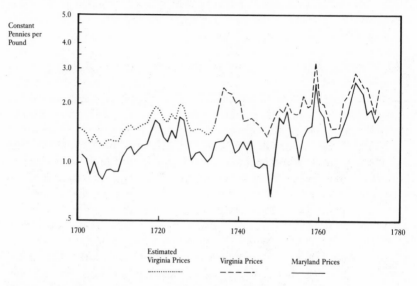

Estimated
Virginia Prices   Virginia Prices   Maryland Prices

Sources: U.S., Bureau of the Census, *Historical Statistics of the United States, Colonial Times to 1970* (Washington, D.C., 1975), II, 1198, as corrected by additional prices collected by the St. Mary's City Commission (for Maryland) and prices collected by Harold Gill of the Research Department of Colonial Williamsburg (for Virginia). Virginia prices, 1701–1734, estimated from regression equation.

tobacco, especially of newly popular snuff. Chesapeake planters, rushing to supply this new demand, settled thousands of new acres and bought thousands of African slaves to grow the crop.[3]

Chesapeake planters gained few benefits from increased exports of tobacco. They sustained heavy new costs to grow more tobacco: not only did they buy many African slaves, but the price of chattels rose substantially in the 1730s and 1740s.[4] Farm prices rose to cover some of these expenses,

3. Allan Kulikoff, "The Economic Growth of the Eighteenth-Century Chesapeake Colonies," *Journal of Economic History*, XXXIX (1979), 284, provides full documentation. The argument can be formally stated as a downward shift in transaction costs, given an unchanging demand curve. The "staple thesis," the theoretical perspective that underlies this analysis, is cogently presented in David W. Galenson and Russell R. Menard, "Approaches to the Analysis of Economic Growth in Colonial British America," *Historical Methods*, XIII (1980), 3–10.
4. Southern Maryland slave prices reported in Allan Kulikoff, "Tobacco and Slaves: Population, Economy, and Society in Eighteenth-Century Prince George's County, Maryland" (Ph.D. diss., Brandeis University, 1976), 485–488, adjusted by the St. Mary's price index. Slave prices rose .1% a year from 1705 to 1733 and 1.3%–1.4% a year from 1733 to 1776, as computed from 1705, 1733, 1755, and 1776 values from linear regression.

and aggregate farm income from tobacco rose markedly between 1720 and 1750.[5] But most of the rise in income resulted from increases in the number of workers cultivating the crop. Farm income, moreover, declined when poor weather cut output or when tobacco prices were particularly depressed (see fig. 11).

Increasing Continental demand for tobacco led Chesapeake planters to overproduce, and these surpluses magnified the impact of depressions. Each downturn in tobacco prices triggered a similar sequence of events. When prices began to decline, planters responded by attempting to increase their tobacco output. Continued production led to even lower prices, and economic decline accelerated. Marginal producers, unable to cover their costs, dropped out of the market, and total exports stagnated. After several years of level exports, short-term European demand for tobacco usually improved. Prices therefore began to rise, and planters redoubled their efforts to grow tobacco. The stage was set for another depression and a repetition of the entire economic cycle.

The recurring depressions of the first half of the eighteenth century led to economic stagnation, even in a rich area like Prince George's County, Maryland. Planters on the eastern side of the county, along the Patuxent River, often owned many slaves and produced tobacco admired in London. Thousands of undeveloped acres awaited cultivation, and those frontier areas should have provided many opportunities for planters and added to the county's wealth as new households were formed and new fields cleared. Nonetheless, Prince George's families shared the stagnation of the region: per capita wealth in that county declined slowly during the first quarter of the eighteenth century and then rapidly during the depressions of the 1730s and 1740s (see fig. 12).[6]

The rising proportion of children in the population accounted for part of the decline of wealth per capita between 1700 and 1750. Both the size of households and the number of dependents supported by each worker in the county increased by nearly a third between 1705 and 1755. The burden of dependency rose throughout the region: in 1755, the number of dependents per worker along the tobacco coast was nearly identical to the number in Prince George's.[7] These increased levels of dependency resulted from

5. Maryland tobacco prices grew 1% a year, 1706–1732, and .6% a year, 1732–1735.
6. Prince George's Inventories and Land Records, 1725–1750, Maryland Hall of Records, Annapolis (MHR); Lois Green Carr, "County Government in Maryland, 1689–1709" (Ph.D. diss., Harvard University, 1968), chap. 7. Gloria L. Main, *Tobacco Colony: Life in Early Maryland, 1650–1720* (Princeton, N.J., 1982), 92–94, presents data consistent with this interpretation.
7. The dependency ratio ([person − taxables] ÷ persons) was 1.5 in Prince George's in 1704, 1.6 in 1733, and 1.9 in 1755, and it was 1.8 along the tobacco coast of Maryland and Virginia

Fig. 11. *Production and Income from Tobacco, 1705–1775*

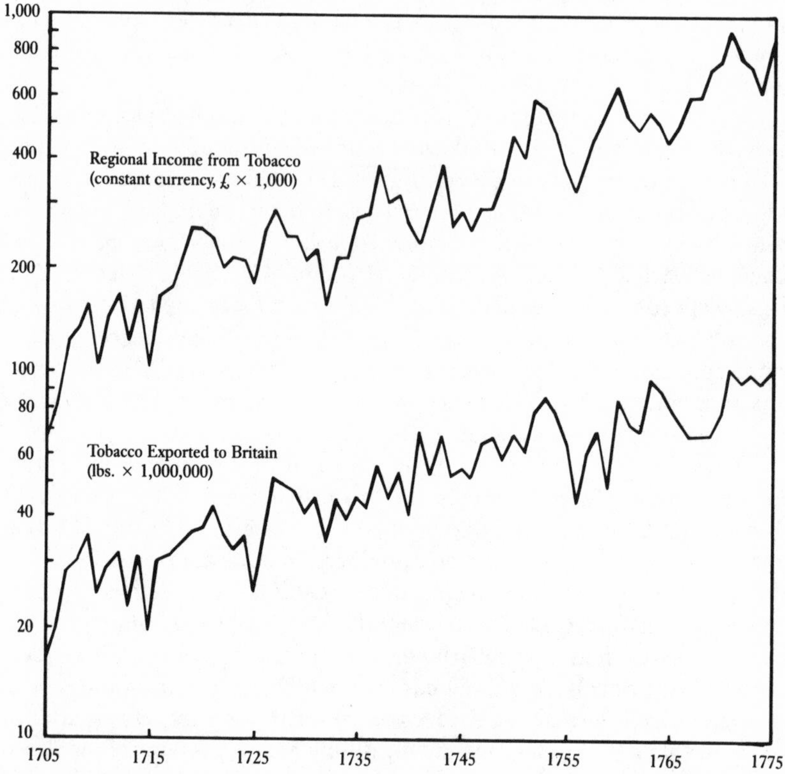

Source: U.S., Bureau of the Census, *Historical Statistics of the United States, Colonial Times to 1970* (Washington, D.C., 1975), II, 1189–1191. Income estimated by multiplying output by prices found in fig. 9, above.

higher birthrates among both whites and blacks and from the out-migration of former servants, which lowered the proportion of adult workers without children. If the relative number of children in the population had not increased, the decline of wealth per capita would have been greatly abated.[8]

White families in Prince George's attempted to overcome depressed economic conditions by expanding tobacco cultivation, and to this end they

___

in 1755. Calculated from data in Evarts B. Greene and Virginia D. Harrington, *American Population before the Federal Census of 1790* (New York, 1932), 129, 150–151; Black Books, II, 110–124, MHR; "Number of Inhabitants in Maryland," *Gentleman's Magazine, and Historical Chronicle*, XXXIV (1764), 261.

8. When the size of household is held constant at the level of 1705, mean per capita wealth becomes £25 in 1733 and £23 in 1755.

Fig. 12. *Wealth in Prince George's County.* Includes real estate, capital, and consumption goods.

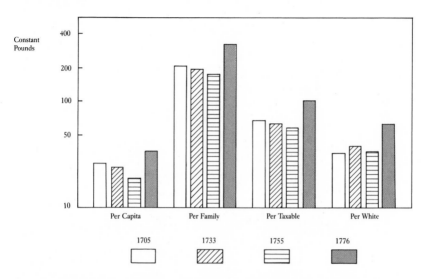

Source: Allan Kulikoff, "The Economic Growth of the Eighteenth-Century Chesapeake Colonies," *Journal of Economic History*, XXXIX (1979), 278. Constant pounds determined from items found in inventories, with land prices stated in pounds sterling as par.

purchased African slaves. Planters invested nearly every bit of spare capital in slaves, and the value of personal property such as livestock declined during the 1730s and 1740s (see fig. 13). Even the poorest planters wanted slaves. This preference resulted in an increase in the number of men of declining wealth who owned slaves but rented land. In 1733 such families had owned physical property (exclusive of slaves) worth £51 10s., but in 1755 their counterparts possessed goods worth only £18 8s.[9]

The purchase of slaves, however, led new masters into a double bind. They needed productive workers to increase tobacco output, which would allow them to pay their creditors and enjoy a higher standard of living. But new African slaves apparently were not particularly productive: wealth per taxable person, a proxy for the value of goods made by the labor force, declined in Prince George's over the first half of the century. Africans had little incentive to work diligently and be productive, and the poor living conditions for those who belonged to marginal planters further lowered their productivity. Tobacco prices often fell so low that planters used all

9. Calculated from Prince George's Inventories, 1731–1734 and 1755–1758; this group rose from 9% to 13% of the living population between 1733 and 1755.

Fig. 13. *Composition of Household Wealth in Prince George's County*

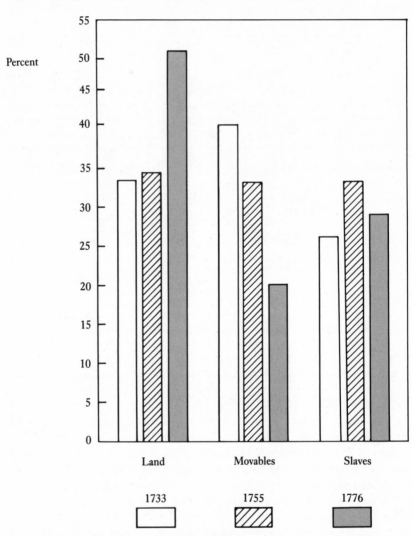

Source: Allan Kulikoff, "The Economic Growth of the Eighteenth-Century Chesapeake Colonies," *Journal of Economic History*, XXXIX (1979), 279.

their income from tobacco for their own subsistence. According to Gov. William Gooch, many of Virginia's planters could not afford to buy cloth during the severe depression of the early 1730s, and he described the result: "Their Negroes go naked all the Winter, have not proper tools to work with, and their Quarters for want of Nails are tumbling down."[10]

Declining per capita wealth, however, does not imply a reduced standard of living for most white families. Between 1705 and 1733, mean household wealth changed little, but wealth per white person rose because the number of whites in households declined as servants left the county. Although the wealth owned by white households declined between 1733 and 1755, living standards, by other measures, may have improved. For example, poor and middling planters in St. Mary's County (a poor neighbor of Prince George's) began buying amenities like earthenware, forks, and spices for the first time in the 1730s and 1740s.[11] A decline in the price of some imports and a heavy investment in slaves explain this apparent contradiction. When slaves are included as wealth, the wealth of white families rose from 1733 to 1755.[12]

Opportunity in a Tidewater County

The economic stagnation of the early eighteenth century decreased economic opportunity and increased the importance of inheritance in determining ultimate success, even in counties like Prince George's where substantial frontier land lay open for development. Youths who migrated to the county searching for employment were the least successful county residents, often unable even to form their own households. Men born in the county usually formed households there, but their chances of eventually owning land or slaves depended on the wealth their fathers had accumulated. Children of tenants inherited little from their fathers and rarely saved enough money from their crops, once the rent was paid, to buy cheap land in the county. Sons of wealthier men, in contrast, formed households, married, lived on their fathers' land rent-free, and inherited land and slaves after their fathers died.

The formation of a household was the initial step in gaining a foothold

10. Fig. 12; Gooch to Board of Trade, May 27, 1732, C.O. 1323/5, 12–13, Public Record Office (microfilm at Colonial Williamsburg Research Department [CW]).
11. Lois Green Carr and Lorena S. Walsh, "Changing Life Styles in Colonial St. Mary's County," *Working Papers from the Regional Economic History Research Center*, I, No. 3 (1978), *Economic Change in the Chesapeake Colonies*, 78–113.
12. Fig. 13; comment based upon price indexes for slaves, agricultural goods, and manufactures calculated by the St. Mary's City Commission from probate inventory data.

in the tobacco economy. As long as youths lived at home, they shared the status of their parents, but laborers who resided with their employers competed with slaves for work and thereby risked being identified with the debased status of black people. Many youthful migrants poured into Prince George's during the 1720s to take advantage of frontier land. About two-fifths of the taxable population of the county in 1733 had moved there during the previous fourteen years, but only half of these persisting migrants had formed households by 1733. Even those men who established farms remained marginal planters: nearly two-thirds of them were poor tenants who commanded only their own labor, about a quarter of them owned land or slaves, and only one-seventh of them possessed both land and slaves in 1733.[13]

Opportunities for youths to form households apparently diminished during the 1730s, despite a short recovery during the latter part of the decade. Men born in the county were far more likely to form a household than immigrants. While about half of the adolescent boys who lived with parents and kinfolk in 1733 had their own households by 1743, only a fifth of the migrant agricultural laborers stayed in the county and began their own households. A few of the remaining men formed households later in the 1740s, but most left the county to seek opportunities elsewhere.[14]

Sons of local residents were more successful in establishing independent households than in-migrants because they commanded greater access to capital. Agricultural laborers usually owned few goods other than the clothes on their back and the horse they used to travel from job to job. Since they had come to Prince George's in the 1720s searching for opportunities, they could probably expect no inheritance in the county of their birth. Most sons of local planters, in contrast, could expect to receive an inheritance, and since their families were known to creditors, they could command loans from merchants and gentlemen to help set up households.[15]

The probability that men who stayed in the county would be able to procure land or slaves—the two forms of capital most necessary for successful tobacco plantations—was directly related to the wealth of their fathers. Sons of poorer men were unable to amass sufficient capital to buy slaves or even purchase cheap frontier land on the county's borders. In fact, sons of men who owned both land and slaves were two and a half times

13. Black Books, X, 8–14, II, 109–114 (1719, 1733 tithables lists), MHR, linked to Prince George's Land Records and Inventories. Darrett B. Rutman and Anita H. Rutman, *A Place in Time: Explicatus* (New York, 1984), 148–158, shows similar patterns for Middlesex County and documents declines over time consistent with data presented here.
14. Black Books, II, 109–114, linked to lists of "Crows and Squirrels" returns in Levy Book A, MHR, for 1743.
15. Prince George's Inventories, 1730–1769, provide examples of goods owned by laborers.

as likely to own both forms of capital as sons of men who owned either land or slaves. Fewer than two of every fourteen sons of tenant nonslaveholders procured either land or slaves or both (see table 5).

Though the opportunity of sons was linked to the wealth of their fathers, youths who began families in Prince George's in the 1710s, 1720s, and 1730s had difficulty in attaining the economic position of their fathers. Only half the sons of men who owned land and slaves possessed both in 1733, and a fifth of the sons of such men were slaveless tenants. Some of them, of course, lived rent-free on the father's land or borrowed his slaves, but use of these resources tied a son to his command. Sons of poorer men fared even less well. Nearly half the sons of men who owned land or slaves were tenants in 1733, and only a fifth of them owned both land and slaves (table 5).

Table 5. *Economic Position of Sons and Position of Father in Prince George's County, circa 1733*

| | Percentage of Sons | | |
| | Status of Father | | |
Status of Son	Tenant Owning No Slaves ($N=112$)	Land- or Slave-owner ($N=321$)	Land- and Slave-owner ($N=498$)
Tenant owning no slaves ($N=344$)	85	46	20
Landowner owning no slaves ($N=232$)	9	34	23
Slaveowner owning no land ($N=42$)	0	1	8
Land- and slave-owner ($N=313$)	6	19	49
Total	100	100	100

Sources: Black Books, II, 109–114 (1733 tithables list), linked with Black Books, X, 8–14 (1719 tithables list), Prince George's Land Records, Prince George's Wills and Inventories, Prince George's Rent Roll, MHR; and data in Lois Green Carr, "County Government in Maryland, 1689–1709" (Ph.D. diss., Harvard University, 1968), appendixes.

Note: The percentages are weighted to include cases where the status of the father could not be determined. In each case the son's status was known, and the unknown fathers were distributed in the same frequency as the known fathers. A fifth of each group of sons were assumed to be immigrants. These cross-sectional data compare fathers and sons at different times in the life cycle.

Above all, success in Prince George's early in the eighteenth century depended upon the timing of inheritance. Sons of men who owned land or slaves or both rarely achieved the father's economic position while he was still alive: nearly half the sons of small property owners and a fifth of sons of planters who owned both land and slaves possessed neither kind of property during the father's lifetime. When the father died, they commonly inherited land or slaves or used capital they received to purchase these goods. Nearly all the sons of planters who owned land or slaves inherited or bought land after their fathers died, and almost half owned slaves as well. Three-quarters of the sons of substantial planters owned both kinds of capital after the father's death, and almost all owned land (see table 6).

Only sons of wealthy men could turn their portion into capital to procure land or slaves and thereby ensure their prosperity, because only they received sufficient liquid capital to make such purchases. Planters who owned both land and slaves held property ten times more valuable than the property of nonslaveholding planters at every stage of the life cycle. While the standard of living of men who owned land or slaves or both rose slowly over the life cycle, tenant nonslaveholders lost ground. The wealth of mar-

Table 6. *Inheritance and Social Mobility in Prince George's County, 1733*

	Percentage of Sons			
	Status of Father			
	Land- or Slaveowner		Land- and Slaveowner	
Status of Son	Father Alive (*N* = 69)	Father Dead (*N* = 61)	Father Alive (*N* = 102)	Father Dead (*N* = 151)
Tenant owning no slaves	46	7	21	2
Land- or slaveowner	38	46	36	25
Land- and slaveowner	16	48	43	73
Total	100	101	100	100

Sources: Black Books, II, 109–114 (1733 tithables list), linked with Black Books, X, 8–14 (1719 tithables list), Prince George's Land Records, Prince George's Wills and Inventories, Prince George's Rent Rolls, MHR; and data in Lois Green Carr, "County Government in Maryland, 1689–1709" (Ph.D. diss., Harvard University, 1968), appendixes.

Note: Only known cases are included. There were insufficient cases for a "Father: Tenant without Slaves" group.

ried tenants with minor children was only a tenth higher than the wealth of unmarried men in the group, despite the added financial burdens the birth of children entailed. Tenants slowly accumulated livestock and consumer durables, thereby increasing their wealth when middle-aged, but their assets declined when they paid portions to their children upon marriage, and they had little to leave their descendants when they died (see fig. 14).

Fig. 14. *Wealth Levels over the Life Cycle, Prince George's County, 1730–1769*

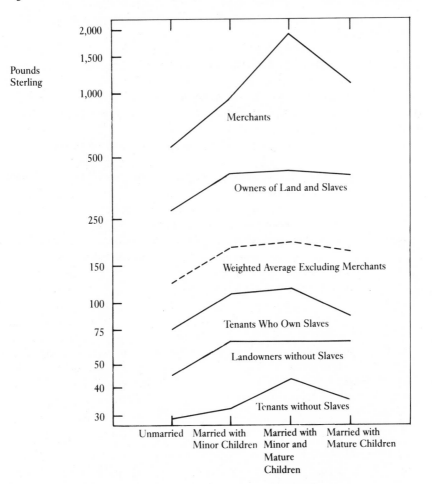

Sources: Prince George's Inventories, 1730–1769, MHR, and methods detailed in Allan Kulikoff, "Tobacco and Slaves: Population, Economy, and Society in Eighteenth-Century Prince George's County, Maryland" (Ph.D. diss., Brandeis University, 1976), 522–526.

Tenant nonslaveholders in Prince George's not only owned far less than their freeholding and slaveowning neighbors, but, in addition, the wealth they possessed and passed on to their heirs could be turned into working capital only with difficulty. These families owned livestock, horses, tobacco, corn, a small quantity of cash, and household items. Consumption goods like bedding, clothing, furniture, and kitchenware accounted for a fifth of their wealth, and another two-fifths was tied up in livestock and grains needed for subsistence. Only a third of their assets was in liquid capital like cash and debts payable (see table 7).

Sons of tenants received little help from their poor parents. A middle-aged tenant with three children, for instance, left his family with an estate of about forty-five pounds; after the debts had been paid and the widow died, each child inherited goods worth only ten pounds, including a cow or two, some swine, a few shillings in cash, and several hundred pounds of crop tobacco, along with a share of the couple's personal possessions. The value and composition of this inheritance was insufficient to purchase land or a slave.[16]

Even if a tenant nonslaveholder added this inheritance to property he had accumulated, he could not buy either a slave or a tract of land. A very frugal tenant might accumulate the fifteen pounds needed to buy a fifty-acre tract only if he enjoyed five years of good crops, received high tobacco prices, and then saved half of his annual profits of about six pounds for five years. That would have been difficult, for he needed to pay his taxes and purchase salt and clothing with his profits. Purchase of a newly arrived African, moreover, was beyond his grasp, for he did not have the sterling bills of exchange that merchants demanded as payment.[17]

Men who owned land but not slaves possessed goods worth five to ten times the value of the goods of tenants without slaves, and half their wealth was concentrated in land, an easily salable form of property. A middle-aged freeholder with three children left his family with about £125 in the 1730s; after his executor had paid his debts and the widow died, each child inherited goods worth £30. The father had owned fewer than two hundred acres; and if all three children inherited a part, one child probably bought out the others with his share of the personal goods of the estate. The children without land had enough property to invest in land or a slave, and half of them owned both land and slaves before they died.[18]

16. Calculations based upon wealth levels reported in fig. 14 for tenants without slaves, about age 45. I assumed that a tenth of the estate was consumed by debts and fees, that the widow lived five years after her husband's death, and that the estate lost two pounds a year.
17. I estimated land prices at 6s. per acre (see fig. 17, below) and calculated income on a crop of 2,000 pounds of tobacco at 1d. per pound (see fig. 10) and land rent at 500 pounds a year (see Earle, *Tidewater Settlement System*, 224–226) for the early 1730s.
18. Table 7; fig. 14. I weighted those who owned land and those who owned slaves by their

Table 7. *Estimated Wealth of Householders in Prince George's County in the 1730s*

Group	Land	Labor	Crops and Live-stock	Other Capital	Consump-tion Items	Total Wealth, Constant £
			Percentage of Assets			
Tenant, owning no slaves	0	2	38	33	22	26
Landowner, owning no slaves	49	1	19	15	16	117
Land- and slaveowner	35	27	13	13	10	596

Sources: Prince George's Inventories and Land Records; Black Books, II, 110–124, MHR.

Note: Assets of all variables but land were calculated from probate inventories. Land value per decedent was estimated by multiplying the average landholdings of men with slaves and land, and of freeholders without slaves by land prices abstracted from the deed books. This value was then added to total estate value, and the proportion of wealth held in various categories determined.

Planters who owned both land and slaves enjoyed a measure of financial security and left their children well equipped to succeed. Two-thirds of their wealth was held in land and slaves, and they could put four or five slave workers into their tobacco fields. Since adult slaves and their offspring were given less to consume than whites, these planters accumulated a good deal of property. A modest planter who owned about two hundred acres of land and two adult slaves, for instance, left a widow and three children with an estate of about two hundred pounds in the 1730s. After the widow died and the estate was settled, each child inherited goods worth about fifty pounds. One child probably received the land, another child the slaves, and the third some personal property and cash from the two siblings. Even the child who received neither land nor slaves gained sufficient capital to buy a small tract of land or one or two slaves, and the other two could use their newly gained land or slaves to increase the size of their holdings. Nearly all the sons of these planters, in fact, eventually owned both land and slaves.[19]

---

weight in the population and then figured their wealth at age 45. I assumed that a tenth of the estate was consumed by fees and debts, that the widow outlived her husband by five years, and that the estate declined in value by three pounds each year.

19. *Ibid.*; £200 was about a third the mean wealth of those with land and slaves. I assumed that 20% of the estate was used to pay fees and debts, that the widow lived five years after her husband, that the estate lost £5 each year, and that the value of the estate's slaves rose £15.

Although substantial planters stayed in Prince George's and tried to consolidate their fortunes during hard times, poor families left the county in large numbers during the 1730s. Men born outside Prince George's, who had no kinfolk in the county, migrated with particularly great frequency. Three-quarters of the men who worked as agricultural laborers in 1733 left by 1743. They were joined by more than half the poor migrant men who managed to form households but who discovered that they could acquire neither land nor slaves. Three-fifths of the men who left the county between 1733 and 1743 belonged to these two groups. Most of the rest of the migrants were either sons of householders (and these men were usually descended from tenants) or long-established tenants who decided to try their luck elsewhere. About two-fifths of both groups left the county. In contrast, fewer than a third of the men who owned land or slaves and fewer than a sixth who possessed both moved out of the county; they were apparently satisfied with the income they and their slaves produced (see table 8).[20]

The Chesapeake Frontier, 1700–1740

Poor families left tidewater to escape the effects of low tobacco prices and relative land scarcity and moved to the frontier to find inexpensive land. But there was no escape from depressed economic conditions. Planters could not begin to exploit large quantities of new land until European demand for tobacco began to grow after 1715. The rate of frontier settlement rose during the 1720s and 1730s and was particularly high during the depression of the late 1720s and early 1730s. Even then success probably eluded most migrants. Although land was cheaper on the frontier than in tidewater, the costs of starting a plantation were still higher than most poor migrants could afford; the most successful families brought some capital with them. Moreover, even after migrants started plantations, their tobacco often commanded low prices because the fragile leaves were damaged during transit.[21]

The inhabited parts of the Chesapeake colonies more than doubled in

20. About 31% of the sons of men with land and slaves, 36% of those whose fathers owned land or slaves, and 65% of the sons of tenants left the county between 1733 and 1743. See table 8 for weighting techniques.
21. See chap. 2 for the relationship of land scarcity to settlement. Taxed land south of the Rappahannock River grew from 2.2 to 2.9 million acres between 1702 and 1723 (growth rate of 1.7% a year) and reached 4.6 million acres by 1735 (3.3% per year, 4.0% from 1726 to 1735). See Quitrent Returns, C.O. 1313–1353/5, and T. 90–503, P.R.O. collected by George Reese and on file at CW.

Table 8. *Migration from Prince George's County, 1733–1743*

Group	Percentage Migrating	Percentage of All Migrants
Laborers without kin ties in the county	75[a]	37
Householders owning no land or slaves, recent migrants to county	58	19
County natives, living with parents or kin	39[a]	15
Long-term residents, owning no land or slaves	39	10
Householders owning either land or slaves	29	13
Householders owning both land and slaves	15	6

Sources: Black Books, X, 8–14, and II, 109–114; Levy Books A, MHR.

Notes: Recent migrants are those on the 1733 tithables list whose families were not in the county in 1719; long-term residents were present, or their families were present, in 1719. [a]The 1743 list includes no nonhouseholders. I estimated that 15% of the 1733 nonheads who were living with parents were still in the county as nonheads in 1743. I similarly estimated that 7.5% of those living with other kin in 1733 and 4% of the unrelated laborers stayed in the county without forming households. Known deaths are excluded from the analysis.

size between 1700 and 1740. In 1700, only a few counties on the Eastern Shore and at the eastern end of the region's peninsulas were filled with plantations, and nearly half the land in tidewater remained unpatented. Since the unpopulated parts of tidewater were located on navigable rivers near centers of population, they quickly filled with planters early in the century, growing from three thousand to nearly fourteen thousand taxable men and women between 1700 and 1730. Once these areas were thickly seated with farms, planters began to settle the parts of piedmont closest to settlements and navigable water. In the 1700s and 1710s, pioneers reached the falls of the James River but settled east of the falls of the Rappahannock and Potomac rivers. Between 1720 and 1740, tobacco planters moved northwest along the Rappahannock and the tributaries of the York River and then followed the courses of the Potomac and James rivers toward the west. Very few families reached southside Virginia, because much of the area was far from white habitation and because streams in the area either were too shallow for navigation or emptied in North Carolina, far from Virginia's tobacco ports (see map 2).[22]

The problem of transporting tobacco around the falls of rivers made piedmont Virginia an undesirable place to settle. Tobacco was a bulky commodity, packed in heavy hogsheads (barrels) and liable to disintegrate if rolled long distances over bumpy roads. Though most tidewater planters easily transported their tobacco the few miles from their farms to nearby landings or warehouses, piedmont planters lived much further from landings. No water vehicle could navigate the falls of rivers that separated tidewater from piedmont, and some planters lived far from any stream that even a flatboat could use. The Virginia assembly refused to establish any inspection warehouse (to which, after 1730, all tobacco had to be taken) in piedmont until the 1780s, apparently on the grounds that travel from piedmont to an oceangoing ship was likely to damage the tobacco and render up-country inspection futile.[23]

Almost as soon as they arrived in piedmont, pioneers tried to solve their transportation problems by making Indian paths into roads and digging roadbeds between the paths. The history of the "three-notch'd road" that linked the Shenandoah Valley to the falls of the James River illustrates the functions of these highways. In 1733 the Goochland County Court ordered that "a road be cleared from the Mountains . . . the most convenient way." Only five thousand people lived in Goochland, which stretched from the falls of the James to the Blue Ridge Mountains, and only a third of the land along the road had been patented by 1733. People and goods moved easily on this well-marked road. Innkeepers ran taverns along its route, and roads were cleared from churches and courthouses to the highway. In the late 1730s, after the highway was completed, planters moved rapidly along the road, farming the countryside.[24]

Planters soon tired of carting their produce around the heads of

22. Richard L. Morton, *Colonial Virginia: Westward Expansion and the Prelude to Revolution* (Chapel Hill, N.C., 1960), II, chaps. 5, 13, 14, details westward migration in Virginia. Calculation of population growth in western tidewater based upon 1710 and 1719 tithables for Henrico, Hanover, Caroline, and Spotsylvania counties (Greene and Harrington, *American Population*, 146–151), with Hanover tithes estimated from the relationship between New Kent (the mother county) and Hanover tithables once Hanover was established.

23. G. Melvin Herndon, "A History of Tobacco in Virginia, 1613–1860" (master's thesis, University of Virginia, 1956), 13–25, and maps of locations of tobacco warehouses appended to it. Inspection laws will be discussed in detail at the end of this chapter.

24. Nathaniel Mason Pawlett and Howard Newton, Jr., *The Route of the Three Notch'd Road: A Preliminary Report* (Charlottesville, Va., 1976), esp. 9 and appended map. See James O'Mara, *An Historical Geography of Urban System Development: Tidewater Virginia in the Eighteenth Century*, Atkinson College, York University, Geographical Monographs, No. 13 (Downsview, Ont., 1983), chap. 3, for a detailed discussion of roads.

Map 2. *The Settlement of Virginia, 1700–1740*

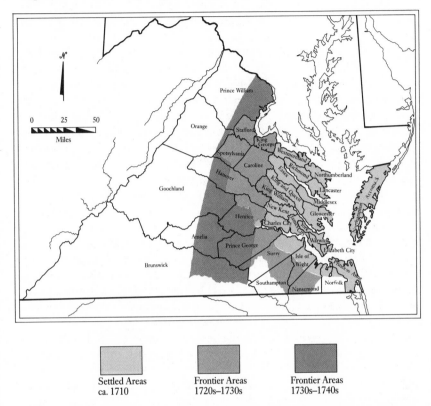

Settled Areas
ca. 1710

Frontier Areas
1720s–1730s

Frontier Areas
1730s–1740s

Sources: Quitrent Returns, C.O. 1313–1353/5, P.R.O. (film at CW); frontiers south of the Rappahannock defined as counties where less than half the land was patented and taxed land grew at a rate of at least 5% a year. Tithables for the Northern Neck in Evarts B. Greene and Virginia D. Harrington, *American Population before the Federal Census of 1790* (New York, 1932), 146–151; and Court Order Books and Parish Registers, VSL. Taxable population of the Northern Neck frontier grew at least 3% a year.

streams and petitioned the assembly and county court to build bridges over small streams and establish ferries over the larger ones. In March 1740, for instance, 103 men petitioned the court of Prince George's to build a bridge over Rock Creek, near the falls of the Potomac River, because the creek was "often very Difficult to pass and the road being much used . . . by the whole County and many others." Similar political pressure led the Virginia assembly to start ferries across the James, Rappahannock, and Potomac rivers soon after white habitation began. The assembly created eleven ferries on the upper reaches of the James River between 1720 and 1748, mostly during the early 1740s, in areas first settled in the 1720s and 1730s; they established three ferries across the Potomac from Fairfax County to Maryland between 1738 and 1742, about twenty years after the first pioneers arrived in Fairfax.[25]

By the early 1740s, planters who lived near the Rappahannock or James rivers ingeniously solved the problem of transporting bulky tobacco to distant markets. Instead of rolling their hogsheads long distances or carrying them on wagons, they connected "two large canoes, each formed out of a solid piece of fifty or sixty feet in length," and placed five or ten hogsheads on the platform between the two canoes, "which from three to five men could convey with ease the distance of one hundred and fifty miles to market, without the help of horses." The tobacco was carried from the falls to a nearby inspection warehouse by wagon.[26]

Wealthier migrants, rather than poor families forced out of tidewater, reaped the benefits of inexpensive land and improvements in transportation. The first pioneers to move to a wilderness area were often poor squatters who did not have sufficient capital to pay to patent the land. As soon as they had built roads and begun small settlements, more prosperous planters, whose families often already owned land in the area, joined these pioneers. An examination of the settlement of frontier areas in Orange County in the late 1730s and Prince George's during the late seventeenth and early eighteenth centuries illustrates these processes.

Orange County, located in a piedmont area between the Potomac and Rappahannock rivers, was first settled in the late 1720s, and its government was first organized in 1734. The original settlers included a number of poor and unpropertied men, nonslaveholders who patented land and formed households, and wealthy men who established slave quarters in the wilderness. Poor pioneers among the settlers found success elusive; tax collectors reported in 1738 that forty-four men, who had not paid their head taxes, either "ran away" or were "not found," and six others apparently died with "no effects." These men represented at least a twelfth of the householders

25. Prince George's Court Records, X, 570, XXV, 280–284, MHR; William Waller Hening, ed., *The Statutes at Large: Being a Collection of All the Laws of Virginia* . . . , 13 vols. (Richmond, Philadelphia, 1809–1823), IV, 362–364, 438–440, 531–533; V, 66–67, 104–106, 189–191, 249–251, 364–365; VI, 13–21, 288–290, 494–496 (hereafter *Virginia Statutes at Large*); Arthur Pierce Middleton, *Tobacco Coast: A Maritime History of Chesapeake Bay in the Colonial Period* (Newport News, Va., 1953), 458–460.

26. William Tatham, *An Historical and Practical Essay on the Culture and Commerce of Tobacco* (London, 1800), repr. in G. Melvin Herndon, ed., *William Tatham and the Culture of Tobacco* (Coral Gables, Fla., 1969), 62–64; Ralph Emmett Fall, ed., *The Diary of Robert Rose: A View of Virginia by a Scottish Colonial Parson, 1746–1751* (Verona, Va., 1977), 53, 250–252.

in the county. Nearly nine-tenths of the taxpayers in 1739 were men of small fortune, who worked the ground with the help of a wife, an adolescent son, or perhaps one or two slaves. At the same time, however, there were at least thirty-seven slave quarters, run by overseers for nonresidents in the county. The owners of these quarters included such prominent families from tidewater counties on the Rappahannock as Talliferro, Baylor, and Taylor.[27]

The first migrants to Prince George's arrived from adjacent areas in Maryland and from abroad in the 1670s and 1680s. They moved northward along the Patuxent River but avoided land near the Potomac River, where only a third of them had settled by 1700. During the early eighteenth century, planters moved further north to the Potomac River and its Eastern Branch. The rate of migration in the 1720s depended upon the concentration of settlers in the area at that time. Most of the land near the Patuxent River was divided into farms by 1720; more people therefore moved into the sparsely peopled Potomac and Eastern Branch watershed, where population doubled from in-migration (see map 3).[28]

Migrants traveled greater distances to reach the frontier than to come to more settled places. Although nearly all the new residents of lands along the Patuxent River had moved from nearby neighborhoods, migrants came from more distant places to reach the Potomac frontier. Nearly half the new residents of the frontier arrived from homes outside Prince George's, and only one-seventh of the native Prince Georgians who moved there had lived in neighborhoods adjacent to their new homes.

The level of success achieved by migrants to the Potomac frontier depended heavily upon the economic resources they could command. Men who arrived from outside the county tended to be poor farmers, searching for opportunities to establish a homestead. Although they apparently began households with ease, nearly two-thirds of them owned neither land nor slaves in 1733, shortly after their arrival, and another fifth held fewer than 150 acres and owned no slaves. The only outsiders who succeeded on the county's frontier in the 1720s were men who brought human or financial capital with them, like George Murdock, pastor of the local parish who

27. John Thomas Schlotterbeck, "Plantation and Farm: Social and Economic Change in Orange and Greene Counties, Virginia, 1716 to 1860" (Ph.D. diss., Johns Hopkins University, 1980), 15–17, 28–30; "Orange County Tithe Lists," *William and Mary Quarterly*, 1st Ser., XXVII (1918–1919), 20–21; reports of tithables, Orange County Order Books, Virginia State Library, Richmond (VSL).

28. Carr, "County Government in Maryland," 562–579; Louise Joyner Hienton, *Prince George's Heritage: Sidelights on the Early History of Prince George's County, Maryland, from 1696 to 1800* (Baltimore, 1977), chap. 4.

Map 3. *Gross Migration into Areas of Prince George's County, 1719–1733*

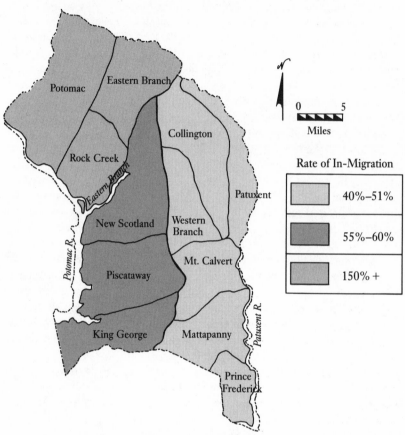

Sources: 1719 and 1733 tithables lists, Black Books, II, 109–114, X, 8–14, MHR.

owned 150 acres and two slaves, or George Buchanan, an immigrant merchant who held four slaves and 1,200 acres.[29]

The rest of the new residents of the Potomac frontier moved ten to forty miles from settled parts of Prince George's or adjacent Anne Arundel County. Nine-tenths of these families owned land or slaves in 1733 and took up family land or purchased frontier acreage with their inheritances. Their families had patented or purchased land early in the century and then established outlying slave quarters or waited until poorer pioneers began farming before setting up a homestead. These families could be divided

29. Prince George's Wills and Land Records, 1725–1735.

into three groups. Thirty-two men, mostly in their forties and fifties, who had operated farms elsewhere in the county for several decades, pulled up stakes and worked frontier lands. A second group of twenty-four youths in their twenties and thirties, sons of substantial freeholders, settled inherited or family land or used family capital to buy a frontier plantation. A final group of twenty-three youths, sons of less wealthy landholders, established farms or worked family land.

Family capital played a crucial role in the development of the Potomac frontier. Prince George's planters owned three-quarters of the slaves brought to the frontier in the 1720s, and they quickly established networks of credit with people in their former neighborhoods. Several examples will illustrate the process. William Ray, born in 1684, grew tired of waiting for his elderly father to die and used capital he had accumulated in his youth to move to 100 acres on the frontier. William Junior, age twenty-eight, formed a separate household and shared his father's land; son John, age twenty-six, moved to lands along Rock Creek owned by his grandfather. William Offutt, who lived near the Patuxent River and owned 4,100 acres and twenty taxable slaves in 1733, shared his bounty with his sons before he died. John Offutt lived on a 250-acre tract near the Potomac and worked three slaves; two of his brothers, William Junior and James, operated two plantations on the frontier granted by their father and between them owned thirteen adult slaves and 2,730 acres in 1733. When William Senior died in 1734, he divided his remaining land among the three younger sons, including Thomas, the youngest, who joined his two brothers on the Potomac frontier when he came of age.[30]

Plantation Management in Tidewater, 1700–1750

Whether they moved to the frontier or stayed in their old homes, planters had to cope with recurring depressions in the tobacco trade. During depressions tobacco growers could choose among limited alternatives. They could grow corn and wheat instead of tobacco, but most planters could not find markets for grain. They could try to operate diversified farms that made sufficient food and cloth for subsistence, but these activities would not produce enough income to pay their debts. Moreover, most planters already raised enough corn, hogs, cattle, and fowl to feed their families, and they usually did not have the money during depressions to invest in home manufacture of cloth.[31] The vast majority of planters continued to grow

30. *Ibid.*; Queen Anne and Prince George's Parish Registers, MHR; Prince George's Wills, box 4, folder 60.
31. Earle, *Tidewater Settlement System*, 120–126.

tobacco hoping to pay their creditors and clothe their families no matter how low tobacco prices fell.

In 1680, nearly every family in the Chesapeake region grew tobacco, but some planters abandoned the crop during each depression from the 1680s through the 1740s. Almost all these planters lived in older tidewater counties where low-quality tobacco was grown and where some substitute staple, no matter how inadequate, had been found. When high prices returned, many of these planters resumed tobacco cultivation, but by 1715, after two downswings and periods of stagnating tobacco exports, only four of every five Chesapeake families regularly cultivated tobacco, and in 1750, after two more severe depressions had passed, only three of every four householders grew tobacco.[32]

The Eastern Shore, tidewater counties south of the James River, and the western James River frontier were especially affected by low prices of the 1690s and 1700s. Virginia's Eastern Shore, which yielded the lowest-quality tobacco in the two colonies, turned to market farming and forest industries and began trading with New England and the West Indies. Further north, planters on Maryland's Eastern Shore bought plows to begin cultivating small grains, and began raising sheep and buying spinning wheels to start manufacturing wool. Planters who lived south of the James River, near to sea-lanes leading to the West Indies, began sending large quantities of corn to those islands. Householders there began experimenting with flax and hemp cultivation and linen production, and men who lived near the Great Dismal Swamp exported naval stores. Finally, some pioneers who lived beyond the falls of the James River raised grains and livestock for their own consumption—the low price of tobacco, combined with high transit costs, precluded the operation of tobacco plantations.[33]

Other defections from tobacco production cut into the growth of tobacco exports during depressions in the 1720s and 1740s. Farmers who lived in the northern half of the Eastern Shore and in northern and western Maryland began shipping grain to the West Indies and Europe. Grain prices declined more slowly than tobacco prices during depressions, and mer-

32. "Inhabitants in Maryland," *Gentleman's Magazine*, XXXIV (1764), 231; Paul G. E. Clemens, *The Atlantic Economy and Colonial Maryland's Eastern Shore: From Tobacco to Grain* (Ithaca, N.Y., 1980), chap. 6. Crude estimates are as follows: 100% in 1680, 81% in 1712–1724 (tidewater south of James, lower Eastern Shore eliminated); 73% in 1750 (these areas plus Shenandoah Valley, two-thirds of Baltimore County, all but 600 Eastern Shore taxables; two-thirds of the slaves and nine-tenths of whites in Frederick County, Maryland, not counted). Speculations here based upon Clemens's work and items cited in nn. 33, 34.

33. Research in Naval Office Records, 1699–1706, by Russell R. Menard; Spotswood to bishop of London, June 13, 1717, *Spotswood Letters*, II, 254; C. G. Gordon Moss, "The Virginia Plantation System: A Study of Economic Conditions in that Colony for the Years 1700 to 1750" (Ph.D. diss., Yale University, 1932), 321–328; Main, *Tobacco Colony*, 73–76.

chants in Philadelphia and Baltimore encouraged farmers to plant and sell more grain.[34]

When depression struck, even planters who continued to grow tobacco tried to reduce expenditures and become more self-sufficient. In a typical prosperous year, planters bought cloth, sugar, iron goods (pots, nails, tools), ceramics, and liquor and hired carpenters and coopers to repair plantation structures and make tobacco hogsheads. Some of these expenses could be postponed during a depression, and planters could save money by growing a wider variety of crops for consumption and local trade, purchasing artisans' tools, or making their own cloth. After tobacco prices started to rise, families kept some of their new tools and added to them during the next depression. As a result, planters were more self-sufficient in 1750 than in 1700.[35]

An examination of the ability of southern Maryland planters to produce homemade cloth shows both the cumulative increase in diversified economic activity on tobacco plantations and the limitations of diversification as a means of fighting depressions. In 1680, few southern Maryland planters owned either sheep or equipment like spinning wheels or looms to process it. By the 1740s, half the families in that area owned sheep or wool-processing equipment, and nearly a third owned both. Most of the progress in diversification, however, came after the severest part of depressions had passed, when planters could afford to buy sheep or spinning wheels. Householders bought equipment and were best able to make cloth just as tobacco prices began to rise in the mid-1710s, mid-1730s, and early 1750s (see table 9 and fig. 15). They tended, however, to let some equipment fall into disuse once recovery was well under way and had to invest in these tools again when the next tobacco depression hit the region.[36]

After 1730, growing numbers of planters owned sheep or wool-making equipment, but most of them could not make a piece of cloth from scratch because they were unwilling or unable to invest four pounds sterling to buy a herd of ten sheep, cards to clean and arrange the fibers of the raw wool, a spinning wheel to make thread and yarn, and a loom to weave the yarn into cloth needed to produce coarse woolens. The sum of all this equaled at least half the tobacco income of a single worker and, when added to taxes and living expenses, was beyond the reach of poorer and middling planters.

---

34. U.S., Bureau of the Census, *Historical Statistics of the United States: Colonial Times to 1970* (Washington, D.C., 1976), 1168, 1190–1191; C.O. 1443–1444/5 (Lower James Naval Office Records); Clemens, *Atlantic Economy*, chap. 6; Clarence P. Gould, "The Economic Causes of the Rise of Baltimore," in *Essays in Colonial History Presented to Charles McLean Andrews by his Students* (New Haven, Conn., 1933), 225–251.

35. Earle, *Tidewater Settlement System*, 106–123; Prince George's Inventories, 1730–1769. Inventories, the basis for this section, indicate ownership of goods at death, but I have assumed that changes in items in inventories reflect real changes in the general economy.

36. Earle, *Tidewater Settlement System*, 122–123.

Table 9. *Wool-Making in Prince George's County, 1730–1769*

Item[a]	Percentage of Householders with Item[b]			
	1730s	1740s	1750s	1760s
Sheep	41	52	62	50
Cards or wheels	45	41	57	47
Looms	5	2	4	7
Sheep & cards or wheels	28	30	41	30
Sheep & looms	1	2	2	5
None	38	43	20	24

Source: Prince George's Inventories, 1730–1769, MHR.

Notes: [a]Several categories are cumulative: those with looms include some who had cards or wheels as well; many of those with sheep and looms also owned cards or wheels. [b]The percentages are weighted averages using all inventories ($N = 751$) probated in these years. The proportions owned by four groups (tenants without slaves, tenants with slaves, landowners without slaves, and landowners with slaves) were counted in each time period by their approximate appearance in the living population.

Instead, planters variously bought sheep, wheels, or looms and had to trade raw materials for services to produce a piece of cloth (table 9).

Wealthy men who owned slaves and farmed their own land were able to weather depressions far better than other planters. Only a quarter of the tenant farmers in Prince George's owned sheep or processing equipment in the 1730s and 1740s, and usually this amounted to just a few head of sheep, a card, or a spinning wheel. In contrast, almost three-quarters of the men who owned both slaves and land also possessed sheep, and almost half owned both sheep and cards or wheels. Although the proportion of tenants who raised sheep or owned processing equipment rose to over two-thirds by the early 1750s, the differential between tenants and wealthier planters remained great.[37]

Although the cost of looms, spinning wheels, and sheep prevented some poorer planters from making cloth (especially during depressions), the labor required to cultivate tobacco and corn also inhibited diversification. "Tobacco," contended Edward Carrington in a letter to Alexander Hamilton late in the century, "requires much labor when growing, and, what with

37. Prince George's Inventories, 1740–1769, show that 42% of the tenants, but 81% of men who owned land and slaves, possessed sheep; 42% of the tenants, but 68% of the landed slaveholders, owned cards or wheels; 22% of the tenants, but 67% of landholding slave-owners, possessed both.

Fig. 15. *Ownership of Wool-Processing Equipment in Maryland, 1680–1770.*
Includes cards, looms, and wheels. Data centered on midpoints of three-
or four-year groups.

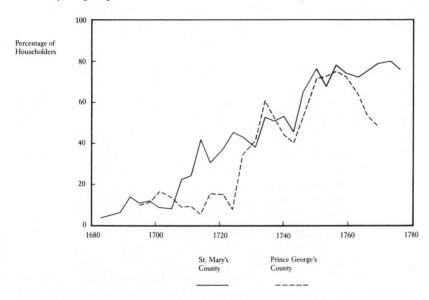

St. Mary's County

Prince George's County

Sources: Prince George's Inventories, 1700–1769 (1700–1729 collected by Lois Green Carr),
MHR: Lois Green Carr and Lorena S. Walsh, "Changing Life Styles in Colonial St. Mary's
County," *Working Papers from the Regional Economic History Research Center,* I, No. 3 (1978),
Economic Change in the Chesapeake Colonies, 107–109.

fitting it for market . . . leaves but little time for the same hands to Manufacture." Only "white females in poor families" and slave women made
cloth, and most of the cloth needed to make garments for slaves had to be
purchased.[38]

Most tobacco planters failed both to diversify their crops and to increase home manufactures. When hard times struck, they responded primarily by trying to increase their tobacco output. Wealthy men bought
African slaves and put them to work raising tobacco, and poor planters
redoubled their own efforts. Since merchants paid for tobacco by the
pound, planters increased the weight of their crop in every possible way,
including packing the trashiest leaves in their hogsheads, "even the very

38. Edward Carrington to Alexander Hamilton, Oct. 4, 8, 1791, with enclosures, in Harold C.
Syrett, ed., *The Papers of Alexander Hamilton,* IX (New York, 1965), 275–282, 299–304 (quote
on 276).

sweepings of their Tobacco Houses." Trashy tobacco brought low prices, but planters persisted in selling it. "This tobacco bad as it is," commented Governor Gooch of Virginia in 1729, "brings the Money or Goods and helps to maintain their Families"; when their tobacco "produces very small returns," they export yet more trash to pay for imports.[39]

The Political Economy of Tobacco Regulation

Tobacco planters unable to cope with the economic devastation of recurring depressions turned to provincial governments to solve their problems. Political leaders in Maryland and Virginia responded to economic crises by attempting to centralize trade, by encouraging diversification, and by trying to raise the price of tobacco by improving the quality and reducing the quantity of the crop exported each year. Ebenezer Cook, the poet laureate of Maryland, described this program in 1730. Cook suggested first that the only way to reverse the market's "ebbing Course" was to limit each worker to "*Six Hundred* Weight, / of *Sotweed* good, and fit for Freight," a two-thirds reduction in output per laborer. But improving the quality of the staple was not enough; Marylanders had to establish towns and build warehouses in them to secure the tobacco crop from the elements. Towns would not grow, and prosperity would not return until planters cultivated "all Sorts of *Grain*." New crops would lead to urban growth, and artisans "of ev'ry Sort" would come to the new towns "When they hear *Money* circulates, / Within our Towns and City Gates."[40]

Political leaders in the Chesapeake colonies experimented with various policies during each depression, searching for an effective solution. The two assemblies emphasized the creation of towns and the centralization of trade, rather than tobacco regulation, during the depression of 1703–1713. Maryland and Virginia legislators enacted similar comprehensive town acts in 1705 and 1706. The laws established towns in nearly every county and were designed to foster manufacturing, provide trades for displaced planters, and encourage farmers to shift from tobacco cultivation to provisioning the towns' awaited inhabitants. The new ports, moreover, would cut the costs of transportation by reducing the number of places ships had to stop to pick up tobacco. In 1712 the Virginia assembly further mandated the

39. Gooch to secretary of state, Feb. 28, 1729, C.O. 1237/5, 130–131. See also Spotswood to Commissioners of Trade, Dec. 29, 1713, *Spotswood Letters*, II, 48.
40. Ebenezer Cook, *[Sotweed Redivivus; or,] The Planter's Looking-Glass* (1730), in Bernard C. Steiner, ed., *Early Maryland Poetry: The Works of Ebenezer Cook* . . . , Maryland Historical Society Fund Publication 36 (Baltimore, 1900), 45–48.

centralization of trade by requiring all tobacco to be taken to central ware-houses before export.[41]

These attempts to create towns, like similar acts of the seventeenth century, ended in failure, and the crown ultimately disallowed the laws. Although towns created by the assemblies between 1680 and 1712 may have attracted a merchant or two, a ferry, or a tavernkeeper, by 1725 only seven small villages contained a resident population. Three tobacco ports— Londontown on the South River near Annapolis, Hampton on the James River across from Norfolk, and West Point located where the York River was formed of the Mattaponi and Pamunkey rivers—had a small population of merchants, innkeepers, doctors, and artisans, numbering from fifty to a hundred souls. In addition, four specialized villages developed in tidewater in the 1700s and 1710s. Williamsburg and Annapolis, the provincial capi-tals, grew because they handled an ever-increasing load of public business. Yorktown and Norfolk, located close to sea-lanes, became ports of entry, attracting merchants, shipmasters, and artisans. The two villages served different functions: Yorktown was the center of the Chesapeake slave trade and exported expensive sweet-scented tobacco, and Norfolk sent an "abun-dance of beef, port, flour, and lumber" to the West Indies, goods collected from farmers south of town and in adjacent North Carolina (see map 4).

Between 1727 and 1732, during the next major depression in the to-bacco trade, the Maryland and Virginia assemblies established twelve new towns, but they were no more successful than earlier urban dreams. None-theless, six new tiny tobacco ports, like those described above, developed on the Rappahannock, Potomac, and Patuxent rivers, and Norfolk and York-town continued to grow. These villages developed because of increased population density in tidewater and continued settlement of piedmont, rather than as a result of legislation.[42]

The geography of the Chesapeake colonies explains the failure of ur-ban development there during the first third of the eighteenth century. There were hundreds of miles of navigable water spread over innumerable

41. *Virginia Statutes at Large*, III, 404–419, IV, 32–36; William Hand Browne *et al.*, eds., *Archives of Maryland . . .*, 72 vols. (Baltimore, 1883–1972), XVI, 636–645 (hereafter *Archives of Maryland*); Francis Makemie, *A Plain and Friendly Perswasive to the Inhabitants of Virginia and Maryland for Promoting Towns and Cohabitation* (orig. publ. London, 1705), in *Virginia Magazine of History and Biography*, IV (1896–1897), 253–271; John C. Rainbolt, "The Absence of Towns in Seventeenth-Century Virginia," *Journal of Southern History*, XXV (1969), 343–360; Edward M. Riley, "The Town Acts of Colonial Virginia," *Jour. So. Hist.*, XVI (1950), 306–323; O'Mara, *An Historical Geography*, 172–177; Darrett B. Rutman and Anita H. Rutman, *A Place in Time: Middlesex County, 1650–1750* (New York, 1984), chap. 7.
42. *Virginia Statutes at Large*, IV, 234–239; *Archives of Maryland*, XXXVI, 456–458, 464–466, 573–576, XXXVII, 167–170, 520–523, 533–540, XXXIX, 490–496.

Map 4. *Villages and Hamlets in the Chesapeake Colonies, circa 1725*

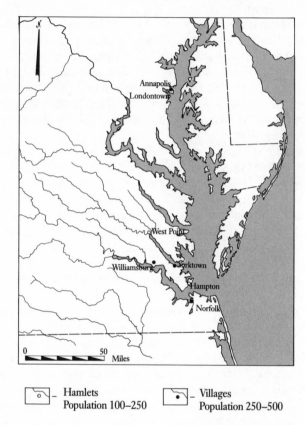

Hamlets
Population 100–250

Villages
Population 250–500

Sources: Carville V. Earle, *The Evolution of a Tidewater Settlement System: All Hallow's Parish, Maryland, 1650–1783,* University of Chicago Department of Geography Research Paper 170 (Chicago, 1975), 83–84, 91; Evarts B. Greene and Virginia D. Harrington, *American Population before the Federal Census of 1790* (New York, 1932), 127–134, 145–153; John W. Reps, *Tidewater Towns: City Planning in Colonial Virginia and Maryland* (Charlottesville, Va., 1972); Edward C. Papenfuse, *In Pursuit of Profit: The Annapolis Merchants in the Era of the American Revolution, 1763–1805* (Baltimore, 1975), 8–16; Elizabeth Donnan, ed., *Documents Illustrative of the History of the Slave Trade to America, IV, The Border Colonies and the Southern Colonies* (Washington, D.C., 1935), 175–206; Louis B. Wright, ed., *The Prose Works of William Byrd of Westover: Narratives of a Colonial Virginian* (Cambridge, Mass., 1967), 173–174.

streams, rivers, and creeks in tidewater. Planters scattered their habitations along all these bodies of water, making relatively compact neighborhoods surrounded by woods. As a result, only one or two families lived on each square mile of land in tidewater and even fewer on the frontier. Gentleman planters and merchants built numerous wharves on all the navigable streams during the seventeenth and early eighteenth centuries, and even the tobacco inspection acts (which forced planters to bring tobacco to designated warehouses) failed to centralize trade. These landings failed to grow into towns because both credit and the manufacture of tobacco originated abroad, with merchants in half a dozen British and European cities profiting from the tobacco trade.[43]

The failure of urban development, combined with the slow progress of plantation diversification and self-sufficiency, led political leaders in the tobacco colonies to attempt to regulate production and export of the crop. Both assemblies passed laws forbidding the growth of seconds and suckers (second-growth tobacco leaves) and the export of trash early in the century, but these laws were rarely enforced because prosecution of charges depended upon the willingness of planters to inform on each other. In seven Virginia counties, only thirty-four cases were brought against planters for tending seconds and exporting trash, and only eight of these resulted in convictions. Then, in 1713, just as the price of tobacco began to rise, the Virginia assembly passed a law that required that all tobacco be inspected in designated warehouses by appointed agents and that trashy tobacco be burned. Gov. Alexander Spotswood apparently bought votes for the measure with promises of lucrative inspectorships for assemblymen. Planters throughout the province bitterly opposed this agents' law. They resented the destruction of previously salable tobacco and the elimination of sales of trash. The burgesses attempted to repeal the act in 1715, and the English Board of Trade disallowed it, after much debate, in 1717.[44]

After 1717 prosperity returned, and tobacco exports rose, but in the 1720s a depression set in again. Since few planters turned to alternative staples, production increased throughout the depression. Faced with in-

---

43. The best analysis is found in Carville Earle and Ronald Hoffman, "Staple Crops and Urban Development in the Eighteenth-Century South," *Perspectives in American History*, X (1976), 11–14, 19–26.
44. Moss, "Virginia Plantation System," 132–134; *Virginia Statutes at Large*, III, 435–440; *Archives of Maryland*, XXXVIII, 175–176, XXX, 260–263; Waverly K. Winfree, comp., *The Laws of Virginia: Being a Supplement to Hening's "The Statutes at Large," 1700–1750* (Richmond, 1971), 75–90, 119–124; Spotswood to Commissioners of Trade, Dec. 13, 1713, *Spotswood Letters*, II, 46–52; Janis M. Horne, "The Opposition to the Virginia Tobacco Inspection Act of 1730" (honors' thesis, College of William and Mary, 1977), 12–16; David Alan Williams, "Political Alignments in Colonial Virginia, 1698–1750" (Ph.D. diss., Northwestern University, 1959), 141–144, 161–162.

creasing exports of tobacco and declining prices, the two assemblies tried to reduce the quantity and improve the quality of exported leaves. In the early 1720s, the legislatures reinstated prohibitions against exporting trash and tending seconds, but the laws were no better enforced than during previous depressions.[45] Between 1723 and 1730, both assemblies sought to reduce exports by limiting, or stinting, the number of tobacco plants each worker could tend. This innovative legislation required that a census be taken, divided workers into categories, and set production limits on each group. Poor men who relied on family labor were permitted to tend more plants per worker than larger operators. The supporters of the law, like Governor Gooch, hoped that it would reduce the quantity of tobacco exported and thereby improve its price, prevent great planters from flooding the market with trashy tobacco, and force farmers to take better care of remaining plants. Unfortunately, the law was difficult to implement because it required careful calculation of both workers and plants. The law was not enforced on the Northern Neck and on the lower Eastern Shore, where low-quality tobacco was grown. Elsewhere, the labor census was in fact taken, but excess plants were rarely destroyed. Only ten cases were brought to court in eight Virginia counties for failure to cut up plants, and only two men were convicted.[46]

A three-sided cacophony of competing interests prevented enforcement of tobacco legislation during the first three decades of the eighteenth century. The English Board of Trade and Maryland's proprietors rejected acts that might reduce the quantity of tobacco shipped to Britain, for such reductions would decrease their income from duties and fees. Planters themselves disagreed about legislative remedies. Governors and their allies in the assemblies, the gentleman planters who produced internationally recognized high-quality tobacco, wanted to eliminate trashy tobacco from the market to protect the value of their own crops. For poor planters, however, a reduction in crop size, without a large and immediate price increase, was a threat to survival. Most poor planters, and nearly every producer who lived where inferior grades of tobacco were grown, feared that their crops

45. *Archives of Maryland,* XXXVIII, 290–294, 300–305, XXXVI, 86–89; *Virginia Statutes at Large,* IV, 87–88. Moss, "Virginia Plantation System," 170–175, documents 38 prosecutions but only 2 convictions in eight Virginia counties from 1720 to 1730 for tending seconds.
46. Winfree, comp., *Laws of Virginia,* 247–253, 295–305; *Archives of Maryland,* XXXVI, 266–275, XXXVII, 138–151; Gooch to Board of Trade, Aug. 9, 1728, C.O. 1321/5, 74–75; William Byrd to Micajah Perry, ca. July 3, 1728, in Marion Tinling, ed., *The Correspondence of the Three William Byrds of Westover, Virginia, 1684–1776* (Charlottesville, Va., 1977) I, 377–378; "An Accompt of the Quantity of Tobacco Planted and Tended in Virginia in the Year 1724," C.O. 1319/5, 220; Moss, "Virginia Plantation System," 176–178; Hemphill, "Virginia and the English Commercial System," 95–96.

would be disproportionately destroyed. These ordinary planters opposed and passively resisted tobacco legislation and continued to plant.[47]

As the depression of the 1720s worsened, planters became desperate. Although most planters wanted to export all the tobacco they grew, richer producers of high-quality leaves insisted on effective regulation. Gentlemen lobbied for severe legislation and intimidated those who opposed regulation. Conflict over tobacco regulation apparently began in Prince George's County, Maryland, in October 1728, just before the Maryland assembly passed a stinting law. Some planters there called for a proregulation meeting "to Assert our Right [for a stinting law] Arm'd in a Suitable Manner." In the same month, Samuel Perrie, one of the wealthiest planter-merchants in the county, and several wealthy friends cursed "the Eastern Shore Burgesses prodigiously, because they was against a Tobacco law," and threatened to "have a hundred Prince George's County men upon Stadt House hill . . . to face the Assembly in Order to Obtain a Tobacco Law."[48]

In Virginia the debate was more peaceful. In 1730 Governor Gooch skillfully organized a coalition of London merchants and wealthy planters, who lobbied successfully for the passage of a new inspection act. Gooch and his allies tried to avoid the problems that had made the 1713 act unenforceable by increasing the number of inspectors, forbidding appointments to members of the assembly, and opening those lucrative posts to middling planters. Even with this change, there was little popular support for the measure among ordinary planters, and some gentlemen preferred the ineffective stinting laws to the new act. The low level of popular and legislative support did not augur well for the reception of the law.[49]

The Virginia Inspection Act of 1730, which resembled the agents' law of 1713, required that all tobacco be taken to a public warehouse and be inspected there by public officials. Only tobacco that proved to be "good, sound, well-conditioned, and merchantable, and free from trash, sand, and dirt" could be passed; the rest had to be burned. The good tobacco was

47. The best analyses of the politics of tobacco are Hemphill, "Virginia and the English Commercial System," chaps. 1, 2, 4; Vertrees J. Wyckoff, *Tobacco Regulation in Colonial Maryland*, Johns Hopkins University Studies in Historical and Political Science, N.S., 22 (Baltimore, 1936), chaps. 6–9; Charles Albro Barker, *The Background of the Revolution in Maryland* (New Haven, Conn., 1940), chap. 3; and Horne, "Opposition to Inspection Act."
48. *Archives of Maryland*, XXV, 499–503; Prince George's Inventories, TB#1, 26–29; Black Books, II, 110–124; Prince George's Land Records, 1720–1739. Perrie's companions were Charles Drury, a factor for Walter Hoxton, who owned six adult slaves in 1733; Bigger Head, a gentleman with three taxable slaves in 1733 and 440 acres of land; and Ligian Wilson, two taxable slaves and 850 acres in 1733.
49. Horne, "Opposition to Inspection Act," chap. 2; Hemphill, "Virginia and the English Commercial System," 149–159.

then weighed, and planters received tobacco notes indicating the weight of each hogshead. The notes could be used as legal tender to pay taxes and private debts. If rigorously enforced, the Inspection Act would have eliminated trashy tobacco from the market, cut the quantity of tobacco exported per worker, centralized tobacco marketing, and created a new currency.[50]

The passage of the Virginia Inspection Act unleashed a torrent of dissent and violence. Planters refused to bring their tobacco to be inspected, and rioters burned four warehouses to the ground in the Northern Neck, destroying substantial quantities of tobacco. After warehouses burned in Lancaster and Northumberland counties in March 1732, planters gathered in Prince William County, on the Northern Neck's frontier, to plan more violence. About fifty "of the meaner sort of People in that County" armed themselves and conspired "to destroy the Public Warehouses in that and the adjacent Counties expecting to be joyn'd by other Malecontents from the neighboring Counties." A week later, this mob burned warehouses in Prince William and King George counties (see map 5).[51]

The ringleaders of the violence were men of small means who owned no slaves and usually only several hundred acres of land; most of their followers were probably slaveless tenants. They produced a hogshead or two of poor-quality tobacco on inferior lands and feared, with some justification, that inspectors would pass the trashy tobacco of their richer neighbors while burning the tobacco they cultivated. The process of inspection seemed arbitrary. "Is it not a clear Case," one small planter asked, "don't we see our Tobacco burnt by the Humour of the Inspectors? Who can bear such Usage?" When it became apparent that no one would listen to their grievances, they burned the warehouses. The destruction was intended to make their opposition to the law and their fear of destitution clear to Gooch and his supporters.[52]

By May 1732 the violence had spread to Maryland, but there wealthy planters who wished to cut exports were the leaders. While the Virginia assembly passed a tough inspection act, even Maryland's ineffective stinting law had lapsed, and wealthy growers of high-quality tobacco took the law into their own hands. Rioters in Prince George's, just across the river from Prince William County, cut tobacco plants of numerous residents. The three leaders included James Magruder, brother of assemblyman John Magruder, and Thomas Waring, who would inherit nine adult slaves and six-

50. *Virginia Statutes at Large*, IV, 247–271 (quote on 251); Horne, "Opposition to Inspection Act," 30–33.

51. This discussion of the tobacco riots is based heavily on Horne's careful research in "Opposition to Inspection Act," chaps. 4–5 and pp. 81, 120–122.

52. *Ibid.*, chap. 4 and pp. 78, 82–83, 109–114; William Gooch, *A Dialogue between Thomas Sweet-Scented and William Oronoco, Planters* (Williamsburg, Va., 1732), 3–7.

Map 5. *Opposition to the Virginia Inspection Act of 1730*

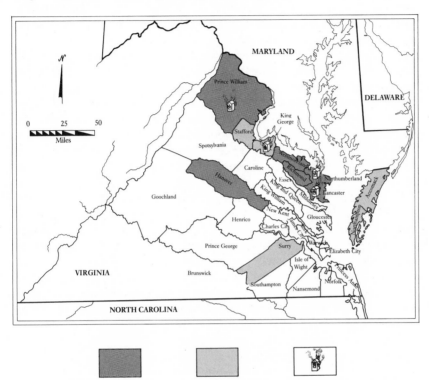

Petitions to 1732 Assembly   Petition to 1732 Assembly   Warehouse Burned
to Repeal Inspection   to Repeal Inspection Act
and to Demand
New Stinting Act

Source: Janis M. Horne, "The Opposition to the Virginia Tobacco Inspection Act of 1730" (honors' thesis, College of William and Mary, 1977), 120–122.

teen hundred acres of land from his father in 1733. Most of the tobacco cutting occurred on poor tobacco land near the Potomac, but these two leaders lived some distance from that area, on good tobacco land near the Patuxent River. To accomplish the cutting, they enlisted the aid of poorer men who lived near the Potomac.[53]

53. *Archives of Maryland*, XLIV, 7–9; Allan Kulikoff, "Tobacco and Slaves: Population, Economy, and Society in Eighteenth-Century Prince George's County, Maryland" (Ph.D. diss., Brandeis University, 1976), 566–567; Black Books, II, 110–124; Prince George's Land Records, 1720–1730. Magruder owned 6 taxable slaves and 300 acres of land in 1733; Warren owned 11 taxable slaves and 680 acres just after his father died; Thomas Owen (the third

The gentleman planters and merchants who governed the two colonies responded swiftly to these challenges to their authority. Anticipating that inspection warehouses might be the target of violence, the Virginia assembly in 1730 had made the destruction of warehouses punishable by death. Now Governor Gooch and the council offered a reward to anyone who named the arsonists and helped bring them to justice, authorized the rebuilding of burned warehouses, and launched a campaign aimed at the barely literate small planters to gain acceptance of the law. To put down the rebellion in Prince William County, Gooch called out the militia. The leaders of the Prince William riot were probably apprehended, but not punished, perhaps because officials feared creating martyrs and further inflaming supporters of the rioters. Nonetheless, those gentlemen who disliked the inspection law resolved to obey it, placing class solidarity above the desire for immediate profit, and the burgesses supported Gooch's program.[54]

Public authorities in Maryland feared disorder more than they feared angering a small number of gentlemen. The governor offered to reward anyone with information about the tobacco cutters, and the Maryland assembly passed a law imposing a one-hundred-pound-sterling fine and six months in prison for anyone convicted of destroying tobacco plants. Though the leaders of the Prince George's riots were captured, they, much like their poorer counterparts in Virginia, were apparently not charged with a crime.[55]

Opposition by poor planters and residents of the Northern Neck did not end, however, when the violence was contained. Citizens of every county in the Northern Neck, of both Eastern Shore counties, and of Hanover County on the James River frontier petitioned the burgesses to repeal the inspection act. Householders in five counties (including four in the Northern Neck) urged that a new stinting law be enacted in its stead, perhaps because they knew that such a law would be ineffective and would permit them to grow as much tobacco as they could. Late in 1732 violence threatened again when Lancaster County planters protested the arbitrary behavior and favoritism of one inspector. Gooch, the council, and the assembly defused the conflict by amending the Inspection Act and firing fourteen particularly capricious inspectors. In 1734, assembly and council renewed the law for four years. Nonetheless, poor and middling planters throughout the province intensely disliked the law and threw out numerous

---

leader) had 3 taxable slaves and 150 acres. The four followers had no taxable slaves and an average of 200 acres.
54. *Virginia Statutes at Large*, IV, 271–273; Horne, "Opposition to Inspection Act," 83–90; Gooch, *Dialogue*.
55. *Archives of Maryland*, XLIV, 7–9, XXXVIII, 530–531.

proregulation assemblymen in the 1734 election. These new legislators, joined by delegates from areas that produced low-quality tobacco, voted to repeal the act by a wide margin. Even though these men were large planters who secretly favored regulation, they voted against it to placate their constituencies. The inspection law stood, however, because the council rejected the repeal bill.[56]

Legislators in Maryland refused to follow Virginia's lead and enact an inspection law. Nearly all planters in the province grew low-quality tobacco, and gentlemen and merchants probably feared massive outbreaks of violence if an inspection law were passed. Yet the tobacco crisis grew worse monthly, and something had to be done. In 1733, the Maryland assembly decided that an issue of paper money, supported by a tax on each hogshead of tobacco exported from the province, would revive the economy by encouraging consumption of manufactured goods. Each householder received thirty shillings of the new money for each taxable person in his home. Every planter, moreover, would have to burn 150 pounds of low-quality tobacco for each of his taxables in 1734 and 1735, a move that legislators hoped would lead to higher prices by reducing exports. In partial payment for the burned tobacco, householders would receive six pennies of the paper money for each 150 pounds burned.[57]

Planters evaded the tobacco regulations of the money law just as they had ignored other tobacco legislation. Small planters who obeyed the law would have been badly hurt: they would have lost about 5s. 5d. for every 150 pounds of trashy tobacco burned, a small sum that would have served to reduce their already low standard of living. Numerous poor planters in Prince George's refused to burn tobacco, but the law was enforced only along the Potomac River, where the cheapest tobacco in the county was grown.[58]

Both the Virginia Inspection Act and Maryland's paper money law seemed to work, for the price of tobacco rose in the mid-1730s in both provinces. Opposition to the inspection system slowly dissipated in Virginia, and the protests of poor planters received less support. In 1736, planters from six counties urged that a new stint law be enacted. In 1742 residents

56. Horne, "Opposition to Inspection Act," 90–91, 121–122; Williams, "Political Alignments," 241–246, 281–287.
57. *Archives of Maryland*, XXXVII, 337–346, XXXIV, 92–113.
58. Prince George's Inventories, 1730–1748; Prince George's Court Records, V, 97–104; Black Books, II, 110–124. The lost income (minus the 6d. bounty) was calculated assuming that trashy tobacco was worth 34% the value of good tobacco (three observations from inventory prices). Proportions not burning tobacco: New Scotland Hundred: 1 taxable, 22%; 2 taxables, 16%; 3 + taxables (excluding those where overseers failed to burn tobacco), 8%; Piscataway Hundred: 1 taxable, 11%; 2 taxables, 13%; 3 + taxables, 5%.

of five counties demanded repeal of the inspection system, but planters in five counties—including three in the previously rebellious Northern Neck—supported retention of inspection, and a renewal passed the assembly easily. Producers who grew sweet-scented tobacco were probably especially pleased with the law. After trashy tobacco was eliminated from Virginia's exports, the relative price difference between Virginia sweet-scented and good Maryland tobacco rose. Nonetheless, Maryland's planters were also satisfied. They now monopolized markets for low-quality tobacco, and many of them began to pack and sell good tobacco, second-quality, and trashy separately.[59]

Once more in the 1740s, tobacco prices fell disastrously. Virginians, satisfied with the inspection system, barely reacted, merely establishing ten new towns, and did not revise their tobacco regulations. Maryland's planters, however, saw the price of their tobacco drop far more steeply than Virginia's price, and by 1745, it was far below the costs of production. Some wealthy planters vowed to change the province's tobacco laws. Although a few of them wanted to reinstate a burning law and again require each planter to burn 150 pounds of tobacco for each of his tithables, most urged the assembly to adopt Virginia's inspection system. Maryland planters could make better tobacco than Virginians, Governor Bladen complained in 1744, but they were "under no kind of Restraint" and "put all manner of Trash, tho' unfit for anything but manure" in their hogsheads and thereby made "the whole of little Value." When demand for tobacco stagnated, merchants refused to buy it in Maryland if inspected Virginia leaves could be found. The Virginia law had "Stood a Tryal of many Years . . . to the General Satisfaction of All Parties," Bladen asserted in 1747; a similar Maryland law would raise the price of the staple and ensure prosperity.[60]

Throughout May and June 1747, the Maryland assembly debated tobacco regulation. They turned down a burning law and decided to debate an inspection act by a margin of better than two to one. Despite the depression, many assemblymen remained opposed to inspection, but an inspection law, modeled on Virginia's, finally passed by a vote of twenty-five to twenty-two. Most opposition came from three lower Eastern Shore counties where little tobacco was grown and what was produced was of low quality. Farmers in this area feared they would not be able to make sufficient inspected tobacco to pay their taxes. Planters elsewhere uniformly supported the law,

59. Fig. 10; Williams, "Political Alignments," 291–292; Moss, "Virginia Plantation System," 240–242; Prince George's Inventories, 1730–1748; Earle, *Tidewater Settlement System*, 24–27; Horne, "Opposition to Inspection Act," 103–108.
60. Wyckoff, *Tobacco Regulation*, chap. 8, esp. 169–173, details the 1746-1747 debate in the *Maryland Gazette* that preceded passage of the law. All but one essayist supported the law. See *Archives of Maryland*, XXVIII, 308–311, for Bladen's speech.

but some local merchants—men who might have feared the law would reduce their business or encourage competition from large Scottish firms—voted against the law.[61]

Legislators repeatedly renewed tobacco inspection laws. The laws created a new currency to pay taxes and debts, and they centralized trade by requiring all tobacco to be brought to a few public warehouses. Supporters hoped, of course, that the inspection system would increase the price of the staple by improving the quality of tobacco each worker made, but the system would work, given constant demand, only if planters obeyed the law and inspectors diligently burned all trashy tobacco.[62]

Poor planters and those who produced inferior grades of tobacco attempted to subvert the inspection system by putting trashy tobacco in their hogsheads. Knowing that inspectors would destroy some of their trash, planters excluded the worst leaves, but packed many poor leaves in their hogsheads and hoped that the inspectors would overlook most of them. When planters brought these hogsheads to the warehouse, an inspector opened each one, inspected the tobacco, burned the trash, and resealed the hogshead. If he found trashy tobacco scattered throughout the hogshead, the planter or his agent (a "picker") had to repack the entire barrel, keeping only the good leaves. There was intense pressure on inspectors to pass the maximum quantities of their neighbors' tobacco; and remembering the tobacco riots, they probably burned only the worst trash. Tobacco pickers apparently often repacked some trash and second-quality tobacco, especially when crops were short or prices low. Inspectors at different warehouses, moreover, used varying standards for passing tobacco, and planters sent their worst tobacco to inspectors with a reputation for passing low-quality leaves.[63]

61. *Archives of Maryland*, XLIV, 516–517, 595–638; Wyckoff, *Tobacco Regulation*, 173–177; Mary McKinney Schweitzer, "Economic Regulation and the Colonial Economy: The Maryland Tobacco Inspection Act of 1747," *Jour. Econ. Hist.*, XL (1980), 556–557. The vote to debate the inspection law was 31 to 14.

62. The best analysis of the economic impact of the act will be found in Schweitzer, "Economic Regulation," *Jour. Econ. Hist.*, XL (1980), 557–565; for renewals, see *Virginia Statutes at Large*, IV, 380–392, V, 10–15, 124–160, VI, 154–193, 222–227, 351–354, 572–575, VII, 387–393, VIII, 69–111, 318–325, 507–511; and *Archives of Maryland*, L, 303–367, LVI, 128–129, LVIII, 433–497, LXI, 222–223, LXII, 123.

63. These speculations are based upon the laws cited *ibid.*; H. R. McIlwaine, ed., *Executive Journals of the Council of Colonial Virginia* (Richmond, 1930), IV, 310–311, 334–338, 423–426, 431, 437; Gooch, *Dialogue*; John Rainbolt, ed., "The Case of the Poor Planters in Virginia under the Law for Inspecting and Burning Tobacco," *VMHB*, LXXIX (1971), 314–321; *Virginia Statutes at Large*, IV, 507–508, VI, 51–53; Purdie and Dixon's *Virginia Gazette*, July 28–Aug. 4, Nov. 11–24, 1738, Jan. 17, 1771; *Archives of Maryland*, XLVI, 453–455, 603–607; *Maryland Gazette*, June 17, 1746; Robert Dinwiddie to Council and Burgesses, 1753, in R. A. Brock, ed., *Official Records of Robert Dinwiddie, Lieutenant-Governor of the Colony of Vir-*

Despite these pressures, the inspection acts were enforced in both Chesapeake colonies. Inspectors burned substantial quantities of trash, and as a result, the output of tobacco per worker probably fell by a fifth or a fourth. Output declined far more in areas producing cheap oronoco tobacco than in places making high-quality sweet-scented tobacco where planters had already reduced production to make tobacco that would achieve the best prices in London.[64] This reduction in output had a mixed impact on the income of planters. On the one hand, tobacco prices rose somewhat because of the inspection system, and the differential between Virginia and Maryland prices diminished greatly. Planters who grew high-quality tobacco could take full advantage of the price increase. On the other hand, poor planters who grew marginal crops saw a disproportionate percentage of their output destroyed by inspectors not easily swayed by men of little status.

The Legacy of Depression

The pressure of recurring depressions, combined with continued population growth, altered the economic structure of the Chesapeake region. After more than half a century of depressed tobacco prices, about one family in four in the region no longer relied upon tobacco as its primary staple, and planters who continued to grow it had learned to diversify their output and had become more self-sufficient. By the middle of the eighteenth century, moreover, the two assemblies successfully regulated tobacco production, centralized tobacco marketing, and created a new commodity currency.

When prosperity returned to the region after 1740, wealthy planters were ready to take advantage of rising tobacco prices and new European demand for grain. These planters, who owned diversified farms and could produce some home manufactures, commanded much new British credit, and that credit, in turn, fueled the greatest spurt of economic growth the Chesapeake region had seen since the middle of the seventeenth century. (The consequences of this prosperity provide the theme of chapter 4.)

---

ginia, 1751–1758 (Virginia Historical Society, *Collections*, N.S., III [Richmond, 1883]), I, 37–39; Wyckoff, *Tobacco Regulation*, 177–207; Thomas M. Preisser, "Eighteenth-Century Alexandria, Virginia, before the Revolution, 1749–1776" (Ph.D. diss., College of William and Mary, 1977), 80–81; Alexander Hamilton to James Brown and Co., Aug. 6, 1774, in Richard K. MacMaster and David C. Skaggs, eds., "The Letterbooks of Alexander Hamilton, Piscataway Factor," Pt. II, "1774–1775," *Maryland Historical Magazine*, LXI (1966), 308.

64. *Md. Gaz.*, Apr. 7, May 19, 1747; Rutman and Rutman, *Place in Time: Explicatus*, 18–24. Higher estimates (Earle, *Tidewater Settlement System*, 26–27, 97–99; Clemens, *Atlantic Economy*, 170–171; Kulikoff, "Tobacco and Slaves," 168) reflect local conditions but are inconsistent with export data in fig. 11, which show no substantial downturn after either inspection act.

Finally, a new gentry class emerged from the politics of depression. These wealthy men had fought a winning battle against poor planters and, in doing so, had increased their own class solidarity. Both the culture they created and the alliances they formed with ordinary yeoman planters developed after gentlemen won the battles over tobacco regulation. The poorest group of planters saw their income diminished by tobacco regulation, lost the most, and came to count for very little in the political realm.[65]

65. See chap. 7 for an analysis of the rise of the gentry class.

4

The Perils of Prosperity, 1740–1800

When Price Davies arrived in Virginia in 1763 to take charge of an Anglican parish near Williamsburg, he was very impressed with the wealth of the country. "The people in general live in luxury," he wrote a Welsh friend, and "their equipages here are many and grand, commonly drawn by six fine horses." Three years later, John Wayles, an agent for a Bristol tobacco merchant, sent similar impressions to his employer. "In 1740," he contended, "I don't remember to have seen . . . a turkey Carpet in the Country except a small thing in a bed chamber, Now nothing are so common as Turkey or Wilton Carpetts, the whole Furniture of the Roomes Elegant & every appearance of Opulence."[1] Although both Davies and Wayles exaggerated the wealth of the Chesapeake region, many observers noted the prosperity of the area, and especially of its wealthy planters.

A remarkable rise in the price of tobacco between 1740 and the American Revolution explains this newfound prosperity. That increase in prices, combined with growing demand for Chesapeake grain in Europe in the 1760s, gave planters greater disposable income, which they used to increase their standard of living, improve their land, and expand the size of their labor force. Moreover, their rising income and the higher price for their staples gained Chesapeake planters far greater access to credit from Britain.

Planters considered this growth of credit between 1750 and 1775 to be both burdensome and beneficial. It was burdensome because it made planters dependent upon foreign creditors, who might call in their debts at any time, and because it increased the consumption of luxuries. But credit enabled planters to improve their living conditions and expand their farm operations. Moreover, Scottish merchants, who provided much of the credit, started new towns and purchased tobacco grown in the far reaches of piedmont that no one else would buy, thereby encouraging frontier settlement.

Wealthy planters reaped most of the benefits of high tobacco prices and increased credit. In tidewater, the most successful planters used loans

1. Price Davies to William Conway, June 30, 1763, in David Evans, ed., "Price Davies, Rector of Blisland Parish: Two Letters, 1763, 1765," *Virginia Magazine of History and Biography*, LXXIX (1971), 159; John Wayles to Farrell and Jones, Aug. 30, 1766, in John M. Hemphill II, ed., "John Wayles Rates his Neighbours," *VMHB*, LXVI (1958), 305.

to improve their plantations. As a result, land prices multiplied rapidly, and tenants' slim opportunities to buy land disappeared. At the same time, the slowly increasing price of slaves drove such labor out of the reach of most poor planters. Even in the prosperous 1760s and 1770s, poor tidewater planters could improve their status only by migrating to the frontier.

Small planters enjoyed greater opportunities on the piedmont frontier, where land was inexpensive and improving gentlemen were scarce. But because the cheapest land was located far from transportation routes and markets, most poor migrants set up subsistence farms, not tobacco plantations. Many of these men could not accumulate even the minimal cash needed to patent land and usually left the region after a few years, only to be replaced by sons of yeomen and richer planters. Even these opportunities disappeared after the Revolution, when nearly all the good land in piedmont had been taken up and dissatisfied poor planters had to leave for Kentucky to find greater opportunities.

Prosperity and Development on the Tobacco Coast

Rising tobacco prices were the main cause of the tobacco colonies' prosperity in the 1750s and 1760s. Although the boom-and-bust cycle characteristic of tobacco production continued, depressions were less severe and recoveries more forceful than they had been earlier in the century. Prices rose in the 1750s after the depression of the late 1740s and peaked in 1759; they declined again in the early 1760s, increased later in the decade, and again fell after the British debt contraction of 1772. The overall level of tobacco prices, however, rose between 1750 and the Revolution. As a result, income from tobacco per laborer rose more than twice as rapidly after 1750 as before that year.[2]

Improving economic conditions in Europe led to higher demand for tobacco products and accounted for much of this rise in farm prices. Both total output and population in Europe began to increase after 1750, and a surge in economic activity in Britain during the 1760s and 1770s provided consumers with greater disposable income. Continental demand for tobacco grew despite an increase in European tobacco prices during the Seven Years' War (1756–1763), which interrupted transatlantic shipments, and the nearly stagnant prices of times of peace.[3]

2. For tobacco prices, see fig. 10; for calculation of the rise in income per laborer from tobacco, see Allan Kulikoff, "The Economic Growth of the Eighteenth-Century Chesapeake Colonies," *Journal of Economic History*, XXXIX (1979), 282–286.
3. *Ibid.*, 284–285; Brinley Thomas, "The Rhythm of Growth in the Atlantic Economy of the Eighteenth Century," *Research in Economic History*, III (1978), 19–35.

Chesapeake planters had some difficulty in meeting this new demand for tobacco because planters in large parts of Maryland and Virginia had shifted to grain production. Tobacco planters began growing corn and wheat when population pressure and crop failures in Europe created new demand and higher prices for Chesapeake grain in the 1760s and 1770s. Eastern Shore and James River farmers who had occasionally planted tobacco shifted almost exclusively to grain, and even planters in prime tobacco-growing areas reduced their tobacco output to take advantage of the spiraling demand for corn and wheat.[4] Proceeds from grain sales, which had constituted less than 5 percent of Virginia tobacco planters' income in 1760, provided 10 percent of their income by 1770. This rapid growth in grain production cushioned the depression of the early 1760s and fueled the boom of the late 1760s.[5] When European agriculture recovered in the early 1770s, some planters shifted out of grain production. Nonetheless, by 1775 only two of every three residents of Maryland and Virginia regularly planted tobacco (see fig. 16).

Higher tobacco prices and this rise in the demand for grain led to substantial economic growth along the tobacco coast during the 1760s and 1770s. Wealth per capita in Prince George's County, Maryland, nearly dou-

---

4. Gaspar J. Saladino, "The Maryland and Virginia Wheat Trade from Its Beginnings to the American Revolution" (master's thesis, University of Wisconsin, 1960), chaps. 2, 3, 5; David C. Klingaman, "The Significance of Grain in the Development of the Tobacco Colonies," *Jour. Econ. Hist.*, XXIX (1969), 268–275; Klingaman, "The Development of the Coastwise Trade of Virginia in the Late Colonial Period," *VMHB*, LXXVII (1969), 26–45; Paul G. E. Clemens, *The Atlantic Economy and Colonial Maryland's Eastern Shore: From Tobacco to Grain* (Ithaca, N.Y., 1980), chap. 6; Clarence P. Gould, "The Economic Causes of the Rise of Baltimore," in *Essays in Colonial History Presented to Charles McLean Andrews by His Students* (New Haven, Conn., 1931), 225–251; James O'Mara, *An Historical Geography of Urban System Development: Tidewater Virginia in the Eighteenth Century*, Atkinson College, York University, Geographical Monographs, No. 13 (Downsview, Ont., 1983), 89–94; T. H. Breen, "The Culture of Agriculture: The Symbolic World of the Tidewater Planter, 1760–1790," in David D. Hall *et al.*, eds., *Saints and Revolutionaries: Essays on Early American History* (New York, 1984), 275–284.

5. This statistic calculated from data in Naval Office Returns, C.O. 1442–1449/5 and Customs 16/1, Public Record Office (film at Colonial Williamsburg Research Department [CW]); and James H. Soltow, *The Economic Role of Williamsburg*, Williamsburg Research Studies (Williamsburg, Va., 1965), table 3, for South Potomac, Rappahannock, York, and Upper James Naval Districts, and adjusted for missing quarters and divided by number of taxables found in Evarts B. Greene and Virginia D. Harrington, *American Population before the Federal Census of 1790* (New York, 1932), 150–151, and in Court Order Books, Virginia State Library, Richmond (VSL). The correlation between pounds of tobacco and bushels of grain exported per worker in fig. 16 was .105 before 1760 and −.663 after 1760. Klingaman's figures for income from grain in "Significance of Grain," *Jour. Econ. Hist.*, XXIX (1969), 272–274, are much higher because he included the Lower James Naval District, an area I excluded because it grew little tobacco.

Fig. 16. *Labor Productivity and Income along Virginia's Tobacco Coast,*
1726–1774

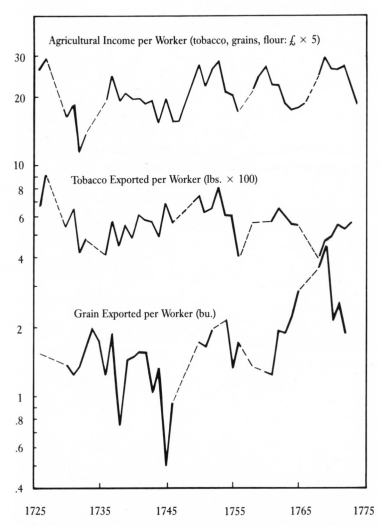

Sources: Calculated from sources in n. 5, and from data in "List of Tithables in Va. Taken
1773," *Virginia Magazine of History and Biography*, XXVIII (1920), 81–82, and Allan Kulikoff, "Tobacco and Slaves: Population, Economy, and Society in Eighteenth-Century Prince
George's County, Maryland" (Ph.D. diss., Brandeis University, 1976), 428–430. I have not
included tidewater south of the James, the Eastern Shore (except for 550 tithables), the Shenandoah Valley, two-thirds of Baltimore County, or any of Maryland from Frederick County
west, in tobacco cultivation.

bled between 1755 and 1776, and the value of householders' real and personal property more than doubled during the same period. Other counties in the region probably grew at a similar rate, for the wealth of householders in nine tobacco counties in 1774 was nearly equal to that of Prince George's.[6]

Credit and Economic Development

England's economic boom during the 1760s and 1770s not only increased demand for tobacco but also produced substantial capital for investment. Chesapeake tobacco firms and farmers looked like good credit risks because prices and imports of their crop were both rising. In 1757 Chesapeake residents owed £1,000,000 sterling to British merchants. These merchants borrowed vast sums of money from private lenders and banks over the next two decades, and they in turn extended credit amounting to millions of pounds sterling to Chesapeake planters. By 1776, planters' debt had more than doubled, reaching more than £2,000,000 sterling. The Scottish debt was particularly important: from 1766 to 1772, money lent by Glasgow firms increased from £500,000 to £1,100,000.[7]

Chesapeake planters went on a buying spree with the credit they received from Britain, and imports of consumer goods skyrocketed. During the first half of the eighteenth century, imports had grown, at best, as rapidly as population. But after 1750 imports rose a third faster than the region's population. Importers rushed so many consumer goods to the region that the market was soon glutted. Since the level of imports of consumer goods rose more rapidly than the demand for them, the price of imports like cloth decreased relative to the value of slaves and land, and these capital goods were used as collateral for the purchase of imports.[8]

6. For Prince George's, see fig. 12, and Kulikoff, "Economic Growth," *Jour. Econ. Hist.*, XXXIX (1979), 277–280; for other Chesapeake counties in 1774, see Alice H. Jones, "Wealth Estimates for the Southern Colonies about 1770," *Claremont Economic Papers*, LXXVI (1973), 35.

7. Jacob M. Price, *Capital and Credit in British Overseas Trade: The View from the Chesapeake, 1700–1776* (Cambridge, Mass., 1980), chap. 1; Soltow, *Economic Role of Williamsburg*, table 6; Richard B. Sheridan, "The British Credit Crisis of 1772 and the American Colonies," *Jour. Econ. Hist.*, XX (1960), 161–186; Edward C. Papenfuse, *In Pursuit of Profit: The Annapolis Merchants in the Era of the American Revolution, 1763–1805* (Baltimore, 1975), 40–41.

8. Allan Kulikoff, "Tobacco and Slaves: Population, Economy, and Society in Eighteenth-Century Prince George's County, Maryland" (Ph.D. diss., Brandeis University, 1976), 110–111; Ronald Hoffman, *A Spirit of Dissension: Economics, Politics, and the Revolution in Maryland* (Baltimore, 1973), 86–88.

British credit also financed the development of frontier areas and towns throughout the Chesapeake region. Large Scottish firms that had expanded their capital in the 1760s by forming multiple partnerships played a particularly important role. By the early 1770s, the top three Glasgow firms—the Spiers, Cuningham, and Glassford groups—were worth £350,000 sterling, held nearly half the assets of all Scottish tobacco firms, and imported almost half the Virginia tobacco that reached Scotland. They attracted business in the Chesapeake by opening at least sixty large and diversified general stores and by extending easy credit to customers.[9]

Scottish firms were especially important in the settlement of southside Virginia, an isolated section of piedmont located far from the area's major rivers, tobacco ports, and inspection warehouses. The three dominant Scottish companies established businesses throughout southside in the 1760s and 1770s and thereby accelerated settlement and tobacco cultivation. They stocked general stores near centers of frontier settlement, sent representatives to more remote areas, granted credit to planters, and bought and transported tobacco. The three firms were so successful that they exported a third of the tobacco the upper James region sent to Britain by 1774. Spiers alone bought a sixth of the district's tobacco and operated six stores in rural southside.[10]

Scottish capital was also partially responsible for the rapid growth of Chesapeake towns in the third quarter of the eighteenth century. The number of villages and towns more than doubled, from fifteen in 1750 to thirty-four in 1780, and their population nearly quintupled, from six thousand to thirty-one thousand inhabitants. Most of the new towns were tobacco ports, located on every navigable river in the region, and they gained resident population when Scottish and local merchants began to compete for business of nearby planters. However, the majority of town residents were clustered in nine small cities, each with over a thousand inhabitants. The availability of credit, combined with ideal locations for marketing tobacco and grain, explains the continued growth of most of these places. Four cities—

9. Jacob M. Price, "The Rise of Glasgow in the Chesapeake Tobacco Trade, 1707–1775," *William and Mary Quarterly*, 3d Ser., XI (1954), 191–197; Sheridan, "British Credit Crisis," *Jour. Econ. Hist.*, XX (1960), 180–183; and Robert P. Thomson, "The Merchant in Virginia, 1700–1775" (Ph.D. diss., University of Wisconsin, 1955), 198, detail the operation of Scottish stores; I counted Glassford, Cuningham, and Spiers stores in works listed here and in n. 7 and in "British Mercantile Claims, 1775–1803," *Virginia Genealogist*, VI–XXIV (1962–1980); "Preliminary List of Glasgow Men Resident Temporarily or Permanently in the American Colonies to 1790," Maryland Hall of Records, Annapolis (MHR).

10. Price, "Rise of Glasgow," *WMQ*, 3d Ser., XI (1954), 183–199; Soltow, *Economic Role of Williamsburg*, 48–63; "British Mercantile Claims," *Va. Gen.*, VI–XXIV (1962–1980).

Alexandria, Fredericksburg, Richmond, and Petersburg—huddled close to the head of navigation of the region's rivers; they commanded the business of a vast hinterland that sent them tobacco and grain and received manufactures in return. Norfolk, Portsmouth, and Baltimore each sent grain and provisions to the West Indies and southern Europe from their vantage point close to the Chesapeake Bay. In contrast, Annapolis and Williamsburg, the colonial capitals, grew into cultural and social centers for newly rich gentlemen (see maps 6, 7).[11] A short analysis of the growth of Richmond, Alexandria, and Annapolis suggests the ways credit and location led to town development.

Richmond developed as a marketing center for the tobacco farms of central piedmont Virginia. Planters from that area sent their tobacco hogsheads down the James River to the falls, where wagoners carted the tobacco to nearby Richmond warehouses. The town grew slowly during the first two decades after its founding in 1737. But by 1769, about six hundred people lived in Richmond (with Manchester, its suburb across the James), and its population reached eighteen hundred by 1782. The town's growth spurt coincided with its increasing tobacco trade: by the 1770s and 1780s, around ten thousand hogsheads of tobacco—nearly a sixth of Virginia's crop—were inspected in Richmond. Much of the crop was purchased by Richmond branches of the Spiers, Glassford, and Cuningham chains.[12]

Alexandria, like Richmond, was founded as a tobacco-shipping center for the surrounding countryside, but most farmers who lived north and west of town grew only wheat or corn. Although Alexandria exported much larger quantities of tobacco than other Potomac river towns, it rarely sent more than three thousand hogsheads of tobacco to Britain. In fact, Alexandria did not become a large port until the 1760s, when European crop failures raised the demand for Chesapeake grain. As soon as area farmers switched to grain or migrated to nearby piedmont areas to grow it, Alexandria merchants began to organize this trade, and by 1770 about twenty grain merchants exported wheat and flour to the West Indies and Europe. New

11. I assumed that the population of hamlets and villages of maps 6, 7, averaged the mean number within the category. In 1750, 30% (2,000 of 6,575) of the urban population lived in large towns, but that figure rose to 76% in 1780 (23,600 of 30,875), or 63% if Baltimore and Norfolk, on the edge of the tobacco Chesapeake, are excluded (12,600 of 19,875).

12. Marianne Patricia Buroff Sheldon, "Richmond, Virginia: The Town and Henrico County to 1820" (Ph.D. diss., University of Michigan, 1975), chap. 1; and "Tobacco Exported from Octo 1782 to Octo 1799," VSL, show that the Richmond area (Byrd's, Manchester, Osborne's, Rocky Ridge, and Schokoe's warehouses) exported 7,501 hogsheads in 1782–1783, 9,908 in 1783–1784, and 13,391 in 1784–1785, accounting for 15%, 19%, and 20% of Virginia's crop, respectively; U.S., Bureau of the Census, *Heads of Families at the First Census . . . , Virginia* (Washington, D.C., 1908), 111–119.

people moved to the town to store and process wheat, and Alexandria's population grew from around 1,000 in 1770 to 2,750 by 1790.[13]

The larger populations of Alexandria and Richmond supported a wider range of businesses than was found in smaller settlements. At the time of the Revolution there were about 250 householders in Richmond and 150 in Alexandria. Although a quarter of the householders in Richmond and two-fifths in Alexandria were merchants and shopkeepers, another two-fifths of the employed men in both towns worked as artisans in a variety of trades or worked in the towns' seven or eight taverns.[14]

Annapolis catered to affluence in the 1760s and 1770s. Although the population of this capital city grew slowly after it reached one thousand during the 1760s, its wealth increased rapidly. At least twelve gentleman planters, lawyers, and merchants built extravagant town houses there between 1764 and 1776. The entire town was organized to serve these gentlemen, legislators, and their friends; there were far more tavernkeepers, lawyers, and makers of luxury goods like coaches and watches in Annapolis than in Alexandria or Richmond. In 1782 the employed men in town could be divided into three groups of roughly equal size: (1) merchants, shopkeepers, and mariners who shipped and traded tobacco and other goods; (2) gentlemen and professionals who ran the government or served each other; and (3) artisans and tavernkeepers who made consumer goods for gentlemen or who housed legislators when the assembly was in session.[15]

Credit, in sum, encouraged economic development in two ways. First, large planters used loans to improve their plantations and standard of living and in turn lent money to other area residents, thereby multiplying the effects of the original credit. As long as credit continued to flow, it could be invested continually in local goods and services, for most debts did not have

13. Thomas M. Preisser, "Eighteenth-Century Alexandria, Virginia, before the Revolution, 1749–1776" (Ph.D. diss., College of William and Mary, 1977), chaps. 1–3. The tobacco export figure is based upon Preisser's assertion that seven or eight tobacco merchants worked in Alexandria, the average exports of one of them, and an assumption that the typical merchant exported only two-thirds of that quantity.

14. Partial occupational distributions for 81 men in Alexandria in 1772–1775 (Preisser, "Eighteenth-Century Alexandria," table 4) and 136 men in Richmond in 1782 (Bureau of Census, *Heads of Families, Virginia*, 111–119) show the following: merchants and shopkeepers, 24% in Richmond and 38% in Alexandria; artisans, 44% in Richmond and 38% in Alexandria; innkeepers, 7% in Richmond and 10% in Alexandria; professionals, 6% in Richmond and 10% in Alexandria; wagoners, 5%; and government officials, 6% in Richmond (the new state capital); and the rest scattered.

15. Papenfuse, *In Pursuit of Profit*, 16–34, 250–256. An occupational distribution for 1783 shows 14% professional and government services (and 5% lawyers); 29% artisans; 21% merchants and shopkeepers; 13% innkeepers; 10% mariners; and the rest scattered ($N = 172$).

Map 6. *Town Development on the Tobacco Coast of the Chesapeake, 1750*

Hamlets
100–250 Residents

Villages
250–500 Residents

Small Towns
500–1,000 Residents

Larger Towns
1,000 + Residents

Sources: Evarts B. Greene and Virginia D. Harrington, *American Population before the Federal Census of 1790* (New York, 1932), 131–134, 150–155; John W. Reps, *Tidewater Towns: City Planning in Colonial Virginia and Maryland* (Charlottesville, Va., 1972); Carville Earle and Ronald Hoffman, "Staple Crops and Urban Development in the Eighteenth-Century South," *Perspectives in American History*, X (1976), 10, 7–78; Jedediah Morse, *The American Gazetteer...* (Boston, 1797); Lester Cappon et al., eds., *The Atlas of Early American History: The Revolutionary Era, 1760–1790* (Princeton, N.J., 1976); Edward C. Papenfuse, *In Pursuit of Profit: The Annapolis Merchants in the Era of the American Revolution, 1763–1805* (Baltimore, 1975), 14; Allan Kulikoff, "Tobacco and Slaves: Population, Economy, and Society in Eighteenth-Century Prince George's County, Maryland" (Ph.D. diss., Brandeis University, 1976), 349–350; U.S., Bureau of the Census, *Heads of Families at the First Census, ... Virginia* (Washington, D.C., 1907), 5. Other places, mostly hamlets without a resident population, are listed by James O'Mara, *An Historical Geography of Urban System Development: Tidewater Virginia in the Eighteenth Century*, Atkinson College, York University, Geographical Monographs, No. 13 (Downsview, Ont., 1983), 213–217 and chap. 5.

Map 7. *Town Development on the Tobacco Coast of the Chesapeake, 1780*

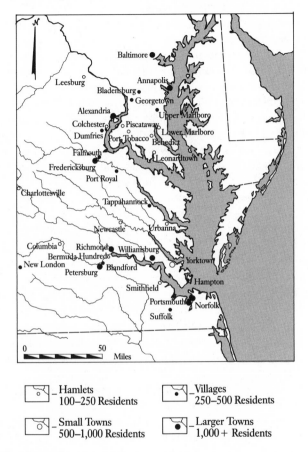

⬚ Hamlets 100–250 Residents	⬚ Villages 250–500 Residents
⬚ Small Towns 500–1,000 Residents	⬚ Larger Towns 1,000+ Residents

Sources: Cited in map 6.

to be fully repaid for four years. Second, merchant creditors aided the settlement of the frontier, thereby encouraging tobacco cultivation, and founded towns that centralized trade and attracted productive artisans.

The Political Economy of Debt

Most families in the Chesapeake region, except those locked in poverty, took advantage of the increased credit of the 1760s and 1770s. By 1776, debt to Britain per household had reached an average of about twenty pounds sterling, and the burden of debt had probably been even greater before 1772, when many merchants called in their loans.[16] Planters invested this money in housing, land, or slaves and thereby markedly increased the wealth of the region.

Wealthy gentleman planters and merchants—those men who owned many slaves, several thousand acres of land, and other property totaling perhaps five thousand pounds in the 1770s—held far more than their share of available British credit. They had excellent collateral for loans because their land and slaves were appreciating rapidly in value. Local merchants owed about a tenth of Virginia's British debt, and local gentleman planters a little over a third of it. These merchants and gentlemen, 2 or 3 percent of Virginia's householders, commanded credit that ranged from one hundred pounds to nearly twenty thousand pounds sterling.[17]

Middling planters, who owned just a couple of hundred acres of land and a few slaves, also found credit easy to obtain. These planters, who owned goods worth from one hundred pounds to six hundred pounds in the 1770s, often borrowed money from both Scottish and local merchants to set up households or to finance modest improvements in their standard of living. In total, middling planters, who composed perhaps three-fifths of the region's families, owed about half the debt owed by Virginians to British merchants in 1776. Most owed sums under twenty-five pounds, and few borrowed more than a few pounds at a time. Borrowing larger sums to expand their operations required mortgaging their land or slaves, and they knew that a drop in tobacco prices or poor weather could then cause them to lose both land and slaves, the basis of their prosperity.[18]

About a third of the households in the region were headed by poor men who owned neither land nor slaves. These men, who owned property worth just twenty-two pounds in the 1770s, benefited little from the expansion of credit. They often borrowed money from Scottish merchants to purchase necessities, but, in return, their crops belonged to the merchant. More than half the tenant nonslaveholders in Prince George's County, for instance, owed money to Scottish merchants by the late 1760s. Despite the

16. Price, *Capital and Credit*, 12–15.
17. Sheridan, "British Credit Crisis," *Jour. Econ. Hist.*, XX (1960), 167. Exact totals were 11% to merchants and 36% to gentlemen. Data on wealth levels and proportions of population in various groups in this and succeeding paragraphs come from sources cited in tables 10, 11, 14.
18. Sheridan, "British Credit Crisis," *Jour. Econ. Hist.*, XX (1960), 67, shows that 53% of the debt was for sums under £100 (and usually £25); table 14. When the wealthiest tenth of Prince George's planters are excluded, others who owned land and slaves had goods worth £586. This group and those who owned land or slaves constituted 57% of the county's householders. The proportion of men who owned land and slaves in the county owing money to Scottish merchants rose from 13%, 1745–1759 ($N = 93$), to 38%, 1760–1764 ($N = 37$), to 75%, 1765–1769 ($N = 45$), Prince George's Inventories, MHR.

credit these small planters received, their wealth declined both absolutely and relative to other groups in the county in the 1750s and 1760s.[19]

Since so many planters and gentlemen relied on British credit, debts became a major political issue when credit contracted in Britain. Problems of credit and indebtedness, unlike the issue of tobacco regulation (discussed in chapter 3), united the large majority of planters. Ordinary planters indebted to merchants for a few pounds owed proportionately as much of their wealth to creditors as did gentlemen who borrowed hundreds of pounds sterling. Anyone could lose his land, his slaves, and even his freedom if he could not pay his debts. Even large planters borrowed beyond their means, indulging in "Idleness Luxury and Extravagance." Debts owed by these men, Thomas Jefferson claimed in 1786, "had become hereditary from father to son for many generations, so that planters were species of property annexed to certain mercantile houses in London."[20]

As long as tobacco prices remained high and the British economy prospered, planters could easily pay their debts and borrow on future crops. Planters, however, unrealistically anticipated that the tobacco market would rise indefinitely and therefore borrowed beyond their means. When tobacco prices declined or British merchants called in their debts, planters were unable to pay and asked for more time to settle their accounts. Severe credit contractions hit the Chesapeake colonies from 1761 to 1765 and again in 1772. Debts owed to merchants increased rapidly during these crises. At Glassford's store at Colchester on the Potomac, for example, currency debts rose from £975 in 1760 to £5,000 in 1764. Even after prosperity returned, customers refused to pay their bills: debtors owed £8,550 in 1769, and the storekeeper considered nearly a fifth of that sum either "doubtful" or "desparate."[21]

The months following the British credit collapse of 1772 were particularly bad. Several British tobacco firms went bankrupt, and London and Glasgow merchants demanded payment of overdue debts from Chesapeake customers. With little new credit available and with the price of tobacco falling, planters could not pay. Merchants, forced to pay their own creditors

19. *Ibid.*; the percentage of nonslaveholding tenants who owed money to a merchant in Prince George's rose from 62%, 1745–1759 ($N = 37$), to 75%, 1760–1769 ($N = 16$), and the proportion indebted to Scottish merchants rose from 3% to 38% over the same period.

20. Emory G. Evans, "Planter Indebtedness and the Coming of the Revolution in Virginia," *WMQ*, 3d Ser., XIX (1962), 517–525 (first quote at 519); Price, *Capital and Credit*, chaps. 1, 7 (Jefferson quote, 5–6); Hemphill, ed., "Wayles Rates His Neighbours," *VMHB*, LXVI (1958), 302–306.

21. Joseph Albert Ernst, *Money and Politics in America, 1755–1775: A Study in the Currency Act of 1764 and the Political Economy of Revolution* (Chapel Hill, N.C., 1973), 66–70, 329–334; Sheridan, "British Credit Crisis," *Jour. Econ. Hist.*, XX (1960), 161–186; Price, *Capital and Credit*, chap. 7; Thompson, "Merchant in Virginia," 312–313.

and unable to extend more time to debtors, brought increasing numbers of planters to court. The number of debt cases in Prince George's County rose from about 50 in 1769, 1770, and 1771 to about 80 in 1772 and 1773 and reached a peak of nearly 120 in 1774. In Pittsylvania County, Virginia, at the edge of the southside frontier, about a third of the families were brought into court on debt charges in 1772, 1773, and 1774, a substantial rise from earlier years. The proportion of cases reaching judgment with executions (permitting the creditor to seize property) rose from less than two-thirds between 1767 and 1772 to nearly three-quarters from 1772 to 1774, and the proportion of cases brought by large Scottish and Virginia merchants doubled.[22]

The credit contraction of 1772–1774 triggered substantial conflict between planters and merchants. As the credit crisis deepened, courts sided with creditors, issued execution orders, and sent increasing numbers of men to prison, but these remedies rarely led to repayment. While in jail the debtor could not pay, and if he declared bankruptcy, each creditor would be paid only a portion of what he was owed. Merchants who seized property often discovered that the estates of poorer planters were too small to cover the entire debt, and the land and slaves of larger planters brought low prices when sold in times of depression. Perhaps for these reasons, a small and declining percentage of creditors in Pittsylvania took debtors' property or received any payment after execution orders.[23]

Since assemblymen in Chesapeake colonies could find no legislative remedy for credit contractions during the 1760s and 1770s, debts owed to British merchants remained a live issue for decades. Colonists stopped paying British creditors during the Revolution, of course, but after the war these merchants demanded repayment of old debts before they would grant

22. Sheridan, "British Credit Crisis," *Jour. Econ. Hist.*, XX (1960), 170–179; Price, *Capital and Credit*, chap. 7; Tommy R. Thompson, "Personal Indebtedness and the American Revolution in Maryland," *Maryland Historical Magazine*, LXXIII (1978), 19–21; Michael Nicholls, "Credit Crisis and Court Closures: Judgment Debt and Collection in Pittsylvania County, Virginia, 1767–1775" (paper presented at the 1978 meeting of the American Historical Association, West Coast Branch), tables 1, 3 (number of debt cases per 1,000 taxables, 1768–1774: 167, 157, 254, 162, 304, 314, 357 [half-year rate]): executions rose from 65%, 1768–1771, to 74%, 1772–1774, and the proportion of cases brought by large merchants rose from 8%, 1767–1771, to 15%, 1772–1774.

23. John Pendleton Kennedy, ed., *Journals of the House of Burgesses of Virginia, 1761–1765* (Richmond, 1907), 234–235, 245, 263; Ernst, *Money and Politics*, 48–51, 66–67, 87–88, 144–145; Alexander Hamilton to James Brown and Co., May 28, 1774, in Richard K. MacMaster and David C. Skaggs, eds., "The Letterbooks of Alexander Hamilton, Piscataway Factor," Pt. I, "1774," *MHM*, LXI (1966), 158–161; Tommy R. Thompson, "Debtors, Creditors, and the General Assembly in Colonial Maryland," *MHM*, LXXII (1977), 72–77. Nicholls, "Credit Crisis," table 5, shows a decline in executions returned "satisfied" from 29%, 1768–1771, to 14%, 1772–1774.

new credit to planters. Nascent political parties in the two states grew out of disputes over the repayment of British debt. Legislators and voters in areas like southside Virginia, where those indebted to Scottish merchants were concentrated, adamantly opposed repayment, while residents from areas where debt was less burdensome wanted to reestablish lines of credit broken by war. The issue of repayment was finally settled in favor of the British creditors by Jay's treaty, but even in the 1790s and 1800s debt collection remained difficult and sporadic.[24]

The Decline of Opportunity in Tidewater

Despite high tobacco prices and easy credit, many tobacco planters failed to improve their economic position in the 1760s and 1770s. In July 1773, Samuel Graham, a Scottish visitor to Charles County, Maryland, wrote home to his father about opportunity along the tobacco coast. "I have heard," he commented, "of several people by marrying advantageously with great industry in making good Crops come from nothing to something, but I have heard too of more whose predecessors have been a long while in the Country and yet are in straiting enough circumstances."[25] This decline of opportunity in tidewater can be traced to the intersection of three trends. First, continued population growth reduced the quantity of land available for purchase and at the same time increased its price. Second, freeholders improved their land with British credit, further increasing land prices. And third, the relative value of goods owned by poor people diminished as the price of land and slaves rose; accordingly, small planters' ability to purchase these two critical means of production decreased. The vicissitudes of opportunity in Prince George's County provide a useful case study.

Despite the declining availability of land, most men born in Prince George's during the second third of the eighteenth century eventually married and formed households. Youths worked on their parents' farms or on nearby plantations, accumulated property, and waited for an opportunity to marry. Although three-quarters of all men between twenty and twenty-four residing in the county in 1776 lived with their parents or neighbors, only a quarter of those in their thirties and a tenth of those over forty had not formed their own households, and merely a twentieth of the men over fifty

24. Emory G. Evans, "Private Indebtedness and the Revolution in Virginia, 1776 to 1796," *WMQ*, 3d Ser., XXVIII (1971), 349–374; Norman K. Risjord, *Chesapeake Politics, 1781–1800* (New York, 1978), 78–82, 110–118, 150–155, 452–464; Charles F. Hobson, "The Recovery of British Debts in the Federal Circuit Court of Virginia, 1790 to 1797," *VMHB*, XCII (1984), 176–200.
25. Chancery Records, XXVI, 68–69, MHR.

had never married.[26] As the number of youths who migrated to Prince George's declined in the 1750s and 1760s, the probability that boys born in the county would establish homes there may have improved. Between a third and a half of the youths in their twenties, but few older men, left the county in the 1770s.[27]

Although youths who stayed in Prince George's formed households with ease, the increasing population of the county severely limited further opportunities to acquire land. White population density nearly doubled between 1733 and 1776, thereby reducing the potential supply of land available to each white resident. Since the number of households continued to grow and the number of acres owned by typical freeholders did not decline, the proportion of landowners among householders decreased, and fewer youths could expect to own land unless they inherited it.[28]

Although the price of improved land in Prince George's rose imperceptibly between 1720 and 1750, it more than tripled between the mid-1750s and mid-1770s (see fig. 17).[29] Some of the increased value of land rested on the growing value of tobacco, but land prices rose three times as fast as the price of tobacco. County families used income from their crops and British credit to improve their lands, houses, and barns, and such improvements drove up farm prices. In addition, declining quantities of unimproved frontier acreage near the county's borders pushed land prices higher. The rising value of land accentuated the significance of inheritance: the son of a prosperous planter could expect to receive valuable land when his father died, but the son of a small landowner or tenant had to purchase increasingly expensive land in order to become a freeholder.

Despite this decline in opportunity, sons of poor men in Prince George's and in adjacent counties could still form households where they

26. Kulikoff, "Tobacco and Slaves," 129.
27. Calculation based upon a comparison of white adult male ages in Prince George's found in Gaius Marcus Brumbaugh, ed., *Maryland Records: Colonial, Revolutionary, County, and Church, from Original Sources*, I (Baltimore, 1915), 1–88, with West Level 8 model life table in Ansley J. Coale and Paul Demeny, *Regional Model Life Tables and Stable Populations* (Princeton, N.J., 1966), 88–89, 136–137, assuming no men over 50 had migrated and adjusting the estimated number of men under 50 for those who had migrated. Darrett B. Rutman and Anita H. Rutman, *A Place in Time: Explicatus* (New York, 1984), 148–154, shows declining opportunity in Middlesex County, Virginia, for sons maturing 1700–1720 and those maturing 1720–1750, a finding consistent with arguments here.
28. Kulikoff, "Tobacco and Slaves," 323; Kulikoff, "Economic Growth," *Jour. Econ. Hist.*, XXXIX (1979), 278; and table 10 show that population density in Prince George's rose from 21 to 37 people per square mile between 1733 and 1776 and that density in Maryland's lower Western Shore (region including Prince George's) rose from 31 to 42 people per square mile from 1755 to 1782.
29. Land prices rose .7% a year, 1720–1742, and .5% a year, 1731–1753 (based upon values from linear regressions for those years) before exploding in the 1760s and 1770s.

Fig. 17. *Land and Slave Prices in the Chesapeake, 1720–1775*

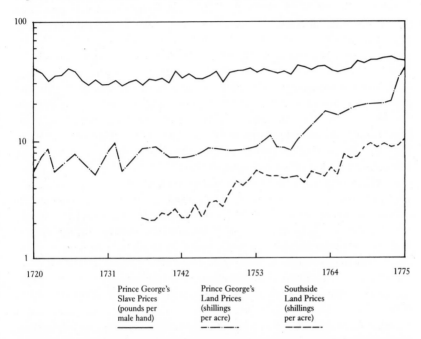

| | Prince George's
Slave Prices
(pounds per
male hand) | Prince George's
Land Prices
(shillings
per acre) | Southside
Land Prices
(shillings
per acre) |

Sources: Prince George's Land Records, MHR, for 35 selected years between 1720 and 1775; southside land records (collected by Michael Nicholls for the St. Mary's City Commission) from deed books of Amelia and Prince Edward counties (coupled together) and Lunenburg and Pittsylvania counties (coupled together), 1736–1775, with sales under 50 acres excluded; Allan Kulikoff, "Tobacco and Slaves: Population, Economy, and Society in Eighteenth-Century Prince George's County, Maryland" (Ph.D. diss., Brandeis University, 1976), 485–488 (slave prices). Maryland series were placed into constant money with consumer price indexes calculated by the St. Mary's City Commission; the Virginia series was changed into sterling values from data in John J. McCusker, *Money and Exchange in Europe and America, 1660–1775: A Handbook* (Chapel Hill, N.C., 1978), 210–215.

were born because they could lease land from rentiers controlling thousands of acres of land. Since the proprietors of these regions, the Calverts in Maryland and the Fairfaxes in Virginia's Northern Neck, had not imposed limits on the number of acres a planter could patent, a few men had accumulated large tracts in the seventeenth and early eighteenth centuries. These speculators had leased their land to tenants rather than selling small parcels for profit. Despite abundant frontier land nearby, tenancy developed very early in these areas. A third of the householders in Prince George's were tenants in 1705, and as the area's frontiers came under cultivation, the proportion of tenants rose to more than half the county's householders by the 1770s. At least half—and possibly more—of the families in southern Maryland and the Northern Neck rented land in the 1780s, probably farming far less land than the two hundred acres owned by typical freeholders (see table 10).[30]

As population density increased in proprietary areas, the character of tenancy changed. Frontier landlords often granted leases for three lives or many years at nominal rent. In return, tenants were required to improve the land by building structures and planting orchards. After most of the land had been developed, landlords usually rented land for short periods and charged substantial rents, amounting to a third or even a half of a single worker's tobacco crop. Tenants in these areas could barely afford high rents and could not accumulate much savings.[31]

Youths who lived south of the Rappahannock River in tidewater Virginia did not share even in these opportunities, for extensive tenancy did not develop there. Only three of every ten families in James City County, organized in 1637, rented land in 1768, and the average landowner possessed more than two hundred acres. Nearly two-thirds of the householders in the region still owned land in 1787. Most sons of small landowners had to move out of the area because neither their fathers nor their neighbors would subdivide their holdings into small parcels. Only a quarter of all the landowners in ten tidewater Virginia counties in 1787 held fewer than a hundred acres, and these were mostly located in a few places that had not produced tobacco for decades.[32]

Once tidewater youths married, their opportunities depended heavily on the economic position of their fathers. Although the supply of slave labor increased through the eighteenth century, most slaves were native-born by the 1750s; most creole slaves were passed between generations of white families and never reached the marketplace. While the slave trade remained strong in the 1720s and 1730s, planters could purchase new Negroes for about thirty pounds sterling, but prices for available creole slaves rose after

30. The size of plots leased to tenants is suggested by median landholdings, assuming that those who rented land held less than the median. Median landholdings, including tenants, was 90 acres in Fairfax and Prince George's counties and 71 acres in Charles and Calvert counties (table 10 and sources there).

31. Gregory A. Stiverson, *Poverty in a Land of Plenty: Tenancy in Eighteenth-Century Maryland* (Baltimore, 1977), chap. 1; Willard F. Bliss, "The Rise of Tenancy in Virginia," *VMHB*, LVIII (1950), 427–441; Aubrey C. Land, *The Dulanys of Maryland: A Biographical Study of Daniel Dulany the Elder (1658–1753) and Daniel Dulany the Younger (1722–1797)* (Baltimore, 1968), chap. 11.

32. Jackson Turner Main, "The Distribution of Property in Post-Revolutionary Virginia," *Mississippi Valley Historical Review*, XLI (1954–1955), 248; Sara S. Hughes, "Elizabeth City County, Virginia, 1782–1810: The Economic and Social Structure of a Tidewater County in the Early National Years" (Ph.D. diss., College of William and Mary, 1975), chap. 8.

Table 10. *Landownership in the Tidewater Chesapeake, 1705–1790*

Place and Year	Percentage of Householders Owning Land	Median No. of Acres Owned by Freeholders	No. of House- holds
	Proprietary Areas		
Prince George's			
1705	65	260	459
1733	58	200	1,204
1755	56	—	1,337
1776	45	200	1,669
Southern Maryland[a]			
1783	47	150	2,805
Northern Neck			
1787	42	—	—
Fairfax Co.			
1782	36	250	831
Richmond Co.			
1782[b]	70	200	511
1790	56	200	655
	Nonproprietary Areas		
James City Co.			
1768[c]	70	210	268
Tidewater Virginia			
1787	64	—	—

Sources: Lois Green Carr, "County Government in Maryland, 1689–1709" (Ph.D. diss., Harvard University, 1968), 581, 588, 597; Black Books, II, 110–124, and Gaius Marcus Brumbaugh, ed., *Maryland Records: Colonial, Revolutionary, County, and Church, from Original Sources*, I (Baltimore, 1915), 1–88, linked with Prince George's Land Records and Debt Books (1755, 1772), MHR; "Number of Inhabitants in Maryland," *Gentleman's Magazine, and Historical Chronicle*, XXXIV (1764), 261; Gregory A. Stiverson, *Poverty in a Land of Plenty: Tenancy in Eighteenth-Century Maryland* (Baltimore, 1977), 144–145; Jackson Turner Main, "The Distribution of Property in Post-Revolutionary Virginia," *Mississippi Valley Historical Review*, XLI (1954–1955), 248; Norman K. Risjord, *Chesapeake Politics, 1781–1800* (New York, 1978), 23, 25; "James City County, Virginia, Sheriff's Tax Books, 1768," *Virginia Genealogist*, VI (1957), 18–22, 69–70.

Notes: [a]Charles and Calvert counties. [b]The 1782 figure is probably too high. [c]Excludes men who owned carriages, but not land; these taxpayers lived outside James City but maintained a residence in Williamsburg.

1740, reaching forty-five pounds by the early 1770s (fig. 17). Men whose fathers owned many slaves therefore had a great advantage over sons of nonslaveholders, who had to buy expensive chattels.

Nevertheless, slaves were widely distributed among planters in tidewater because most slaveholders divided their slaves among all their children and because a disproportionate number of poor men's sons left the region. By the middle of the century, from half to two-thirds of the householders in several tidewater counties owned slaves, each typically holding around three slaves of working age. Slaveholding spread further in the pre-Revolutionary decades. By the 1780s, about two-thirds of the planters in nine tidewater counties owned slaves, with most owning about six slaves of all ages (or three or four slaves of working age). Very few men possessed as many as ten slaves in these counties at any time in the century (see table 11).[33]

These transformations of the region's economy differentially affected various social groups. In Prince George's, for instance, economic change reduced opportunity for sons of middling planters, but left the substantial opportunities for sons of wealthy men and the poor chances of sons of tenants remarkably unchanged. A new group of slaveholding tenants emerged, composed mostly of sons of planters who owned both land and slaves. As the price of land rose and frontier land disappeared, many planters no longer owned acreage near their homes that they could pass on to their sons. Since their slaveholdings kept growing through natural increase, they gave their offspring a slave or two after they had established new tobacco farms. These youths joined sons of slaveholding tenants, who often inherited slaves but rarely purchased land. At the same time, the relative size of the group of men who owned land, but not slaves, declined by half, because most of these men owned too little land to divide it into farms for each of their sons. Two-thirds of their sons joined the ranks of slaveless tenants (see table 12).[34]

Patterns of inheritance accentuated the economic decline of sons of men who owned land or slaves while strengthening the position of sons of men who owned both forms of capital. The proportion of sons of land- or slaveholders who remained tenants without slaves after their fathers died

33. The summary figure given in the text calculated from table 11, counting southern Maryland, 1782–1790; the peninsula, 1782; and other tidewater Virginia, 1782–1783, equally (mean = 65%).

34. Compare table 5 (economic position in county ca. 1733) with table 12. The proportion of householders in Prince George's who owned slaves, but not land, rose from 9% in 1733 to 17% in 1776, while the proportion who owned land, but not slaves, declined from 24% to 10%, and the proportion of slaveless tenants rose from 32% to 38%. Black Books, II, 110, MHR; and Brumbaugh, ed., *Maryland Records*, I, 1–88, linked with Land Records and Debt Books, MHR.

Table 11. *Slaveholding in the Tidewater Chesapeake, 1733–1790*

Place and Year	Percentage of Householders Owning Slaves	Median No. per Slaveowner[a]	No. of House- holds
Calvert			
1733	45	3	553
Prince George's			
1733	39	3	1,123
1776	52	—	1,667
Lancaster Co.			
1745	68	3	245
1776–1777	77	4	204
Southern Maryland[b]			
1782–1790	52	5	4,724
Peninsula, Virginia[c]			
1782	78	6	754
Other tidewater Virginia[d]			
1782–1783	67	6	742

Sources: Charles Francis Stein, *A History of Calvert County, Maryland* (Baltimore, 1960), 375–381; Black Books, II, 110–124, MHR; Gaius Marcus Brumbaugh, ed., *Maryland Records: Colonial, Revolutionary, County, Church, from Original Sources*, I (Baltimore, 1915), 1–88, adjusted for missing half of Prince George's; Robert E. Brown and B. Katherine Brown, *Virginia, 1705–1786: Democracy or Aristocracy?* (East Lansing, Mich., 1964), 75; Gregory A. Stiverson, *Poverty in a Land of Plenty: Tenancy in Eighteenth-Century Maryland* (Baltimore, 1977), 146–147; personal property tax lists for Charles City, James City, and Warwick counties, 1782–1783, VSL, Norman K. Risjord, *Chesapeake Politics, 1781–1800* (New York, 1978), 20, 23; Nancy L. Oberseider, "A Sociodemographic Study of the Family as a Social Unit in Tidewater, Virginia, 1660–1776" (Ph.D. diss., University of Maryland, 1975), 202–203.

Notes: [a]Taxable (adult) slaves before 1780, all slaves after 1780. [b]Calvert and Charles counties, 1782; Anne Arundel County, 1790. [c]Charles City, James City, and Warwick counties. [d]Richmond and Middlesex counties.

rose from less than a tenth in the 1730s to a third by the 1770s, and the proportion who used their inheritance to buy land and slaves declined from nearly half to about a third. At the same time, the proportion of sons of substantial planters who inherited their fathers' position rose from less than three-quarters to nearly nine-tenths (see table 13).

The rising price of land and slaves explains the debased value of the inheritances of poor men, for they received goods of relatively less value in

Table 12. *Economic Position of Sons and Position of Father in Prince George's County, circa 1776*

	Percentage of Sons			
	Status of Father			
Status of Son	Tenant Owning No Slaves (*N* = 130)	Landowner Owning No Slaves (*N* = 131)	Slaveowner Owning No Land (*N* = 64)	Land- and Slaveowner (*N* = 394)
Tenant owning no slaves (*N* = 300)	90	65	42	18
Landowner owning no slaves (*N* = 58)	3	14	3	9
Slaveowner owning no land (*N* = 126)	5	7	50	20
Land- and slave- owner (*N* = 235)	2	15	5	53

Sources: Gaius Marcus Brumbaugh, ed., *Maryland Records: Colonial, Revolutionary, County, and Church, from Original Sources*, I (Baltimore, 1915), 1–88 (census for Potomac half of the county) linked with Prince George's Land Records, Debt Books, and Inventories, MHR, and with data from table 5.

Note: The percentages were weighted to include cases where the status of the father was unknown, using a method similar to that for table 5, but assuming that a tenth of each group of sons were immigrants.

the 1770s than in the 1730s. The proportion of the estates of tenants and nonslaveholders tied up in consumer durables like clothing and furniture rose from a fifth in the 1730s to a third in the 1770s, the portion tied up in livestock and crops stayed about the same, and the share consisting of cash and other capital declined from a third to a fourth of their meager resources (see table 14). All these goods bought less in the 1770s than in the 1730s. In 1735, a tenant could purchase a full field hand for about nineteen head of cattle, but in 1770 the same slave cost about thirty head. Similarly, he could buy fifty acres of average land in the county for about nine head in 1735, but he needed twenty-six head in 1770.[35]

It was extremely difficult for a tenant in Prince George's in the 1760s and 1770s to add inheritance to current income and purchase either land or slaves. His profits from tobacco rose from about £6 to £8 a year, but the

35. Calculations based upon slave and cow-and-calf prices for 1735 and 1770 found in Kulikoff, "Tobacco and Slaves," 485–492, and land prices reported in fig. 17, adjusted by a consumer price index.

Table 13. *Inheritance and Social Mobility in Prince George's County, 1776*

	Percentage of Sons			
	Status of Father			
	Land- or Slaveowner		Land- and Slaveowner	
Status of Son	Father Alive (N=34)	Father Dead (N=31)	Father Alive (N=61)	Father Dead (N=153)
Tenant owning no slaves	44	32	25	1
Land- or slaveowner	38	36	46	11
Land- and slaveowner	18	32	30	88
Total	100	100	101	100

Sources: Gaius Marcus Brumbaugh, ed., *Maryland Records: Colonial, Revolutionary, County, and Church, from Original Sources*, I (Baltimore, 1915), 1–88, linked with Prince George's Land Records, Debt Books, and Inventories, MHR, and with data from Table 5.

Note: Only known cases are included. There were insufficient cases in the "Father: Tenant without Slaves" group.

price of a fifty-acre tract jumped from £15 to £38.[36] An enterprising tenant might have bought a slave child born in the county, for he probably needed only £4 4s., but he would have found financing the £8 6s. down payment for a full hand difficult. Since slave children added to a tenant's burden of dependency until they started to work and since household expenses consumed all the income of most tenants, fewer than two in twenty bought a slave in the 1770s.[37]

As the number of slaves in the county rose, some planters came to own surplus hands, and in the 1760s slave hire became common. A nonslaveholder who hired a slave improved his family's standard of living, but he

36. Figs. 10, 17; Carville V. Earle, *The Evolution of a Tidewater Settlement System: All Hallow's Parish Maryland, 1650–1783*, University of Chicago Department of Geography Research Paper 170 (Chicago, 1975), 224–226. Land price estimated here at 15s. (circa 1770), tobacco at 2d. a pound, and land rental at 500 pounds of tobacco.
37. Table 12; estimate assumes that a planter who sold a slave in the 1770s required a down payment at least as great as the 1,000 pounds of tobacco he would receive for hiring out the slave (see sources cited in fig. 31) and that hire rate for children was half that for adults (who were worth half the adult price; see Kulikoff, "Tobacco and Slaves," 253).

Table 14. *Estimated Wealth of Householders in Prince George's County in the 1770s*

			Percentage of Assets			
Group	Land	Labor	Crops and Live-stock	Other Capital	Consump-tion Items	Total Wealth, Constant £
Tenant, owning no slaves	0	0	40	25	35	22
Landowner, owning no slaves	75	0	11	7	8	253
Slaveowner, owning no land	0	52	17	15	16	121
Land- and slaveowner	53	29	6	6	5	990

Sources: Prince George's Inventories and Land Records, MHR; Prince George's Debt Books, 1772, MHR; Gaius Marcus Brumbaugh, ed., *Maryland Records: Colonial, Revolutionary, County, and Church, from Original Sources*, I (Baltimore, 1915), 1–88.

Note: For methods of calculation, see note to table 7.

gained too little additional income to purchase a slave or land. In 1770, a full male hand produced goods worth £16 4s., but the owner received nearly three-quarters of that sum as rent, leaving the renter with some corn and salable tobacco worth about £3 6s. Corn grown by the slave was eaten by the master's family, fed to hogs, or sold locally at low prevailing prices.[38]

Though the wealth of men who owned slaves or land rose between the 1730s and 1770s, their relative economic position deteriorated, and their children's opportunity declined. A middle-aged freeholder with three children might leave his family with about two hundred pounds in the 1760s or 1770s; after his executor had paid his debts and his widow died, each child would inherit goods worth about fifty pounds if the estate were divided evenly. A father with an estate of two hundred pounds would have owned fewer than two hundred acres of land or a couple of taxable slaves. One child might inherit land, but the amount of the inheritance would be too small for others to purchase a plantation in Prince George's. Slaves were readily available for those with cash to buy them, and most descendants in

38. Assumes that a slave produced 1,400 pounds of tobacco at 2d. a pound, 16 barrels of corn at 6s. each (Earle, *Tidewater Settlement System*, 128; Kulikoff, "Tobacco and Slaves," 493–496), cost 1,000 pounds of tobacco for hire, and consumed 3 barrels of corn, 25 pounds of pork (at half the bacon price, 4s.), and 12s. in clothing (Prince George's Accounts, DD#6, 301–303, and Testamentary Papers, box 54, folder 10, MHR, give expenses in current money).

this group would probably use their inheritance to buy one. But slaveownership would entail considerable risks for small planters. Most of these men owned but one taxable slave, and a third held only slave children. These small planters ran the risk that the slave child might die before he became productive or that the adult slave might run away if pushed too hard.[39]

The prospects of sons of substantial planters improved between the 1730s and 1770s because the value of their fathers' property nearly doubled as the value of slaves and land they owned appreciated. The three children of a planter who owned two hundred acres of land and two taxable slaves would inherit about one hundred pounds each in the 1770s, double the amount their fathers received in the 1730s. As a result, the proportion of sons of men who owned both land and slaves who attained their fathers' economic position once the fathers died rose from three-quarters to nearly nine-tenths between 1733 and 1776.[40]

In summary, opportunity in tidewater during the prosperous years of high tobacco prices of the 1760s and 1770s was tied to the ownership of land and slaves. Men who owned both these assets commanded a disproportionate share of available credit and used it to improve their plantations and their standard of living. Poor men, cut out of the market for land and slaves by increasing costs, gained little from high tobacco prices and had to leave for the frontier if they sought to improve their station.

The Peopling of Piedmont Virginia

Pushed from old tidewater areas by shrinking economic opportunity, thousands of migrants settled a vast area of piedmont Virginia between 1740 and 1775 and, with the help of credit supplied by Scottish merchants, turned hundreds of thousands of acres of land into tobacco plantations. Settlers reached the sources of the Potomac and James rivers in the mountains in the 1740s, and they followed the Appomattox, Roanoke, and Nottoway rivers toward piedmont North Carolina in the 1750s and 1760s. At least three-quarters of the land in piedmont Virginia was patented by 1770, and rapid settlement continued only in Halifax and Pittsylvania, located in the southwest corner of piedmont (see map 8).[41]

39. For computational procedures for estate value, see chap. 3, n. 18, except that I have increased the loss of the estate to four pounds a year. Brumbaugh, ed., *Maryland Records*, I, 1–88, gives slave distributions.
40. For computational procedures for estate value, see chap. 3, n. 19, except that I assumed that the value of land rose £25 and of slaves £40 between the father's and the widow's death. The initial value of the estate was £330.
41. Richard L. Morton, *Colonial Virginia: Westward Expansion and the Prelude to Revolution* (Chapel Hill, N.C., 1960), II, chaps. 13, 14, details frontier settlement.

Map 8. *The Virginia Frontier, 1740s–1770s*

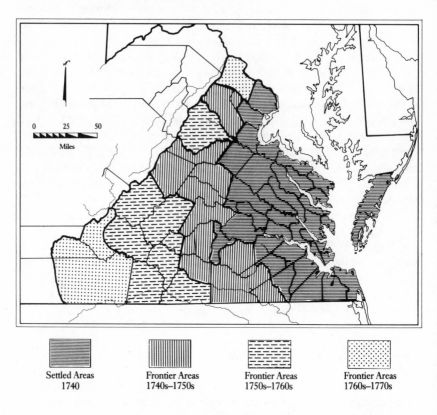

| Settled Areas 1740 | Frontier Areas 1740s–1750s | Frontier Areas 1750s–1760s | Frontier Areas 1760s–1770s |

Sources: Quitrent Returns, C.O. 1313–1353/5, P.R.O. (film at CW), counties south of the Rappahannock River; tithables collected from Court Order Books, VSL, and Evarts B. Greene and Virginia D. Harrington, *American Population before the Federal Census of 1790* (New York, 1932), 151–155 (Northern Neck). Frontier counties are those where less than half the land is patented and taxed land grows at a rate of at least 5% a year (counties south of the Rappahannock River), or where tithable population grows at more than 3% a year (Northern Neck).

The process of settlement of the piedmont Virginia frontier can be divided into four stages. Almost as soon as Virginians drove the Indians from an area, a few pioneers arrived, squatting on the land and raising crops for their own subsistence. Second, speculators discovered the region and patented thousands of acres. Their activities began a land rush, and hundreds of planters soon patented smaller parcels of land or bought unimproved acres from the speculators. Most of the good land was taken within a decade or two, but population continued to grow at a slower pace until nearly all the land had been divided into farms. Finally, as population density increased, out-migration began, and population growth slowed to a trickle.[42]

The history of southside Virginia, a section of piedmont located south of the James River, illustrates this process. Few whites ventured to southside early in the century, for several hundred Indians still lived there, and Virginians were proscribed from settling beyond the Nottoway River until 1714. Intensive development of the region began in the 1720s. Between 1727 and 1745, the quantity of land taxed in the region jumped five and a half times, and the working population nearly quadrupled. Taxed land rose at one and a half times the rate of population during these years because speculators patented thousands of acres but only slowly attracted settlers to buy it. Though population nearly tripled between 1745 and 1760, the quantity of taxed land merely doubled. The rate of growth of newly taxed land diminished in the 1760s, but the population continued to rise (see fig. 18). During the 1770s and 1780s the last plots of unimproved land were patented, and the residents of the entire southside then faced a potential land shortage.

This process was repeated in every southside county. Land speculators moved into Amelia County, located on the Appomattox and Nottoway rivers, in the early 1730s, and acreage taxed in the county nearly quadrupled between 1732 and 1740. At the same time, the number of taxables tripled. Although the growth of taxed land slowed in the 1740s and nearly ended by 1750, population rose by three-quarters between 1755 and 1770 as planters improved previously unused land. Settlers first arrived in Lunenburg County, which included nearly all the southern border of the province, during the early 1740s. Speculators bought thousands of acres in the 1740s and 1750s, and the quantity of taxed land tripled between 1746 and 1760 and began to slow down only in the 1760s. Since much land was still unused in the 1770s, rapid population growth continued unabated. Over the 1750s and 1760s, however, the focus of settlement shifted toward the south and west, where the legislature carved four new counties out of the original boundaries of Lunenburg.[43]

Land speculators played a vital role in the settlement of southside. Perhaps a quarter of the land patented there between 1703 and 1753 was held by speculators for later sale. A few men grabbed thousands of acres of land beyond the limits of settlement and hoped that low prices would attract poor farmers. In 1735 William Byrd, the largest land speculator in south-

42. See chap. 2 for the demographic determinants of this process.
43. *Ibid.*; Michael Lee Nicholls, "Origins of the Virginia Southside, 1703–1753: A Social and Economic Study" (Ph.D. diss., College of William and Mary, 1972), chap. 2.

Fig. 18. *The Settlement of Southside Virginia, 1700–1770*

Taxables :	Southside	Amelia	Lunenburg
Acres (÷ 10) :	Southside	Amelia	Lunenburg

Sources: Quitrent Returns, C.O. 1313–1353/5, P.R.O. (film at CW), and tithables from Court Order Books, VSL.

side, patented 100,000 acres along the Roanoke River, over a hundred miles from the nearest frontier settlement. Though Byrd opened this vast area for development, he sold little of it; as late as 1750—when the frontier had moved much closer to the Roanoke—four-fifths of the land remained unsold. Most speculators attracted purchasers to buy smaller parcels of land they had patented near centers of population. Samuel Cobbs, for instance, sold a third of the 17,819 acres he patented from 1732 to 1750 in Amelia County to fifteen planters by 1748.[44]

44. Nicholls, "Origins of Virginia Southside," 82–83, 91–94; Maud Carter Clement, *The History of Pittsylvania County, Virginia* (Lynchburg, Va., 1929), 35–38. I have called each person who patented a tract of 2,000 acres or more a speculator.

The southside frontier, as we have seen, attracted thousands of land-hungry migrants. The first pioneers often traveled long distances to newly opened areas, but they were quickly followed by others who moved from counties that bordered frontier areas. A majority of the initial settlers of southside in the 1730s and 1740s came from adjacent counties, usually traveling less than fifty miles. One-third traveled greater distances, and an eighth had moved from north of the James River, at least a hundred miles distant.[45] When inexpensive land in any part of the region had disappeared, some planters moved on to newer frontiers, but others continued to come from nearby counties, taking over already-improved plantations. Even the older areas that provided migrants attracted some new residents, usually men who moved from adjacent counties.

The movement of Virginia's Revolutionary War soldiers (found on muster rolls) as children and youths from about 1755 to 1775 clearly illustrates these migration patterns and places southside settlement into a larger regional context. Half of those who migrated moved within the Chesapeake region with their parents or left home to search for opportunities as young adults, another third arrived as immigrants from Britain and Europe in the 1770s, and the rest came from northern colonies. They moved in distinctive migration streams around tidewater, central piedmont Virginia, the southside, and the Shenandoah Valley. The newer the frontier, the greater the distance migrants traveled, and the larger the gain in population from the entry of settlers. The more densely peopled the region, in contrast, the shorter was the distance migrants traveled, and the greater the loss of population from out-migration (see maps 9, 10, 11).[46]

Nearly all of tidewater Virginia lost population in the 1760s and 1770s from out-migration, and very few new settlers arrived from outside the colony. Nonetheless, families that stayed in tidewater moved within the region, and between a tenth and a quarter of county enlistees from tidewater had been born in another county. More soldiers left than came to Caroline County, located on the Rappahannock River, for instance, yet more than a third of Caroline's soldiers had migrated to that county. Nearly all of those who migrated within tidewater moved short distances, with three-fifths of the migrants moving between adjacent counties.[47]

In contrast, many future soldiers and their parents moved from tide-

---

45. Nicholls, "Origins of Virginia Southside," 46–55.

46. Calculations in this and succeeding paragraphs are based upon Chesterfield Supplement and Revolutionary War Records, I, VSL, both muster rolls that give data on age, birthplace, and residence at enlistment in the late 1770s or early 1780s. I am indebted to Georgia Villaflor and Kenneth Sokoloff for allowing me to use their compilation of these data.

47. *Ibid.*; 59% of the 122 internal migrants in tidewater (except tidewater south of James) moved between adjacent counties.

Map 9. *Migration Flows of Revolutionary War Soldiers in Virginia, 1755–1775*

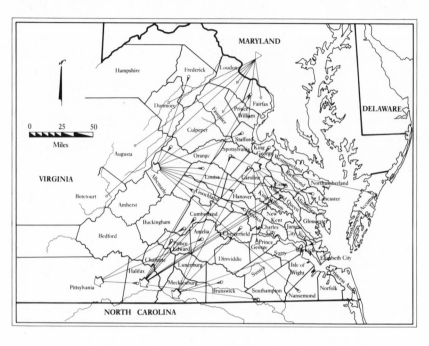

Sources: Chesterfield Supplement and Revolutionary War Records, I, both at VSL. Migration patterns determined from notations of place of birth and place of residence found in these two muster roles.

water to central piedmont Virginia in the 1760s and 1770s to take advantage of the modest quantities of unimproved land still found there. Half the men who enlisted in this area had been born outside their county of residence. Central Virginia attracted families from hundreds of miles away: one-sixth of the migrants had been born outside of the Chesapeake colonies. Only a quarter of those born in the Chesapeake region came from adjacent counties, and many of the others had moved from tidewater counties bordering on the Potomac or Rappahannock rivers, often more than a hundred miles away.[48]

48. *Ibid.*; there were 112 total immigrants: 21% were immigrants from abroad, 29% were born in adjacent counties, 38% were born elsewhere in the Chesapeake, and 17% were born in other colonies.

Map 10. *Net Migration into Virginia Counties by Revolutionary War Soldiers, 1755–1775*

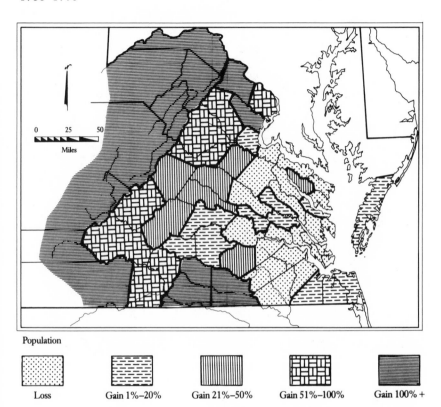

Population

Loss	Gain 1%–20%	Gain 21%–50%	Gain 51%–100%	Gain 100% +

Sources: Cited in map 9.

Every county in southside Virginia except long-settled Amelia and Prince Edward gained substantially from the migration of future soldiers, and the soldier population of four frontier counties doubled through in-migration in the 1760s and 1770s. Between half and three-quarters of the soldiers enlisting in southside counties had been born outside their county of residence. While fewer than a tenth of the area's enlistees came from outside the Chesapeake colonies, planters and their children did move long distances to reach southside. Only a fifth of the Virginia-born migrants came from adjacent counties; the others moved from northern and eastern parts of the colony, from piedmont counties settled earlier in the century, or

Map 11. *Gross Migration Flows into Virginia Counties by Revolutionary War Soldiers, 1755–1775*

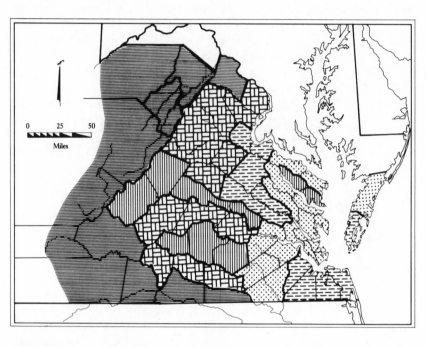

76% +
Migrants

51%–75%
Migrants

41%–50%
Migrants

26%–40%
Migrants

10%–25%
Migrants

Sources: Cited in map 9.

from the peninsulas of tidewater, located more than a hundred miles from their new homes.[49]

The Virginia Southside: The Best Poor Man's Country?

The thousands of people who left tidewater for piedmont moved in search of economic opportunity. But poor folk enjoyed only limited opportunities

49. *Ibid.*; there were 89 migrants to the area: 10% were foreign-born, 16% were born in adjacent counties, 69% were born elsewhere in the region, and 6% were born in other colonies.

once they arrived in frontier piedmont, despite the availability of inexpensive land, high tobacco prices, and easy credit. The process of frontier settlement explains some of their difficulties. The first pioneers to reach the wilderness were often poor folk who squatted on frontier land and grew food for their own subsistence, for roads to market were too poor to permit transport of tobacco hogsheads. Pioneers in Brunswick and Lunenburg counties, for instance, sent only about five hundred hogsheads of tobacco (150 pounds per taxable worker) to the nearest tobacco warehouses on the Appomattox River in the late 1740s. More prosperous planters followed poor men into southside as soon as roads were built. These men chased squatters off the land and patented it themselves. They took full advantage of high tobacco prices and the expanding credit granted by Scottish merchants. By 1769 Brunswick and Lunenburg planters sent ten thousand hogsheads of tobacco to Appomattox River warehouses, about 750 pounds for each worker in the area.[50]

Whites migrated easily from tidewater to southside Virginia, no matter how poor they were. Tidewater residents usually moved the hundred or more miles to southside in small steps, working as laborers or tenants along the way and trying to accumulate sufficient capital to purchase or patent land when they arrived on the frontier. For this journey, a migrant needed a horse and perhaps a cart to carry the goods he owned. Nearly everyone, even laborers, owned a horse, and almost all migrants had sufficient money to buy a cart. Travel costs were probably minimal: the migrant could carry food with him, might stay at a planter's house some evenings, and could find cheap room and board at an inn the rest of the time. If he ran short of cash, he might work as a day laborer to gain money to continue his journey.[51]

The first settlers of southside brought little wealth with them. The resources migrants brought to Amelia County in 1736 and to Lunenburg County in 1750, both at the edge of the frontier, were scanty: only one-sixth of the white men over age sixteen and only one-quarter of the heads of household possessed taxable slaves. Nearly half of these slaveowners possessed only one adult slave. Most migrants had either owned little land and no slaves or had been laborers in their former homes. A tenth of the white

---

50. Roger Atkinson to Lyonel and Samuel Lyde, Aug. 25, 1772, in A. J. Morrison, ed., "Letters of Roger Atkinson, 1769–1776," *VMHB*, XIV (1907–1908), 352–353; Calvin B. Coulter, "The Virginia Merchant" (Ph.D. diss., Princeton University, 1944), 8–11; Clement, *Pittsylvania County*, 107–113; William Waller Hening, ed., *The Statutes at Large: Being a Collection of All the Laws of Virginia . . .* , 13 vols. (Richmond, Philadelphia, 1809–1823), V, 57–58 (hereafter *Virginia Statutes at Large*).

51. Kulikoff, "Tobacco and Slaves," 326; Nicholls, "Origins of Virginia Southside," 46–55; Earle, *Tidewater Settlement System*, 145.

men, most probably youths, worked as agricultural laborers in these two counties, despite the great landed riches that surrounded them. Men of substance, who owned land and slaves, would lose more than they would gain by moving to a new frontier like southside. They could easily bear the cost of patenting land and might patent several hundred acres for their children; but they did not move to southside, for they would lose substantial income for each slave sent to develop the land (see table 15).[52]

Once a migrant reached the southside frontier, his major expenses began. He had to purchase a cow and some swine for subsistence, buy food for himself and his family to last until his corn and vegetables were harvested, and begin the difficult job of clearing his land of trees, bushes, or thick grass. Nearly all migrants could bear the eight pounds to nine pounds needed for subsistence the year of their arrival, but they had to face the prospect of patenting or buying land while losing income until they improved their holdings. A migrant had two choices: he could go to a totally unsettled area or move to a rapidly developing frontier. In the first case, he would pay a low price for land but could not grow tobacco until roads connected his farm to distant markets. If he chose the second option, he would pay much more for land, but he could begin planting tobacco his second year because roads to markets already existed. The initial costs of settling a developing area were greater than staking a claim in a raw frontier, but the ultimate benefits soon made up the difference. The choice a migrant made depended upon his ability to meet the initial costs of getting land.

A poor laborer tended to move to an unsettled area, squatting on unimproved land, because he could not afford to purchase land even at nominal prices. Since few families lived nearby, the migrant faced little pressure to establish a legal claim to the land by surveying and patenting it. The poor squatter might build his cabin, clear what he chose to call his land, and plant crops for several years. After a few years, however, other settlers would reach the area and begin surveying and patenting land around his farm; the squatter would have to follow suit or lose his investment. If he had worked diligently, he might have earned enough money to pay these costs, but he would more likely have been forced to move yet further into the backcountry. He still could not grow tobacco, for there were still no roads built to markets, and his income from corn depended upon finding new neighbors. In addition, he had to use his limited income to clothe his family

52. Nicholls, "Origins of Virginia Southside," 113, 120–123, 203. Commodity prices reported in Kulikoff, "Tobacco and Slaves," 474–504; figs. 10, 17; data on land system of southside in chap. 3; data on production in Earle, *Tidewater Settlement System*, 27; and Clemens, *Atlantic Economy*, 190–195.

Table 15. *Conjectured Costs and Benefits of Moving to Southside Virginia, 1750–1770*

Cost or Benefit	Value in £ Sterling	
	Totally Unsettled Area	Developing Frontier Area
Costs of moving		
Out-of-pocket expenses		
Purchasing 100 acres of land	£ 5 0s.	£10 0s.
Horse and cart to move goods	10 0	10 0
Travel to new area	1 0	1 0
Livestock needed for subsistence[a]	5 0	5 0
Food for one year[b]	3 0	3 10
Total out-of-pocket expenses	24 0	29 10
Forgone income, first 3 years		
From tobacco[c]	20 0	6 14
From corn[d]	7 0	6 6
Total forgone income	27 0	13 0
Total expenses	51 0	42 10
Benefits of moving		
Income from corn, first 3 years[e]	24 0	12 10
Income from tobacco, first 3 years[f]	0 0	20 0
Total income	24 0	32 10
Capital gains from improving land	5 0	15 0
Total benefits	29 0	47 10
Balance after three years	−22 0	5 0

Sources: Cited in n. 52.

Notes: The migrant is a married tenant (to unsettled area) with one child (to developing frontier area). [a]Two cows and several pigs. [b]Assumes that no crops can be grown the first year, that adults consume 3 barrels of corn a year, that a child consumes 1.5 barrels of corn annually, and that corn is worth 10 s. a barrel. [c]Counts income tenant would have received if he had remained a tenant. Tobacco crop estimated at 1,500 pounds (for the family), with 500 pounds rental at 1.6d. per pound. No tobacco can be grown in the first three years on the new frontier, but tobacco can be marketed after the first year in the developing frontier area. [d]Assumes a total production of 20 barrels a year, subtracting what has been consumed. [e]Value of corn (at 10s. a barrel) grown during second and third years, at 30 barrels a year in the totally unsettled area and 20 barrels a year in the developing frontier area, with home consumption subtracted. [f]Assumes no tobacco produced on new frontier, but 1,500 pounds a year, at 1.6d. per pound, for second and third years on developing frontier.

and buy essential consumer goods. Finally, even if he had enough cash, he might not be able to find a surveyor or to pay someone to go to Williamsburg to enter his patent.[53]

Former tenants, who were far wealthier than laborers, could move to either a raw frontier or to a rapidly developing area. A tenant who moved to an unsettled area probably had sufficient capital when he arrived to have his new land surveyed and patented. If he successfully survived his first year, he would gain a surplus of £24 from his corn crops over the next two years. This income, with the capital gains from improving his land, gave him a large stake in the new community. A tenant who moved instead to a developing area took greater risks but eventually enjoyed greater benefits. The migrant bought land instead of livestock and thereby risked malnutrition if inexpensive corn could not be found. A former tenant who survived his first year, however, earned £32 10s. from his tobacco and corn crops and £15 in capital improvements on his land during the next two years. With this income and credit from a Scottish merchant, he could buy a slave and precariously enter the yeoman class. Success in either area depended upon high corn and tobacco yields and good prices for both commodities. Poor yields and low prices, however, all too often wrecked these poor men's hopes for success (table 15).

A remarkably large proportion of the initial settlers of southside Virginia failed in their quest for wealth and security. More than two-thirds of the original settlers of Amelia County left between 1736 and 1749, including half the dependent sons and laborers, nearly half of the nonslaveholders, and a fifth of the slaveowners. Although many of these men had paid to have their land surveyed, most probably did not hold title to it because they had failed to patent it. When their debts became burdensome or their crops were short, they "absconded so that the process of law cannot be served against" them and moved further into the backcountry. Between 1735 and 1748, more than a third of the defendants in debt cases in Amelia left the county without paying their creditors.[54]

Most of those who stayed in Amelia achieved a degree of success. Many long-term residents eventually patented several hundred acres of land and saw the value of their holdings double as they improved it. These improvements gave pioneers new working capital they could use to buy a slave. About two-fifths of householders without slaves in 1736 owned a slave by 1749, and most of the small slaveholders saw their work force grow through natural increase. Although these men increased their income, their standard of living remained low. The small slaveholder typically owned a

53. *Ibid.*, 36, 73–79; fig. 17.
54. *Ibid.*, 113–119 (quote on 119), 120–123.

single slave, a few head of cattle and swine, a horse, and a few personal possessions.[55]

As southside Virginia developed, new groups came to farm already productive lands. Almost as soon as settlement began, wealthy planters established slave quarters in the wilderness. A fifth of the slaveholders in Lunenburg County in 1750—only four years after that county was organized—were nonresidents. After initial settlement began, sons of these substantial planters moved onto the already-developed quarters and brought yet more slaves with them. More than a third of the residents of Amelia County in 1749 owned slaves, and a fifth of them held five or more taxable men and women. Gentleman planters continued to set up quarters in Amelia, however, for a quarter of all slaveholders and a third of those who owned at least five adult slaves lived outside the county.[56]

The opportunities for success in southside began to diminish within a generation after the beginning of rapid development. Substantial slaveholders, both residents and nonresidents, took up and improved the best land, and a small group of indigenous slaveholders descended from the original group of poor migrants joined them. Four-fifths of the heads of households of Lunenburg County in 1764 had migrated there after 1750, sometimes bringing substantial capital with them; the rest, who had stayed in the county for fourteen years, slowly improved the land they owned and purchased a slave or two. At the same time, poor men left the region: two-fifths of the heads of household migrated from Lunenburg between 1764 and 1769, and only one-fifth of the white laborers in the county between 1750 and 1769 ever established households there.[57]

The out-migration of poor families, the in-migration of men of substance, and slow improvements in the fortunes of a few original settlers led to a rapid diffusion of slaves and land among southside's planters. More than two-thirds of the heads of household in Amelia County in 1768 and nearly half of those in Lunenburg County in 1764 owned slaves, a substantial increase over earlier decades. A similar process occurred in other counties in the region, and by the 1780s, six of every ten families held slaves, usually owning five chattels and working three adults in their tobacco fields (see table 16).

Although many poor pioneers had squatted on land they did not own, the proportion of legal landowners rose greatly in southside as development

---

55. *Ibid.*, 124–126, 131–132; Richard R. Beeman, *Cavaliers and Frontiersmen: The Cultural Development of Lunenburg County, Virginia, 1746–1832* (Philadelphia, 1984), 64–67.

56. Nicholls, "Origins of Virginia Southside," 203–206; Beeman, *Cavaliers and Frontiersmen*, chap. 3; Beeman, "Social Change and Cultural Conflict in Virginia: Lunenburg County, 1746 to 1774," *WMQ*, 3d Ser., XXXV (1978), 455–476.

57. Beeman, *Cavaliers and Frontiersmen*, chap. 3.

Table 16. *Slaveholding in Piedmont Virginia, 1736–1815*

Place and Year	Percentage of Householders Owning Slaves	Median No. per Slaveholder[a]	No. of Households
Amelia			
1736	23	2	308
1749	45	2	901
1768	70	3	869
1778	77	3	839
1782	76	6	1,211
1788	64	4	1,264
1794	64	—	1,327
Prince Edward			
1755	35	3	219
1782	61	5	691
Charlotte			
1764	42	2	349
1783	64	5	710
1790	58	4	1,057
Lunenburg[b]			
1750	27	2	1,113
1764	45	3	1,313
1769	53	3	398
1782	57	4	881
1783	67	5	575
1795	54	4	1,138
1815	70	4	978
Central Virginia[c]			
1763–1767	62	4	630
Other piedmont[d]			
1782	51	4	1,741
Southside[e]			
1782–1783	60	5	4,949

Sources: Cited in n. 63.

Notes: [a]Tithable (adult) slaves before 1780; all slaves, 1780–1783; slaves 12 and older, 1788–1794; slaves 9 and older, 1815. [b]Includes entire county as of 1764; e.g. including Charlotte. The 1783 partial returns probably overstate slaveownership, but the 1782 returns (like many in the state) missed a number of slaves. [c]Goochland County, 1763, and Louisa County, 1767. [d]Albemarle and Fairfax counties. [e]Amelia, Pittsylvania, Prince Edward, Halifax, Lunenburg, and Charlotte counties.

proceeded, and tenancy never took hold. In 1750 only half the household-ers in Lunenburg County held land, but only fourteen years later, three-quarters held legal title to the land they farmed. Nearly three-quarters of the families in five nearby counties owned land in the 1760s (see table 17), and a similarly high proportion held land in eight piedmont counties in 1787. Some of the nonlandowners, moreover, were sons of owners who lived rent-free on parental land. Landownership or access to rent-free land was therefore nearly universal in southside in the 1780s; perhaps as few as a tenth of the region's planters rented land.[58] The relative isolation of south-side made tenancy difficult for most families. They had to bear the extra cost of hauling their produce long distances to market over poor roads as well as high costs of consumer goods carted from tidewater ports.

As planters developed their holdings, the price of southside land jumped. The cost of land in Amelia and Lunenburg rose dramatically in the 1740s and early 1750s, stagnated as new frontiers opened in the late 1750s and early 1760s, and increased again in the late 1760s. Land prices in the region as a whole, in fact, tripled between 1750 and 1775 (fig. 17). Al-though higher land prices brought capital gains to resident planters, mi-grants found purchase of land far more costly. Moreover, the costs of mov-ing further into the southside frontier increased as well. Land in newly established Pittsylvania County between 1767 and 1769 cost more than twice as much as similar acreage had cost in Amelia County in 1735, imme-diately after its founding: the hundred acres of unimproved land a migrant purchased for ten pounds in Amelia in the 1730s cost twenty-four pounds in Pittsylvania by the late 1760s.[59]

The economic development and declining opportunities of southside during the 1750s and 1760s transformed the social structure of the region from one of small landowners and squatters to one dominated by landed slaveowners. In Lunenburg County, for instance, the proportion of heads of household who owned both land and slaves rose from about two-fifths to more than half during the 1760s, and the relative number of slaveless ten-ants declined from more than a fifth to just a seventh of all planters. County planters bought cheap land before they purchased expensive slaves: nearly a third of the householders owned land but not slaves, but only one in twenty farmed rented land with his own slaves.[60] Families who worked their own

58. Table 17; Nicholls, "Origins of Virginia Southside," 72–77. The tenancy estimate assumes that 70% of the families owned land, 10% squatted on the land, and 12% were sons of landholders waiting for inheritances (see Kulikoff, "Tobacco and Slaves," 125–126, for ratios applied here).

59. Fig. 17. The Amelia price, 1736–1738, was 2s. per acre; the Pittsylvania price, 1767–1769, was 4s. 10d. per acre.

60. In Lunenburg, landless tenants accounted for 20% of the heads of household in 1764 and

Table 17. *Landownership in Piedmont Virginia, 1750–1815*

Place and Year	Percentage of Householders Owning Land	Median No. of Acres per Freeholder	No. of House- holds
Lunenburg[a]			
1750	55	—	1,012
1764	75	340	393
1769	80	—	398
1782	75	—	881
1795	65	—	1,138
1815	77	—	1,078
Amelia			
1749	70	—	800
1768	78	250	862
1788	76	250	1,864
Charlotte			
1764	70	360	349
1790	67	275	1,057
Mecklenburg			
1764	69	320	571
Central Virginia[b]			
1763–1767	76	350	630
Prince Edward			
1783	68	250	691
Piedmont Virginia			
1787	72	—	—

Sources: Michael Lee Nicholls, "Origins of the Virginia Southside, 1703–1753: A Social and Economic Study" (Ph.D. diss., College of William and Mary, 1972), 66–68; Landon C. Bell, ed., *Sunlight on the Southside: Lists of Tithes and Tithables, Lunenburg County, Virginia, 1748–1783* (Philadelphia, 1931), 213–269; Richard R. Beeman, *Cavaliers and Frontiersmen: The Cultural Development of Lunenburg County, Virginia, 1746–1832* (Philadelphia, 1984), chap. 7; Paula Jean Martinac, "'An Unsettled Disposition': Social Structure and Geographical Mobility in Amelia County, Virginia, 1768–1794" (master's thesis, College of William and Mary, 1979), 26; tithable lists, Goochland County, 1763 and Louisa County, 1767, VSL; Edward Ayres, "Migration and Social Structure in Prince Edward County, Virginia, 1782–1792," MS (1969), charts 5, 6.

Notes: [a]Lunenburg in 1764 includes only those within the post-1764 bounds. [b]Louisa County, 1767; Goochland County, 1763.

land without slaves fared even less well than those in tidewater, because their land was worth a third of tidewater acreage, and they had to travel greater distances to get their crops to market.

The Chesapeake Frontier Disappears, 1780–1800

The economic system of the Chesapeake colonies during the mid-eighteenth century had been based upon the market production of tobacco and the continual exploitation of unimproved land on the region's frontiers. The rising price of tobacco in the 1750s and 1760s generated increasing credit from Britain that allowed planters to improve their land and their standard of living. Although poor men had few opportunities in old tidewater areas where land was scarce, they had better chances if they moved to the frontier. Moreover, sons of substantial planters remained wealthy because some offspring moved to the frontier, while others inherited the home plantation.

This economic system began to break down in the 1780s and 1790s. In the first place, tidewater planters no longer found tobacco cultivation profitable, and turned to general farming. The Revolutionary War disrupted tobacco markets so severely that less tobacco reached Britain and Europe in the period 1776–1782 than during any single year before the war. Planters had to shift from tobacco to grain farming and herding in order to survive. After the war, the tobacco trade revived, reaching levels attained in the best years before the war, but not all planters returned to tobacco cultivation. Farmers in tidewater counties in the York and James river basins exported 15 percent of the region's tobacco in the 1760s, but only 4 percent in 1784. Piedmont Virginia's share of the market, in contrast, rose from about a quarter to nearly half the total exports.[61]

The wars of the French Revolution in the mid-1790s again plunged tobacco markets into a depression, cutting Virginia's exports by more than half, from seventy-two million pounds in 1790 to thirty-four million in

14% in 1769, tenants with slaves for 5% in 1764 and 6% in 1769, landowners without slaves for 32% in 1764 and 28% in 1769, and land- and slaveholders for 44% in 1764 and 52% in 1769 (N = 393 in 1764 and 362 in 1769). Similar figures for Mecklenburg and Charlotte counties, 1764, were 26%, 5%, 30%, and 39% (N = 920), while these groups numbered 19%, 14%, 20%, and 48% in Prince Edward County in 1782 (N = 219). See Landon C. Bell, ed., *Sunlight on the Southside: Lists of Tithes, Lunenburg County, Virginia, 1748–1787* (Philadelphia, 1931), 213–269; and Edward Ayres, "Migration and Social Structure in Prince Edward County, Virginia, 1782–1792," MS, 1969, charts 5, 6.

61. Customs 16/1, P.R.O. (film at CW); "Tobacco Exports from Octo 1782 to Octo 1799," Auditor's Item 49, VSL; Jacob M. Price, *France and the Chesapeake: A History of the French Tobacco Monopoly, 1674–1791, and of Its Relationship to the British and American Tobacco Trade*, 2 vols. (Ann Arbor, Mich., 1973), chap. 28.

1796. While output declined by two-fifths in piedmont Virginia, it nearly disappeared north of the James River. When tobacco markets recovered after the wars, farmers in these regions did not resume tobacco cultivation, because new tobacco lands in North Carolina, Kentucky, and Tennessee produced better and less expensive tobacco. Tobacco production in the Chesapeake was limited to a few counties in southern Maryland, the central Virginia piedmont, and the Virginia southside, even in years of good weather and high prices, throughout the first half of the nineteenth century.[62]

Not only did tobacco cultivation disappear from tidewater, but economic opportunity continued to diminish in southside and reached the low levels common in tidewater by the end of the century. As the number of families increased, the average landholdings of planters declined, and there was insufficient land available for all sons of freeholders to achieve their fathers' status. In both Lunenburg and Charlotte counties, landownership declined from about three-quarters to two-thirds of heads of household between the early 1780s and 1790s. Some of these nonlandowers were sons of freeholders, temporarily living on their fathers' acreage; others were tenants, who survived because the legislature finally placed numerous inspection warehouses in southside, near their homes. At the same time, the proportion of householders who owned slaves also declined from about two-thirds to about half. Only in the early nineteenth century, after large numbers of men left the area and the number of local families declined, did land and slave ownership again increase.[63]

By the 1780s, inheritance had become nearly as important for the increasing numbers of southside natives as it had been in tidewater. In Amelia County, for instance, men of small means who could expect to inherit neither slaves nor land left the area. Two-thirds of the native fami-

62. *Ibid.*; J.D.B. DeBow, *Statistical View of the United States ... Being a Compendium of the Seventh Census ...* (Washington, D.C., 1854), 324, 330.
63. Tables 16, 17; maps appended to G. Melvin Herndon, "A History of Tobacco in Virginia, 1613–1860" (master's thesis, University of Virginia, 1956); Beeman, *Cavaliers and Frontiersmen*, chap. 7, table 8, sees greater opportunities than indicated here. Robert E. Brown and B. Katherine Brown, *Virginia, 1705–1786: Democracy or Aristocracy?* (East Lansing, Mich., 1964), 75; tithable lists, Goochland County, 1763, Louisa County, 1767, personal property tax list, Amelia County, 1782, VSL; Risjord, *Chesapeake Politics*, 25, 50; Nicholls, "Origins of the Virginia Southside," 113, 202, 205; Paula Jean Martinac, "'An Unsettled Disposition': Social Structure and Geographical Mobility in Amelia County, Virginia, 1768–1794" (master's thesis, College of William and Mary, 1979), 39; W. S. Morton, [Prince Edward tithables, 1755], *Tyler's Historical and Genealogical Magazine*, XVII (1936), 50–54; Ayres, "Migration and Social Structure in Prince Edward County," chart 9; Bell, *Sunlight on the Southside*, 213–285; Lester J. Cappon, ed., "Personal Property Tax List of Albemarle County," Albemarle County Historical Society, *Papers*, V (1944–1945), 47–73; Bureau of the Census, *Heads of Families, Virginia*, 22–24, 40–42.

lies of that county, however, owned slaves, and nearly a third of them worked with at least six adult slaves. Three-quarters of these long-term residents owned at least a hundred acres of land, and nearly a third of them possessed more than five hundred acres. These men usually passed their wealth on to their children and often gave them land or slaves before they died. Nearly two-thirds of the sons of long-term residents who came of age in the 1770s and 1780s owned slaves by the early 1790s, but they did not possess as many as their parents. Similarly, nearly all these sons owned land, but two-fifths of them had fewer than a hundred acres (see table 18).

Opportunities for poor newcomers, slight enough in the 1750s and 1760s, disappeared in the 1780s and 1790s. The high prices of land in Amelia and Prince Edward kept many poor migrants away but attracted slaveholders and freeholders who wanted to live in a developed society. More than a third of the men who moved into Prince Edward County in the 1780s and early 1790s owned slaves before they arrived. Poor migrants, in contrast, could rarely build their fortunes in southside. Even though many migrants to Amelia County, for instance, brought slaves with them or owned

Table 18. *Career Social Mobility in Amelia County, 1768–1794*

Group, by Ownership	Percentage in Group			
	Persisting Families	Sons	In-migrants	Out-migrants
	Slaveholding			
	(N = 181)	(N = 228)	(N = 161)	(N = 145)
0–1 slaves	32	39	58	55
2–5 slaves	40	48	32	36
6+ slaves	28	13	11	9
Total	100	100	101	100
	Landholding			
	(N = 181)	(N = 127)	(N = 96)	(N = 145)
0–100 acres	24	42	70	39
100–500 acres	46	50	24	55
500+ acres	30	8	6	7
Total	100	100	100	101

Source: Paula Jean Martinac, "'An Unsettled Disposition': Social Structure and Geographic Mobility in Amelia County, Virginia, 1768–1794" (master's thesis, College of William and Mary, 1979), 68–69.

Table 19. *Migration and Social Mobility in Prince Edward County, 1782–1792*

Group	Percentage among Taxpayers[a]	Percentage of Group Owning Slaves
Persisters	79	63
In-migrants	9	35
New native taxpayers	18	38
Out-migrants	21	39
In-migrants and new native taxpayers who move out	10	—

Source: Edward Ayres, "Migration and Social Structure in Prince Edward County, Virginia, 1782–1792," MS (1969), charts 9–11.

Note: [a]These are averages based on separate calculations for 1782–1784, 1784–1786, 1786–1788, and 1788–1792; persisters plus out-migrants equal 100%; persisters plus in-migrants and new native-born taxpayers do *not* equal 100 because of differences in the base used to calculate the numbers. There were, on average, 721 taxpayers in the years covered, the number rising from 681 to 845.

land before they came to the county, more than half the newcomers were unable to purchase slaves, and more than two-thirds of them owned fewer than a hundred acres of land after they had lived in the county a number of years.[64]

Though men still came to older southside counties like Prince Edward in the 1780s, they soon discovered that the chances for success were slight and decided to leave. Nearly a tenth of the taxpayers in Prince Edward in the 1780s had come to the county in the previous two years, and another fifth were sons of taxpayers. About a fifth of all the taxpayers left the county every other year, but half these migrants were sons of taxpayers or recent arrivals to Prince Edward. Whereas nearly two-thirds of the persisters owned slaves in the county, only two-fifths of the newcomers and men who left the county had slaves (see table 19).

Most of southside, and indeed the entire Chesapeake region, had become a land of opportunity only for men born to wealth. The prosperity of the second half of the eighteenth century, based upon high tobacco prices and abundant credit, had permitted planters to upgrade their plantations and thereby increased the price of land so much that only an inheritance would guarantee youths their own property. At the same time, slave prices rose and increased the wealth of slaveowners (and their offspring), but

64. Tables 16, 17, and sources cited there.

threw many nonslaveholders out of the market for bound labor. This process occurred first in tidewater, where little land remained unimproved
by mid-century and where population pressure, as well as improvements,
pushed land prices higher. Sons of modest planters, born in tidewater, did
find opportunities in piedmont between the 1730s and 1770s. There they
purchased unimproved land cheaply, built equity in their acreage, found
credit, and perhaps bought slaves. As population density increased and
piedmont planters improved their holdings, the piedmont came to resemble
tidewater. By the 1780s, just a few counties, located at the western edge of
southside, remained a good poor man's country. Poor migrants from southside moved from county to county or migrated to the raw frontiers of backcountry Georgia or Kentucky.[65] Expansion and opportunity—so characteristic of the frontier areas of the Chesapeake region through most of the
eighteenth century—had ended.

65. Beeman, *Cavaliers and Frontiersmen*, chap. 7; and "Social Change and Cultural Conflict,"
WMQ, 3d Ser., XXXV (1978), 455–476; Martinac, "'An Unsettled Disposition,'" 47–59.

II
White Society

5
The Origins of Domestic Patriarchy among White Families

In March 1729 Ann Thomas urged the Prince George's County court in Maryland to permit her "to tend such a Quantity of Tobacco for herself, her labouring girls and her [sickly] slave as may be Sufficient for a maintenance for herself and them." Her request ran counter to current law—meant to improve tobacco prices—which permitted slaves and white men and boys to tend tobacco plants but forbade white women to tend them. In support of her petition to waive the law, Thomas recounted her attempts to provide for her family. Her husband's "Several Mismanagements and ill Conduct" had "reduced [her] to so great want and necessity that for some time she had relief by a pension from the Court." About ten years before, her husband left her, but she was "a Constant hard Labourer in Tobacco" and had "made an honest shift to Maintain herself and family of Several Small children without putting the County to charge of a pension." She purchased a slave, but he was too sick to work and drained her resources. Despite her husband's departure, she "had frequently done the part of wife by him in his Sickness and been at great expense on his account and never has had any benefit of his Labour for many years." The new law, however, prevented her from making a crop and supporting her three daughters, ages eleven, thirteen, and fifteen, and she would soon require county assistance again.

The justices refused Thomas's request. They probably investigated her claim and discovered that the family had greater resources than Thomas admitted. In the first place, she owned a healthy slave woman who could work in the ground. Two sons, both in their late teens, worked as laborers on nearby plantations and could assist their mother, and a married son resided with his family nearby and might take in his mother and sister. Families as poor as Thomas's survived on similar allotments of tobacco plants, the justices may have reasoned, and there was little reason that Thomas could not emulate them.[1]

Although Thomas and the justices agreed in principle about the fundamentals of family government—that women should nurture children and

1. Prince George's Court Records, liber O, fols. 410–411; Prince George's Wills, box 6, folder 26, and box 7, folders 7, 8; King George Parish Register; and Black Books, II, 109–124, Maryland Hall of Records, Annapolis (MHR).

comfort their husbands in sickness and health while men supported their families by growing tobacco for the market—Thomas's independence challenged the subservient behavior that the justices expected of women. While Thomas explained that her husband's incompetence and departure from the home and her slave's illness forced her into the fields, the justices wanted her husband and sons to return home and fulfill their obligations. To gain these ends, the justices refused to waive the rarely enforced stinting law.

This case suggests the acceptance of a kind of partriarchalism as the ideal form of family government by some early eighteenth-century Chesapeake planters. Although these planters rejected the connection between male supremacy in the family and royal absolutism in government that lay at the heart of European patriarchal theory, they sought to retain patriarchal control over their families. This *domestic patriarchalism* was both a set of beliefs about power relations within families and households and a description of behavior within the family. The ideology of domestic patriarchalism placed husbands over wives within the family, asserted that women were legally inferior to men, and separated the economic roles of men and women into distinct spheres, with men responsible for the economic well-being of the family and for civic participation outside it and women responsible for child nurture and household management. In a patriarchal family system, one would expect to find husbands controlling the distribution of family assets (and preferring sons over daughters), the separation of public and private roles, distinctive economic roles for men, women, and children, and paternal control of their children's marriage decisions. Children and wives willing to accept their place could expect affectionate and even companionate fathers and husbands, especially in wealthy families where servants and slaves lightened the workload of both women and men. This domestic patriarchy was very different from the kind of bourgeois family government that slowly developed in England and the American North. Although both systems of family government ensured male supremacy by keeping women out of public life and by enforcing a sexual division of labor, the equality of husbands and wives in domestic relations and the elevation of women's roles of child nurture and family management to a position of great ideological importance never occurred in the eighteenth-century Chesapeake region.[2]

2. The literature on patriarchalism is vast. I am indebted to Elizabeth Fox-Genovese and her article, "Placing Women's History in History," *New Left Review*, No. 133 (May-June, 1982), 5–29, esp. 22–24, for clarifying the issues and suggesting the "domestic patriarchy" formulation. The definition here was also influenced by Michelle Zimbalist Rosaldo and Louise Lamphere, eds., *Women, Culture, and Society* (Stanford, Calif., 1974); Lawrence Stone, *The Family, Sex, and Marriage in England, 1500–1800* (New York, 1977), chaps. 4–9; and Gordon J. Schochet,

Although some white immigrants brought patriarchal ideals with them when they came to the Chesapeake, they found the practice of domestic patriarchalism difficult. Since adult life expectancy was quite low in the Chesapeake colonies during the seventeenth century and generational continuity was difficult to maintain, few men lived long enough to impose their will upon their children. Planters' wives, moreover, often had to work in the fields beside their husbands because of the growing shortage of labor during the middle and late seventeenth century, a practice that reduced the economic differentiation of men and women at the heart of patriarchal theory.

When demographic conditions improved at the end of the seventeenth century and the growing slave trade eased the labor shortage, many more families took on patriarchal characteristics. Since men lived longer, they could more readily impose their will upon their wives and children, and the acquisition of slaves permitted them to take their wives out of the tobacco fields and set them to domestic tasks. Men who owned slaves not only could afford this division of labor but knew they should not debase their wives by setting them to do slaves' work. Poor families, in contrast, still needed the wives' labor and probably continued the system of family labor common in the seventeenth century throughout the succeeding generations.

The Demographic Basis of Domestic Patriarchy

Immigrant men and women, who constituted a majority of the white adult population until the end of the seventeenth century, married late, died young, and left numerous orphans to the care of their heirs and the community at large. After English men and women left home, about age twenty, and came to the Chesapeake, they worked four or five years as servants; and those who survived their seasoning could expect to live only about twenty years after completion of their term. Since at least two men migrated for every woman, men had to postpone marriage until nearly age thirty, well after they had become freedmen, and they often married women ten or more years younger than themselves.[3]

Patriarchalism in Political Thought: The Authoritarian Family and Political Speculation and Attitudes, Especially in Seventeenth-Century England (New York, 1975). Daniel Blake Smith, *Inside the Great House: Planter Family Life in Eighteenth-Century Chesapeake Society* (Ithaca, N.Y., 1980), chaps. 1–4, 8, argues for the increasing modernity of family life in the eighteenth-century Chesapeake; while Jan Lewis, *The Pursuit of Happiness: Family and Values in Jefferson's Virginia* (Cambridge, 1984), argues that the personal life of late-eighteenth-century gentry families became very affective and emotional (see esp. chap. 5).
3. See above, chap. 1, and Lois Green Carr and Lorena S. Walsh, "The Planter's Wife: The

In such a demographic environment, a woman could anticipate little long-term support from her first husband, nor could a husband expect to maintain lengthy patriarchal authority over his wife. Very few immigrant marriages were long: in two Maryland counties, for instance, marriages lasted, on average, only eleven to thirteen years before one spouse died (see table 20). Since widows and widowers soon remarried, several husbands exercised authority sequentially over a woman who lived to age fifty. Because men married much younger women, a wife was likely to become a widow; she probably learned the tobacco business while her husband was alive so she could take over once he died. During the interval between marriages, a widow gained some independent power and sometimes retained control over her first husband's property even after she remarried.[4]

The high ratios of men to women among immigrants and the shortage of labor in the region after 1660 accelerated the development of more egalitarian relations between husbands and wives than were common in rural English families. With so many men clamoring for wives among the few women in the region, women could choose their spouses. Women and men, moreover, performed similar tasks and worked together growing tobacco because there was insufficient labor on most plantations to meet European demand for tobacco.[5]

Although women on the tobacco coast thus had some advantages over their English counterparts, they lost the paternal protection common in the mother country. Native-born women commonly married in their middle to late teens during the seventeenth century, often as soon as they reached menarche. Some of these girls may have been forced into marriage by fathers or guardians before they were willing to begin their own families, and they had to bear the risk of reduced immunity to disease that each pregnancy brought. Setting up a household with a new husband did not offer a woman any remission of exploitation. Not only was she expected to work in the fields, but she had to maintain the cabins, bear and nurse infants, and take care of children.[6]

Short marriages and frequent parental death meant great uncertainty

Experience of White Women in Seventeenth-Century Maryland," *William and Mary Quarterly*, 3d Ser., XXXIV (1977), 542–571, esp. 542–553; and Russell R. Menard, "Immigrants and Their Increase: The Process of Population Growth in Early Colonial Maryland," in Aubrey C. Land *et al.*, eds., *Law, Society, and Politics in Early Maryland* (Baltimore, 1977), 96, 100.

4. See sources cited for table 20, and Lorena S. Walsh, "Charles County, Maryland, 1658–1705: A Study of Chesapeake Social and Political Structure" (Ph.D. diss., Michigan State University, 1977), 69.

5. Carr and Walsh, "Planter's Wife," *WMQ*, 3d Ser., XXXIV (1977), 542–555.

6. *Ibid.*, 550–563; Russell R. Menard and Lorena S. Walsh, "The Demography of Somerset County, Maryland: A Progress Report," *Newberry Papers in Family and Community History*, 81-2 (1981), 34.

Table 20. *Length of Marriages in Colonial Maryland*

County, Date, and Origin of Spouses	Mean Length (Years)	No. of Marriages
Somerset, 1665–1695		
Both immigrant	13.3	36
One immigrant, one native	19.8	33
Both native	26.3	24
Charles, 1658–1689		
Both immigrant	11.4	176
Both native	16.5	35
Prince George's[a]		
1700–1724	21.9	114
1725–1749	22.4	80
1750–1775	25.3	72

Sources: Russell R. Menard and Lorena S. Walsh, "The Demography of Somerset County, Maryland: A Progress Report," *Newberry Papers in Family and Community History*, 81-2 (1981), 34; data provided by Walsh, summarized in "Charles County, Maryland, 1658–1705: A Study of Chesapeake Social and Political Structure" (Ph.D. diss., Michigan State University, 1977), 68; Allan Kulikoff, "Tobacco and Slaves: Population, Economy, and Society in Eighteenth-Century Prince George's County, Maryland" (Ph.D. diss., Brandeis University, 1976), 59.

Note: [a]Calculated from marriage-length distributions.

for children. Children born in the Chesapeake region during the seventeenth century could anticipate that one or both parents would die before they could fend for themselves. Step-parents, siblings, uncles, and neighbors often succeeded to parental authority before children reached adolescence: the proportion of children in seventeenth-century Middlesex County, Virginia, who lost at least one parent rose from a quarter of the five-year-olds to more than half of the thirteen-year-olds (see table 21). Guardians on occasion despoiled the estates of orphans (in law, those without fathers), deprived their charges of necessities, or even physically abused them. Children who lost one or both of their parents must have matured early and learned to accept responsibility for their own sustenance at an early age.[7]

The legislators of the Chesapeake colonies understood well the risks that orphans faced and accordingly passed laws giving local justices of the

7. Darrett B. Rutman and Anita H. Rutman, " 'Now-Wives and Sons-in-Law': Parental Death in a Seventeenth-Century Virginia County," in Thad W. Tate and David L. Ammerman, eds., *The Chesapeake in the Seventeenth Century: Essays on Anglo-American Society* (Chapel Hill, N.C., 1979), 153–182.

Table 21. *Orphanage in the Chesapeake*

	Percentage of Children					
	Both Parents Alive		One Parent Alive		Neither Parent Alive	
Achieved Age of Child	17th Century, Middlesex	18th Century, Prince George's[a]	17th Century, Middlesex	18th Century, Prince George's	17th Century, Middlesex	18th Century, Prince George's
1	93	97	7	3	0	0
5	77	88	21	12	3	b
9	59	74	32	25	10	2
13	46	65	34	31	20	4
18	33	47	36	43	31	10
21[c]	27	38	37	47	36	15

Sources: Darrett B. Rutman and Anita H. Rutman, "'Now-Wives and Sons-in-Law': Parental Death in a Seventeenth-Century Virginia County," in Thad W. Tate and David L. Ammerman, *The Chesapeake in the Seventeenth Century: Essays on Anglo-American Society* (Chapel Hill, N.C., 1979), 159–161 (for Middlesex); Prince George's estimates calculated from data on the age of children at the father's death found in Prince George's Wills and the Queen Anne, Prince George's, and King George Parish Registers, MHR (with father's death as first and last parent counted equally), and the age of children at the mother's death (rarely found in the records) calculated from the formula in Alfred J. Lotka, "Orphanage in Relation to Demographic Factors: A Study in Population Analysis," *Metron*, IX (1931), 37–109.

Notes: [a]These estimates are deliberately biased in favor of higher levels of parental death (that is, to show higher levels of orphanage). The age of children at their fathers' deaths, calculated using the Lotka formula, was greater than with the empirical data, and the mean age at childbirth was calculated from the lower fertility levels of the 1730–1775 data in fig. 5, with the higher mean ages at maternity of that schedule. [b]Less than .5%. [c]Age at marriage in Middlesex data, if less than 21.

peace, sitting as an orphans' court, greater authority over the estates and lives of orphans than was usual in England. The orphans' court, in both Chesapeake colonies, bound out poor children, appointed or registered the names of guardians of freeholders, oversaw the operation of orphans' plantations, and adjudicated disputes between orphans and their guardians. Justices took these responsibilities seriously. The children of more than four-fifths of the men who died in Prince George's County, Maryland, for instance, came under the jurisdiction of the orphans' court of the county: security was taken from guardians of children with landed estates, and the children of tenants were bound out to local planters. More than one-sixth of the children in neighboring Anne Arundel County—246 in all—were under the jurisdiction of the orphans' court in 1706 and probably accounted for nearly nine of every ten children who had lost their fathers in the county.[8]

The demographic conditions that prevented the development of patriarchal family government disappeared at the end of the seventeenth century. As white immigration declined, the proportion of native-born adults in the white population rose, reaching half by 1700. These natives lived longer and married at younger ages than their immigrant parents.[9] Family life in the eighteenth century therefore became more secure than it had been previously. Women could expect economic support for many years, since the marriages that natives contracted lasted longer than those of immigrants. Fathers could more readily control the economic destiny of their children because they more often lived to see them married. And children could expect more sustained parental care and were less likely to live in families with step-parents and step-siblings than their ancestors.

Marriages celebrated by native-born couples often lasted twice as long as those of immigrants. In Somerset County, Maryland, for instance, marriages between two native-born spouses lasted twenty-six years on average, nearly twice as long as those between two immigrants and a third longer than those between an immigrant and a native. In Prince George's County during the eighteenth century, these longer marriages became typical, lasting, on average, from twenty-two to twenty-five years, with first marriages probably continuing another ten years (table 20). One in three recorded marriages was extraordinarily long, lasting more than thirty years—forty-one years on average.[10]

8. *Ibid.*, 160–167; Lois G. Carr, "The Development of the Maryland Orphans' Court, 1654–1713," in Land *et al.*, eds., *Law, Society, and Politics*, 41–62 (data on 51); Dorothy H. Smith, ed., "Orphans in Anne Arundel County, Maryland, 1704–1709," *Maryland Magazine of Genealogy*, III (1980), 34–42, compared with Evarts B. Greene and Virginia D. Harrington, *American Population before the Federal Census of 1790* (New York, 1932), 128 (1704 census), and using parental death schedules in Rutman and Rutman, "'Now-Wives and Sons-in-Law,'" in Tate and Ammerman, *Chesapeake in the Seventeenth Century*, 159, and the age schedule in Ansley J. Coale and Paul Demeny, *Regional Model Life Tables and Stable Populations* (Princeton, N.J., 1966), 38 (female West Level 7, 2.5% growth rate).

9. See chap. 1 for this transition; for proportions native-born, see Darrett B. Rutman and Anita H. Rutman, "'More True and Perfect Lists': The Reconstruction of Censuses for Middlesex County, Virginia, 1668–1704," *Virginia Magazine of History and Biography*, LXXXVIII (1980), 58–63; Lorena S. Walsh, "Mobility, Persistence, and Opportunity in Charles County, Maryland, 1650–1720" (paper presented at the annual meeting of the Social Science History Association, Bloomington, Ind., Oct. 1982), table 1.

10. Allan Kulikoff, "Tobacco and Slaves: Population, Economy, and Society in Eighteenth-Century Prince George's County, Maryland" (Ph.D. diss., Brandeis University, 1976), 59, 437–441; table 2 and fig. 7, above; Coale and Demeny, *Regional Model Life Tables*, 5. Length of first marriage was estimated by using the minimum life expectancy of men or women at the

The increased duration of marriage substantially altered the lives of women. A husband could, if he desired, establish and maintain continuous authority over his wife and children, and his wife could count on his economic support for many years. Many wives died before their husbands, and women who lost their husbands tended to be older than forty and, since the surplus of men had disappeared, found remarriage increasingly difficult. Although widows in their twenties and thirties who lived in Prince George's in the 1770s remarried as frequently as widowers of the same age, widowers in their forties and fifties remarried four to seven times more frequently than widows.[11]

When the duration of marriages rose during the first third of the eighteenth century, the probability that children would lose their parents declined substantially. There were both fewer orphans and more children with both parents alive at every age in eighteenth-century Prince George's than in seventeenth-century Middlesex. Two-thirds of the eighteen-year-old youths in Middlesex, but only half in Prince George's, for instance, had lost at least one parent; and nearly a third of that group in Middlesex, but only a tenth in Prince George's, had lost both parents (table 21). The proportion of fathers who lived to see their sons reach twenty-one increased from less than half in seventeenth-century Middlesex to nearly two-thirds in Prince George's during the eighteenth century.[12]

Children of native-born parents lived more secure lives than earlier generations in the Chesapeake region. Even though a child still usually lost a parent before maturity, he was older when that event occurred than his ancestors had been, and he probably had adult siblings willing to protect his interests. As the number of orphans declined and their ages increased, the orphans' courts lost much of their importance. The number of poor, fatherless orphans bound out by the Prince George's orphans' court declined from 8.5 per year during the 1720s to 4.6 a year during the 1730s and 1740s, and the number of children brought to court to choose their guard-

---

mean age of marriage, and the results ranged from 34 years (early in the century) to 32 years (1730–1775 marriage cohorts).

11. Since the greater life expectancy of men, combined with their higher age at marriage, suggests similar numbers of widows and widowers at the same age, the relative number of unmarried widows and widowers should indicate the relative propensity to remarry. In Prince George's County in 1776, there were 16 widows, ages 20–39, and 14 widowers, ages 24–43; 33 widows, 40–49, and 5 widowers, 44–53; 26 widows, 50–59, and 7 widowers, 54–63; 16 widows, 60–69, and 7 widowers over 73. The ages are lagged because of the earlier ages of female marriage, but ending the lag does not change the pattern (except to add widows to the first category). For the 1776 census, see Gaius Marcus Brumbaugh, ed., *Maryland Records: Colonial, Revolutionary, County, and Church, from Original Sources*, I (Baltimore, 1915), 1–88, linked with local land records, probate records, and parish registers, at MHR.

12. See table 21 and sources cited there.

ians barely rose from 1720 to 1750, despite a doubling of the number of white children in the county. Parents relied less on the courts and more on informal arrangements with kin and neighbors to care for their orphaned children, and mothers uniformly retained custody of children when their husbands died. The orphans' court became a last resort to adjudicate disputes rather than a pervasive influence over orphan children.[13]

Not only did parents live longer, but fathers retained control over both land and slaves, valuable property that their children needed to prosper. During the seventeenth century, life expectancy was so low that most sons of freeholders inherited land in their early twenties, but as life expectancy rose in the eighteenth century, sons waited longer for their portions. Two-fifths of the fathers of freeholders in Prince George's County, for instance, maintained plantations long after their sons had married. Though fathers often set up their sons on family land when they married, older sons of long-lived fathers usually waited ten or fifteen years after marriage before gaining title to their farms: fewer than a fifth of fathers under seventy gave any land to their sons, and only half of those over seventy began to distribute it. Older planters held on to their land to support their families, to ensure their maintenance if they fell ill, and to strengthen paternal authority over their sons. About half of tidewater planters owned fewer than two hundred acres and had to retain title to their farms to support their families, but even the largest landowners, who could well afford to give land to their children, usually kept title to most of it until they died, perhaps wishing to ensure the continued deference of their sons. The increase in slaveholding added to the power planters held over their children, for slaveholders could offer their offspring (both sons and daughters) the added capital and prosperity that title to slaves would yield, in return for good behavior.[14]

The increased length of marriage, with the reduction in the number of remarriages it brought, helped streamline authority in plantation households. Conflicts within families, between step-children and step-parents, or between guardians and their charges may have been common in the

13. Dorothy H. Smith, ed., *Orphans and Infants of Prince George's County, Maryland, 1696–1750* (Annapolis, Md., 1976), spot-checked with original court records, MHR. Smith usually found orphans' bonds but sometimes missed guardianships. I have therefore used only years when some guardian was chosen or appointed to reach this conclusion.

14. See tables 3, 11, above, for slave ownership. These comments are based on table 21; Prince George's Wills, 1730–1769, linked with biographical data from Land Records and the 1733 tithables list, Black Books, II, 109–124. Transmission of property before death is sometimes documented by will, but often must be inferred from other data. Evidence from the 1730s, which shows greater distribution before death, is probably more reliable than later wills. In the 1730s, 3 of 13 men under 70 with mature children and 7 of 16 men over 70 gave land away before their death; in the 1740–1769 period, 8 of 70 men under 70 and 17 of 39 over 70 gave land away.

seventeenth century, when most households contained a wide variety of kin, including step-parents, step-siblings, and half-siblings. These conflicts probably diminished, and the authority of fathers probably increased during the eighteenth century because most planter households contained only parents and their own children. The composition of households in Prince George's County in 1776 may have been representative. Although about half the planters owned slaves, these chattels rarely lived in the master's house. Only one-seventh of all householders owned servants, hired laborers, or boarded guests. Nearly half of all county households included only husband, wife, and their own children, and another tenth were headed by widows or widowers and housed the surviving spouse and the children. A third of the households included people other than parents and children, but even these were not particularly complex, with most adding a laborer or two, step-children, or an orphan assigned to the family by the county. Only a tenth of the families were extended generationally or laterally, mostly by widowed mothers of the husband or wife (see table 22).[15]

Husbands and Wives in the Domestic Economy

Although many unmarried men started households in the Chesapeake region during the seventeenth century, married couples were the center of plantation businesses and of family government during the eighteenth century. Unmarried men headed only one household in fourteen in Prince George's County in 1776, and only a tenth of the single men in their twenties ran farms that year. Once a new couple married, they set up a plantation almost immediately, only rarely living with the bride's or groom's family.[16] Husbands increasingly ran these domestic commonwealths in ways consistent with the principles of domestic patriarchalism, sometimes responding violently when wives challenged their authority.

Planters and their wives realized that a prosperous farm business and a successful marriage supported each other. "Two young persons who marry without a reasonable prospect of an income to support them and their family," a Virginia essayist wrote in 1770, "are in a condition as wretched as any I know of." As soon as a couple decided to wed, negotiations between their fathers ensued to ensure that the couple would have a good chance to succeed. These negotiations were the most protracted among the gentry class, where parents wished to be certain that bride and groom would bring

15. Households for the purpose of this chapter are defined as including all *whites* living under the same roof, and families are those household members related by blood or marriage.
16. See chap. 2, n. 11, for stem families in Prince George's.

Table 22. *Household Structure in Prince George's County, 1776*

Type of Household[a]	Percentage in Type ($N = 889$)[b]
Unmarried head	
Coresident siblings	1
Others never married	6
Total	7
Elementary family	
Husbands and wives	3
Parents and children	48
Widows and children	7
Widowers and children	2
Total	60
More complex	
Step-parents and their children	7
Elementary families and boarders, laborers, or orphans	14
Extended family households[c]	11
Total	33
Grand total	100

Sources: Gaius Marcus Brumbaugh, ed., *Maryland Records: Colonial, Revolutionary, County, Church, from Original Sources*, I (Baltimore, 1915), 1–88 (1776 census), linked with the King George Parish Register, Prince George's Wills, Inventories, and Land Records, all MHR.

Notes: [a]Categories adapted from Peter Laslett's scheme in "Introduction: The History of the Family," in Laslett and Richard Wall, eds., *Household and Family in Past Time* (Cambridge, 1972), 28–34. [b]Of the 918 households in the census, 29 could not be classified. [c]Households presumed to be either extended or just augmented by boarders or laborers distributed between groups according to the relative number of known extended or augmented households.

equal wealth into the marriage, but yeoman families also insisted that portions and dowries be paid to the new couple. Ignatious Doyne of Calvert County followed this custom in 1749 when James Brooke asked for one of Doyne's "Daughters in Marriage." Since he had no objection to the match, he "went to Madame [Sarah] Brooke to know what she would give her Son." Widow Brooke insisted that she did not have "anything in the world," but Doyne persisted and complained that James Brooke had "but one Negro." "I hope you will contrive to give him one at least." She refused and even asked to use the Negro girl she had given to James as her servant. Joseph Wheat of Montgomery County had better luck when his daughter married Zephaniah Prather, son of William, in 1761. After the wedding, Wheat visited Prather and told him "what he intended to give his said Daughter." Prather "appeared well Satisfied" and in turn took Wheat to a "small plantation" near his home, "and said this place I intend to give unto my son Zephaniah Prather Together with my Negro Boy Tobey."[17]

A man and a woman should not contemplate marriage unless they loved and respected each other, for "mutual love and esteem" were "the very cement of matrimonial happiness." This writer would have approved the 1759 marriage of Sarah Lee and Philip Fendall, both members of the Maryland gentry, for they not only possessed "every natural Endowment, and needful Accomplishment to . . . promise them Happiness in private Life," but they were sure to reap "the Benefit of their early and Constant Affection for each other."[18]

Since men and women possessed different sensibilities and performed different roles within marriage, they brought contrasting social qualities into their new homes. Men should enjoy the esteem of other men of their station, possess an upright character and be fair and honest in all their economic dealings, be careful and industrious in their daily tasks, and be courteous in their relationships with both men and women. The *Maryland Gazette* eulogized Robert Boone of Anne Arundel County when he died in 1759, for instance, because he was "an honest and industrious Planter, who Died on the same Plantation where he was Born in 1680, . . . and has left a Widow, to whom he was married 57 Years." While men were expected to possess qualities that prepared them for the marketplace, wives were encouraged to practice submissiveness to authority. A well-accomplished woman should above all be agreeable, affable, amenable, and amiable; she should practice charity and benevolence to her neighbors and the poor; and she should always behave virtuously. A woman who possessed these attributes was "endow'd with every Qualification to render a man happy in the Conjugal State."[19]

17. Rind's *Virginia Gazette*, Feb. 4, 1773; Testamentary Proceedings, XXXVI, 225, and Montgomery County Land Records, B, 2–3, MHR. See Smith, *Inside the Great House*, 140–150; Lewis, *Pursuit of Happiness*, 24–28, 36–37; and Neil Larry Shumsky, "Parents, Children, and the Selection of Mates in Colonial Virginia," *Eighteenth-Century Life*, II (1975–1976), 83–88, for marriages in the gentry class.

18. *Ibid.*, *Maryland Gazette*, Oct. 4, 1759; see Smith, *Inside the Great House*, 135–143, and Lewis, *Pursuit of Happiness*, chap. 5, for the importance of love and affection (Lewis dates significance of emotion to the post-Revolutionary era).

19. *Md. Gaz.*, Feb. 15, 1759, Sept. 5, 1750. This analysis is based upon marriage and death notices in the *Md. Gaz.*, 1745–1767, reprinted in Christopher Johnston, comp., " 'News' from the 'Maryland Gazette,' " *Maryland Historical Magazine*, XVII (1922), 364–377, XVIII (1923), 150–183, checked with the originals. Eighty-six notices listed at least one ideal male characteristic (41, worthy or esteemed; 29, fair, upright, honest, candid; 11, beloved; 11, good, upright

Gentlemen insisted that wives be submissive to their husbands, and women tolerated, and even on occasion supported, a subordinate role within the family because that was the only way they could gain status as an adult. Marriage reduced the legal rights a single woman enjoyed but, at the same time, made her mistress over her husband's home, permitted her to bear legitimate children, and entitled her to economic support from her husband. An essay published in the *Virginia Gazette* in 1738 urged a wife to be "a faithful Friend, one who has no Views or Interest different from his, and makes his Joys and Sorrows all her own." Edith Cobb, the wife of the county clerk of Amelia County, Virginia, followed this advice during her long marriage, and her husband Samuel showed his appreciation by bequeathing her most of his estate in 1757. He gave "a very considerable Power" to her because "she has been my Wife near Forty Years during which Time hath always been kind, loving, and obedient to me without affectation." Mary Ambler, another Virginia lady, copied a passage from Fordyce's advice book into her diary in 1770 that counseled "christian meekness" to avoid the danger of "putting your-selves forward in company, of contradicting bluntly, of asserting postively," and instructed her daughter "to observe it well all her Life."[20]

English common law and the statute law of Maryland and Virginia legitimated the subservience of wives by granting husbands legal dominion over them. They controlled their wives' property (unless a premarital agreement was signed), and the wife could rarely sell property, buy goods, sign contracts, or make a will while her husband lived. Even though wives—to protect their dower rights to a third of the family land—had to give their consent before their husbands could sell land, husbands often informed their wives of land sales only after the transaction was completed. In Louisa County, Virginia, between 1765 and 1812, for instance, women gave their consent to land transfers more than seven days after the sale in half of the transactions. Women in Louisa had few choices and always agreed to the sale. One wife, when presented with a completed deed, wished that "the land . . . mentioned not be sold, but since it is the case she is entirely willing that the conveyance . . . should be recorded."[21]

---

character; 12, careful, industrious, diligent, skillful; 10, amenable, courteous; 6, good Christian; 5, charitable), and 60 listed ideal female characteristics (33, agreeable, affable, amenable, amiable; 13, charitable, benevolent; 13, esteemed; 14, virtuous; 15, well accomplished, of whom 12 agreeable as well; 7, pious, Christian; 7, sensible; 5, every quality to make a man happy).

20. *Va. Gaz.*, Feb. 10–27, 1738; Smith, *Inside the Great House*, 67–68, 159–164; Linda E. Speth, "Women's Sphere: Role and Status of White Women in Eighteenth-Century Virginia" (master's thesis, Utah State University, 1980), 31.

21. See Speth, "Women's Sphere," chap. 2; Joan R. Gundersen and Gwen Victor Gampel,

Ideally, the division of labor within marriage was supposed to sustain the authority of men in the family. A husband's most important responsibility was to provide food, clothing, and other necessities for his wife and children to the limit of his ability and economic station. That Chesapeake planters considered this task the very essence of manhood is suggested by the sad case of John Jackson. He had rented "a plantation at a very dear rate" in Prince George's County from 1724 to 1731 and had used "his honest Endeavours to maintain himself his Wife and a small Child now but eight years old" despite an illness that had left his wife lame and "altogether helpless" since 1727. Now, in 1731, Jackson found himself and his family destitute, and his "Endeavours fruitless," and begged of the county court to grant him "such relief as your Worships Compassion and charity shall think fit." If Jackson—a tenant who owned no slaves and hired no labor—was ashamed of his predicament, the court was hostile and rejected his petition and waited three years before it granted him a pension.[22]

Not only did planters cultivate tobacco to support their families, but they sold the crop, did all the shopping and marketing, and kept the plantation's books. Husbands, who could expect long marriages in the eighteenth century, refused to share responsibility for plantation management with their wives. From time to time, husbands therefore tried to instruct their wives about plantation work in their wills. In 1758 Thomas Bowie, a wealthy planter with three small children, bequeathed land to his wife "Provided she does not Clear or Cutt down above twenty thousand Tobacco Hills in any one year"; similarly, in 1740 Capt. Charles Beall told his wife "not to Sel or Destroy any timber of . . . moor than what may bee for the Plantations Use and the Mill."[23]

Planters usually worked in the ground as well as directed the labor of their mature sons, slaves, and white hired men in the cultivation of tobacco and in the maintenance of the farm. Although most planters could muster two or three workers to help them, many newly married men, tenants, and small freeholders relied only on their own efforts to support their families. A small proportion of planters owned or hired enough workers to stand

---

"Married Women's Legal Status in Eighteenth-Century New York and Virginia," *WMQ*, 3d Ser., XXXIX (1982), 114–134; and Julia Cherry Spruill, *Women's Life and Work in the Southern Colonies* (Chapel Hill, N.C., 1938), chap. 16, for convenient summaries of women's legal rights. For Louisa data, see Ransom True, "Land Transactions in Louisa County, Virginia, 1765–1812: A Quantitative Analysis" (Ph.D. diss., University of Virginia, 1976), 138–142, 156–157.

22. Prince George's Court Record, R, 282–283; Levy Book A (1734), MHR.

23. Prince George's Wills, box 9, folder 1 and liber 1, fols. 311–312; Testamentary Papers, box 78, folder 27, MHR.

back and oversee farm operations, and only the richest gentlemen could afford to hire overseers and manage their plantations from afar. Most slave-holders found themselves in circumstances similar to those of Jeremiah Pattison's, who complained in 1737 that he had labor enough to "enable him with a good deal of pain and Industry to support himself and Family by making Tobacco Corn and Other grain having no more than three taxable Slaves of which Two are almost past their Labour . . . and six young Slaves some of which do Jobs and the rest are but a . . . Burthen."[24]

While the great majority of men living in counties like Prince George's continued to labor in their fields throughout the eighteenth century, the economic position of planters slowly improved as more of them used slaves to increase the standard of living of their families. The proportion of plant-ers in Prince George's who toiled alone declined from two-fifths in 1733 to a third in 1776. At the same time, the number of householders who could direct a gang of five to nine workers rose from a tenth to a seventh, and the proportion of men who worked ten or more laborers grew from one in twenty-five to one in fourteen.[25]

While men managed the plantation, women took care of their homes. They prepared the family's food, washed clothes, tended gardens, made clothes, spun thread, wove cloth, milked cows, and churned butter. Though a few wives of wealthy gentlemen directed a retinue of slave women in these tasks, most planters kept slave women in the field, leaving their wives to complete household chores by themselves until their daughters were old enough to help them. Each of these tasks had to be repeated week after week, and wives sometimes envied the more varied jobs their husbands performed.[26]

Cloth and clothes production was the wife's most important economic contribution to the household economy. Although women infrequently spun thread, carded wool, or wove cloth from fiber during the seventeenth cen-tury, planters responded to recurring depressions in the tobacco trade by purchasing sheep, cards, and spinning wheels for their wives, and cloth-making became a very important domestic activity during the first half of the eighteenth century. Women universally made clothes from imported cloth, knitted bulky items, and repaired damaged wearing apparel, thereby saving the household from the great expense of importing ready-made

---

24. Chancery Records, VI, 210, MHR.
25. Black Books, II, 110–124; Brumbaugh, ed., *Maryland Records*, I, 1–88, adjusted to take into consideration slaveholdings on the Patuxent side of the county (missing in the census).
26. Mary Beth Norton, *Liberty's Daughters: The Revolutionary Experience of American Women, 1750–1800* (Boston, 1980), chap. 1; Spruill, *Women's Life and Work*, chap. 4; Smith, *Inside the Great House*, 58–60.

clothing. Cloth production from scratch or, more commonly, local trade of wool, flax, thread, and cloth among farms possessing one part of the production process further added to the value of the wife's production.[27]

Seventeenth-century wives served their families and occasional guests at crude tables or barrels, and the family ate from wooden (or sometimes earthen) bowls with fingers or spoons and knives. Housewives added more formal meal preparation and service to their numerous chores during the eighteenth century, when meals became far more ceremonial and hospitality more common. This change is most clearly documented in St. Mary's County, the poorest county on Maryland's tobacco coast. Planters there began purchasing earthenware plates and bowls and table linen during the seventeenth century, and all but the poorest householders owned all of those items by the 1720s. Knives and forks reached a majority of substantial planters in the 1720s and 1730s and less prosperous folk by the 1750s and 1760s. Finally, county families increasingly livened their meals with spices and tea. Though none but the wealthiest families added spices to their food early in the century, a majority of middling planters and a third of poorer freeholders used them by the 1750s and 1760s. And while fewer than a tenth of the planters' wives served tea before 1740, the proportion who used it thereafter rose steadily, reaching nearly three-quarters of the households by the 1770s.[28]

Child care was the most time-consuming task assigned to Chesapeake wives. A woman could expect to give birth once every two to three years from marriage to menopause, and she assumed the burdens of childbearing, nursing, weaning, and child care with little assistance from her husband. This division of labor tied younger women to their homes, although it freed men to work in the fields or visit neighbors and nearby villages without concern for the safety or care of their offspring.

No Chesapeake family could possibly attain the harmony and complete separation of tasks that the domestic patriarchal ideal demanded. Husbands and wives bickered, argued, and occasionally even separated. From time to time, husbands and wives brought their difficulties to local or provincial courts. The two cases examined below paint a vivid picture of marital expectations and roles and suggest the limits of patriarchal domestic economy.

When John Abington, a wealthy Prince George's merchant, died in 1739, he left his widow Mary and their six children an estate of two thou-

27. Norton, *Liberty's Daughters*, 15–20; and above, chap. 3, esp. fig. 15.
28. Lois Green Carr and Lorena S. Walsh, "Changing Life Styles in Colonial St. Mary's County," *Working Papers from the Regional Economic History Research Center*, I, No. 3 (1978), *Economic Change in the Chesapeake Colonies*, 83–89, 99–103.

sand pounds sterling and several thousand acres of land. Unable to manage this fortune, she soon married Dr. Andrew Scott, a man of high status but small fortune. The couple paid almost all of Abington's personal estate to his creditors but collected few debts owed to him. They soon began bickering, and in 1746 Mary Scott sued her husband in Maryland's chancery court for separate maintenance. She claimed that she had behaved properly toward her husband; when he "prevailed upon" her to "joyne in a Deed" to break entail on some of Abington's land and have it assigned to him, she "had in all things . . . Complyed with the Request . . . and had thereby put every thing out of her Power." After he received the land, he treated her "with so much Cruilty and Inhumanity" that she "could not live or Cohabit with him without running a Manifest hazard of her Life." Finally, he turned her "out of Doors almost naked and quite Destitute of all the Necessaries of Life," forced her to turn to neighbors, and refused to give her the thirty pounds he promised her for her support.

Dr. Scott painted a far different picture. While he admitted taking the land, he claimed the estate was otherwise too small to support her and added that he had given Abington's children the land bequeathed to them. He denied treating her "with any Cruielty" but claimed he had suffered from her "indecent, Disorderly, Abusefull and Turbulent" behavior caused by her "common and frequent Drunkedness" until he had to leave the house and stay with neighbors. They urged him to "Seperate from her," but he "was Resolved to bear with her as Long as he could and to endeavour by all easy and Moderate means to Reclaim and reform her." When he learned that "she had been guilty of the worst and most Scandalous of Crimes which a Wife could be guilty of to a husband," of bringing "a Disease upon him which for Decency and the Shamefullness of it he forbears to give a name," he finally forced her from the house. After listening to both sides, the court ordered Scott to pay his wife thirty pounds as long as she lived apart from him.[29]

A decade before the Scotts separated, Jane Pattison of Calvert County sued her second husband, Jeremiah, a middling planter, for separate maintenance in chancery court. From the start of her marriage, she had "behaved herself in a virtuous and respectful manner toward" him despite his appropriation of "a considerable Estate" left by her first husband to her and her children. Notwithstanding her good behavior, within a year of the wedding he "conceived so very great Dislike and Aversion to" her that "not only he used her very cruelly by beating her with Tongs . . . without any just or

29. Chancery Records, VIII, 237–243 (quote on 237–238, 241); Prince George's Wills, box 5, folder 39; Inventories, XXVII, fol. 345.

reasonable provocation . . . but also turned her out of Doors about Six years ago destitute of Cloaths and almost naked" and cut off her credit when she tried to replace them. Friends witnessed repeated beatings before the couple separated and later helped find her clothing, but Pattison still refused to support her "suitable to what he could afford." And Mrs. Pattison therefore sued for an annual allowance.

Jeremiah Pattison vehemently disagreed with his estranged wife. While he "was not wealthy" when he married her, he lived "in a comfortable and decent manner." After he paid her first husband's debts and distributed part of the remainder of the estate to her children, little was left. Mrs. Pattison "treated him not only with the greatest . . . Contempt" but even threw firebrands and iron candlesticks at him, all the while shouting "the most horrid and shocking Imprecations" at him. He responded with "the most gentle and persuasive Means he could think of to reclaim" her, and when that did not work, he "corrected her in a very moderate Manner." She abandoned him voluntarily, despite his attempts to "prevail on her to stay at home and manage her household Affairs which she absolutely refused to do." After she left home a second time, he urged her to return, writing: "My Dear I am Sorry that you should be so ill advised to desert your Habitation and send this to desire you would return home and behave Yourself as a loving Wife ought if you'l do that you shall always by me be used Lovingly. I am your Loving Husband." Mrs. Pattison refused to return, and the court ordered him to pay her thirty pounds a year.

Disagreement over the financial operation of the plantation lay at the root of Pattison's unhappiness. Samuel Abbot, her first husband, left a small personal estate with no taxable slaves but farmed four hundred acres of excellent land. Pattison lived on the edge of respectability, working as an itinerant carpenter before his marriage in 1724, but he too owned land. After the marriage, Pattison supported his family on his wife's land and rented his property to tenants, netting about two thousand pounds of tobacco each year. He used the profits from his two estates to buy five adult slaves by 1733. Mrs. Pattison, who wanted this bounty for her children, asked him to "dispose of all that he had at his Death to her Children" and was "much dissatisfied" when he refused. The couple argued repeatedly over this, calling each other vile names and usually concluding with Mrs. Pattison's throwing household implements at him and Pattison's beating his wife so severely that she left home to recover. Finally, since he would not bequeath his property to her children or stop beating her, she resolved to "take no Care of his Affairs but would make all she Could for her Children." She made good on her threat, forcing him to "put out" his linen "to be washed, his Stockings to be knit and his Negroes Cloaths to be made," and refused to serve him when he "asked for victuals," insisting that if he "was above taking it himself he might go without" and at the same time feeding "some very good meat" to a male neighbor.[30]

Although the behavior reported by these two cases may have become increasingly unrepresentative as the number of second marriages diminished, the cross section of ordinary and wealthier planters and their wives who testified in court agreed about the principles of family government. They agreed, for instance, that wives owed their husbands obedience and smooth operation of the household in return for the financial support needed to purchase the necessities of life. The litigants claimed to follow these norms. While Scott and Pattison insisted that they properly supported their wives, their wives claimed fidelity and obedience. Mrs. Pattison even asked her witnesses about her first marriage, and they all agreed that she had been "a very dutiful good wife." Since the husband ruled the household, he had the right to correct his wife moderately when she went astray and punish her more harshly if necessary. Even the wives agreed with this idea, insisting that they gave their husbands no provocation but implying that clear reason would justify punishment.

Landed families generally accepted these principles of family government and the power relations they entailed throughout the eighteenth century. The emotional sensibilities of relations between gentry husbands and wives, however, probably began to soften during the last quarter of the eighteenth century. The slaves owned by these wealthy families performed all the plantation's heavy labor, thus freeing gentlemen and their wives from much of the work of ordinary white women and men. Freed from servile labor, these wealthy women and men increasingly emphasized emotion, love, individual feelings, and companionship within their marriages. Child rearing took on a heightened importance, especially for women. A new and highly charged emotional and possessive language began to appear in family correspondence. These new sensibilities were incorporated into patriarchal family government. Plantations remained units of production. Gentry women did not create a new, semiautonomous sphere dominated by child nurture for themselves. Even the wealthiest women retained important productive functions, for they directed and participated in gardening, cloth production, and candlemaking.[31]

---

30. Chancery Records, VI, 207–239; Inventories, IX, 260–263; Charles Francis Stein, *A History of Calvert County, Maryland* (Baltimore, 1960), 376. The first two paragraphs on the Pattisons draw mainly on the charge and response (quotes on 207–210); the last, on the depositions (quotes on 230, 232, 236).
31. This paragraph reinterprets data in Smith, *Inside the Great House*, chaps. 1–4, 8; and in Lewis, *Pursuit of Happiness*, chap. 5, in ways they might not accept.

The Family Life Cycle in the Domestic Economy, 1720–1800

Unlike the Scotts and Pattisons, nearly every Chesapeake couple had children soon after marriage, who modified relations between husbands and wives, gave each spouse added responsibilities, and created new layers of authority in the household. Since women bore children regularly until menopause, some children remained at home throughout their parents' lives.[32] Variations within family government probably hinged upon the ages of spouses and their children: young parents with small children, middle-aged couples with adolescents, and widows and widowers with their unmarried children faced varying problems. This life-cycle approach sheds light on the economy of the family and the changing nature of domestic patriarchy within it.

The birth of children during the early years of marriage increased the work load wives sustained. A woman, age thirty-three, who had married when she was twenty-one, would probably be pregnant with her sixth child. She had spent 4 of her first 12 years of marriage pregnant and perhaps another 4.5 years nursing the surviving children, a task which sometimes made her ill. Each new child, moreover, forced her to make more clothing for her growing family. Few women could call on any help in these tasks in the early years of marriage. Daughters were too young to help with child care and sewing, and only the wealthiest planters owned enough slaves to put one or two to work as domestics. Even the wealthiest wives, furthermore, nursed their own children, sometimes refusing to send them out to wet nurse, even if in delicate health themselves.[33]

The work of all but the wealthiest slaveholders intensified when children began to arrive. Whatever help their wives had provided in the fields was reduced when their domestic duties increased, and infants had to be fed and clothed without providing compensating field work. Poorer men struggled to maintain their standard of living, but might fail during the periodic depressions that hit the tobacco trade. Men who owned slaves possessed greater resources, but unless their labor force grew when their children were born, they probably had to push their slaves harder to sustain the same standard of living.

32. In Prince George's in 1776, nine-tenths of the ever-married heads of household had children in their homes, and children lived with three-quarters of the men and two-thirds of the women over 65. Data exclude probable stepchildren and dependent men and women. In total, 9 of 39 of the men and 9 of 27 of the women over 65 lived without any of their children. Calculated from Brumbaugh, ed., *Maryland Records*, I, 1–88.
33. Smith, *Inside the Great House*, 34–39; Spruill, *Women's Life and Work*, 55–57; Norton, *Liberty's Daughters*, 90–91.

While women in their thirties and early forties continued to bear and nurse children, their maturing daughters assumed some responsibilities for child care and domestic industry. Parents sometimes left young children with older siblings when they went out. John Hatherly and his wife, for instance, allowed their fourteen-year-old daughter to watch her nine-year-old brother while they attended a funeral in Anne Arundel County in 1751. Daughters copied their mothers' household chores even before they learned the necessary skills. In 1773 Philip Fithian saw little girls—daughters of gentlemen—"imitating what they see in the great House; sometimes tying a String to a Chair and then run buzzing back to imitate the Girls spinning." Adolescent girls, even the daughters of wealthy gentlemen, spent much of their day making clothes. Frances Hill may have been typical of gentlemen's daughters. Throughout 1797 this adolescent girl sewed, knitted, or made clothes nearly every day but Sunday. In January, for example, she knit a stocking for herself, darned her stockings, hemmed a handkerchief for a friend, lined her brother's coat sleeves, mended her brother's breeches and her father's drawers, and made her mother an apron.[34]

Sons joined their fathers in cultivating tobacco and grain at the age of ten to twelve. When the Virginia and Maryland assemblies wished to limit the production of tobacco by permitting only certain groups to tend plants, they allowed white boys over ten (in Virginia) or over twelve (in Maryland) to tend half the number of a full taxable laborer over sixteen. Sons of ordinary planters, age ten or twelve, often joined their fathers in the fields. John Hatherly, age twelve, and his brother Benjamin, age ten, had helped their father with the 1751 tobacco crop; and when their parents attended a funeral in 1751, they stayed at home helping a servant make tobacco hills. "When one of them asked if he thought they could make a Thousand before night," the servant went on a rampage and killed two family members. More happily, John Evans remembered "that when he was a little boy just able to pick up wheat" in the early 1730s, "he was reaping wheat at Samuel Whites," his uncle, but since he was only twelve or thirteen, he soon stopped working to join his cousins in play.[35]

34. *Md. Gaz.*, Apr. 10, 1751; Hunter Dickinson Farish, ed., *Journal and Letters of Philip Vickers Fithian, 1773–1774: A Plantation Tutor of the Old Dominion*, new ed. (Williamsburg, Va., 1957), 189; William K. Bottorff and Roy C. Flannagan, eds., "The Diary of Frances Baylor Hill of 'Hillsborough,' King and Queen County, Virginia (1797)," *Early American Literature Newsletter*, II, No. 3 (Winter 1967), 3–53 (she knitted or sewed 22 of 31 days in Jan., skipping only 5 Sundays and 4 other days [see 6–17]); Smith, *Inside the Great House*, 56–61.

35. William Hand Browne *et al.*, eds., *Archives of Maryland . . .* , 72 vols. (Baltimore, 1883–1972), XXXVII, 138–139; Waverly K. Winfree, comp., *The Laws of Virginia, Being a Supplement to Hening's "The Statutes at Large," 1700–1750* (Richmond, 1971), 247–248, 296; *Md. Gaz.*, Apr. 10, 1751; Court of Appeals Record, TDM#1 (1788), 84, MHR.

Parents enjoyed their children's help on the plantation until the children left home to marry, set up a household, or work on a nearby farm. Few adolescents lived with or worked for neighbors or kin; in Prince George's in 1733, for instance, three-quarters of sons whose fathers were alive lived at home, and nearly every youth waited until he reached his majority at twenty-one before leaving home. Similar numbers of sons remained at home in southside Virginia in the 1750s and 1760s, and the proportion of sons living at home until marriage in Prince George's probably increased in the 1770s.[36]

The birth of children modified the distribution of authority in the household. Fathers expected sons and daughters to obey them while at home, insisted upon the right to approve marriage partners they chose, and demanded their respect even after they matured. Mothers shared parental authority with their husbands and gained sole authority over minor children if their husbands died. Siblings also sustained mutual obligations to each other. Peter Dent, a gentleman and justice, suggested the power of this family hierarchy when he wrote his will in Prince George's County in 1757. He urged of his "Dear Children that they be Dutifull to their Mother During her Life and Loving and Obligeing to Each other the youngest always Submitting to the Eldest in reason and the Eldest bearing with the Infirmitys of the youngest and advising them in the best manner they can that they may Live in Concord all their Lives."[37]

As children were born and matured, the bundle of mutual duties and responsibilities that tied the family together grew more complex. Since few children in Prince George's in 1776 left home before marriage, the number of children directed by parents grew, reaching a peak of five or six when the mother was in her early forties and her husband was near fifty, and declined slowly thereafter, diminishing to four children when mothers were in their mid-fifties and fathers were sixty. Older children may have eased the burdens of child nurture. Although only three or four children lived in a typical household in the county in 1776, the typical child grew up with four or five siblings.[38]

36. Black Books, II, 110–124; and tables 3, 4, above. There were 154 sons over 16 living with fathers in 1733 and 49 whose fathers were probably alive who lived with kin or neighbors. Of 48 sons living at home whose ages were known, 33 were between 16 and 20, and their average age was 19.2 (standard deviation 2.4). The mean age of eight sons with known age who lived away from home was 22.8 (standard deviation 4.4).

37. Prince George's Wills, box 8, folder 56.

38. The 1776 census (Brumbaugh, ed., *Maryland Records*, I, 1–88) shows the mean number of children, for the marriage reported in the census, for women rose from .6 at ages 17–19 to a peak of 5.6 at ages 41–43, then declined to 4.5 at ages 53–55. Men age 21–23 had 1.0 children with them, and this number rose to 5.2, ages 45–47, before declining to 4.5 at ages

Children's obligations to parents and siblings sometimes dictated financial sacrifice. Fathers often insisted that sons allow their mothers full use of the land they would ultimately inherit. Francis Waring, a gentleman of great wealth who died in Prince George's in 1769, bequeathed his home farm to his son Leonard, "provided he Suffers his Mother to Enjoy the Land which I have Alloted her." Similarly, Thomas Wilson gave son Josiah the home plantation only if he did not interrupt "his Mother during her Life for making use of the Land as she shall think proper." Reciprocal obligations between siblings became especially important after both parents died. Edward Willett, a pewterer, gave all his pewterer's molds and tools to his son William when he died in Prince George's in 1744, "provided he Doth make what necessary pewter the rest of my Children shall want." William Young especially wanted to ensure that his son William find a home after he died. He knew that William was "not Capable of himself to Act soe in the world as to Gitt a Liveing," and accordingly he gave William's part of the estate to his son John in his 1760 will, with the request that John "Assist the Said William," his brother.[39]

Fathers held a potent lever over their children. They rarely turned over ownership of land or slaves to their children before they died, even if they permitted use of this capital during their lifetime. If children failed to obey their fathers, they might find themselves cut out of the parental estate. Robert White, of Prince George's County, refused to bequeath land to his son James in 1768 that he had let him farm for thirty years, because the two argued about religion. James had converted to Anglicanism from Catholicism and served as a vestryman and considered his father an "Ignorant Illerate man wholy Biggotted to all the Follies and Superstitions of the Roman Church." Thirteen years earlier John Anderson of Charles County told his daughter Mary Burch that "his Son James and Daughter Caty were running about and took no Care of him," and though "they expected a great Deal when he died, . . . they should find little of it."[40]

Although couples farmed their land together as long as the marriage lasted, the number of children remaining at home diminished greatly when the couple grew older. In Prince George's in 1776, fewer than two children lived at home with mothers over sixty years old, and between two and three children lived with fathers (who had more often remarried) of the same

---

57–59. The mean number of children per household was 3.6, but the mean family size (excluding parents) of children was 5.3, and the mean sibling group size was 4.3. For these measures, see Daniel Scott Smith, "Averages for Units and Averages for Individuals within Units: A Note," *Journal of Family History,* IV (1979), 84–86.

39. Prince George's Wills, box 11, folder 13; box 6, folders 53, 54; box 9, folder 31.

40. Testamentary Proceedings, XLII, 378–384, XXXVI, 258, MHR.

age.[41] Most of the children in these households were adolescents and young adults, well able to take care of themselves and help provide their parents with a comfortable living in their old age.

Married men and widowers, even those of advanced ages, maintained a household and continued working the ground. Only one of every seven men above sixty in Prince George's in 1776 lived as a dependent in the home of kin or neighbors. Two-thirds resided with their wives, and the rest, only a seventh of the total, were widowers. These proud men usually refused to seek aid from loved ones. Ninian Beall of Thomas, a widower of eighty, headed a household on a small plantation near Bladensburg town but worked no slaves. Two children still lived with him, including a daughter and her husband, but whatever help they provided for him was under his direction as the master of the family. In 1773, Robert Thompson, then eighty-three, considered himself "very Antient and Infirm and not able to Look after my Business and withall much in debt," and he therefore gave his daughter Agnes, age fifty-two, his fourteen slaves and all his stock and household furniture in return for "paying my debts, finding me Accomodations, and paying me . . . the sum of twenty pounds common Current money a Year." Two years later, when the census taker came to the Thompson home, Robert Thompson claimed to be the head of his household and relegated his daughter to the position of a dependent.[42]

Women faced far greater problems when their husbands died, because of their inferior social status and lack of experience in operating a plantation. Though widows possessed the legal right of the feme sole to buy and sell property and act for themselves, most widows in their twenties and thirties probably remarried, thereby losing their legal rights. Older women, whose numbers increased as the century progressed, usually did not remarry but remained widows the rest of their lives. However long a widow stayed single, she needed more than legal rights to support her children. Husbands recognized the economic problems their widows would have and tried to ease their burdens in two ways. First, they often appointed their wives executors of their estate, thereby guaranteeing that they would control all the familial property while the estate passed through probate. And, second, they bequeathed their wives sufficient property to ensure that profitable farming would continue.

Although planters almost always named wives as executors of their

41. The 1776 census (Brumbaugh, ed., *Maryland Records*, I, 1–88) shows 1.5 children living with women 59–61 and 1.7 children living with women 62 +; 3.5 lived with fathers 60–62, and 2.6 lived with fathers 63 +.

42. Beall family records in the hands of Mrs. Margaret Cook; Brumbaugh, ed., *Maryland Records*, I, 1–88; Prince George's Land Records, CC#2, 63. Of 110 men over 58, 16 were dependents in the households of others, 66 were married, and 28 were widowers.

estates during the first half of the eighteenth century, they began to question their wives' ability to administer their property as the century progressed. Between 1710 and 1760, planters in tidewater York, St. Mary's, and Prince George's counties sometimes appointed a mature son or, less frequently, another kinsman or friend as coexecutor, but men excluded widows from executorships in only a tenth of the wills in the three counties. In the 1760s and 1770s, however, the proportion of planters in St. Mary's County who appointed adult sons or kinsmen to help wives administer their estates doubled. Husbands in Albemarle County, in the Virginia piedmont, behaved in a more patriarchal manner than those in tidewater from the beginnings of settlement. Frontiersmen used their wills to assert an authority over their wives that might have been more contested in the less-settled piedmont, and sought to protect their children from second husbands. Though two-thirds of these men named wives as executors in the 1750s and 1760s and nearly half continued this practice through the 1790s, they usually appointed a son or friend to help administer the estate. As the county developed and more older men with adult sons died, fathers turned to their sons rather than to their wives and named them sole executors twice as often in the 1790s as in the 1750s (see table 23).

Eighteenth-century tidewater planters usually gave their wives sufficient property to support their children and live comfortably after the children left home. Despite the increasing age of widows (and the growing number of adult sons), there was remarkable continuity in the powers tidewater planters gave their widows throughout the colonial era. Widows, by law, were entitled to a third of the husband's estate, and they could reject any smaller bequest and demand to receive their thirds.[43] Only about a third of the planters in tidewater Maryland during the colonial period limited their wives to their dower rights or attempted to have them accept less, and only a tenth granted them property on the condition that they remained widows. Six of every ten married testate decedents used their wills to increase their widows' rights beyond the dower third, either by granting them control of the dwelling plantation and all its stock, labor, and implements during their natural life or by giving them the equivalent in land, slaves, and movable property. Though widows could operate the farms as they saw fit, their husbands often limited their control by bequeathing the property to a particular child or children after the death of their mother (see table 24).

Although settlers in piedmont Virginia were more generous to their widows than their tidewater cousins, they placed somewhat greater con-

---

43. The best summary of common law, practice, and statute law can be found in Elie Vallette, *The Deputy Commissarry's Guide within the Province of Maryland* (Annapolis, Md., 1773), esp. 69–70, 119.

Table 23. *Executors of Married Men in Eighteenth-Century Virginia and Maryland*

	Percentage of Executors Named in Wills					
				Prince		
	York[a]	St. Mary's Co.[b]		George's[c]	Albemarle[d]	
Person	1710– 1749	1710– 1759	1760– 1777	1730– 1769	1750– 1769	1770– 1799
Chosen	(N=93)	(N=344)	(N=169)	(N=258)	(N=74)	(N=139)
Wife alone	55	71	53	73	11	6
Wife and sons	22	11	22	12	24	22
Wife and others	16	7	12	4	30	20
Wife included	92	89	87	89	65	48
Sons alone	5	—	—	7	15	27
Kin or friends alone	3	—	—	4	20	25
Wife excluded	9	10	13	11	35	52
Total	101	99	100	100	100	100

Sources: Prince George's Wills, 1730–1769; Lois Green Carr and Lorena S. Walsh, "Woman's Role in the Eighteenth-Century Chesapeake" (paper presented at the Colonial Williamsburg Conference on Colonial Women, 1981), table 10; Daniel Blake Smith, *Inside the Great House: Planter Family Life in Eighteenth-Century Chesapeake Society* (Ithaca, N.Y., 1980), 237–239.

Notes: [a]Includes only the 1710s, 1720s, and 1740s; and the proportions of "wife alone," "wife included," and "wife excluded" found in the data; other categories estimated from overlapping categories of "wife and all others," "sons," "wife excluded," and "friends." [b]"Sons" and "kin or friends" not separately computed. [c]"Others" includes kin and friends; "sons" includes wills where sons were joined by kin or friends of decedent. [d]Estimated in same way as York County.

straint upon them. Two-thirds of the planters in Amelia and Albemarle counties (a third more than in tidewater) granted their wives a plantation, and fewer limited them to their dower or less, but nearly three times as many gave them a plantation only as long as they remained widows. Since piedmont planters typically owned farms of three hundred acres (50 percent larger than in tidewater), they could more often afford to give their wives control of an entire plantation.[44] Husbands feared, however, that the plantation would quickly attract fortune hunters and wished to protect their children by forestalling the potential control of a second husband (table 24).

Although widows usually possessed legal authority over the husband's estate, any widow's actual power depended more upon the age of her sons than on the legal terms of her husband's will. As long as all the children remained minors, the widow as executor controlled most of her husband's estate, but as sons came of age, they took their portions with them or stayed at home uneasily waiting for their mothers to die so they could inherit the

44. Calculated from tables 10, 16, above.

Table 24. *Bequests to Wives in Wills in the Chesapeake*

	Percentage of Total Bequests in Counties				
Extent of Bequest	St. Mary's and Charles, 1640–1710 (*N* = 308 Wills)	St. Mary's, 1710–1776 (*N* = 470 Wills)	Prince George's, 1730–1769 (*N* = 278 Wills)	Amelia, 1735–1775 (*N* = 238 Wills)	Albemarle, 1750–1779 (*N* = 204 Wills)
All estate or dwelling plantation for life[a]	39	36	43	37	41
All estate or dwelling plantation for widowhood[b]	11	8	11	26	26
More than dower in another form[c]	20	24	17	11	17
Dower or less or unknown	30	32	29	26	17
Total	100	100	100	101	101

Sources: Lois Green Carr and Lorena S. Walsh, "The Planter's Wife: The Experience of White Women in Seventeenth-Century Maryland," *William and Mary Quarterly*, 3d Ser., XXXIV (1977), 556, 558; Prince George's Wills, 1730–1769, MHR; Linda E. Speth, "Women's Sphere: Role and Status of White Women in Eighteenth-Century Virginia" (master's thesis, Utah State University, 1980), 25; Daniel Blake Smith, *Inside the Great House: Planter Family Life in Eighteenth-Century Chesapeake Society* (Ithaca, N.Y., 1980), 240.

Notes: [a]Includes "all estate" category in Charles, St. Mary's, and Amelia samples. [b]Includes "all or dwelling plantation for minority of child" in Charles, St. Mary's, and Albemarle samples. [c]"Personal property for widowhood" in Albemarle sample. [d]Includes "maintenance or home room" in Charles and St. Mary's samples and "dwelling house for life" and "dwelling house for widowhood" in the Amelia sample.

home plantation. Tensions between widows and their adult sons over the use of property occurred because of unresolved tensions within domestic patriarchalism between the authority of mothers (whom sons were bound to obey) and the dominance of adult men over women.

Wealthy planters in Prince George's County sometimes tried to prevent this discord between widows and sons by provisions in their wills. In 1751 Daniel Carroll, a wealthy merchant and gentleman planter, urged his wife and children to consult several neighboring kinsmen and friends "In case any Difference or Dispute shou'd hereafter unfortunately happen Between my said loving Wife and any of my Dear Children, either about the management or Division of any part of the Estate." Other planters admonished widows and sons to allow each other to live peaceably on their allotted plantations. In 1744 William Tannehill of Prince George's ordered his wife not to "hinder my son James to get all upon the back branch if he is so minded." Similarly, Charles Walker granted his wife her dower rights in land in 1730 if she permitted their son Joseph, age fifteen, "to have Liberty to live on some part of" it "and theron Work and have the benefit of his Labour, He no ways Interrupting . . . his Mother."[45]

Adult sons usually gained control of property from their widowed mothers in Prince George's. Fathers often permitted their sons to work for themselves when they reached their middle or late teens and allowed them to inherit property at age twenty-one.[46] As sons took their portions and daughters married and depleted the estate yet further, widows found themselves unable to earn a subsistence and dependent upon their children for their bread. Only a quarter of the widows in the county in 1776 over the age of fifty-seven maintained their own households. The rest lived with sons or neighbors. Widows frequently lost control even over their own plantation when the son who would inherit the property came of age. Unmarried sons as young as twenty or twenty-one who lived at home assumed the position of head of household from their widowed mothers nearly two-thirds of the time.[47]

Some women, ill prepared to operate plantations, gladly turned over the farm to their sons in return for support. When Thomas Richardson of Prince George's came "of age to receive his fortune by his Fathers Will," his mother Susannah said "that she did not care to put herself to the Trouble of paying him his Fortune" but "had agreed to go Equally halfs in every thing." She was apparently satisfied with the arrangement: not only did Thomas reopen the family tavern, but his mother felt that "her son Thomas Richardson was very Carefull and that if he continued to be so and took care of the House, she would take care in the House and would not begrudge him the half of every thing that should be made and raised on the plantation."[48]

45. Prince George's Wills, box 7, folder 62; box 4, folders 9, 28.
46. Fourteen Prince George's decedents granted their sons property or the profits of their own labor at an average age of 18.4. Prince George's Wills, 1730–1769.
47. Of 99 women 58 and over, 37 lived with husbands, 16 were widows who headed households, 39 were dependents in homes of others, and 7 were widows in households headed by their unmarried sons. Of 39 widows with sons over 21 at home, 16 headed their own household; 9 of the 23 unmarried sons who headed households that included their mothers were 21 or under.
48. Testamentary Papers, box 73, folder 33; "Preliminary List of Tavernkeepers in Prince George's County," copy at MHR. Quotes are from deponent testimony in the case.

A son's assertion of authority might, however, leave his mother resentful and force her to find ways to maintain some autonomy. Sarah Brooke, widow of John of Calvert County, lived with her son Roger in the 1740s and 1750s, when she was in her fifties and sixties. Though Roger operated the plantation, his mother still nominally owned much of it. When he complained that "she did not give his two Negroes Meat enough," she replied that he should "kill Meat of his own as he had Hoggs and then he might give them what he pleased as he was not contented with what She gave them." She wanted "to keep the Staff in her own Hand better her Children should come to her than she to go to them," but her attempts at autonomy were not very successful. She distrubuted all her property to her sons James and Roger, and Roger "made use of all the crops every Year . . . without any Division and disposed of it as he thought proper for his own use" despite the desires of his mother. She depended upon him for subsistence, and without him would have to "beg my Bread from Door to Door," yet even this minimal care was given only grudgingly, for she complained that she had "no Body to do anything for me not so much as to bring me a Coal of Fire to light my Pipe."[49]

Morality, Virtue, and the Family Economy

Parents in the eighteenth-century Chesapeake were responsible for training their children to take their proper place in adult society and teaching them the reciprocal responsibilities of parents and children, husbands and wives, masters and slaves, and magistrates and citizens. All education in the region, whether formal literacy training in schools or informal instruction in the home, aimed at this end. Sons who learned proper behavior in this society were ultimately rewarded with sufficient property from their fathers' estates to permit them to start their own patriarchal families.

Although tidewater planters infrequently expressed emotional religious commitments, they understood the necessity of strong moral education. The Reverend Thomas Craddock of Baltimore County probably expressed the common Anglican view on moral training in a sermon in 1752 on a murder in his parish. The murderers both ignored moral education *and* deprived the victim's children of that training by killing a nurturing parent. If the murderers had "been trained up in the ways of religion and virtue, they wou'd never have been guilty of this wickedness," Cradock told his

49. Testamentary Proceedings, XXXVI, 224–226; Christopher Johnson, "The Brooke Family," *MHM*, I (1906), 188. Quotes are from deponent testimony, which concerns Roger Brooke's administration of his mother's estate.

congregation. But the deed was done, and "a young, defenseless tribe of children" lost "the care and assistance of their father or mother," the adults responsible "for their *spiritual*, as well as temporal interest," and reduced them "to a state of indigence, who, had their parents liv'd, might have had a sufficient competency." To prevent similar acts in the future, masters and fathers ought to be "conspicuous in the worship of God, in acts of justice and charity to man; in a *Spiritual* care of your families ... ; and such a conduct, with the blessing of God, may have a happy influence o'er many of them."[50]

Planters and their wives shared and on occasion expressed this concern. The *Maryland Gazette* eulogized Rebeccah Sanders, when she died at seventy-five in 1752 in Anne Arundel County, not only because she had "a just Sense of Religion herself" but also because "she instilled the Principles of it thro' her numerous Family; and having educated her Children in the Paths of Virtue and Piety, had the inexpressible satisfaction ... to reflect that they were each an Honour to her." Several planters in Prince George's County admonished their wives in similar tones in their wills. In 1734, Archibald Edmonston asked his widow and son James to "inspect into the behavior and deportment of my Son Thomas Edmonston," who was to be under their control during his minority. When James Adams, a middling planter, died in 1750, he asked that his son John "be bound till he arrive at the Age of twenty-one years to Some good honest Man, that will Endeavour to Instruct him in his Duty to God, himself, and his Neighbour[s]."[51]

In an ideal society, each person knows how to behave in the presence of social inferiors and superiors. The children of slaveholders—a majority of the white populace—saw their parents deprive slaves of freedom, expropriate their labor, and barter them from hand to hand and learned thereby that they could treat black people with contempt they should never use on their white peers. Thomas Jefferson best captured the consequences of this training in a well-known passage: "The whole commerce between master and slave is a perpetual exercise in the most boisterous passions, the most unremitting despotism on the one part, and degrading submissions, on the other." As "the parent storms," Jefferson insisted, "the child looks on, catches the lineaments of wrath, puts on the same airs in the circle of smaller slaves, gives a loose to the worst of passions, and thus ... educated and daily exercised in tyranny, cannot but be stamped by it."[52]

50. [Thomas Cradock], "A Sermon Preached in My Own Parish Church in the Year 1752 on Account of a Most Barbarous Murder Committed on the Body of *Ann Clark*," Cradock Papers, Maryland Historical Society, Baltimore (MHS). I am greatly indebted to David Curtis Skaggs for sending me a typescript of this manuscript sermon and for permitting me to quote from it.
51. *Md. Gaz.*, Apr. 2, 1752; Prince George's Wills, box 4, folder 51, box 7, folder 51.
52. Thomas Jefferson, *Notes on the State of Virginia* (1785), ed. Thomas Perkins Abernethy (New York, 1964), 155–156. See chap. 10, below, for work and race relations.

Parents instructed their children to take their proper place in white society by training them to perform tasks appropriate to their sex. Fathers took their sons with them when they went abroad from the plantation and sent them on errands to nearby farms or to the general store as soon as they could ride horses and accept responsibilities. Most important, they introduced them to the world of male work by teaching them how to cultivate tobacco and grains and instilled in them the male ethic of aggressive behavior by taking them hunting.[53]

Daughters stayed closer to home and learned both housewifery and their inferior place in the family order from their mothers. The daughters of Robert Carter of Nomini Hall, one of Virginia's richest gentlemen, imitated woman's work at a young age, and Philip Fithian, their tutor, even discovered them one day "stuffing rags and other Lumber under their Gowns just below their Apron-Strings, . . . prodigiously charmed at their resemblance to Pregnant Women!" Mothers were particularly responsible for training their daughters to sew, knit, and spin so they could engage in necessary plantation labor. When Margaret Gough of Calvert County charged her guardians with improperly maintaining her, she considered the fact that she "never was taught to sew and would not have known how to make her own Shifts had her [step-]sister not taught her" to be potent evidence of neglect.[54]

White children learned to identify themselves not only by race and gender but by their position in the social hierarchy. Devereux Jarratt, the son of a prosperous carpenter and slaveholder, grew up in New Kent County, Virginia, in the 1730s and 1740s. He learned as a child that his place was inferior to that of a gentleman's son, and he soon could identify gentlemen both by their demeanor and by the wigs they wore and the coffee and tea they drank, goods not used by his own, somewhat poorer family. "We were accustomed to look upon, what were called *gentle folks*, as beings of a superior order," he wrote in his autobiography. "For my part," he added, "I was quite shy of *them*, and kept off at a humble distance."[55]

Children learned to read and write in order to understand their moral obligations and to help them perform the work demanded of them. Substantial planters sometimes reflected upon these twin goals of formal education. Samuel Pottinger, who died in Prince George's in 1742, directed that his son "be taught to Read write and cast Accompts and my Daughter to

53. Smith, *Inside the Great House*, 82–85.
54. *Ibid.*, 56–61; Farish, ed., *Journal of Fithian*, 193; Chancery Records, XII, 234 (1773; Gough was born in the late 1730s).
55. *The Life of the Rev. Devereux Jarratt, Rector of Bath Parish, Dinwiddie County, Virginia, Written by Himself* (Baltimore, 1806), 13–15; David L. Holmes, "Devereux Jarratt: A Letter and Reevaluation," *Historical Magazine of the Protestant Episcopal Church*, XLVII (1978), 38–40; see chap. 7, below, for an analysis of white class relationships.

Read." Before he died in 1730, Thomas Brooke, a gentleman with many children, similarly requested that his "two youngest Sons . . . be well educated in reading writing and arithmetick and That they shall be brought up in the doctrine and principles of the Church of England."[56]

Since most Chesapeake planters and their wives were barely literate, they had to send their children to school to learn how to read, write, and cipher. Before the middle of the eighteenth century, there were few free schools in Virginia, and private schoolmasters, paid by parents, were in short supply. There was but one schoolteacher for every hundred white families in eight tidewater Virginia parishes in 1724, a figure that implies that each child might attend one short school term. At the same time, only four teachers, each responsible for more than four hundred families, ran schools in two piedmont parishes, and at best they reached a quarter of the children entrusted to their care.[57]

As areas developed, more schools sprang up. In Elizabeth City County, one of Virginia's original shires, the number of schoolmasters grew from two in 1670, to three in 1724, and five in 1782; and at the same time, the number of families each teacher had to serve declined from about eighty-five to sixty-five. The parish schools, furthermore, included an academy where boys might study Latin as well as English. Though Prince George's County was not founded until 1697, there were already several private schools within its borders in 1724, and a free parish school joined them in the 1740s. By 1755, there were between ten and fourteen schoolmasters in the county, each responsible for eighty-five to a hundred families. County schools at that date attracted various kinds of students: although most teachers ran reading schools, one operated a Latin school, another taught practical and advanced mathematics as well as reading and writing, and two women instructed girls in French, sewing, and knitting.[58]

56. Prince George's Wills, box 6, folder 24, box 4, folder 11.
57. William Stevens Perry, ed., *Papers Relating to the History of the Church in Virginia, 1650–1776* (Geneva, N.Y., 1870), 261–318. Calculations based upon answers to query on schools and on numbers of families in each parish. I assumed that there were three children per family and that each teacher taught 25 pupils a year. In Williamsburg, there were 4 schools, or 1 for each 28 families; in the tidewater parishes, 18 schools, or 1 for each 97 families; in the piedmont parishes, 4 schools, or 1 for every 408 families.
58. For Elizabeth City, see Lawrence A. Cremin, *American Education: The Colonial Experience, 1607–1783* (New York, 1970), 530–534; Perry, *Papers Relating to Church in Virginia*, 294; and Greene and Harrington, *American Population*, 150–155; for Prince George's, see William Stevens Perry, ed., *Historical Collections Relating to the American Colonial Church* (Davenport, Iowa, 1878), IV, 200–209; Black Books, X, 39; Prince George's Court Records, XXIII, 493; Louise Joyner Hienton, *Prince George's Heritage: Sidelights on the Early History of Prince George's County, Maryland, from 1696 to 1800* (Baltimore, 1972), chap. 10; and "Number of Inhabitants in Maryland," *Gentleman's Magazine, and Historical Chronicle*, XXXIV (1764), 261.

Educational resources were unevenly spread through the white population. Wealthier parents, who could better afford to pay for schooling, more frequently wished to educate their children, and planters, no matter what their economic condition, educated sons more thoroughly than they did daughters. Parents and magistrates in Prince George's followed these expectations. The wealthier the father with young children, the more likely he was to mention education in his will. While only one planter in ten in the county whose wealth totaled less than four hundred pounds directed that his children be educated, more than one in three with more than one thousand pounds included a similar provision.[59]

The schooling that the Prince George's orphans' court required masters or guardians to provide orphans and apprentices suggests the minimal educational expectations of ordinary planters. The court ordered some education for three-quarters of the girls and seven-eighths of the boys brought before it between 1720 and 1750. However, the justices differentiated the content of education by gender, insisting that more than half the boys given an education be taught to read and write (and the rest just to read), while asking that only one girl in sixteen be taught to read and to write. Orphans' courts in Lancaster County, Virginia, in the 1720s and Anne Arundel County, Maryland, 1770–1779, ordered similar training, but added ciphering to the boys' education.[60]

The educational experience of most planters' children closely followed these prescriptions. Orphans of middling and substantial planters in three Virginia counties between 1731 and 1808 enjoyed one or two years of formal education after their fathers died. While boys received two years of training, more than half the girls probably had none, and girls who attended a reading school usually went for only one year. Since school terms lasted only a few weeks to a few months, boys probably learned to read and write during their attendance, while girls learned only to read.[61]

59. Smith, *Inside the Great House*, 61–65, 88–108. An analysis of Prince George's Wills, 1730–1769, linked to inventories, selecting only those decedents under 60 who had children under 15, yielded the following proportions of decedents with educational clauses in their wills: 1 of 20 with estates under £100, 6 of 39 with estates of £100–£250, 1 of 20 with estates of £250–£400, 2 of 18 with estates of £400–£650, 4 of 20 with estates of £650–£1,000, and 11 of 29 with estates of over £1,000.
60. Smith, ed., "Orphans and Infants of Prince George's County," shows that the orphans' court required some education for 99 of 114 boys and 41 of 54 girls brought before it between 1720 and 1750. The content of education was specified for 68 boys (37 to read and write, 31 to read) and 33 girls (31 to read, 2 to read and write, 6 to spin or sew). Alice Elaine Matthews, "Pre-College Education in the Southern Colonies" (Ph.D. diss., University of California at Berkeley, 1968), 118 (Lancaster, $N = 21$), 121 (Anne Arundel, $N = 23$).
61. Thomas K. Bullock, "Schools and Schooling in Eighteenth Century Virginia" (Ed.D. diss., Duke University, 1961), 200–204, analyzes data in Guardian Accounts for Accomack, Cum-

Schools in colonial Virginia did teach their more privileged male students to read and write. About two-thirds of the men born in three tidewater Virginia counties and three-fifths born in five piedmont counties during the first half of the eighteenth century could sign their names as adults. Men with wealthy parents were more likely to learn to sign. Although literacy was nearly universal among planters who owned land and slaves, only two of every five poor tenants could read and write.[62]

Once children learned to read, they had access to a few books. Nearly six of every ten householders living in Prince George's between 1730 and 1769 owned at least one book. Literate parents not only sent their children to school more frequently than their less wealthy, illiterate neighbors, but they also owned books with far greater regularity. Although only a third of the tenant nonslaveholders and about half of the planters who owned land or slaves possessed books, three-quarters of freeholders who worked slaves on their own land owned a book or two.[63]

A majority of literate parents owned a few edifying or practical volumes that they used to teach morality and farm management to their children. Anglican parents used the Bible and the Book of Common Prayer, supplemented by such patriarchal tomes as Richard Allestree's seventeenth-century *Whole Duty of Man* as guides for proper behavior. The Bible was the most important book in most plantation libraries; nearly all literate families owned one, and sometimes they possessed no other book.[64] Parents and schoolmasters commonly taught children to read "distinctly in the Bible," because the Bible was God's literal word and, moreover, no other book contained so many edifying stories and moral principles or had such a prominent role (along with the prayer book and psalter) in divine services.

---

berland, and Essex counties that show that the median years of education was 2 for boys (mean = 2.4; $N = 102$) and 1 for girls (mean = 1.8; $N = 48$). Since there were similar numbers of boys and girls among orphans, only 45% as many girls as boys were educated.

62. Kenneth A. Lockridge, *Literacy in Colonial New England: An Enquiry into the Social Context of Literacy in the Early Modern West* (New York, 1974), chap. 2, esp. 80–81.

63. Prince George's Inventories, 1730–1769, show that 36% of tenants without slaves ($N = 148$), 60% of freeholders without slaves ($N = 72$), 48% of tenants with slaves ($N = 33$), 75% of planters who owned both slaves and land ($N = 342$), and 86% of merchants ($N = 63$) owned at least one book at their death. When these groups are weighted by their number in the living population (see chap. 4, n. 34), then between 55% and 57% owned books.

64. Of 81 planter libraries precisely inventoried, 1745–1769, in Prince George's, 69% contained a Bible, 32% had a Book of Common Prayer, and 6% held the *Whole Duty of Man*; 19% of those who owned books at death in Baltimore and Talbot counties owned only a Bible (or Bible and prayer book) between 1720 and 1776 (see Joseph Towne Wheeler, "Books Owned by Marylanders, 1700–1776," *MHM*, XXXV [1940], 337–343); and in St. Mary's County, 1703–1776, 29% of estates of less that £50, 57% with estates of £50–£225, and 76% with estates over £225 owned religious books (see Carr and Walsh, "Changing Life Styles in St. Mary's County," *Working Papers from Reg. Econ. Hist. Res. Center*, I, No. 3 [1978], 84, 90).

Planter families commonly counted an almanac among their small bundle of books. Nearly two-thirds of the ten thousand volumes sold in the 1750s and 1760s at the *Virginia Gazette* office in Williamsburg were almanacs. Almanacs contained a broad collection of information useful to planters, including monthly calendars, data on the time of sunrise and sunset, weather predictions, the distance between the colony's villages and towns, and essays on scientific and medical topics. Moreover, planters could jot down their thoughts or farm accounts in the volume's margins and blank pages. And finally, a Virginia almanac cost only 7.5 pennies each year—a cheap price every planter could afford![65]

Since most boys received only a brief introduction to literacy, and girls often none, few people in the Chesapeake region read for pleasure or intellectual stimulation. Only sons of the wealthy gentlemen, many of whom attended Latin schools or the College of William and Mary, could participate in a high literary culture or understand the political and philosophical articles found in the region's two newspapers. (Less-educated men, of course, read almanacs, Bibles, and newspaper advertisements.) This lack of childhood training and the subsequent minimal adult interest were reflected in planters' libraries: only magistrates owned law books, and only one literate planter in six possessed a Latin classic, political tract, or volume of history.[66]

White children in the Chesapeake were trained to take their place in society through repeated instruction by adults. Parents taught their children patriarchal principles at home and sent them to school and church to reinforce the lesson. When preachers alluded to biblical passages to sustain a moral principle, parish children understood what they meant; when parents wished to explain the social hierarchy of the Chesapeake to their offspring, they chose to read the Bible or the *Whole Duty of Man*. Children observed and learned to emulate the fundamentals of proper deportment every day at home, in the tobacco fields, at school and church, and in visiting kindred.

Children needed property as well as moral lessons to be able to take their appropriate place in white society. The ownership of land and slaves

---

65. These data are from the *Va. Gaz.* daybooks (1751–1753, 1764–1766) at CW and were collected by Gregory and Cynthia Stiverson and taken from their important unpublished manuscript on books and reading in Virginia with their kind permission. See Cynthia Z. Stiverson and Gregory A. Stiverson, "The Colonial Retail Book Trade: Availability and Affordability of Reading Material in Mid-Eighteenth-Century Virginia," in William L. Joyce *et al.*, eds., *Printing and Society in Early America* (Worcester, Mass., 1983), 132–173, esp. 146–147, for a summary of some of this work.

66. Only 16% of the planter libraries cited in n. 64 contained legal books, and only 16% owned a history, the *Spectator*, or any other nonreligious book. For a similar pattern in St. Mary's, see Carr and Walsh, "Changing Life Styles in St. Mary's County," *Working Papers from Reg. Econ. Hist. Res. Center*, I, No. 3 (1978), 85.

buttressed the moral order of the region by making the perpetuation of domestic patriarchy possible. Parents therefore tried to ensure that all their children possessed enough property to replicate the family government of their childhood, a goal that led some planters to reject primogeniture (still a part of the law of intestacy) in their wills. In societies where patriarchy and political order were strongly connected, primogeniture maintained the social and political hierarchy that linked king and father, but chattel slavery helped sever that link by making each person a potential master as well as parent. Since servile work and dependence were identified with slaves, all men ideally should have owned land, the hallmark of independence. Planters who lived in frontier areas could readily distribute land to all their sons, and sometimes to their daughters. Wealthy planters gave each of their sons a fully stocked plantation, thereby maximizing the number of men able to behave like patriarchs in their own families. Poorer men favored one or two of their sons, hoping thereby that at least one son could emulate his father, but, of course, thereby reducing the total number of men who could play patriarchal roles in the future. Increased population density reduced the size of landholdings so much that primogeniture began to rise even among middling yeomen. This increased favoritism in the redistribution of resources to eldest sons created a gap between the expectation that all children ought to form their own domestic patriarchies and their ability to do so.

From the outset of colonization, planters favored older sons over their sisters and younger brothers, but most planters who made wills owned enough land to give each son a plantation. About three-quarters of the testators in St. Mary's County during the seventeenth century, and in Prince George's and Albemarle counties during the next century, gave some land to all their sons; only a third of these men, however, bequeathed land to any of their daughters. The rest of the testators, more than a quarter of the total, owned so little land that they had to favor several sons or give all their land to their oldest son (see table 25).

As population density increased in tidewater during the eighteenth century, the typical size of landholdings diminished, and more and more planters excluded one or more of their sons from land distribution in order to give working plantations to the remaining sons. Only one testator in seven in Prince George's County favored one or two sons or practiced primogeniture during the 1730s, when frontier land was still available; but after 1740, nearly all the lands were soon taken, and the proportion of men who favored older sons doubled.[67] Planters who gave all their land to their

---

67. The trend toward primogeniture is accentuated when intestate decedents, whose land was all given to the eldest son after the widow's death, are included. An estimate of the number of

Table 25. *Division of Land in Families with Two or More Children in the Chesapeake, 1640–1799*

	Percentage of Wills in County			
Type of Division	St. Mary's, 1640–1710 (N = 135 Wills)	Prince George's, 1730–1739 (N = 45 Wills)	Prince George's, 1740–1769 (N = 150 Wills)	Albemarle, 1750–1799 (N = 165 Wills)
Primogeniture	8	2	16	
One son receives all or most of land[a]				20
Some sons favored at the expense of others	19	13	15	
All sons receive some land	47	40	43	53
Land divided among all children	26	44	27	27
Total	100	99	101	100

Sources: Lorena Seebach Walsh, "Charles County, Maryland, 1658–1705: A Study of Chesapeake Social and Political Structure" (Ph.D. diss., Michigan State University, 1977), 147–148; Prince George's Wills, 1730–1769 (linked to other local records), MHR; Daniel Blake Smith, *Inside the Great House: Planter Family Life in Eighteenth-Century Chesapeake Society* (Ithaca, N.Y., 1980).

Note: [a]This is the best equivalent of "primogeniture" and "some sons favored" that the data allow.

oldest son owned an average of only 180 acres; and if they had divided their land equally among all their sons, each son would have received only 54 acres, about half the minimum needed to make tobacco. Similarly, planters who gave land to their two or three oldest sons, excluding the rest, bequeathed an average of only 101 acres to each favored son. If they had given all their sons an equal share, each son would have farmed 57 acres. Since the price of land increased more rapidly than any other commodity during the 1760s and 1770s, sons of a small freeholder who inherited land enjoyed a great advantage over their landless brothers, no matter how equitably the rest of their father's assets were disbursed.[68]

---

men with two or more sons who died intestate raises the proportion practicing primogeniture to 19% in Prince George's, 1730–1739, and to 41%, 1740–1769.

68. Prince George's Wills, 1730–1769; fig. 17, above. Data on size of holdings and number of children found on 18 men who gave land to one son and on 12 who excluded some sons, but included others.

Fathers gave each daughter and son a portion of their personal estate sufficient to set up housekeeping, sometimes specifically granting each some livestock, kitchen utensils, bedding, and slaves. While sons received a stocked plantation, daughters took personal goods bequeathed to them as a dowry. Most testators in Prince George's County attempted an equitable distribution of their personal goods: more than half of them divided their movable property equally among all their children, including those who inherited land; another quarter granted landless children a larger share than children with land; and the remaining planters favored some sons at the expense of other children. An equal distribution of movable goods often favored older sons over their siblings because much of the personal property, but not the land, could be used to pay debts the decedent owed. Parents in neighboring Charles County, Maryland, attempted to equalize bequests by granting land almost exclusively to sons, but gave somewhat greater numbers of slaves to daughters. Fathers bequeathed most male field hands to sons and most female slaves to daughters. These slaves, of course, became the personal property of the daughters' husbands when they married, but fathers apparently expected that some of the female slaves bequeathed to daughters would remain with them as personal servants.[69]

When men died before they had disbursed their property to their heirs, they entrusted their widows with this task. Younger widows, however, often remarried, and the family's land and other property fell into the hands of their new husbands. A few widows sought to protect their children's legitimate portions by signing a prenuptial agreement with their prospective grooms that allowed them to retain control of family property. Ann Smallwood, born in Prince George's in 1735, owned neither land nor slaves but wished to give what little she had to her two daughters. She twice retained control over her property, by signing prenuptial contracts with John Wynn in 1779 and Thomas Blacklock in 1783, but both times she had to relinquish her dower rights. Sarah Elson, more typically, owned 140 acres and fifteen slaves, along with other property, before she married John Kirby in Montgomery County, Maryland, in 1784. The agreement she signed before her marriage gave her control over this property, at least half the farm's prof-

---

69. The distribution of personal property can be determined from 201 wills of Prince George's planters: 107 (53%) divided their property equally among all children (46, or 23% of them, had excluded daughters or sons from land); 52 (26%) divided property equally among those who did not receive land, excluding or giving smaller portions to those who did; 27 (13%) divided personal property unequally, favoring sons over daughters; and 15 (8%) divided it unequally, favoring either a son or a daughter at the expense of others. For Charles County, see Jean Butenhoff Lee, "Land and Featherbeds: Parents' Bequest Practices in Charles County, Maryland" (paper presented at conference, "The Colonial Experience: The Eighteenth-Century Chesapeake," Baltimore, Sept. 1984), 19–37.

its, and the right of support "suitable to her Rank and Station" by her husband.[70]

Domestic Patriarchy within Chesapeake Society

Although seventeenth-century immigrants to the Chesapeake colonies found the practice of domestic patriarchy difficult, by the early eighteenth century landed families in the tidewater region had developed a distinctive patriarchal form of family government and refined it as the century progressed. In these landed and slaveholding families, women obeyed their husbands and kept to their proper place, and children deferred to both parents, but especially to their fathers. Planters educated their children to behave respectfully and used their control of property that adult children wanted to reinforce this lesson.

Even though patriarchal behavior was limited to the family, it did restrain the competitive way that men behaved in informal groups and in political discourse. Although political relations between gentlemen and yeomen were based upon principles of reciprocity rather than upon any analogies with paternal power in the family, when men associated, they replicated the hierarchy of the family by dividing themselves into groups based upon wealth, status, and education. Yeomen learned the habit of deference in their own families and therefore understood the superior place of gentlemen in the political order.

The influence of domestic patriarchy was most strongly felt by freeholding families in tidewater, where resources were becoming scarce. Tidewater slaveholders, whose families stayed on the land for generations, wielded a substantial influence over the behavior of wives and children. But men needed land and slaves in order to follow patriarchal norms. Poor tenants had too few resources to hold their children to the ancestral home and needed all the labor they could muster, including that of their wives, to survive economically, and the poorest freeholders were not much better situated. Migrants to piedmont Virginia, in contrast, lived in a raw society with abundant resources, where a son could always find cheap land just beyond his father's plantation, and he therefore had less incentive to defer to his father.

Since patriarchal norms were not always clear, conflicts between members of patriarchal families sometimes occurred. Three kinds of conflict may have been particularly common. Because patriarchalism only weakly

70. Prince George's Land Records, CC#2, 570–571, FF#1, 382–384, FF#2, 142–144; Brumbaugh, ed., *Maryland Records*, I, 1–88.

proscribed violence against wives, husbands sometimes tried to whip their wives into submission, a practice that eventually could lead even the most deferential wife to run away from home. Second, fathers who wanted to hold on to their land may have fought with sons who wished to be fully independent. And third, patriarchal norms did not rank the authority of widowed mothers and adult sons in the family—and once the patriarch had died, the struggle for authority that ensued sometimes led to conflict between mothers and sons.

Patriarchalism, finally, weakened the bonds between slave and master. Fathers distributed slaves among all their children when they died, much like other kinds of personal property. Since few men owned enough slaves to bequeath entire families to each child, they inevitably separated black husbands from wives and parents from children. Those masters who separated families broke one of the primary rules of a paternalistic relationship by arbitrarily breaking up families and thereby lost some of the power they had over the personal lives of their slaves.

6
From Neighborhood to Kin Group
The Development of a Clan System

In 1777 the Maryland assembly, uncertain of the loyalty of the people, required every free man over eighteen to swear an oath of allegiance to the new government. In Prince George's County, where the oath was popular, kinsmen often decided to support the new political order and to take the oath together. Families from every economic group in the county participated. William Selby, a middling slave- and landowner, and his five sons, all tenant householders who may have lived on their father's land and used his slaves, each swore the oath. William and his three sons swore together at Bladensburg, where the other two soon added their voices. Ignatious Digges, a Catholic gentleman, and his brother Thomas, a Jesuit priest who lived with him, met their kinsman Clement Hill and his son Clement at Upper Marlboro, where they took the oath. And eight sons, grandsons, and other relations of eighty-two-year-old Ninian Beall, all yeomen, came in groups of two and three to Bladensburg: Ninian and Thomas Beall, sons of the patriarch, swore the oath with their nephew Ignatious Price; three sons of Ninian Junior appeared together; and John Beall of Ninian Junior and his uncle, John Brown, went together.[1]

This activity suggests that kinspeople were used to acting together as a component of the broader community in the tidewater Chesapeake. Since counties, the only significant units of local government, usually covered far too vast a territory to constitute a single community, planters and their families had to create other patterns of association. Although white adults created informal social networks with men or women, yeomen or gentlemen, and church members in their neighborhoods, they increasingly organized their community life with kindred. Planters and their wives chose to associate with kinfolk of similar status who lived in their neighborhood and joined them in prayer every Sunday. Moreover, these kinship networks me-

---

1. William Kilty, *Laws of Maryland* . . . (Annapolis, 1799–1800), Feb. 1777, chap. 20, Oct. 1777, chap. 20; Louise J. Hienton and Helen W. Brown, comps., "1778 Oaths of Fidelity, Prince George's County, Maryland," bound typescript, Maryland Hall of Records, Annapolis (MHR); Gaius Marcus Brumbaugh, ed., *Maryland Records: Colonial, Revolutionary, County, and Church, from Original Sources,* I (Baltimore, 1915), 1–88; Prince George's Land Records and Debt Books, MHR.

diated between competitive planters and powerful justices of the peace in ways difficult for unrelated neighbors to achieve.[2]

Networks of kindred had not always played such an important role in white society. Even though families began to interact with their neighbors at nearby mills, churches, and homes and men escaped to meet other men at musters, horse races, and taverns as soon as settlement began, extensive kinship networks failed to develop until the late seventeenth century. The late marriages and high death rates experienced by the immigrants who settled the region made kinship and family nearly coterminous, with step-parents, half-siblings, and other relations inhabiting the same home.[3]

The increase in population density in settled areas at the end of the seventeenth century permitted creole whites to create ever more numerous social networks based upon gender, class, neighborhood, and kinship. Three stages governed the development of communities in the tobacco colonies during the eighteenth century. When an area was first occupied, farmers built small settlements in the wilderness. The population of these widely scattered settlements was far too small to sustain any community activity save rudimentary neighborliness. As migrants filled in the woodlands between plantations, creating denser neighborhoods, they devised informal groups of neighbors, men, women, church members, and kindred. As the children and grandchildren of early settlers grew up and married their neighbors, increasingly large proportions of the population were related by blood or marriage and focused their attention on the growing clans of kindred in their neighborhood, thereby excluding other neighbors from their social world.

The entire transition from frontier society to neighborhood groups to kin networks was probably complete before 1700 in places settled by the 1650s and 1660s, like Middlesex County, but it had barely started in some remote areas of southside Virginia by the time of the Revolution.[4] This

2. A *community* is composed of individuals who interact regularly; that is, communities are social networks that theoretically can be measured. *Kinship networks* and *neighborhoods* are special kinds of communities, the first based on blood and marriage, the second on geographic space delimited by the technology of transportation. See Darrett B. Rutman, "Community Study," *Historical Methods*, XIII (1980), 29–42.

3. Darrett B. Rutman and Anita H. Rutman, " 'Now-Wives and Sons-in-Law': Parental Death in a Seventeenth-Century Virginia County," in Thad W. Tate and David L. Ammerman, eds., *The Chesapeake in the Seventeenth Century: Essays on Anglo-American Society* (Chapel Hill, N.C., 1979), 153–175; Lorena S. Walsh, "Community Networks in Early Maryland" (paper presented at the Third Hall of Records Conference on Maryland History, "Maryland, a Product of Two Worlds," May 1984); T. H. Breen, "Horses and Gentlemen: The Cultural Significance of Gambling among the Gentry of Virginia," *William and Mary Quarterly*, 3d Ser., XXXIV (1977), 239–257.

4. Darrett B. Rutman and Anita H. Rutman, *A Place in Time: Explicatus* (New York, 1984), 107–116; Rutman and Rutman, *A Place in Time: Middlesex County Virginia, 1650–1750* (New

chapter explores these developments in Prince George's County, Maryland, first settled in the late seventeenth century, and pays some attention to Lunenburg County, located in the southside and settled fifty years later.

Not every white family enjoyed an equal opportunity to associate with neighbors, kinfolk, and communicants. Gentleman and yeoman planters whose families had lived in an area for generations provided the core of these social networks. About a third of the families in most long-settled areas participated only fitfully in social networks: sickly men and women, most widows, and destitute families were excluded from them and had to rely on the charity of wealthy neighbors or on the county court or Anglican vestrymen for subsistence; transients, servants, and poor planters depended upon each other for companionship and often left an area before they could form many friendships.[5]

Neighborhood Communities on the Tobacco Coast

Social networks in neighborhoods shifted continually as areas grew and people came and left the vicinity. Planter families formed, destroyed, and re-formed neighborhood communities in response to population density and the changing economic composition of the area's households. As the population density of an area rose, planter families could find companionship, places to congregate, and economic services in smaller and smaller areas, and they therefore steadily reduced the effective size of their neighborhoods.

Neighbors lived far from each other on the frontier and had to cover great distances to visit even a few other families. Frontier areas were so sparsely peopled that local government, either ecclesiastical or secular, barely existed. Farmers traveled on Indian paths to reach distant churches, taverns, stores, and courthouses. When William Byrd came to southside Virginia in 1733, he complained, "We were quite out of Christendom," and as a result, "very little devotion went forward" on Sundays. A month later, he made a "Sunday's journey to Brunswick Church, which lay about eight miles off," probably a two-hour ride over miserable trails. Justices of the peace lived scattered among the people in frontier counties and possessed the same power to settle small-debt cases and punish infractions by slaves as justices in more densely settled tidewater, but they were as undistin-

---

York, 1984), chap. 4; Richard R. Beeman, "Social Change and Cultural Conflict in Virginia: Lunenburg County, 1746 to 1774," *WMQ*, 3d Ser., XXXV (1978), 455–476.

5. Frederick H. Schmidt, "Looking for the Lesser Sort in Eighteenth-Century Virginia" (paper presented at the Eleventh Conference of the East-Central American Society for Eighteenth-Century Studies, 1980); see chap. 7 below.

guished as the people they served and could not hope to maintain order in tiny frontier settlements.[6]

The increases in the number of taxing districts in Prince George's County (called hundreds) and of processioning districts (to check land bounds) in Lunenburg County suggest that when neighborhoods became thickly peopled, their legal areas diminished, thereby symbolizing more compact neighborhoods. When Prince George's was founded in 1696, the county court established six hundreds, but it formed three new hundreds over the next thirty years and seven new hundreds between 1768 and 1777, for a total of sixteen. Rapid population growth in Lunenburg County similarly led the vestry of Cumberland Parish to increase the number of processioning districts from nine in 1764 to twenty in 1768 and thirty by 1772.[7]

Economic differentiation between neighborhoods started soon after the first pioneers arrived. Different kinds of planters, for instance, settled, respectively, the Patuxent and Potomac river watersheds of Prince George's. The rich tobacco lands along the Patuxent attracted middling and wealthy men who owned slaves and land. Gentlemen patented thousands of acres along the Potomac River, and later their heirs leased much of it to poor tenants. Yeoman planters and tenant farmers moved to lands along the Potomac River and its Eastern Branch. By 1719, forty years after the first settlers arrived in the county, between a third and a half of the families who lived near the Patuxent owned slaves, but only a quarter of the householders on the Potomac side of the county held any slaves.[8]

As population density increased, that neighborhood differentiation intensified. Slaveholders moved north of the Eastern Branch in the 1720s, and in 1733 about two-fifths of all householders there owned taxable slaves. So many of these families purchased land that nearly two-thirds of them were freeholders. At the same time, half or more of the families around the Patuxent River owned slaves, and more than two-thirds of them worked their own land. In contrast, fewer than a third of the whites who lived south

6. Beeman, "Social Change and Cultural Conflict," *WMQ,* 3d Ser., XXXV (1978), 455–463; William Byrd, "A Journey to the Land of Eden Anno 1733," in Louis B. Wright, ed., *The Prose Works of William Byrd of Westover: Narratives of a Colonial Virginian* (Cambridge, Mass., 1966), 385, 409.

7. Louise Joyner Hienton, *Prince George's Heritage: Sidelights on the Early History of Prince George's County, Maryland, from 1696 to 1800* (Baltimore, 1972), chap. 4; Landon C. Bell, *Cumberland Parish, Lunenburg County, Virginia, 1746–1816: Vestry Book, 1746–1816* (Richmond, Va., 1930), 511–565.

8. Allan Kulikoff, "Tobacco and Slaves: Population, Economy, and Society in Eighteenth-Century Prince George's County, Maryland" (Ph.D. diss., Brandeis University, 1976), 368–371; *Black Books,* X, 8–14 (1719 tithables list), MHR. Slaveholding was estimated from the distribution of total taxables.

of the Eastern Branch but near the Potomac held any taxable slaves, and few of them owned land (see map 12).

After several generations of development, neighborhoods became even more homogeneous. Land values in 1783 were nearly twice as high near Upper Marlboro as in the Piscataway region, and the further that one traveled from the Western Branch of the Patuxent, the less valuable land became. Tax assessments per capita for whites in 1783 show the same pattern: each white person was worth £132 in the northern Patuxent hundreds, £69 in the southern Patuxent hundreds, and £76 along the Potomac River and Eastern Branch.[9]

Economic differentiation proceeded more slowly in Lunenburg County than in Prince George's. The squatters and poor planters who came to Lunenburg in the 1740s either left the county soon after arrival or accumulated sufficient capital to purchase land or slaves, and later migrants brought slaves with them. Even though three-quarters of the county's families owned land and two-thirds held slaves by 1783—fifty years after the first pioneers arrived—distinctive neighborhoods did develop. Only two-fifths of the planters in one taxing district, with a seventh of the county's white population, owned slaves that year, but well over three-quarters of the households in four other districts, with a quarter of the whites, held slaves. Slaveholding in the rest of the districts approximated the county average.[10]

As neighborhoods became more compact, densely populated, and internally homogeneous, local families could associate with numerous folk similar to themselves in wealth, status, and religion. Planters, in fact, met a number of their social and economic needs within their neighborhood. Neighbors banded together to petition the county court to clear new public roads that made it easier for them to get to church, market, and courthouse. They relied upon each other for companionship, chose marriage partners from neighboring families, and sought aid from neighbors in times of distress. And when neighbors disagreed, their conflict was far more vehement than what any strangers might provoke.

Not only were planter settlements separated by thick forests, but planters found it difficult to visit neighbors because roads were so inadequate. There were only fifty miles of public pathways in Prince George's County in the early 1700s, just after the county was founded. Most roads cleared in the county before 1710 linked scattered neighborhoods along the Potomac

9. Kulikoff, "Tobacco and Slaves," 371–374, 203–205, 534–537; Summary List of Prince George's County Assessments of 1783, Executive Papers, MHR.
10. Landon C. Bell, ed., *Sunlight on the Southside: Lists of Tithes, Lunenburg County, Virginia, 1748–1783* (Philadelphia, 1931), 386–417. Data could not be compiled for one district, and the percentage of householders holding any slaves for two districts was determined from a regression of percentage slaves with percentage with taxable slaves.

Map 12. *Ownership of Taxable Slaves and Land in Prince George's County,*
1733

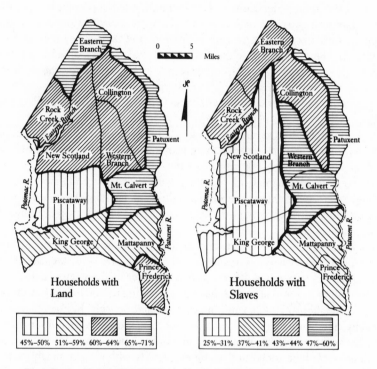

Sources: Black Books, II, 109–124 (1733 tithables list), linked to Prince George's Land Records and Rent Rolls, MHR.

River and Eastern Branch with more densely populated areas on the Patuxent River, but there were few roads within neighborhoods that linked communities.[11]

Planters united first along the frontier to improve transportation. Like other newly settled areas, neighborhoods in eastern New Scotland Hundred in Prince George's lacked roads and bridges, and after the area's white population doubled in the 1720s, local planters demanded public improvements. James Edmonston, a gentleman who owned four adult slaves and 2,350 acres of land, brought four petitions to the county court demanding improvements on area streams. In 1730 Edmonston and twenty-three oth-

11. Lois Green Carr, "County Government in Maryland, 1689–1709" (Ph.D. diss., Harvard University, 1968), 578, 377n; Prince George's Court Records, XXIX, 474, MHR.

ers successfully urged the court to build a bridge over the Northeast Branch because "the freshes had Spoil'd the Fording place . . . which render it many times unpassable." Two years later Edmonston and his neighbors petitioned the court three times, twice urging bridge construction (with thirty-two and thirty-eight neighbors) and once demanding that a creek be cleared of fallen trees. The court had one bridge built and cleared the creek but refused to construct the other bridge, perhaps tiring of Edmonston's continual demands.[12]

Edmonston gained support for his petition from a huge frontier neighborhood. Only five of the seventeen families who lived in a 5-square-mile area that surrounded his home supported him. Though most of the rest of the petitioners lived near the proposed bridges, Edmonston solicited support over an area of 175 square miles and even enticed fourteen men who lived further away to sign. These strangers included two wealthy merchant planters, four kinsmen of one of the merchants, and a schoolteacher, all of whom came to the area on business (see table 26).

The signers represented a cross section of every economic group in the area except transients and nonslaveholders. These two groups represented half the population of the region but only an eighth of the signers. Nonetheless, Edmonston solicited support from all who had lived in the county for several decades and showed that they had a stake in society through the ownership of land or slaves. Nearly three-tenths of the householders in this group signed the petitions, and they represented more than half the petitioners. Most of these men owned a couple hundred acres of land and perhaps an adult slave or two. Edmonston less frequently asked freeholders among recent arrivals in the area to sign, but, nonetheless, nearly a quarter of the men in this group added their names to the list.

Neighborhood demands for improvements in public roadways, like Edmonston's, led to an explosion of road building in Prince George's. There were 295 miles of public roads in the county in 1739, five times more than in 1700. Road construction slackened in the 1740s and 1750s, but by 1762, an additional 188 miles entered the system. These new roads linked neighborhoods and plantations throughout the county so well that demand for new projects disappeared, and only 46 new miles were built between 1762 and 1828 (see map 13).

Although most roads built from 1700 to 1740 connected new settlements with older areas, the functions of new roads changed after 1740 from serving long-distance travelers to providing families with neighborhood paths. In the Patuxent watershed, and to a lesser extent along the

12. Table 26 and sources cited there. It seems clear that Edmonston instigated the petitions, because his name appears first on three of them.

Table 26. *Wealth of Petitioners for Improvements along the Eastern Branch, Prince George's County, 1730–1733*

Socioeconomic Group, by Residence[a]	Percentage Signing Petition	Percentage of Petitioners (N = 65)	Percentage of Family Heads in Region (N = 329)
Near the Eastern Branch[b]			
Established families owning land or slaves or both	28	52	37
New arrivals owning land or slaves or both	23	15	13
Tenant nonslaveholders	6	6	20
Established families who left county, 1733–1743	4	3	14
All transients	2	2	16
Elsewhere in county			
Land- and slaveowners in the Patuxent watershed[c]	5	15	
All others	—	6	

Sources: Black Books, II, 106–124, X, 8–14 (1733 and 1719 tithables list), and Prince George's crow and squirrel levy for 1743 in Levy Book A, and Prince George's Land Records and Rent Rolls linked to Prince George's Court Records, VIII, 17, 136, 399, IX, 165, all MHR.

Notes: [a]Established families lived in the county from before 1719 to after 1743; new arrivals came to the county between 1719 and 1733 but stayed to 1743 or later; transients arrived after 1719 and left before 1744 (this group includes tenant nonslaveholder transients). [b]Includes Eastern Branch, New Scotland, Rock Creek, and Potomac hundreds (administrative units). This is the "region" of the third column. [c]Patuxent Watershed includes Patuxent, Mt. Calvert, Western Branch, Mattapanny, and Prince Frederick hundreds.

Eastern Branch, a complex local network emerged because wealthy planters demanded them. Around Upper Marlboro, the second county seat, for example, the distance between intersections decreased, shortcuts between major roads appeared, and the county constructed alternative routes during the 1740s and 1750s (see map 14).

This system of public roads facilitated both communication between neighbors and the marketing of crops. Although steep banks and washed-out fording places made small streams treacherous and major highways turned into muddy rutted messes when too many wagons passed over them, planters readily rolled tobacco on almost all county roads. Planters caused some problems themselves when they enclosed a portion of their land surrounding roadbeds and erected gates or stopped up roads to protect their

Map 13. *Public Roads in Prince George's County, 1739, 1762*

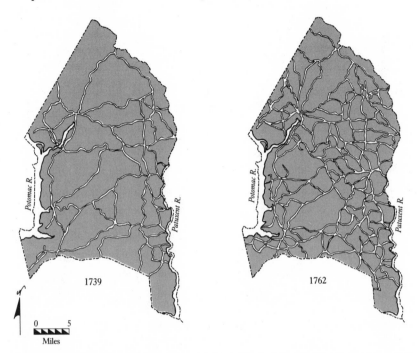

1739

1762

Miles

Sources: Allan Kulikoff, "Tobacco and Slaves: Population, Economy, and Society in Eighteenth-Century Prince George's County, Maryland" (Ph.D. diss., Brandeis University, 1976), 329–330; Prince George's Court Records, X, 338–340, XXV, 280–284, MHR. Drawn in collaboration with Margaret Cook.

crops. Despite these impediments, people rode on horseback, at a brisk pace: sustained speeds of up to five miles an hour were probably common, and travelers covered about forty miles in a day.[13]

Once the road system had been fully developed, other neighborhood concerns took on greater importance. Neighbors befriended each other, visited one another's homes, and watched their children grow up together. When children reached adulthood and began searching for a spouse, they naturally turned to neighborhood friends they and their parents had known for years. The geographic extent of the marriage market in Prince George's—a good indicator of the impact of neighborhood friendships— barely changed over the eighteenth century despite a 50 percent increase in

13. Kulikoff, "Tobacco and Slaves," 336–338.

Map 14. *Changes in Upper Marlboro Road Network, 1739–1762*

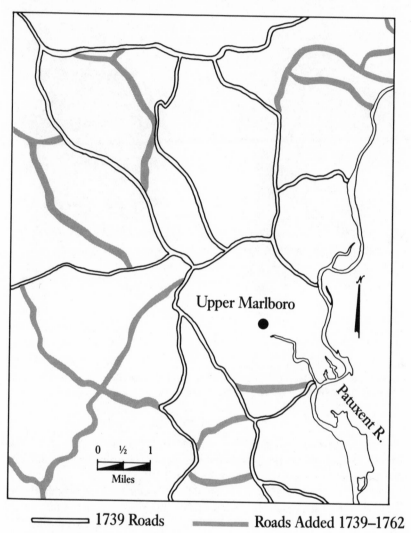

Upper Marlboro

Patuxent R.

0   ½   1
Miles

══════ 1739 Roads   ▬▬▬▬▬ Roads Added 1739–1762

Source: Detail from map 13.

the density of white households in the county. About a quarter of brides and grooms lived in the same neighborhood of thirty or forty white families, within two miles of their intended mates. Another fourth of these men and women had to search further afield, yet they found spouses within five miles of their parental homes, an area in which perhaps 90 families lived early in the century and 130 lived by the time of the Revolution. Nearly all the rest married into families who lived ten to twenty miles from home.[14]

Even though the county court in Maryland and the Anglican vestry in Virginia were legally obligated to help the deserving poor, neighbors often banded together to help ill, destitute, widowed, or orphaned neighbors until court or vestry could meet. In Prince George's this aid took three forms: alms to needy folk, shelter for old and ill men and women, and testimony before the justices about the worthiness of a supplicant.

Widows and ill or elderly men asked neighbors for help most often. Before 1750, for instance, Mary Chapel had "subsisted for many years by your Worships Bounty and the charity of good Neighbours, who while she was able to Present herself to their sight, bestowed many Charitable Favours upon her," but now, unable to walk, she could no longer beg neighbors for help and needed—and received—a larger pension from the county. And in 1749, John Knight, sixty-eight years old and "very Ill with a Plurisee," urged the justices of Prince George's Court to grant him a pension to pay his neighbor and benefactor, Anne Atchinson, who had taken care of him. Atchinson was a "poor Woman with a charge of 5 Children, and she cannot afford to Keep him for nothing."[15]

Neighbors felt some responsibility toward local orphans and servant children, and they intervened with the justices if they witnessed violent treatment of them. After Ann Brown, mother of Mary and Diana Tracy, and Mary and Richard Brown, died in the early 1730s, her three oldest children objected to the appointment of John Wilson as Richard's guardian and produced "some of their near Neighbours to testify as to the useage" of Richard by Wilson. The court listened to the testimony and named Thomas Hill and Mary Tracy as Richard Brown's guardians. When neighbors saw Rich-

---

14. Kulikoff, "Tobacco and Slaves," 375–376, 323–324; Black Books, II, 109–124; Brumbaugh, ed., *Maryland Records*, I, 1–88. The distribution of marriage distances of 147 couples, 1700–1790, is as follows: 26% lived less than 2 miles apart, 27% lived 2–5 miles apart, 20% lived 5–10 miles apart, 18% lived 10–20 miles apart, 8% lived 20–50 miles apart, and 1% lived 50–100 miles apart. To calculate the size of the marriage market, I computed the number of households per square mile in 1733 and 1776 and then multiplied these totals by 2.0 miles and by 3.5 miles (midpoint of 2–5 miles). In 1733, the number of families equaled 28 for the 2.0 mile category and 87 for the 2–5 mile category; in 1776, the number of families equaled 42 and 129, respectively.

15. Prince George's Court Records, XX, 236, 177.

ard Lane, a servant boy, mistreated by Thomas Dawson in 1767, they sheltered him, and his mother claimed that "he would not be Able to Subsist if it was not, for some of the good Neighbours."[16]

Neighbors rallied around friends when they fell on hard times. When John Elson, a tenant who owned a five-year-old slave child, petitioned Prince George's court to be free from local taxes in 1749 because of rheumatism, his neighbor William Smith, a large slaveowner, appended a note verifying Elson's story. Similarly, when Isaac Downes, a freeholder with 232 acres of land, requested to be tax-free in 1747 because a rupture made it impossible for him to earn a living, eight landowners, six of them neighbors, signed his petition.[17]

Since neighbors paid such close attention to each other's business, bitter disagreements among them sometimes erupted. Conflicts between neighbors over roads, for example, were probably common. Two cases brought before the Prince George's justices during the early 1730s show how jurists solved conflict through arbitration by disinterested parties. When Philip Evans petitioned the court in 1732 to reopen a road he claimed was "frequently used by the Neighbourhood when they going a Training and . . . to Broad Creek Church," the justices chose two slave-holding neighbors of Evans to view the road. "Being unwilling to displease one Neighbour more than another," they consulted "the Neighbours dwelling most convenient to the . . . road." After seeing two neighbors who objected to reopening the road because two nearby pathways led to the church, they concluded that "it would be a great hardship on them to clar[e] a road for the convenience of on[e] Neighbour." In 1733, when neighbors Groves Tomlinson and James Gore turned the main road leading from the western frontier to the Eastern Branch, some neighbors denied that they had agreed the road be turned as Tomlinson claimed and asked that the old road be maintained. Gore replied that he had turned the road but a hundred yards to protect his cornhills. Four freeholders that lived in the general vicinity of the road, including a merchant and a land speculator, viewed the road and voted three to one to permit its new course.[18]

In a society in which surveys of land were often inexact, disputes over boundaries were also common. In 1766 Clement Hill, a wealthy gentleman, wrote a neighbor that he "saw your People getting fence logs I think on my Land" and offered to send him the courses of the tract to prevent further poaching. Similarly, cousins Ninian and Thomas Beall argued heatedly with

16. *Ibid.*, VIII, 387, 398, XXVIII, 320.
17. *Ibid.*, XVII, 614, XX, 237; Prince George's Debt Book, 1750; Prince George's Inventories, DD#2, MHR.
18. Prince George's Court Records, IX, 125, 292–293, 400.

Stephen Lewis over ownership of a five-hundred-acre tract in Frederick County in 1747 and 1748. Ninian Beall insisted that Lewis, his nephew, and others had so frequently "laboured with many of the Inhabitants of the County . . . in acquainting them with his Cause" to "the prejudice of the Defendents" that he could not receive a fair trial. In 1748, however, when Lewis failed to appear in court, the case was dropped.[19]

One feud between neighbors kept families in southeastern Prince George's upset for several years in the late 1740s. An area tenant, Thomas Weston, began the feud when he accused John Wilson, son of neighboring freeholder Joseph Wilson, of assaulting his three sons. After Wilson's dog had chased and bit his children, Wilson hit them with "clubs, Sticks, and Staves" until "their lives were despaired of." The grand jury indicted John Wilson in March 1747, four months after Weston swore the peace against him, but the case was continued. In November 1747, Joseph Wilson insisted in a petition to the court, signed by twelve of his friends, that the dispute between his son and the Westons was trivial, yet Weston had threatened him with a "Continuation of the same hard useage in the future" and more court action. Even though Wilson's supporters included seven neighbors and five freeholders, the court rejected his petition. When the case finally came to trial in 1748, the charges were dismissed.[20]

Manly Competition, Female Cooperation

White men and women lived separate lives in eighteenth-century Chesapeake society. While men marketed crops and competed with other men in sports or diversions, women stayed at home or visited neighboring plantations. When Edward Kimber visited the tobacco coast in the 1740s, he noticed that local women exhibited "an Air of Reserve . . . that looks at first . . . like Unsociableness, which is barely the Effect of living at a great Distance from frequent Society, and their thorough Attention to the Duties of their Stations." "Their Amusements are quite innocent," he added, "and within the Circle of a Plantation or two, they exercise all the Virtues that can raise one's Opinion of the too light Sex." This segregation of public and private spheres into male and female worlds was strong from the outset of colonization, but until tidewater was thickly seated with plantations and villages, men often remained at home with their wives or joined them in

19. Clement Hill Papers, in possession of Dr. Robert Sascer of Upper Marlboro, Md.; *Stephen Lewis* v. *Thomas Beall*, ejectment papers, box 19, MHR.
20. Prince George's Court Records, XVII, 180, 380, XVIII, 91, 23, 276, 301, 305, XIX, 5–8. Names linked with Prince George's Debt Book, 1750, and Black Books, II, 109–124.

rounds of visits. During the second half of the eighteenth century, men left their wives at home when they visited newly founded villages to fight, drink, talk politics, or watch races at the taverns, general stores, and racetracks of the village.[21]

Outsiders contrasted innocent female amusement with the dissolute sports of men. In 1769 James Reid, a Presbyterian immigrant, contended that the typical Chesapeake gentleman "drinks, fights, bullies, curses, swears, whores, games, sings, whistles, dances, jumps, capers, runs, talks baudy, visits Gentlemen he never saw, has the rendez-vous with Ladies he never spoke to, . . . eats voraciously, sleeps, snores, and takes snuff." Other commentators seconded Reid's satire in more serious writings. Eight years later, Ebenezer Hazard, son of a Philadelphia merchant, noted that Virginians were "much addicted to Gaming, drinking, swearing, horse-racing, [and] cockfighting." About the same time, J. F. D. Smyth, an English visitor, found middling planters "all excessively attached to every species of sport, gaming, and dissapation, particularly horse-racing, and that most barbarous of all diversions, . . . cock-fighting."[22]

A social ethic shared by most men in the region lies buried in these acerbic comments. All the activities enumerated involved competition between planters of equal rank. The racetrack, cockpit, tavern, or forest became a field of battle where virile men competed to see who owned the fastest horse or most vicious rooster or who could hold the most liquor or bag the most game. Any participant considered an attack on his performance to impugn his honor, and he could defend his virtue only by fisticuffs, slashing newspaper articles, or court fights. To be a complete man, one had to participate in these events, and anyone, like James Reid, who refused to join in found himself excluded from the company of other men. A brief examination of four fields of honor—the woods, the racetrack, the tavern, and the general store—suggests the ways male solidarity strengthened over the eighteenth century.[23]

21. "Eighteenth-Century Maryland as Portrayed in the 'Itinerant Observations' of Edward Kimber," *Maryland Historical Magazine*, LI (1956), 331–334. See Michelle Zimbalist Rosaldo, "Women, Culture, and Society: A Theoretical Overview," in Rosaldo and Louise Lamphere, eds., *Women, Culture, and Society* (Stanford, Calif., 1974), 17–42, for an excellent analysis of public and domestic roles of men and women.
22. James Reid, "The Religion of the Bible and Religion of K[ing] W[illiam] County Compared" (1769), in Richard Beale Davis, ed., *The Colonial Virginia Satirist: Mid-Eighteenth-Century Commentaries on Politics, Religion, and Society* (American Philosophical Society, *Transactions*, N.S., LVII, Pt. i [Philadelphia, 1967]), 48 (cited hereafter as Reid, "Religion of the Bible"); Fred Shelley, ed., "The Journal of Ebenezer Hazard in Virginia, 1777," *Virginia Magazine of History and Biography*, LXII (1954), 414; J.F.D. Smyth, *A Tour in the United States of America . . .* , 2 vols. (London, 1784), I, 67.
23. Reid, "Religion of the Bible," 48–50. The best theoretical analysis of these issues is in Clifford Geertz, "Deep Play: Notes on the Balinese Cockfight," *Daedalus* (Winter, 1972), 1–37.

Hunting was a necessity as well as a sport in much of the region. Frontier planters had to kill wild boars (which they had set loose themselves), wolves, crows, and squirrels that endangered their crops and livestock. These pests, moreover, sometimes persisted long after the frontier had passed. Both assemblies paid bounties for wolves' heads throughout the colonial era because wolves "very much obstruct the raising and increase of cattle, sheep, and hogs." Each householder in Maryland and parts of Virginia was required to produce three squirrel scalps or crows' heads per taxable. If more were returned, the province paid a bounty; planters who submitted fewer had to pay a small fine.[24]

Planters took these responsibilities seriously, killing crows, squirrels, and wolves in great profusion. In 1746, about half of all the heads of household in Prince George's County, for instance, returned more than their quota of crows and squirrels, and nearly a quarter of this group killed fifty or more animals beyond their allotted number. These regular hunters included a few gentlemen, but most were yeomen who owned a couple of slaves or several hundred acres of land.[25]

Until the second half of the eighteenth century, most hunting was an informal diversion, not a sport with recognized rules. Several examples suggest the informality of the game. Sometime in 1720 Francis Marbury—a justice of the peace and wealthy planter of Prince George's County—went hog hunting with two less wealthy neighbors. They soon "met with a body of them ... [;] the Hogs furiously Attacked them, [and] obliged them to shoot one." Thirty-five years later, fifteen-year-old Peter Bycraft "went to Thomas Cleland's Mill" near Rock Creek in Frederick County, Maryland, "and when there Mr. Cleland was standing in the Millyard with his Gun in his hand and asked him ... if his Dog would go in the water" to retrieve a duck Cleland had shot.[26]

The most complete discussion of male activities in the Chesapeake is in Jane Carson, *Colonial Virginians at Play* (Charlottesville, Va., 1965); but the best analyses of them are in Rhys Isaac, *The Transformation of Virginia, 1740–1790* (Chapel Hill, N.C., 1982), chap. 5.

24. Carson, *Virginians at Play*, 137–141; William Waller Hening, *The Statutes at Large: Being a Collection of All the Laws of Virginia . . .*, 13 vols. (Richmond, Philadelphia, 1809–1823), III, 42–43, 282–283, IV, 89–91, 353–355, 446, V, 203–204, VI, 152–154, VIII, 147–148, 200, 380–381 (hereafter *Virginia Statutes at Large*); William Kilty, *The Laws of Maryland* (Annapolis, 1799), chap. 7, 1728.

25. Kilty, *Laws of Maryland*, chap. 7, 1728; Prince George's Levy Book, A, 312–348, MHR, lists the crows' and squirrels' returns for 1746. I excluded residents of Frederick County (created in 1748). There were 457 names on the list disbursing money for surplus animals (35 with more than 100 extra; 105 with more than 50 extra), and 507 people fined for bringing in insufficient numbers. The social status of regular hunters was determined by linking them with the 1733 tithables list (Black Books, II, 106–124).

26. Prince George's Land Records, HH, 173; Montgomery County Land Records, A, 328–329, MHR.

Game slowly disappeared from tidewater. In 1724 Hugh Jones reported that wolves and bears no longer endangered travelers in tidewater, and the Virginia woods had become so depleted of deer by 1738 that the assembly limited the hunting season to October and November. As game disappeared, planters searched for animals on their neighbors' land, often ignoring signs that prohibited hunting. In 1764 three Prince George's gentlemen complained that they had "frequently suffer'd great Injury in their Stock, etc. by Persons going through their Plantations with Dogs and Guns under Pretence of Hunting and Fowling" and gave notice that they would prosecute trespassers. Thirty-five years later, George Washington had similar problems with his neighbors and informed them that his "Lands have been Posted, according to Law, many years" and ordered them to stop "hunting or driving Deer on my land."[27]

As impediments to hunters increased, the activity turned into a gentleman's sport. Gentlemen began to ride with hounds in the English manner in the 1730s, and fox hunters became common after the Revolution. John Bernard exquisitely described hunting rituals during the 1790s: the company would "enter the wood, beat up the quarters of anything, from a stag to a snake, and take their chance for a chase." "If the game went off well ..., at every hundred yards up sprung so many rivals that horses and hunters were puzzled which to select, and every buck, if he chose, could have a deer to himself," a possibility that "enabled the worst rider, when all was over, to talk about as many difficulties surmounted as the best."[28]

Chesapeake planters competed for honor in horse races as well as in hunting. Racing began during the last decades of the seventeenth century, and by 1700 there were at least a dozen tracks in tidewater Virginia. Gentlemen raised racehorses, rode their own mounts on a quarter-mile straight track, and made large wagers with each other to raise a purse. The size of the bets and entrance fees sometimes precluded active participation by ordinary planters, but many yeomen were in the large crowds that watched the races.[29]

During the middle third of the eighteenth century, horse races became more frequent, better organized, and longer (up to five miles) and attracted even greater numbers of spectators. Crowds at eighteenth-century races included gentlemen, yeomen, youths, and, occasionally, women of all classes. While the richest men imported steeds from England, many Chesa-

27. *Virginia Statutes at Large*, III, 328, V, 60–63, 480–481; Carson, *Virginians at Play*, 138–149; *Maryland Gazette*, May 3, 1764.
28. Carson, *Virginians at Play*, 138–149; John Bernard, *Retrospections of America, 1797–1811*, ed. Bayle Bernard (New York, 1887), 156–157.
29. Isaac, *Transformation of Virginia*, 98–101; Breen, "Horses and Gentlemen," *WMQ*, 3d Ser., XXXIV (1977), 239–257.

peake gentlemen raised studhorses. Although the races with the largest audiences and the highest wagers were held in towns like Williamsburg and Annapolis, gentlemen organized races in every little village in tidewater Maryland and Virginia each year, often as part of a two- or three-day fair.[30]

Taverns, or ordinaries, became ever more important fields of honor for gentlemen and yeomen alike during the eighteenth century. Early ordinaries had been established to serve travelers, but as population density increased, local planters flocked to public houses. Even the poorest taverns, "mere shelters from the weather," gave planters a respite from the drudgery of agriculture, and the most elegant of them provided a great contrast to the small, crowded cabins where most planters lived. One tavern in Leeds in the 1750s was filled with mahogany tables and chairs and "stuft with fine large glaized Copper Plate Prints"; as men entered William Wirt's tavern in Bladensburg in the early 1770s, they saw portraits of the king and queen and twelve paintings of the seasons.[31]

Men visited public houses to escape from home, wife, and crying infants, and while they were there, they ate, drank, gambled, argued politics, and proved their worthiness as men in fisticuffs and games. The most frequent patrons of Wirt's public house in the early 1770s were men between the ages of twenty-six and forty-five, almost all of whom had children under five at home. When they arrived at his tavern, they saw few women but barmaids and, rarely, the wife of a patron. One clergyman complained in 1751 that these havens for men had become places "where not only Time and Money are squandered away, but where prohibited and unlawful Games . . . abound to the greatest Excess."[32]

These activities, of course, attracted ever more men to ordinaries. Patrons consumed vast quantities of alcohol at Chesapeake taverns, often without food. An evening at a public house sometimes began with a series

30. Carson, *Virginians at Play*, 105–132; Hienton, *Prince George's Heritage*, 129–130, 134–136, 140; Aubrey C. Land, *Colonial Maryland: A History* (Millwood, N.Y., 1981), 195–196; Isaac, *Transformation of Virginia*, 98–101.

31. Lorena Walsh's research on a 17th-century St. Mary's County tavern; Smyth, *Tour in the United States*, I, 49–50; "Narrative of George Fisher Commencing with a Voyage from London, May 1750 . . . ," *WMQ*, 1st Ser., XVII (1908–1909), 170; Prince George's Inventories, box 24, folder 22.

32. Prince George's Inventories, box 24, folder 22; Brumbaugh, ed., *Maryland Records*, I, 1–88; Patricia Anne Gibbs, "Taverns in Tidewater Virginia, 1700–1744" (master's thesis, College of William and Mary, 1968), chaps. 2–3 (quote on 39). I identified the age in 1776 of 205 patrons of Wirt's tavern (on the list of sperate debts or listed as "good" on list of desperate debts) and discovered the 10% of the men on the census age 16–20 in 1772 were on the list along with 15% of those 21–25, 29% of those 29–35, 34% of those 36–45, 26% of those 46–55, 27% of those 56–60, and 16% of those over 60. The proportions of these patrons who had children under 5 in 1772 were, age 16–20, 0%; 21–25, 37%; 26–35, 68%; 36–45, 83%; 46–55, 40%; 56–60, 8%; and above 60, 0%.

of toasts. When Landon Carter visited a local ordinary in 1775 to settle an old dispute with Dr. Nicholas Flood, he began by drinking "to this devil, ... but he would not take notice of me." The toasts continued: Carter "drank a Hercules to clear the Augean stable of Britain," but Flood countered with "a Hercules to clear all our Courts everywhere of the rascals," including, presumably, Justice Carter. Besotted with liquor, men sometimes challenged each other in manly games. In September 1755, "some people at *Queen-Anne* Town, in *Prince-George*'s County, having drank too much, got to making Sport, ... with one of their Company, by tripping his Heels, and throwing him down on a Floor, till they gave him a Fall which kill'd him." Six years later, in Dorchester County, Maryland, "*Roger Addams*, having Drank too much, laid a Wager that he could then Drink all the Wine there left in a Decanter, at one Draught. He won the Wager; but Died a few Minutes after."[33]

Conversation often turned to politics in this congenial atmosphere. A lengthy discussion about an upcoming election among six freeholders, one justice of the peace, and the servant of a candidate in Robert Munford's 1770 play *The Candidates* took place on "A Porch of a tavern." During June 1765 a French traveler heard seditious talk about the Stamp Act in both Chesapeake colonies. At a tavern in Hanover County, Virginia, "we had nothing talked of but the stamp Dutys," and one militia major said "freely he'l sooner Die than pay a farthing, and is shure that all his Countrymen will do the Same." Later that month, he dined at a tavern at Upper Marlboro, the county seat of Prince George's, during court days, and his "large Company" talked "Continually on the Stamp Dutys."[34]

As population increased, men demanded still more places to drink and cavort, forcing county courts to grant new ordinary licenses, especially in small villages where men congregated. When planters failed to find a tavern, they badgered local planters for drink and food, thereby driving the victim to request an ordinary license. For instance, James Chapman of Upper Marlboro asked his county court in 1727 for a license because he had been "prodigiously agrieved by the multitude of people that come to Court." Similarly, Mary Cramphin complained in 1749 that "she is very much Troubled with Travellors that cross at the Eastern Branch Ferry and has been at Expense in Providing Things Necessary to Keeping Ordinary."

33. "Narrative of George Fisher," *WMQ*, 1st Ser., XVII (1908–1909), 173; Jack P. Greene, ed., *The Diary of Colonel Landon Carter of Sabine Hall, 1752–1778*, 2 vols. (Charlottesville, Va., 1965), II, 937–938; *Md. Gaz.*, Sept. 18, 1755, Mar. 5, 1761.
34. "Journal of a French Traveller in the Colonies, 1765," *American Historical Review*, XXVI (1920–1921), 747, XXVII (1921–1922), 73; Jay B. Hubbell and Douglass Adair, eds., "Robert Munford's *The Candidates*," *WMQ*, 3d Ser., V (1948), 233–235.

After justices licensed hundreds of taverns, a vast network of public houses could be found in tidewater and piedmont. The number of ordinaries in Prince George's, for example, rose from 10 in 1735 to 21 in the early 1760s, and at the same time, the number of households per tavern declined from 120 to 90. In 1786 there were at least 170 ordinaries in Virginia south of the Rappahannock River. The longer an area was settled, the lower the ratio of taverns to white men: there was a tavern for every 150 men in tidewater, for every 125 men in central Virginia (including Richmond), but only one for every 250 men in sparsely populated southside Virginia.[35]

Each tavern attracted a regular clientele. When Benjamin Henry Latrobe visited the tiny village of Newcastle in Hanover County in 1797, he discovered such a congenial group. The "whole town . . . assembled every evening at the billard room," and "as every face is known, and every acquaintance intimate, ceremony and even politeness have disappeared." Similar gatherings could be found in Prince George's County earlier in the century. Regular customers visited their neighborhood tavern about three times a month, ten months each year, and found close to thirty of their neighbors there when they arrived. An eighth of them came once a week or even more often (see fig. 19). Schoolmasters, who traveled the county tutoring children of gentlemen, visited six times a month; gentlemen imbibed four times a month; but ordinary planters, who ran their farms with little help, managed to come only twice monthly.[36]

William Wirt's public house and billiard room may have been the finest in Prince George's, and when he died in 1772, more than seven hundred patrons still owed him for drink and gaming. Nearly three-fifths of his customers lived in town or in nearby neighborhoods. They constituted a cross section of freeholders in the area: two-thirds of townsmen and planters who owned land and slaves, two-fifths of those who held land or slaves,

35. Prince George's Court Records, N, 491, XX, 236; Prince George's Ordinary Licenses, *ibid.*, MHR, and in Kulikoff, "Tobacco and Slaves," 349–350. Virginia licenses and white men over 21 found in "A State of the Inspectors Accounts from Oct 1786 to Oct 1787 . . . ," Auditor's Item XLIX, Virginia State Library, Richmond (VSL), underrecords the number of taverns. I used the ratio of white tithes to licenses (excluding counties with no listed license and the Northern Neck, where data were too scanty) to estimate the number of licenses of counties outside the Northern Neck with no license or one. This raised the number of public houses from 170 listed to 234.

36. Edward C. Carter II *et al.*, eds., *The Virginia Journals of Benjamin Henry Latrobe, 1795–1798* (New Haven, Conn., 1977), II, 327–328. Three Prince George's tavernkeepers owned an average of 28 chairs; source for number of patrons: Prince George's Inventories, box 24, folder 22, and GS#2, 153–155; Inventories, XLIII, 253–255. Mean number of visits per year for 55 customers was 39.5; for 28 planters, 25.8 (excludes largest case); for 8 gentlemen, 44.9; for 4 schoolmasters, 72.3.

Fig. 19. *Visits by Customers to Tavern, 1742–1769, and General Store, 1769*

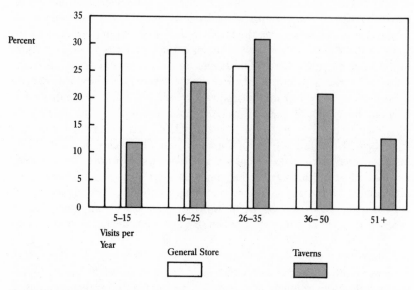

Sources: Ledgers, Piscataway Store, Simpson-Baird Company, Glassford Papers, Library of Congress; Prince George's Court Records, libri 18–30, MHR. Regular customers were those who sold one hogshead or more of tobacco to the store or those whose 1768 balance plus 1769 purchases at the store was £15 current money or more. A customer equals any year for any tavern account (submitted as evidence in court suits) in which four or more consecutive months were not skipped. If any account listed more than one year, it was counted as more than one case: one account, three years, equals three customers.

and a quarter of the tenant nonslaveholders visited Wirt's establishment. The further a planter lived from Bladensburg and the poorer he was, the less likely he was to frequent Wirt's tavern.[37]

From the beginnings of settlement, men sold their tobacco and corn crops to planter-merchants or merchants and purchased manufactured

37. Prince George's Inventories, box 24, folder 22, linked with Brumbaugh, ed., *Maryland Records*, I, 1–88, Prince George's Debt Books, 1772, and Prince George's Land Records. I found 218 of 719 men who owed Wirt money when he died (sperate plus good debts) on the 1776 census; many of the others were from county families who lived just beyond the census area. In Bladensburg, New Scotland, and Eastern Branch hundreds (adjacent to Bladensburg), 66% of those who owned land and slaves ($N = 101$), 39% of those with land or slaves ($N = 65$), and 26% of the nonslaveholding tenants ($N = 95$) were patrons. In Oxon and Rock Creek hundreds, 5 or more miles distant, 49% of the landed slaveholders ($N = 43$), 31% with either ($N = 51$), and 10% of the tenant nonslaveholders ($N = 108$) owed Wirt. And in Piscataway and King George hundreds on the Potomac, 10 or more miles distant, 18% of those with land and slaves ($N = 132$) but only 5% of the rest ($N = 284$) came to Wirt's.

goods with the proceeds. Men excluded women from these exchanges during the seventeenth century because marketing usually involved selling tobacco to a planter-merchant or consigning it to a London merchant and waiting for a ship laden with dry goods to dock to pick up the orders. By the early eighteenth century, however, year-round stores began to appear in the region, and the number of these emporiums rose rapidly through the century. During the 1760s and 1770s, a village store carried hundreds of different items, including many types of cloth, axes and hoes, Bibles and prayer books, carpentry and smithing tools, drugs and spices, and liquor of all kinds.[38]

Even though women might have patronized these stores, buying items for their own use without interfering with male prerogatives of marketing tobacco, men appropriated general stores for themselves. Women rarely visited their neighborhood store, even when they purchased goods in their own name. Almost a tenth of the account holders but only one of every thirteen customers (those who picked up goods in the store) at the Simpson-Baird store in Piscataway in 1769 were women; widows who held store accounts sent their sons or unrelated men to the store to gather their goods three times as frequently as they ventured there themselves. Elizabeth Kelley, a Piscataway tavernkeeper, for instance, kept an account at the store to supply her tavern but rarely visited the place, instead sending her slave Watt to pick up her purchases (see table 27).

More than two-thirds of the customers at the Simpson-Baird store were men buying goods on their own account. Men came to stores like this one to haggle over tobacco prices, purchase cloth, farm implements, or rum, and talk with other male customers. Planters typically visited the Simpson-Baird store twice a month, but a sixth of the store's regular patrons came at least three times a month (table 27). In June and August they sold the previous year's crop, paid their bills, and bought dry goods and plantation necessities. They visited the store in the fall and winter to buy a quart of rum or a few ells of cheap cloth. Then they probably looked for friends among the other thirteen to twenty-five customers and drank rum with them before taking off for a nearby public house or their own plantations.[39]

The growth of villages in the Chesapeake region in the eighteenth century increased the opportunities men had to gather, drink, and argue. A

---

38. Prince George's Court Records, S, 179–184, W, 74–75, 226, Z, 296, 596–598, document year-round stores in that county in the 1720s and 1730s; Jacob M. Price, "The Rise of Glasgow in the Chesapeake Tobacco Trade, 1707–1775," *WMQ*, 3d Ser., XI (1954), 179–199, details the consignment and store trades.

39. Simpson-Baird Day Books and Journals, Glassford Papers, Library of Congress, Washington, D.C.; Kulikoff, "Tobacco and Slaves," 359–361.

Table 27. *Gender of Customers at the Simpson-Baird Store,*
Prince George's County, 1769

Customer's Relationship to Holder of Store Account	Percentage of Total Visits to Store[a]		
	Men ($N=967$)	Women ($N=75$)	Overall ($N=1,042$)
Same person	70	2	72
Kindred[b]	11	4	15
Unrelated whites	7	2	9
Slaves	4	c	4
Total	92	8	100

Source: Day Books and Journal, Piscataway Store, Simpson-Baird and Company, January, April, and July 1769, Glassford Papers, Library of Congress. The daybooks list both the account-holder and the customer if the latter was a different person.

Notes: [a]Each trip by each customer is counted *except* trips to rival merchants, trips where only the account-holder but not the person who picked up the goods was mentioned, and trips when payment was made by note, letter, or order. [b]Male kindred include 5% sons for fathers, 3% sons for mothers, 2% brothers for brothers, and 1% other; female kindred include 3% wives for husbands, and 1% other. [c]Less than .5%.

short analysis of Prince George's County illustrates this development. In 1700 there was just one village in the county, and nearly all the taverns, ship landings, and artisans' shops that planters frequented were scattered across the landscape. Between 1715 and 1730, four small market towns (three on the Patuxent River and one on the Eastern Branch) and three tiny crossroads emerged in the county. Although the crossroads each contained just one or two businesses (like a tavern and ferry), the villages attracted increasing numbers of planters. By the 1730s, six of ten county tavernkeepers and about half the merchants had set up shop in these villages and crossroads (see map 15).[40]

As the county's population increased and Scottish merchants began to compete for local trade, the number and size of villages increased. By 1760, six market towns, arranged in regular patterns along the Potomac and Patuxent rivers, could be found in the county, and three others could be found nearby in adjacent counties. Nine-tenths of the stores and two-thirds of the taverns in the county could be found in the towns, and nearly all the rest were located at crossroads. Other businesses men frequented also located

40. Hienton, *Prince George's Heritage*, chaps. 2, 8–9; various issues of the *Md. Gaz.*, 1747–1775; Kulikoff, "Tobacco and Slaves," 323–324, 349–350.

Map 15. *Market Towns and Crossroads in Prince George's County, 1715–1765*

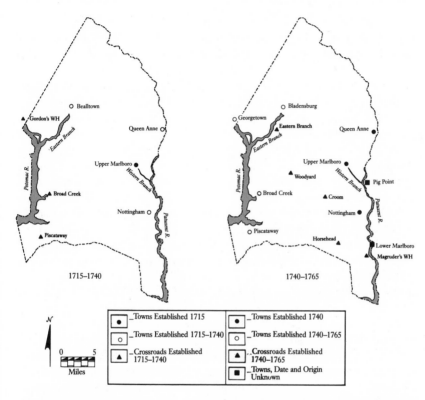

Sources: Louise Joyner Hienton, *Prince George's Heritage: Sidelights on the Early History of Prince George's County, Maryland, from 1696 to 1800* (Baltimore, 1972), chaps. 2, 8–9; *Maryland Gazette*, 1747–1775; Allan Kulikoff, "Tobacco and Slaves: Population, Economy, and Society in Eighteenth-Century Prince George's County, Maryland" (Ph.D. diss., Brandeis University, 1976), 323–324, 349–350.

in towns: a third of the mills and two-fifths of the artisans' shops were located in the towns.[41]

The number of businesses that would entice a planter to spend a day in town increased greatly over the second half of the century. There were already four taverns, two stores, and a blacksmith shop in Bladensburg in the early 1740s, for instance, but Scottish storekeepers made it into "a great place of export" by the 1770s. The thirty-five householders in Bladensburg in 1776 included seven merchants, six tavernkeepers, two doctors, and four

---

41. Kulikoff, "Tobacco and Slaves," 349–351.

artisans, and the town also boasted a smith's shop, a shipyard, and a rope-walk.[42]

Although nearly every tidewater planter lived within easy commuting distance of a small village like Bladensburg by 1770, men in piedmont lived far from any town. The only crossroads found in most piedmont counties surrounded the courthouse and usually contained only a tavern and a general store, and few men lived close enough to visit there regularly. Planters in piedmont, like those of tidewater earlier in the century, ran their social lives on plantations and at churches, stores, courthouses, and taverns scattered through the countryside.[43]

The informal gatherings of tidewater men at muster, courthouse, hunt, cockfight, horse race, tavern, and store became more exclusive and regular over the eighteenth century. Symbolic occasions, such as races and musters, where relative strangers competed for honor diminished in significance when small villages proliferated and taverns and stores began serving neighborhoods each working day. Tidewater planters chose their compatriots carefully during pre-Revolutionary decades, seeking out the same small group of men weekly at tavern and general store and monthly when crowds gathered at courthouse, muster, or racetrack. The cumulative impact of this heightened intercourse among men was ambiguous. Though members of each informal group knew each other well and probably closed ranks when challenged by strangers, male solidarity never turned into daily cooperation, because groups of men formed only to assert their individuality and compete among themselves. Such competition did not establish status, but only temporarily reordered it among men of similar standing in the community. Two examples of feuds, one between tenants and the other between gentlemen, illustrate male competitiveness.

William Radwell and Jonas Dawson, two tenants who lived just north of Annapolis, bickered several times during the summer of 1760 "about their skill in Dancing a Jigg." They continued to exchange insults at a "petty Horse-Race" that August until "the Constable . . . told them, *Not to Swear; but they might Fight and be D——mn'd.*" In response to this command, "*Radwell* challeng'd *Dawson* to try then who was the *best Man*, as he term'd it, by Boxing." The fight began, but "after a few Blows, *Dawson* own'd he had enough, or that his Antagonist was the *best Man*." Both men accepted

42. *Ibid.*; *Md. Gaz.*, 1759–1762; Hienton, *Prince George's Heritage*, chap. 9; Brumbaugh, ed., *Maryland Records*, I, 1–88, linked to Prince George's Land Records; William Wirt Papers, II, 4904, Library of Congress.

43. Carville Earle and Ronald Hoffman, "Staple Crops and Urban Development in the Eighteenth-Century South," *Perspectives in American History*, X (1976), 60–61; *Journal of Du Roi the Elder . . .*, trans. Charlotte S. J. Epping (New York, 1911), 147–149.

the result of their battle, and after the fight was over, "they wash'd, shook Hands, and drank as Friends; but a few Minutes after *Dawson* dropp'd down Dead, and is suppos'd to have got his Death from a Blow he receiv'd on his Left Side." An ordinary competition thus turned into homicide: Radwell was convicted of manslaughter, and Dawson left "a poor Widow and five small Children" to fend for themselves.[44]

Robert Tyler and John Hepburn, both wealthy descendants of gentry families in Prince George's, became friendly after Tyler married a daughter of one of Hepburn's friends in the 1750s. Some years later, after a session of the county court where both men sat, they shared "the Jollity of the Night; and he [Hepburn] having drank much deeper than any one else," Tyler insisted that "he would either leave off Stammering, or direct his Discourse to some one else." The rest of the company joined in, and he "was soon laughed out." Tyler insisted that Hepburn held a grudge for this attack on his honor, an incident Hepburn considered "too trifling and ridiculous . . . to merit the least Notice." Hepburn claimed his revenge, if he sought it, during Tyler's 1765 campaign for a seat in the Maryland assembly. After the 1764 races at Piscataway, Tyler had "made some idle Expression . . . at a drinking Frolic." Though Tyler believed his drunken condition excused his behavior, Hepburn, who was not present, felt the comments suggested "Blasphemy and Treason" and reported them to the governor and urged Tyler to withdraw from the contest or "the Transaction wou'd probably be . . . urged against him at the Election." When Hepburn saw that Tyler would win the election despite this incident, he pretended to support him at the polls but didn't. The final act of this feud was played out in 1769, when both men carried their dispute to the *Maryland Gazette*.[45]

Women lived in a world often removed from the competition and violence their husbands and brothers shared. They responded to their relative powerlessness and frequent exclusion from some public places by forming their own social circles and by devising an alternative set of values based upon cooperation and charity. An exchange between Prize, a freeholder, and Lucy Twist, wife of a freeholder, at a racetrack barbecue before an election in Robert Munford's *Candidates* evokes these gender differences. Prize declares that he would not support Wou'dbe even though he "is a civil gentleman," for "he can't speak his mind so boldly as Mr. Strutabout, and commend me to a man that will speak his mind freely." Lucy Twist dissents from this male view: "Commend me to Mr. Wou'dbe, I say,—I nately like

44. *Md. Gaz.*, Aug. 21, Sept. 18, 1760. I found no land for either party in Anne Arundel Debt Books or Land Records.
45. *Md. Gaz.*, July 22, Aug. 31, 1769.

the man; he's mighty good to all his poor neighbours, and when he comes into a poor body's house, he's so free and so funny, is'nt he?"[46]

During the second half of the eighteenth century, daughters of gentry couples created strong social ties with their peers, continually exchanging visits and attending barbecues and balls together. When Maria Carter visited New England in 1764, she expected her married cousin Maria Beverley to write her an "account of every alteration in the Circle of Young Ladies" since she left, and Beverley did not disappoint her, relating three engagements as well as the birth of Carter's sister in one letter alone. The wealthiest gentry girls spent weeks with female kindred and friends. Eighteen-year-old Lucinda Lee Orr, for instance, paid extended visits to three aunts from September to November 1782. Nearly every day, she visited female neighbors, had female guests, dined with friends, or played with her female cousins. She entertained suitors at dances and formal dinners but otherwise viewed male attention as an unwanted intrusion.[47]

Wealthy adolescent girls often made deep and lasting friendships with young ladies they visited. When away from home, Lucinda Orr wrote a journal for her friend Polly Brent and frequently lamented the days she spent away from her. One evening, for instance, after her cousin Nancy Lee had commented that the "moonlight . . . reminded us of our absent Friends," Orr "joined in thinking so, and my thoughts were at that instant with my Polly." When a lady married, these friendships diminished in importance because the new wife had to please her husband and supervise the care of her children. Nonetheless, married women continued to visit friends, and their friendships were probably vigorously renewed when their daughters reached adolescence and required chaperons on their rounds of visits.[48]

Wives of poorer planters, who cared for children, kitchen, and garden, had less time for visiting, yet they occasionally went to a neighbor's home to see female friends, saw other women at church each Sunday, and provided aid in times of need. The tribulations of Jane Pattison of Calvert County, wife of a middling planter whose husband (as we have seen) repeatedly whipped her during the 1730s, document the activities of a female social

46. Hubbell and Adair, eds., "Munford's *The Candidates,*" *WMQ*, 3d Ser., V (1948), 240.
47. Daniel Blake Smith, *Inside the Great House: Planter Family Life in Eighteenth-Century Chesapeake Society* (Ithaca, N.Y., 1980), 73–79; Maria Beverley to Maria Carter, Apr. 20, 1764, in "Some Family Letters of the Eighteenth Century," *VMHB*, XV (1907–1908), 433–434; Emily Virginia Mason, ed., *Journal of a Young Lady of Virginia, 1782* (Baltimore, 1871); William K. Bottorff and Roy C. Flannagan, eds., "The Diary of Frances Baylor Hill of 'Hillsborough,' King and Queen County, Virginia (1797)," *Early American Literature Newsletter*, II, No. 3 (Winter 1967), 4–53; J. Hall Pleasants, ed., "Letters of Molly and Hetty Tilghman: Eighteenth-Century Gossip of Two Maryland Girls," *MHM*, XXI (1926), 20–39, 123–149, 219–241.
48. Mason, ed., *Journal of a Young Lady of Virginia*, 43.

network in admittedly extraordinary circumstances. A small circle of women aided Pattison; she showed her bruises to at least seven neighborhood women. Though Pattison was in her forties, her friends ranged in age from eighteen to fifty. She had known her older friends an average of twenty-four years and the younger women since they were children. She sought refuge at the home of Ann Smith, her neighbor and childhood friend, nine or ten times, complaining of beatings and showing "several Violent Bruises" each time. Once, after Dr. James Somerville treated her, several neighborhood women saw she "was then very bare of Cloaths" and persuaded her to go with them to a local store "to take necessaries for herself."[49]

Even when men and women gathered at dances, weddings, funerals, christenings, and church services, they sometimes huddled in their own groups. Husbands and wives witnessed weddings together but separated when the nuptial parties began. While men stood outside the church on Sundays discussing politics or organizing barbecues, women planned visits. At least three Anglican churches in tidewater Virginia institutionalized this practice by assigning men and women to separate pews. At Pohick Church in Fairfax County in the 1770s, for instance, magistrates and their wives sat on opposite sides of the communion table. Similarly, the "most respectable inhabitants and housekeepers" were divided by sex, with the men on the right side and their wives on the left side of the church.[50]

Men and women held such different values that they sometimes related to each other in awkward ways. Although boys and girls attended reading schools together, they met infrequently thereafter. Meanwhile, they learned their respective roles from adults of their own sex. Courtship could be an especially trying time: men competed for women, seeking to prove their worth or show their skill in dancing, and women searched for compassionate men or indulged in romantic fantasies. Gentry and yeoman children attended dancing school and, when they began courting, organized numerous dances where they could minimize conversation and mask social insecurity. After they married, men and women often went their separate ways and returned to their old social circles.[51]

49. Chancery Records, VI, 207–239, MHR. See chap. 5 for more on this case.
50. William Wirt to his children, June 25, 1825, Wirt Papers, II, 4913–4915; Allan Kulikoff, ed., " 'Throwing the Stocking,' A Gentry Marriage in Provincial Maryland," *MHM*, LXXI (1976), 520–521; Donald Sweig, "1649–1800," in Nan Netheron *et al.*, *Fairfax County, Virginia: A History* (Fairfax, Va., 1978), 74–76; C. G. Chamberlayne, ed., *The Vestry Book of Stratton Major Parish, King and Queen County, Virginia, 1729–1783* (Richmond, Va., 1931), 166–171; George Carrington Mason, *Colonial Churches of Tidewater Virginia* (Richmond, Va., 1945), fig. following 132.
51. Smith, *Inside the Great House*, 71–73, 130–139; Carson, *Virginians at Play*, 21–35; Isaac, *Transformation of Virginia*, 80–87; Chancery Records, XXX, 254, 257, 262, 269, 295; see chap. 5, above, for education.

The Parish Community

The Anglican parish church, often the first neighborhood institution on the frontier, remained an important community center long after the frontier had passed. The church was supposed to be the center of the community, where neighbors met weekly to join in communion with God and each other. All adults were required to attend church services monthly to participate in the rituals of the faith. This sense of community was symbolized by the insistence that every family report each birth, marriage, and death of a member to the parish so it could be recorded. And each household had to pay taxes to support parish activities and to construct and maintain churches.[52]

The parish community, ideally, was both universal and hierarchical. A self-perpetuating board of elders, called vestrymen, was responsible for allocating parish taxes and overseeing morality. Virginia vestrymen, or the churchwardens chosen from this group, were required to "present Persons not coming to Church; those who prophane the Sabbath, by Working, Traveling, Tipling at Ordinaries, ... Cursing, and all Persons who shall transgress any Penal Laws"—like those against blasphemy, bastardy, or fornication—"made for the Restraint of Vice and Immorality."[53]

Most parishes hardly fitted this image during the seventeenth and early eighteenth centuries, but the situation improved slowly thereafter. One writer complained in 1662 that Virginia parishes often lacked both church and minister. Moreover, families "of such Parishes" lived "at such distances from each other" and were so "remote from the House of God" that they often failed to attend church, "being discouraged, by the length or tediousnesse of the way, through extremities of heat in Summer, frost and Snow in Winter, and tempestuous weather in both." Though parishes built new churches, nearly a third of Chesapeake parishes still lacked a rector in 1700. Vacancies declined to one in eight by the mid-1720s and nearly dis-

52. Darrett B. Rutman, "The Evolution of Religious Life in Early Virginia," *Lex et Scientia*, XIV (1978), 190–213, esp. 197–200; Isaac, *Transformation of Virginia*, 58–65; Jan Lewis, *The Pursuit of Happiness: Family and Values in Jefferson's Virginia* (Cambridge, 1983), 43–48.

53. George Webb, *The Office and Authority of a Justice of Peace* ... (Williamsburg, Va., 1736), 71–83 (quote on 71); William H. Seiler, "The Anglican Church: A Basic Institution of Local Government in Colonial Virginia," in Bruce C. Daniels, ed., *Town and County: Essays on the Structure of Local Government in the American Colonies* (Middletown, Conn., 1978), 134–159; Joan Rezner Gundersen, "The Myth of the Independent Virginia Vestry," *Historical Magazine of the Protestant Episcopal Church*, XLIV (1975), 134–141; Gerald E. Hartdagen, "The Vestry as a Unit of Local Government in Colonial Maryland," *MHM*, LXVII (1972), 363–388; Hartdagen, "The Vestries and Morals in Colonial Maryland," *MHM*, LXIII (1968), 360–378.

appeared thereafter, but provincial assemblies never created enough parishes in frontier areas. In 1725 and 1775, tidewater Virginia parishes averaged between eighty and a hundred square miles and served between 200 and 250 families, but the area covered by frontier parishes increased from three hundred to nearly six hundred square miles, and the number of families in each rose from 450 to 550 between 1725 and 1775. Parishioners partially solved this problem by erecting one chapel of ease (a secondary house of worship for the parish) in tidewater parishes and one or two chapels in frontier areas where services were held on alternate weeks or where lay readers presided, or by appointing curates to assist the parish minister.[54]

Vestrymen enforced neither Anglican polity nor Christian morality in their parishes. They left discovery of fornication and bastardy to constables and rarely accused anyone of other transgressions of the moral code. Nor did they oversee adequate vital registration. When Henry Addison, rector of a parish in Prince George's, looked back on the system of parish registration in 1786, he concluded that it "is almost universally neglected." And he added that "if the rule were Established here that no marriage Should be deemed valid that had not been registered in the parish Book it would, I am persuaded, bastardize nine tenths of the people in this Country."[55]

Though Virginia vestrymen could have enforced conformity by reporting those who missed church, they pursued miscreants only when politically necessary. Those who lived far from church could not get there, and even if they did, there would be no room for them in already-crowded buildings. Between 1734 and 1774 Caroline County vestrymen brought only eighty-two people to court for not attending church, and nearly three-quarters of them were charged in only five of those years. The most concerted cam-

54. R. G., *Virginia's Cure; or, An Advisive Narrative concerning Virginia* . . . (London, 1662), 3–4, reprinted in Peter Force, ed., *Tracts and Other Papers Relating Principally to the Origin, Settlement, and Progress of the Colonies in North America* . . . , III (Washington, D.C., 1844); George MacLaren Brydon, *Virginia's Mother Church and the Political Conditions under Which It Grew* (Richmond, Va., 1947), I, 363–364, 374–382; Carol L. van Voorst, "The Anglican Clergy in Maryland, 1692–1776" (Ph.D. diss., Princeton University, 1978), 98–101, 150–165, 183–187, 199–201; William Stevens Perry, ed., *Papers Relating to the History of the Church in Virginia, 1650–1776* (Geneva, N.Y., 1870), 261–318; "'A List of Parishes and the Ministers in Them [1774],'" *WMQ*, 1st Ser., V (1896–1897), 200–202; Nelson W. Rightmyer, *Maryland's Established Church* (Baltimore, 1956), 45–46, 135–152; Robert Beverley, *The History and Present State of Virginia* (1705), ed. Louis B. Wright (Chapel Hill, N.C., 1947), 253. Parish vacancies include all of Virginia and Maryland; tidewater Virginia includes only the James and Rappahannock river watersheds.
55. Kulikoff, "Tobacco and Slaves," 574; for a different view, see Hartdagen, "Vestry as a Unit of Local Government," *MHM*, LXVII (1972), 363–388; and "The Vestries and Morals," *MHM*, LXIII (1968), 360–378.

paigns came in 1738, when a local woman reported seventeen neighbors for missing church, and in late 1768, when the vestry prosecuted sixteen Baptists, including the preacher, for missing Anglican services.[56]

Only about two-fifths of the white families in the Chesapeake region participated regularly in Anglican worship early in the eighteenth century, and as piedmont Virginia was settled, that proportion dropped to just over a third by the 1770s (see fig. 20). In tidewater Virginia, an area well supplied with parishes, about half the whites came to services during the middle third of the century, but only a third participated in piedmont Virginia, and only a seventh at the edge of the frontier, despite the creation of twenty-one new parishes there between 1725 and 1775.[57]

The failure of Anglicans to attract most white families gave dissenters ample opportunity to convert the unchurched, but Anglicans had little competition until the 1750s. Even in 1750, about half of Chesapeake whites were unchurched, and only one in ten practiced the Catholic, Presbyterian, or Quaker faith, and they constituted only a fifth of the active Christians in

56. Hartdagen, "Vestry as a Unit of Local Government," *MHM*, LXVII (1972), 365; Brydon, *Virginia's Mother Church*, I, 366–368, II, 156–158, 173; T. E. Campbell, *Colonial Caroline: A History of Caroline County, Virginia* (Richmond, Va., 1954), 96–97, 133–134, 200–205, 435–437. A. G. Roeber, *Faithful Magistrates and Republican Lawyers: Creators of Virginia Legal Culture, 1680–1810* (Chapel Hill, N.C., 1981), 141–142, shows that grand jury presentments for missing church ranked as one of the three most common offenses, but he does not give number of presentments and includes Caroline County among his counties.

57. Numerical estimates made in this and succeeding paragraphs are based upon these sources and use the methods of fig. 20. Evarts B. Greene and Virginia D. Harrington, *American Population before the Federal Census of 1790* (New York, 1932), 128–129, 149–151; "Number of Inhabitants in Maryland," *Gentleman's Magazine, and Historical Chronicle*, XXXIV (1764), 261; Kulikoff, "Tobacco and Slaves," 428–430; "Inspector's Accounts, 1786," VSL; Edwin Scott Gaustad, *Historical Atlas of Religion in America*, rev. ed. (New York, 1976), 11, 20; Lester J. Cappon *et al.*, eds., *Atlas of Early American History: The Revolutionary Era, 1760–1790* (Princeton, N.J., 1976), 36, 39; Patricia U. Bonomi and Peter R. Eisenstadt, "Church Adherence in the Eighteenth-Century British American Colonies," *WMQ*, 3d Ser., XXXIX (1982), 245–286; "A List of Parishes and the Ministers in Them [1774]," *WMQ*, 1st Ser., V (1896–1897), 200–202; Rightmyer, *Maryland's Established Church*, 135–152; Thomas Hughes, *History of the Society of Jesus in North America, Colonial and Federal* (London, 1908–1917), Text, II, *From 1645 till 1773*, 541–542; William Hand Browne *et al.*, eds., *Archives of Maryland* ... (Baltimore, 1883–1972), XXV, 258; Lois Green Carr and David William Jordan, *Maryland's Revolution of Government, 1689–1692* (Ithaca, N.Y., 1974), 33–34; Rufus M. Jones, *Quakers in the American Colonies* (New York, 1911), xvi; Kenneth L. Carroll, ed., "Robert Pleasants on Quakerism: 'Some Account of the First Settlement of Friends in Virginia ... ,'" *VMHB*, LXXXVI (1978), 7–8; Carroll, *Quakerism on the Eastern Shore* (Baltimore, 1970), 202; Beverley, *History and Present State of Virginia*, ed. Wright, 261–262; Richard L. Morton, *Colonial Virginia: Westward Expansion and the Prelude to Revolution* (Chapel Hill, N.C., 1960), I, 388–391; "An Account of All the ... Meetings of the People Called Quakers in the several Provinces in America ... , 1776," Quaker Collection, Haverford College, Haverford, Pa.; Robert B. Semple, *A History of the Rise and Progress of Baptists in Virginia* (Richmond, Va., 1894), esp. 78–79.

Fig. 20. *Religious Communions in the Chesapeake*

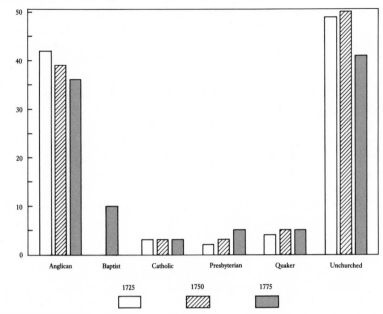

Sources: Cited in n. 57.

Note: Estimates are of adult adherents and exclude Frederick County, Maryland, and Virginia west of the mountains. The Anglican estimate for 1725 is based upon reported numbers attending services and for 1775 on number of parishes, assuming 600 people came regularly. The 1750 estimate is an average of the 1725 and 1775 numbers, and the population base includes all whites over the age of 10. The 1725 estimate of Catholics was based on a 1708 Maryland census, and the estimates of 1750 and 1775 assumed a direct relationship between the percentage of land held by Maryland Catholics and their share of its population. The Quaker estimate for 1775 follows a conjecture by Rufus Jones, and the 1725 and 1750 estimates were calculated from the number of meetings and the ratio of members to meetings in 1775. All Presbyterian estimates assumed that there were 50 households per church. The 1775 Baptist estimate was calculated by applying the ratio of known members to known churches to the total number of churches, a number then doubled to take into account adherents who were not baptized members and then divided by adult population.

the two colonies. Most dissenters lived in Maryland, where the Anglican church was not established until the 1690s, but even there only a third of practicing Christians were dissenters. Maryland's Catholics were concentrated in just two counties; most of her Quakers lived on the Eastern Shore; and Presbyterians worshiped wherever Scots or Scots-Irish immigrated.

Unchurched folk may have known the rudiments of Christianity, but they cared little for organized religion. Devereux Jarratt, the Methodist divine, grew up in nonreligious households. Though he read religious texts in school and memorized chapters of the Bible, he lived with irreligious brothers as an adolescent after his parents died. "During the 5 or 6 years, I continued with my brothers," Jarratt recalled, "I do not remember ever to have seen or heard any thing of a religious nature." Even though "there was a church in the parish, within three miles of me, and a great many people attended it," he continued, "I went not once in a year."[58]

After 1750, evangelical preachers repeatedly attacked irreligion in Virginia, focusing particularly upon unchurched planters in piedmont, men the Anglican ministry ignored. New Light Presbyterians worked over the land in the late 1750s and 1760s, and Baptists joined them in the late 1760s, and together they converted thousands of people. Anglican ministers soon recognized this assault. In 1769 a congregation in the Northern Neck piedmont urged division of their parish because "many of the Inhabitants reside so far from their Parish Churches that they can but seldom attend Public Worship; from which causes Dissenters have . . . encouragement to progate their pernicious Doctrines." But the Anglican response came too late; by 1775 only a third of piedmont's families actively participated in the established church, but another third belonged to evangelical churches, and a twentieth worshiped at Quaker meetings.[59]

Despite the inroads made by dissenters in piedmont, a large majority of practicing Christians in tidewater prayed at Anglican churches, where they formed a community of believers. When the vestry of Queen Anne Parish in Prince George's randomly laid out pews in the parish chapel in 1742, throwing parishioners out of their accustomed seats, some parishioners complained that it would disrupt the good communal relations they had developed over the past thirty years. Ever since the chapel opened, the minister had "read the Prayers of the Church" and preached there on alternate Sundays, and the petitioners "did attend divine Service, and at their own Cost provided themselves with handsome Seats," which they had used for twenty-five years.[60]

The weekly sabbath service was both a religious and a social occasion. It was the largest regular gathering of whites in dispersed tidewater society, attracting two hundred people or more in good weather, but many fewer during the winter, when inclement weather and illness kept many away. The

58. *The Life of the Rev. Devereux Jarratt, Rector of Bath Parish, Dinwiddie County, Virginia, Written by Himself* (Baltimore, 1806), 17–21.

59. H. C. Groome, *Fauquier during the Proprietorship: A Chronicle of the Colonization and Organization of a Northern Neck County* (Richmond, Va., 1927), 141–143; for the spread of revivalism, see Wesley M. Gewehr, *The Great Awakening in Virginia, 1740–1790* (Chapel Hill, N.C., 1930), chaps. 3–6.

60. Browne *et al.*, eds., *Archives of Maryland*, XXVIII, 285–289 (quote on 285).

minister of Albemarle Parish in Sussex County, Virginia, made a unique record of the number of communicants in his parish in the 1750s and 1760s. As the number of parish families grew by about 50 percent in those decades, the attendance at each of the four parish churches rose from about 225 to 300. While the throngs at church during spring and summer grew from 250 to 350 from 1749 to 1771, winter attendance increased from about 200 to just 225.[61]

Only freeholders regularly attended Anglican services. During the 1730s about a quarter of the white families of Prince George's County, an area with both frontier and long-established parishes, were Anglicans, while another tenth were Catholics, Quakers, or Presbyterians. Wealthy and long-established families came to church more often than their poorer and more transient neighbors. Nearly two-thirds of the established families who owned land and slaves prayed at Anglican services, and they constituted half the congregation. Most of the rest of the active members owned land or slaves. Fewer than two in forty tenant nonslaveholders came to church, filling only a tenth of the seats, and many of them were sons of freeholders, waiting for their inheritances (see table 28).

Philip Fithian, a tutor in the home of Robert Carter of Nomini Hall, captured the swirl of action when members arrived at a church in Westmoreland County in 1774. There were, he wrote, "three grand divisions of time at the Church on Sundays, Viz. before Service giving and receiving letters of business, reading Advertisements, consulting about the price of Tobacco . . . and settling either the lineage, Age, or qualities of favourite Horses." Then the congregation entered the church, with "prayrs read over in haste, a Sermon seldom under and never over twenty minutes, but always made up of sound morality, or deep studied Metaphysics." When the service ended, the people spent "three quarters of an hour . . . in strolling round the Church among the Crowd, in which time you will be invited by several different Gentlemen home with them to dinner."[62]

Eighteenth-century planters applied their ideas of social order to church activities, irretrievably mixing the profane and sacred. Ordinary

---

61. Bonomi and Eisenstadt, "Church Adherence," *WMQ*, 3d Ser., XXXIX (1982), 254–262; Albemarle Parish estimates derived from number of communicants, 1749–1771, determined from linear regression each of the four times communion was given each year (divided by four [churches], and multiplied by four [ratio of communicants to those attending, 1724]) found in Gertrude Richards, ed., *Register of Albemarle Parish, Surry and Essex Counties, Virginia, 1738–1778* (Richmond, Va., 1958), 1–6.
62. Hunter Dickinson Farish, ed., *Journal and Letters of Philip Vickers Fithian, 1773–1774: A Plantation Tutor of the Old Dominion*, new ed. (Williamsburg, Va., 1967), 167–168. A brilliant evocation of the Virginia Anglican communion is found in Isaac, *Transformation of Virginia*, 58–68.

Table 28. *Active Anglican Church Membership in Prince George's County in the 1730s*

Socioeconomic Group[a]	Probability of Active Membership[b] (Percentage)	Percentage of Church Members ($N=297$)	Percentage of Population ($N=1,034$)
Established families owning land and slaves	65	47	21
More transient families owning land and slaves	41	13	9
Established families owning land or slaves	37	21	16
More transient families owning land or slaves	21	10	14
Tenant nonslaveholders long resident in county	14	5	10
All other tenants	3	3	29
Overall	26[c]	99	99

Sources: Vestry Books of St. Paul's, Queen Anne's, Prince George's, and Piscataway parishes, MHR (lists of church officers; pew lists for Piscataway [1724], St. Paul's [1735], and Queen Anne's [1735, 1742]; and a subscription list for a new church in Prince George's [1726]) compared with data from Black Books, II, 110–124 (1733 tithables list), X, 8–14 (1719 tithables list) and Prince George's Land Records and Court Records, all MHR.

Notes: [a]Established individuals are those whose families lived in the county in 1719 and continued to live there at least through 1743; more transient families moved to the county after 1719 or left before 1743. Those members of families who died before 1743 but lived in the county from 1719 are counted as established. [b]Active church members were those that (1) served in church office, (2) held a pew, (3) signed the subscription list, or (4) were the parent, child, or sibling of a pew holder. The base population excludes those whose land- and slave-holding status could not be determined and all known Catholics, Presbyterians, and Quakers. Since many dissenters and Catholics probably escaped notice, the known dissenters were multiplied by two, and the additional people subtracted from the base population as they appeared in the entire population. [c]All the percentages but the "overall" are calculated after excluding Catholics and dissenters, but the 26% represents the part of the entire population that actively participated in the Anglican church.

planters entered the church first and found their way to their pews or to unassigned seats in the gallery. Gentlemen arrived late and made a grand entrance just as the service began and left in a body after all others had departed. The seating arrangements of several eighteenth-century churches symbolically represented the prevailing social structure. Wealthy gentlemen purchased the best pews and, each Sunday, sat apart from their less prestigious neighbors. The Pohick Church in Fairfax County, where George Washington worshiped, established a seating hierarchy as soon as it opened in 1772. Magistrates, vestrymen, and invited guests sat across from the communion table. The wealthiest gentlemen and merchants, including George Washington and George Fairfax, owned pews in front of the communion table, and other important men, including George Mason, sat behind the vestry. Less wealthy but respectable planters owned pews behind the pulpit in the rear of the church. A similar seating plan could be found at the new church of Stratton Major Parish, King and Queen County, in 1767. Distinguished gentlemen and their families sat at the front of the church, followed by vestrymen, gentlemen, and yeomen.[63]

Once they were seated, parishioners heard the ancient liturgy of the Church of England, a service that connected each listener to God, neighbors, and the high culture of England. Services began with morning prayers and the litany and ended with a sermon. Every Sunday the minister or lay reader spent close to an hour leading the congregation through responsive prayers from both testaments, psalms, benedictions, the creed, and the Lord's Prayer—all meant to remind parishioners of the sinfulness of men and the need for repentance. Members followed along in prayer books and responded in unison when called upon. Most regular communicants probably memorized much of the lyrical and elevating language they heard so often.[64]

The minister addressed his sermon, the high point of the service, to educated men rather than to the majority of semiliterate people in his audience. He typically expounded for half an hour on Christian virtue or Christian doctrine, sometimes citing Greek or Latin texts and always pointing frequently to the Bible. Thomas Cradock, a clergyman from Baltimore County, explained in a 1767 sermon that it was necessary to preach repeatedly on virtue because "the Life of every sincere Christian is a warfare against a great number of Enemies, some of them very potent, and others very politick. Virtue is a rich Prey rescued narrowly out of the Fire, the purchase of Labor and sweat of Care and Vigilance."[65]

63. Farish, ed., *Journal of Fithian*, 29; Isaac, *Transformation of Virginia*, 59–65; Sweig, "1649–1800," in Netherton *et al.*, eds., *Fairfax County*, 74–77; Chamberlayne, ed., *Vestry Book of Stratton Major*, 166–171.
64. Marion J. Hachett, "A Sunday Service in 1776 or Thereabouts," *Hist. Mag. Prot. Epis. Ch.*, XLV (1976), 369–385; Isaac, *Transformation of Virginia*, 58–68. The time the service took and the contents of the prayer book were checked in John E. Booty, ed., *The Book of Common Prayer, 1559: The Elizabethan Prayer Book* (Charlottesville, Va., 1976), 49–60, 68–76, 247–268 (assuming two to three minutes per page).
65. The fullest description of sermons is found in Richard Beale Davis, *Intellectual Life in the Colonial South, 1585–1763*, 3 vols. (Knoxville, Tenn., 1978), II, chap. 6; but David Curtis

Virginia ministers celebrated communion just before the sermon four times a year, but their Maryland colleagues administered the Sacrament bimonthly. Despite the slender requirements for receiving communion—a person had to be confirmed and of sound moral character—some adults and most children who attended services were not communicants. In 1724 about a quarter of those present took communion. Some of them may have taken communion irregularly, but age, ignorance, and poverty also kept many parishioners from the communion table. Though children were supposed to learn the catechism and then be confirmed when adolescents, ministers catechized youths only during Lent, and many may have skipped confirmation. Adults, even if confirmed, may have felt uncomfortable receiving communion with their social superiors, especially since the collection preceded the ritual.[66]

Parishioners went to Sunday services to enjoy the liturgy, to affirm their position in the social hierarchy, and to conduct business. Participants held prescribed seats that showed them their place in the society, and the sermon often reinforced the hierarchy by extolling the duties that servants owed to their masters or that citizens paid to magistrates. After the service concluded, everyday concerns exploded. Each parishioner, an acerbic Presbyterian complained in 1769, "attends worship . . . only to make bargains, hear and rehearse news, fix horse races and cock matches, and learn if there are any barbecued Hogs to be offered in sacrifice Gratis to satisfy a voracious appetite." This mixture of secular and sacred activities appealed to those white freeholders and their families who formed a community each Sunday at church.[67]

Circles within Circles: Kinship in the Colonial Chesapeake

Although white families ultimately made kinship, rather than gender or church membership, the basis of social intercourse, initially the conditions

---

Skaggs, "Thomas C. Cradock and the Chesapeake Golden Age," *WMQ*, 3d Ser., XXX (1973), 93–116, is also valuable (quote from 101). The length of sermons is estimated from seven Cradock sermons, six found in the Maryland Diocesan Archives, Baltimore, and used with the kind permission of David Curtis Skaggs, and the other in Skaggs, "Thomas Cradock's Sermon on the Governance of Maryland's Established Church," *WMQ*, 3d Ser., XXVII (1970), 637–653, assuming two to three minutes per manuscript page.

66. Bonomi and Eisenstadt, "Church Adherence," *WMQ*, 3d Ser., XXXIX (1982), 260–262, 277–283; Brydon, *Virginia's Mother Church*, I, 372–373, 380–382; Booty, ed., *Book of Common Prayer*, 405–406; Hachett, "Sunday Service in 1776," *Hist. Mag. Prot. Epis. Ch.*, XLV (1976), 376–383.

67. Reid, "Religion of the Bible," 50.

of life (and death) had seriously reduced the numbers of living kin. Continued immigration kept the proportion of blood relatives living in each neighborhood small. The persistence of this pattern depended upon the time of settlement. For instance, there were few large kin groups in Middlesex County, Virginia, settled in the mid-seventeenth century, until early in the eighteenth century. Although four-fifths of the heads of households in that county were linked by ties of friendship to other, unrelated families in 1704, half the heads had no kinship ties to other households in the county. By 1724, four-fifths of county householders were kindred to at least one other county family. But in the Patuxent River watershed of Prince George's in 1719, forty years after the first pioneers arrived, only one in eleven families shared its name with even four other households, and many of the rest had no patrilineal kindred at all.[68]

Since most kindred of early settlers either lived in England or had died, planters relied upon the conjugal family rather than the lineage. Parents tended to give first-born sons and daughters their own names, highlighting the importance of the nuclear family unit, rather than the name of a grandparent, aunt, or uncle, which would have symbolically linked the child with the paternal or maternal lineage. Nearly two-thirds of a group of gentry and prosperous freeholder families in Prince George's named first sons for fathers in the 1680s and 1690s, and two-fifths named first daughters for mothers. Such practices were not confined to prosperous families. First-born sons were named for their fathers four times more often than for paternal grandfathers in seventeenth-century Middlesex County, and first-born daughters were two and a half times more likely to bear the mother's than the maternal grandmother's name.[69]

With the decline of immigration and the increase in life expectancy at the start of the eighteenth century, concentration of kindred in neighborhoods rose sharply. In response, planters and their families became more aware of extended kin, a pattern documented by the increasing proportion of parents who honored the family line of both husband and wife by giving first (and subsequent) children the names of grandparents, uncles, and aunts. In addition, families interacted more frequently with local kin, rather than with unrelated neighbors. Extended kin drew ever closer, exchanging rounds of visits, sharing church pews, and marrying blood relatives with rising regularity. Grandparents, in particular, appeared for the first time in

68. Rutman and Rutman, " 'More True and Perfect Lists,' " *VMHB*, LXXXVIII (1980), 40–42, 67–74; Hienton, *Prince George's Heritage*, 37–41; Lois G. Carr, "County Government in Maryland," 566–575; Black Books, X, 8–14.
69. Rutman and Rutman, *A Place in Time: Explicatus*, 88–95; figs. 21, 22, and sources cited there.

the region and often gave grandchildren property in their wills. Indeed, kindred viewed neighborhood needs and even questions of political loyalty (as we have seen) in light of the desires of extended kindred.

The number of patrilineal kindred living near each other rose in the eighteenth century through a process of selective migration. A motley group of freeholders, tenants, and laborers moved from settled areas to frontiers, but only those planters who patented enough land for themselves and their sons could start family networks. Some kinfolk moved to adjacent tracts on the frontier, and after a couple of generations their sons, nephews, and grandchildren farmed the lands they had acquired. The complexity of neighborhood kin relationships grew as children and grandchildren of the pioneers married neighbors.[70]

The settlement of the Potomac River basin of Prince George's and of Lunenburg County illustrates this process. Planters began farming land near the Potomac River in the late 1690s, and by 1719 nearly 250 families lived there. Kinfolk sometimes moved together, for about two of every five householders shared surnames with other families, but half of these patrilineal groups contained only two households, usually a father and adult son or two brothers. The area's population more than doubled during the 1720s as families moved further into the interior, but concentrations of kinfolk nonetheless began to proliferate. Nearly three of every five families living in the area in 1733 shared surnames with other families, and one-eighth of them were members of just nine family groups. At least one member of eight of these nine families had formed a household in the area during the 1710s (see fig. 21).

The pioneers who carved out farms in the Potomac wilderness patented great quantities of land and held much of it for future generations. As the descendants of these men reached maturity, they established plantations on this land and inadvertently built ever larger patrilineages. By 1776 more than two-thirds of the families in the area shared surnames with other householders, and most of them lived close to brothers, sons, or cousins. Two-thirds of the planters who had paternal kin in the area lived within two miles of blood relations, nearly half of them residing on land next to a kinsman. Almost a tenth of area residents belonged to six patrilineages containing at least ten households each. Members of these large and established families lived even closer together; more than a third were near neighbors, and three-quarters of the rest lived just a couple of miles away.[71]

70. See chap. 4 for the operation of this migration system.
71. Of 611 households that shared surnames in 1776, 28% lived within five names of another blood relative on the 1776 census (listed geographically), and 68% lived in the same taxing district. Similar figures for larger family groups were 36% residing on adjacent farms and 85% living in the same taxing district.

Fig. 21. *Patrilineal Kinship in Prince George's County, 1719–1776*

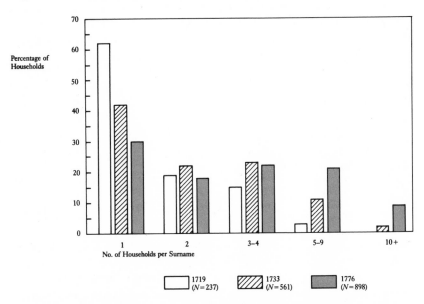

Sources: Black Books, X, 8–14, II, 109–124 (1719, 1733 tithables lists), MHR; Gaius Marcus Brumbaugh, ed., *Maryland Records: Colonial, Revolutionary, County, and Church, from Original Sources*, I (Baltimore, 1915), 1–88. I excluded common names from the figure, but undoubtedly a few of those who shared surnames with others were not paternal kin. Wife's blood relations could not be counted.

Pioneers reached Lunenburg County, in Virginia's southside, in the 1730s and 1740s, forty years after they reached the Potomac in Prince George's. So many farmers moved there during the 1740s that the county taxed nearly two hundred families in 1750. Patrilineal kin flocked together to the county, for in 1750 four of every ten families already shared surnames with others in the county, and one in every eight belonged to paternal groups of five or more families—a proportion four times as great as in Prince George's at a similar point in its history. Ever-growing proportions of the county's households were members of paternal kinship groups. By 1783 the extent of patrilineal kinship in Lunenburg equaled that of Prince George's. Only a quarter of the heads of household in that year had no patrilineal kin living in the county, and more than a tenth of them counted nine or more families among their paternal blood relations (see fig. 22).

The history of a neighborhood near the Eastern Branch in Prince George's suggests how settlement and marriage patterns turned unrelated neighbors into close kindred. In the 1710s ten families settled a five-

Fig. 22. *Patrilineal Kinship in Lunenburg County, 1750–1783*

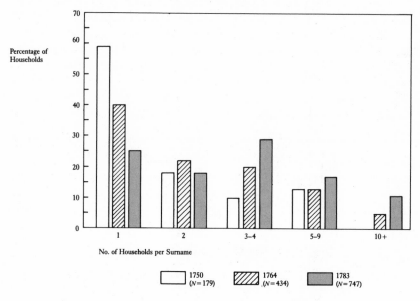

Sources: Landon C. Bell, ed., *Sunlight on the Southside: Lists of Tithes, Lunenburg County, Virginia, 1748–1783* (Philadelphia, 1931), 387–417. This figure includes only taxed families living within Lunenburg's post-1764 bounds. Richard Beeman permitted me to use his alphabetical printout of the 1750 and 1764 lists.

square-mile area several miles from the source of the Eastern Branch. At least five of the families moved from the same neighborhood, but only Ninian Beall and his second cousin James Edmonston were blood relations. In 1733, when seventeen families lived on the same land, the number of kin ties had increased substantially. Robert Brasshers's sons were children in 1719, but Robert and two sons farmed adjacent homesteads in 1733. Similarly, young Lancelot Wilson started a plantation near his father's during the 1720s. One Traile and one Nicholls lived in the neighborhood in 1719, but two of each family resided there in 1733. And Jonathan Waddams, related to Beall and Edmonston, moved to the area in the 1720s.

The number of kin ties between these neighbors continued to rise as Ninian Beall and his wife Catherine Duke reared twelve children, born between 1723 and 1746. These children grew up with each other and with the children of unrelated neighbors; no Dukes lived in the county, and only one Beall aunt, with her children, lived within five miles of the farm. Two daughters and four sons married and farmed land adjoining the family plantation between 1745 and 1771. Four of the six children married close neighbors, and another wed a remote cousin who lived just outside the area. During the 1770s, Ninian's grandchildren associated with the many cousins, aunts, uncles, and in-laws who lived on adjacent plantations.

A census in 1776 provides a benchmark for assessing the impact of kinship on neighborhood organization (see map 16). Twenty-four freeholders and some tenants lived on a six-square-mile area surrounding the plantation of Ninian Beall, Sr. All but four of the landowners were related to at least one other family in the neighborhood, and these four lived near the bounds of the area and probably had kinfolk nearby. Twelve Bealls or Beall relations dominated a three-square-mile area around Ninian Senior's farm. Each of these twelve families owned 150–200 acres of land and held a slave or two, and they were connected in a web of kinship that bound each family to nearly every one of the other eleven.[72] Zachariah Brown and his wife Margery Beall lived with her father, Ninian Senior, and Ninian's near neighbors included families of four sons, two daughters, two grandsons, and two in-laws of Beall's children.[73]

As soon as the number of kindred living in tidewater neighborhoods increased, the lineage took on increased symbolic importance. Eighteenth-century parents, for instance, named first sons for grandfathers and uncles far more frequently than did their immigrant ancestors and waited to name a later son for his father, thus stressing the importance of lineage over the conjugal family. In Middlesex County, parents generally named first sons for paternal grandfathers and second sons for their fathers. The proportion of yeoman and gentry parents naming first sons for fathers in Prince George's declined continually from two-thirds in the seventeenth century to only a quarter by the 1770s. At the same time, the proportion of first sons named for grandfathers rose from less than one of six to around half (see fig. 23).[74]

72. The history of the Beall family and its neighborhood was compiled with the help of Margaret Cook and her Beall genealogical files. Mean acreage of the 12 households equaled 234 acres, and mean number of taxable slaves was 1.3 and of total slaves was 2.6. Two of the families were slaveless, and one was a tenant. Six owned between 160 and 260 acres, and eight owned one or two taxable slaves.
73. Kulikoff, "Tobacco and Slaves," 538–541, details these relationships. J. A. Barnes, *Social Networks*, Addison-Wesley Module in Anthropology, No. 26 (Reading, Mass., 1972), 6–11, defines social network zones as the sum of "all the relations" between all the members of a network, and that sum divided by the number of participants as the "density" of the zone. There were 66 possible pairs of relationships between the 12 members of the Beall network. If one includes parents, siblings, blood uncles and aunts, and first cousins along with sons-in-law, fathers-in-law, and siblings-in-law, then the density of the network was 38 of 66, or 58%. If relations of spouses of heads of household are included, the density was 47 of 66, or 71%.
74. For Middlesex, see Rutman and Rutman, *A Place in Time: Explicatus*, 88–95; for Prince George's, see figs. 23, 24. Daniel S. Smith's sophisticated essay, "Child-Naming Patterns,

Map 16. *Ninian Beall's Relatives in His Neighborhood, 1776*

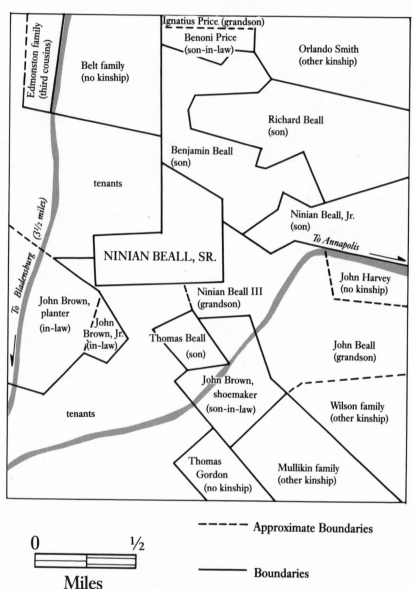

Source: Margaret Cook, Beall Genealogical Files.

Fig. 23. *Names Given First Sons in Prince George's County, 1680–1820*

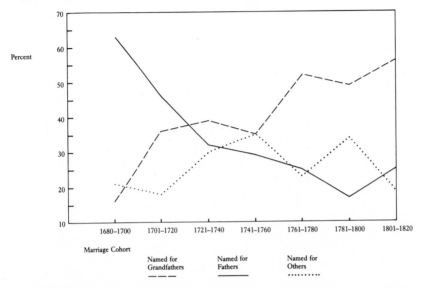

Sources: Harry Wright Newman, *Mareen Duvall of Middle Plantation* (Washington, D.C., 1952); Effie Gwynn Bowie, *Across the Years in Prince George's County* (Richmond, Va., 1947); Margaret Cook, Beall genealogy files. Christopher Johnston, "Sprigg Family," *Maryland Historical Magazine*, VIII (1913), 74–84; "Belt Family," *MHM*, VIII (1913), 195–202; "Brooke Family," *MHM*, I (1906), 66–73, 184–188, 284–289, 376–380. Data on the Duvalls were compiled by Michele M. Donovan, "Child-Naming Patterns of the Mareen Duvall Family through 1860" (paper, Bryn Mawr College, 1981). The smallest number of families in a cohort was 19, and the other cohorts ranged from 28 to 58.

A similar pattern can be seen in the names given first daughters. Parents in eighteenth-century Middlesex usually named first daughters for maternal grandmothers and second daughters for their mothers. Fewer than two of every five first daughters held the names of their mothers in the 1680s and 1690s in Prince George's, and that proportion declined to around one in five by the 1760s and 1770s, similar to that for first sons. Mothers reached back into the lineage and increasingly gave first daughters the name of a grandmother. As many firstborn daughters held the names of grandmothers as of mothers during the seventeenth century, but two to four times as many were named for grandmothers during the eighteenth century (see fig. 24).

Most parents wished to see their names carried into future genera-

Kinship Ties, and Change in Family Attitudes in Hingham, Massachusetts, 1641 to 1800," *Journal of Social History*, XVIII (1985), 541–566, serves as a model for this analysis.

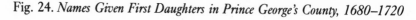

Fig. 24. *Names Given First Daughters in Prince George's County, 1680–1720*

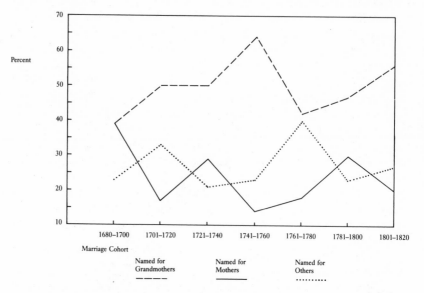

Sources: Harry Wright Newman, *Mareen Duvall of Middle Plantation* (Washington, D.C., 1952); Effie Gwynn Bowie, *Across the Years in Prince George's County* (Richmond, Va., 1947); Margaret Cook, Beall genealogy files. Christopher Johnston, "Sprigg Family," *Maryland Historical Magazine,* VIII (1913), 74–84; "Belt Family," *MHM,* VIII (1913), 195–202; "Brooke Family," *MHM,* I (1906), 66–73, 184–188, 284–289, 376–380. Data on the Duvalls were compiled by Michele M. Donovan, "Child-Naming Patterns of the Mareen Duvall Family through 1860" (paper, Bryn Mawr College, 1981). The smallest cohort of families was 13, and the rest ranged from 22 to 45.

tions, and eventually named children after themselves. Nine-tenths of the couples married in Prince George's during the 1680s and 1690s gave a son his father's name, and two-thirds named a daughter for her mother. As life expectancy improved, couples often waited and named later children for themselves. But since some adults died while still young, fewer families had children who carried on the parental name. Between the 1740s and the 1820s, only three-fifths of the families named a son for his father, and only one-half of them gave a daughter her mother's name.[75]

75. The proportions of families naming sons for fathers by 20-year marriage cohorts, beginning with 1680–1700, were 90%, 77%, 67%, 57%, 61%, 60%, and 59%; similar percentages for daughters were 68, 58, 62, 54, 46, 52, and 48. The smallest group of men was 30, of women, 28. The data were weighted by the number of children of that sex, with those with one or two children counted as one-third, and those with three or more counted as two-thirds.

Even though parents named fewer children for themselves, they gave the names of grandparents to their children with undiminished vigor throughout the eighteenth century. When parents named children for grandparents, they rarely sought future inheritances. Fathers gave most land to sons; if parents had sought to elicit a gift of land or slaves for their children, they would have named children primarily after paternal grandparents. Yet Prince George's families particularly remembered maternal grandparents, thereby symbolically reinstating the wife's tie with her parents that she severed at marriage. About three of every five firstborn sons and daughters named for grandparents received the name of a maternal grandparent. Although parents chose equally between maternal and paternal grandmothers, nearly twice as many first sons received the name of their mother's father as of their father's father. As mothers bore more children, they continued to name offspring for grandparents not yet honored, but the bias toward the female lineage continued. Though nearly two-thirds of all parents named a son for a maternal grandfather, only half named a daughter for her paternal grandmother.[76]

As new children were born and took their place in the family, they too received kin names. More than three-quarters of the children born into large families in Prince George's during the eighteenth century were named for blood relations. Parents first ensured that their names and those of their parents would be perpetuated and then selected favorite brothers and sisters to serve as namesakes for their children. A typical family of seven children included one child named for a parent, two for grandparents, and two for aunts and uncles. Parents alternated between the lineages of father and mother, choosing half their children's names from each. This naming system placed infants into a vast network of grandparents, aunts, and uncles, and, by implication, the children of aunts and uncles, their first cousins.[77]

76. The proportions naming first children for paternal grandparents of those named for grandparents for 20-year marriage cohorts beginning in 1680 were 45% ($N = 22$), 37% ($N = 38$), 26% ($N = 27$), 49% ($N = 39$), 27% ($N = 33$), and 48% ($N = 58$), an alteration without trend. Data on naming for mothers' fathers and fathers' mothers are from Michelle M. Donovan, "Child-Naming Patterns of the Mareen Duvall Family through 1860" (seminar paper, Bryn Mawr College, 1981), 3–4.

77. These data cover the 1725–1775 marriage cohorts and exclude the Duvalls. Families entered the sample when there were three or more children of one sex and when the names of all grandparents, uncles, and aunts were known. This 50-family sample, which contains 341 children, is heavily weighted toward wealthy gentlemen, but there were no changes over time or between larger and smaller families within the group: 17% were named for parents, 32% for grandparents, 13% for parents' siblings, 5% for more remote kin; and 23% for people outside the family.

Revolutionary practices and republican ideology bent but failed to undermine this naming system. During the 1780s and 1790s, parents added *George, Martha,* and *Benjamin* to their list of acceptable names, even when they had never been used by the family. These names particularly appealed to the Duvall family of Prince George's and their many kindred. While the proportion of parents in these families naming children for themselves dropped to low levels after the Revolution, more than a quarter of them named children for national heroes, and two-fifths of this group named a son for George Washington![78]

Even though parents gave children middle names with ever greater frequency after 1760, a practice that suggested that each child was a discrete individual and not just a member of a lineage, the middle names they received usually came from within the family. This tendency was particularly pronounced among the Duvalls: three-quarters of the middle names given children during the 1760s and 1770s were lineage surnames, and that proportion never dropped below one-half before the Civil War. Parents favored the maiden names of mothers and grandmothers: about one-half of the Duvalls named for a maternal grandfather between the 1760s and 1820s, for instance, bore both his forename and his surname.[79]

The heightened intensity of kin naming suggests that landed Chesapeake families conceived of their lineages as social groups and sought to perpetuate them. In fact, established gentry and yeoman families, about a third of the whites in tidewater, created close-knit kinship networks during the eighteenth century. Grandparents, uncles, aunts, and cousins attended the baptism of each newborn member, and their families often exchanged visits. When youths began to court, they often chose to marry kin, especially cousins they had known since infancy.[80]

Grandparents, who held these networks together by providing neutral ground for relations to congregate, appeared in increasing numbers in the Chesapeake region by the mid-eighteenth century. At least one grandparent could attend the christening of each child born in Prince George's in 1776, and two grandparents might have witnessed two-thirds of these events.

---

78. Donovan, "Child-Naming Patterns," 3–4.

79. *Ibid.,* 5–6, 12.

80. Smith, *Inside the Great House,* chap. 5; Elizabeth Bott, *Family and Social Networks: Roles, Norms, and External Relationships in Ordinary Urban Families* (New York, 1971), chap. 5, defines close-knit families. Smith argues that Chesapeake families were not close-knit, but his evidence, except for an analysis of four diaries, supports the view documented here. All four diarists were atypical even of gentlemen: two (William Byrd and Landon Carter) were members of the greater gentry, a group with less intensive kin relations than the rest of their class; one (James Gordon) was an immigrant with few blood kin in Virginia; and the other (Francis Taylor) was single.

Even though many grandparents died while their grandchildren were infants, seven of every eight children aged ten to fourteen in 1776 still had one living grandparent, and one-half of them could visit two grandparents.[81]

Grandparents shared intimate moments with grandchildren and often remembered several of them in their wills. Fewer than half of all grandfathers in Prince George's between 1730 and 1769 made a bequest to any grandchild, because they had to take care of their own children, but three-quarters of their widows gave part of their estate to favored grandchildren. When a married child predeceased a father, the grandfather often distributed the dead child's portion of his estate to the grandchildren. Otherwise, grandparents treated male and female children of sons and daughters equally, favoring several of them with a slave, a cow, or tokens like mourning rings.[82]

Brothers and sisters remained close after they married, and that affection extended to their children. Uncles took special interest in nephews; aunts sometimes guided the activities of nieces. Gentlemen sought advice on child rearing from their brothers and occasionally sent their children to live with them. Children spent most of their time on family visits with cousins, often becoming close friends; cousins who lived near each other not only visited frequently but attended school and church together.[83]

Adults sometimes cemented their relations with siblings, nephews, and nieces by remembering them in their wills. In York County, one in four adults with minor children bequeathed a small part of his estate to siblings, nieces, or nephews during the first half of the century, and one in five followed that practice in Albemarle County. Although only one in fourteen married men with small children in Prince George's gave any property to a sibling, niece, or nephew, unmarried men usually divided their estate

81. These assertions are based upon knowledge of the paternal grandfather of 30% (729 of 2,418) of children, 0–14, in the 1776 Prince George's census (Brumbaugh, ed., *Maryland Records*, I, 1–88). I discovered that 49% of the children aged 0–4, 44% aged 5–9, and 40% aged 10–14 had living paternal grandfathers. I assumed that the age of a child at the death of each grandparent was statistically independent of the others and that all grandparents followed the mortality schedule of the paternal grandfather. These assumptions yielded crudely accurate findings: about 94% of those 0–4 years old had one live grandparent, and 69% had two alive; about 87% of those 10–14 had one live grandparent, and 53% had two live grandparents.

82. Smith, *Inside the Great House*, 32–33, 44–45, 234–235; Prince George's Wills, 1730–1769, MHR. Of 49 known grandparents (with three grown children or two married daughters), 37 bequeathed goods to grandchildren. There was no statistical difference in either the distribution of goods by men and women or in the distribution of grandchildren who received gifts: 25% of the 232 grandchildren were sons' sons; 28% were daughters' sons; 16% were sons' daughters; and 31% were daughters' daughters.

83. Smith, *Inside the Great House*, 72–78, 83–84, 114–115, 178–189.

among siblings, and more than a third of them gave a portion to nephews or nieces, favoring nephews over nieces and the daughters of brothers over those of sisters.[84]

Even though youths chose their own spouses, the broader community, and especially the kin group, played important roles in eighteenth-century marriages. Parents sought to keep family property within the kinship group, and the growing incidence of marriages between relations suggests that they were successful. Once the choice had been made, banns were published in church preceding the wedding, thereby announcing the prospective bride and groom to kinfolk, friends, and neighbors, as well as giving church members an opportunity to object to the match. Kindred, moreover, attended both the wedding and the festivities that followed it.[85]

Marriages between cousins and other kin were increasingly common among both gentlemen and yeomen. When Benjamin Henry Latrobe visited Amelia County in southside Virginia in 1796, he reported that "half the Gentlemen of the county seem to be married at least to second or third cousins," an exaggeration he documented by examples, including that of Captain Murray who "is married to a first cousin of his own, the daughter of an own cousin on both sides, and *her* parents were first cousins." The intermarriages of the yeoman Bealls of Prince George's with the Brown family were equally intense. In 1745 Ninian Beall's daughter Eleanor married John Brown's son John, and only five years later Ninian Beall, Jr., wed Catherine Brown, his neighbor and sister-in-law. Children born to these two couples were both maternal and paternal first cousins. The kin tie between the Beall and Brown families was cemented in the 1770s when two sons of Ninian Beall, Jr., married two daughters of John Brown, Jr.[86]

Cousins like these couples married each other at an extremely high rate. Gentlemen and prosperous yeomen in Prince George's, for instance, married only within their groups, and rising numbers of them chose to wed blood relations. Between 1700 and 1730, when inbreeding in the county was already high, a tenth of the marriages in these groups were between

84. *Ibid.*, 231–236; Prince George's Wills, 1730–1769. Of 127 younger Prince Georgians, 11 gave goods to relatives outside the household, and 56 of 127 men with grandchildren bequeathed goods to them, with married men over 60 and those with two or more married daughters assumed to be grandfathers. I excluded those decedents from Smith's samples who bequeathed items to grandchildren, so as to make them comparable with the Prince George's group. In Prince George's 20 of 29 unmarried male decedents willed goods to brothers, 18 to sisters, 10 to parents, 5 to cousins, and 14 to nieces and nephews (9 to brothers' sons, 6 to sisters' sons, 5 to brothers' daughters, and 2 to sisters' daughters).

85. A fuller version of these rituals and more details about weddings will be found in Kulikoff, "'Throwing the Stocking,'" *MHM*, LXXI (1976), 516–521.

86. Carter *et al.*, eds., *Virginia Journals of Latrobe*, I, 113–128.

first cousins or more remote kin, but more than one-quarter of the brides and grooms were blood relations by the 1760s. The proportion of first-cousin marriages among consanguineous marriages rose from less than a third early in the century to more than a half by the 1760s (see table 29).[87]

Cousins deliberately chose to marry each other, because the size of the marriage pool grew faster than the number of kindred within the marriage market.[88] The center of the marriage market for the children of freeholders in Prince George's was located within a two-mile radius of the parental home, an area that included many kinfolk. As youths searched more remote places for spouses, the relative number of kindred diminished. While about two-fifths of all marriages between 1730 and 1790 were between relations, more than half the brides and grooms who lived within two miles of each other were kindred, and only a third of those who lived beyond that point were previously related.[89]

The high incidence of cousin marriage disturbed a few commentators. Peter Fontaine, an Anglican cleric, attempted to prevent his daughter from marrying a first cousin, and in 1754 he defended his stand. Marriage between strangers divided "in many degrees by descent" created a new circle of relationships upon their wedding, but "confining these alliances within our own family is straitening the circle greatly, making a circle within a circle, a state within a state . . . which is not only of pernicious consequence to the government, but contrary to the true spirit of Christianity." Latrobe, who saw "nothing *morally* wrong" in cousin marriage, nonetheless contended that from "a political point of view, I think it not expedient that

87. Frequency of cousin marriages in a variety of places is reported in Stanley L. Engerman, "Studying the Black Family," review of *The Black Family in Slavery and Freedom, 1750–1925*, by Herbert G. Gutman, *Journal of Family History*, III (1978), 89–90; L. L. Cavalli-Sforza and W. F. Bodmer, *The Genetics of Human Populations* (San Francisco, 1971), 350–353; and C. M. Woolf *et al.*, "An Investigation of the Frequency of Consanguineous Marriages among the Mormons and Their Relatives in the United States," *American Journal of Human Genetics*, VIII (1956), 236–252. My data can be viewed in two ways: either the numbers in table 29 ought to be divided by about 3 (assuming that unrecorded groups never married kin), or they can be compared with isolate populations. The inbreeding coefficients for Prince George's (.0023, .0086, .0197 for the three cohorts of the table) approximate the "special cases of high inbreeding coefficients in isolates" cited by Cavalli-Sforza and Bodmer (353).
88. J. Hajnal, "Concepts of Random Mating and the Frequency of Consanguineous Marriages," Royal Society of London, *Proceedings*, Ser. B (Biological Sciences), CLIX (1964), 125–177, esp. 145; and L. L. Cavalli-Sforza, "Some Notes on the Breeding Patterns of Human Populations," *Acta Genetica*, VI (1956–1957), 395–397.
89. Table 29 and sources cited there; cross-tabulations of kin marriages and marriage distance were based upon 118 marriages between 1730 and 1790: 19 of 33 of the marriages where spouses' parents lived less than two miles apart were kin, but only 30 of 65 of those more distant.

Table 29. *Kinship Ties between Brides and Grooms, Prince George's County, 1700–1790*

Relationship[a]	Percentage of Marriages, by Marriage Cohort		
	1700–1730 ($N=59$)	1730–1760 ($N=96$)	1760–1790 ($N=113$)
Blood relatives			
First cousins	3	6	15
Second cousins	0	4	6
More remote blood kin	7	12	7
Total	10	22	28
Affinal ties			
Sibling exchange	3	6	4
Step-siblings and cousins	0	2	2
More remote affinal ties	5	10	7
Total	8	19	13
No known kin ties	81	59	58
Grand total	99	100	99

Sources: Effie Gwynn Bowie, *Across the Years in Prince George's County* (Richmond, Va., 1947); Harry Wright Newman, *Mareen Duvall of Middle Plantation* . . . (Washington, D.C., 1954); and Margaret Cook, Beall Genealogical files, MSS in her possession.

Note: [a]Affinal ties are relationships by marriage. In sibling exchange, two siblings from one family marry two siblings from another family. Only the last of the two marriages is included in the "sibling exchange" category because only the last couple was previously related by marriage. If spouses were both blood kin and in-laws, the marriage is counted only under the proper blood tie category.

relations in a near degree should marry" because "society ought to be like a coat of Mail composed of rings, in which none can be strained without dividing and communicating the force throughout the whole texture."[90]

After a marriage the blood relations of bride and groom merged to form a single kinship group. Jacob Henderson, for instance, rector of a parish in Prince George's, was an Irish immigrant who married twice into the Duvall family. Though he had no children by either wife, he welcomed Benjamin Duvall, the step-grandson of his first wife, into his home for

90. Carter *et al.*, eds., *Virginia Journals of Latrobe*, I, 128; Peter Fontaine to John and Moses Fontaine, Apr. 15, 1754, in Ann Maury, ed. and trans., *Memoirs of a Huguenot Family* (New York, 1853), 341–342.

eighteen years beginning in 1735. Similarly, the marriage of Benjamin Young and Mary Dulany pulled Benjamin and his sister Letitia into the Dulany kin network. When Letitia's marriage to Stead Lowe was contested by Lowe's English heirs in the 1780s, Henry Addison, Mary Dulany's brother-in-law and rector of a Prince George's parish, insisted that the marriage was legitimate. "If any Such Suspiction had prevailed," he wrote, "I must unavoidably have Known it . . . as there was a family Connection, a brother of Mrs. Lowe . . . having married my wifes Sister a Daughter of the Hon. Daniel Dulany of the Council." Furthermore, Addison had baptized one of Lowe's children and remembered that Benjamin Young, the child's uncle, had acted as godfather.[91]

In-laws, as members of the same kin group, became potential mates for unmarried youths in the two families. The proportion of marriages between in-laws in Prince George's rose from one in twelve early in the eighteenth century to one in eight at the century's close. The siblings of bride and groom were especially close, and marriages between siblings-in-law were common, constituting about a third of all marriages between affinal kindred (table 29).

Fontaine and Latrobe had reason to fear the social consequences of marriages between kindred. Groups of relations increasingly separated themselves from unrelated neighbors. They made weddings the centerpiece of a Christmas season characterized by rounds of family visits, inviting only kinfolk and a few close neighbors to the festivities. Kinfolk went to church as much to see relatives sitting nearby as to listen to the service. Finally, kindred united politically to petition for public facilities such as roads and bridges.

Although marriage celebrations were nearly unknown in the seventeenth century, they became very common by the 1760s. The marriage ceremony, a brief exchange of vows, took place at the home of the bride's parents or at a local minister's house. The celebration after the ceremony was the most important part of the affair. The wealthier the parents of bride and groom, the more lavish the parties. At the least, a number of guests were invited, liquor flowed freely, and a large meal was served, but more lavish celebrations that continued for several days or even a week were not uncommon.[92]

Guests at wedding parties included relatives of both families and un-

---

91. Anne Arundel Land Records, NH#10, 379–380; Hienton, *Prince George's Heritage*, 60–61, 30–36; Effie Gwynn Bowie, *Across the Years in Prince George's County* . . . (Richmond, Va., 1947), 35–36; Montgomery County Land Records, C, 330.

92. Kulikoff, "'Throwing the Stocking,'" *MHM*, LXXI (1976), 519; Carson, *Virginians at Play*, 12–21; Revolutionary War Pension Applications of Joseph Duvall and John O'Hara, National Archives, Washington, D.C.

related close friends. John T. Lowe's brother, sister, and uncle were present when he married Susan Riddle in 1784. Ralph Basil, Sarah Duvall, Mary Carroll (née Duvall), and Gabriel Duvall witnessed the nuptials of kinspeople Mary Duvall and Joseph Duvall. Basil, Carroll, and Sarah Duvall were neighbors of the newlyweds and were "raised boys and girls together and went to school" with both of them. Close neighbors attended the ceremony and brought kinsfolk with them. Elizabeth Watters, a bridesmaid at the nuptials of Thomas Jones and Elizabeth Duvall in 1777, had known Duvall since "early in life as they were raised near neighbors and went to School together." Watters came to the celebration with her brother and sister.[93]

Increasing numbers of weddings were integrated into family celebrations at Christmas, a time when Chesapeake families visited each other, held parties, and exchanged gifts.[94] Between 1650 and 1750, couples tended to wed in the winter months, avoiding the heat of summer (when the labor of tobacco cultivation was intense), and Lent (when Anglican marriages were proscribed), but otherwise spread weddings randomly over the year. During the second half of the eighteenth century, the Lent prohibition on marriages disappeared, and couples increasingly celebrated their weddings in December and January. The proportion of Anglicans in Prince George's, for instance, who wed in December rose from one-seventh between 1700 and 1724 to more than a fifth from 1786 to 1798. There were similar trends in Middlesex County, Virginia, and in several southside Virginia counties. In all three places December weddings occurred at a rate two and a half times the daily average for marriages, and in addition, January marriages in southside and Prince George's were twice the daily average.[95]

Kin, both blood relations and in-laws, gathered for sabbath observances. Catholic, Presbyterian, and Anglican services were family affairs in Prince George's. Roman Catholic chapels were established on plantations of wealthy Catholic gentlemen, but these places were so small that only a few families could attend. Jesuit Thomas Digges lived with his brother Ignatious and celebrated mass during the 1780s for the Digges family at

93. Pensions of John T. Lowe, Joseph Duvall, and Thomas Jones, National Archives.
94. Carville V. Earle, *The Evolution of a Tidewater Settlement System: All Hallow's Parish, Maryland, 1650–1783*, University of Chicago Department of Geography Research Paper 170 (Chicago, 1975), 157–160; Farish, ed., *Journal of Fithian*, 39–40; Carson, *Virginians at Play*, 8–11.
95. Kulikoff, "Tobacco and Slaves," 356–358; Darrett B. Rutman *et al.*, "Rhythms of Life: Black and White Seasonality in the Early Chesapeake," *Journal of Interdisciplinary History*, XI (1980), 29–31, 36–38, 42–45; *The Parish Register of Christ Church, Middlesex County, Va., from 1653 to 1812*, Parish Records, 1st Ser. (Richmond, Va., 1897); "Rev. John Cameron's Register: A Register of Marriages for Bristol Parish," in Bell, *Cumberland Parish*, 304–312.

their chapel. The Bealls and a few related families dominated both Presbyterian churches in the county, and when the Bealls moved from near Marlboro to the Eastern Branch, the Upper Marlboro church withered away, only to be replaced by one in Bladensburg, near the new homes of most of the Bealls. Anglicans, too, worshiped with their extended kin. The Duvalls built one of the chapels of Queen Anne Parish for their relations and friends, and the Brookes and Lees similarly dominated worship at a chapel of Saint Paul's Parish.[96]

Henderson's chapel of Queen Anne Parish was the Duvall family church. Various Duvalls and their neighbors had worshiped there since it opened in the 1710s, but sometime before 1740 Jacob Henderson, the parish rector who owned the building, donated it to the parish. It became an official chapel, and pews were distributed by lot in 1741. More than three-quarters of the forty-seven families who bought parts of eighteen pews were related by blood or marriage to at least one other parishioner. The Duvalls, their kindred, and a few close friends gathered at the chapel on a typical Sunday in the 1740s: pewholders included seventeen Duvalls, five Spriggs, and five Hillearys. When Lewis Duvall, son of Elizabeth Jacob Duvall, came to church, he was surrounded by kindred. He shared pew sixteen with two brothers. Nearby, in pew twelve, sat his sister Elizabeth Denine and her husband William, another sister Susannah Fowler and her husband William, and Mark Brown, the brother of his wife. In addition, his cousin Benjamin Jacob and his son Mordecai (who married into another branch of the Duvall family) occupied pew fourteen.[97]

Once kin groups were fully established in a neighborhood, its members often organized for political purposes. When James Edmonston circulated petitions through many Eastern Branch frontier neighborhoods in the early 1730s demanding public improvements, he did not limit his search to kindred. Even though nearly half the 68 signers were related by blood or married to other signers, Edmonston found kinfolk by chance. Although 6 of his own relatives signed a petition, Edmonston overlooked his father, a brother, an uncle, and a second cousin, all of whom lived in the neighborhoods Edmonston canvassed. Later petitions to the court were more strictly limited to overlapping kin groups. Between 1744 and 1752, six groups of neighbors and kindred from long-settled parts of the county presented road petitions to the court. The largest had 55 signatures, the smallest only 12.

96. Bowie, *Across the Years*, 275–276; Hienton, *Prince George's Heritage*, chap. 6; Queen Anne and St. Paul's parish vestry books, MHR.
97. Hienton, *Prince George's Heritage*, 78–80; Queen Anne Parish Vestry Book; Harry Wright Newman, *Mareen Duvall of Middle Plantation . . .* (Washington, D.C., 1952), 148, 167, 179, 210.

Only a third of the 136 signers were unrelated to at least one other petitioner: one-half had blood ties, a third were in-laws, and nearly a quarter were linked by both blood and marriage to fellow signers.[98]

The best example of kin group pressure on the county court can be seen in a petition presented in November 1747 by thirteen neighbors living near the Patuxent River. They urged the court to build a bridge over the Patuxent at Sturgeon Shoals, "for it will be very convenient for the people of the Middle and Upper part of Prince George's County and Sundry Inhabitants of Annarundel County to pass to each other for their mutual correspondence and business." By June 1748 the bridge and road leading to it were built. The bridge was constructed more for the convenience of the Duvalls, who had numerous relatives on the other side of the river, than for other residents of the area. Five of the signers were descendants or affines of Mareen Duvall. Three petitioners, two Beall brothers and their nephew, lived eight miles from the bridge. They probably signed because Regnall Odell, their brother-in-law and uncle, lived near the river. Odell and the Bealls through him were remotely connected to the Duvalls by an affinal tie to Baruch Williams (see map 17).[99]

Kin group solidarity was maintained with some difficulty because these networks had no internal mechanisms to resolve conflicts between relations. Relatives who bickered and could not quietly compromise divided kin groups into warring factions. The Catholic Brooke and Waring families of Prince George's and the Carroll family of Anne Arundel County all split apart when one branch of each joined the newly established Anglican church at the end of the seventeenth century. The Brooke and Carroll families, moreover, were involved in bitter disputes over the devolution of family property when members of the Catholic branches of their families joined the Jesuits and sought to give their property to the order. Later in the century Jacob Henderson regularly argued with kindred. Not only did he approve the distribution of pews by lot in 1740, but several years later he "turned the Main Road passing by his Plantation to Queen Anne Town from a Commodious and Inter Level Way into a most desparate uneven broken hill Road," inciting fifty-five of his neighbors, including many parishioners and ten of his own in-laws, to complain to the county court about his behavior.[100]

---

98. Table 26 and sources cited there; Prince George's Court Records, XV, 504, XVII, 394–395, XIX, 176, XXII, 196. Of the signers, 44 had blood ties to other petitioners; 18 had affinal ties; 25 had both affinal and blood ties; and 49 had neither.

99. Prince George's Court Records, XVIII, 289–290. Kulikoff, "Tobacco and Slaves," 542–544, details the relationships. The density of this network is 18 of 78, or 23%. When 3 unrelated signers are eliminated, the density rises to 18 of 45, or 40%.

100. Hughes, *History of the Society of Jesus*, Text, II, 560–561; research of Lois Green Carr; Prince George's Court Records, XV, 504.

Map 17. *Kinship Connections among Petitioners of the Bridge at Sturgeon Shoals.* Only main roads are shown.

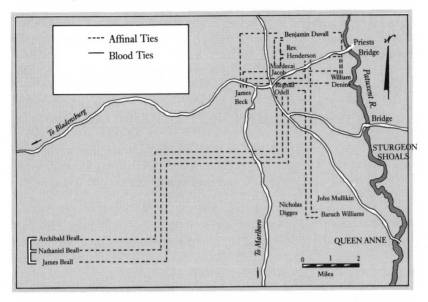

Sources: Prince George's Court Records, XVIII, 289–290, MHR; Allan Kulikoff, "Tobacco and Slaves: Population, Economy, and Society in Eighteenth-Century Prince George's County, Maryland" (Ph.D. diss., Brandeis University, 1976), 542–544.

Kinship and Class in the Chesapeake

From the outset of settlement, white adults in the Chesapeake participated in neighborhood social networks based upon gender, religion, and kinship. At first, these informal groups were independent: family members associated with different neighbors at home, church, courthouse, and tavern. But as population density increased and the web of kinship grew, social networks based upon gender and religion tended to be organized around kin relations. This transition was complete in much of tidewater before the mid-eighteenth century, but since kinship networks took several generations to mature, close-knit family networks did not appear on the piedmont frontier until the end of the century.[101]

101. The persistence of this kin system in general, and of cousin marriage in particular, in the antebellum South is suggested by Bertram Wyatt-Brown, *Southern Honor: Ethics and Behavior in the Old South* (New York, 1982), chap. 8 (esp. 217–225), and 380–385; and by Catherine Clinton, *The Plantation Mistress: Woman's World in the Old South* (New York, 1982), 57–58, 240–241.

Although families of local gentry and substantial freeholders formed close-knit kinship networks with ease, poor and unsettled folk lived in any neighborhood too short a time to join a church, and their children left their parents' neighborhood long before they married and began a household. Poor folk probably gathered in temporary groups segregated by gender, the men at taverns or cockfights, the women at farmhouses of nearby tenants.

The growth of kinship networks among gentry and yeoman families provided meaningful social interchange for members but at the same time separated white society into exclusive clans that were unable to unite planters against slaves or regulate relations among white strangers. Planters increasingly turned to the local bench, and the gentry class it represented, to arbitrate disputes and take care of the dependent classes. The social rules that guided the interaction of gentlemen and yeomen did succeed, as we shall see in the next chapter, in unifying various groups of kindred and in maintaining white male control of local society.

7

The Rise of the Chesapeake Gentry

George Washington and Thomas Jefferson inhabited a society in which gentlemen of generations standing dominated the economy and polity and passed their dominion on to their sons undiminished. Justices of the peace administered county government and punished miscreants, with the consent but hardly the advice of lesser men. These gentlemen thought it their duty to provide moral guidance and political leadership as stewards of the entire society. Ordinary yeoman planters usually deferred to their gentry neighbors in political matters, but insisted that gentlemen protect their property and asserted the right to choose between gentlemen who stood for seats in provincial assemblies.[1]

Though the Chesapeake gentry class was strongly entrenched in power by the mid-eighteenth century, it matured late in the colonial era. A few gentlemen migrated across the ocean, but some commoners turned themselves into gentlemen almost as soon as they arrived, and a few of them made it to the top. Men found and lost fortunes; indentured servants finished their term, married heiresses, and sat at the right hand of governors. Those who made it to the top, however, left few sons to perpetuate their authority, for mortality was high and fertility low among immigrants. As a result, justices and assemblymen did not constitute a tightly organized ruling class, but were amorphous gatherings of immigrants who inspired too little confidence to gain the respect of poorer whites and had too little power to suppress their demands. Class conflict therefore broke out between rulers and upwardly mobile freed servants during the third quarter of the seventeenth century.

1. Charles S. Sydnor, *Gentleman Freeholders: Political Practices in Washington's Virginia* (Chapel Hill, N.C., 1952), is still a remarkably perceptive account of gentility and deference. Rhys Isaac, *The Transformation of Virginia, 1740–1790* (Chapel Hill, N.C., 1982), adds new dimensions to our understanding of tidewater deferential society; while Jack P. Greene, "Society, Ideology, and Politics: An Analysis of the Political Culture of Mid-Eighteenth-Century Virginia," in Richard M. Jellison, ed., *Society, Freedom, and Conscience: The American Revolution in Virginia, Massachusetts, and New York* (New York, 1976), documents the ideology of Virginia's gentry class. For dissenting views, see Robert E. Brown and B. Katherine Brown, *Virginia, 1705–1786: Democracy or Aristocracy?* (East Lansing, Mich., 1964), a work that insists that 18th-century Virginia was a middle-class democracy; and Darrett B. Rutman and Anita H. Rutman, *A Place in Time: Middlesex County, Virginia, 1650–1750* (New York, 1984), chap. 5; and Rutman and Rutman, *A Place in Time: Explicatus* (New York, 1984), chap. 10, which view Virginia through the prism of social stratification theory, rather than class analysis.

Economic stagnation, an increase in life expectancy among whites, and the decline of white servitude and its replacement by slavery at the end of the seventeenth century permitted gentlemen to consolidate their power. When tobacco prices plummeted and tobacco production stagnated in the 1680s and 1690s, opportunities for ordinary men greatly diminished. The servant trade dried up, and large-scale slavetrading began at the same time, raising the cost of labor and reducing the access of most planters to unfree workers. Wealthy men, however, took advantage of slave markets to build their fortunes, and since they lived longer, they passed greater wealth on to their sons, leaving them in good position to follow their fathers in office. Finally, unruly ex-servants left the region, thereby reducing conflicts between wealthy and poor planters.[2]

By the second third of the eighteenth century, the slave system cemented gentry control.[3] Gentlemen chose not to work on their farms, because their slaves produced all they needed and left them free to assume political leadership. These gentlemen, perhaps a twentieth of the region's white men, had the self-confidence, based on their power and wealth, to maintain interdependent relationships with yeoman planters. About half the white men were yeomen, and many of them owned a slave or two, or hoped to someday, and they counted on their patrons, the gentleman justices, to enforce good order and prevent slave uprisings. If they needed money to buy land or slaves, they turned to their patrons. In return for these services, yeomen assented to gentry authority.

services defined

Once the gentry class gained the assent of the yeomanry, it could safely ignore the rest of white society, groups of people who lacked the independence required to participate in public life. Wives submitted to the rule of husbands; tenants owed landlords heavy rents that kept them dependent; laborers and servants depended upon their masters for work and food; and the deserving poor had to beg justices for the bread they ate. In a society in

2. Russell R. Menard, "From Servant to Freeholder: Status Mobility and Property Accumulation in Seventeenth-Century Maryland," *William and Mary Quarterly*, 3d Ser., XXX (1973), 37–64; Bernard Bailyn, "Politics and Social Structure in Virginia," in James Morton Smith, ed., *Seventeenth-Century America: Essays in Colonial History* (Chapel Hill, N.C., 1959), 90–115; David W. Jordan, "Maryland's Privy Council, 1637–1715," in Aubrey C. Land *et al.*, eds., *Law, Society, and Politics in Early Maryland* (Baltimore, 1977), 65–87; Jordan, "Political Stability and the Emergence of a Native Elite in Maryland," in Thad W. Tate and David L. Ammerman, eds., *The Chesapeake in the Seventeenth-Century: Essays on Anglo-American Society* (Chapel Hill, N.C., 1979), 243–273; and William A. Reavis, "The Maryland Gentry and Social Mobility, 1637–1676," *WMQ*, 3d Ser., XIV (1957), 418–428, all show early high opportunity and the slow development of a closed native elite.
3. My views on social class have been influenced by Marxist writings. See particularly Stanislaw Ossowski, *Class Structure in the Social Consciousness*, trans. Sheila Patterson (New York, 1963); and Raymond Williams, *Marxism and Literature* (Oxford, 1977).

which slaves constituted the largest group of adult dependents, white dependents enjoyed a precarious position indeed.

If gentlemen implicitly relied upon a hierarchical vision of society to sustain their control, their authority also rested upon reciprocal, and sometimes even equal, exchanges with the yeomanry. Any challenge to either the hierarchical authority of gentlemen or to these reciprocal relations would challenge gentry authority. In fact, a generation after the tidewater gentry class gained effective control, it faced two political threats. During the 1760s and 1770s, Baptist and Presbyterian preachers and their followers in piedmont—where the gentry class was barely established—rejected gentry religion and culture and refused to accept their patronage. And the American Revolution in Virginia and Maryland was a gentry revolt against England that both destroyed the chain of authority that linked the crown with local justices and to the people and required great sacrifices from ordinary folk. The reciprocal ties between gentlemen and yeomen were so strong, however, that the gentry class survived both these crises and came into the 1780s with a strengthened position.

The Making of the Gentry Class

During the eighteenth century, gentlemen in the tidewater Chesapeake became a self-conscious ruling class that not only increasingly monopolized power and wealth but formed its own culture as well. Since the maintenance of political authority required great wealth, rich planters devised a series of inheritance and marriage strategies designed to maintain the family's wealth. As a result, gentlemen and their sons increasingly controlled the bench and assemblies of the Chesapeake. At the same time, gentlemen distinguished themselves from ordinary folk by pursuing a classical education that placed them in the center of the high culture of England.

As early as 1733 the wealthiest planters and merchants in Prince George's County, for instance, belonged to a nearly self-perpetuating oligarchy. Although two of every five sons of men of great wealth inherited sufficient property to rank among the richest men in the county and an equal proportion of immigrant merchants and professional men made it to the top, only one of every twenty immigrants or sons of native freeholders achieved great wealth. About two-thirds of the county's richest men built on inheritances from wealthy fathers, and another sixth were immigrants who came over with capital or education, but fewer than a fifth of the group had more humble origins (see table 30).

The great opportunities of sons of wealthy men and the slender chances of other planters did not change between 1733 and 1776, but the

Table 30. *Sources of Wealth of the Richest Men in Prince George's County,*
1733–1776

Wealthholders and Source of Wealth[a]	Percentage of Group Joining Richest Families		Percentage of Richest Families	
	1733 (N=278)	1776 (N=225)	1733 (N=59)	1776 (N=31)
Built on inheritance from wealthy father	42	41	67	61
Accumulated as immigrant with capital or education[b]	38	50	17	16
Built on wealth of freeholder father[c]	5	5	9	23
Accumulated as ordinary immigrant	—	—	7	0
Total			100	100

Sources: Black Books, II, 106–124, MHR, and Gaius Marcus Brumbaugh, ed., *Maryland Records: Colonial, Revolutionary, County, and Church, from Original Sources*, I (Baltimore, 1915), 1–88, linked with Prince George's Land Records, Debt Books, and Wills and Inventories, MHR.

Notes: Five unknowns in 1733 and four in 1776 are included in number of cases, but excluded from percentages. [a]In 1733 men with more than eight taxable slaves or more than 1,500 acres of land (or fewer than five slaves and more than 4,000 acres) were included; in 1776 those with more than eight taxable slaves or more than 800 acres were included (the price of land more than doubled in the interval). [b]Merchants, factors, lawyers, doctors, and clergymen are included. [c]Ordinary immigrants and freeholder fathers are combined in "Percentage Joining" columns in 1733; 1733 and 1776 "Percentage Joining" columns exclude those whose fathers had land *or* slaves, but they are included in the "percentage of richest families."

generational depth of the wealthiest families increased. The only wealthy immigrants in 1776 were merchants with access to British capital. Most wealthy men came from rich families that had maintained their wealth for generations. About half the wealthy native whites in 1733 were the sons of immigrants, and the fathers of two-fifths of these men had been indentured servants or ordinary free immigrants. The vast majority of native sons in 1776, in contrast, could trace their wealth as far back as their grandfathers, and a third had wealthy fathers, grandfathers, and great-grandfathers.[4]

Much of the wealth of the region slowly devolved upon a few families. The hundred richest men in Virginia in 1787 each owned land, slaves, and

4. Table 30. There were 14 known second-generation sons in 1733 (fathers included 3 indentured servants, 3 free immigrants, 4 sons of English gentlemen, and 4 professional men); 11 third-generation sons; and 2 of the fourth generation (great-grandfather immigrants). In 1776, 3 of 19 known wealthy men had wealthy fathers, 9 had wealthy fathers and grandfathers, and 7 had wealthy fathers, grandfathers, and great-grandfathers.

other goods worth about fifteen thousand pounds sterling, ran plantations in several counties, and invested heavily in frontier land. These hundred men were members of fifty-one family groups, and twenty of them were Carters, Randolphs, Cockes, and Fitzhughs. Many families with one representative among the hundred were related to other wealthy families, like George Washington and his in-law John Custis, and others like Robert Beverley were descended from a long line of wealthy Virginians.[5]

Men built great fortunes and passed them on to their children by pursuing mercantile activity, by arranging good marriages for those children, and by disposing of their estates in ways guaranteed to keep their fortunes together. Wealthy men ideally insisted that their children marry into other rich families, a strategy that combined two substantial fortunes or brought new money into the family when daughters married immigrant merchants. Ideal inheritance strategies depended upon family size: a man with few children might divide his fortune in a relatively equal manner and expect that that portion, along with a good marriage, would permit each child to remain wealthy; a man with many children, however, had to favor a few children or encourage several sons to stay single if even part of the family was to retain the family fortune.

Mercantile activity and land speculation were quick roads to wealth. Robert Carter, the richest man in early eighteenth-century Virginia, built on an inheritance of one thousand pounds and one thousand acres of land by engaging in the slave trade and by running the Fairfax proprietary lands in the Northern Neck and patenting more than three hundred thousand acres there. Men of lesser wealth also reaped great profits as merchants. Nearly a third of the wealthy sons of rich men in Prince George's were merchants in 1733, and a fifth of that group in 1776 still traded tobacco despite the increasing dominance of large stores run by Scottish merchants.[6]

The marriages of Robert Carter's children were among the most successful in maintaining the family fortune. Carter ensured his children's prosperity by approving solid matches for them with other prominent families worth thousands of pounds sterling, including the Burwells, Fitzhughs, Pages, Harrisons, Wormleys, and Hills. By linking his children to these

5. Calculated from Jackson Turner Main, "The One Hundred," *WMQ*, 3d Ser., XI (1954), 354–384, with a reduction of total wealth to pre-Revolutionary values.
6. Louis Morton, *Robert Carter of Nomini Hall: A Virginia Tobacco Planter of the Eighteenth Century*, 2d ed. (Williamsburg, Va., 1945), chap. 1; in Prince George's there were 7 immigrant merchant-planters in 1733 and 13 native merchant-planters, and 5 immigrant and 5 native merchant-planters in 1776. The mercantile origins of the gentry class were first detailed by Aubrey C. Land in "Economic Behavior in a Planting Society: The Eighteenth-Century Chesapeake," *Journal of Southern History*, XXXIII (1967), 469–485, and in "Economic Base and Social Structure: The Northern Chesapeake in the Eighteenth Century," *Journal of Economic History*, XXV (1965), 639–654.

families, he not only added land and slaves to the family coffers but built a dynasty that included most of the province's first families. Carter's descendants continued to build fortunes and marry well, and by 1787 fourteen of his grandsons and great-grandsons were among the hundred wealthiest Virginians.[7]

Since eighteenth-century families usually included four or five children who survived into adulthood, the fortunes of even the richest families would soon be dissipated unless they could find new capital. Immigrants with capital were welcomed into gentry families because they brought new sources of income into the family enterprises. James Russell, for instance, a consignment merchant and storekeeper in Prince George's in the 1730s, married Ann Lee, daughter of a wealthy member of the Maryland council. Russell turned Ann's dowry and his own capital into a thriving business and left for London in the early 1750s, where he became the foremost tobacco importer of his day. While Russell used his Lee connections to establish his business, he repaid the family handily, leaving his Prince George's business in the hands of a brother-in-law and entering into a partnership with his wife's nephew. Other Maryland gentry families emulated Lee. Three immigrant merchants in Bladensburg married into prestigious local families. Christopher Lowndes, who arrived in 1738 as a factor for a Liverpool firm, married Elizabeth Tasker, daughter of the president of the Maryland council, after he had developed a thriving business. And two daughters of John Brice, chief justice of Maryland, married Richard Henderson, a factor for a Scottish firm, and David Ross, a doctor who dabbled in the dry goods trade.[8]

Men needed inheritances as well as good marriages to perpetuate family fortunes. Fewer than a sixth of the sons of wealthy Prince Georgians managed to acquire great riches while their fathers were alive, but once their fathers had died, about half of them achieved their fathers' economic standing.[9] Fathers played a balancing act, trying to ensure that each child received a fair portion while keeping the family wealth relatively intact. The Addisons of Prince George's were very successful in planning for the fu-

7. Morton, *Robert Carter of Nomini Hall*, chap. 1; Main, "The One Hundred," *WMQ*, 3d Ser., XI (1954), 354–384.

8. Jacob M. Price, "One Family's Empire: The Russell-Lee-Clerk Connection in Maryland, Britain, and India, 1707–1857," *Maryland Historical Magazine*, LXXII (1977), 167–179; Prince George's Land Records, T, 623, Maryland Hall of Records, Annapolis (MHR); Louise Joyner Hienton, *Prince George's Heritage: Sidelights on the Early History of Prince George's County, Maryland, from 1696 to 1800* (Baltimore, 1972), 138–139, 162–163.

9. Of 53 sons in 1733 whose fathers had died, 30 gained great wealth, as did 17 of 39 in 1776; 13 of the rest owned both land and slaves in 1733, as all the rest did in 1776; but only 4 of 26 whose fathers were alive in 1733 and 1 of 8 in 1776 reached this status, while 8 in 1733 and 3 in 1776 owned land *or* slaves.

ture. Thomas Addison, the only son of an immigrant merchant, was born in 1697 and received most of his father's estate of more than eighteen hundred pounds and sixty-five hundred acres. His oldest son, John, inherited the bulk of his estate and married well. Son Henry Addison received clerical training as part of his portion and then married an extremely wealthy widow, thereby combining his inheritance, his clerical income, and his wife's wealth. Addison's two other sons stayed single, made careers as ship captain and military officer, and left their worldly goods to their brothers and nephews.[10]

Men with large families who practiced partible inheritance and failed to arrange good marriages for their children could not ensure the continued wealth of their descendants. Mareen Duvall, a Huguenot exile who became a merchant in Anne Arundel County, for instance, accumulated a personal estate worth fifteen hundred pounds and 2,350 acres of land by the time he died in 1697, but he divided his estate relatively equally among his twelve children, sums that in themselves attracted few wealthy suitors. Three of his children wed rich planters, six married well-off yeomen, but the other three found more humble mates. Although the men that two of his daughters married built substantial fortunes, none of Duvall's other children maintained the father's status. Son Mareen Duvall, for instance, married well but fell into economic difficulty by "Mismanagement of his Affairs" and in 1718 had to sell most of his property to pay his debts, and the wealthiest of his brothers managed to accumulate only four slaves and 210 acres of land by 1733.[11]

Wealthy men sought to control the offices of justice of the peace, sheriff, vestryman, and assemblyman to protect their hold on the economy and to cement their social prominence. County justices performed both judicial and administrative functions. They decided issues of law, determined guilt or innocence of those charged with crimes such as bastardy, set the tax rate and allocated county funds, appointed overseers for orphans, and ordered roads built and bridges maintained. Sitting alone, justices adjudicated minor local disturbances, settled small debt cases, and punished slaves. Sheriffs kept order in the county, collected local and provincial taxes (for a fee), and impaneled juries. Virginia vestrymen not only ran the parish and spent county taxes as those in Maryland did but disbursed poor relief, a function granted justices in Maryland. Although assemblymen debated public policy

10. Lois Green Carr and David William Jordan, *Maryland's Revolution of Government, 1689–1692* (Ithaca, N.Y., 1974), 232–234; Effie Gwynn Bowie, *Across the Years in Prince George's County* . . . (Richmond, Va., 1947), 32–56.

11. Harry Wright Newman, *Mareen Duvall of Middle Plantation* . . . (Washington, D.C., 1952), 20–61, 97–102 (quote on 100), 141–143, 162–167, 209–212, 366–368, 385–388, 455–457, 472–473; Black Books, II, 106–124, MHR, linked with Prince George's Land Records.

with their peers and passed laws that regulated economic development and local government, they also championed local issues of importance to their county's magistrates and yeomanry.[12]

The wealthiest planters and planter-merchants dominated local benches and provincial legislatures from the 1650s to the Revolution. During the late seventeenth century, Virginia justices and burgesses—already wealthy men—used their offices to patent thousands of acres of frontier land. By 1705, three-fifths of Virginians who owned two thousand or more acres of land were justices or burgesses. Maryland officeholders were similarly wealthy. More than a third of the men who served on the Maryland council between 1660 and 1699 owned more than five thousand acres of land, and only about a quarter of them held fewer than two thousand acres. Although Maryland justices owned less land during the seventeenth century and the exclusion of Catholics from the bench after 1689 prevented a number of wealthy men from serving, justices in Charles and St. Mary's counties appointed between 1660 and 1720 held, on average, at least seven hundred acres of land, far more than most planters. The landholdings of officeholders in Maryland rose during the early and middle eighteenth century, when much frontier land was patented, but then declined during the 1770s. Since land prices jumped fiercely after 1770, the landed wealth of these men actually increased. Though the landholdings of justices in piedmont Virginia approximated those of yeoman planters when settlement began, justices soon pulled away from their neighbors, patenting hundreds of new acres (see table 31).[13]

12. The best summary of the duties of local officers is found in Lois Green Carr, "The Foundations of Social Order: Local Government in Colonial Maryland," in Bruce C. Daniels, ed., *Town and County: Essays on the Structure of Local Government in the American Colonies* (Middletown, Conn., 1978), 72–110; but see also George Webb, *The Office and Authority of a Justice of the Peace* . . . (Williamsburg, Va., 1736), 200–207.

13. Jordan, "Emergence of a Native Elite," in Tate and Ammerman, eds., *Chesapeake in the Seventeenth Century*, 264–265; Martin Herbert Quitt, "Virginia House of Burgesses, 1660–1706: The Social, Educational, Economic Bases of Political Power" (Ph.D. diss., Washington University, St. Louis, 1971), 133–146; Lorena S. Walsh, "The Development of Local Power Structures on Maryland's Lower Western Shore in the Early Colonial Period" (paper presented at the 1980 meeting of the Organization of American Historians), supplemented with data kindly provided by author; Edward C. Papenfuse *et al.*, eds., *A Biographical Dictionary of the Maryland Legislature, 1635–1789*, I (Baltimore, 1979); Lois Green Carr, "County Government in Maryland, 1680–1709" (Ph.D. diss., Harvard University, 1968), 619–621; Black Books, II, 110–124, and Gaius Marcus Brumbaugh, ed., *Maryland Records: Colonial, Revolutionary, County, and Church, from Original Sources*, I (Baltimore, 1915), 1–88, linked with Prince George's Land Records and Prince George's Debt Books; William D. Armstrong, "The Justices and Burgesses of Fauquier County, Virginia, 1759–1776" (master's thesis, University of Virginia, 1968), 13; Daniel B. Smith, "Changing Patterns of Local Leadership: Justices of the Peace in Albemarle County, Virginia, 1760–1820" (master's thesis, University of Virginia, 1972), 42–47; Richard R. Beeman, "The Creation of an Elite Ruling Tradition in the Virginia

Table 31. *Wealth of Justices of the Peace and Legislators in the Chesapeake,
1660–1795*

Place and Group	N	Median No. of Adult Slaves[a]	Median No. of Acres[a]
St. Mary's Co., justices of peace[b]			
1660–1679	33	—	1,200
1680–1710	49	—	700
Charles, justices of peace[b]			
1660–1679	29	—	700
1680–1720	51	—	900
Southern Maryland, legislators[c]			
1700–1724	39	10	800
1725–1749	23	10	1,100
1750–1773	32	12	2,000
1774–1789	55	11	1,100
Prince George's, justices of peace			
1696–1709[b]	27	—	900
1728–1738[d]	28	8	1,000
1771–1781[d]	14	12	600
Fauquier, justices of peace			
1759–1776[e]	22	10	—
Albemarle, justices of peace[e]			
1760–1780	38	8	1,100
1780–1800	44	6	700
Lunenburg, justices of peace[f]			
1770	17	8	900
1782	16	8	600
1795	15	8	700

Sources: Cited in n. 13.

Notes: [a]Acres to nearest hundred; slaves count only those over age 16, dividing examples of
total slaves by half. [b]Wealth at time of appointment. [c]Wealth at time of election or appointment
or as soon thereafter as possible. [d]All justices serving between the listed dates; wealth totals as
of 1733 and 1776; the 1771–1780 group includes only the Potomac half of the county. [e]All
justices serving between listed dates; wealth data from contemporary inventories and tithable
lists. [f]All justices serving at dates indicated, with wealth from tax lists.

Many seventeenth-century legislators and justices probably found labor to farm their lands with some difficulty, but eighteenth-century holders of high office owned numerous slaves. The median number of slaves of all ages owned by Virginia burgesses rose from five in the late seventeenth century to seven by the 1710s and 1720s; at the same time, the proportion of burgesses who owned no slaves fell from a quarter to a tenth. Assemblymen in eighteenth-century Maryland owned, on average, between ten and twelve adult slaves, and most of them probably hired an overseer to discipline slaves and run their plantations. Justices in both tidewater and piedmont owned about eight adult slaves, just about enough to hire an overseer, and the number of taxable slaves remained high after the Revolution (table 31).

Although seventeenth-century officeholders were men of great wealth, few of them founded dynasties, because most were immigrants who left no male heirs. More than two-thirds of the members of the Virginia House of Burgesses first elected between 1677 and 1686 were immigrants, and that proportion dropped only slightly, to three-fifths, in the 1690s. Nearly all Maryland justices and assemblymen were immigrants until 1670, and a twelfth of the legislators, along with a fifth of the justices, had been indentured servants. When the proportion of native-born officials rose in the late seventeenth century, the first political dynasties were founded. The proportion of natives among Virginia burgesses rose from less than a third in the 1670s to half by the late 1690s, and, at the same time, grandsons of immigrants began to serve in that body. By the 1700s and 1710s, three-fifths of Maryland legislators and three-quarters of justices in four southern Maryland counties were natives. These men were often the sons of officials: the fathers of a third of Maryland assemblymen, 1700–1715, and between a third and a half of the southern Maryland justices had preceded their sons in higher offices.[14]

Most eighteenth-century officials left several male heirs who survived to adulthood, and service in higher office became their birthright. Families that maintained their wealth over generations came to dominate local benches and county delegations to the assemblies. The men that ruling families placed on the bench or in the assembly represented their kindred as well as their less affluent neighbors. Newly wealthy men found it difficult to serve unless they married daughters of justices and legislators, and even

---

Southside: Lunenburg County as a Test Case" (paper presented at the 1980 meeting of the Organization of American Historians), 26–30.

14. Walsh, "Development of Local Power Structures," tables 1–3; and Jordan, "Emergence of a Native Elite," in Tate and Ammerman, eds., *Chesapeake in the Seventeenth Century*, 267; Quitt, "Virginia House of Burgesses," 10–18.

that did not guarantee a seat, because incumbents tended to hold on to their offices for ever longer periods of time.[15]

The history of the bench in Prince George's County suggests how a few gentry families consolidated their hold on local political power during the eighteenth century. Though the area was first settled during the 1660s, a new county was not organized until 1696. Few of the justices appointed from 1696 to 1708 were related to earlier justices. Half of the justices appointed by 1725 were immigrants, and the grandfathers of only one-thirteenth of them had lived in Maryland. Kinship was of little importance in determining appointment, for nearly every wealthy Anglican served, and neither close blood relations nor in-laws preceded more than a third of the justices on the bench. Still, wealthy immigrants often married the daughters of justices, and wealthy sons of justices sometimes received a commission. In total, two-fifths of the fathers-in-law and one-fourth of the fathers of justices appointed before 1725 had served on the court of Prince George's or of a nearby county (see fig. 25).

As county population increased and the number of wealthy Anglicans began to exceed the number of slots for justices, family background rose in importance as a criterion for selection. Only a seventh of the justices and sheriffs appointed in Prince George's between 1725 and 1775 were immigrants, and most of them were wealthy merchants. Nearly one-third of officials were third-generation natives, and more than a quarter of them traced a Chesapeake genealogy back to their great-grandfathers. Native-born justices and sheriffs were usually related to men who had served on the bench: the fathers, grandfathers, or fathers-in-law of two-fifths of them had been justices or assemblymen, and a fifth had a brother or uncle who had served before them. The proportion of men who were the first in their family to hold higher local office, moreover, declined from more than a third to about a fifth after 1725 (fig. 25).[16]

Members of a few extended families dominated the county bench and the office of sheriff in Prince George's. Nearly two-fifths of the men appointed to these offices between 1725 and 1775 were members of just

---

15. Jack P. Greene, "Legislative Turnover in British America, 1696–1775: A Quantitative Analysis," *WMQ*, 3d Ser., XXXVIII (1981), 442–463, shows falling rates of turnover in both Maryland and Virginia from 1700 to 1775.

16. The distribution by generation of sheriffs and justices (excluding those whose genealogy could not be traced) is as follows:

Generation	1696–1724	1725–1749	1750–1774
Immigrant	20	5	5
Second	17	16	5
Third	2	15	6
Fourth	1	4	14

Fig. 25. *Prior Service in Major Office by Kindred of Justices and Sheriffs in Prince George's County, 1696–1775*

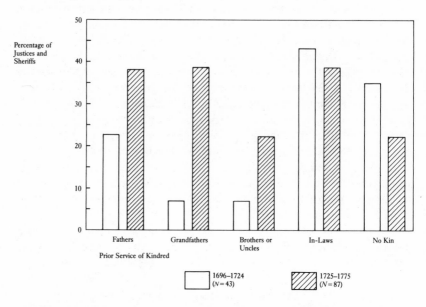

Sources: Lois Green Carr, "County Government in Maryland, 1689–1709" (Ph.D. diss., Harvard University, 1968), 617–621, and appendix 6, table 5; Maryland Commission Books, MHR (abstracted by Randall Miller), linked to data in Prince George's Wills, Land Records, and Parish Registers, MHR, and to data in Edward C. Papenfuse *et al.*, eds., *A Biographical Dictionary of the Maryland Legislature, 1635–1789* (Baltimore, 1979–1984), I; and Effie Gwynn Bowie, *Across the Years in Prince George's County* (Richmond, Va., 1947). Major offices here are justice of the peace, sheriff, provincial justice, legislator, or councillor. Categories are not exclusive: a man whose father and grandfather served is counted in both places. There is no double counting: if both grandfathers served, the man is counted only once in the grandfather group.

seven family groups. Two families, the Magruders and Spriggs, alone provided fifteen justices. The record of public service by the Magruder family was especially full. Alexander and Samuel Magruder, sons of Alexander (a Scottish rebel and ex-servant who never achieved high local office), became justices in 1697 and 1706, respectively. Eight other Magruders served the county as justices during the half-century after 1725, including one grandson of Alexander Junior and one son and three grandsons of Samuel.[17]

Men who reached the Prince George's bench or became sheriffs be-

17. There were 8 Magruders, 7 Spriggs and Belts, 5 Hawkins and Frasers, 4 Bealls, and 3 each of Addisons, Gantts, and Lees. Two justices served from 10 other families.

tween 1725 and 1775, but did not belong to officeholding families, were chosen from two groups. About half these men were immigrant merchants or lawyers, selected because of their familiarity with the law or their facility with complicated accounts. The others tended to be sons of wealthy men who had never achieved high public office or men remotely related to former justices. Nathaniel Offutt, for instance, was the son of wealthy merchant William Offutt, who had not been chosen, because he was illiterate; John Fraser was the son of a well-known Virginia-born clergyman whose calling precluded appointment; and Mordecai Jacob married the daughter of Robert Tyler, Jr., whose father had served on the court many years earlier.[18]

Similarly strong political dynasties of interrelated families dominated courthouses all over the Chesapeake. Three families, for instance, the Taylors, Taliferros, and Buckners, provided more than a fifth of the justices appointed in Caroline County, Virginia, between the founding of the county in 1728 and 1781. And more than a quarter of the sixteen hundred justices appointed in Virginia between 1757 and 1775 belonged to only fifty-five patrilineages, each of which had at least five justices, and many others were related to these families by marriage. The most prominent and prestigious families in the colony, including Washington, Carter, Lee, Mason, and Randolph, were among those who served repeatedly as justices.[19]

Though kinship became even more thoroughly embedded in the Maryland assembly than on local benches by the mid-eighteenth century, political dynasties developed slowly early in the century. Nearly two of every five southern Maryland assemblymen or councillors first elected or appointed between 1700 and 1724 were immigrants, and an equal proportion had immigrant fathers. Not surprisingly, wealthy immigrants and relatively undistinguished natives found marriage into gentry families a good way to qualify for high office. More than two-fifths of these early eighteenth-century legislators married women whose fathers had served in the assembly. Blood lineages grew slowly in importance among legislators. Though few sons succeeded their fathers into the assembly before 1700, nearly a third of the members elected or appointed between 1700 and 1724 served a generation after their fathers. Another eighth followed their grandfathers into office, and a fifth of them served after brothers or uncles (see fig. 26).

When the generational depth of southern Maryland legislators rose during the middle half of the eighteenth century, kin ties among legislators

18. Of the 20 men who were the first in their families to serve between 1725 and 1775, 6 were immigrant merchants, 3 were immigrant doctors, 5 had remote kin on the bench or were from wealthy families of long standing, and 5 could not be traced.
19. T. E. Campbell, *Colonial Caroline: A History of Caroline County, Virginia* (Richmond, Va., 1954), 345–351; Sydnor, *Gentlemen Freeholders*, 60–73, 146.

Fig. 26. *Prior Service in Major Office by Kindred of Southern Maryland Legislators, 1700–1789*

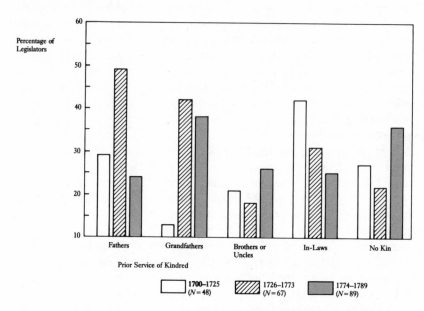

Sources: Edward C. Papenfuse *et al.*, eds., *A Biographical Dictionary of the Maryland Legislature, 1635–1789* (Baltimore, 1979–1984), I, for Prince George's, Anne Arundel, Calvert, Charles, and St. Mary's counties and Annapolis town. It includes both houses for all legislators whose names end in the letters A–H and all Prince George's legislators. Higher offices here are legislator, councillor, and provincial justice. General procedures are the same as for fig. 25.

dramatically increased. Only one-sixth of legislators first selected between 1725 and 1773 were immigrants, and more than half counted Maryland grandfathers among their ancestors. More than a third of this group traced a Maryland ancestry back at least to their great-grandfathers.[20] As the generational continuity of legislators rose, the importance of marriage diminished, and the significance of bloodlines grew in determining who would reach the legislature. Almost half the legislators selected between 1725 and 1773 followed their fathers into office, and nearly an equal number had grandfathers who had served. At the same time, fewer than a third of the members married a daughter of a legislator.

20. Between 1700 and 1724, 17 of 46 legislators were immigrants, 20 were second-generation natives, 8 were third-generation, and 1 was fourth-generation. Of 64 selected from 1725 to 1773, 11 were immigrants, 19 were second-generation, 22 were third-generation, 9 were fourth-generation, and 3 were fifth-generation.

A few families dominated the delegation from Prince George's County between 1725 and 1773. Since each county sent four men to the assembly and since there were nineteen elections between 1725 and 1773, the county's voters could have chosen seventy-six different men. Yet they elected only nineteen men during these years, and members of only four families served seven-tenths of the terms. For instance, six descendants of Thomas Sprigg, who represented the county from 1712 to 1714, filled nearly a third of these terms. The first of them, Ralph Crabb, married one of Sprigg's daughters and served between 1719 and 1733. He was followed by two of Thomas's sons: Edward Sprigg, who sat from 1728 to 1754 and was assembly speaker, and his brother Osborne, who served from 1739 to 1745. Both Sprigg brothers married daughters of Joseph Belt, their stepfather, who represented the county from 1725 to 1737. Two other Spriggs served shorter terms.[21]

Justices, sheriffs, and assemblymen formed an almost hereditary caste by the mid-eighteenth century. The youthful age when men first reached high office documents the dominance of ascription over economic or educational achievement in the selection of officeholders. Wealthy men married in their mid-twenties and reached their greatest prosperity after age forty. Men who became justices in Middlesex County between 1680 and 1750 first entered that office when they were thirty-three. More than four-fifths of the fathers of men who served in high provincial and local office (justice, legislator, sheriff, colonial official) had preceded them in high office. These men achieved their highest position at age thirty-one, but the few men who reached high office without kin ties did not gain high office until age thirty-seven. Southern Maryland legislators whose fathers served in the assembly gained their first major office when they were twenty-eight, several years after they married, and men whose fathers-in-law served were selected at an average age of thirty. In contrast, legislators who were the first in their family to serve were chosen for their first high office at age thirty-seven, and nearly a third were over forty. Blood relationships were even more important on the Prince George's bench: men whose fathers had been justices were appointed at age twenty-eight, those whose grandfathers or uncles (but not fathers) had served became justices when they were thirty-four, but men who relied only on their fathers-in-law to secure a judgeship waited until they were forty before joining the bench.[22]

21. Compiled from Papenfuse *et al.*, eds., *A Biographical Dictionary*, I.
22. For Middlesex, see Rutman and Rutman, *A Place in Time: Explicatus*, 144–148. See fig. 26 for Maryland. Only those Marylanders with known birth years are included. The Maryland legislators cover years from 1725 to 1789: where the father served, mean age at first service was 28.0 ($N = 36$, SD [standard deviation] = 6.6; excluding highest age, mean = 27.2, SD = 4.3); where other blood kin served, mean = 32.6 ($N = 15$, SD = 4.8); where in-laws

Though wealthy families in the tidewater Chesapeake had gained political and economic control of their counties by the 1720s, wealth and high
office alone did not turn these ruling groups into a cohesive ruling class
with a distinct culture that set them apart from ordinary planters. In fact,
they shared the competitive culture of gambling, horse races, and blood
feuds of their poorer neighbors and failed to pursue the education that
might set them apart from other planters, probably because before mid-
century most of their workers were rebellious African slaves who required
continual supervision.[23]

Nonetheless, by the 1750s and 1760s wealthy officeholders and their
kindred and friends constituted a distinctive class. As native slaves replaced
Africans in the work force, the productivity of slaves may have increased
and the need for continual supervision diminished. Unlike yeomen, gentlemen no longer had to choose between consumption and leisure. Even those
yeomen who owned a slave or two had to spend most of their time working
with their slaves and sons in making their crops. Any time they spent away
from their farm potentially reduced their income and, with it, their ability to
consume. Gentlemen, in contrast, did not work with their hands, but used
the wealth their slaves produced to establish high status, to purchase luxury
goods, or to seek learning or office.[24]

The increased use of personal servants by the gentry after the mid-
eighteenth century, when native slaves replaced Africans, perhaps best
documents the desire of gentlemen to set themselves apart from ordinary
planters. African slaves poured into the region during the first forty years of
the century, but they were usually placed on small units and forced to tend
tobacco. Robert "King" Carter, who owned more than seven hundred slaves
when he died in 1732, did not have any black personal servants and used
only a single black domestic. By mid-century, gentlemen had to have slave
personal servants to establish their status when they appeared in public.
Charles Carroll of Carrollton, who owned more than three hundred slaves
in 1773, employed two waiting men, two grooms, and a cook on his main
plantation and six household servants in his Annapolis home. Similarly,
Robert Carter of Nomini Hall, a grandson of King Carter, owned three
housemaids, a cook, a waiter, and two postilions at Nomini Hall in 1791.

---

served, mean = 37.1 (N = 32, SD = 8.8). Prince George's data cover the years 1725–1775.
If father served, mean = 28.4 (N = 21, SD = 4.0); if grandfather served, mean = 34.3 (N
= 8, SD = 7.2); if in-laws served, mean = 40.0 (N = 12, SD = 10.1; when highest age
excluded, mean = 38.4, SD = 8.7); there were only four known ages where no kin served.
23. See above, chap. 6, for the male competitive ethic.
24. The idea of a leisure class was, of course, developed by Thorstein Veblen in *The Theory of
the Leisure Class* (1899), but I am indebted to Stanley Engerman for pointing out the importance of the trade-off between consumption and leisure in the South.

Men of less wealth, who owned more than ten adult slaves, emulated the richest gentlemen by using one or two slaves as servants.[25]

Gentlemen spent income generated by their slaves to establish a standard of living that further separated them from ordinary planters. A middling planter lived in a two- or three-room house and owned a couple of sheets and a tablecloth; a gentleman lived in a mansion and stocked a linen closet. Gentlemen used tea and coffee regularly and ate from fine china; other planters drank tea or coffee only intermittently and used earthenware utensils. Every planter owned a horse or two and often a simple cart, and gentlemen raised racing steeds and drove fine carriages to church or courthouse.[26]

Gentlemen also increased the social distance between themselves and yeomen by participating in a written culture closed to less wealthy men. Most men gained only minimal literacy. Sons of ordinary planters attended school for a year or two and learned to read and write, while some of their sisters learned only to read and others stayed unlettered. In contrast, children of gentlemen began their education with private tutors or at local reading schools, and the sons of gentlemen continued their education at private schools, where they studied English composition and Latin. Donald Robinson's grammar school in King and Queen County, Virginia, may have been typical of these institutions. He taught 214 students between 1758 and 1773, instructing about 40 percent of them in Latin for an average of 2.7 years and 60 percent in English for 1.7 years. A fifth took both subjects, but only a tenth studied mathematics or Greek.[27]

Sons of gentlemen continued their education at the College of William and Mary, at other North American colleges, or abroad. William and Mary was founded in the 1690s, just when the Chesapeake population was beginning to increase naturally, and the college started to educate large numbers of students in the 1720s, when the first large generation of white natives came of age. About fifteen students matriculated at the college each year in the 1750s and 1760s, and this number increased to around twenty a year in the 1770s. Most classes at William and Mary included representatives of

25. Robert Carter Inventory, Carter Papers, Virginia Historical Society, Richmond (VHS); Charles Carroll of Carrollton Inventory, Carroll Account Book, Maryland Historical Society, Baltimore (MHS); Robert Carter Deed of Manumission, Duke University, Durham, N.C., film at Colonial Williamsburg Research Department (CW); Gerald W. Mullin, *Flight and Rebellion: Slave Resistance in Eighteenth-Century Virginia* (New York, 1972), 62–78; chap. 10, below.
26. Isaac, *Transformation of Virginia*, 70–79; Lois Green Carr and Lorena S. Walsh, "Changing Life Styles in Colonial St. Mary's County," *Working Papers from the Regional Economic History Research Center*, I, No. 3 (1978), *Economic Change in the Chesapeake Colonies*, 73–118.
27. Thomas K. Bullock, "Schools and Schooling in Eighteenth Century Virginia" (Ed.D. diss., Duke University, 1961), chaps. 3, 4, esp. 132–140; Daniel Blake Smith, *Inside the Great House: Planter Family Life in Eighteenth-Century Chesapeake Society* (Ithaca, N.Y., 1980), 88–108.

major tidewater families like the Burwells, Byrds, and Carters. For example, five sons and at least eight paternal grandsons and great-grandsons of Robert "King" Carter attended the college between 1720 and 1780.[28]

Students often spent only a year or two at William and Mary, and yet they established lifelong contacts with other tidewater gentlemen. When the Revolution began, college alumni naturally picked others who had attended the college to serve with them on important committees. Twelve of the twenty members of the committees of correspondence and safety of Virginia appointed in 1773 and 1775 had attended William and Mary. In fact, two-fifths of the sixty-four Virginians who served on seven important Revolutionary-era bodies, including the Continental Congress and the Constitutional Convention, were alumni of William and Mary.[29]

This cadre of educated men supported newspapers and patronized the arts and letters. Though a few men with literary talents wrote in the Chesapeake colonies in the seventeenth century, they gained little local support for their work. But eighteenth-century gentlemen wanted a fuller intellectual life. In 1727 William Parks founded the *Maryland Gazette*, and a year later he printed *The Mousetrap*, a poem translated by Richard Lewis. This book, the first literary work published in the South, gained wide support among Maryland's gentry: 149 men, about 1 percent of the householders of the province, subscribed to copies of the poem. In Prince George's County, for instance, nearly a fifth of the men who owned more than a thousand acres of land and almost a third of those who held ten or more taxable slaves purchased the volume. In 1734 Parks moved to Virginia, where he founded the *Virginia Gazette*. When Parks left Maryland, the local newspaper folded, but it was revived by Jonas Green in 1745. Both newspapers published for the educated public. They were filled with foreign news, learned essays first published in England, belles lettres, and poetry. Few articles, except for an occasional piece of local news or advertisements for runaways or local stores, appealed to ordinary planters. Despite its limited audience, the *Virginia Gazette* reached almost two thousand readers in the 1760s and 1770s.[30]

28. *The History of the College of William and Mary . . . from its Foundation, 1693 to 1874* (Richmond, Va., 1874), 83–96; "Notes Relating to Some of the Students Who Attended the College of William and Mary, 1753–1770," *WMQ*, 2d Ser., I (1921), 27–41; "Notes Relative to Some of the Students Who Attended the College of William and Mary, 1770–1778," *WMQ*, 2d Ser., I (1921), 116–130; *A Provisional List of Alumni, Grammar School Students, Members of the Faculty, and Members of the Board of Visitors of the College of William and Mary from 1693 to 1888* (Richmond, Va., 1941).
29. "Education in Colonial Virginia," Pt. 5, "Influence of William and Mary College," *WMQ*, 1st Ser., VII (1898), 2–5.
30. Richard Beale Davis, "The Intellectual Golden Age in the Colonial Chesapeake Bay

A brief study of the gentry of Prince George's suggests that education spread through much of the gentry class by the time of the Revolution. Members of seven of the sixteen wealthiest families in the county received training as doctors or clergymen during the middle half of the century, and daughters married educated men in another two families. Education slowly permeated these families. Henry Addison, for instance, was the son and grandson of members of the Maryland council. The first man in his family to receive a higher education, he was trained at Oxford, took clerical orders, and became rector of a parish a couple of miles from his family's home. His niece Eleanor married Jonathan Boucher, a learned Anglican cleric, in 1772. The Clagett family began educating their sons at about the same time. Eleanor Clagett, a fourth-generation Marylander, married John Eversfield, an English immigrant and longtime rector of a local parish, in 1730. Eversfield built a tidy fortune from Clagett land and his own income. Her successful marriage prompted her younger brother Samuel to seek clerical training, and he served in several Maryland parishes in the 1740s and 1750s. His son Thomas John Clagett, born in 1745, was educated at the College of New Jersey (later Princeton), took Anglican orders, and in 1792 became the first Episcopal bishop consecrated in America.[31]

These educated men lived in two worlds: they associated with other gentlemen at home, and they communicated with friends abroad by letter or through their publications. Seven residents of Prince George's, three of them native-born Marylanders and the rest immigrants who married into gentry families, published articles or pamphlets during the eighteenth century. Dr. Richard Brooke, a fifth-generation Marylander who reported on the climate, constitution, and population of Maryland to English readers, most closely approximated the educated gentry ideal.[32]

Although few gentlemen enjoyed an extensive education, educated men influenced their entire class. They debated public policy with other gentlemen at church, tavern, and race track. Moreover, all gentlemen, and not just those few who possessed great learning, sought knowledge of the

---

Country," *Virginia Magazine of History and Biography*, LXXVIII (1970), 131–143; Joseph A. Leo Lemay, *Men of Letters in Colonial Maryland* (Knoxville, Tenn., 1972), 111–116, 126–131, 193–202; Richard Lewis, trans., *The Mouse-Trap; or, The Battle of the Cambrians and Mice: A Poem* (Annapolis, Md., 1727), subscriber's list, linked to data in Black Books, II, 109–124, and Prince George's Deeds and Rent Rolls, MHR; William P. Black, "The Virginia Gazette, 1766–1774: Beginnings of an Indigenous Literature" (Ph.D. diss., Duke University, 1971), 17–20.

31. Bowie, *Across the Years*; Hienton, *Prince George's Heritage*. Wealthy families are defined as those with at least two members with 1,000 acres of land, £1,000 estates, or eight or more taxable slaves.

32. *Ibid.*; Newman, *Mareen Duvall of Middle Plantation*; Lawrence C. Wroth, *A History of Printing in Colonial Maryland, 1686–1776* (Baltimore, 1922); and Lemay, *Men of Letters*.

world beyond their neighborhood. They consigned tobacco to England, wrote letters to London merchants, visited provincial capitals on business or to sit in the assembly, and joined social clubs with other gentlemen.

The formation of exclusive social clubs by gentlemen symbolizes their growing class consciousness. By the early eighteenth century, the two assemblies had become gentlemen's debating societies, and after the day's legislative business was completed, they retired to taverns and eating clubs with their friends. More formal orga nizations sprang up by the 1730s and 1740s. The history of three Maryland clubs suggests the reasons gentlemen sought each other's company. The South River Club, begun by gentleman planters and merchants who lived near Annapolis, met monthly for dinner from the 1730s to the nineteenth century. The Tuesday Club of Annapolis, organized by Dr. Alexander Hamilton in 1744, required high intellectual achievement for membership, but members invited a cross section of Maryland's gentry class to participate in its dinners and to help write its satirical history of Maryland politics. When Hamilton died in 1756, the club disbanded, but the Homony Club, in existence from 1770 to 1773, continued its traditions.[33]

Gentlemen formed a self-confident, self-conscious, and powerful ruling class throughout tidewater by the mid-eighteenth century, yet their authority did not extend to most of piedmont. Most piedmont counties were too new to be ruled by a hereditary class of gentlemen, and some of the region's justices were nouveaux riches of undistinguished lineage. Even the wealthiest men of these counties often lived in crude cabins, possessed few amenities and no luxuries, and considered education a frill. Not until after the Revolution did a gentry ruling class, similar to that of tidewater, first appear in this region.[34]

The Rule of Gentlemen

Although wealthy gentlemen dominated the polity and economy of the tidewater Chesapeake by the early eighteenth century, they struggled with poorer planters over tobacco regulation. As we have seen, during each depression from the 1680s to the 1730s, wealthy men sought to impose limits

33. Jane Carson, *Colonial Virginians at Play* (Charlottesville, Va., 1965), 260–270; Elaine G. Breslaw, "Wit, Whimsy, and Politics: The Use of Satire by the Tuesday Club of Annapolis, 1744 to 1756," *WMQ*, 3d Ser., XXXII (1975), 295–306; *The Ancient South River Club: A Brief History by the Historical Committee of the Club* (Menasha, Wis., 1952).

34. Richard R. Beeman, *Cavaliers and Frontiersmen: The Cultural Development of Lunenburg County, Virginia, 1746–1832* (Philadelphia, 1984), chaps. 1–3.

on tobacco production by legislation and, when that failed, sometimes led rioters to cut the tobacco plants of their neighbors. This conflict culminated in the 1720s and 1730s when Governor Gooch of Virginia and his gentry allies forced the tobacco inspection law through the Virginia assembly, requiring planters to take their tobacco to warehouses and watch while their trashy leaves were destroyed. Poor planters, who bitterly opposed the law, burned several warehouses and forced their representatives to support repeal of the law.[35]

When tobacco prices rose after 1735 and conflict over tobacco regulation diminished, gentlemen finally legitimated their authority over the landed and slaveowning planters just below them in the social structure. Gentlemen no longer dominated these men by using their political or economic power but gained the support of yeomen by seeking their advice and serving as their patrons. County gentlemen sought the votes of yeomen in elections and their service on juries; they supported yeomen when they wanted to form a new county or parish in their neighborhood; they broke bread with their kindred among the yeomanry at church, tavern, and family gatherings; and they extended credit to yeoman neighbors.[36]

A class of yeoman planters formed in tidewater during the middle half of the eighteenth century as a result of these reciprocal exchanges between gentlemen and the freeholders they sought to incorporate into civil society. Independence, usually documented by the ownership of land or slaves, was required for political participation, but not all property owners were yeomen. A man who wanted to become a member of civil society had to earn that right by deferring to his betters and by maintaining a good reputation. An examination of jury service and voting, two critical symbolic acts performed by citizens in Chesapeake society, suggests that only freeholders and slaveowners of long standing in the community were recognized by other planters as yeomen.

The local economy and government could not have functioned without grand and petit jurors, men conscripted to serve the public good. Grand jurors returned indictments in criminal cases and responded to accusations from vestrymen and constables, while petit jurors decided both criminal and civil cases. Since most civil proceedings revolved around credit, jurors frequently adjudicated disputes between merchants and planters. This task took on great importance in the Chesapeake colonies, where neither government nor banks regulated the distribution and repayment of credit. Only

---

35. Conflict over tobacco is examined in detail in chap. 3 above.
36. The most thorough theoretical examination of these issues can be found in Williams, *Marxism and Literature*, chap. 6.

male freeholders could serve as jurors. Even after they were chosen, petit jurors could be challenged for "Partiality; where there is express Malice, or Favour, or Kindred . . . tho' ever so remote" to either of the parties.[37]

Since men gained prestige from service on juries, the rate of planter participation on these panels suggests the degree of equality among white men. As long as most planters were immigrants or migrants and white population density was low, sheriffs had little choice but to select nearly every eligible male landowner for service on juries. Such widespread participation gave planters a stake in society and may have helped maintain order in a society that lacked a strong ruling class. But after white immigration declined and population increased in tidewater at the beginning of the eighteenth century, sheriffs became more selective in choosing jurors. Jury service changed from a universal social obligation to a form of patronage by the sheriff and a way of distinguishing worthy freeholders from the mass of men.[38]

The history of jury selection in Prince George's County, Maryland, from the founding of the county in 1696 to the 1770s suggests that this transition from civic responsibility to patronage could begin quickly. About three-quarters of county landowners were called for jury duty between 1696 and 1709, and most of the rest were Catholics, who could not take the oaths required of jurors. In fact, a typical Protestant freeholder served on a jury every two to five years. Nor did sheriffs exclude tenants: despite laws requiring freeholder status for jury service, about a third of the county's tenants were jurymen at least once between 1696 and 1709.[39]

Widespread participation on juries in Prince George's disappeared by the 1720s and 1730s. Since the number of heads of family rose from fewer than three hundred in 1706 to more than eleven hundred in 1733, even the most egalitarian sheriff could not have chosen everyone. Sheriffs, however, turned to a small group of men, from families of good reputation long resident in the county, when they sought jurors. Nearly three-quarters of planters from established families who owned land and slaves served on a jury between 1725 and 1741, and they constituted more than half the county's jurymen. Once sheriffs put these substantial yeomen on juries, they incorporated newcomers who owned land and slaves and established men who held slaves or land into the body politic. Nearly half the heads of family in these groups served on a jury, and they accounted for a third of the jurymen. Other newcomers rarely served on juries, even if they owned land,

37. Webb, *Office of Justice of Peace*, 192–197 (quote on 196).
38. This paragraph owes much to Carr, "Foundations of Social Order," in Daniels, ed., *Town and County*, 89–91.
39. Carr, "County Government in Maryland," 604–609, 655–658.

and tenants (except sons of landowners) nearly disappeared from juries (see table 32).

The growth of patrilineal kinship in the county reinforced this increased selectivity for jury service. Nearly three-fifths of the men who sat on juries in Prince George's between 1725 and 1741 were related to at least one other juror. Fathers and sons, uncles and nephews, and pairs of cousins and brothers frequently followed each other into the jury box. Two kinds of families supplied many jurors. Yeoman families long resident in the county sometimes contributed large numbers of jurors, and one or two men from every large kinship group of freeholders served on juries. All nine Brassherses in the county, for instance, sat on a jury. These men, descendants of Robert Brasshers of Calvert County, held from fifty to four hundred acres of land but owned no slaves. One-fifth of the jury terms were served by members of magistrate families, usually brothers or nephews of judges, though justices and their sons sometimes sat on prestigious juries impaneled by provincial assize courts held in the county. Twelve members of the wealthy Magruder family, for instance, served eighty-eight terms on both petit and grand juries.[40]

Jury service in Prince George's became even more restrictive in the 1770s, in part because the number of households grew from eleven hundred to nearly seventeen hundred between the 1730s and the 1770s. Sheriffs limited civic participation to sons of substantial yeomen and excluded poorer freeholders who had served frequently earlier in the century. The proportion of jurymen who owned both land and slaves rose from about three-fifths in the 1730s to three-quarters in the 1770s. Nonetheless, the proportion of men in this group who served diminished from two-thirds between 1725 and 1741 to only one-half from 1768 to 1784. Sheriffs infrequently asked planters who owned a small parcel of land or a slave or two to sit on juries: participation by this group declined from more than a third in the 1730s to only one-seventh in the 1770s.[41]

Tidewater counties with smaller populations than Prince George's continued to call on a high proportion of their freeholders to serve in public office. From three-tenths to one-half of the landowners of Elizabeth City,

---

40. See table 32 and sources there. These data exclude service by affines.

41. This analysis is based upon a 1776 census for half the county in Brumbaugh, ed., *Maryland Records*, I, 1–88, linked to data in Prince George's Levy Book A, Land Records, and Debt Books, MHR. In total, 20% of the white male heads of household served as jurors ($N = 789$, excluding Quakers and Catholics). That included 2% of the tenant nonslaveholders ($N = 320$), 14% of those who owned land or slaves ($N = 202$), 48% of those who owned land and slaves ($N = 251$), and 19% of the sons of men who owned land and slaves but had not yet received their inheritance ($N = 16$).

Essex, and Charles City counties were chosen as jurors, as overseers of the highways, or for other minor offices in a sample year during the 1740s and 1750s. These three counties averaged about four hundred households each, only a third the number in Prince George's. Nonetheless, civic participation apparently declined even in these tiny counties. Even though the number of householders in Middlesex County fluctuated around 370 throughout the first half of the eighteenth century, officeholding by landowners in the county declined from four-fifths between 1705 and 1710 to only half from 1745 to 1750.[42]

Although poor men, servants, and women often came to court, sheriffs chose jurors from the crowds of men of substance who witnessed court proceedings. As the size of these gatherings increased, sheriffs restricted their choice to the most substantial of these men. About a twentieth of the jurymen in Prince George's from 1696 to 1708 made up one-quarter of the total service on jury panels, and each of these men sat on at least sixteen juries. About a fifteenth of the jurors in Caroline County from 1732 (when the county was formed) to 1745 made up a similar group, and each of these men sat on eleven or more panels. Sheriffs continued to select just a few men, despite the increasing number of men eligible to serve as jurors. A tenth of the jurors in Prince George's between 1725 and 1741, for instance, sat on juries in eleven or more court sessions, and they served a quarter of all the jury terms. A similar concentration could be found in that county in the 1770s.

Although the wealth of men who sat repeatedly on juries in Prince George's changed little over the first half of the century, their social standing improved substantially. The median landholdings of men who sat on at least sixteen juries between 1696 and 1709 were 250 acres, and men who served on panels during eleven or more court terms from 1725 to 1741 owned, on average, 200 acres and two adult slaves. Nonetheless, sheriffs paid more attention to a family's social standing during the 1730s than earlier in the century. Although they chose indiscriminately among freeholders in the 1700s, about a third of the frequent jurors during the 1730s were related to other frequent jurors, and many other members of their extended families served on a few panels.[43]

42. D. Alan Williams, "The Small Farmer in Eighteenth-Century Virginia Politics," *Agricultural History*, XLIII (1969), 98–99. Population data are taken from Darrett B. Rutman and Anita H. Rutman, "'More True and Perfect Lists': The Reconstruction of Censuses for Middlesex County, Virginia, 1668–1704," *VMHB*, LXXXVIII (1980), 55; Evarts B. Greene and Virginia D. Harrington, *American Population before the Federal Census of 1790* (New York, 1932), 150–151.

43. Prince George's Levy Book A; Prince George's Land Records; Prince George's Wills; Prince George's Inventories; Black Books, II, 110–124, all MHR; Carr, "County Govern-

Table 32. *Service on Juries in Prince George's County, 1725–1741, of Resident Householders in 1733*

Group[a]	Probability of Serving (Percentage)	Percentage of Jurors ($N=353$)	Percentage of Householders ($N=1{,}093$)[b]
Established men owning land and slaves	71	49	22
Established men owning land or slaves	44	23	17
Less-established men owning land and slaves	52	11	7
Less-established men owning land or slaves	25	8	11
Established tenant families	11	6	16
More transient tenants	2	2	23
All other transients	11	1	4
Overall	32	100	100

Sources: Lists of jurors (both petit and grand) in Levy Book A and Prince George's Court Records, MHR, linked with Black Books, II, 110–124 (1733 tithables list), X, 8–14 (1719 tithables list), and 1743 Crow's lists in Levy Book A and to land data in Prince George's Rent Rolls and Land Records, MHR.

Notes: Includes prior service of men, 1697–1720, of older men, compiled by Lois G. Carr, "County Government in Maryland, 1689–1709" (Ph.D. diss., Harvard University, 1968), appendix. [a]Established men are those listed (or those whose families are listed) on the 1719 tithables list and are still in the county in 1743, except for tenant nonslaveholders, where the group includes all those in the county in both 1719 and 1733. Less-established men were those who were in the county in 1719 and left before 1743 or who came after 1719 and stayed until at least 1743. More transient tenants were those who arrived after 1719 and either left before 1743 or were still in the county that year. All other transients are those who came after 1719 and left before 1743. [b]Excludes women heads of household and all known Catholics and Quakers.

Voting, like jury service, separated white men into two groups, free-holders welcome to participate in political discourse, and men too poor or unsettled to be full members of civil society. Eighteenth-century elections were contests between representatives of gentry families rather than ideological battles. Voters examined the positions of candidates on such local issues as the location of a new courthouse, reviewed the reciprocal obliga-

---

ment," 662; Campbell, *Colonial Caroline*, 351–356. Caroline and early Prince George's data are for juries served; Prince George's data, 1725–1741, are for court sessions served, and for 1768–1784, for years served.

tions that bound them to each candidate, and then voted orally in front of candidates and neighbors.[44]

Though sheriffs often failed to enforce the exclusion of tenants from the polls, men from well-established families voted far more often than tenants and transients. As a result of this exclusion of poor men from the polls, only about half the family heads usually turned out for elections in the tidewater Chesapeake during the mid-eighteenth century.[45] Although more than half the heads of household in Lancaster County voted in 1748 and 1752, for instance, nearly four-fifths of the landholders voted, and only a quarter of the tenants were permitted to cast a ballot, many of whom may have been sons of freeholders. Men who owned a slave or two but rented land on short-term leases voted less frequently than even the poorest freeholders. Most voters, moreover, had already found a place in local society by civic participation: more than three-fifths of the voters in five elections in tidewater and piedmont Virginia held between 1748 and 1752 had served in local office before the election.[46]

Voters participated in elections to establish credentials as citizens worthy of attention from the gentry class. Candidates sought out potential voters at taverns, churches, and horse races and feted them at innumerable barbecues, plying them with food and drink while discreetly soliciting their votes. Although tidewater elections were often placid affairs, piedmont candidates, who were less distinguished and not yet entrenched in power, continued to treat voters at the polls and sometimes overstepped the bounds of acceptable gentry behavior, promising to support specific legislation or bribing men for their votes.[47]

Candidates seeking support listened carefully to the complaints of yeomen assembled at political gatherings. Robert Munford's play *The Candidates* suggests how proper candidates ought to behave. Nearly all the char-

44. The literature on elections in the Chesapeake colonies is vast and often contentious. The debate can be followed in Sydnor, *Gentlemen Freeholders*, chaps. 2–4; Brown and Brown, *Virginia, 1705–1786*, chaps. 7–9; Lucille Griffith, *The Virginia House of Burgesses, 1750–1774*, rev. ed., (University, Ala., 1970), chap. 3; David Curtis Skaggs, *Roots of Maryland Democracy, 1753–1776* (Westport, Conn., 1973), chap. 1; and Isaac, *Transformation of Virginia*, 110–114.

45. Computed from data in Brown and Brown, *Virginia, 1705–1786*, 141–147, and table following 73; in Griffith, *Virginia House of Burgesses*, 157–168; and in Sydnor, *Gentlemen Freeholders*, 121–124, assuming that there were 1.4 white taxables per household.

46. Data from Brown and Brown, *Virginia, 1705–1786*, 189–190; and Williams, "Small Farmer in Virginia Politics," *Ag. Hist.*, XLIII (1969), 100. Lancaster tenancy estimated from crude number of households (at 1.4 taxable per household) and number of landholders.

47. Sydnor, *Gentlemen Freeholders*, chap. 4; Brown and Brown, *Virginia, 1705–1786*. The difference between tidewater and piedmont is astutely analyzed by Richard R. Beeman in "Robert Munford and the Political Culture of Virginia," *Journal of American Studies*, XII (1978), 169–183.

acters in the play are either candidates and their servants or yeomen and their wives. Mr. Wou'dbe, a proper gentleman and eventual victor in the race, condescends to consult with the electorate at a race track barbecue but refuses Guzzle's intemperate request that he "get the price of rum lower'd." In contrast, he defers to yeomen on local issues and promises to consider fairly their demands for changes in economic policy. When yeoman Stern complains about paying ferryage rates to attend church and contemplates petitioning the assembly to "get us clear of that expense," Wou'dbe says the request is "just; and make no doubt but it would pass into a law." Yeoman Prize brings up a more volatile issue, the behavior of men who pick trashy tobacco from hogsheads. "Why don't you burgesses," he yells, "do something with the damn'd pickers? If we have a hogshead of tobacco refused, away it goes to them; and after they have twisted up the best of it for their own use, and taken as much as will pay them for their trouble, the poor planter has little for his share." Wou'dbe judiciously answers, "There are great complaints against them; and I believe the assembly will take them under consideration." When Prize, dissatisfied with this response, asks whether Wou'dbe would vote against the pickers, the candidate answers that he "will, if they deserve it."[48]

Yeomen entered into a multitude of reciprocal but often unequal relationships with gentlemen. Gentlemen attended the parish church with yeomen and joined the family activities of kindred among the yeomanry. Yeomen borrowed money from gentlemen in times of distress but, in return, behaved deferentially around the gentry. And yeomen expressed their political views vigorously and insisted upon legal support for dominion over their dependents but, in return, supported the political authority of the gentry.

Kinship ties linked gentry to yeomanry, for nearly all gentry families included numerous yeomen. Often only one member of a family was a gentleman; the rest were yeomen. Gentry families attended church with their yeomen kindred, named children after them, lent them money, and solicited their political support. The gentry Tylers of Prince George's, for instance, attended Henderson's Chapel with their yeoman cousins, the Duvalls; gentry and yeoman Bealls all came to the Presbyterian church in Bladensburg. Robert Tyler, a justice and assemblyman, named a child Mareen, after his father-in-law; and there were Ninians in every Beall line.[49]

48. *Ibid.*; Jay B. Hubbell and Douglass Adair, eds., "Robert Munford's *The Candidates*," *WMQ*, 3d Ser., V (1948), 217–251, quote on 243–244.

49. Newman, *Mareen Duvall of Middle Plantation*, 162–163; Beall Genealogical Files, MSS in possession of Margaret Cook.

Justices, who valued their yeoman kindred, enforced the patriarchal rule of yeomen over their families, assuring masters of dominion over their slaves and control of their wives and children. Masters could punish slaves as they saw fit, sell or bequeath them at will, and demand sustained labor from them, subject only to the customary rules they made themselves. Slaves had no recourse to the courts, and justices took slaves from masters only when the latter committed a felony. Gentry support for patriarchal dominion in yeoman families combined with the prosperity of the second half of the eighteenth century to secure planters' dominion over their dependents. High tobacco prices, along with vigorous grain markets, permitted yeomen to improve their standard of living and better fulfill their economic obligations to wives and children. As long as husbands did not overstep the bounds of decency, they could rule their families as they saw fit. Wives brought husbands to court only if they failed to support them or if they beat them severely. Once gentry magistrates guaranteed yeomen this familial autonomy, other forms of reciprocity between yeomen and the ruling class were used to sustain gentry authority.[50]

Yeomen and gentlemen established intricate reciprocal networks of credit before 1700, but the quantity of credit available to them grew rapidly after 1750, when Scottish merchants poured thousands of pounds sterling into the region and competed for planter business with local shopkeepers, London consignment houses, and each other. Nearly all credit originated in Britain and took the form of loans or advances on future crops. Gentlemen and prosperous yeomen took advantage of competition among merchants and often borrowed from several of them.[51] Local merchants and gentleman planters reinvested the money borrowed from British creditors in loans to less wealthy neighbors, creating and sustaining a vast multiplication of monetary loans and payments in kind that ultimately involved every freeholder in the region.[52]

Planters who needed money to purchase slaves or land or to pay off debts after a poor harvest often mortgaged land or slaves to a local merchant or gentleman. Between two-thirds and seven-eighths of the mort-

---

50. See chap. 5 for patriarchalism and chap. 10 for master-slave relations.

51. *Maryland Gazette*, June 2, 1763. Prince George's Inventories, Accounts, and Land Records show that the proportion of decedents who owed money to both Scottish factors and local or London merchants rose from one-seventh in the 1750s to one-quarter in the 1760s.

52. The best general analyses of the credit system are found in Jacob M. Price, *Capital and Credit in British Overseas Trade: The View from the Chesapeake, 1700–1776* (Cambridge, Mass., 1980), chaps. 1, 7; and Robert Forster and Edward C. Papenfuse, "Les grands planteurs du Maryland au dix-huitième siècle: Une élite politique et économique," *Annales: Économies, sociétés, civilisations*, XXXVI (1982), 552–573, esp. 558–563, document the social and political context of debt relationships.

gages in four Virginia counties from 1738 to 1779 were held by merchants and gentlemen. About two-thirds of this group were merchants. Although wealthy men sometimes borrowed large sums from each other, more than two-thirds of the debtors were ordinary planters who borrowed one hundred pounds or less to retire their debts or buy land or slaves.[53]

In addition, both yeomen and gentlemen continually traded goods and services to increase their output and improve their standard of living. They thereby became both creditors and debtors, usually borrowing small sums from neighbors and lending them equally small sums in return. Nearly every householder who died in Prince George's between 1730 and 1769 owed money to creditors at his death, and the heirs of three-quarters of them collected money owed to the estate. A person's wealth determined the level of his participation in credit networks. Although four-fifths of all tenants without slaves owed money to one—or, more likely, several—creditors, more than half neither lent money nor provided services to other planters. Men who owned land or slaves owed money to more creditors and were somewhat more likely to lend money themselves than tenants without slaves, and three-quarters of the planters who owned both land and slaves had others indebted to them and usually owed money to at least five creditors (see table 33).

Justices of the peace regulated the credit system, recording debts when creditors brought cases to them and attaching property when necessary to ensure payment. Since only judicial procedures could guarantee payment, merchants frequently sought a place on the bench, where they could deal with minor debt cases themselves and oversee the credit system. Two of the initial eighteen justices appointed in Caroline County in 1728 were merchants, and another ten merchants joined the bench between 1732 and 1765, about a sixth of the justices selected during those years. Merchants not only sought judicial office in Prince George's County, but they often stayed on the bench for years: twelve of the twenty-eight men appointed between 1725 and 1773 who served more than ten years were merchants.[54]

These merchant justices, like their planter colleagues, knew the limits of their power. In good times, they recorded debts for merchants to ensure repayment; in times of credit contraction, they increasingly attached property for merchants who sought immediate repayment. Yet they were debtors too, and they rarely took the further step of sending debtors to prison. Only about 300 men were imprisoned for debt in Maryland between 1707 and 1764, and even during the next decade, when the British credit system collapsed twice, only 750 men were put behind bars. Most of them soon

53. Brown and Brown, *Virginia, 1705–1786*, 99–105.
54. Campbell, *Colonial Caroline*, 345–351; for Prince George's, see fig. 25 and sources there.

Table 33. *The Web of Credit in Prince George's County, 1730–1769*

No. of Creditors of Estate	Percentage of Decedents					
	No. Indebted to Estate					
	0	1–2	3–5	6–10	11+	Overall
Tenants without Slaves (*N*=107)						
0–1	17	6	2	0	1	26
2–4	22	12	2	2	2	39
5+	12	12	6	2	3	35
Total	51	30	9	4	6	
Land- or Slaveowners (*N*=68)						
0–1	9	1	7	5	0	22
2–4	15	9	6	0	1	31
5–9	13	3	3	4	7	31
10+	7	1	1	2	4	16
Total	44	15	17	12	13	
Land- and Slaveowners (*N*=287)						
0–1	4	2	2	0	0	9
2–4	7	5	5	1	3	22
5–9	11	9	6	2	5	32
10–15	2	5	2	3	6	18
16+	1	2	6	4	6	20
Total	25	23	21	11	19	

Sources: Prince George's Inventories and Accounts, MHR.

Note: Excluded are merchants, tavernkeepers, and those decedents where no account was filed. Estates with "sundry" persons indebted to it were distributed among the known groups as they appeared.

petitioned the assembly for release, and more than four-fifths of their petitions were accepted.[55]

Although yeomen were equal to gentlemen as masters of families and of slaves and often participated as equals with gentlemen in reciprocal exchanges of goods and services, they participated infrequently in govern-

55. See chap. 4, above, for the impact of credit crises on debtors, and Tommy R. Thompson, "Debtors, Creditors, and the General Assembly in Colonial Maryland," *MHM*, LXXII (1977), 59–77, esp. 71–73.

mental administration and the resolution of provincial political issues. Gentlemen in colonial assemblies made decisions about the formation of new counties and parishes, the tobacco economy, and the relationship of colony and mother country without consulting the yeomanry. Virginia's governors, moreover, appointed justices only from lists of gentlemen submitted by the local bench, and Maryland governors consulted only with local gentlemen (and especially the county's assemblymen) before selecting justices.[56]

The yeomanry partially resolved this tension between equality and hierarchy by insisting upon equitable administration of government. For instance, they urged sheriffs and tobacco inspectors to bend rules on tax collection and on burning low-quality tobacco in times of poor crops or low prices. Furthermore, they successfully pressured their justices and assemblymen to support their petitions for founding new counties and parishes. Gentlemen acquiesced in these pressures to maintain social harmony.

Gentlemen sometimes responded to the needs of the yeomanry when they recommended men for the bench. Magistrates and governors made sure that at least one justice lived in every county neighborhood who could adjudicate minor disputes and settle small claims of the yeomanry. From time to time, gentlemen supported the judicial appointment of yeomen. The eighteen members of Caroline's first court included two yeoman planters and a trader who supported ordinary planters, and another four yeomen served as justices in the county from 1732 to 1765.[57]

Since tobacco inspectors decided how much of a planter's crop had to be destroyed, all planters had an important stake in their selection. Although vestrymen chose inspectors in Maryland, planters often lobbied for men they preferred. The contest between Andrew Beall, a merchant, and his first cousin John Beall, carpenter, for an inspectorship in 1769 in Bladensburg vividly illustrates planter concerns. Andrew Beall, the incumbent inspector, learned shortly before the election that three Scottish merchants in Bladensburg opposed his selection, and he set about rallying support. He circulated a petition that derided his opposition, insisting that these men had "not more that an equal right with the Planters, to recommend an Inspector" and urged his own election as a "Man independent and free" of mercantile interests. One of the first signers was James Wilson, a fifty-nine-year old gentleman from the neighborhood who owned ten adult slaves and 1,350 acres of land. Armed with this endorsement, Beall went to the local Anglican church the Sunday before the election to gain support from the

---

56. Little is known about the selection process. These comments are based upon the kinds of men who served and upon personal communications from John Hemphill (on Virginia) and Lois Carr (on Maryland).

57. Campbell, *Colonial Caroline*, 345–349.

parishioners. He first approached William Berry, a gentleman who lived some miles away. Berry skimmed the petition, looking for names of other gentlemen, and signed it without understanding that three Bladensburg merchants wanted to replace Beall. Berry and Beall together persuaded three yeomen to add their names. Their effort came to naught, however, for Berry soon learned that "Andrew Beall would be disagreeable to all the Merchants, as an Inspector, and also to many Planters," and he changed sides, supporting John Beall, who won the election.[58]

Since planters wanted church and courthouse located near their farms, the creation of new parishes and counties and the relocation of churches and courthouses were major political issues throughout the Chesapeake. The power of ordinary planters to create or move public facilities, however, was limited. They could mount a campaign for change, but without gentry aid their cause was doomed. Although frontier planters, for instance, regularly sought new counties or more centrally located courthouses, justices, who often lived in old neighborhoods, usually opposed their request. Frontiersmen persisted and eventually gained sufficient gentry support to petition the assembly for redress. The Virginia assembly typically granted petitions for three new parishes per legislative session during the middle half of the eighteenth century. That body also received requests for the creation of three new counties per session as well, but opponents sometimes counterpetitioned, and legislators formed only one new county per term. The successful campaign by freeholders of frontier Albemarle County, Virginia, to create a new county and the unsuccessful attempt by freeholders in Prince George's to prevent the rebuilding of a distant courthouse illustrate the need for unified gentry support to build new public facilities.[59]

Like other backwoodsmen, planters who lived in the southern end of Albemarle County felt isolated from the county seat, located thirty-five miles to the north. By 1777, when a quarter of the county's families lived in that area, local planters petitioned the assembly for the division of the

58. *Md. Gaz.*, Feb. 20, Mar. 30, 1769; information on participants can be found in Brumbaugh, ed., *Maryland Records*, I, 1–88, as linked with Prince George's Land Records, Debt Books, and Court Records, and in Bowie, *Across the Years*, 59–60. Andrew Beall owned 12 taxable slaves and 215 acres of land in 1776, and his cousin John Beall owned 4 slaves and at least 80 acres of land. Berry inherited substantial land from his father in 1769 and later served on the Prince George's court. Poorer signers included Thomas Craufford, 32, son of James, 72, who had not yet distributed any of his 8 taxable slaves and 450 acres to his three sons; Shadrick Lanham, 40, who owned 100 acres of land; and Zachariah Scott, 32, who probably owned a small tract of land.

59. Raymond C. Bailey, *Popular Influence upon Public Policy: Petitioning in Eighteenth-Century Virginia* (Westport, Conn., 1979), chaps. 4, 7, esp. tables 8, 9; E. Lee Shepard, " 'The Ease and Convenience of the People': Courthouse Locations in Spotsylvania County, 1720–1840," *VMHB*, LXXXVII (1979), 279–289.

county. They suffered "great Hardships and inconveniences" in reaching the courthouse, they contended, including "the Roads extremely bad," studded with "Craggy" mountains, and "two Rivers and many Creeks that are Rapid." In fact, they could not "Attend to their business without Riding The Day before and the day after" the court met.

The campaign to establish this new county, called Fluvanna, began when justices who lived in the southern part of the county tired of the trip to court and of complaints by their neighbors. Before they petitioned the legislature, they gained support from Albemarle's assemblymen and even persuaded Thomas Jefferson (then one of the delegates) to draw a map of the proposed division of the county. At the same time, they mobilized dissatisfied yeomen in their neighborhoods. They wrote the petition, carefully entering their names in the first column, and then circulated it widely, quickly collecting 133 signatures representing almost one-third of the families in the proposed county. The signers were a cross section of the area's freeholders. Although only a sixth of the men who labored without slaves signed, almost three of every ten men who owned one to five slaves supported the drive, and nearly half of those who possessed six or more slaves added their names. Although few planters from older parts of the county supported the campaign, they and their representatives acquiesced, and Fluvanna was born.[60]

Debate over the location of the Prince George's courthouse began in the 1740s when the old courthouse began to fall apart. Justices started to agitate to rebuild the courthouse in 1741, and in 1747 they let contracts for rebuilding it and assessed the populace one hundred thousand pounds of tobacco to pay for it. This action unleashed a torrent of controversy. Not only had the court levied a vast sum, but they had ignored the long-standing grievance of Eastern Branch planters. The population of that area, located about twenty miles from the courthouse, had grown rapidly in the 1720s and 1730s. James Edmonston, a justice who lived near the Eastern Branch, dissented from the levy and insisted that his view be recorded. Area gentlemen urged the court to "forbear to agree with any workmen 'till the meeting

---

60. William H. Gaines, Jr., ed., "An Unpublished Thomas Jefferson Map with a Petition for the Division of Fluvanna from Albemarle County, 1777," Albemarle County Historical Society, *Papers*, VII (1946–1947), 22–27; Julian P. Boyd *et al.*, eds., *The Papers of Thomas Jefferson*, II, *1777 to June 1779* (Princeton, N.J., 1950), 14–15. Names on the petition were linked to the 1782 assessment for Fluvanna in U.S., Bureau of the Census, *Heads of Families at the First Census . . . , Virginia* (Washington, D.C., 1908), 18–19; and to Lester J. Cappon, ed., "Personal Property Tax List for Albemarle County, 1782," Albemarle Co. Hist. Soc., *Papers*, V (1944–1945), 47–73. I found 84 of 130 names on these lists: 3 nonslaveholders in Albemarle; and in Fluvanna, 23 of 165 without slaves signed; 32 of 114 with one to five slaves; and 26 of 58 with more than six slaves.

of the Assembly" so the issue could be debated, but the court ignored their wishes. These men so firmly believed that the behavior of the court was injurious to their interests that they penned a complaint to the assembly, claiming that the levy "is not warrented by Law and . . . may be of dangerous consequences" to their "rights and Liberties." Most of the sixty-nine men who signed their petition were prosperous yeomen from neighborhoods along the Eastern Branch who owned a couple of slaves and several hundred acres of land.[61]

Educated gentlemen of the Eastern Branch continued their campaign with a long debate in the *Maryland Gazette* over the constitutionality of the tax. Although they realized that the rebuilding of the courthouse was a local issue, they insisted that the court's behavior violated the rights of Englishmen. To give a county court unlimited power to tax would place in their hands the right to confiscate property. Even the assembly had no right to "invest a County Court with an unlimited Power of Taxing the People at Pleasure, on every frivolous Pretence they may think proper to call a *public Charge*." Since the Maryland assembly had given courts only limited rights to tax for specific purposes, the justices should have asked the assembly to authorize the extraordinary tax to rebuild the courthouse.[62]

A supporter of rebuilding the courthouse responded that his opponents, a mere local interest, were a faction that spread dissension "not only in private Companies and public Meetings only, but in Print also." The law clearly gave the county bench the right to tax the people for any legitimate purpose. Since the law granted "discretionary power" to justices to tax, those opposed to rebuilding the courthouse should show, he added, "that under this general Power Bridges are to be built, Ferrys to be kept, and the Poor to be maintained, and yet a Court-House not to be repaired."[63]

Eastern Branch gentlemen won the constitutional argument but lost the political battle. The assembly passed a law that permitted the courthouse to be finished, probably prompted by Edward Sprigg, the senior justice on the Prince George's bench, the speaker of the lower house, and a resident of a neighborhood near the courthouse. Even the division of Prince George's in 1748 failed to satisfy Eastern Branch planters, because the new county's courthouse was located forty miles from their neighborhoods.

61. The politics of this controversy can be followed in Carr, "Foundations of Social Order," in Daniels, ed., *Town and County*, 96–97; and Hienton, *Prince George's Heritage*, 124–125. The quotes can be found in the *Md. Gaz.*, Dec. 16, 1747, Jan. 20, 1748; and in William Hand Browne *et al.*, eds., *Archives of Maryland . . .* , 72 vols. (Baltimore, 1883–1972), XLVI, 75–77 (hereafter cited as *Archives of Maryland*). The petition can be found in *Calendar of Maryland State Papers*, No. 1, *The Black Books* (Annapolis, Md., 1943), 79.
62. *Md. Gaz.*, Jan. 20, Feb. 10, Mar. 16, Apr. 20, 1748.
63. *Ibid.*, Mar. 23 (supplement), Apr. 20.

Their petitions in 1751, moreover, to create another new county in their area failed to win acceptance.[64]

This debate in Prince George's vividly illustrates the necessity of gentry leadership and unity to gain political change. Although ordinary planters suffered the most from the inconvenient location of the courthouse, they had to allow gentlemen to lead the campaign. The Eastern Branch forces insisted that "Numbers of Gentlemen, Natives of this Province, of good Credit and Fortune" were "amongst the most forward, in the Opposition to the Measures of the Court." Only gentlemen participated in the constitutional debate in the courthouse fight, and in the end, the power of the speaker of the house and his allies decided the issue.[65]

Though tidewater gentlemen incorporated yeomen into the political and economic system, they paid little attention to white women or poor white men. These people, who worked as wives, servants, laborers, or tenants, depended upon the head of the family for their keep, subsisted on the charity of gentleman justices or vestrymen, or owed their livelihoods to landlords who could expel them at will. Since poor folk shared nothing but their dependence, they rarely united against their overlords, and gentlemen could safely ignore their needs. But gentlemen did distinguish among poor folk. Although they exploited the labor of the dependent poor, they gave public charity to deserving widows, orphans, and old and sick people.

Servants and laborers subsisted at the bottom of white society. Since they depended upon a master for food, clothing, and shelter, they had to follow his orders and endure corporal punishment for slights real or imagined. Until they left the master's home, their political identities were subsumed under his, and even after they set up their own farm, they rarely gained enough property to vote or serve on juries. Most of them soon decided to seek their fortunes elsewhere.

The sad tale of Humut Godfrey and his wife Margaret in Prince George's during the tobacco depression of the 1740s suggests how little political recourse laborers had when masters exploited them. In 1744 Godfrey indented himself and his wife to John Cook, a justice and gentleman planter, for seven years because he could no longer support himself, his wife, and their two small children. Until 1746, when Godfrey sprained his back, the term was uneventful. This injury made work difficult, but Cook responded with "Indignation and hatred" by reducing his rations and ignoring "his Wife in her Travails or Miscarriages, his Children in their Sickness." Finally, a terrible incident in April 1748 led Godfrey to petition the

64. *Archives of Maryland*, XLVI, 155–156; *Black Books*, 103–104; Hienton, *Prince George's Heritage*, 124–125.
65. *Md. Gaz.*, Apr. 13, 1748.

court for redress. One day that month, after Cook left home on business, his wife told Godfrey that "nothing ailed him but Laziness and Deceit" and threatened to "Send the Overseer to whip him to work." Despite the "incredible pain," Godfrey worked "in the Anguish" to avoid a whipping. His wife, who toiled beside him, told their mistress that she was "not Sensible of the pain he is in." The overseer, hearing her complaint, called her a damned bitch and threatened to beat her. Much insulted by his language, she insisted that she was "not a slave" who could be whipped and added that she had "never yet receiv'd a Blow from my Master." This angered the overseer even more, and he took "a great hiccory Switch," called her a bitch again, and "gave her Several Blows," to which she responded, "I no more look like a B——ch than you look like the Son of one." He then tied her up and beat her again. Godfrey watched helplessly but finally asked his mistress "if she would suffer his Wife to be tied like a Dog," but the mistress replied that "the overseer may do with her as he pleases." With that, he started to untie her even "If it cost me my life . . . for she is my lawfull Wife." But the overseer and another servant caught him and beat him so badly that "blood gushed out of his Ear." The next morning Godfrey complained to a neighborhood gentleman, who gave him a supportive letter about the incident for Cook. Meanwhile, the overseer beat his wife again, and when Godfrey showed the letter to Cook, who had returned, he had her whipped a third time. In June 1748 the court listened to Godfrey's story, but rejected his plea.[66]

The Godfreys' experience shows how little control servants and laborers had over their own lives. Even though they were white adults, they had to behave subserviently and accept punishment otherwise reserved for the most powerless—slaves and children. A servant should not have tried to circumvent his master's authority, even to protect his wife from bodily harm. Cook was incensed when Godfrey reported his wife's behavior to a neighbor and probably considered the petition—which Godfrey, unlike a slave, had a right to make—a challenge to his own authority. The court, in its turn, upheld Cook's authority by rejecting the petition.

Though tenants lived independently, they relied upon landlords for land, structures, and tools and often for marketing crops. Most tenants paid a portion of their crop as rent and accumulated little property. They usually owned a horse and a little livestock and lived in a small house, but had few outbuildings like kitchens to improve their standard of living. These farmers rarely stayed in the same neighborhood more than a few years before moving away to search for greater opportunities.[67]

66. Prince George's Court Records, XIX, 165–168, MHR.
67. The best works on tenancy are Gregory A. Stiverson, *Poverty in a Land of Plenty: Tenancy in*

The market relations of production complicated the dependence of tenant upon landlord. Each tried to gain the greatest income from the land, but the landlord, who could raise rents at will and dispose of the land as he saw fit even while the tenant farmed it, held the upper hand. Ann Kitchen, a "distressed widow with two young Children" who rented land from Joseph Chew of Prince George's in 1729, discovered his power when she tried to enforce an oral contract in court. When she moved onto Chew's land, the tobacco house was "very much out of repair," and Chew promised to fix it quickly. But he failed to keep his promise, thereby forcing Kitchen to spend "another twenty shillings for the use of a house to live in and two hundred pounds of Tobacco . . . to cure my Tobacco." Moreover, Chew let his horse run wild through her cornfield, reducing her output from sixty to twelve bushels. And when she tried to pay her rent, Chew refused to accept the tobacco she offered because of its alleged low quality, making it impossible for her to "make any other Satisfaction." The court, however, refused to hear her cry for "Charitable redress."[68]

While laborers and tenants depended upon masters or landlords for their subsistence, the deserving poor relied upon aid from local officials. In Virginia, the parish vestry granted money to "indigent Persons, disabled by Age, Sickness, or Corporal Infirmities and incapable of maintaining themselves by their own Labour." Common forms of relief included exemption from taxes, cash payments, and deliveries of food and manufactured goods. Vestries also paid for child care for the indigent and medical expenses of poor folk who fell ill. Justices of Maryland's county courts dispensed similar forms of relief.[69]

Those unfortunate people who sought aid had to debase themselves before vestrymen or justices by relating tales of woe in the most servile manner. Though most recipients were women, old and ill men qualified. The Prince George's court, for instance, made Hugh Riley levy-free in 1726 after he told the justices that he was "between seventy and Eighty years of age and not able to work to maintain his family having no servants to work for him and having five small children not able to work." Four years later the court granted identical tax relief to William King, age sixty, who claimed to be "very Crazy and almost lost his Eyesight is Scarcely able to

---

Eighteenth-Century Maryland (Baltimore, 1977); and Willard F. Bliss, "The Rise of Tenancy in Virginia," *VMHB*, LVIII (1950), 427–442. Unfortunately, both deal with privileged long-term tenants rather than more typical and poorer tenants-at-will.

68. Prince George's Court Records, R, 6–7, S, 116.

69. Webb, *Office of Justice of Peace*, 250–252; Howard Mackey, "The Operation of the English Old Poor Law in Colonial Virginia," *VMHB*, LXXIII (1965), 29–40; Mackey, "Social Welfare in Colonial Virginia: The Importance of the English Old Poor Law," *Historical Magazine of the Protestant Episcopal Church*, XXXVI (1967), 357–382.

get his Livelyhood." Other men, once granted aid, had to return if they needed more. Thomas Bushell received two hundred pounds of tobacco in 1730 from the county court, but came back in November 1730 because the sum was so small that he could not "live on it"; nor could he "get any person to take him in which now constrains him most humbly to begg that your worships would be pleased" to consider his plea. On hearing him, the justices increased his allowance to five hundred pounds of tobacco per year.[70]

Planters avoided petitioning for relief because they recognized that such a request made them into servile dependents and outcasts from civil society. Ralph Fisher of Prince George's, for instance, suffered years of misery without help. In 1724, at about age thirty-seven, he "broke his Arm and has Ever Since Lost the use of it but not being Willing to Trouble your Worships or to be a Charge to the County has Industriously Endeavoured Ever Since Very hard for a Livelihood and Maintainance for himself and his family." But he finally, and successfully, petitioned to be levy-free in November 1736 after a fire broke out "in his Tobacco house, it being also his Dwelling house which Burnt Together with his goods [and] all his then housed Tobacco." Since he lost his curing barn, he found that "the Remainder of his Tobacco is Rotting in the field," further impoverishing him and forcing him to rely on "the Aid of his good Neighbours" and of the county. Fisher apparently never recovered from his misfortunes. In 1752, he successfully petitioned the county court for a pension, again complaining about his broken arm and the fire. By then, age sixty-five and "very Infirm" and "unable to Work," he was "totally incapable of Supporting himself or Assisting his Wife . . . without Relief."[71]

This system of poor relief began to break down in the 1750s and 1760s. As youths migrated to the piedmont frontier, the proportion of older adults among tidewater's population increased. At the same time, tobacco inspection laws reduced production on marginal lands farmed by the poor and further added to poor rolls. The number of people on the dole in Sussex County, Virginia, grew from one family in thirty in 1742 to one in seventeen in 1774. And nearly a seventh of the families in Anne Arundel County, Maryland, received aid during the late 1760s.[72]

70. Prince George's Court Records, L, 643, P, 595–596.

71. *Ibid.*, W, 245, XXII, 196.

72. For Sussex, see Amanda Jane Townes, "The Care of the Poor in Albemarle Parish, Surry and Sussex Counties, Virginia, 1742–1787" (master's thesis, College of William and Mary, 1976), 46–49. The Anne Arundel data are found in *Archives of Maryland*, LXIII, 124; the numerical importance of the 180 families receiving aid was determined using census data in Allan Kulikoff, "Tobacco and Slaves: Population, Economy, and Society in Eighteenth-Century Prince George's County, Maryland" (Ph.D. diss., Brandeis University, 1976), 428–429.

The assemblies of both Chesapeake colonies responded to the rising tide of poor people by authorizing the construction of almshouses. A number of counties established poorhouses during the pre-Revolutionary decades, thereby further degrading the status of the poor. In Maryland, any justice could place "Rogues, Vagrants, Vagabonds, Beggars and other Dissolute and Disorderly" persons in the almshouse, and the trustees of these institutions could put "the Poor to work" and punish the beggars and vagabonds. All who entered the poorhouse had to wear a badge with "a large Roman P" to mark them as poor, and anyone refusing to wear such a letter could be whipped or given hard labor.[73]

Though as many as a third of the white families of tidewater were poor on the eve of the Revolution, they were unable to influence public policy. They were segregated from each other: laborers traveled from plantation to plantation searching for work, but servants had to remain on the master's farm unless given permission to leave. Tenants spent most of their time minding their farms or drinking with friends, and the lame and elderly could travel only with difficulty. Even if they could have gathered, their interests diverged. Laborers and servants wanted to find the best employer, tenants sought easy terms from landlords and hoped to accumulate capital to buy their own place, and the deserving poor relied on the dole for their survival. Gentlemen, who saw that the poor were without influence, either pitied or ignored them.

A series of favorable circumstances permitted the tidewater gentry to maintain firm control over the region's polity during the mid-eighteenth century. A strong and nearly hereditary ruling class, confident of its place in society, developed during the first third of the century. At the same time, slaves replaced servants in the tobacco fields, thereby reducing the potential for dissatisfaction among poor whites. Gentlemen debased poor people, who were unable to demand redress of their grievances, but favored the politically important yeomanry. Gentlemen not only listened to the political grievances of yeomen but were bound together with them in numerous mutually beneficial ways.

Few interlocking relations tied gentry to yeomanry in the new societies of southside Virginia during the 1760s and 1770s. Southside gentlemen, the younger sons of tidewater gentlemen or undistinguished nouveaux

---

73. The 1768 Maryland law, found in *Archives of Maryland*, LXI, 486–495 (quotes on 488, 493), LXIV, 219, 259, 380, show that four of five old lower Western Shore tobacco counties had poorhouses and that two of three farming counties in the north and west and only two of six Eastern Shore counties had similar institutions. For Virginia's 1755 law, see William Waller Hening, *The Statutes at Large: Being a Collection of All the Laws of Virginia . . .* , 13 vols. (Richmond, Philadelphia, 1809–1823), VI, 475–478 (hereafter cited as *Virginia Statutes at Large*); and Mackey, "Operation of the English Old Poor Law," *VMHB*, LXXIII (1965), 39.

riches, were surrounded by transient and unruly freeholders. There were many fewer taverns, churches, and villages where they could exchange obligations, and Scottish merchants controlled a large share of the available credit, thereby reducing the hold of local gentlemen over yeomen needing loans.[74]

The wealthy planters of southside, unlike those of tidewater, suffered a grave challenge to their authority during the 1760s and 1770s. Apostles of evangelical religion converted thousands of previously unchurched yeomen and their families to the Baptist faith and persuaded them that the drinking, dancing, hunting, and gambling so much a part of the exchanges between gentry and yeomen were sinful activities. Baptists replaced these ceremonies with religious fellowship, insisted that all Christians, even wealthy gentlemen, were equals in God's universe, and paid deference to their own brethren rather than to their gentry neighbors. Gentlemen responded with intermittent persecution, but they could not eliminate the group.[75]

The Crisis of the Gentry Class

During the American Revolution, just a generation after the tidewater gentry consolidated its authority, substantial tension arose both within the gentry class and between gentlemen and yeomen. The revolt against England required gentlemen to put aside political differences and unite around new, independent governments. Like their northern counterparts, these men adopted a republican ideology of popular sovereignty to legitimate their revolution. Any division over the rebellion or its ideology within the ruling class might have encouraged ordinary planters to follow tory gentlemen to the English side. To make their revolution, gentlemen had to enlist support from the yeomanry as taxpayers and soldiers. But the ideology of popular sovereignty that gentlemen used against the British implicitly promised much wider participation in political and ideological debate and thereby threatened the gentry class with a loss of control of their own revolt. The gentry ruling class maintained and even strengthened its position after the war by accepting yeoman demands for more democratic and less hierarchical social relations between the two classes.

Although pre-Revolutionary gentlemen considered participation in political debate to be a right granted their social class as the stewards of social order, they rarely disagreed about the fundamentals of class, gender, and race relations. Maryland assemblymen divided themselves into shifting

74. Beeman, *Cavaliers and Frontiersmen*, chaps. 1–3.
75. This is brilliantly documented in Isaac, *Transformation of Virginia*, chaps. 8, 11.

proprietary and country factions; Virginia assemblymen formed personal cliques or united to fight governors or their gentry colleagues among the clergy over taxes. Planters and merchants sometimes debated the utility of indebtedness, and lawyers and justices fought over the operation of local courts. The Revolution, however, raised fundamental issues of political allegiance. Whig gentlemen sought to replace the sovereignty of king and Parliament with a republican polity and popular sovereignty, an ideology bound to create dissent and division. Some gentlemen agreed with patriot grievances but insisted on maintaining political ties to Britain. Whig leaders, however, managed to control ideological dissent in their own ranks by spreading officeholding and political responsibility very broadly. At the same time, they reduced the number of loyalists among conservative gentlemen to a scattered few (with the regional exception of the southern Eastern Shore and the area around Norfolk) by using various forms of coercion, from forced recantations to exile and confiscation of property.[76]

Gentlemen had to mobilize the yeoman population both to form a new government and to fight the war. But political mobilization was fraught with danger and ambiguity. Ever since the conflict over tobacco regulation in the 1730s and 1740s, gentlemen had kept ordinary planters out of politics and ruled as benign stewards of the public good. Most planters not only left government to gentlemen but probably considered imperial conflicts in far-off New England during the 1760s and 1770s as barely relevant to their own concerns. Since whig theory asserted that new governments could be formed only with the direct consent of the governed, gentlemen mobilized the yeomanry in public meetings and petition campaigns and insisted that they sign loyalty oaths. Once mobilized, however, yeomen began to insist upon a voice in political and war policies such as military recruitment and procurement, taxation, and religious toleration. Gentlemen slowly learned to accommodate the political positions of their yeoman constituents, decisions that ultimately led to a broader sharing of political authority under gentry leadership than the ruling class had allowed before the war.

Gentlemen developed class solidarity by opening up political office to less prestigious gentry families, a strategy that gave new men a stake in the

---

76. Charles Albro Barker, *The Background of the Revolution in Maryland* (New Haven, Conn., 1940), esp. chaps. 4, 7; Greene, "Society, Ideology, and Politics," in Jellison, ed., *Society, Freedom, and Conscience*, 35–43; and Thad W. Tate, "The Coming of the Revolution in Virginia: Britain's Challenge to Virginia's Ruling Class, 1763–1776," *WMQ*, 3d Ser., XIX (1962), 323–343, summarize pre-Revolutionary legislative politics. A. G. Roeber, *Faithful Magistrates and Republican Lawyers: Creators of Virginia Legal Culture, 1680–1810* (Chapel Hill, N.C., 1981), esp. chaps. 3, 4, stresses conflicts between lawyers and magistrates; Herbert Sloan and Peter Onuf, "Politics, Culture, and the Revolution in Virginia," *VMHB*, XCI (1983), 259–284, raise questions about class, culture, and revolution similar to those covered in this section.

outcome of the war and turned them into fervent whigs. The election of local committees of safety, mandated by the Continental Congress in 1774, gave gentlemen their first chance to supplement their own ranks. The committees enforced the strictures of the Continental Association against trade with Britain, solicited patriotic speeches to instill loyalty to the new regime, raised militias for local defense, and censured dissenters.[77]

Though the most distinguished families dominated local committees in the Chesapeake colonies, many less distinguished men also served. At least fifty-four of the wealthiest hundred men in Virginia sat on local committees along with fifty leaders of the House of Burgesses. Nonetheless, most were not that rich. Like typical justices, they owned from seven hundred to eighteen hundred acres of land and eleven to fifteen slaves.[78] Many committeemen, moreover, had never served in high office. About half the justices of fourteen tidewater and piedmont counties joined committees, but since these bodies were larger than the bench, only two-fifths of the committeemen had judicial experience. Another fifth of them were close blood kin of justices, but the rest included more remote relations, wealthy merchants, and molders of public opinion like doctors and clergymen.[79]

An examination of three counties shows that committees varied in their inclusiveness, from a reconstruction of the local bench that gave all power to a few men to the election of nearly the entire gentry class, with power delegated to a much smaller but more prestigious group. During the 1760s

77. The operation of the committee system is detailed in Dale Edward Benson, "Wealth and Power in Virginia, 1774–1776: A Study of the Organization of Revolt" (Ph.D. diss., University of Maine, 1970); Larry Bowman, "The Virginia County Committees of Safety, 1774–1776," *VMHB*, LXXIX (1971), 322–337; and Richard A. Overfield, "The Loyalists of Maryland during the American Revolution" (Ed.D. diss., University of Maryland, 1968), chaps. 3–5.

78. Median landholding and slaveholding of committeemen in seven counties (Isle of Wight, Southampton, Albemarle, Westmoreland, Caroline, and Cumberland, Virginia, and Prince George's, Maryland) were calculated from data in Benson, "Wealth and Power," 399–425; Hienton, *Prince George's Heritage*, 175, linked to Prince George's Land Records and Debt Books; Brumbaugh, ed., *Maryland Records*, I, 1–88; and Papenfuse *et al.*, eds., *Biographical Dictionary*. The number of Virginia slaves was divided in half to determine taxable slaves. Median landholding was 700 acres in two counties, 900 acres in two, 1,000 acres in one, and 1,800 acres in two; median taxable slaves held ranged from 11 (1 county) to 12 (4 counties) and 13 and 15 (1 each). These data should be compared to table 31, above.

79. Counties include those of n. 78, above, and Prince Edward, Charles City, James City, King and Queen, Spotsylvania, Lancaster, and Pittsylvania counties, Virginia, as well. See sources in n. 78, and Charles Washington Coleman, "The County Committees of 1774–'75 in Virginia," *WMQ*, 1st Ser., V (1896–1897), 94–106, 245–255, linked to "Justices of the Peace of Colonial Virginia, 1757–1775," Virginia State Library, *Bulletin*, XIV (1921), 43–130. Mean size of last court before the Revolution in these counties was 17.6 (SD = 1.8), and mean size of the committees, including replacements, was 26.2 (SD = 5.7). Although 55% of sitting justices joined committees (SD = 16%), only 42% (SD = 12%) of the committeemen had prior service as a justice.

and 1770s, the justices of Albemarle's court were very wealthy and intricately tied together by kinship. County voters placed fourteen of them, who owned, on average, eighteen hundred acres of land and fifteen adult slaves, on the committee. The freeholders of Caroline County elected a more representative committee. They owned, on average, nine hundred acres of land and thirteen adult slaves. Although seventeen of the twenty-one men elected in 1774 were either justices or related to them, the new committee chosen in 1775 was more diverse. The six new members included the parish minister, a radical lawyer of modest wealth, and a self-made planter.[80]

In contrast, the freeholders of Prince George's County, Maryland, elected 170 men, including every county justice and nearly all men who owned more than ten working slaves, to a Committee of Inspection at mass meetings in December 1774 and January 1775. These officeholders included a few yeomen, at least fifteen Catholic gentlemen and two Quakers whose faith had kept them off the bench, and eleven merchants. County voters selected twenty-one men from this group as a Committee of Correspondence to enforce the association and in September 1775 replaced them with a thirty-two-member Committee of Observation. Although eight members of the Committee of Correspondence had been justices and six others came from magistrate families, the other six men included two Catholic gentlemen. Only thirteen of these men joined the Committee of Observation, but the new members were similar to those they replaced, including five justices, eight men from magistrates' families, three Catholic gentlemen, and four yeomen.[81]

New men continued to serve in the revolutionary governments that replaced the committees. Maryland's new governments initiated nine conventions between 1774 and 1776. Until the ninth meeting, conventions seated whomever voters sent, and freeholders typically chose eight or nine men, double the four allotted each county in the assembly. The impact of expanding participation can be seen among southern Maryland members. The proportion of new legislators elected from 1774 to 1789 whose fathers had preceded them dropped from a half to a quarter, and though many of these new members could still point to legislator grandfathers, the number

---

80. Benson, "Wealth and Power," 119–123, 136–139, 403–404, 412–414; "Justices of Virginia," Va. St. Lib., *Bull.*, XIV (1921), 89, 106, 109; Mary M. Sullivan, "The Gentry and the Association in Albemarle County, 1774–1775," Albemarle Co. Hist. Soc., *Magazine*, XXIII (1964–1965), 33–44; Campbell, *Colonial Caroline*, 343–351, 231–235, 256–262.

81. Hienton, *Prince George's Heritage*, 172–175; *Md. Gaz.*, Dec. 1, 1774, Jan. 26, 1775, linked to sources cited in fig. 25, above. Data on slave ownership cover half the county and are found in Brumbaugh, ed., *Maryland Records*, I, 1–88. In all, 19 of 26 men in that area who owned more than 10 slaves served on the Committee of Inspection. A least 2 members of 33 families were chosen, and of these 110 men, 68 came from gentry families and 33 from yeoman stock.

lacking any close kin ties to previous assemblymen rose from a quarter to more than a third (fig. 26).[82]

A similar pattern could be seen on the Prince George's court. In 1777 nine new justices replaced nine who had died, resigned, or joined the army. While the new justices included one former justice, two men whose fathers had been magistrates, and three kinsmen of former justices, three of them were of yeoman stock, a much higher proportion than had been common for half a century.[83]

Though most gentlemen joined the whig cause, a few merchants, clergymen, lawyers, and placemen insisted that revolution was rebellion against the legitimate authority of king and Parliament. Since these men could defeat the economic purposes of the association, and, even worse, turn yeomen away from the rule of whig gentlemen, they posed a grave danger to revolutionary government. Committees spent much time inspecting the records of merchants who imported goods from England, and when they completed that task, they opened mail of suspected tories, sought to persuade traitors of their errors, and when all else failed, demanded public contrition or exile.[84]

Revolutionary committees gave tory gentlemen every chance to recant their views. In October 1775, Thomas Johnson, rector in Charlotte County, "drank success to the British arms" at a local tavern. Johnson confessed at a committee meeting later that month, but "in the most equivocal and insulting manner." He insisted, furthermore, on continuing to trade with a merchant accused of violating the association. The committee sought to "receive him again into friendly communion" and therefore "expostulated with him on the impropriety of his conduct," but his confession was insufficiently contrite, and the committee judged him "an enemy to America" and urged all citizens to shun him. Three months later Johnson, tired of his isolation, wrote a requisite confession. He admitted he "drank success to the British army," but he did "solemnly declare it was done inadvertently." "All my dependence, my nearest and dearest connexions, are in this country," he said, and he expected "to share with the Americans in the present unhappy contest."[85]

Anyone with public influence and tory opinions faced immediate cen-

82. Papenfuse *et al.*, eds., *Biographical Dictionary*, I, 65–78.
83. Commission Books, MHR, abstracted by Randall Miller, and sources cited in fig. 25, above.
84. The best analysis of these activities is in Benson, "Wealth and Power," chaps. 4–8; but Isaac, *Transformation of Virginia*, 248–255, expounds brilliantly on ceremonies of contrition.
85. William J. Van Schreeven *et al.*, eds., *Revolutionary Virginia: The Road to Independence*, 7 vols. (Charlottesville, Va., 1973–1983), VI, 37–38, 299–300. Similar cases are scattered in Vols. II–VI of this collection, and in Benson, "Wealth and Power," chaps. 7, 8.

sure. After Westmoreland County schoolmaster David Wardrobe published a letter critical of whig policy in a Glasgow newspaper, the county committee insisted he apologize. Until then, the committee urged the parish vestry to bar him from his vestryhouse school and asked parents of children he taught to "immediately take them away" from school and consider him "a wicked enemy to America." Wardrobe refused to appear before the committee in November 1774, but instead wrote an "insulting" letter, and the committee kept him on their blacklist. Several months later, however, Wardrobe "came to Westmoreland courthouse, and, in the presence of a considerable number of people," admitted his article contained "falsehoods and misrepresentations." To regain communal approval he chose to "most heartily and willingly, on my knees, implore the forgiveness of this country."[86]

These two strategies, placing many gentlemen on committees and censuring dissenters, worked remarkably well. Whig gentlemen persuaded reluctant friends to join the patriot cause. Despite the presence of tory gentlemen in Caroline County, for instance, all but two of the justices supported the whig government. Patriot success extended even to sheriffs and clerics who depended upon governors for patronage. In Maryland, only friends of the proprietor or men the governor placed in office became tories, and nine-tenths of officials with local ties joined the whigs. Furthermore, three-fifths of Maryland's clergymen, often tied to England by birth or education, became patriots.[87]

Tories nonetheless contested the southern half of the Eastern Shore and counties around Norfolk. Civil war in those areas proved the damage that division among gentlemen could generate. A substantial majority of the gentry class in those areas stayed loyal to the king, and they and their kindred attracted many yeomen to loyalist units and encouraged untold others to sell goods to the British or sign oaths supporting the monarchy.[88]

While gentlemen consolidated their own ranks, they devised ways to gain yeoman support. They held mass meetings, circulated anti-English petitions, made patriotic speeches and sermons to persuade ordinary planters that their cause was just and that the behavior of the British was unfair, urged yeomen to vote in elections for extralegal committees, and coerced

86. Van Schreeven *et al.*, eds., *Revolutionary Virginia*, II, 165, 179–180.
87. Campbell, *Colonial Caroline*, 262–266; Anne Alden Allan, "Patriots and Loyalists: The Choice of Political Allegiances by Members of Maryland's Proprietary Elite," *Jour. So. Hist.*, XXXVIII (1972), 283–292.
88. Adele Hast, *Loyalism in Revolutionary Virginia: The Norfolk Area and the Eastern Shore* (Ann Arbor, Mich., 1982); Overfield, "Loyalists of Maryland"; Ronald Hoffman, "Popularizing the Revolution: Internal Conflict and Economic Sacrifice in Maryland, 1774–1780," *MHM*, LXVIII (1973), 125–139.

them to sign loyalty oaths. Although yeomen willingly supported whig gentlemen, they often insisted upon a more open political system in return.

Popular mobilization began slowly. The first mass meetings in the region occurred in Virginia's Northern Neck, after Archibald Ritchie, an unsympathetic merchant, announced in February 1766 that he would use tax stamps, required by Parliament, on a cargo lying in Leedstown. Even though he soon changed his mind, local gentlemen led by Richard Henry Lee demanded he recant and called a mass meeting to confront him. At that meeting, 115 men, half of them gentlemen (including eight assemblymen) and the other half a tiny part of the yeomanry, signed a document that attacked the Stamp Act and agreed to prevent its execution even at the risk of "Danger or Death." The next day 400 men marched to Ritchie's house and made him sign the resolution on pain of tarring and feathering.[89] Four years later, George Mason and other Fairfax County gentlemen revived this strategy to bolster support for the faltering nonimportation league. These gentlemen circulated their petition throughout the county, gaining support from merchants, the entire county bench, two-thirds of the county's vestrymen, and a cross section of about a ninth of the freeholders.[90]

Until mid-1774, few Chesapeake gentlemen save those of the Northern Neck sought to rouse ordinary planters, but after Parliament closed the port of Boston and banned town meetings in the wake of the Boston Tea Party, the gentry class began to mobilize the yeomanry. From late May to early July 1774, gentlemen called massive public meetings in at least forty-eight counties and three towns in tidewater and piedmont. These meetings, meant to generate support for the association among yeomen, often attracted several hundred people. Meetings were particularly common in tidewater Virginia north of the James River and in central piedmont Virginia, but there was far less activity on the southside frontier, where vast

89. David W. Eaton, *Historical Atlas of Westmoreland County, Virginia* (Richmond, Va., 1942); Van Schreeven *et al.*, eds., *Revolutionary Virginia*, I, 22–26. I identified 92 of 115 men by status from Eaton's data, counting 43 justices, burgesses, and large slaveholders as gentlemen and the others as yeomen. Of the signers, 30 had kindred among the petitioners. Eaton listed counties for 97 men: 36 from Westmoreland, 13 from Richmond, 12 from Essex, 11 from Stafford and King George, 4 from Northumberland, 3 from Lancaster and Spotsylvania, and 2 from Prince William and Caroline.

90. Donald M. Sweig, "The Virginia Nonimportation Association Broadside of 1770 and Fairfax County: A Study in Local Participation," *VMHB*, LXXXVII (1979), 316–325. I counted all signers of petitions 1 and 2 (Colechester and Alexandria) and justices and vestrymen (eliminating duplicates) as gentlemen ($N = 65$). I assumed that there were 100 gentlemen in the county, then subtracted total gentlemen from Sweig's estimate of white tithes and gentlemen who signed from the 333 petitioners. That yielded a ratio of 268 yeoman signers among 2,285 tithes.

distances made public meetings difficult, and on the loyalist-dominated Eastern Shore.[91]

In late 1774, gentlemen continued to mobilize the citizenry by calling elections for the selection of Revolutionary committees. These elections, mandated by the Continental Congress, gave ordinary planters their first opportunity to choose local officials. The gentry, as we have seen, controlled elections, placing assemblymen, justices, and other wealthy planters on the committees. Voters sometimes even ranked the gentry by prestige and wealth. Two very rich burgesses and a wealthy justice from a prominent family won the first three places in the 1774 Caroline elections. In Albemarle County, where there was a strong relationship between wealth and standing at the polls, voters gave Thomas Jefferson the most votes; John Walker, an assemblyman and justice, and Nicholas Lewis, justice and sheriff, followed close behind.[92]

Despite mass meetings and local elections, many planters remained apathetic. Only a fifth to a third of white adult men voted in committee elections in Albemarle, Caroline, and Cumberland counties. And voters sometimes misunderstood the issues. In August 1775, seventy-two freeholders of Chesterfield County, including some large slaveholders, urged new elections be held because "Very Few had it in Their Power to Vote in the choice of the committee, at that time not well Understanding what they Ware to do, or the Intent of Associating, and Then not being Associates" had been barred from voting.[93]

Mass meetings, furthermore, sometimes endangered the very gentlemen who called them. Caroline and Cumberland voters replaced gentlemen with men of lesser stature in the second round of committee elections. In

91. Meetings compiled from Van Schreeven *et al.*, eds., *Revolutionary Virginia*, I, 109–168; and J. Thomas Scharf, *History of Maryland from the Earliest Period to the Present Day* (Baltimore, 1879), II, 140–162. There were meetings in 9 Maryland counties and Baltimore Town and in 37 tidewater and piedmont counties and towns in Virginia (5 of 10 in Norfolk and tidewater south of James and Eastern Shore; 5 of 10 in southside; 10 of 11 in Northern Neck; 9 of 11 in rest of tidewater; 8 of 12 in central piedmont Virginia and Fredericksburg).

92. Campbell, *Colonial Caroline*, 231–235, 344; Sullivan, "Gentry and Association in Albemarle," Albemarle Co. Hist. Soc., *Magazine*, XXIII (1964–1965), 37, 42–43; Benson, "Wealth and Power," 403–404, 412–413. The correlation between number of votes and number of slaves in Albemarle is .543.

93. *Ibid.*; Van Schreeven *et al.*, eds., *Revolutionary Virginia*, IV, 469–470, 483–484; Greene and Harrington, *American Population*, 150–151; Bureau of the Census, *Heads of Families, Virginia*, 49–51; "Justices of Virginia," Va. St. Lib., *Bull.*, XIV (1921), 92. Turnout of white males over 21 was 23% in Albemarle, 22% and 26% in Caroline, and 34% in Cumberland. To calculate turnout, I assumed that three-quarters of men voting cast ballots for the man with the greatest number of votes. Of 72 signers of the Chesterfield petition, 39 could be identified: 4 men had no slaves; 12 owned 1–9 slaves, 23 had 10 or more slaves; and one justice signed the petition.

Caroline County, a tavernkeeper rose from ninth to first place in the poll, and several wealthy gentlemen lost votes; seven justices left the Cumberland committee but were replaced by just two justices and other, less important gentlemen. Freeholders occasionally even demanded radical change. In Anne Arundel County, Maryland, representatives of several militia companies wrote a radical constitution in June 1776, and one month later, 855 men met and demanded universal white manhood suffrage.[94]

Gentlemen defused radicalism and built public opinion favorable to the whig cause by sponsoring patriotic speeches. One address, by Lt. George Gilmer to Albemarle County's independent volunteers in April 1775, survives. A choice, Gilmer insisted, was now "before us, either to become the voluntary and abject slaves of a wicked administration, or to live free." He urged soldiers to "exert to the utmost Valour, prudence, and love for our Country" and unite "to oppose any power that shall attem[pt to subvert] our lives, liberties, or properties," as the British did in Boston, and ended with a plea for financial support for the company and sound military discipline from the soldiers.[95]

Governor Dunmore of Virginia, the last royal governor of that colony, ironically boosted whig mobilization while fighting patriots for control of the government. In November 1775, he proclaimed that all rebels' slaves willing to fight for Britain would be freed. About eight hundred slaves joined Dunmore's army, a number sufficient to arouse great fears among slaveholders that their slaves would run away and thereby deprive them of their livelihood and independence. Whig polemicists lost no time in using this British threat to their property to recruit planters to the patriot cause.[96]

The signing of the Declaration of Independence triggered celebrations throughout the Chesapeake region. The Maryland Council of Safety asked local committees to "proclaim it in your County"; the Virginia council ordered sheriffs to put the Declaration "at the door of the Court-House." Public festivities in towns were quite vigorous. In Williamsburg, the Declaration "was solemnly proclaimed . . . admidst the acclamation of the people, accompanied by firing of canon and musketry"; in Richmond, a similar celebration ended with fireworks and a dinner for a thousand people, complete with "many patriotic toasts." The army encampment near Hampton town celebrated too. "There was much excitement and great rejoicing in the camp," one veteran remembered. "They had a barrel of very bad West-

94. Campbell, *Colonial Caroline*, 256–258, 344–345; Benson, "Wealth and Power," 405–407; Skaggs, *Roots of Maryland Democracy*, 183–186, 220–226.
95. Van Schreeven *et al.*, eds., *Revolutionary Virginia*, III, 49–53, IV, 227.
96. Mullin, *Flight and Rebellion*, 130–136. Jeannie Ford Dissette, "Slavery and the Coming of the Revolution in Virginia, 1774–1776" (seminar paper, University of Pennsylvania, 1972), 28–49.

indie rum. About dark they kicked the head out of the barrel and set the rum on fire. It blazed terribly and for a time enlightened the whole camp."[97]

Whig gentlemen not only tried to influence the yeomanry through appeals to patriotism and self-interest but also insisted that all white men swear an oath to commit themselves to defend the new regime. The oath demanded that every man "yield any allegiance to the King of Great Britain," be loyal to his state, and report "all Treasons or Treaterous Consperacies" to appropriate authorities. Revolutionary authorities, at least in Maryland, gained assent to the new government from a majority of white men. More than three-quarters of white men living on the lower Western Shore and half the men living in the rest of the state, even on the loyalist Eastern Shore, swore the oath. Propertyholders of some standing in the community almost universally took the oath, motivated by patriotism, ties to whig kinsmen, or fear of ostracism or double or triple taxation if they refused to swear. But poorer, less-settled men often ignored the law. In Prince George's County, for instance, nine of every ten men who owned land and slaves supported the government, but only half their tenant nonslaveholding neighbors joined them. Only half the heads of household of ages nineteen to twenty-four signed, but three-quarters of those in their fifties took the oath.[98]

Once gentlemen managed to entice or cajole a majority of the yeomanry to the patriot cause, they discovered that yeomen insisted upon gaining an important role in making public policy. Gentlemen had unknowingly invited such a demand by adopting the republican rhetoric of independence and popular sovereignty. Conservative gentlemen feared that these radical innovations in political economy would encourage ordinary planters to take over government from their betters. They were rightfully concerned. A flurry of petitions on every important issue of the day began to reach the Virginia House of Delegates soon after the Revolution began. These documents differed from earlier petitions of planters that asked for county or

97. Peter Force, ed., *American Archives* . . . , 5th Ser., I (Washington, D.C., 1848), cols. 364, 464, 633; Dixon and Hunter's *Virginia Gazette*, July 26, Aug. 10, 1776; John Frederick Dorman, ed., *Virginia's Revolutionary War Pension Applications* (Washington, D.C., 1958–), IV, 32.

98. William Kilty, *Laws of Maryland* . . . (Annapolis, 1799), Feb. 1777, chap. 20, Oct. 1777, chap. 20; *Virginia Statutes at Large*, IX, 281–283, 351, X, 104; Overfield, "Loyalists of Maryland," 209–234. I linked Brumbaugh, ed., *Maryland Records*, I, 1–88, to Louise J. Hienton and Helen W. Brown, comps., "1778 Oaths of Fidelity, Prince George's County, Maryland," bound typescript, MHR, and found that the number who signed varied from 46% of those without land and slaves ($N = 308$), to 64% of men with land or slaves, to 88% of men with land and slaves; and the percentage by age was 54%, 19–24 ($N = 63$); 58%, 25–29 ($N = 116$); 61%, 30–39 ($N = 202$); 64%, 40–49 ($N = 171$); 73%, 50–55 ($N = 117$); and 59%, 55+ ($N = 123$). For kin ties and oath taking, see above, chap. 6.

parish divisions, for they attempted to advise and even instruct their representatives on public issues. Residents of Orange County, in the northern piedmont, for instance, sent remonstrances to the legislature between 1777 and 1790 on the inequities of land taxation, the necessity of home manufactures for the internal defense of Virginia, the operation of the militia system, freedom of religion, and the disposition of episcopal glebes. More than a hundred citizens, a tenth of the white adults in the county, signed most petitions. Although petitioners addressed the legislature respectfully, they insisted that they had every right, "as good Inhabitants of the Commonwealth in general, and being moved With a Zeal for the prosperity of our Country," to debate public issues.[99]

Virginia's military manpower policies during the Revolutionary war illustrate the heightened impact of the yeomanry on politics. Political leaders in Virginia tried to make and implement manpower policies consistent with principles of equity (meaning that all white men faced an equal risk of serving) and voluntarism (meaning that men ought to enlist freely). These goals were potentially contradictory: unless enough men volunteered to defend the state and new nation, some would have to be drafted against their will. Two issues, the definition of who was at risk to serve and the ways men would be chosen for military service, were resolved only after much debate between gentlemen and the yeomanry.[100]

Since only militiamen were at risk to be drafted into the army or mobilized for state service, the fewer the men who could obtain exemptions from militia service, the larger would be the pool eligible for draft. It was therefore not surprising that ordinary planters took great interest in making militia membership universal for men between ages sixteen and fifty. Nearly all exemptions from militia musters common before the war—including those for doctors, slave overseers, tobacco inspectors, millers, and boat pilots— were withdrawn for the war, and only men with physical disabilities, ministers, Quakers, and Mennonites consistently avoided militia membership during the war.[101]

99. See Ronald Hoffman, *A Spirit of Dissension: Economics, Politics, and the Revolution in Maryland* (Baltimore, 1973), for gentry fears; William H. B. Thomas, *Patriots of the Upcountry: Orange County, Virginia, in the Revolution* (Orange, Va., 1976), prints nine political petitions that had an average of 88 signatures (114 when the three concerning glebes are combined), quote on 125.

100. These issues are documented in detail in my essay, "The Political Economy of Military Service in Revolutionary Virginia," in John Murrin, ed., *Warfare and Society in Early America from the Aztecs to the Civil War* (forthcoming).

101. Arthur J. Alexander, "Exemption from Military Service in the Old Dominion during the War of the Revolution," *VMHB*, LIII (1945), 163–171; John David McBride, "The Virginia War Effort, 1775–1783: Manpower Policies and Practices" (Ph.D. diss., University of Virginia, 1977), 29–30, 43–44, 69–84.

At the beginning of the war, gentlemen, fearing slave rebellion, had exempted overseers from militia membership. This law raised such severe criticism from yeomen of its inequitable effects that it was abandoned in May 1776, less than a year after it first passed. Hundreds of planters from five counties in piedmont Virginia, mostly poor to middling planters who owned few slaves, railed against the exemption in petitions to the fifth Virginia convention. All the petitions complained that the law exempting overseers "from bearing arms in the Militia, and also Excus'd them from being Drafted as Soldiers" led youths to "become Overseers that Otherways would not ... to Screen themselves from Fighting in defence of their Country as well as their own Property." Poorer planters among the petitioners considered the exemption unjust because if overseers, mostly youths, did not enlist, poor family men would be drafted, thereby forcing their families to go "up and down the County abegging, or [stay] at home starving."[102]

Whig gentlemen not only responded to yeoman pressure by eliminating the exemption of overseers but allowed local planters and their sons to control the process of selecting men to serve in activated militia units and in the Continental army. After experimenting with a volunteer army and a draft lottery of bachelors, legislators left the choice of men to be enlisted to militia units themselves. After local officials had divided the county militia into a number of classes equal to their quota of men, each class chose one man for the draft, offering him any inducement they wished. If a class refused to select a man, justices either chose a man "who in their opinion can be spared" or held a draft lottery to determine who would go.[103]

All white men, including heads of families, could be chosen to serve in the army by militia units, but once selected, any draftee could procure a substitute for himself or his class. When married men and men over thirty were chosen by their militia class, they rarely enlisted, but found substitutes for themselves (often their sons or brothers or a neighbor's teenage son) that thereby permitted them to continue to support their families while sharing the costs of warfare. The system of substitution was very widespread; at least a sixth of all Virginia soldiers were substitute draftees sometime in the war.[104]

This manpower procurement system enjoyed widespread support until nearly the end of the war. About half of the white men in Virginia over

102. Petitions found in Van Schreeven *et al.*, eds., *Revolutionary Virginia*, VI, 474–477, VII, pt. i, 47–48, 87–88, 114–115 (quote), 236–239; analysis of the status of petitioners found in Kulikoff, "Political Economy," in Murrin, ed., *Warfare and Society*.
103. Kulikoff, "Political Economy," in Murrin, ed., *Warfare and Society*; McBride, "Virginia War Effort," chap. 3.
104. See Kulikoff, "Political Economy," in Murrin, ed., *Warfare and Society*, for details.

sixteen saw active duty, and nearly four-fifths of all youths between sixteen and twenty-five served. Youths expected to spend about eighteen months under arms, but were usually activated for only six months to a year during each tour of duty; these soldiers spent most of their time defending their county or state. After completing a term on active duty, a youth could return home and help on the farm before entering the militia or army again.[105]

Ordinary planters willingly enlisted as long as they were not asked to serve long tours of duty or could find substitutes when drafted. But in 1780 and 1781, when hyperinflation and the English invasion of Virginia reduced the number of men willing to be substitutes, poorer planters could no longer afford substitutes. In March 1781, 132 men from Orange County, most of whom were nonslaveholders or owned one or two slaves, complained that a recent call to draft men by class was unfair, even though they had "Liberty to hire a man for three years or during the War." They had failed to hire substitutes and felt they should serve three-month militia terms rather than provide a man for eighteen months because their families would "in all human probability come to misery and ruin" during the two crop seasons they would be under arms.[106]

Men who felt the draft unfair and soldiers needed at home deserted in ever-increasing numbers in 1780 and 1781. About a tenth of Virginians mobilized to fight in 1780 deserted even before reaching the Continental army. Virginia gentlemen tolerated a good deal of draft evasion and desertion because they understood that the military system was not entirely equitable. Legal penalties for draft evasion and desertion were quite moderate. Draft evaders were merely sent to join their units; deserters were supposed to serve an additional six to eight months under arms, after their current term was finished. Local authorities, mindful of possible unrest, sometimes refused to enforce even these moderate penalties and allowed deserters to live peaceably in their communities.[107]

The Legacy of the Revolution

During the middle decades of the eighteenth century, tidewater gentlemen had anchored their power upon hierarchical principles and at the same time developed political and economic authority over the yeomanry through

105. *Ibid.*
106. Thomas, *Patriots of the Upcountry*, 125–127, prints the petition; Kulikoff, "Political Economy," in Murrin, ed., *Warfare and Society*, details the economic status of the signers.
107. Arthur J. Alexander, "A Footnote on Deserters from the Virginia Forces during the American Revolution," *VMHB*, LV (1947), 137–146; Alexander, "Desertion and Its Punishment in Revolutionary Virginia," *WMQ*, 3d Ser., III (1946), 383–397; Joseph A. Goldenberg *et*

thousands of reciprocal exchanges. There was substantial tension between hierarchical theory and the rough equality that reciprocity sometimes implied. Gentlemen traced their right to govern from the king, in whose name commissions for justices were signed and court sessions opened. Because they received authority from the king and dominated economic life, they could command deference from ordinary planters. Nonetheless, gentlemen treated deferential yeomen with some respect and gained their consent for gentry rule through reciprocal exchanges at courthouse and church.

The Revolution accentuated the tension between hierarchy and equality. Whig gentlemen justified their revolt by referring to popular sovereignty, and the yeomanry took them at their word. Yeomen expected to be consulted by gentlemen and even to instruct their representatives. The gentry class not only endorsed the rhetoric of republicanism, substituting "the expressions *Executive* or *Commonwealth* and *citizens*" for words like "*King and subject*," but accepted, perhaps with less grace, the decline in overt deference paid them. "In our high *republican times*," Devereux Jarratt, the Methodist divine, lamented in 1804, "there is more *levelling* than ought to be, consistent with good government," and "too little regard and reverence paid to magistrates and persons in public office."[108]

The adoption of the ideology of popular sovereignty by the yeomanry temporarily challenged gentry rule, but once the gentry class accepted political compromises, it reconstituted its authority. The steps in this reassertion of power, detailed in the Afterword, can be briefly stated. After a long political fight, gentlemen would disestablish the Episcopal church. They would even expand the franchise, theoretically permitting most white men to vote. Yet they would retain firm control over local government and keep the office of justice of the peace an appointive one. And despite the development of political parties and the increasing size of the electorate, voter turnout would diminish over the early nineteenth century. The gentry class had won the war—and the peace.[109]

al., "Revolutionary Ranks: An Analysis of the Chesterfield Supplement," *VMHB*, LXXXVII (1979), 185, 189; McBride, "Virginia War Effort," 246–260.

108. William Waller Hening, *The New Virginia Justice: Comprising the Office and Authority of a Justice of the Peace . . .* (Richmond, Va., 1799), preface; *The Life of Devereux Jarratt, Rector of Bath Parish, Dinwiddie County, Virginia, Written by Himself . . .* (Baltimore, 1806), 14–15.

109. For an elucidation of these themes, see the Afterword.

III
Black Society

8

From Africa to the Chesapeake
Origins of Black Society

Although the eighteenth-century Chesapeake planter looked upon newly enslaved Africans as strange and barbaric folk, he knew that American-born slaves could be taught English customs. Hugh Jones, a Virginia cleric, commented in 1724 that "the languages of the new Negroes are various harsh jargons" but added that slaves born in Virginia "talk good English, and affect our language, habits, and customs." How readily did slaves in Maryland and Virginia accept English ways? Did the preponderance of whites in the region's population and their power force slaves to accept Anglo-American beliefs, values, and skills? Or did slaves succeed in creating their own institutions despite white repression? This chapter attempts to answer these questions.[1]

How readily slaves could form their own culture depended upon both the pattern of forced African immigration to the Americas and the economic and demographic environment that awaited new slaves. Black forced immigrants came from hundreds of different communities and did not have a common culture. Their religious beliefs, kinship systems, and forms of social organization differed substantially. Nevertheless, West Africans did share some values and experiences. For example, each West African group developed different kinship practices, but throughout the region each person located his place in society by his position in his kin group and lineage. When Africans arrived in the New World, their cultural differences were initially of greater significance than the values they shared. They shared only their experience as slaves and labored to make a new society out of their common beliefs and values. The features of the society they formed depended upon the demands of the white masters, the characteristics of the economy, the demography of slave and white populations, and the extent of ethnic divisions among blacks. As they interacted daily, slaves learned to cope with ordinary problems of working, eating, marrying, and child rearing under the adverse conditions of slavery. The social institutions they developed were neither imposed by Europeans nor directly taken from African

1. Hugh Jones, *The Present State of Virginia, from Whence Is Inferred a Short View of Maryland and North Carolina*, ed. Richard L. Morton (Chapel Hill, N.C., 1956 [orig. publ. London, 1724]), 75–76.

communities, but were a unique combination of elements borrowed from the European enslavers and from the common values of various African societies. As soon as slaves formed social institutions, internal conflict diminished, and blacks could place a new Afro-American culture into a settled social context.[2]

The size of working units that masters organized, the number of Africans they bought from slavetraders, and the crops they grew, as well as the rules they required their slaves to follow, influenced the kind of communities their slaves could form. Economic decisions by thousands of masters determined both the density of the black population and the proportion of whites in the population, and these demographic patterns in turn set limits on the intensity of slave community life. The choice of crops was crucial. Some crops required large plantations; others could be grown on small farms. Since large plantations needed more slaves than small farms, large planters purchased greater numbers of African slaves, and consequently, regions dominated by large plantations had greater concentrations of slaves and a larger proportion of Africans in their slave population than regions dominated by farms. Slaves who lived on a large plantation in a region where a substantial majority of the people were enslaved and the density of the slave population was high probably had more opportunities to worship their gods, begin stable families, and develop their own communities than did slaves who lived on small quarters in a preponderantly white country. A slave who lived with many Africans in a place where continual heavy importation of blacks kept the proportion of Africans high was more likely to adopt African customs than the slave who lived where importation was sporadic, the proportion of immigrants among black adults low, and the numbers of whites great.[3]

2. Sidney W. Mintz and Richard Price, *An Anthropological Approach to the Afro-American Past: A Caribbean Perspective*, Institute for the Study of Human Issues, Occasional Papers in Social Change, No. 2 (Philadelphia, 1976), 1–21, provides a valuable theoretical framework adopted in this chapter. See Gerald W. Mullin, *Flight and Rebellion: Slave Resistance in Eighteenth-Century Virginia* (New York, 1972), chaps. 2–3, for an argument that native slaves in Virginia assimilated white norms. *Society*, as used here, concerns social institutions such as family, government, or churches; *culture* includes values and beliefs that motivate and justify behavior in a society.

3. Mintz and Price, *Anthropological Approach*; Richard S. Dunn, *Sugar and Slaves: The Rise of the Planter Class in the English West Indies, 1624–1713* (Chapel Hill, N.C., 1972); Orlando Patterson, *The Sociology of Slavery: An Analysis of the Origins, Development, and Structure of Slave Society in Jamaica* (London, 1967); Peter H. Wood, *Black Majority: Negroes in Colonial South Carolina, from 1670 through the Stono Rebellion* (New York, 1974); Mullin, *Flight and Rebellion*; and Russell R. Menard, "The Maryland Slave Population, 1658 to 1730: A Demographic Profile of Blacks in Four Counties," *William and Mary Quarterly*, 3d Ser., XXXII (1975), 29–54, together suggest these patterns.

This model explains the development of black society in the Chesapeake colonies quite well. African and Afro-American slaves developed a settled life there very slowly. Three stages of community development can be discerned. From roughly 1650 to 1690, blacks assimilated the norms of white society, but the growth of the number of blacks also triggered white repression. The period from 1690 to 1740 was an era of heavy slave imports, small plantation sizes, and social conflicts among blacks. The infusion of Africans often disrupted newly formed slave communities. Finally, from 1740 to 1790, imports declined and then stopped, plantation sizes increased, the proportion of blacks in the population grew, and divisions among slaves disappeared. Consequently, native blacks formed relatively settled communities.

The Africans Arrive

Between 1650 and 1690 two demographic patterns shaped black life. Tobacco was the region's cash crop, and most planters were men of moderate means who could afford few slaves. Therefore, blacks constituted a small part of the Chesapeake population, only about 3 percent of the people in 1650 and 15 percent in 1690. Most lived on small plantations of fewer than eleven blacks. Moreover, almost all slaves were immigrants, and most came to the Chesapeake from the West Indies. Some had recently arrived in the islands from Africa; others had lived there a long time or had been born there.[4]

These characteristics led blacks toward assimilation in the Chesapeake colonies in the decades before 1660. Natives of the islands and longtime residents knew English and were experienced in slavery; new African slaves soon learned English in order to communicate with masters and most other slaves. Blacks and whites cultivated tobacco together, and blacks learned to imitate white servants by occasionally challenging the master's authority. Seventeenth-century Englishmen perceived Africans as an alien, evil, libidinous, and heathen people, but even they saw that their slaves did not fit this description, and many whites treated blacks as they did white servants. Some black residents became and remained free, even considering themselves to be like yeomen.[5]

4. Wesley Frank Craven, *White, Red, and Black: The Seventeenth-Century Virginian* (Charlottesville, Va., 1971), 84, 93–95, 97; U.S., Bureau of the Census, *Historical Statistics of the United States, Colonial Times to 1970* (Washington, D.C., 1975), 1168 (hereafter cited as *Historical Statistics*); Menard, "Maryland Slave Population," *WMQ*, 3d Ser., XXXII (1975), 34–35.
5. The two most thorough examinations of the social status of black people in the seventeenth-

After 1660 the lot of blacks deteriorated; stringent racial laws were passed in Virginia each year between 1667 and 1672 and in 1680, 1682, and 1686.[6] The timing of these laws was due in part to the growth and changing composition of the black population. The numbers of blacks in the Chesapeake colonies doubled every decade except one from 1650 to 1690, but the white population grew more slowly.[7] Slaves began to be imported directly from Africa for the first time in the 1680s. These Africans seemed to Englishmen to be the strange, libidinous, heathenish, and disobedient people they believed typical of black people.

Africans continued to pour into the Chesapeake: from 1700 to 1740, slavers brought fifty-four thousand blacks into Virginia and Maryland, about forty-nine thousand of whom were Africans. The proportion of Africans among all slave immigrants rose from nearly three-quarters from 1710 to 1718 to more than nine-tenths between 1727 and 1740. More than half, and perhaps three-quarters, of these Africans went to a few lower tidewater counties, while some of the rest worked in the upper tidewater.[8] The proportion of recent arrivals among black slave adults fluctuated with trade cycles: about one-half in 1709, one-third in 1720, one-half in 1728, and one-third in 1740 had left Africa or the West Indies within ten years. This rhythm of imports affected every facet of black life, for every few years

century Chesapeake are Joseph Douglas Deal III, "Race and Class in Colonial Virginia: Indians, Englishmen, and Africans on the Eastern Shore during the Seventeenth Century" (Ph.D. diss., University of Rochester, 1981), esp. chap. 3 and pt. 2; and T. H. Breen and Stephen Innes, *"Myne Owne Ground": Race and Freedom on Virginia's Eastern Shore, 1640–1676* (New York, 1980); but see also Edmund S. Morgan, *American Slavery, American Freedom: The Ordeal of Colonial Virginia* (New York, 1975), 154–156, 310–315; Winthrop D. Jordan, *White over Black: American Attitudes toward the Negro, 1550–1812* (Chapel Hill, N.C., 1968), chap. 1; Ross M. Kimmel, "Free Blacks in Seventeenth-Century Maryland," *Maryland Historical Magazine*, LXXI (1976), 19–25; Warren M. Billings, "The Cases of Fernando and Elizabeth Key: A Note on the Status of Blacks in Seventeenth-Century Virginia," *WMQ*, 3d Ser., XXX (1973), 467–474; James H. Brewer, "Negro Property Holders in Seventeenth-Century Virginia," *WMQ*, 3d Ser., XII (1955), 575–580.

6. Jordan, *White over Black*, 71–82; Betty W. W. Coyle, "The Treatment of Servants and Slaves in Colonial Virginia" (master's thesis, College of William and Mary, 1974), 100–108.

7. The sources for the demographic statistics cited in this and succeeding paragraphs will be found in figs. 8, 9, and Allan Kulikoff, "A 'Prolifick' People: Black Population Growth in the Chesapeake Colonies, 1700–1790," *Southern Studies*, XVI (1977), 394–409.

8. This assertion is based upon an analysis of slave ages judged in the York and Lancaster counties Court Order Books, 1710–1740, in the Virginia State Library, Richmond (VSL). The name and age of every black immigrant under 16 had to be registered with the local court, and a comparison of the numbers brought into court, adjusted for age structure extended to similar counties and compared with immigration totals, was used to construct the estimate. For the laws, see William Waller Hening, ed., *The Statutes at Large: Being a Collection of All the Laws of Virginia . . .* , 13 vols. (Richmond, Philadelphia, 1809–1823), II, 479–480, III, 258–259, VI, 40–41 (hereafter cited as *Virginia Statutes at Large*).

native blacks and earlier comers had to absorb many recently imported Africans into their ranks.

The demographic composition of slave cargoes suggests that Africans had a difficult time establishing a regular community or family life after their arrival in the Chesapeake. The slave ships usually carried two men for every woman. Children composed fewer than one-fifth of imported slaves, and there was a similar surplus of boys over girls. Nearly all the children were youths aged ten to fourteen, and almost all the rest were eight or nine (see fig. 9).

Nonetheless, newly enslaved Africans possessed a few building blocks for a new social order under slavery. Many did share a similar ethnic identity. About half the African arrivals at Port York during two periods of heavy immigration were Ibos, Ibibios, Efkins, and Mokos from Nigeria, and another fifth came from various tribes in Angola.[9] From 1718 to 1726, 60 percent came from the Bight of Biafra (the Ibo area); between 1728 and 1739, 85 percent were imported from Biafra or Angola (see table 34). Most new slaves spoke similar languages, lived under the same climate, cultivated similar crops, and shared comparable kinship systems.[10] When they arrived in the Chesapeake, they may have combined common threads in their cultures into new Afro-American structures.

Before Africans could reconstruct their lives, they had to survive the middle passage, the demoralizing experience of being sold, and the stress of their first year in the Chesapeake. The terrible hardships of the middle passage are well known. Africans were often packed naked into crowded and unsanitary ships, coffled together much of the time, and fed a starchy diet. Perhaps one in five died en route. Although they sometimes managed to develop friendships with shipmates that mitigated their misery, these fragile connections were usually destroyed after the ships made port.[11] The

9. Philip D. Curtin, *The Atlantic Slave Trade: A Census* (Madison, Wis., 1969), 157–158, 161, 188, 245; Roger Anstey, *The Atlantic Slave Trade and British Abolition, 1760–1810* (Atlantic Highlands, N.J., 1975), 60, 70–72.

10. C. K. Meek, *Law and Authority in a Nigerian Tribe: A Study in Indirect Rule* (London, 1937), chap. 1; Ikenna Nzimiro, *Studies in Ibo Political Systems: Chieftaincy and Politics in Four Niger States* (Berkeley, Calif., 1972), 25–29; "The Early Travels of Olaudah Equiano" (1789), in Philip D. Curtin, ed., *Africa Remembered: Narratives by West Africans from the Era of the Slave Trade* (Madison, Wis., 1967), 69–88; Jan Vansina, *Kingdoms of the Savanna* (Madison, Wis., 1966), chap. 1 and 191–197.

11. Daniel Pratt Mannix and Malcolm Cowley, *Black Cargoes: A History of the Atlantic Slave Trade, 1518–1865* (New York, 1962), chap. 5; Mintz and Price, *Anthropological Approach*, 22–23. Nantes traders lost about 19% of their slaves in transit between 1715 and 1741 (mean of five-year cohorts), and the Dutch West India Company lost about 20% between 1700 and 1739 (mean of ten-year cohorts). See Curtin, *Atlantic Slave Trade*, 277; and Johannes Postma, "Mortality in the Dutch Slave Trade, 1675–1795," in Henry A. Gemery and Jan S. Hogen-

Table 34. *Geographic Origins of Africans Entering Port York,*
Virginia, 1718–1739

	Percentage of Slaves Entering	
Port of Origin	1718–1726 (*N* = 8,400)[a]	1728–1739 (*N* = 5,818)[b]
Bight of Biafra	60	44
Angola	5	41
Gold Coast	13	5
Senegambia	4	10
Madagascar	9	0
Windward Coast	7	0
Sierra Leone	1	0
Total	99	100

Sources: Elizabeth Donnan, ed., *Documents Illustrative of the History of the Slave Trade to America*, IV, *The Border Colonies and the Southern Colonies* (Washington, D.C., 1935), 183–185, 188–204. The categories are taken from Philip D. Curtin, *The Atlantic Slave Trade: A Census* (Madison, Wis., 1969), 128–130.

Notes: [a]Of 8,613 total entering; origin of 3% unknown. [b]Of 8,786 total entering; origin of 34% unknown.

survivors arrived tired, weak, and sick from their long voyage. Between 1710 and 1718, about one-twentieth of them died before they could be sold. The sales took place aboard ship, and the slaves were bought one by one, in pairs, or in larger groups over several afternoons. The buyers were strange white men and women, fully clothed and healthy and speaking an alien tongue, who peered and poked all over the Africans' bodies. After the sale, some shipmates left with different masters; others were returned to their chains to be sold another day.[12]

Many slaves had to endure the indignity of slave sales numerous times before they were finally purchased. Early in the century, some slave ships sold Africans in Barbados and then came to Yorktown; in the 1720s and 1730s, slavers first went to Yorktown and then upriver to West Point or to

---

dorn, eds., *The Uncommon Market: Essays in the Economic History of the Atlantic Slave Trade* (New York, 1979), 255.

12. Elizabeth Donnan, ed., *Documents Illustrative of the History of the Slave Trade to America*, IV, *The Border Colonies and the Southern Colonies* (Washington, D.C., 1935), 175–181; Robert Carter Diary, 1722–1727, Sept. 18, 20, 21, 27, 29, 1727, Alderman Library, University of Virginia, Charlottesville; Mullin, *Flight and Rebellion*, 14; Gregory A. Stiverson and Patrick H. Butler III, eds., "Virginia in 1732: The Travel Journal of William Hugh Grove," *Virginia Magazine of History and Biography*, LXXXV (1977), 31–32.

ports on the Rappahannock River.[13] Once they arrived in Virginia, slave ships took about two and a half months to sell their cargoes and leave the province, and slaves were shown to customers for an average of two to five days before being bought.[14] How often an African was placed on sale depended upon the individual's age, sex, and health and the state of the market for slaves. Planters purchased healthy men first; women and children were second and third choices; unhealthy slaves were sold last. Women and children were sometimes bought by middlemen who took them from the ship and sold them in the interior of the province.[15]

Despite the degradation of the slave sale, Africans made a small beginning toward a new community life as they traveled several days to the master's plantation. Although they had left most of their shipmates behind, they usually walked in small groups and could use the trip to renew old friendships or make new ones. Only about one-third of the Africans in four groups purchased from 1702 to 1721 were purchased singly; another third left in pairs, and the rest left in larger groups (see table 35). Furthermore, slaves destined for different masters may have traveled together whenever a planter who lived more than a day's trip from the sale site asked a neighbor going to the sale to buy a slave for him.[16]

13. Between 1710 and 1718, 41% of all Africans stopped first in the islands; 15% from 1732 to 1739 were displayed there first. From 1710 to 1733, from 72% to 81% of African immigrants entered York, and from 17% to 20% came to Rappahannock (grouped years); 1735–1740, 58% to York, 18% to Rappahannock, 12% to upper James. Donnan, *Documents of Slave Trade*, II, *The Eighteenth Century* (Washington, D.C., 1931), 299–300, 427–432, compared with IV, 175–206. For West Point, see IV, 101, and *Virginia Gazette*, June 1, 1739. For Yorktown, see *Va. Gaz.*, Apr. 8, 1737, June 8, 1739. For Yorktown to West Point, see *Va. Gaz.*, Aug. 19, 1739. For York to Rappahannock, see Augustus Moore to Isaac Hobhouse, May 3, 1723, in Walter E. Minchinton, ed., "The Virginia Letters of Isaac Hobhouse, Merchant of Bristol," *VMHB*, LXVI (1958), 294.

14. Walter E. Minchinton, "The Triangular Trade Revisited," in Gemery and Hogendorn, eds., *The Uncommon Market*, 341 (data from 1725–1738); sale data from two ships consigned to Robert Carter: the *John and Betty* (2.2 days) and the *Rose* (5.3 days), the third and the last ships at Rappahannock in 1727. Both ships had high proportions of women and children. Robert Carter Diary, July 17–Aug. 3, Sept. 18–Oct. 5, 1727; Carter to John Pemberton, July 26, 1727 (added to June 28 letter), and Carter to George Eskridge, Sept. 21, 1727, Robert Carter Letterbooks, 1727–1728, Virginia Historical Society, Richmond (VHS).

15. "Sale of the Charfield Slaves Begun July 23, 1717 Belonging to Samuel Jacobs and Company, Bristol," Stephen Loyd–John Tayloe Account Book, VHS; John Baylor Account Book, 1719–1721, Baylor Papers, 139, 162–164, Alderman Library; Robert Carter to Francis Chamberlayne and Francis Sitwell, July 26, 1720, Sept. 27, 1727, in Louis B. Wright, ed., *Letters of Robert Carter, 1720–1727: The Commercial Interests of a Virginia Gentleman* (San Marino, Calif., 1940), 41–43, 52–53.

16. Even Robert Carter had slaves delivered to him on occasion. Carter to ———— [May 21, 1728], Carter Letterbooks. I estimated distance of purchasers from the *Charfield*, which was berthed at Urbanna on the Rappahannock (John Tayloe to Samuel Jacobs and Co., July 1727,

Table 35. *Size of African Slave Purchases in Virginia,*
1702–1721

Size of Purchase (No. of Slaves)	Percentage of Slaves ($N=318$)
1	34
2	32
3	6
4	8
5+	21
Total	101

Sources: Elizabeth Donnan, ed., *Documents Illustrative of the History of the Slave Trade to America*, IV, *The Border Colonies and the Southern Colonies* (Washington, D.C., 1935), 71–72 (African Galley, 53 Slaves, 1702); "Sale of Charfield Slaves," Loyd-Tayloe Account Book, VHS (124 slaves; excludes those sold to merchants); John Baylor Account Book, 1719–1721, Alderman Library, University of Virginia (83 personal sales; 58 women and children from the *Prince Eugene*, 1719). Each group counted in proportion to the numbers of slaves sold.

Once they entered the plantation world, African immigrants had to begin to cope with their status. The absolute distinction between slavery and freedom found in the Chesapeake colonies did not exist in West African societies. African communities and kin groups possessed a wide range of rights in persons. A captive in war might end up as anything from a chattel, who could be sold, to the wife of one of the victorious tribesmen; he might become an agricultural laborer, a soldier, or a domestic servant. At first, such outsiders were treated harshly, especially in societies with numerous slaves, but eventually their children or grandchildren could move from marginality to partial or full membership in a kin group or community.[17]

When they reached their new homes, Africans were immediately put to work making tobacco. Most were broken in on the most routine tasks of

Loyd-Tayloe Account Book), from data in Clayton Torrence, comp., *Virginia Wills and Administrations, 1632–1800* . . . (Richmond, Va., 1930). I identified 75 of 128 slaves sold at this sale to planters (those probably resold excluded), and the mean distance traveled was 37 miles, a trip of about two days.

17. Igor Kopytoff and Suzanne Miers, "African 'Slavery' as an Institution of Marginality," in Miers and Kopytoff, eds., *Slavery in Africa: Historical and Anthropological Perspectives* (Madison, Wis., 1977), 3–81; Martin Klein and Paul E. Lovejoy, "Slavery in West Africa," in Gemery and Hogendorn, eds., *The Uncommon Market*, 181–212.

production. Nearly two-thirds of them arrived between June and August, when the tobacco plants had already been moved from seedbeds and were growing rapidly. The new slaves' first task was weeding between the rows of plants with hands, axes, or hoes. These jobs were similar to those that Ibos and other Africans had used in growing other crops in their native lands. After a month or two of such labor, slaves could be instructed in the more difficult task of harvesting. Some Africans refused to accept this new work discipline, either not understanding or pretending not to understand their masters. Edward Kimber, a visitor to the Eastern Shore in 1747, wrote that a "new Negro" (a newly enslaved African) "must be broke. . . . You would really be surpriz'd at their Perseverance; let an hundred Men shew him how to hoe, or drive a Wheelbarrow, he'll still take the one by the Bottom, and the Other by the Wheel."[18]

Not only were Africans forced to work for harsh masters in a strange land, but masters usually stripped them of their names, their last personal possession. Africans imbued names with great meaning, and naming often followed a ceremony at birth or coming of age. They often possessed several names, each to be used on a different occasion. Masters in the Chesapeake, without ceremony, forced Africans to adopt English names and required that they be used in daily exchanges between whites and blacks.[19] At least four-fifths of African youths age ten to fifteen, whose ages and names were recorded in York and Lancaster counties at the peak of the slave trade, received English names. Only 3 percent of these 465 slaves kept African names. Six maintained day names, used in many African communities to indicate the day of birth: four were *Cuffy* (male name for "Friday"), one was *Jacko* (*Quacko*, male name for "Wednesday"), and one *Juba* (female name for "Monday"). Eighty slaves, however, might have persuaded their masters to allow them to retain Anglicized versions of African names. Three names were especially common. Twenty-four boys were named *Jack*, an English version of *Quacko*, and twelve were named *Jemmy*, probably an Anglicized version of *Quame* (male name for "Saturday"). The most common name among African girls in this group was *Phyllis* (often spelled *Fillis*), a name rarely employed by whites. The name is phonetically close to *Fili*, an African word meaning "losing one's way" in Mandingo and "to abandon" or "to

---

18. Donnan, ed., *Documents of Slave Trade*, IV, 188–243; Herbert S. Klein, "Slaves and Shipping in Eighteenth-Century Virginia," *Journal of Interdisciplinary History*, V (1974–1975), 396–397; "Eighteenth-Century Maryland as Portrayed in the 'Itinerant Observations' of Edward Kimber," *MHM*, LI (1956), 327–328.
19. J. L. Dillard, *Black English: Its History and Usage in the United States* (New York, 1972), 123–135; Wood, *Black Majority*, 181–186; John S. Mbiti, *African Religions and Philosophy* (New York, 1969), 154–157.

deceive" in Bambora. Perhaps these girls had not been named *Fili* before their capture, but adopted the name to describe their current low condition.[20]

Enslaved Africans almost never gave their children African names, but apparently had to accept the names masters chose for them. First-generation native-born slaves in Middlesex County, Virginia, received the diminutive form of English names (*Jack, Will, Betty, Moll*) that whites gave their children or (much less frequently) names from classical mythology. African parents in Middlesex infrequently persuaded their masters to allow slave children to be named for African kindred, even in some highly Anglicized form. Instead, masters wanted to be able to distinguish readily among slaves and therefore never gave precisely the same name to two children in the same generation.[21]

Under these conditions, Africans were often struck with loneliness and illness. For example, Ayuba (Job) Suleiman was brought to Maryland's Eastern Shore in 1730. He was "put . . . to work in making tobacco" but "every day showed more and more uneasiness under this exercise, and at last grew sick, being no way able to bear it; so that his master was obliged to find easier work for him, and therefore put him to tend the cattle." A new slave might become so ill that he could not work. Thomas Swan, a planter in Prince George's County, Maryland, bought two Africans in the summer of 1728; in November of that year he asked the county court to refund one poll tax because "one of them has been sick ever since he bought him and has done him little or no Service."[22]

One in four new Negroes died during his first year in the Chesapeake; in some years, mortality seems to have been especially high. In 1727 Robert Carter lost at least seventy hands, perhaps a quarter of all his slaves born abroad and more than half of his new Negroes. Because Africans possessed some native immunities against malaria, most survived the malarial attacks of their first summer in the region, but respiratory illnesses struck them hard the following winter and spring. Planters considered late spring "the best time of buying them by reason they will be well season'd before the

20. Records of slave ages judged found in York County Order Books, 1710–1749, and Lancaster County Order Books, 1717–1740. There were 278 boys and 187 girls in the samples. For *Fili* and other slave names, see Lorenzo Dow Turner, *Africanisms in the Gullah Dialect* (Chicago, 1949), 40–190 (86 for *Fili*).

21. Darrett B. Rutman and Anita H. Rutman, *A Place in Time: Explicatus* (New York, 1984), 97–103.

22. Thomas Bluett, "The Capture and Travels of Ayuba Suleiman Ibrahima" (1734), in Curtin, ed., *Africa Remembered*, 41; Prince George's Court Record, liber O, fol. 355, Maryland Hall of Records, Annapolis (MHR).

winter."[23] Blacks living in New Kent County, Virginia, between 1714 and 1739 died infrequently in the summer, but deaths rose somewhat in the fall, increased from December to February, and peaked in March and April. The county undoubtedly included many Africans. Whites in the same parish died more frequently in autumn and less often in spring than did their slaves. A similar pattern could be found in Middlesex County. Deaths of slaves in that county between 1651 and 1746 rose in the fall months and peaked in February before beginning a long decline that ended with the harvest season.[24]

Despite disease and death, new Negroes soon began to develop friendships with other slaves and to challenge the authority of their masters by attempting to make a new life for themselves off their quarters. They were able to oppose their masters because so many of their fellow workers were also recent immigrants who shared their new experiences under slavery. In the mid-1700s, late 1710s, mid-1720s, and mid-1730s, when unusually large numbers of blacks entered Virginia, these Africans, united by their common experiences and able to communicate through the heavily African pidgin they probably created, ran off to the woods together, formed temporary settlements in the wilderness, and several times conspired to overthrow their white masters.

First, Africans had to find or create a common language because there were few speakers of any common African tongue in any neighborhood. Some new slaves may have devised a form of sign language soon after arrival, but the large concentrations of Ibos and Angolans among the Africans suggest that many spoke similar languages and that others could have become bilingual. Others probably spoke some West African pidgin that they had learned in Africa in order to communicate with Europeans. A new

23. Robert Carter to William Dawkins, May 13, 1727, Carter Letterbooks, VHS; Carter to Dawkins, June 3, 1727, Carter Letterbooks, Univ. Va.; Conquest Wyatt to Richard Wyatt, June 1, 1737, July 20, 1743; Earl of Romney's Deposit, Loan 15, British Library (CW); Robert Bristow to Thomas Booth, Oct. 30, 1710, Sept. 15, 1711, Robert Bristow Letterbooks, VSL; Elizabeth Suttell, "The British Slave Trade to Virginia, 1698–1728" (master's thesis, College of William and Mary, 1965), 58–59; Robert Carter Inventory, 1733, VHS. The estimates of mortality among Carter's slaves are based on inferences from his purchasing practices and the composition of his slave population in 1733.

24. See the death register printed in C. G. Chamberlayne, ed., *The Vestry Book and Register of St. Peter's Parish, New Kent and James City Counties, Virginia, 1684–1786* (Richmond, Va., 1937). The presence of Africans is suggested by high black adult sex ratios in the register: the adult sex ratio was 151 men per 100 women (and 157, excluding mulattoes), the black child sex ratio was 100, and the white adult sex ratio was 115. For Middlesex, see Darrett B. Rutman *et al.*, "Rhythms of Life: Black and White Seasonality in the Early Chesapeake," *Jour. Interdisc. Hist.*, XI (1980–1981), 36–37.

creole language may have emerged in the Chesapeake region combining the vocabulary of several African languages common among the immigrants, African linguistic structures, and the few English words needed for communication with the master.[25]

Almost as soon as Africans landed, they attempted to run away together. Seven of Robert Carter's new Negroes did so on July 7, 1727. They took a canoe and may have crossed the Rappahannock River. Carter sent men "sev[era]l ways" for them, and on July 15 they were returned to him. Enough new Negroes ran away to persuade the Virginia assembly to pass laws in 1705 and 1722 detailing procedures to follow when Africans who did not speak English and could not name their master were recaptured.[26]

A few Africans formed communities in the wilderness in the 1720s, when black immigration was high and the frontier close to tidewater. In 1725 the Maryland assembly asserted that "sundry" slaves "have of late Years runaway into the Back-Woods, some of which have there perished, and others . . . have been entertained and encouraged to live and inhabit with the Shewan-Indians." Other slaves, who heard of their success, were "daily making Attempts to go the same Way." Any slave who ran beyond the Monocacy River, at the edge of white settlement, was to have an ear cut off and his chin branded with an *R*. The assembly, recognizing that Africans habitually ran away, withheld this punishment for new Negroes during their first year in the colony.[27]

Africans established at least two outlying runaway communities during the 1720s. Fifteen slaves began a settlement in 1729 on the frontier near present-day Lexington, Virginia. They ran from "a new Plantation on the head of the James River," taking arms, tools, clothing, and food with them. When captured, "they had already begun to clear the ground." Before they submitted to the whites, they exchanged "a shot or two by which one of the Slaves was wounded." Governor Gooch claimed that the government's stern reaction prevented the creation of a strong, independent black community similar to the Maroons in Jamaica. Another small community evidently developed on the Maryland frontier in 1728 and 1729. Early in

25. "Capture of Ayuba Suleiman," in Curtin, ed., *Africa Remembered*, 42–43; "Travels of Olaudah Equiano," *ibid.*, 88–89; Menard, "Maryland Slave Population," *WMQ*, 3d Ser., XXXII (1975), 35. The problem of language was first discussed by Mullin, *Flight and Rebellion*, 44–47; for pidgin, see Wood, *Black Majority*, chap. 6, and Dillard, *Black English*, 73–93.

26. Carter Diary, July 17, 24, 1727; *Virginia Statutes at Large*, III, 456, IV, 168–175; Waverly K. Winfree, comp., *The Laws of Virginia, Being a Supplement to Hening's "The Statutes at Large,"* *1700–1750* (Richmond, 1971), 212–222; Mullin, *Flight and Rebellion*, 40–45.

27. William Hand Browne *et al.*, eds., *Archives of Maryland . . .* , 72 vols. (Baltimore, 1883–1972), XXXVI, 583–586, XXXV, 505–506, XXXVII, 211, XXV, 394–395 (hereafter cited as *Archives of Maryland*); Prince George's Court Records, L, 515.

1729, one of the runaways living there returned to southern Prince George's County to report on the place to his former shipmates and attempted to entice them to join the group.[28]

As soon as Africans arrived in the Chesapeake colonies in large numbers, government officials began to complain about their clandestine meetings. In 1687 the Virginia council asserted that masters allowed blacks to go "on broad on Saterdays and Sundays . . . to meet in great Numbers in making and holding of Funeralls for Dead Negroes." Governor Francis Nicholson of Maryland wrote in 1698 that groups of six or seven slaves traveled thirty or forty miles on weekends to the sparsely inhabited falls of the Potomac.[29]

Whites suppressed clandestine meetings primarily because they feared slave violence and rebellions. Perhaps there was reason for their concern. Poisonings were not uncommon in the two Chesapeake colonies, and slaves sometimes conspired to poison their masters. For example, fourteen slaves who lived on five plantations scattered over a seventy-five-square-mile area of Prince George's County, Maryland, near the Potomac River met together in January 1738 and "Sev[er]al other days as well before and after" to plan, it was alleged, the murder by poison of John Beall, who owned four of the conspirators. Though only one slave, Beall's Bess, was convicted and sentenced to hang, all the masters had to post bond to ensure the good behavior of their slaves.[30]

Africans pushed to suicidal actions might instead revolt against the slave system. Revolts were rare in the Chesapeake colonies, where whites heavily outnumbered slaves, but Africans apparently participated in conspiracies in Surry, James City, and Isle of Wight counties in Virginia in 1710, and in Prince George's County, Maryland, in 1739 and 1740. The 1739–1740 conspiracy, which is the best documented, was organized by slaves who lived in St. Paul's Parish, an area of large plantations where numerous slaveholders had recently bought Africans. The Negroes spent eight months in 1739 planning to seize their freedom by killing their masters and other white families in the neighborhood. Their leader, Jack Ran-

28. Mullin, *Flight and Rebellion*, 43–44; quotation from Michael Mullin, ed., *American Negro Slavery: A Documentary History* (New York, 1976), 83; Prince George's Court Records, O, 414–415.

29. H. R. McIlwaine, ed., *Executive Journals of the Council of Colonial Virginia*, I (Richmond, 1925), 86–87; *Archives of Maryland*, XXIII, 498–499, also cited in Menard, "Maryland Slave Population," *WMQ*, 3d Ser., XXXII (1975), 37–38; *Virginia Statutes at Large*, IV, 128–129.

30. Philip J. Schwarz, "Slave Criminality and the Slave Community: Patterns of Slave Assertiveness in Eighteenth-Century Virginia" (paper presented at the annual meeting of the Organization of American Historians, New York, April 1978), 10, table 1; Prince George's Court Records, W, 661–663.

som, was probably a native, but most of the conspirators were Africans, for it is reported that the planning was done by the slaves in "their country language." The revolt was postponed several times, and finally white authorities got wind of it. Stephen Boardley, an Annapolis lawyer, reported that whites believed that two hundred slaves planned to kill all the white men, marry the white women, and then unite both shores of Maryland under their control. Ransom was tried and executed, four other slaves were acquitted, and the furor died down.[31]

Every attempt by Africans to establish an autonomous social life off the plantation failed because whites, who held the means of terror, insisted that their slaves remain at home. Running to the woods, founding outlying communities, or meeting in large groups challenged work discipline and cost the planter profits. Nevertheless, substantial numbers of Africans probably participated in activities off the plantation. Slaves from many different African communities proved that they could unite and live together. Others, though unable to join them, must have heard of their exploits and discovered that a new social life might be possible. Sooner or later, however, Africans had to turn to their plantations to develop communities.

But as late as the 1730s, plantations were not conducive places in which to create a settled social life. A major deterrent was the size of the slave populations on plantation quarters. On quarters of fewer than ten slaves, completed families of husbands, wives, and children were uncommon, and the slaves, who lived in outbuildings, did not control enough space of their own to run their own lives apart from the master. In tidewater, plantations were small (see table 36). No plantations with more than twenty slaves were inventoried in seventeenth-century Anne Arundel County, Maryland. Only 28 percent of the slaves on Maryland's lower Western Shore before 1711 lived on plantations of more than twenty slaves, and some of them resided in quarters distant from the main plantation. Quarters were similarly small in York and Lancaster counties in the 1710s. From 1700 to 1740, plantation sizes in Anne Arundel and Prince George's increased. But plantations failed to grow in York and St. Mary's, and frontier units in Virginia's piedmont were as small as those in tidewater at the beginning of the century. If these counties were typical of the Chesapeake in the 1730s, then half of the slaves lived on quarters of ten or fewer, and only a quarter resided on units of more than twenty.[32]

31. Herbert Aptheker, *American Negro Slave Revolts* (New York, 1943), 169–170, and sources cited there (Aptheker calls one conspiracy two); Stephen Boardley Letter Books, 1738–1740, Maryland Historical Society, Baltimore; *Archives of Maryland*, XXVII, 188–190, 230–232, XL, 425, 428, 457, 523; Prince George's Court Records, X, 573–576; Chancery Records, VIII, 38–39, MHR (shipment of 320 Africans in 1734 to Benedict near the site of the conspiracy).
32. Kulikoff, "Origins of Afro-American Society," *WMQ*, 3d Ser., XXXV (1978), 241. Lorena

Table 36. *Plantation Size in Maryland and Virginia, 1658–1745*

| | Percentage of Slaves | | | | |
| | Size of Unit (No. of Slaves) | | | | |
Place and Time	1–5	6–10	11–20	21+	Total
Maryland, lower Western Shore[a]					
1658–1710 (*N*=1,618)	29	22	21	28	100
1721–1730 (*N*=794)	17	19	20	44	100
Prince George's					
1731–1740 (*N*=842)	17	26	34	24	101
St. Mary's Co.					
1721–1730 (*N*=484)	26	21	25	28	100
1731–1740 (*N*=524)	32	22	35	11	100
Anne Arundel					
1658–1699 (*N*=305)	36	17	47	0	100
1700–1719 (*N*=1,050)[b]	16	13	22	50	101
1720–1739 (*N*=1,549)[b]	12	18	20	51	101
York					
1711–1720 (*N*=618)	28	20	22	30	100
1721–1740 (*N*=905)	27	25	31	17	100
Lancaster Co.					
1711–1725 (*N*=248)	29	22	31	17	99
1726–1745 (*N*=821)[b]	14	18	22	48	102
King Carter's plantations					
1733 (*N*=733)	2	14	40	45	99
Virginia piedmont cos.[c]					
1720–1739 (*N*=345)	21	39	21	19	100

Sources: see n. 32.

Notes: [a]St. Mary's, Charles, Calvert, and Prince George's, 1658–1710; Prince George's and Charles, 1721–1730. [b]Unusually large numbers of planters with major slaveholding (21+) died. [c]Spotsylvania, Goochland, and Orange.

African social structures centered on the family, but slaves in the Chesapeake had difficulty maintaining family life. Men who lived on small quarters often had to find wives elsewhere, a task made more difficult by the high ratio of men to women in much of tidewater. As long as adult sex ratios remained high, men had to postpone marriage, and women might be forced to marry early. Even on large plantations men could not count on

---

S. Walsh, "Changing Work Roles for Slave Labor in Chesapeake Agriculture" (paper delivered at conference, "The Colonial Experience: The Eighteenth-Century Chesapeake," Baltimore, Sept. 1984), table 1; and Philip Morgan, "Slave Life in the Virginia Piedmont: A Demographic Report" (paper at conference, "The Colonial Chesapeake"), table 5.

living in family units, for sex ratios there were higher than on small quarters. During the 1730s the adult sex ratio in Prince George's was 187, but on nine large plantations in the county, each having ten or more adult slaves, it stood at 249. A similar pattern could be found in both York and Lancaster counties at times between 1710 and 1740.[33]

Since most slaves lived on small plantations, the development of settled black community life required visiting between quarters. Sometimes slaves met on larger plantations getting "Drunke on the Lords Day beating their Negro Drums by which they call considerable Numbers of Negroes together." On one Sunday in 1735, Edward Pearson's Negroes with some of his "Neighbours Negroes was Beating a Drum and Danceing but by my Consent" in Prince George's. Slaves probably did not regularly visit friends on nearby plantations, however. Visiting networks could develop only where blacks were densely settled and constituted a large part of the population. Before 1740 the population in tidewater was never more than half slave except in a few counties between the James and York rivers. Only 16 percent of the people in the Chesapeake colonies were black in 1690, but this proportion grew to 25 percent in 1710 and 28 percent in 1740.[34]

The large plantations in tidewater housed masters, overseers, native blacks, new Negroes, and less recent immigrants, but smaller units, with only a few natives or immigrants, tended to be more homogeneous. The concentration of men on large plantations suggests that most African adults were bought by the gentry, a pattern documented by the composition of John Mercer's and Robert Carter's plantations. Mercer bought 69 slaves between 1731 and 1746. These purchases included 6 seasoned Africans or natives in 1731 and 1732, 25 new Negroes from 1733 to 1739, and 20 new Negroes and 15 seasoned slaves in the 1740s. By 1740 Mercer owned a mixed group of new Negroes, seasoned immigrants, and native children and adults. The composition of Carter's quarters in 1733 shows the culmination

33. Allan Kulikoff, "Tobacco and Slaves: Population, Economy, and Society in Eighteenth-Century Prince George's County, Maryland" (Ph.D. diss., Brandeis University, 1976), 77; York County Wills and Orders, XIV–XVII, and Lancaster County Wills, X–XIII, VSL. York adult sex ratios in 1711–1720 were 126, and 145 on large plantations (numbering five) with 10 or more adult slaves, the sex ratio on Robert Carter's plantations in 1733 (Carter Inventory, VHS) was 153, and the sex ratio in Lancaster Inventories, 1726–1735, was 113. Menard, "Maryland Slave Population," *WMQ*, 3d Ser., XXXII (1975), 37; Prince George's Court Records, V, 618, 630.

34. *Historical Statistics*, 1168; Russell R. Menard, "Economy and Society in Early Colonial Maryland" (Ph.D. diss., University of Iowa, 1975), 412; Menard, "Maryland Slave Population," *WMQ*, 3d Ser., XXXII (1975), 35. Slave concentrations in the James-York area are inferences from later data in Evarts B. Greene and Virginia D. Harrington, *American Population before the Federal Census of 1790* (New York, 1932), 150–151.

of this process. More than half of Carter's 734 slaves lived on plantations where one-fifth to one-half were recent immigrants, and another third resided on quarters composed predominantly of natives or older immigrants. Only one-seventh of his slaves lived on quarters dominated by new Negroes. About one-half of the quarters of over 20 slaves included numerous immigrants, but natives formed a majority of the rest. Most of the eighteen farms with 11–20 slaves included Africans and creoles, but five others were peopled by natives. Nine of the eleven quarters where new Negroes formed a majority were small units of fewer than 10 slaves.[35]

Most new Negroes learned to be slaves on such diversified plantations. Nearly two-thirds of Carter's recent immigrant slaves lived on plantations with numerous native adults and children, and white overseers resided at almost every quarter. Other slaves, owned by middling planters, were directed in their labor daily by their masters. Africans had to learn some English in order to communicate with masters, overseers, and native slaves, and they were put into the fields with other slaves who had already learned that they had to work to avoid punishment and that resistance had to be indirect. Africans saw that a few slaves were given responsibilities—and power—over other slaves or were taught new skills. Slaves born in Africa apparently were well acculturated on Robert Carter's quarters. While the great majority of his adult slaves were agricultural laborers, some Africans (who had probably been in the country for a number of years) joined their native friends as foremen who worked under white overseers. Perhaps nineteen of the thirty-three foremen on these plantations were born in Africa. Four other men, possibly Africans, became sloopers (boatmen) on Carter's main plantation.[36]

Nonetheless, Africans and native slaves quarreled on occasion because of the great differences in their respective experiences. Natives had not been herded into ships and sold into bondage. They were probably healthier than forced immigrants. Many of them were baptized Christians, and some became believers. To Africans, by contrast, Christianity was an alien creed, and they sometimes tried to maintain their own Islamic or African religions in opposition to it. Ben, for example, was brought from Africa to Charles County, Maryland, about 1730. According to his grandson, Charles Ball, Ben "always expressed great contempt for his fellow

---

35. John Mercer's Ledger B, 12, Bucks County Historical Society, Doylestown, Pa. (film copy at Colonial Williamsburg Research Department [CW]); Carter Inventory, VHS. I identified as immigrants all men, women, and children age 10–14 who did not live in a family and all husband-wife households.

36. Carter Inventory, VHS. There were resident overseers on all but two quarters with 9 slaves. Two overseers supervised two quarters; 63 slaves lived on these four farms.

slaves, they being . . . a mean and vulgar race, quite beneath his rank, and the dignity of his former station." Ben never attended a Christian service but held that Christianity was "altogether false, and indeed no religion at all."[37]

The most significant difference between recent immigrants and creole blacks can be seen in their family life. A native-born slave on Robert Carter's plantations in 1733 usually lived in a family composed of husband, wife, and children, whereas new Negroes were placed in sex-segregated barracks and seasoned immigrants lived in conjugal units without children. Conditions at Carter's plantations were optimal; elsewhere, high sex ratios and competition from creole men limited the marriage opportunities of African men. Furthermore, newly enslaved African women often waited two or three years before taking a husband, thus further reducing the supply of prospective wives. The reluctance of Afro-American women to marry Africans may have been one of the grievances of the Prince George's conspirators in 1739–1740.[38]

Several incidents on Edmond Jennings's plantations in King William County, Virginia, in 1712–1713, suggest that Africans competed among themselves for wives, sometimes with tragic results. George, who lived at Beaverdam Quarter, complained in November 1712 that "his country men had poysened him for his wife," and he died the following February, reputedly from the poison. Roger, of Silsdon Quarter, apparently wanted more than one wife. In December 1712 or January 1713, he "hanged himself in ye old 40 foot Tob. house not any reason he being hindred from keeping other negroes men wifes beside his owne." The overseer ordered Roger's "head cutt off and stuck on a pole to be a terror to the others."[39]

Slaves in the Chesapeake colonies failed to establish a settled community life in the times of heavy immigration in the 1710s, 1720s, and 1730s. Conflicts between Africans and between African and native slaves could never be fully resolved as long as large numbers of Africans were forced into slavery in the two colonies. On the other hand, the rate of immigration, the proportion of Africans in the slave population, and the proportion of blacks in the population were never great enough to permit successful communities based mostly upon African institutions and values to develop either on the plantation or away from it.

---

37. Charles Ball, *Fifty Years in Chains*, ed. Philip S. Foner (New York, 1970 [orig. publ. as *Slavery in the United States: A Narrative of the Life and Adventures* . . . (New York, 1837)]), 22–23; "Capture of Ayuba Suleiman," in Curtin, ed., *Africa Remembered*, 42.

38. Carter Inventory, VHS; Stephen Boardley thought the conspirators planned to kill black women as well as white men. Boardley Letter Books, 55–58.

39. Inventories of the Negroes on the Estate of Edmond Jennings, 1712–13, Francis Porteus Corbin Papers, Duke University, Durham, N.C. (film at CW).

Toward Afro-American Slave Communities

The demographic conditions that prevented blacks from developing a cohesive social life before 1740 changed during the quarter of a century before the Revolution, as immigration of Africans to the Chesapeake declined sharply. Only 17 percent of Virginia's adult blacks in 1750 and 15 percent in 1755 had arrived within the previous ten years, and these newcomers went in relatively greater numbers to newer piedmont counties than had their predecessors. For instance, wealthy planters in Amelia County in Virginia's southside region bought so many slaves between 1734 and 1754 that 59 percent of that county's black adult population in 1755 had been born in Africa.[40] The proportion of adult blacks in 1755 who had entered Virginia since 1750 ranged from 4 percent in Lancaster County and 8 percent in York County in tidewater Virginia to 15 percent in Caroline County and 21 percent in Fairfax County, both near the fall line. After 1755, almost all of Virginia's black immigrants went to piedmont counties.[41]

As the number of enslaved Africans in tidewater declined, the internal division among blacks diminished. These recent arrivals were under greater pressure than their predecessors to acquire the language, values, and beliefs of the dominant native majority. Like new Negroes before them, they sometimes ran away, but with less success. On arrival, they found themselves isolated and alone. Olaudah Equiano, for example, was brought to Virginia in 1757 at age twelve. "I was now exceedingly miserable," he later wrote, "and thought myself worse off than any ... of my companions; for they could talk to each other, but I had no person to speak to that I could understand. In this state I was constantly grieving and pining, and wishing for death." But once slaves like Equiano learned English, they became part of the Afro-American community. Bob, twenty-nine, and Turkey Tom, thirty-eight, were new Negroes who lived on the home plantation of Charles Carroll of Carrollton in 1773. Since Bob and Tom were apparently the only two recent immigrant slaves on any of Carroll's many plantations, they both could participate fully in plantation life. Bob was a smith, a position usually reserved for natives; he married the daughter of a carpenter and lived with her and their two children. Tom, a laborer, also found a place

40. Kulikoff, "A 'Prolifick' People," *So. Stud.*, XVI (1977), 422–423; Donnan, ed., *Documents of Slave Trade*, IV, 202–224, shows that in the 1740s, York remained the major slave port (53% arrived there), but upper James (where most new settlement occurred) received 22% of the slaves. For Amelia County, see Philip Morgan, "Slave Life in the Virginia Piedmont," table 4.
41. Computed from the ages of slaves judged found in Lancaster, IX–X, York Judgments and Orders, 1746–1752, 1752–1754, Fairfax Orders, 1749–1754, 1754–1756, all found in VSL; and T. E. Campbell, *Colonial Caroline: A History of Caroline County, Virginia* (Richmond, Va., 1954), 331.

in the plantation's kinship networks: his wife was at least a third-generation Marylander.[42] Very few Africans probably ever became artisans, but so few Africans were imported that most Africans in tidewater could find wives among the native majority.

The internal divisions among slaves reappeared, to a degree, in piedmont Virginia. The slave trade centered in the region: by the 1760s, nearly all Africans who arrived in Virginia landed at Bermuda Hundred, a small settlement located near present-day Petersburg and close to the expanding southside region. Newly enslaved Africans made up as much as a third of the total black population of the region.[43] Nonetheless, the proportion of Africans in piedmont's adult slave population rapidly diminished, for both small and large planters brought many slaves from their tidewater plantations into new areas, and by the 1780s, when the children of these slaves reached maturity, only about a tenth of adult slaves had been born in Africa. Even in Amelia County, the center of a vigorous African slave trade, the proportions of Africans in the adult slave population declined from 59 percent in 1755 to 20 percent by 1782. As the number of Afro-American slaves in the region increased, the surplus of men disappeared. In Amelia County, founded in southside in 1736, for instance, the adult slave sex ratio declined from 234 men for each 100 women in 1736 to 158 in 1749 and reached 116 by 1778. Similarly, the adult slave sex ratio in Lunenburg County, founded in 1746, declined from 350 in 1750 to 110 a decade later and then fluctuated between 100 and 140 during the 1760s. By the Revolution, then, most slave men in piedmont could find wives without great difficulty, and a major cause of dissension among blacks diminished.[44]

42. John W. Blassingame, *The Slave Community: Plantation Life in the Antebellum South* (New York, 1972), 16; "A List of Negroes on Doohoregan Manor Taken in Familys with Their Ages Decr. 1, 1773," Charles Carroll (of Carrollton) Account Book, MHS.

43. Donnan, ed., *Documents of Slave Trade*, IV, 219–231, shows that upper James became the dominant slave port (50% of slaves, 1750–1754; 62%, 1760–1764), while York faded into insignificance (42%, 1750–1754; 4%, 1760–1764). For Bermuda Hundred, see Hunter's *Va. Gaz.*, Sept. 12, 1751, July 10, 30, 1752, Aug. 12, 1752; Royle's *Va. Gaz.*, Nov. 4, 1763; Purdie and Dixon's *Va. Gaz.*, June 27, Aug. 1, Sept. 5, 1766, Aug. 11, 1768, May 18, 1769. As well, ages judged disappear from tidewater court records: from 1755 to 1770, there were 6 ages judged in York (1755–1758 missing), 3 in Lancaster, 15 in Caroline, 41 in Fairfax, and 46 in Prince Edward (1754–1758 and 1765–1769) on the southside frontier. York Judgments and Orders, 1759–1763, 1763–1765, 1765–1768, 1768–1770; Lancaster Orders, 10–14; Fairfax Orders, 1754–1756, and Minutes, 1756–1763; Campbell, *Caroline County*, 331. The estimate of immigrants in piedmont population is reported by Morgan in "Slave Life in the Virginia Piedmont," 5, and n. 11.

44. Greene and Harrington, *American Population*, 150–155; Jackson Turner Main, "The One Hundred," *WMQ*, 3d Ser., XI (1954), 354–384, esp. 356–359; Kulikoff, "'Prolifick' People," *So. Stud.*, XVI (1977), 405; Philip David Morgan, "The Development of Slave Culture in Eighteenth Century Plantation America" (Ph.D. diss., University College, London, 1977),

The size of quarters increased after 1740 throughout tidewater, providing greater opportunities for slaves to develop a social life of their own. The proportion who lived on units of more than twenty slaves doubled in St. Mary's County, increased by half in York and Anne Arundel counties, and grew, though more slowly, in Prince George's. In the 1780s, one-third to two-thirds of the slaves in eleven tidewater counties lived on farms of more than twenty slaves, and only a sixth to a tenth lived on units of fewer than six. If these counties were typical, 44 percent of tidewater's blacks lived on farms of more than twenty slaves, and another 26 percent lived on medium-sized units of eleven to twenty (see table 37). The number of very large quarters also grew. Before 1740 few quarters housed more than thirty slaves, but by the 1770s and 1780s the wealthiest gentlemen ran home plantations with more than one hundred slaves and quarters with thirty to fifty.[45]

Since middling planters brought few slaves with them when they migrated to piedmont and since wealthy planters established small quarters, a larger proportion of slaves in piedmont resided on smaller units than in tidewater. Although the number of slaves on small quarters diminished in four piedmont counties in the 1750s, the creation of new counties, with small plantations, limited further reductions during the 1760s and 1770s. But plantation sizes did increase in older piedmont counties, and the size of units in piedmont approximated the size in tidewater. The earlier a county was settled, the greater the proportion of slaves who resided on large quarters. By the early 1780s, more than two-fifths of the slaves who resided in eight piedmont counties organized before 1760 lived on plantations with twenty or more other slaves. In contrast, more than two-fifths of the slaves

---

289–290; Michael Lee Nicholls, "Origins of the Virginia Southside, 1703–1753: A Social and Economic Study" (Ph.D. diss., College of William and Mary, 1972), 121–122; Morgan, "Slave Life in the Virginia Piedmont," figs. 2–3.

45. Quarter-by-quarter lists of slaves of Robert Carter in 1733 (Carter Inventory, VHS), Charles Carroll of Carrollton in 1773 ("Negroes on Doohoregan Manor"), and the manumission record of Robert Carter of Nomini in 1791 (Louis Morton, *Robert Carter of Nomini Hall: A Virginia Tobacco Planter of the Eighteenth Century*, 2d ed. [Williamsburg, Va., 1945], table 9 in appendix, 285) provide rare glimpses of the internal organization of plantations. Only 9% of King Carter's slaves in 1733 lived on plantations of more than 30 slaves, but 44% of Carroll's and 53% of Carter's of Nomini lived on quarters that large; 34% of Carroll's slaves and 22% of Carter's of Nomini slaves resided on units of more than 100. Kulikoff, "Origins of Afro-American Society," *WMQ*, 3d Ser., XXXV (1978), 248–249 (Prince George's, St. Mary's except 1790, York, tidewater except St. Mary's, Essex, Gloucester); U.S., Bureau of the Census, *Heads of Families at the First Census, . . . Virginia* (Washington, D.C., 1908), 49–54; Bayly Ellen Marks, "Economics and Society in a Staple Plantation System: St. Mary's County, Maryland, 1790–1840" (Ph. D. diss., University of Maryland, 1979), 159 (St. Mary's, 1790); Walsh, "Changing Work Roles for Slave Labor," table 1 (Anne Arundel); and Morgan, "Slave Life in the Virginia Piedmont," tables 5, 6 (piedmont, frontier).

Table 37. *Plantation Size in the Chesapeake, 1740–1790*

Place and Time	Percentage of Slaves				
	Size of Unit (No. of Slaves)				
	1–5	6–10	11–20	21+	Total
Prince George's					
1741–1770 (*N*=3,360)[a]	13	19	27	42	101
1771–1779 (*N*=1,099)	10	17	18	55	100
St. Mary's Co.					
1741–1750 (*N*=580)	39	24	27	11	101
1751–1760 (*N*=892)	21	27	30	23	101
1761–1777 (*N*=2,284)[a]	19	21	23	35	98
Anne Arundel					
1740–1759 (*N*=2,139)[a]	14	19	40	27	100
1760–1777 (*N*=2,530)[a]	12	14	29	45	100
York					
1741–1750 (*N*=689)	19	24	36	22	101
1751–1760 (*N*=803)[b]	12	13	26	49	100
1761–1780 (*N*=1,451)[a]	10	17	36	38	101
Tidewater					
1782–1790 (*N*=46,547)[c]	13	17	26	44	100
Piedmont Virginia[d]					
1740–1749 (*N*=646)	22	22	35	21	100
1750–1759 (*N*=1.381)	14	25	31	30	100
1760–1769 (*N*=1,583)	15	22	37	26	100
1770–1779 (*N*=2,223)	14	28	34	24	100
1782–1785 (*N*=34,226)[e]	13	18	28	41	100
Frontier Virginia[f]					
1782–1785 (*N*=10,307)	21	23	28	29	101

Sources: Cited in n. 45.

Notes: [a]Decades are grouped together when no substantial changes occurred or to smooth out random change between decades. [b]Greater than usual number of major planters died. [c]Includes Anne Arundel (1790), Prince George's (1783), and St. Mary's (1790) counties in Maryland, and Essex, Gloucester, Lancaster, Middlesex, James City, Warwick (all 1783), Charles City (1784), and York (1785) in Virginia. [d]Counties 1740–1779 include Goochland, Orange, and Spotsylvania (all 1740–1779), Chesterfield (1750–1779), and Loudoun (1760–1770). [e]Only counties formed before 1760; includes Albemarle, Amelia, Amherst, Chesterfield, Cumberland, Goochland, Louisa, and Orange. [f]Piedmont counties formed after 1760; includes Amherst, Fluvanna, Halifax, and Pittsylvania.

of four frontier piedmont counties (organized after 1760) still lived on small units of ten or fewer during the early 1780s.[46]

Because plantation sizes increased, more lived on quarters away from the master's house and his direct supervision. On small plantations the quarter could be located in an outbuilding or in a single dwelling. On large plantations, the quarters resembled small villages. Slave houses and the yards that surrounded them were centers of domestic activity. The houses were furnished with straw bedding, barrels for seats, pots, pans, and usually a grindstone or handmill for beating corn into meal. Agricultural tools and livestock were scattered outside the houses, and the quarter was surrounded by plots of corn and tobacco cultivated by the slaves.[47]

Afro-Americans made the quarters into little communities, usually organized around families. Because the African slave trade largely ceased, the adult sex ratio decreased. Almost all men and women could marry, and by the 1770s many slaves had native grandparents and great-grandparents. The quarter was the center of family activity every evening and on Sundays and holidays, for except during the harvest, slaves had these times to themselves. Nonresident fathers visited their wives and children; runaways stayed with friends or kinfolk. In the evenings native men sometimes traveled to other quarters, where they passed the night talking, singing, smoking, and drinking. On occasional Sundays they held celebrations at which they danced to the banjo and sang bitter songs about their treatment by the master.[48]

The economy of the quarters was partially controlled by the slaves, since distance from the master allowed them a little autonomy in small matters. Slaves occasionally slaughtered stock without permission, ate some of the meat, and traded the surplus. Chickens, sheep, and swine were

---

46. See tax lists and census records cited in n. 45.

47. "'Itinerant Observations' of Kimber," *MHM*, LI (1956), 327; Isaac Weld, Jr., *Travels through the States of North America and the Provinces of Upper and Lower Canada* (London, 1799), 84–85. A plat of a quarter, surrounded by fields, can be found in *Moore v. Meek*, Ejectment Papers, box 30, MHR. A quarter located in a kitchen is described in Provincial Court Judgments, EI#4, 110–112, MHR. The furnishings and implements at quarters are listed in Prince George's Inventories, TB#1, 93–94 (1726); PD#1, 6–10, 26–28 (1729), 247–248 (1734), 426 (1738); DD#1, 56–68, 82–83 (1741), 363 (1744); DD#2, 128–129, 219, 322 (1752); GS#1, 245–246 (1758); and GS#2, 257–258 (1772), 357–359 (1775), MHR.

48. See chap. 9 below; *The Journal of Nicholas Cresswell, 1774–1777* (New York, 1924), 18–19; *Archives of Maryland*, XLIV, 647–648; Ferdinand-M. Bayard, *Travels of a Frenchman in Maryland and Virginia* . . . , ed. and trans. Ben C. McCary (Williamsburg, Va., 1950), 96; Thomas Bacon, *Four Sermons, Preached at the Parish Church of St. Peter, in Talbot County* . . . (Bath, 1783 [orig. publ. London, 1753]), 56–58; Carville V. Earle, *The Evolution of a Tidewater Settlement System: All Hallow's Parish, Maryland, 1650–1783*, University of Chicago Department of Geography Research Paper 170, (Chicago, 1975), 160–161.

traded to fellow slaves, as well as to peddlers, merchants, and other whites; slaves sold part of their provisions, seeds, and crops from their gardens and sometimes traded these goods for liquor. Slaves in practice owned the plantation's chickens and dunghill fowl. The danger and excitement of stealing the master's livestock were shared by all the quarter's families. This illegal activity was apparently widespread. A Prince George's planter complained in 1770, "In the Neighbourhood where I live, it is almost impossible to raise a stock of Sheep or Hogs, the Negroes are constantly killing them to sell to some white people who are little better than themselves." Masters tended to overlook, or even condone, this activity as long as slaves otherwise worked diligently.[49]

After 1740, the density of the black population and the proportion of slaves in the population of tidewater both increased, and, as a result, the area's slave society gradually spread out to embrace many neighboring plantations in a single network. Ironically, masters provided slaves with several tools they could use to extend these cross-quarter networks. Slave sales tore black families asunder, but as masters sold and transferred their slaves, more and more kinfolk lived on neighboring quarters, and naturally they retained ties of affection after they were separated. Whites built numerous roads and paths to connect their farms and villages, and their slaves used these byways to visit friends or run away and evade recapture. By the 1770s and 1780s, Afro-Americans numerically dominated many neighborhoods and created many cross-plantation networks.

The density of black population and the proportion of slaves in the population increased in both Chesapeake colonies. The number of slaves per square mile rose by more than one-third between 1755 and the early 1780s in three tidewater areas. Slaves composed 26 percent of the population of the lower Western Shore of Maryland in 1710, 38 percent in 1755, and 46 percent in 1782. A similar change occurred on Maryland's Eastern Shore, and by 1775 the results were visible in tidewater Virginia. In that year, nearly every county between the Rappahannock and James rivers as far west as the heads of navigation was more than one-half black; more than half of Virginia's slaves lived in these counties. Between 40 and 50 percent of the people were black in 1775 in the Northern Neck and in piedmont counties adjacent to tidewater.[50]

49. Morgan, "Development of Slave Culture," 213–226; Mullin, *Flight and Rebellion*, 60–62; *Archives of Maryland*, XXIV, 732–733, XXVII, 155–158, L, 436; *Maryland Gazette*, Oct. 12, 1758, Oct. 18, 1770, Mar. 13, 1777; Rind's *Va. Gaz.*, Mar. 17, 1768; Dunlap's *Md. Gaz.* (Baltimore), Nov. 4, 1777; Prince George's Court Records, EE#2, 99, 543 (1778).

50. "Number of Inhabitants in Maryland," *Gentleman's Magazine, and Historical Chronicle*, XXXIV (1764), 261; Greene and Harrington, *American Population*, 154–155; Kulikoff, "To-

Quarters were connected by extensive networks of roads and paths, which grew remarkably complex during the eighteenth century. For example, Prince George's County had about 50 miles of public roads in 1700, but 478 in 1762, or one mile of public road for every square mile of taxed land in the county. This elaboration of roads made it easier for slaves to visit nearby plantations. Whites could not patrol all these roads, let alone private paths not maintained by the county, without a general mobilization of the white population.[51]

Two Maryland examples from the 1770s and 1780s illustrate the demographic characteristics of places where Afro-American slaves were able to develop cross-plantation social networks. The area around Upper Marlboro, Prince George's county seat, was more than three-fifths black and had more than 25 slaves per square mile in 1783. The region, which covered about 130 square miles, extended to the Patuxent River and included an adjacent area across the river in Anne Arundel County. Perhaps half the blacks in this region lived on quarters of more than 20 slaves and another fourth on farms of 11–20. The road network here was the most developed in the county. Elk Ridge was located near Baltimore town. In 1783 its population was about half black, with 14 slaves per square mile. About three-fifths of the Elk Ridge slaves lived on farms of more than 20 blacks, and another one-fifth on units of 11–20. One neighborhood in this area was very heavily black. In 1774, 330 of Charles Carroll's slaves lived at Doohoregan Manor on the main plantation and at nine other quarters spread over the ten-thousand-acre tract. Many social activities could occur in the village of 130 slaves on the main plantation, and somewhat fewer activities among the 143 who lived on farms of 21–40 slaves. The rest of Carroll's slaves resided on small quarters of fewer than 21 people. Visiting among slaves on Carroll's various quarters must have been common, however, because slaves on one quarter were frequently related by blood and marriage to those on another.[52]

These ideal conditions could not be found everywhere in the region. From just north of the Patuxent to just south of the James, plantations were large, black population density was high, few whites were present, and

---

bacco and Slaves," 202–203, 323, 428–432; Bureau of the Census, *Heads of Families, Virginia*, 9–10; Lester J. Cappon *et al.*, eds., *Atlas of Early American History: The Revolutionary Era, 1760–1790* (Princeton, N.J., 1976), 24, 67, 100, 102.

51. See above, chap. 6; Earle, *Tidewater Settlement System*, 154–157.

52. Kulikoff, "Tobacco and Slaves," 205, 532–536; Anne Arundel Summary of 1783 Tax Lists, Executive Papers, MHR; Lyons Creek and Elk Ridge Hundred 1783 Tax List, MHS; "Negroes on Doohoregan Manor," Carroll Account Book; Prince George's Inventories, 1750–1790.

road networks were well developed. Slaves in these areas could create a rudimentary cross-plantation society. Some parts of piedmont, like Amelia County, approached these conditions by the 1780s. By contrast, in other regions on the Eastern Shore and upper Western Shore of Maryland and in much of southside Virginia, blacks were a minority, and small planters tilled the soil with their sons and perhaps several slaves. Here whites controlled the environment, and slaves had fewer opportunities to pursue their own activities.[53]

Even within areas of high black population and large plantations, the opportunities of slaves for social life outside their own plantations varied from place to place. In twenty-eight taxing districts of Anne Arundel and Prince George's counties in 1783, blacks constituted from 27 to 66 percent of the population. Large plantations tended to be located where the population was predominantly enslaved, but the relationship was not exact; in Anne Arundel in 1783, 18–58 percent of the slaves in eight hundreds whose population was more than half black lived on quarters of more than twenty slaves.[54] Neighborhoods near each other could have very different racial compositions. Taxing districts along the Potomac River in Prince George's, about fifteen miles from Upper Marlboro, were only about 40 percent enslaved; and around Oxon Creek, where most of the householders were white tenants, only 30 percent of the people were enslaved. Only one-third of the slaves along the Potomac lived on farms of more than twenty slaves. In Virginia, both James City and York counties were more than 60 percent enslaved in the 1780s. Most of the large plantations in these counties were located in upper Yorkhampton Parish, where more than half the slaves lived on quarters larger than twenty slaves. Only one-third to one-fourth of the slaves lived on big quarters in the rest of these counties.[55]

Even on large plantations, social life was often insecure. Some slaves were sold or forced to accompany their masters to the piedmont, far away from family and friends: about a fifth of all slaves in southern Maryland and a third in the tobacco-growing regions of Virginia left the area of their birth between 1755 and the 1780s. It probably took several decades for these slaves to repair the disruptions in their lives and create new communities. Even when a slave remained the property of the same white family, he might not live on the same farm for more than a few years. For example, after the

53. These generalizations are based upon study of tax lists cited in table 37 and summaries of 1783 tax lists for all Maryland counties, MHR.
54. The Pearson Product Moment Correlation between percentage black and percentage living on farms of more than 20 slaves for 12 hundreds (27%–61% black) was .744.
55. Kulikoff, "Tobacco and Slaves," 205; James City Personal Property Tax List, 1783, and York County Personal Property Tax List, 1785, VSL.

Revolution, large planters in Elizabeth City County, Virginia, tended to hire out their slaves to tenants and small landowners. A slave might live on a different plantation every year, suffering separations from spouse, children, and friends.[56]

Nevertheless, one-half to three-quarters of the Afro-Americans who lived in tidewater in the 1780s enjoyed some sort of social life not controlled by their masters. Perhaps 44 percent lived on large quarters, and another 4 percent were men who lived in neighborhoods with many large quarters and could visit nearby farms. Another 26 percent lived on farms of eleven to twenty blacks and could participate in the family and community activities of their quarters. The remaining 26 percent of the slaves were women and children who lived on small plantations. They usually did not travel from quarter to quarter but had to wait for husbands and fathers to visit them.

The Afro-Americans made good use of these opportunities to create their own society. In the years before the Revolution, they developed a sense of community with other slaves both on their own plantations and in the neighborhood. This social solidarity can be shown in several ways. In the first place, Afro-Americans often concealed slaves from within the neighborhood on their quarters. Since masters searched the neighborhood for runaways and placed notices on public buildings before advertising in a newspaper, many runaways, especially truants who were recaptured or returned voluntarily after a few days' absence, were not so advertised. The increasing appearance of such advertisements in the *Maryland Gazette* during the thirty years before the Revolution suggests that slaves were becoming more successful in evading easy recapture. The numbers of runaways in southern Maryland rose in each five-year period between 1745 and 1779, except the years 1765–1769, and the increase was especially great during the Revolution, when some escaped slaves were able to reach British troops.[57]

Most runaways required help from other blacks. Only a small minority were helped by whites, and about three-quarters (twenty-two of twenty-nine) of those so helped in southern Maryland were artisans, mulattoes, or

---

56. Kulikoff, "Tobacco and Slaves," 84–88; Greene and Harrington, *American Population*, 151–155 (compares 1755 tithables and 1790 population, divided by two, and assumes a 2% rate of natural increase); Sarah S. Hughes, "Slaves for Hire: The Allocation of Black Labor in Elizabeth City County, Virginia, 1782 to 1810," *WMQ*, 3d Ser., XXXV (1978), 260–286.

57. Table 38; Jeannie Ford Dissette, "Landon Carter of Sabine Hall: A Master of Slaves" (seminar paper, University of Pennsylvania, 1971), 36–39; *Md. Gaz.*, Mar. 9, 1758 (notices put up for runaway); Benjamin Quarles, *The Negro in the American Revolution* (Chapel Hill, N.C., 1961), chap. 2.

women. Women infrequently ran away, and there were few slave mulattoes and artisans.[58] The majority of runaways traveled from plantation to plantation through a quarter underground. Some joined family members or friends on nearby or even distant plantations; others attempted to pass as free in small port towns, find employment, or leave the region. About one-half of southern Maryland runaways (see table 38) and nearly one-third (29 percent) of Virginia's advertised runaways before 1775 stayed with friends or kinfolk. Since most unadvertised truants probably visited nearby quarters, the proportion of visitors among *all* runaways may well have been much higher. They hid on quarters or in surrounding woods for a few days or weeks and then returned voluntarily or were recaptured. Many of the other slaves, who wanted to pass as free, also had to use the plantation underground to reach their destination, and at least half of them stayed within visiting distance of their family and friends. Only one runaway in four in southern Maryland and one in three in Virginia before 1775 left his home province and tried to begin a new life as a free person.[59]

The slave community, of course, had its share of conflicts, and on occasion a slave assaulted or stole from another slave. Nonetheless, accounts of several of these incidents suggest that the rest of the slave community united against the transgressors. Slaves sometimes refused to testify against their fellows, especially when blacks stole goods from whites, but when a member of the black community was hurt, slaves testified against the guilty person to protect themselves or their property. In May 1763 Jack poisoned Clear with a mixture of rum and henbane; she became ill and died the following February. Six slaves who belonged to Clear's master informed him of the act and testified against Jack in Prince George's court. They were joined by three slaves who lived on nearby plantations. The jury found Jack guilty, and he was sentenced to hang. Similarly, when Tom (owned by Richard Snowden, a prominent ironmaker) broke into Weems's quarter (near the Snowden ironworks) in Anne Arundel County and took goods belonging to Weems's slaves, six men and women owned by James and David Weems testified against him. He was found guilty and hanged.[60]

There were limits to slave solidarity. Though native-born slaves often remained loyal to immediate kinfolk and friends on their own quarters, to more distant kinfolk, and to slaves on nearby or distant plantations, these loyalties sometimes clashed with each other or with the demands of the

58. Mullin, *Flight and Rebellion*, 112–116; *Md. Gaz.*, Apr. 9, 1772, Jan. 29, 1767, Feb. 14, 1771.
59. Table 38; Mullin, *Flight and Rebellion*, 108, 129. Since the number of unknowns is so large, it is difficult to be more precise.
60. Prince George's Court Records, XXVI, 343, 357; Anne Arundel Judgments, IB#6, 347–348, 355; *Md. Gaz.*, Dec. 14, 1774.

Table 38. *Motives of Runaway Slaves in Southern Maryland, 1745–1779*

Known Motives of Runaways[a]	Percentage $(N=117)$[b]
To visit	54
To pass as free, to work	26
To escape Maryland	21
Total	101

Sources: All runaway ads published in the *Maryland Gazette* (Annapolis), 1745–1779, the *Maryland Journal* (Baltimore), 1773–1779, and Dunlap's *Maryland Gazette* (Baltimore), 1775–1779, from Prince George's, Charles, Calvert, Frederick (south of Monocacy River), and Anne Arundel counties and any slave born in or traveling to those areas.

Notes: [a]Of 244 runaways, the motives of 127, or 52%, are not known. [b]A division of the ads by time (1745–1759, 1760s, 1770s) shows no significant differences.

master. Then slaves had to choose sides in intricate master-slave conflicts. The development of these alliances can be seen in the response of Landon Carter and of his slaves when Simon, Carter's ox-carter, ran away in March 1766. Carter had Simon outlawed, and joined the militia to hunt for him. Simon was aided directly by at least six residents of his quarter, including an uncle, a brother, and a sister-in-law. Nonetheless, several other kinfolk, who lived on other quarters, were forced by Carter to inform against him. Finally, after two weeks, Talbot (another of Carter's slaves who lived some distance from Simon) shot Simon in the leg and, with the aid of several other slaves, recaptured him.[61]

The Origins of Afro-American Culture

Slaves in the Chesapeake, unlike those in the West Indies, took several generations to form a semiautonomous Afro-American culture. West Africans needed settled communities to develop the bundle of common values and beliefs they brought over with them into a syncretic culture, but the demographic environment of the early eighteenth-century Chesapeake was extremely hostile to the formation of settled communities. Heavily white populations, high black sex ratios, continually declining proportions of Africans among slaves, conflicts between African and creole slaves, and small unit sizes all made the development of both slave communities and slave

61. This incident is brilliantly portrayed in Rhys Isaac, *The Transformation of Virginia, 1740–1790* (Chapel Hill, N.C., 1982), 332–345.

culture difficult. African forced migrants did not forget these values, however, but used behavioral symbols of them whenever they could. These Africans practiced their beliefs in disconnected and often private episodes, not in daily social interaction with many other slaves. African slaves in the Chesapeake made tribal drums, strummed on their banjos, poisoned their enemies as did African witches and cunning men, passed on a few African words to their descendants, and sometimes engaged in private devotions to Allah or their tribal gods.[62]

Afro-American slaves had developed strong community institutions on their quarters by the 1760s and 1770s, but the values and beliefs they held are difficult to ascertain. Since blacks in the Chesapeake region did not achieve a settled social life until after a heavy African slave trade stopped and since whites continued to live in even the most densely black areas, one would expect slave culture in the region to reflect white values and beliefs. Even native-born slaves had little choice either about their work or about the people who lived with them in their quarters. Nevertheless, they had a small measure of self-determination in their family life, in their religion, and in the ways they celebrated and mourned. When they could choose, Afro-American slaves simultaneously borrowed from whites and drew on the values and beliefs their ancestors brought from West Africa to form a culture not only significantly different from that of Anglo-Americans but also different from the culture of any West African group or any other group of North American slaves.

The ways Afro-American slaves organized their family life indicates most clearly how they used both African and Euro-American forms to create a new institution compatible with their life under slavery. By the time of the Revolution, most slaves lived in families, and slave households were similar to those of their white masters. About as many creole slaves as whites lived in two-parent and extended households. Whites lived in monogamous families, and only scattered examples of the African custom of polygyny can be found among creole blacks. Slavery forced the kinfolk of extended families to live very close to one another on large plantations, where they played and worked together. By contrast, whites only occasionally visited their extended kinfolk and worked in the fields only with their children, not with adult brothers and sisters. This closeness fostered a sense of kin solidarity among Afro-Americans. They named their children after both sides of the family (but interestingly enough, daughters were not often named after their mothers). And they sometimes refused to marry within the plantation even when sex ratios were equal: many of the available

62. See sources cited in nn. 17, 18, 25–31, this chapter; table 36; and Morgan, "Development of a Slave Culture," chap. 5.

potential partners were first cousins, and black slaves apparently refused to marry first cousins. This may have represented a transformation of African marriage taboos that differed from tribe to tribe but tended to be stricter than those of Chesapeake whites, who frequently married first cousins.[63]

West African religions varied remarkably among themselves, yet enslaved Africans shared a similar way of viewing the world, which they passed on to their native black children. All activities, Africans believed, were infused with sacredness, each in its own particular way. Religion was not universal but was practiced only within a communal context. God, spirits, animals, and plants were all seen in relation to people in the community, and certain men—rainmakers, medicine men, priests, sorcerers—had special powers over spirits or material life not available to most people.[64]

In contrast, the Anglican faith practiced by most slaveholders in the Chesapeake before the Revolution radically separated the sacred from the secular: Anglicans attended church services in isolated buildings on Sundays but often ignored religious ceremonies the rest of the week. Although native slaves occasionally accepted the outward signs of Christian belief, few became convinced Protestants. Their children were baptized, and sometimes they received religious instruction. All three Anglican clergymen of Prince George's County reported in 1724 that they baptized slave children and adults (especially native-born adults) and preached to those who would listen. In 1731 one Prince George's minister baptized blacks "where perfect in their Catechism" and "visit[ed] them in their sickness and married them when called upon." Similar work continued in Virginia and Maryland in the generation before the Revolution. Nonetheless, Thomas Bacon, a Maryland cleric and publisher of a compendium of the colony's laws, believed that these baptized slaves were often "living in as profound Ignorance of what Christianity really is, (except as to a few outward Ordinances) as if they had remained in the midst of those barbarous Heathen Countries from whence their parents had been first imported."[65]

63. See below, chap. 9; Herbert G. Gutman, *The Black Family in Slavery and Freedom, 1750–1925* (New York, 1976), 88–90, chaps. 3–5; for evidence of extensive kin naming among slaves owned by Charles Carroll and Thomas Jefferson during the 18th century, see Mary Beth Norton *et al.*, "The Afro-American Family in the Age of Revolution," in Ira Berlin and Ronald Hoffman, eds., *Slavery and Freedom in the Age of the American Revolution* (Charlottesville, Va., 1983), 178–181.

64. Mbiti, *African Religions and Philosophy*, esp. chaps. 2–3, 15–16; Mechal Sobel, *Trabelin' On: The Slave Journey to an Afro-Baptist Faith* (Westport, Conn., 1979), chap. 1.

65. William Stevens Perry, *Historical Collections Relating to the American Colonial Church*, IV (Davenport, Iowa, 1878), 201, 206, 304, 306–307; Bacon, *Four Sermons at St. Peter*, 4; Thad W. Tate, *The Negro in Eighteenth-Century Williamsburg*, 2d ed. (Williamsburg, Va., 1972), 65–75; Thomas Bacon, *Four Sermons, upon the Great and Indispensible Duty of All Christian Masters and Mistresses to Bring up Their Negro Slaves in the Knowledge and Fear of God* (London, 1750), v, vii.

Native-born slaves continued to observe African forms of mourning and celebrating, but they did not place these forms within the structure of Anglican religion, nor did masters give them time enough to expand these occasional ceremonies into an indigenous Afro-American religion. Whites sometimes observed these strange practices. Thomas Bacon, for instance, preached to blacks on Maryland's Eastern Shore in the 1740s at services they directed "at their *funerals* (several of which I have attended)—and to such small congregations as their *marriages* have brought together." Two early nineteenth-century observers connected similar services they saw to the slaves' remote African past. Henry Knight, who traveled to Virginia in 1816, explained that masters permitted slaves a holiday to mourn the death of a fellow slave. The day of the funeral, "perhaps a month after the corpse is interred, is a jovial day with them; they sing and dance and drink the dead to his new home, which some believe to be in old Guinea," the home of their grandparents and great-grandparents. A Charlotte County, Virginia, cleric saw more solemn but equally emotional services. He contended that there were "many remains . . . of the savage customs of Africa. They cry and bawl and howl around the grave and roll in the dirt, and make many expressions of the most frantic grief . . . sometimes the noise they make may be heard as far as one or two miles."[66]

The slaves' music and dance, though often unconnected to their religion, displayed a distinctly African character. Afro-American slaves continued to make and to play two instruments (the banjo and balafo) of African origin. In 1774 Nicholas Cresswell, a British visitor, described slave celebrations in Charles County, Maryland. On Sundays, he wrote, the blacks "generally meet together and amuse themselves with Dancing to the Banjo. This musical instrument . . . is made of a Gourd something in the imitation of a Guitar, with only four strings." "Their poetry," Cresswell reported, "is like the music—Rude and uncultivated. Their Dancing is most violent exercise, but so irregular and grotesque. I am not able to describe it." Cresswell's reaction to the dancing suggests that it contained African rhythms unknown in European dance. If the form was African, it was placed in an American context: the slave songs Cresswell heard "generally relate the usage they have received from their Masters or Mistresses in a very satirical stile and manner."[67]

Native slaves retained folk beliefs that may have been integral parts of

66. Bacon, *Four Sermons, upon the Great Duty*, v, vii; Arthur Singleton [Henry C. Knight], *Letters from the South and West* (Boston, 1824), 77; Morgan, "Development of Slave Culture," 385. Morgan's extensive research, 248–255 and chap. 5, is the best analysis of slave religion in early Virginia.

67. *Journal of Cresswell*, 18–19; Dena J. Epstein, *Sinful Tunes and Spirituals: Black Folk Music to the Civil War* (Urbana, Ill., 1977), 34, 39, 48, 57; Blassingame, *Slave Community*, 27–32.

West African religions. Slaves sometimes turned to magic, sorcery, and witchcraft to resolve conflicts within their own community or to strike back at harsh or unreasonable masters. Some African medicine men, magicians, sorcerers, and witches migrated and passed on their skills to other slaves. These men were spiritual leaders (or powerful, if evil men) in many African communities, including those of the Ibos, and they continued to practice among creole slaves who believed in their powers. Several examples suggest the prevalence of these beliefs. William Grimes was born in King George County, Virginia, in 1784; his narrative of his life as a runaway suggests that he was terrified by a woman he thought was a witch, that he feared sleeping in the bed of a dead man, and that he consulted fortune-tellers. Dissatisfied slaves might consult conjurers to discover how to poison their masters. In 1773, for instance, Sharper was accused by his master, Peter Hansbrough of Stafford County, Virginia, of "Endeavouring to Procuring Poison from a Negroe Doctor or Conjurer as they are Call'd" for an unknown but dangerous purpose after Hansbrough had "discovered Some behaviour in ... Sharper which occasioned [him] to be more Strict in inquiring into ... where he Spent his time in his absent hours." Similarly, two slave blacksmiths in Spotsylvania County were convicted of attempting to poison their master in 1797, but seventy-six local residents petitioned the state for clemency because the slaves had been influenced by "a Negro Wench, or conjuror of Mr. James Crawford."[68]

Afro-American slaves did not transform these disparate fragments of African cultures into a new slave religion until the development of white evangelical religion during the decades before and after the Revolution. Revivalist preachers permitted and even encouraged slaves to adapt African forms to the Christian faith. The most intensive black religious activity was in southside and central piedmont Virginia, areas with the Chesapeake's highest concentrations of new Negroes. The first evangelical mission to slaves began in 1755, when two white Baptists organized a black congregation on William Byrd's plantation in Mecklenburg County; that group of Christians lasted until the Revolution. Samuel Davies, a Presbyterian clergyman who practiced in Hanover County, and several of his colleagues converted as many as a thousand slaves to evangelical Protestantism in the 1750s. Davies thought that these blacks were true Christians, not only acquainted with "the important doctrines of the Christian Religion, but also a deep sense of things upon their spirits, and a life of the strictest Morality and Piety." They placed African music into Protestant liturgy: "The *Ne-*

---

68. Charles H. Nichols, Jr., "The Case of William Grimes, the Runaway Slave," *WMQ*, 3d Ser., VIII (1951), 556–558; "Miscellaneous Documents, Colonial and State," *VMHB*, XVIII (1910), 394–395; Morgan, "Development of Slave Culture," 387–395 (quote on 392).

groes," Davies commented, "above all of the human species that ever I knew, have an ear for Music, and a kind of delight in Psalmody." Some of his converts even "lodged all night in my kitchen; and sometimes, when I have awakened about two or three a-clock in the morning, a torrent of sacred harmony poured into my chamber, and carried my mind to heaven."[69]

The numbers of Afro-Americans attracted to evangelical Protestantism rose slowly in the 1770s and then increased rapidly during the awakenings of the 1780s and 1790s. By 1790, about 7 percent of Virginia's black adults were members of Baptist or Methodist churches, and far more were affected by the revivals in both piedmont and tidewater counties. Slave work patterns and the authority of masters might be affected by this new and all-encompassing religiosity. For instance, some members of the Episcopal church in King George County complained in the mid-1780s that "Preachers or Exhorters" daily gathered "together Multitudes of People in the Woods most of them Slaves, alienating their minds from their Daily Labour and their Masters Interest."[70]

Blacks accepted the exhortations of Baptist and Methodist preachers in the 1780s and 1790s far more enthusiastically than did whites. They answered the preacher's call with crying, shouting, shaking, and trembling. Their reaction was perhaps in part dictated by their African past: the ceremonies of revivals were similar to those of some African religions, and African forms meshed well with the emerging theology of evangelical Protestantism. Revivals, unlike the liturgy of rational religion, allowed slaves to reduce the distinctions between sacred and secular and return to a holistic, African kind of religiosity.[71]

Afro-American slaves developed their own social institutions and indigenous culture during the second half of the eighteenth century. A period of great disruptions among blacks early in the century was followed by a time of settled communities. Newly enslaved Africans came to the Chesapeake colonies in large enough numbers to cause conflicts between native slaves and new Negroes, but the migration was too small to allow Africans

69. Samuel Davies, *Letters from the Rev. Samuel Davies, etc., Shewing the State of Religion in Virginia (Particularly among the Negroes)* . . . (London, 1757), 4–7, 12–17, 42–43; Sobel, *Trabelin' On*, 102, 296.

70. Morgan, "Development of Slave Culture," 248–255 (quote on 253), 400–408.

71. *Ibid.*; see Sobel, *Trabelin' On*, chaps. 3–4; Donald G. Mathews, *Religion in the Old South* (Chicago, 1977), chap. 5; and Lawrence W. Levine, *Black Culture and Black Consciousness: Afro-American Folk Thought from Slavery to Freedom* (New York, 1977), chaps. 1, 3, for descriptions of the later development of Afro-American religion and culture. Eugene D. Genovese, *Roll, Jordan, Roll: The World the Slaves Made* (New York, 1975), bk. 2, pt. 1, brilliantly describes how slaves transformed white Protestant religion in the antebellum period.

to develop syncretic communities and cultures. It was only when native adults began to predominate that earlier conflicts among blacks were contained and families and quarter communities began to emerge. The culture these creole slaves forged put African forms of behavior into Euro-American familial and religious structures. Creole slaves by that time were two or three generations removed from Africa and (except in southside Virginia) infrequently saw Africans. They may not have been aware of the complicated origins of their behavior.

For the slaves, the origins of their culture were less important than its autonomy. White observers agreed that the music, dance, and religiosity of black slaves differed remarkably from those of whites. The emergence of black culture, and especially the beginnings of Afro-Christianity, played an important role in the development of slave solidarity. Slaves possessed little power over their lives: they suffered the expropriation of the fruits of their labor by their masters; they could be forced to move away from family and friends at a moment's notice; they were subject to the whip for any perceived transgressions. The practice of a distinctive culture within their own quarters gave them some small power over their own lives and destinies they otherwise would not have possessed.[72]

The development of an indigenous black community life and culture had a great impact upon the social structure of the entire region. Afro-Americans became both an enslaved working class and a racial caste, separate from their white masters. They had their own system of social relations among themselves, within the context of slavery. Even though whites continued to possess remarkable power over blacks, they had to relate to slaves as a group with a structure and culture they could not entirely control. Afro-American communal life and culture, then, set minimal bounds on white behavior and encouraged black solidarity.

72. See Levine, *Black Culture*, 24–25, for somewhat similar comments.

9
Beginnings of the Afro-American Family

Sometime in 1728, Harry, a recently imported African, escaped from his master in southern Prince George's County, Maryland, and joined a small black community among the Indians beyond the area of white settlement. The following year, Harry returned to Prince George's to urge his former shipmates, the only sort of kinfolk he had, to return there with him. More than forty years later, another Harry, who belonged to John Jenkins of Prince George's, ran away. The Annapolis newspaper reported that "he has been seen about the Negro Quarters in *Patuxent*, but is supposed to have removed among his Acquaintances on Potomack; he is also well acquainted with the Negroes at Clement Wheeler's Quarter on Zekiah, and a Negro Wench of Mr. Wall's named Rachael; a few miles from that Quarter is his Aunt, and he may possibly be harboured thereabouts."[1]

These two incidents, separated by two generations, are suggestive. African Harry ran away *from* slavery to the frontier; Afro-American Harry ran *to* his friends and kinfolk spread over a wide territory. The Afro-American runaway could call on many others to hide him, but the African had few friends and, seemingly, no wife. These contrasts raise many questions. How readily did African immigrants begin families once they reached the Chesapeake colonies? How did Afro-Americans organize their families, and what role did these families serve in sustaining slave communities and culture? Who lived in slave households? What was the impact of arbitrary sale and transfer of slaves upon family life? How did an Afro-American's household and family relations change through the life cycle? This chapter attempts to answer these questions.[2]

Almost all blacks who lived in Virginia and Maryland before 1780 were slaves. Because their status precluded them from enjoying a legally secure

1. Prince George's County Court Record, O, 414, Maryland Hall of Records, Annapolis (MHR); *Maryland Gazette*, Mar. 12, 1772.
2. Pioneering essays by Russell R. Menard, "The Maryland Slave Population, 1658–1730: A Demographic Profile of Blacks in Four Counties," *William and Mary Quarterly*, 3d Ser., XXXII (1975), 29–54; Peter Wood, *Black Majority: Negroes in Colonial South Carolina, from 1670 through the Stono Rebellion* (New York, 1974), chap. 5; and Mary Beth Norton et al., "The Afro-American Family in the Age of Revolution," in Ira Berlin and Ronald Hoffman, eds., *Slavery and Freedom in the Age of the American Revolution* (Charlottesville, Va., 1983), 175–191, suggest some characteristics of colonial black families. Herbert G. Gutman, *The Black Family in Slavery and Freedom: 1750–1925* (New York, 1976), is the standard work on slave families in the 19th century.

family life, slave households often excluded important family members. Households, domestic groups, and families must therefore be clearly distinguished. A *household*, as used here, is a coresidence group that includes all who shared a "proximity of sleeping arrangements" or lived under the same roof. *Domestic groups* include kin and nonkin, living in the same or separate households, who share cooking, eating, child rearing, working, and other daily activities. *Families* are composed of people related by blood or marriage. Several distinctions are useful in defining the members of families. The *immediate family* includes husband and wife or parents and children. *Near kin* includes the immediate family and all other kin, such as adult brothers and sisters or cousins who share the same house or domestic tasks with the immediate family. Other kinfolk who do not function as family members on a regular basis are considered *distant kin*.[3]

The process of slave family formation can perhaps best be understood as an adaptive process, based upon relations between masters and slaves and among black kinfolk themselves. Slaves structured their expectations about family security around what they knew the master would permit. No slaves enjoyed the security of legal marriage, but had to accept whatever protection individual masters were willing to provide for their sexual unions. (These unions will be called "marriages" in this chapter, even though they lacked legal status.) Although masters sometimes sanctioned slave marriages and encouraged slave family formation, they could withdraw those privileges whenever they desired and separate slave family members through sales, bequests, or gifts. Masters determined the outward bounds of slave family life, but Africans, and especially their descendants, gave meaning to the relations between members of slave families. In particular, slaves tried to mitigate the insecurity of family life by giving kindred outside the immediate family responsibilities in child rearing and by devising extensive kinship networks.[4]

African Slaves and Their Families

Africans who were forced to come to the Chesapeake region in the late seventeenth and early eighteenth centuries struggled to create viable fami-

3. I have borrowed my definitions of household and domestic group from Donald R. Bender, "A Refinement of the Concept of Household: Families, Co-residence, and Domestic Functions," *American Anthropologist*, LXIX (1967), 493–504 (quote on 498). The use of *immediate family*, *near kin*, and *distant kin* was suggested to me by Herbert Gutman.
4. Sidney W. Mintz and Richard Price, *An Anthropological Approach to the Afro-American Past: A Caribbean Perspective*, Institute for the Study of Human Issues, Occasional Papers in Social Change, No. 2 (Philadelphia, 1976).

lies and households, but often failed. They suffered a great loss when they were herded into slave ships. Their family and friends, who had given meaning to their lives and structured their place in society, were left behind, and they found themselves among strangers. They could neither recreate their families nor devise a West African kinship system in the Chesapeake. The differences between African communities were too great. Some Africans lived in clans and lineages; others did not. Some traced their descent from women, but others traced descent from men. Mothers, fathers, and other kin played somewhat different roles in each community. Initiation ceremonies and puberty rites, forbidden marriages, marriage customs, and household structures all varied from place to place.[5]

Though African immigrants did not bring a unified West African culture with them to the Chesapeake colonies, they did share important beliefs about the nature of kinship. Africans modified these beliefs in America to legitimate the families they eventually formed. They saw kinship as the principal way of ordering relations between individuals. Each person in the tribe was related to most others in the tribe. The male was father, son, and uncle; the female was mother, daughter, and aunt to many others. Because their kinship system was so extensive, West Africans included kinfolk outside the immediate family in their daily activities. For example, adult brothers or sisters of the father and mother played an important role in child rearing and domestic activities in many African societies.[6]

Second, but far less certainly, African immigrants may have adopted some practices associated with polygyny, a common African marital custom. A few men on the Eastern Shore of Maryland in the 1740s, and perhaps a few others scattered elsewhere, lived with several women. However, far too few African women (in relation to the number of men) arrived in the Chesapeake to make polygynous marriages common. Only one of the 249 men on Robert "King" Carter's many quarters in 1733, for instance, had more than one wife living with him. Despite the absence of polygyny, the close psychological relations between mothers and children found in African polygynous societies might have been repeated in the Chesapeake colonies. In any event, African slave mothers played a more important role than fathers in teaching children about Africa and about how to get along in the

5. The following works suggest variations in African kinship systems: A. R. Radcliffe-Brown, "Introduction," in Radcliffe-Brown and Daryll Forde, eds., *African Systems of Kinship and Marriage* (London, 1950), 1–85; Meyer Fortes, "Kinship and Marriage among the Ashanti," *ibid.*, 252–284; Jack Goody, *Comparative Studies in Kinship* (Stanford, Calif., 1959), chap. 3; Robert Bain, *Bangwa Kinship and Marriage* (Cambridge, 1972); William J. Goode, *World Revolution and Family Patterns* (New York, 1963), 167–200.

6. Mintz and Price, *Anthropological Approach*, 22–26, 32–43 (esp. 34–35); John S. Mbiti, *African Religions and Philosophy* (New York, 1970), 104–109.

slave system. Both African custom and the physical separation of wives and husbands and fathers from their children played a role in this development.[7]

African forced migrants faced a demographic environment hostile to most forms of family life. At first, older slaves could have become uncles to younger Africans, and Africans of the same age could have acted as brothers, but African men had to find wives in order to begin a Chesapeake genealogy. That task was difficult: most blacks lived on small farms of fewer than eleven slaves, the small black population was spread thinly over a vast territory, and the ratio of men to women was high (and especially high on large plantations where Africans were likely to live).[8]

Africans had competition for the available black women. By the 1690s, some black women were natives, and they may have preferred Afro-American men, who were healthy, spoke English, and knew how to act in a white world, to unhealthy or unseasoned Africans. White men were also competitors. Indeed, during the seventeenth and early eighteenth centuries, white adult sex ratios were as high as, or higher than, black adult sex ratios. At any period whites possessed a monopoly of power, and some of them probably took slave women as their common-law wives.[9] African men competed for the remaining black women, who were mostly recently arrived Africans. These immigrant women often waited two or three years before marrying. Since the number of women available to African men was so small and immigrant men died frequently soon after arrival, many probably died before they could find a wife.

Foreign-born male slaves in Virginia and Maryland probably lived in a succession of different kinds of households. Newly imported Africans had no black kin in the Chesapeake. Since sex ratios were high, most of these men probably lived with other, unrelated men. African men may have substituted friends for kin. Newly enslaved Africans made friends with their nearest shipmates during the middle passage, and after their arrival in the

7. "Eighteenth-Century Maryland as Portrayed in the 'Itinerant Observations' of Edward Kimber," *Maryland Historical Magazine*, LI (1956), 327; Robert Carter Inventory, Carter Papers, Virginia Historical Society, Richmond (VHS); Goode, *World Revolution*, 167–168, 196; Mbiti, *African Religions*, 142–145. Women in polygynous societies nursed infants for three to four years and abstained from intercourse during part of that period. If this pattern was repeated in the Chesapeake, it was partially responsible for the low birthrate among Africans discussed in chap. 2. See Mbiti, *African Religions*, 111.

8. See above, chaps. 1, 8, for data on black demography, plantation size, and other associated issues.

9. P.M.G. Harris, "The Spread of Slavery in the Colonial Chesapeake, 1630–1775" (paper presented at the Third Hall of Records Conference on Maryland History, "Maryland, A Product of Two Worlds," May 1984), 14–15, presents demographic evidence for possible miscegenation.

Chesapeake, some of them lived near these men. New Negroes could live with other recent immigrants because migration from Africa occurred in short spurts from the 1670s to the late 1730s. The high sex ratios of large plantations indicate that wealthy men bought many of these Africans. Even if his shipmates lived far away, the new immigrant could share the experiences of others who had recently endured the middle passage.[10]

Despite difficulties, most Africans who survived a few years eventually found a wife. In societies with a high sex ratio, women tend to marry young, but men tend to postpone marriage. This shortage of women prevented most recently arrived African men from finding a wife on the plantation. For them the opportunity to live with a wife and children was rare. Nonetheless, high sex ratios probably increased the opportunity of older, more established African men to marry younger women. (The sexual imbalance is reduced; that is, there are as many younger women as older men.) By the 1690s, large numbers of Afro-American slave women entered their mid-teens and married. Because plantation sizes were small and individual farm sex ratios were likely to be uneven, the wives and children of married African men very often lived on other plantations. These men still lived mainly with other unrelated men, but at least they had begun to develop kin ties. Though few African men lived with their wives and children, the longer an African lived in the Chesapeake, the more likely he was to live with his immediate family.[11]

Robert "King" Carter, the largest slaveholder in the Chesapeake colonies in the 1720s and 1730s, purchased many Africans in the years before he died. The scale of his operations and the large size of his quarters presented enslaved African men with more opportunities to begin families than most of their fellows. Even though Carter apparently encouraged marriage and family life among his slaves, many of his men probably had no kindred on their quarters when he died in 1732. Over half the men and a similar proportion of boys age ten to fourteen lived with unrelated men. These men were probably recently arrived Africans unable to find wives because of the high sex ratios on Carter's holdings. If a man survived a few years on a Carter plantation, he probably married. About a tenth of Carter's adult male slaves had recently married women who resided on or moved to

10. Mintz and Price, *Anthropological Approach*, 22–23; Prince George's Inventories, 1730–1769, MHR. Large plantations were those with 11 or more adult slaves.

11. Prince George's Wills, 1730–1749, MHR, and Inventory of the plantation of Daniel Carroll of Duddington, Charles Carroll of Annapolis Account Book, Maryland Historical Society, Baltimore (MHS). The inventory was taken in 1735 (but never probated), a time of high slave imports, but Carroll sold rather than bought slaves. There were only 2 men between 15 and 29 years of age (but 12 women) on his plantations, and 7 above 60; 2 of the 4 men in their 40s, 2 of the 3 in their 50s, and 6 of 7 who were 60 or older lived with wives and children.

their quarters, but did not yet have children in 1733. Older slave men, whether immigrants or creoles, often lived with their wives and children, and more than a quarter of Carter's men were in this group (see table 39).[12]

A greater proportion of African women than African men lived with kindred, especially on large plantations. There was such a surplus of men on these units that African women who lived on them could choose husbands from among several African or Afro-American slave men; women who found husbands on nearby plantations soon had children living with them. On Robert Carter's plantations, for instance, more than half of the men but only a quarter of the women lived in households that contained no kindred. About three-fifths of the women but only two-fifths of the men lived with their spouses. Proportionately, a third more of Carter's women than his men lived with both children and spouse, and women lived in mother-children households five times more frequently than men lived in father-children units.

Even on small plantations, African women commonly lived with their children. Some African women may have been so alienated that they refused to have children, but the rest raised several offspring, protected by the master's reluctance to separate very young children from their mothers. Since the children were reared by their mothers and eventually joined them in the tobacco fields, these households were domestic groups although incomplete as families.

Because spouses of African-born slaves were usually separated, African mothers reared their Afro-American children with little help from their husbands. Even when the father was present as on large plantations like those of Robert Carter's, the extended kin so important in the life of African children was missing. Mothers probably taught them the broad values that they brought from Africa and related the family's history in Africa and the Chesapeake. When the children began working in the fields, they learned from their mothers how to survive a day's work and how to get along with master and overseer.

Each group of Africans repeated the experiences of previous arrivals. The social position of Africans may have slowly improved, however. As the African slave trade peaked and then declined, adult sex ratios also decreased: the sex ratio on large plantations in Prince George's County, Mary-

---

12. Robert Carter Inventory, VHS, shows an adult slave sex ratio of 153 (excluding old people) and a sex ratio among youths 10–14 of 150. Although 51% of the boys lived in households without kindred, only 19% of the girls similarly lacked kin. One can identify those who had been in the country a number of years by the age of their children. The new Negro status of couples without children (30 in total, 3 formed by old people) was inferred from the high fertility of slave couples and the absence of such households on large plantations later in the century.

Table 39. *Slave Household Structure on Robert "King" Carter's Quarters, 1733*

	Percentage Occupying, by Age				
Household Type	Males, 15+ (*N*=249)	Females, 15+ (*N*=175)	Children, 0–9 (*N*=212)	Children, 10–14 (*N*=91)	Overall (*N*=733)
Husband-wife	12	18			8
Husband-wife-children	28	39	57	33	40
Mother-children	a	21	31	23	17
Father-children	4	0	6	3	4
Extended	1	2	1	1	1
No family present[b]	54	20	5	39	30
Total	99	100	100	99	100

Source: Robert Carter Inventory, Robert Carter Papers, VHS.

Notes: [a]Less than .5%. [b]Slaves apparently living alone or in barracks, with no other kindred found in household.

land, declined from 249 (men per 100 women) during the years of heavy immigration of the 1730s to 142 in the 1740s after immigration decreased. More new Negroes could therefore take wives after 1740 than in previous decades.[13]

Afro-American Slave Households and Families

Afro-American slaves had a more stable family life than their imported African parents. As children they almost always lived with their mothers and siblings and sometimes with their fathers. When the black population began to grow through a surplus of births over deaths in the 1720s and 1730s, the proportion of native-born adults among slaves rose, and slave family life changed remarkably.

The changing composition of the slave population combined with other changes to restructure Afro-American slave households and families. Alterations in the adult sex ratio, the size of plantations, and slave population density provided slaves with opportunities to enjoy a more satisfying family life. The way masters transferred slaves from place to place limited the size and composition of black households, but slave family members

13. Prince George's Inventories, 1730–1744.

separated by masters managed to establish complex kinship networks over many plantations. Afro-American slaves used these opportunities to create a kind of family life that differed from African and Anglo-American practices.

Demographic changes permitted slaves to create more complex households and families. As the number of adult Africans in the population decreased, the sex ratio declined to between 100 and 110 by the 1750s. This decline gave most men an opportunity to marry by about age thirty. The number of slaves who lived on plantations with more than twenty blacks increased, and the density of the black population and the proportion of blacks in the entire population both rose. The number of friends and kinfolk whom typical Afro-American slaves saw every day or visited with regularity increased, while their contact with whites declined because extensive areas of the Chesapeake became largely black counties.

How frequently masters sold or bequeathed their Afro-American slaves and where they sent them affected black household composition. Three points seem clear. First, planters kept women and their small children together but did not keep husbands and teenage children with their immediate family. Slaveowner after slaveowner bequeathed women and their increase to sons or daughters. However, children of Chesapeake slaveowners tended to live near their parents. Thus, even when members of slave families were so separated, they remained in the same neighborhood.[14] Second, slaves who lived on small farms were separated from their families more frequently than those on large plantations. At their death small slaveowners typically willed a slave or two to the widow and to each child. They also frequently mortgaged or sold slaves to gain capital. If a slaveowner died with many unpaid debts, his slaves had to be sold.[15] Finally, relatively few slaves were forced to move long distances. More slaves were affected by migration from the Chesapeake region to the new Southwest in the nineteenth century than by long-distance movement in the region before the Revolution. These points should not be misunderstood. Most slaves who lived in Maryland or Virginia during the eighteenth century experienced forced separation from members of their immediate family sometime in their lives, and about twenty-six thousand tidewater slaves (a quarter of all the region's slaves) were forced to move to piedmont or to the valley of Virginia between 1755 and 1782, usually over such long distances that they could no longer see their kindred. More than two-thirds of all of

14. These statements are based upon Prince George's Wills, 1730–1769, and court cases discussed below.
15. Prince George's Wills, 1730–1769; mortgages in Prince George's Land Records, libri T, Y, PP. Estate sales were sometimes advertised in the *Md. Gaz.* Slaves could not be sold from an estate until all other movable property had been used to pay debts. Elie Valette, *The Deputy Commissarry's Guide within the Province of Maryland* (Annapolis, 1774), 91, 134–135.

tidewater's slaves, however, probably lived close enough to visit most family members.[16]

These changes led to a new social reality for most slaves born in the 1750s, 1760s, and 1770s. If unrelated people and their progeny stay in a limited geographic area for several generations, the descendants of the original residents must develop kin ties with many other people who live nearby. Once the proportion of adult Africans among slaves declined, this process began. African slave women married and had children; the children matured and married. If most of them remained near their birthplace, each was bound to have siblings, children, spouses, uncles, aunts, and cousins living in the neighborhood. How these various kinspeople were organized into households, families, and domestic groups depended not only upon the whims of masters but also upon the meaning placed on kinship by the slaves themselves.

The process of household and family formation and dissolution was begun by each immigrant black woman who lived long enough to have children. The story of Ann Joice, a black woman who was born in Barbados, taken to England as a servant, and then falsely sold into slavery in Maryland in the 1670s, may have been similar to that of African women once they became slaves. The Darnall family of Prince George's owned Ann Joice. She had seven children with several white men in the 1670s and 1680s; all remained slaves the rest of their life. Three of her children stayed on the Darnall home plantation until their death. One was sold as a child to a planter who lived a few miles away; another was eventually sold to William Digges, who lived about five miles from the Darnall plantation. Both the spatial spread and the local concentration of kinfolk continued in the next generation. Peter Harbard, born between 1715 and 1720, was the son of Francis Harbard, who was Ann Joice's child. Peter grew up on the Darnall farm, but in 1737 he was sold to George Gordon, who lived across the road from Darnall. As a child, Peter lived with or very near his grandmother Ann Joice, his father, and several paternal uncles and aunts. He probably knew his seven cousins (father's sister's children), children of his aunt Susan Harbard, who lived on the William Digges plantation. Other kinfolk lived in Annapolis but were too far away to visit easily.[17]

16. Migrations of slaves in the 18th century are discussed above, chaps. 4 and 8, and by Philip Morgan, "Slave Life in the Virginia Piedmont: A Demographic Report" (paper presented at conference, "The Colonial Experience: The Eighteenth-Century Chesapeake," Baltimore, Sept. 1984), 3–4, and table 3. Slave movement in the 19th century is analyzed in Allan Kulikoff, "Uprooted Peoples: Black Migrants in the Age of the American Revolution, 1790–1820," in Berlin and Hoffman, eds., *Slavery and Freedom*, 143–171.

17. Court of Appeals of the Western Shore, BW#10 (1800–1801), 456–483, esp. 459–460, MHR.

As Afro-American slaves were born and died and as masters sold or bequeathed their slaves, slave households were formed and reformed, broken and created. Four detailed examples illustrate this process. Daphne, the daughter of Nan, was born about 1736 on a large plantation in Prince George's owned by Robert Tyler, Sr. Until she was two, she lived with her mother, two brothers, and two sisters. In 1738, Tyler died and left his slaves to his wife, children, and grandchildren. All lived on or near Tyler's farms. Three of Daphne's siblings were bequeathed to granddaughter Ruth Tyler, who later married Mordecai Jacob, her grandfather's next-door neighbor. Daphne continued to live on the Tyler plantation. From 1736 to 1787, she had six different masters, but she still lived where she was born. Daphne had lived with her mother until her mother died, and with her ten children until 1779. Children were eventually born to Daphne's daughters; these infants lived with their mothers and near their maternal grandmother. When Robert Tyler III (the grandson of Robert Tyler, Sr.), Daphne's fifth master, died in 1779, his will divided Daphne's children and grandchildren between a son and a daughter. Daphne was thus separated from her younger children, born between 1760 and 1772. They were given to Millicent Beanes (the daughter of Robert III), who lived several miles away. Daphne continued to live on the same plantation as her four older children and several grandchildren. An intricate extended family of aunts, uncles, nieces, nephews, and cousins resided in several households on the Tyler plantation in 1778, and other, more remote kinfolk could be found on the neighboring Jacob farm.[18]

Family separations might be more frequent on smaller plantations. Rachael was born in the late 1730s and bore ten children between 1758 and 1784. As a child she lived on the plantation of Alexander Magruder, a large slaveowner in Prince George's. Before 1746, Alexander gave her to his son Hezekiah, who lived on an adjoining plantation. Hezekiah never owned more than ten slaves, and when he died in 1769, he owned only two, including one willed to his wife by her brother. Between 1755 and 1757, he mortgaged nine slaves, including Rachael, to two merchants. In 1757, Samuel Roundall (who lived about five miles from the Magruders) seized Rachael and six other slaves mortgaged to him. In 1760 Roundall sold Rachael and her eldest daughter to Samuel Lovejoy, who lived about nine miles from Roundall. At the same time, four other former Magruder slaves were sold: two to planters in Lovejoy's neighborhood, one to a Roundall neighbor, and one to a planter living at least fifteen miles away in Charles County.

18. Chancery Papers no. 5241 (1788); Prince George's Wills, I, 280–285; Prince George's Original Wills, box 7, folder 66, box 13, folder 51; Prince George's Inventories, DD#1, 22–24, DD#2, 379–386, GS#1, 246–248, ST#1, 96–100, all at MHR.

Rachael's separation from friends and family members continued. In 1761, Lovejoy sold Rachael's eldest child, age three, to his neighbor George Stamp. By the time Samuel Lovejoy died in 1762, Rachael had two other children. She and her youngest child went to live with John Lovejoy, Samuel's nephew and near neighbor, but her second child, age two, stayed with Lovejoy's widow. Her third child was sold at age six, but Rachael and her next seven children lived with John Lovejoy until at least 1787 (see map 18).[19]

Hundreds of large and middling slaveholders living in older tidewater counties established plantations in piedmont areas for their children or themselves in the 1750s, 1760s, and 1770s. Perhaps a third of the adult slaves in tidewater Virginia (and a fifth in southern Maryland) were forced to migrate to piedmont to operate these distant quarters. Since masters required some (but rarely all) of their slaves to leave, Afro-American slaves were inevitably separated from kindred. These separations were permanent, for their new homes were at least fifty and often several hundred miles away from their former quarters.[20]

In the late 1750s or early 1760s, Peyton Randolph, a member of the Virginia House of Burgesses (and eventually its speaker), organized a plantation in Charlotte County, deep in the southside frontier, located about 150 miles from his homes in Williamsburg and James City County. At first, he transferred a number of youths in their late teens and early twenties to the new quarter. By 1764, sixteen adult slaves and an overseer lived on the thirty-four-hundred-acre tract in Charlotte. Nearly a generation passed before Randolph's slaves rebuilt the kinship networks they had left behind. The young migrants married and had children, and by the 1780s *their* children had matured and begun to marry. There were thirty-two adult slaves on the plantation in 1784, perhaps twenty of them children of the original migrants. Sarah's experience illustrates the process of family destruction and rebuilding. At age twenty she was forced to leave her kindred in James City for Charlotte. Though her three children came with her, her husband was left behind. After she arrived in Charlotte, she remarried and had three more children. In 1784 Sarah lived in Charlotte surrounded by her six children and two grandchildren. Two daughters had married slaves who lived on the Charlotte quarter, and each new family included an infant.[21]

19. Chancery Records, XVI, 298–304; Prince George's Land Records, PP (2d part), 4, NN, 407; Prince George's Original Wills, box 7, folder 3, box 9, folder 52; Prince George's Inventories, DD#1, 438–441, GS#2, 111–112, all MHR.
20. Jackson Turner Main, "The One Hundred," *WMQ*, 3d Ser., XI (1954), 355–384; migration data reported in chap. 8, above.
21. Data on Randolph taken from Randolph Papers (film at Colonial Williamsburg Research

Map 18. *Sale and Later Transfer of Hezekiah Magruder's Slaves, 1755–1780*

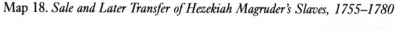

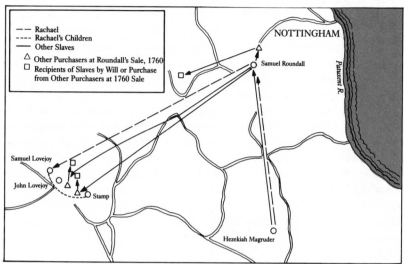

These four examples suggest how Afro-American slave households and families developed in the eighteenth century. Three demographic processes combined to create and destroy complex households and families. Husbands and wives, and parents and children were frequently separated by the master's transfers of family members. A young man tended to receive slaves from his parents or purchase them on the open market, thereby separating family members. If economic disaster did not intervene, his slaveholdings grew through natural increase, slave families were reestablished, and extended family networks developed. When the master died, the family's slaves were divided among heirs, and the process began again. Only during the second stage were slave families even relatively secure. At the same time, as generation followed generation, households, or adjacent huts, became increasingly complex and sometimes included grandparents, uncles, aunts, or cousins as well as the immediate family. Since other kin lived on nearby plantations, geographically dispersed kinship networks that connected numbers of quarters emerged during the pre-Revolutionary era.

Department [CW]), as reported in Eileen Starr, "Slaves Belonging to Peyton Randolph" (undergraduate paper, College of William and Mary, 1976); and Landon C. Bell, ed., *Sunlight on the Southside: Lists of Tithes, Lunenburg County, Virginia, 1748–1783* (Philadelphia, 1931), 223. The date of settlement inferred from the ages of Randolph's slaves in 1784 and the appearance of Randolph in the 1764 tax list (but not on the 1753 list).

This second process of building kinship networks had to be started all over again when slaves were forced to migrate to frontier regions.[22]

How typical were the experiences suggested by these examples? How were families organized into households and domestic groups on large and small quarters? Data from the records of four large planters taken between 1759 and 1775 and a census of Prince George's slaves taken in 1776 permit a test of these hypotheses concerning changes in household structure, differences between large and small units, and the spread of kinfolk across space. The data cover both large quarters and small farms and provide a good test of these ideas because by the 1770s most Afro-American slaves could trace a Chesapeake genealogy back to immigrant grandparents or great-grandparents.

Kinfolk (immediate families and near kin) on large plantations were organized into three kinds of residence groups. Most of the slaves of large quarters were related by blood or marriage. Domestic groups included kinfolk who lived on opposite sides of duplex slave huts and who shared a common yard and eating and cooking arrangements. Finally, most households included members of an immediate family.

The kinship structures of slaves on large plantations are illustrated by a household inventory taken in 1773–1774 of 385 slaves owned by Charles Carroll of Carrollton on thirteen different quarters in Anne Arundel County. Because Carroll insisted that the inventory be "taken in Familys with their Ages," the document permits a detailed reconstruction of kinship networks.[23] Though the complexity and size of kinship groups on Carroll's quarters were probably greater than on other large plantations, the general pattern could easily have been repeated elsewhere.[24]

The ten men and three women who headed each list were probably leaders of their quarters. Five of the quarters were named for these individuals. They tended to be old slaves who had been with the Carroll family

22. See Gutman, *Black Family in Slavery and Freedom*, 137–139, for a brilliant exposition of much of this model.
23. "A List of Negroes on Doohoregan Manor Taken in Familys with Their Ages Decr. 1, 1773," and other lists of slaves at Popular Island, Annapolis Quarter, and Annapolis taken in Febr. and July 1774, Carroll Account Book, Maryland Historical Society, Baltimore (MHS). I am greatly indebted to Edward Papenfuse for calling this list to my attention. For another, and compatible, analysis of Carroll's slaves, see Norton *et al.*, "Afro-American Family," in Berlin and Hoffman, eds., *Slavery and Freedom*, 177–180.
24. Only a handful of people in the Chesapeake colonies owned as many slaves as Carroll. He could therefore afford to keep his slave families together, an option not open to most slaveholders. Nonetheless, two-thirds of Carroll's slaves lived on units with fewer than 40 people, and 57% of them on quarters with fewer than 30. Only the 130 slaves who lived at Riggs (the main plantation at Doohoregan) developed more extensive kinship networks than was possible for slaves of other large planters.

for many years. While the mean age of all adults was thirty-seven years, the mean age of the leaders was forty-nine, and six of the thirteen were over fifty-five.[25] The leader often lived with many kinfolk and was closely related to 36–38 percent of all the other slaves on the quarter. For example, Fanny, sixty-nine years of age, was surrounded by at least forty near kinfolk on the main plantation at Doohoregan, and Mayara James, sixty-five years of age, lived with twenty-three relatives on his quarter.

Slave genealogies at Annapolis Quarter and at Doohoregan Manor provide detailed examples of the kinds of kinship networks that could develop on quarters after several generations of relative geographic stability (figs. 27, 28). Because most slave quarters had between fifteen and thirty slaves, the network included only two or three households. The kin group at Annapolis Quarter may have been typical. Thirteen of the seventeen slaves who lived there in 1774 were descendants of Ironworks Lucy, ten of them children and grandchildren of Lucy's daughter Sall. One of Sall's sons-in-law and his brother also lived there. Peter and Charles, other descendants of Lucy, lived on the quarter but had families elsewhere.

Nearly half the slaves who resided on Riggs Quarter, Carroll's main plantation, were kinfolk (63 of 130). A slave kinship network of this size could develop only on the home plantations of the largest Chesapeake planters.[26] Each of the members of the group was either a direct descendant or an affine (in-law) of old Fanny. She was surrounded on her quarter by five children, nineteen grandchildren, nine great-grandchildren, four children-in-law, and three grandchildren's spouses. The network grew through the marriage of Fanny's children and grandchildren to children of other residents of the quarter. For example, Cooper Joe, his wife, and thirteen children and grandchildren were closely related to Fanny's family. By the early 1750s Cooper Joe had married Nanny of Kate, and about 1761 Fanny's son Bob married Frances Mitchell of Kate. Joe and Nanny's children were first cousins of the children of Bob and Frances and thereby more remotely connected to all the rest of Fanny's descendants. The alliance of the two families was cemented in 1772, when Dinah, the daughter of Kate of Fanny, married Joe, the son of Cooper Joe.[27]

25. There were 139 married adults (all ages) and single people over 21 in the group. Although 46% of the leaders were over 55, only 11% of all adults had reached that age.
26. For example, only a maximum of 6% of slaves in Prince George's, Anne Arundel, Charles, and St. Mary's counties, Md., lived on units of more than 100 in 1790. The 6% is a maximum number because the census taken sometimes combined several of the master's quarters. See U.S., Bureau of the Census, *Heads of Families at the First Census . . . , Maryland* (Washington, D.C., 1907), 9–16, 47–55, 92–98, 104–109. The growth of large units (more than 40 slaves) in Prince George's, 1776–1810, is documented by Richard S. Dunn, "Black Society in the Chesapeake, 1776–1810," in Berlin and Hoffman, eds., *Slavery and Freedom*, 68–70.
27. Joe married his mother's sister's husband's mother's grandchild.

Fig. 27. *Kinship Ties among Charles Carroll's Slaves at Annapolis Quarter,*
1774

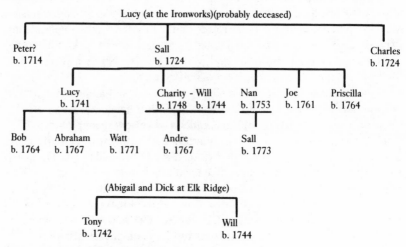

Source: Charles Carroll Account Book, Carroll Papers, MHS.

Note: Will (Charity's Husband), son of Abigail and Dick, appears twice. Peter may not be Lucy's son, but probably is. Mark (b. 1758) and Jem (b. 1754) apparently were not related to others on the quarter but had relatives elsewhere on Carroll's plantations.

The intraquarter kinship network was also a work group. Fanny's and Lucy's adult and teenage kinfolk worked together in the fields. Masters separated their slaves by sex, age, and strength and determined what each would do, but blacks judged each other in part by the reciprocal kinship obligation that bound them. Afro-American slaves worked at their own pace and frequently thwarted their masters' desires for increased productivity. Part of this conflict can be explained by the desires of kinfolk to help and protect each other from the master's lash, the humid climate, and the malarial environment.[28]

Landon Carter's attitude toward his old slave Jack Lubbar suggests the dimensions of kinship solidarity in the fields. Lubbar had been a foreman over many groups of slaves and often directed his kindred in their work. Lubbar alternately protected and pushed those who labored under him. He was "blessed with his children's company," perhaps because he drove his charges lightly. In 1766 Carter complained, "Old Jack is both too easy with those people and too deceitfull and careless himself." When Lubbar died in 1774, Carter remembered only his loyalty. In Jack's old age, he wrote,

28. See below, chap. 10, for work and work discipline.

Fig. 28. *Fanny and Some of Her Kinfolk on Doohoregan Manor, 1773*

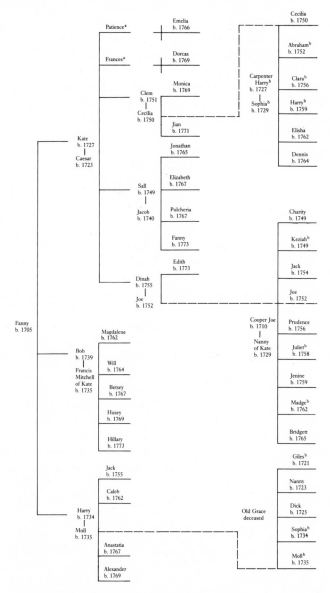

Source: Charles Carroll Account Book, Carroll Papers, MHS.

Notes: [a]Those without a birthdate not resident on any Carroll farm. [b]Did not live at Rigg's Quarter (Fanny's Quarter). [c]This family lived at the sawmill at the main quarter of Doohoregan Manor. Frances Mitchell was a sister of Nanny, who was the wife of Cooper Joe.

Lubbar worked at the Fork quarter "with 5 hands and myself; in which service he so gratefully discharged his duty as to make me by his care alone larger crops of Corn, tobacco, and Pease twice over than ever I have had made by anyone." Other slaves did not share Lubbar's occasional desire to produce a large crop for Carter. "At this Plantation," Carter wrote, "he continued till his age almost deprived him of eyesight which made him desire to be removed because those under him, mostly his greatgrandchildren, by the baseness of their Parents abused him much." Lubbar's grandchildren and great-grandchildren were related in intricate ways: parents and children, maternal and paternal cousins, uncles and aunts, and brothers and sisters. They united against Lubbar to slow the work pace and conserve their energy.[29]

When Afro-Americans came home each night from the fields, they broke into smaller domestic groups. Their habitat set the scene for social intercourse. On large plantations "a Negro Quarter, is a Number of Huts or Hovels, built at some Distance from the Mansion-House; where the Negros reside with their Wives and Families, and cultivate at vacant Times, the little Spots allow'd them."[30] Slaves lived in two kinds of housing. Four early nineteenth-century slave houses still standing in southern Maryland, as well as three homes at Doohoregan Manor, Charles Carroll's home plantation, were duplexes. Each of the southern Maryland houses included two rooms, of about sixteen by sixteen feet, separated by a thin wall. In three of the surviving houses, the two huts shared the same roof but had separate doorways. Two had separate fireplaces, the residents of one duplex shared a fireplace, and one quarter (which was over a kitchen) did not have a fireplace. Neither family had much privacy, and communication must have been commonplace. Most slaves, however, apparently wanted more privacy and built single-family cabins. Slave houses in St. Mary's County at the end of the eighteenth century, for instance, were single-family structures that averaged sixteen by sixteen feet; similarly, sixteen slave houses on Doohoregan Manor were slightly larger, averaging twenty by fifteen feet. Even when slave families lived in separate houses, they were built very close together and surrounded a common yard, where residents could talk, eat, or celebrate.[31]

29. Jack P. Greene, ed., *The Diary of Colonel Landon Carter of Sabine Hall, 1752–1778*, 2 vols. (Charlottesville, Va., 1965), I, 301, 303, 575, II, 836, 840.
30. Kimber, "'Itinerant Observations' of Kimber," *MHM*, LI (1956), 327; references cited in chap. 8, n. 47, above.
31. The best analysis of slave housing (mostly in the antebellum period) will be found in George W. McDaniel, *Hearth and Home: Preserving a People's Culture* (Philadelphia, 1982), chap. 2. I examined the four structures, three in St. Mary's County and the other in Prince George's County. I am indebted to Cary Carson for his data on the St. Mary's buildings and to

On the quarters the smallest local residence unit to contain kinfolk was the household. Household members were not isolated from other kinfolk. They worked with their relatives in the fields, associated with neighbors in the common yard, and cooked meals or slept near those who lived in neighboring huts. Even youths who lived in barracks with other unrelated youths were never far from kindred.[32] Nevertheless, kinfolk who lived in the same household were spatially closer when at home than any other group of kin. Who lived in typical households on slave quarters? How many husbands lived with their wives and children? How many children were separated from their parents? Did kin other than the immediate family live in many households?

Nearly half of all the Afro-Americans owned by four large planters resided in households that included both parents and at least some of their children. More than half of the young children on all four plantations lived with both parents, but a far higher proportion of adults and children ten to fourteen years of age lived in two-parent households on the Carroll quarters than on the other three groups of quarters. About half of the men, women, and youths ten to fourteen lived in two-parent households on Carroll's plantations, but only a third of the women, a quarter of the men, and two-fifths of the youths could be found in two-parent homes on the other farms. Almost all the other children lived with one parent, usually the mother; but more than a quarter of those ten to fourteen years of age lived with siblings or with apparently unrelated people (see table 40).[33]

The differences between Carroll and the other three large slaveowners is striking. Carroll, unlike all but a few other Chesapeake gentlemen, was able to provide his people with spouses from his own plantations and chose to keep adolescent children with their parents. More than half the men (56 percent) and a quarter of the women on Addison's, Wardrop's, and Jerdone's plantations were either unmarried or lived away from spouses and children. On Carroll's quarters only 27 percent of the men and 12 percent of the women were similarly separated from wives and children.

Many slaves on the Carroll, Addison, and Wardrop quarters lived with or near kin other than parents or children. Carroll's and Addison's slaves

Margaret Cook for her help with the Prince George's site. For Carroll, see Federal Direct Tax of 1798, Elkridge Hundred, Anne Arundel County, 5–8, MHR. I am indebted to Alexander O. Boulton for calling the Carroll materials to my attention. For St. Mary's, see Bayly Ellen Marks, "Economics and Society in a Staple Plantation System: St. Mary's County, Maryland, 1790–1840" (Ph.D. diss., University of Maryland, 1979), 52–53.
32. Almost all of the boys and men on Charles Carroll's quarters in 1774 had kin on the same or a nearby quarter.
33. Proportions in two-parent households: 49% (Carroll) and 33% (other farms) of women; 51% and 26% of men; 52% and 40% of those aged 10–14.

Table 40. *Afro-American Slave Household Structure on Four Large Plantations in the Chesapeake, 1759–1775*

Household Type	Percentage Occupying, by Age				
	Males, 15+ (N=189)	Females, 15+ (N=158)	Children, 0–9 (N=224)	Children, 10–14 (N=99)	Overall (N=670)
Husband-wife	3	4			2
Husband-wife-children	37	42	53	46	45
Mother-children	2	19	25	10	15
Father-children	7	0	7	6	5
Siblings	5	3	5	9	5
Mother–children–other kin	3	11	6	10	7
Other extended[a]	3	4	2	5	4
No family in household[b]	40	18	2	15	18
Total	100	101	100	101	100

Sources: Prince George's Inventories, GS#1, 73 (James Wardrop's, 32 slaves); and GS#2, 334–336 (Addison's 3 plantations, 109 slaves); Charles Carroll Account Book, MHS (385 slaves); Philip David Morgan, "The Development of Slave Culture in Eighteenth Century Plantation America" (Ph.D. diss., University College, London, 1977), 326 (Francis Jerdone's plantations in piedmont Virginia, rest of slaves).

Notes: [a]Half the slaves lived in two-parent households with other kin; half lived in three-generation households that included grandparents and grandchildren but not the generation in between. [b]Includes some slaves with kinfolk on the plantation, but in other households.

had been with the families for several generations, and extended households thus formed. About 7 percent of these slaves were in the household of a brother or sister, and more than a tenth (13 percent) of parents and children shared their home with another kinsperson. There were several types of these extended households: seven included parents, children, and siblings of the mother; two included a grandmother living with her children and grandchildren; in one household grandparents took care of two young grandchildren; and in one hut, an adult brother and sister lived with her children and one grandchild.

Slave family life on the plantations Francis Jerdone established in piedmont Virginia in the 1740s or 1750s was somewhat less settled than on those in tidewater Maryland. By 1770, when he took a census of his slaves, insufficient time had elapsed to allow the creation of *any* households with extended kindred. Men found marriage on the plantation more difficult than in Maryland: although the sex ratio among black adults was only 110 on the Maryland quarters, it reached 162 on Jerdone's plantations.[34]

Far less can be learned about families on small plantations. On these farms, the slave quarter could be in an outbuilding or in a small hut. All the slaves, whether kin or not, lived together, cooked together, reared their children together, and slept in the same hut. Only 18 percent of the blacks on small units in Prince George's County in 1776 lived in two-parent households. About a third resided in mother-child households, including over half the young children and three-tenths of those ten to fourteen years of age. Nearly three-quarters of the men and two-fifths of the women—some unmarried—lived with neither spouse nor children. More than two-fifths of the youths ten to fourteen years of age lived away from parents and siblings. These differences in the composition of slave households on large and small plantations influenced child-rearing patterns. Although slave fathers played a major role in rearing their children on large units, they were rarely present on smaller farms. On these small units, mothers had to cope with child rearing alone or, perhaps, with the help of an unrelated adult (see table 41).

The Life Cycle of Afro-American Slaves

By the 1750s, a peculiarly Afro-American life cycle had developed. Afro-Americans lived in a succession of different kinds of households. Children under ten years almost always lived with their mothers, and more than half on large plantations lived with both parents. Between ten and fourteen years of age, large numbers of children left their parents' homes. Some stayed with siblings and their families, others were sold, and the rest lived with other kin or unrelated people. Women married in their late teens, had children, and established households with their own children. More than two-fifths of the women on large plantations and a fifth on small farms lived with husbands as well as children. The same proportion of men as women lived in nuclear households, but because children of separated spouses usually lived with their mothers, large numbers of men, even on big plantations, lived only with other men.

These life-cycle changes can perhaps best be approached through a study of the critical events in the lives of Afro-Americans. Those events probably included the following: infancy, leaving the matricentral cell, be-

34. Philip David Morgan, "The Development of Slave Culture in Eighteenth Century Plantation America" (Ph.D. diss., University College, London, 1977), 325–327.

Table 41. *Afro-American Slave Household Structure on Small Plantations in Prince George's County, 1776*

Household Type	Percentage Occupying, by Age				
	Males, 15+ (N=275)	Females, 15+ (N=276)	Children, 0–9 (N=325)	Children, 10–14 (N=162)	Overall (N=1,038)
Husband-wife-children	17	18	22	10	18
Mother-children	2	35	56	29	32
Father-children	2	a	4	1	2
Siblings	7	5	6	17	8
No family	72	42	12	43	41
Total	100	100	100	100	101

Source: Gaius Marcus Brumbaugh, ed., *Maryland Records: Colonial, Revolutionary, County, and Church, from Original Sources*, I (Baltimore, 1915), 1–88.

Notes: The household types were inferred from black age structures on individual farms, and the statistics that result are thus conjectural. [a]Less than .5%.

ginning to work in the tobacco fields, leaving home, courtship and marriage, child rearing, and old age.

For the first few months of life, a newborn infant stayed in the matri-central cell, that is, received his identity and subsistence from his mother.[35] A mother would take her new infant to the fields with her "and lay it uncovered on the ground . . . while she hoed her corn-row down and up. She would then suckle it a few minutes, and return to her labor, leaving the child in the same exposure." Eventually, the child left its mother's lap and explored the world of the hut and quarter. In the evenings, he ate with his family and learned to love his parents, siblings, and other kinfolk. During the day the young child lived in an age-segregated world. While parents, other adults, and older siblings worked, children were "left, during a great portion of the day, on the ground at the doors of their huts, to their own struggles and efforts."[36] They played with age-mates or were left at home with other children and perhaps an aged grandparent. Siblings and age-mates commonly lived together or in nearby houses. In Prince George's

35. For the matricentral cell, see Meyer Fortes, "Introduction," in Jack Goody, ed., *The Developmental Cycle in Domestic Groups*, Cambridge Papers in Social Anthropology, No. 1 (Cambridge, 1958), 1–14, esp. 9; and Sidney W. Mintz, "A Final Note," *Social and Economic Studies*, X (1961), 532–533.
36. Samuel Stanhope Smith, *An Essay on the Causes of the Variety of Complexion and Figure in the Human Species* (1787), ed. Winthrop D. Jordan (Cambridge, Mass., 1965 [orig. publ. New Brunswick, N.J., 1810]), 35, 61–62, 156–157.

County in 1776, 86 percent of those from zero to four years of age and 82 percent of those from five to nine years of age lived on plantations with at least one other child near their own age. Many children lived in little communities of five or more children their own age. Children five to nine years old, too young to work full time, may have cared for younger siblings; in Prince George's in 1776, 83 percent of all children under five years of age lived on a plantation with at least one child five to nine years of age.[37]

Black children began to work in the tobacco fields between seven and ten years of age. For the first time they joined fully in the daytime activities of adults.[38] Those still living at home labored beside parents, brothers and sisters, cousins, uncles, aunts, and other kinfolk. (Even on smaller plantations, they worked with their mothers.) Most were trained to be field hands by white masters or overseers and by their parents. Though these young hands were forced to work for the master, they quickly learned from their kinfolk to work at the pace that black adults set and to practice the skills necessary to "put massa on."

At about the same age, some privileged boys began to learn a craft from whites or (on the larger plantations) from their skilled kinfolk. Charles Carroll's plantations provide an example of how skills were passed from one generation of Afro-Americans to the next. Six of the eighteen artisans on his plantations under twenty-five years of age in 1773 probably learned their trade from fathers and another four from other kinfolk skilled in that occupation. For example, Joe, twenty-one, and Jack, nineteen, were both coopers and both sons of Cooper Joe, sixty-three. Joe also learned to be a wheelwright and, in turn, probably helped train his brothers-in-law, Elisha, eleven, and Dennis, nine, as wheelwrights.[39]

Beginning to work coincided with the departure of many children from their parents, siblings, and friends. The fact that about 54 percent of all slaves in single-slave households in Prince George's in 1776 were between seven and fifteen years of age suggests that children of those ages were typically forced to leave home. Young blacks were most frequently forced from large plantations to smaller farms.[40] The parents' authority was elimi-

---

37. Gaius Marcus Brumbaugh, *Maryland Records: Colonial, Revolutionary, County, and Church, from Original Sources*, I (Baltimore, 1915), 1–88.

38. See below, chap. 10.

39. Carroll Account Book. Elisha and Dennis were sons of Carpenter Harry and Sophia. Joe married Dinah of Kate and Caesar; her brother married Cecilia of Harry and Sophia. Elisha and Dennis were therefore Joe's wife's brother's wife's brothers.

40. Only the children of slaveowners or those who had just bought their first slave were likely to have only one slave, so this data is a useful indicator of the age at which children were first sold. The transfers from large to small plantations can also be seen by comparing the small group (12%) of slaves 10–14 on large plantations who lived away from kin with the large proportion (43%) on small farms (see tables 40, 41).

nated, and the child left the only community he had known. Tension and unhappiness often resulted. For example, Hagar, age fourteen, ran away from her master in Baltimore in 1766. "She is supposed to be harbor'd in some Negro Quarter," he claimed, "as her Father and Mother Encourages her in Elopements, under a Pretense she is ill used at home."[41]

Courtship and marriage (defined here as a stable sexual union) led to substantial but differential changes for slave women and men. The process began earlier for women: men probably married in their middle to late twenties, women in their late teens.[42] Men, who initiated the courtship, typically searched for wives by visiting a number of neighboring plantations and often found a wife near home, though not on the same quarter. Some evidence for this custom, suggestive but hardly conclusive, can be seen in the sex and age of runaway slaves. Only 9 percent of all southern Maryland runaways, 1745–1779, and 12 percent of all Virginia runaways, 1730–1787, were women. Few men (relative to the total population) ran away in their late teens, but numbers rose in the early twenties when the search for wives began and crested between twenty-five and thirty-four, when most men married and began families (see fig. 29). Courtship on occasion ended in a marriage ceremony, sometimes performed by a clergyman, sometimes celebrated by the slaves themselves.[43]

Slave men had to search their neighborhood to find a compatible spouse because even the largest quarter contained few eligible women. Some of the potential mates were sisters or cousins, groups blacks refused to marry.[44] When they were excluded, few choices remained on the quarter, and youths looked elsewhere. Charles Carroll united slave couples once they married, but that usually required either bride or groom to move. Only a fifth of the forty-seven identifiable couples on his plantations in 1773 had lived on the same quarter before they married. Either husband or wife, and sometimes both of them, moved in three-fifths of the cases. The other fifth of the couples remained on different quarters in 1773.[45] Yet most planters

41. *Md. Gaz.*, Oct. 1, 1766.

42. See chap. 1 for slave ages at first conception. Age at marriage cannot be determined with precision but can be approximated from the age differences of husbands and wives. On the Carroll, Addison, and Wardrop plantations, 47 husbands were 6.8 (mean) years older than their wives. Carroll Account Book; Prince George's Inventories, GS#1, 73, GS#2, 334–336.

43. Thomas Hughes, *History of the Society of Jesus in North America, Colonial and Federal* (London, 1908–1917), Text, II, *From 1645 till 1773*, 560–561; William Stevens Perry, ed., *Historical Collections Relating to the American Colonial Church* (Davenport, Iowa, 1870), IV, 306–307; Thomas Bacon, *Four Sermons, upon the Great and Indispensible Duty of All Christian Masters and Mistresses to Bring up Their Negro Slaves in the Knowledge and Fear of God* (London, 1750), v–vii.

44. Gutman, *Black Family in Slavery and Freedom*, 88–89; the current research of Gutman and Mary Beth Norton shows few cousin marriages on large plantations in the 18th century.

45. Carroll Account Book. If the previous residence of only one spouse could be determined, I

owned too few slaves, on too few quarters, to permit a wide choice of spouses within their plantations; furthermore, they could not afford to purchase the husband or wife. Inevitably, a majority of slave couples remained separated for much of their married life.

Marriage was far less important for slave women than for white women; slave women, unlike their white counterparts, neither shared property with their husbands nor received subsistence from them. After the relationship was consummated, the woman probably stayed with her family (parents and siblings) until a child was born, unless she could form a household with her new husband.[46] Childbearing, and the child rearing that followed, however, were highly important rites of passage for most slave women. Once she had a child, she moved from her mother's or parents' home to her own hut. The bonding between the slave mother and her child may have been far more important than her relationship with her husband, especially if he lived on another plantation. Motherhood, moreover, gave women a few valued privileges. Masters sometimes treated pregnant women and their newborn children with greater than usual solicitude. For example, Richard Corbin, a Virginia planter, insisted in 1759 that his steward be "Kind and Indulgent to pregnant women and not force them when with Child upon any service or hardship that will be injurious to them." Children were "to be well looked after."[47]

Marriage and parenthood brought less change in the lives of most men. Many continued to live with other men. Able to visit his family only at night or on holidays, the nonresident husband could play only a small role in child rearing. If husband and wife lived together, however, they established a household. The resident father helped raise his children, taught them skills, and tried to protect them from the master. Landon Carter

---

assumed that there was no change if the known spouse lived on the same quarter after marriage, but that there was a change if the known spouse lived on a different quarter. There were 5 unknowns in the 47 cases.

46. Of all marriages of slave women, 1720–1759, in Prince George's, 70% married before age 20 (see chap. 2). Many of these teenage girls should have been pregnant with their first children between 16 and 19. If they were living with their husbands, then their households would include only a husband and wife. On the three Maryland plantations analyzed in table 40, there were only three husband-wife households, and the women in them were 19, 27, and 56 years old. Of the women age 16–19, about a third were married: about one-half with children lived with sisters; the others about equally lived with husband, with husband and children, or without children separated from husband. Most unmarried lived with parents.

47. Deborah G. White, "Female Slaves: Sex Roles and Status in the Antebellum Plantation South," *Journal of Family History*, VIII (1983), 254–258, argues for the primacy of the mother-child bond over that of husbands and wives; the quoted passage is from William K. Scarborough, *The Overseer: Plantation Management in the Old South* (Baton Rouge, La., 1966), 183–184.

Fig. 29. *Age of Runaway Men in Maryland and Virginia*. Data centered at midpoint.

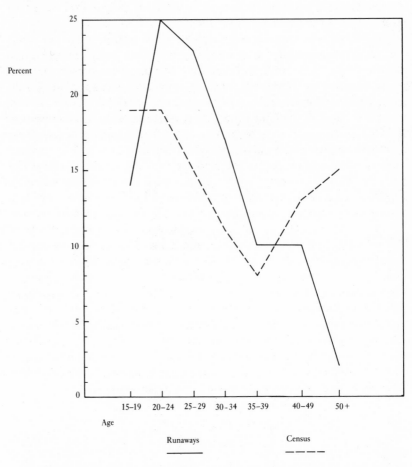

Sources: All runaway slave ads published in the *Maryland Gazette*, 1745–1779, and Dunlap's *Maryland Gazette*, 1775–1779 from Prince George's, Charles, Calvert, Frederick (south of Monocacy River), and Anne Arundel (south of Severn River, excluding Annapolis) counties, and any slave born in or traveling to those areas ($N=72$); all runaway ads (men and women, but few women of reported age) from Virginia newspapers, 1730–1787, reported in Lathan Algerna Windley, "A Profile of Runaway Slaves in Virginia and South Carolina from 1730 through 1787" (Ph.D. diss., University of Iowa, 1974), 80; census for Prince George's County from Gaius Marcus Brumbaugh, ed., *Maryland Records: Colonial, Revolutionary, County, and Church, from Original Sources*, I (Baltimore, 1915), 1–88.

reacted violently when Manuel tried to help his daughter. "Manuel's Sarah, who pretended to be sick a week ago, and because I found nothing ailed her and would not let her lie up she run away above a week and was catched the night before last and locked up; but somebody broke open the door for her. It could be none but her father Manuel, and he I had whipped."[48]

On large plantations, mothers could call upon a wide variety of kin to help them raise their children: husbands, siblings, cousins, uncles, or aunts might be living in nearby huts. Peter Harbard learned from his grandmother, father, and paternal uncles how his grandmother's indentures were burned by Henry Darnall, a large planter in Prince George's County, and how she was forced into bondage. He "frequently heard his grandmother Ann Joice say that if she had her *just right that she ought to be free and all her children. He hath also heard his Uncles David Jones, John Wood, Thomas Crane*, and also his father Francis Harbard declare as much." Peter's desire for freedom, learned from his kinfolk, never left him. In 1748, he ran away twice toward Philadelphia and freedom. He was recaptured but later purchased his freedom.[49]

As Afro-Americans grew older, illness and lack of stamina cut into their productivity, and their kinfolk or masters had to provide for them. On rare occasions, masters granted special privileges to favored slaves. Landon Carter permitted Jack Lubbar and his wife "to live quite retired only under my constant kindness" during the last three years of his life, and after over half a century of service. When Thomas Clark died in 1766, he gave his son Charles "my faithful old Negro man Jack whom I desire may be used tenderly in his old age." Charles Ball's grandfather lived as an old man by himself away from the other slaves he disliked. Similarly, John Wood, Peter Harbard's uncle, was given his own cabin in his old age.[50]

Many old slaves progressed through several stages of downward mobility. Artisans and other skilled workers became common field hands. Although 10 percent of the men between forty and fifty-nine years of age were craftsmen in Prince George's, only 3 percent of men above sixty years of age held similar positions. Mulatto Ned, owned by Gabriel Parker of Calvert County, was a carpenter and cooper most of his life, but he had lost that job by 1750 when he was sixty-five. Abraham's status at Snowden's ironworks in Anne Arundel County changed from master founder to la-

48. Greene, ed., *Diary of Carter*, II, 777.

49. Court of Appeals of the Western Shore, BW#10 (1800–1801), 459–460; *Md. Gaz.*, Nov. 2, 1748.

50. Greene, ed., *Diary of Carter*, II, 840; Prince George's Original Wills, box 10, folder 35; Charles Ball, *Fifty Years in Chains*, ed. Philip S. Foner (New York, 1970 [orig. publ. as *Slavery in the United States: A Narrative of the Life and Adventures* . . . (New York, 1837)]), 21–22; Court of Appeals of the Western Shore, BW#10, 549 (1802).

borer when he could not work full time. As slaves became feeble, some masters refused to maintain them adequately or sold them to unwary buyers. An act passed by the Maryland assembly in 1752 complained that "sundry Persons in this Province have set disabled and superannuated Slaves free who have either perished through want or otherwise become a Burthen to others." The legislators uncovered a problem: in 1755, 20 percent of all the free Negroes in Maryland were "past labour or cripples," while only 2 percent of white men were in this category. To remedy the abuse, the assembly forbade manumission of slaves by will and insisted that masters feed and clothe their old and ill slaves. If slaveholders failed to comply, they could be fined four pounds for each offense.[51]

As Afro-American slaves moved from plantation to plantation through the life cycle, they left behind many friends and kinfolk and established relations with slaves on other plantations. And when young blacks married off their quarter, they gained kinfolk on other plantations. Both of these patterns can be illustrated from the Carroll plantations. Sam and Sue, who lived on Sam's quarter at Doohoregan Manor, had seven children between 1729 and 1751. In 1774, six of them were spread over four different quarters at Doohoregan: one son lived with his father (his mother had died); a daughter lived with her family in a hut near her father's; a son and daughter lived at Frost's; one son headed Moses' quarter; and a son lived at Riggs. Marriages increased the size and geographic spread of Fanny's relations (fig. 28). A third of the slaves who lived away from Riggs Quarter (the main plantation) were kin to Fanny or her descendants. Two of Kate's children married into Fanny's family; Kate and one son lived at Frost's, and another son lived at Jacob's. Cecilia, the daughter of Carpenter Harry and Sophia, married one of Fanny's grandchildren. Harry and Sophia lived with three of their children at Frost's, and two of their sons lived at Riggs, where they were learning to be wheelwrights with kinsperson Joe, son of Cooper Joe.[52]

Since husbands and wives, fathers and children, and friends and kinfolk were often physically separated, they had to devise ways of maintaining their close ties. At night and on Sundays and holidays, fathers and other kinfolk visited those family members who lived on other plantations. Fathers on occasion had regular visiting rights. Landon Carter's Guy, for instance, visited his wife (who lived on another quarter) every Monday eve-

51. Prince George's Inventories, 1730–1760 (age-skill data); Snowden Account Book, Private Accounts; Inventories, XLIII, 320; and Chancery Records, VII, 2–12, 25–34, 50–52, all at MHR; "Number of Inhabitants in Maryland," *Gentleman's Magazine, and Historical Chronicle,* XXXIV (1764), 261. For two examples of ill slaves sold from master to master, see *Maryland Journal, and the Baltimore Advertiser,* Sept. 28, 1779; and Chancery Records, XVI, 469–478 (1789).
52. Carroll Account Book.

ning.[53] These visits symbolized the solidarity of slave families and permitted kinfolk to renew their friendships but did not allow nonresident fathers to participate in the daily rearing of their children.

Even though this forced separation of husbands from wives and children from parents tore slave families apart, slaves managed to create kinship networks from this destruction. Slave society was characterized by hundreds of connected and interlocking kinship networks that stretched across many plantations. A slave who wanted to run away would find kinfolk, friends of kinfolk, or kinfolk of friends along his route willing to harbor him for a while. As kinship networks among Afro-American slaves grew ever larger, the proportion of runaways who were harbored for significant periods of time on slave quarters seems to have increased in both Maryland and Virginia.[54]

There were three different reasons for slaves to use this underground. Some blacks, like Harry—who left his master in 1779, stayed in the neighborhood for a few weeks, and then took off for Philadelphia—used their friends' and kinfolk's hospitality to reach freedom.[55] Others wanted to visit. About 27 percent of all runaways from southern Maryland mentioned in newspaper advertisements from 1745 to 1779 (and 54 percent of all those whose destinations were described by masters) ran away to visit. For example, Page traveled back and forth between Piscataway and South River in 1749, a distance of about forty miles, and was not caught. He must have received help from many quarters along his route. And in 1756, Kate, thirty years old, ran away from her master, who lived near Georgetown on the Potomac. She went to South River (about thirty miles distant), where she had formerly lived. Friends concealed her there. Her master feared that since "she had been a great Rambler, and is well known in *Calvert* and *Anne-Arundel* Counties, besides other Parts of the Country," Kate would "indulge herself a little in visiting her old Acquaintance," but spend most of time with her husband at West River.[56]

Indeed, 9 percent of the southern Maryland runaways left masters to

53. Greene, *Diary of Carter*, I, 329, 348, II, 648, 845, 1109–1110; *Md. Gaz.*, July 11, 1771.

54. Gerald W. Mullin, *Flight and Rebellion: Slave Resistance in Eighteenth-Century Virginia* (New York, 1972), 129 (*cf.* above, table 38), shows that the proportion of visitors increased from 29% before 1775 to 38% of all Virginia runaways whose destinations can be determined from 1776 to 1800. The major problem with the data is the large proportion of unknowns (52% in Maryland and 40% in Virginia).

55. *Md. Gaz.*, July 6, 1779. Other examples of slaves' using the underground to escape slavery are found there, Apr. 28, 1757, July 11, 1771. From 1745 to 1779, 9% of all Maryland runaways (32% of visitors) ran away to visit spouses; 4% (14%) visited other kinfolk; and 15% (54%) visited friends. Total number of visitors was 63 (of 233).

56. *Ibid.*, Oct. 4, 1749, Nov. 11, 1756; for other extensive kinship networks, see Aug. 11, 1751, Mar. 12, 1772, Jan. 30, May 22, 1777.

join their spouses. Sue and her child Jem, eighteen months old, went from Allen's Freshes to Port Tobacco, Charles County, a distance of about ten miles, "to go and see her Husband." Sam, age thirty, lived about thirty miles from his wife in Bryantown, Charles County, when he visited her in 1755. Will had to go more than a hundred miles, from Charles to Frederick County, to visit his wife, because her master had taken her from Will's neighborhood to a distant quarter.[57]

Slave families in the eighteenth-century Chesapeake were often unstable, but Afro-Americans learned to cope with displacement and separation from kindred with some success. Slaves created flexible kinship networks that permitted slaves to adjust to separation. Most slaves were either members of a kin-based household or could call upon kindred on their own or nearby quarters for aid and encouragement. A girl who grew up in a two-parent household on a large plantation, for instance, might be sold in her teens to a small planter, marry a slave from a neighboring farm, and raise her children with minimal help from her husband. She would have learned about alternative child-rearing methods from playmates whose fathers lived elsewhere and would have been familiar with the nocturnal movement of men to visit their families. Her husband's kindred could provide some help and friendship if they lived nearby. If she longed for her old home, she could run away and visit, knowing that kindred and friends would hide her from the whites.

In sum, slave kinship networks provided Afro-Americans with an alternative system of status and authority and thereby set outside limits to exploitation by the master. A slave had not only a place in the plantation work hierarchy, mostly determined by the master, but a position within his kin group. Slave culture and religion developed within this system: blacks participated as kindred at work and in song, dance, celebrations, prayer, and revivals at home.

57. *Ibid.*, Mar. 9, 1758, Feb. 6, 1755, Aug. 12, 1773; John Woolman claimed that husbands and wives were often separated. *The Journal of John Woolman* (1774; 1871 ed.) *and a Plea for the Poor* (1793; orig. publ. as *A Word of Caution and Remembrance to the Rich*), Corinth Books ed. (New York, 1961), 59.

10
Slavery and Segregation
Race Relations in the Chesapeake

Great irony pervades the history of race relations in the Chesapeake colonies. Planters feared and disliked Africans, but when the supply of servants declined at the end of the seventeenth century, they were forced to turn to them. Once planters bought African slaves, they could not avoid contact with them: most planters owned few slaves, and most slaves lived on small units. Masters directed and worked alongside their slaves, lived near them, and sometimes became intimate with them. By the mid-eighteenth century, native-born slaves had replaced Africans in the work force. Like whites, these Afro-American slaves spoke English, practiced Christianity, and grew tobacco. Yet they increasingly lived on their own quarters away from whites, a development encouraged by their masters, who viewed their dark color as a mark of inferiority.

Slaves slowly became a peculiar kind of laboring class. Enslaved Africans refused discipline, worked only when forced, and attempted to run away from slavery. Masters had little choice but to watch them closely and put them to work on the simpler tasks of tobacco cultivation. Native-born slaves, on the other hand, acquiesced in their status and tried to make the best of a bad bargain by gaining some control over the processes of work. Masters understood this change and gave slaves greater plantation responsibilities. By the mid-eighteenth century, slaves not only produced most of the tobacco exported to Britain, but they also completed much of the simple craft work needed on plantations. Slave dominance of the productive processes gave them some leverage. Masters and their native-born slaves engaged in rudimentary negotiations that led to some accommodations in working conditions. Although masters maintained their physical power over slaves and successfully demanded high levels of crop production from them, slaves sometimes were able to control the pace of work.

The wealth, power, and prestige of whites depended upon the ownership of slaves. Once slaves achieved natural increase, masters no longer had to buy slaves to expand their labor force. Mid-eighteenth-century slaveowners, then, possessed both the means of production (land and slaves) and the means of *reproduction* of the means of production. The more slaves one owned, the more one would eventually possess, and the wealthier one would become. Only slaveholders, moreover, possessed high social standing: "The custom of the country is such," wrote a Baptist minister, "that without slaves, a man's children stand but a poor chance to marry in reputation," or even, according to another commentator, "to appear in polite company."[1]

As the social differences between whites and blacks diminished, a new form of racism emerged. Planters needed but disliked blacks. They expropriated their chattels' labor and sold their bodies on the open market, but knew they were humans like themselves. Planters increasingly turned to skin color, now the only immediately noticeable difference between the races, to demonstrate the necessity of slavery. Blacks were innately inferior, could never be full citizens. Nor should whites breach the color line and contaminate their own blood. This racial ideology only accentuated the spatial segregation of the races and hardened the caste barriers between them.[2]

Africans and Englishmen

Both mutual revulsion and daily contact characterized the often-strained relations between whites and the Africans they enslaved in the Chesapeake. Even before Africans arrived in large numbers, whites had judged their dark skin color as evil, and their lack of European culture sustained that impression. Africans practiced heathen religions, spoke incomprehensible tongues, and were reputed to have vast sexual appetites. Most Chesapeake blacks were enslaved in law by the 1660s and 1670s, and when Africans began pouring into the region in the early 1700s, both Chesapeake colonies had already enacted detailed slave codes.[3]

When these strange people refused to work or accept their new status, masters reacted with anger and discipline. "A new Negro, if he must be broke," wrote one commentator, "will require more hard Discipline than a

1. Duncan J. MacLeod, *Slavery, Race, and the American Revolution* (Cambridge, 1974), 73; James Reid, "The Religion of the Bible and the Religion of K[ing] W[illiam] County Compared" (1769), in Richard Beale Davis, ed., *The Colonial Virginia Satirist: Mid-Eighteenth-Century Commentaries on Politics, Religion, and Society* (American Philosophical Society, *Transactions*, N.S., LVII, pt. i [Philadelphia, 1967]), 48.
2. Winthrop D. Jordan, *White over Black: American Attitudes toward the Negro, 1550–1812* (Chapel Hill, N.C., 1968), chap. 7, esp. 304–308; MacLeod, *Slavery, Race, and Revolution*, chap. 2.
3. Jordan, *White over Black*, pt. 1; William Waller Hening, ed., *The Statutes at Large: Being a Collection of All the Laws of Virginia ...*, 13 vols. (Richmond, Philadelphia, 1809–1823), III, 447–462 (hereafter cited as *Virginia Statutes at Large*); William Hand Browne et al., eds., *Archives of Maryland ...*, 72 vols. (Baltimore, 1883–1972), XXX, 283–292 (hereafter cited as *Archives of Maryland*).

young Spaniel." Masters whipped disobedient new Negroes and used other punishment as well. Ann Joice, a Negro born in Barbados, was taken to England as a child and held as a servant; in 1668, she was sent to Maryland and indentured to Henry Darnall. Darnall employed her as a cook and refused to free her at the end of her term. Instead, he "burnt her indentures" and sent her to a neighboring plantation, where "she was kept in a kitchen celler for five or six months." Less acculturated new Negroes, who understood their predicament even less well than Joice, must have suffered similar punishment with some frequency.[4]

Even after new Negroes became reconciled to their status, masters and slaves disagreed about the way slaves ought to work. Planters expected their slaves to work from sunup to sundown at a consistent pace and to produce large quantities of tobacco and grain. New Negroes, however, retained some African attitudes toward work even under slavery. Africans worked for the present, in spurts according to inclination or season, rather than by the clock. They looked to the past rather than the future; the goal of a hereafter in future time, so important in Protestant religion and in the development of industrial work discipline, was missing from West African thought.[5]

Since masters feared their new Negroes' incompetence or sabotage, they forced them to perform the simplest and most repetitive tasks in the tobacco fields and left skilled labor to white artisans and acculturated slaves. Since most Africans arrived during the summer, after tobacco was already growing, masters set newly arrived slaves to work hoeing the ground to keep the tobacco plants free from weeds and worms. Masters or more acculturated slaves taught new Negroes to cut the top leaves from tobacco plants to improve the quality of the crop and to prune the suckers that replaced these leaves. New Negroes helped harvest the crop in August or September, a month or two after they arrived, and then placed it into tobacco houses to be cured for a month. Finally, they learned to strip the leaves from the stalks and to pack the leaves into hogsheads. The more delicate tasks of preparing the ground for sowing the seeds (in January and February), sowing the seeds (in February or March), and the delicate replanting of the young plants into tobacco hills when the crop was two inches high (in May and

4. "Eighteenth-Century Maryland as Portrayed in the 'Itinerant Observations' of Edward Kimber," *Maryland Historical Magazine*, LI (1956), 327–328; Court of Appeals of the Western Shore, BW#10 (1800–1801), 456–483, esp. 459–460 (quote), 470, 483, Maryland Hall of Records, Annapolis (MHR).
5. E. P. Thompson, "Time, Work-Discipline, and Industrial Capitalism," *Past and Present*, No. 38 (1967), 56–97; John S. Mbiti, *African Religions and Philosophy* (New York, 1969), chap. 3; Eugene D. Genovese, *Roll, Jordan, Roll: The World the Slaves Made* (New York, 1975), 285–324; Gerald W. Mullin, *Flight and Rebellion: Slave Resistance in Eighteenth-Century Virginia* (New York, 1972), 42–45.

June) took place at least half a year after the Africans arrived and when the process of acculturation had already begun.[6]

During the first half of the century, nearly all slaves, both African and native, remained agricultural laborers. Nine of every ten male slaves, and probably every female, in Prince George's County worked as field hands in 1733. Most of the others were drivers of small groups of workers or men who operated their own quarter with one or two others. Only 4 percent of the men were artisans, and almost all of those were carpenters and coopers who stayed on their master's plantation repairing outbuildings and making tobacco hogsheads (see table 42).

Even Robert "King" Carter, who owned 390 slaves of working age when he died in 1732, rarely trained his slaves to be craftsmen. Three of every four of them were field hands, and an eighth were "foremen," who apparently assisted the overseers in directing the work force. About 6 percent of Carter's men were sawyers, carters, and boatmen, jobs that distinguished them from ordinary field hands. About 7 percent of the men were artisans, nearly double the proportion in Prince George's, a large majority of whom were Virginia-born carpenters and coopers.

Most artisans who worked for Chesapeake planters before 1740 were white servants or householders, and this fact was particularly true of tradesmen other than carpenters and coopers. More than three-quarters of the artisans in Prince George's in 1733 were white, and even a magnate like Robert Carter chose to employ whites. Although two-thirds of his twenty-six artisans were slaves, seven of his ten tailors, blacksmiths, bricklayers, butchers, ship carpenters, and glaziers were white indentured servants.[7]

However much planters might have disliked the sight of blacks, they came into close contact with them. More than half the masters in tidewater owned fewer than five slaves, and work units were even smaller. Between 1688 and 1744 nearly two-thirds of the slaves in Anne Arundel County, Maryland, worked on units with six or fewer slaves, half of them on units

---

6. For seasonal patterns in tobacco cultivation, see T. H. Breen, "The Culture of Agriculture: The Symbolic World of the Tidewater Planter, 1760–1790" in David D. Hall *et al.*, eds., *Saints and Revolutionaries: Essays on Early American History* (New York, 1984), 255–260; Lewis Cecil Gray, *History of Agriculture in the Southern United States to 1860*, I (Washington, D.C., 1933), 215–216; Philip David Morgan, "The Development of Slave Culture in Eighteenth Century Plantation America" (Ph.D. diss., University College, London, 1977), 89–96; Hugh Jones, *The Present State of Virginia, from Whence Is Inferred a Short View of Maryland and North Carolina*, ed., Richard L. Morton (Chapel Hill, N.C., 1956 [orig. publ. London, 1724]), 76–79; Gregory A. Stiverson and Patrick H. Butler III, eds., "Virginia in 1732: The Travel Diary of William Hugh Grove," *Virginia Magazine of History and Biography*, LXXXV (1977), 67–69.

7. Black Books, II, 109–124, linked to Prince George's Land Records, Court Records, Inventories, and Wills, 1725–1735, MHR; Robert Carter Inventory, Carter Papers, Virginia Historical Society, Richmond (VHS).

Table 42. *Occupations of Male Slaves, 1733*

	Percentage in Group	
Occupation	Prince George's[a] ($N=1{,}323$)	Robert Carter's Plantations ($N=245$)
Agricultural		
Field hands	90	74
Drivers	2	13
Family farmers	3	0
Total	95	87
Semiskilled		
Servants	1	0
Sawyers	0	3
Carters	0	2
Boatsmen	0	1
Total	1	6
Craftsmen		
Carpenters and coopers	4	6
Others	[b]	1
Total	4	7
Grand total	100	100

Sources: Black Books, II, 109–124, and Prince George's Inventories, 1725–1739, MHR; Robert Carter Inventory, Carter Papers, VHS.

Notes: [a]Occupational structure estimated by applying inventory sex ratios to the 1733 tax list in Black Books, weighting slave occupations in the inventories by unit sizes in the tax lists, and determining the numbers of drivers and family farmers from size of units and presence of whites. [b]Less than .5%.

with one or two other laborers.[8] Nearly a third of all adult slaves in Prince George's in 1733 lived on quarters with one or two other adults, and these quarters constituted two-thirds of the units in the county. On these quarters, the master usually worked with his slaves, but a few were permitted to operate small quarters without constant white supervision. Forty-nine black

8. Russell R. Menard, "The Maryland Slave Population, 1658 to 1730: A Demographic Profile of Blacks in Four Counties," *William and Mary Quarterly*, 3d Ser., XXXII (1975), 35, 50; Lorena S. Walsh, "Changing Work Roles for Slave Labor in Chesapeake Agriculture" (paper presented at conference, "The Colonial Experience: the Eighteenth-Century Chesapeake," Baltimore, Sept. 1984), tables 1–3.

adults, a twelfth of those who lived on units of one to three slaves, worked on farms slaves ran. Most of the larger quarters, where two-thirds of the slaves resided, were operated by overseers or by the master and his sons. More than seven-tenths of the planters who owned ten or more adult slaves, but only four-tenths of those who possessed five to nine slaves, employed at least one unrelated white worker who could act as overseer (see table 43).

Even the wealthiest planters divided their working slaves into small groups. Robert Carter, for instance, put his slaves on forty-eight different quarters, scattered over nine counties. More than half his slaves worked on units of fewer than ten workers, and only twenty-three slaves labored on his home plantation. Carter sought supervision for his far-flung slaves, hiring overseers to operate forty-six of his quarters, and only three of them had responsibilities at more than two different units. No overseer lived at either a small quarter with four workers or on the home plantation. Seventeen indentured servants were employed at the home quarter, however, and one of them could have functioned as an overseer (see table 43).

Given the close contact between white men and black women, some interracial sexual intimacy was bound to develop. Some masters, overseers, and servants raped black women, and others established longer relationships with them. Few of these encounters were recorded, however, for neither fornication with a slave woman nor the birth of a bastard mulatto child was a crime. Though rape was not a crime, white men found open cohabitation with black women socially undesirable. When William Hardie of Prince George's accused Daniel Carroll, a wealthy merchant of the same county, of buggery and of keeping mulattoes, since "he ... could use them as he pleased," Carroll sued for slander, finding both charges equally harmful. Legal marriage between the races was forbidden. Only one white man in Prince George's between 1720 and 1780 attempted to marry a mulatto woman, the daughter of a free black man, and he was indicted; the defendant apparently reconsidered or proved his wife to be white, for the case was dropped in 1744.[9]

White women were severely penalized for sexual contact with black men if they were caught. In Virginia, the woman had to pay a stiff fine or suffer being sold into servitude for five years; in Maryland, the term was seven years. Their mulatto children, in both colonies, were sold and had to serve as slaves until they reached age thirty-one. Despite these penalties, a tiny number of white women slept with slave men. Sixteen white women

9. Clinton Ashley Ellefson, "The County Courts and the Provincial Court in Maryland, 1733–1763" (Ph.D. diss., University of Maryland, 1963), 544–546; Prince George's Court Records, AA, 191 and CC, 17.

Table 43. *Size of Working Units, 1733*

Size of Unit (No. of Slaves)	Prince George's		Robert "King" Carter's Plantations	
	Percentage		Percentage	
	Units ($N=514$)	Slaves on ($N=2,024$)	Units ($N=48$)	Slaves on ($N=390$)
1–3	65	30	8	2
4–9	28	42	60	51
10–19	5	19	27	37
20+	1	9	4	11
Total	99	100	99	100

Sources: Black Books, II, 109–124, MHR; Robert Carter Inventory, Carter Papers, VHS.

were convicted of bearing twenty-five mulatto bastards in Prince George's in the 1720s and 1730s. Twelve of these women were indentured servants, new to the country; the other four were daughters of poor planters. Only five of them continued to see their black lovers until they repeated their crime. Mary Wedge, a servant of Thomas Harwood, persisted in a common-law marriage to a slave on a nearby plantation and bore seven children. The uniqueness of her case points to the limits of miscegenation in the Chesapeake.[10]

Slaves as Class and Caste

The Afro-American slaves who dominated the adult black population of the Chesapeake colonies after 1740 had a firmer understanding of the requirements and social rules of chattel slavery than their African ancestors. First, they had to accept the absolute power of their masters over their persons: they could be sold or transferred at any time, thereby suffering separation from kindred and friends. Not only did they have to refrain from assaulting or stealing from whites, they also owed every white complete deference.

10. Prince George's Court Records, 1720–1739; Winthrop D. Jordan, "American Chiaroscuro: The Status and Definition of Mulattoes in the British Colonies," *WMQ*, 3d Ser., XIX (1962), 183–200; *Virginia Statutes at Large*, III, 453; *Archives of Maryland*, XXX, 289–290; Prince George's Court Records, N, 358–359, O, 345–346, S, 297–298, V, 108, 410, W, 505, and X, 192, for Wedge.

Slaves had to obey their masters and work diligently for them and take in return only those goods their master gave them. Finally, slaves had to avoid social contact with whites, and sexual relations with white women were forbidden. These rules constituted a primer of race relations.

Although native-born slaves were subjected to the absolute power of the master, they also belonged to their own families and communities. Masters sometimes recognized these institutions and felt some responsibility for nurturing them. Whites tried to keep members of black families together, for they did not want to risk sullen, unproductive work that might result from separations. Afro-American slaves trained their children in craft skills they had acquired, and masters permitted these new artisans to practice their trades because their skills made them more valuable. Masters believed that they had to feed and clothe their slave families adequately and often looked the other way when their charges augmented the family diet from the farm's fruit, grain, and fowl.

The relations between Afro-American slaves and their white masters were fraught with conflict and tension. Slaves continually tried to stretch their privileges and turn them into rights, while masters resisted encroachments on their authority. Though a slave who ran away to a neighboring plantation to visit friends or kindred would probably be whipped when he returned or was recaptured, he cemented community feeling and undercut the master's authority by leaving the plantation without permission and missing work. Despite the frustration and anger of masters, slaves sometimes refused to work at the pace demanded of them and played master against overseer to try to gain the upper hand. Although neither of these strategies gave slaves much independence, they created living space within the system and defined the boundaries of race relations.[11]

Afro-American slaves knew from early childhood that they would suffer arbitrary separation from kindred and learned that they had little power to stop it. When the master died, he divided his slaves among his children. When a white child left home, his father gave him a slave as a personal servant. If he got into financial trouble, he sold his slaves. For example, Elizabeth Harding, of lower Frederick County, Maryland, gave a slave man and boy to her son Charles just before her death. Charles called some neighbors together to witness the transfer in February 1769, "soon after which three Negroes entered the room one after the other, when . . . Eliza. Harding took . . . Saml. and Geo. by the Arm or hand and thrust them forward to her son Charles." This description of racial relations is suggestive. The slaves allowed themselves to be pushed toward their new master, and they neither protested nor resisted this undignified behavior.[12]

11. This viewpoint is developed in Genovese, *Roll, Jordan, Roll*, bk. 1, pt. I.
12. Testamentary Proceedings, XLIV, 521–524 (quote 522), MHR.

Similar scenes occurred repeatedly, and slave children were particularly vulnerable, for they made splendid gifts for the children of planters. For example, in 1761 Thomas Brooke, a wealthy planter in Prince George's, sent his two-year-old son Isaac to live with Elizabeth Batt, a miller who lived fifteen miles away, and "at the same time had a negroe named Ally brought up to tend him." Ally was probably an adolescent girl, forced to leave home to serve her new master. More frequently, these human gifts did not leave home until their new master matured, but they learned at a young age that they were property that could be deeded from person to person. In 1749, Samuel White of Prince George's gave a five-year-old Negro girl named Murrier to his son Guy, then about twelve, and also distributed other slaves to his children. It was harvest time, and many neighbors were at the White plantation to help cut wheat. White called Murrier to him, in front of these white witnesses, and "laid his hand on her head and said this girl I have given to my son Guy White." Then, with Murrier "in his hand," he said that he "would give Ball to his son Samuel White, Harry to his son Joseph and Pegg to his daughter Casey."[13]

All this and much more, slaves had to accept with good humor. In fact, slaves often showed great deference toward their master and other whites. The most acculturated slaves sometimes stuttered when confronted with strange white people, fearing that they would get themselves or some other slaves in trouble and hoping that the "sharp questioning" would soon cease. A complaining slave had to be particularly deferential. Philip Fithian, tutor on the plantation of Robert Carter of Nomini Hall, remembered one encounter between slave and master vividly. "An old Negro Man came with a complaint to Mr Carter of the Overseer that he does not allow him his Peck of corn a Week," Fithian wrote in 1774. "The humble posture in which the old Fellow placed himself before he began moved me. . . . He sat himself down on the Floor clasp'd his Hands together, and with his face directly to Mr *Carter*, and then began his Narration."[14]

Some of the deference slaves displayed before masters was a facade meant to protect them from retribution. Afro-American slaves learned from each other how to defy while seeming to obey, and psychological warfare between masters and slaves resulted. Field hands forgot their orders, feigned illness, worked only when watched, or pretended they did not understand the assigned task. They continued to practice habits like drinking

13. Testamentary Papers, box 75, folder 15, and Court of Appeals Record, TDM#1 (1788), 83–85, MHR.
14. Mullin, *Flight and Rebellion*, 79–82; Hunter Dickinson Farish, ed., *Journal and Letters of Philip Vickers Fithian, 1773–1774: A Plantation Tutor of the Old Dominion* (Williamsburg, Va., 1957), 129; J.F.D. Smyth, *A Tour in the United States of America . . .* , 2 vols. (London, 1784), I, 39; Robert E. Brown and B. Katherine Brown, *Virginia, 1705–1786: Democracy or Aristocracy?* (East Lansing, Mich., 1964), 66–67.

that they knew would annoy their masters and ignored the inevitable punishment. Even William Sydebotham, a "benevolent and popular" English merchant in Bladensburg, Maryland, eventually tired of his slaves' antics. Sydebotham owned two slaves, "Wat, a house servant: a very sprightly actor, saucy, drinking quarlesome fellow" of about thirty-five, and Jerry, seventeen, "a good natured heavy handed creature." Nat got "drunk every evening while his master was getting as [drunk]" and "contrived to annoy his master . . . by getting up a quarrel with poor Jerry." Sydebotham "bore it as long as he could" but finally punished them by forcing Wat and Jerry to strip and fight each other. Both were knocked down in a long, vicious fight. They learned their lesson well; after the fight, Sydebotham drank "his afternoons' booze in peace."[15]

However artfully they challenged their masters, slaves quickly learned not to attack whites. Capital crimes, other than burglary, rarely occurred in Virginia during the eighteenth century. Slaves there committed only one act of violence (rape, murder, attempted murder, or poisoning) per county every ten years. Rape of white women by slave men was especially rare: only forty-nine men were convicted of rape, one conviction per county every fifty years. Even if numerous black murderers and rapists were lynched, the rate of black violence against white men was still low. Far more burglars were brought to justice: there were three cases every two years in most counties.[16]

Blacks in Prince George's also avoided crimes of violence against whites. There were only three cases of arson, one of perjury, and three assaults against whites by slaves there between 1740 and 1779. Murders and rapes were very rare: blacks were charged with five murders or attempted murders and two rapes of whites during these decades. One can easily understand why few of them killed or raped whites: eight of the nine slaves charged with these crimes were convicted and hanged.[17]

Only a very angry slave would attack a white. In June 1779, Jack Wood, Jack Crane, and Davy murdered their overseer, William Elson. Wood and Crane were descendants of Ann Joice, the Barbados Negro who believed her freedom had been stolen from her. Because of their descent, the two

15. Mullin, *Flight and Rebellion*, 53–57; William Wirt Papers, II, 4909–4910, Library of Congress, Washington, D.C.
16. Philip J. Schwarz, "Slave Criminality and the Slave Community: Patterns of Slave Assertiveness in Eighteenth-Century Virginia" (paper presented at the 1978 Southern Historical Association meeting), tables 1–2. There were 1,244 crimes against property: stealing (1,080), arson (36), receiving stolen goods (20), hog stealing (89), other (19), and 890 convictions (72%) in the group.
17. Prince George's Court Records, 1740–1779, and Provincial Court Records, 1740–1776 (abstracted by Ross Kimmell), MHR.

"thought themselves above the level of common slaves" and were unwilling to tolerate hard usage from an overseer. Elson was murdered while "walking with some of his Negroes in the Woods, and having before threatened to chastise one of them for an offense, was struck with a club." Though Elson begged for his life when he recovered, they "cut his throat from Ear to Ear with an Axe." One of the men confessed, and all three were hanged. This crime was such a singular exception to the general peacefulness of blacks in the county that it was remembered thirty years later.[18]

A slowly increasing number of native-born slaves in Prince George's stole the property of whites. Although African-born thieves stole trinkets worth a shilling or two, native slaves appreciated European consumer goods and risked their lives to take food, clothing, or liquor worth several pounds to supplement their sometimes meager rations. Slaves were whipped by their masters for stealing from their own plantations or brought before a justice of the peace for petty thievery. More serious cases reached the county court: between 1740 and 1779, fifty-eight slaves were indicted for theft. Nearly three-quarters of them were convicted, and more than half were sentenced to hang. At least four of the burglars were pardoned by governor and council, but the rest of the sentences were carried out.[19]

The origin of conflicts between masters and slaves can be found in differing conceptions of the responsibilities of masters held by whites and blacks. Masters felt they had a duty to feed, clothe, and house their slaves; in return they expected unquestioned execution of their orders. In a sermon preached to whites, Thomas Bacon asked: if masters "should keep their Slaves in a starving condition, without allowing them Meat for their Bellies, or Cloathing for their Backs, or Shelter to lie under. . . . Would not all Mankind cry out Shame at such inhuman, and cruel treatment?" Bacon told slaves, in another sermon, that masters would provide their subsistence and, in return, "You are to serve your masters with chearfullness, and humility."[20]

Afro-Americans, in contrast, believed they deserved reciprocity from

18. Prince George's Court Records, XXIX, 589–590; *Maryland Gazette*, June 28, 1770; Court of Appeals of the Western Shore, BW#10, 459, 480; *Archives of Maryland*, XXXII, 370–371.
19. Prince George's Court Records, 1720–1779, and Provincial Court Records, 1720–1776; Schwarz, "Slave Criminality," 5–7; *Archives of Maryland*, XXXII, 107–108, 197–198, 269, 272. For crimes punishable by a single justice, see Ellefson, "County Courts," 175. Between 1740 and 1779, 74% of the accused burglars were convicted, and 54% of them (40% of the accused) were sentenced to hang. In all, 33% of the accused (44% of those convicted) were hanged.
20. Thomas Bacon, *Four Sermons, upon the Great and Indispensible Duty of All Christian Masters and Mistresses to Bring up Their Negro Slaves in the Knowledge and Fear of God* (London, 1750), 49; and *Four Sermons, Preached at the Parish Church of St. Peter, in Talbot County* (Bath, 1783; orig. publ. London, 1753), 39, 83–84.

their masters for their labor. They produced their masters' tobacco and grain, and without their labor, the system would collapse. Slaves expected subsistence—and more. Their families, communities, and work groups were not to be separated arbitrarily. They expected to be allowed to use livestock and poultry raised on the quarters and spend evenings and Sundays as they pleased. Finally, they were to work at a pace set by their black coworkers and not by whites. When masters broke this implicit contract, their native slaves ran away or worked poorly in the fields.[21]

Masters provided slaves with a subsistence diet but permitted them to supplement it on their own initiative. Though food was plentiful, slave diets were not well balanced. Masters gave slaves corn rations, and cornbread or cornbread seasoned with pork was the major slave staple. Although some masters provided slaves only with corn, others included pork frequently and fish and beef on occasion. On larger plantations, slaves added to their diets from the fruits and vegetables grown in the small gardens they tended in their spare time and fowl they raised in their yards.[22] George Washington thought his adult slaves should have eleven pounds of corn, two pounds of fish, and half a pound of meat each week along with whatever milk, fat, and chickens they might find themselves; nonetheless, fish—a major source of protein—often failed to reach them. Landon Carter, a less benevolent master, refused to distribute a meat ration, preferring to "only reward them with a bit now and then as they deserved it by their work and diligence"; and he dismissed complaints of inadequate corn rations as "a contrivance of the people to get more to feed the[i]r fowls."[23] However inadequate the nutritional content of their diets, slaves apparently did not suffer from malnutri-

21. See Genovese, *Roll, Jordan, Roll*, 89–91, 133–137, 142–147, for a provocative development of these ideas.

22. Mullin, *Flight and Rebellion*, 50; Stiverson and Butler, eds., "Virginia in 1732," *VMHB*, LXXXV (1977), 32–33; Testamentary Papers, box 45, folder 26, and Chancery Records, XVI, 318–319, XXVI, 68–69, MHR; Rind's *Virginia Gazette*, Mar. 17, 1768; Smyth, *Tour in United States*, I, 43–45, 69; Isaac Weld, Jr., *Travels through North America and the Provinces of Upper and Lower Canada* (London, 1799), 84–85; marquis de Chastellux, *Travels in North America in the Years 1780, 1781, and 1782*, ed. and trans. Howard C. Rice, Jr. (Chapel Hill, N.C., 1963), II, 432; Charles Ball, *Fifty Years in Chains*, ed. Philip S. Foner (New York, 1970 [orig. publ. as *Slavery in the United States: A Narrative of the Life and Adventures . . .* (New York, 1837)]), 25–26.

23. John C. Fitzpatrick, ed., *The Writings of George Washington from the Original Manuscript Sources, 1745–1799*, 39 vols. (Washington, D.C., 1931–1944), XXXI, 186–187 (gives annual expenditures; in determining weekly ration, I have assumed adults received twice that of children), XXXII, 65, 294, 474–475, XXXIII, 201–202, 303, 336–337; Jack P. Greene, ed., *The Diary of Colonel Landon Carter of Sabine Hall, 1752–1778*, 2 vols. (Charlottesville, Va., 1965), II, 602, 871 (discussed in Jeannie Ford Dissette, "Landon Carter of Sabine Hall: A Master of Slaves" [seminar paper, University of Pennsylvania, 1971], 6–8).

tion: slave women were healthy enough to conceive and bear children throughout the year.[24]

Slave clothing was made of coarse imported linen and homespun wool and cotton. Whites gave male hands shoes, shirts, and trousers once a year, and their female hands received shoes and shifts. Male runaways typically wore shirts, trousers, stockings, shoes, and several jackets, and some owned hats and coats. Ordinary hands often possessed a change of clothes but usually owned only one pair of shoes and stockings. Sometimes slaves had to earn a fuller wardrobe: Landon Carter, for instance, "allowed them but one shirt" and "obliged them to buy linnen to make their other shirt instead of buying liquor with their fowls." Masters dressed their personal servants in waistcoats and petticoat breeches; artisans (and other slaves, on occasion) earned enough money to procure high-quality cloth and make fancy clothing.[25]

As we have seen, slaves who lived on large plantations often dwelt in duplex homes measuring about sixteen by sixteen feet; on smaller plantations, they lived in an outbuilding or in a smaller Negro quarter, usually measuring twelve by sixteen or twenty feet. These were not permanent structures; rather, they were hastily built shacks, with wooden chimneys and earthen floors. The cabins were poorly heated, and slaves insisted on receiving blankets for their straw beds to help ward off the cold. Large planters, like Jefferson and Washington, moved these quarters from field to field when new areas were opened to cultivation.[26]

Although masters encouraged stable family relations, even the wealthiest planter could not avoid separating family members when he went bankrupt, purchased a new plantation, or died. The sale or gift of a slave to kindred, moreover, permitted whites to assert their authority over their

24. Darrett Rutman *et al.*, "Rhythms of Life: Black and White Seasonality in the Early Chesapeake," *Journal of Interdisciplinary History*, XI (1980–1981), 33–35, 51–52. Conceptions, however, did cluster around the period of end of harvest to early winter, with birth peaks in late spring and summer.

25. Mullin, *Flight and Rebellion*, 51; runaway ads in the *Md. Gaz.*, 1745–1779; Prince George's Accounts, DD#6, 175–181, and Testamentary Papers, box 45, folder 26, and box 54, folder 10, MHR; Greene, ed., *Diary of Carter*, I, 484, 299, 242, 281; Dissette, "Landon Carter," 8–10; Fitzpatrick, ed., *Writings of Washington*, XXXIV, 379.

26. Gregory A. Stiverson, "Landless Husbandmen: Tenants on the Maryland Proprietary Manors in the Eighteenth Century: An Economic Study" (Ph.D. diss., Johns Hopkins University, 1973), 101–108, 572–578; 1798 direct tax lists for Prince George's County, Maryland Historical Society, Baltimore (MHS); three slave quarters in St. Mary's County, Maryland, examined by Cary Carson and the author; Edwin Morris Betts, ed., *Thomas Jefferson's Farm Book, with Commentary and Relevant Extracts from Other Writings* (Princeton, N.J., 1953), 6, 337–339, 77 (facsimiles); Fitzpatrick, ed., *Writings of Washington*, XXXIII, 177–178, 196, XXXIV, 217.

blacks. George Washington, for instance, took four men from John Mercer in 1786 in payment of a debt, even though it was "as much against my inclination as it can be against your's, to hurt the feelings of those unhappy people by a separation of man and wife, or of families." Slaves passed from white to white tried to visit family members left behind. More than a fifth of all slave runaways advertised in the *Virginia Gazette* between 1730 and 1787 had been sold or transferred at least once, and many tried to return to their old home.[27]

Since whites did not fulfill black expectations concerning their social lives but merely provided subsistence, Afro-Americans continued to challenge their masters' authority. Petty thievery reached epidemic proportions on the largest plantations. Washington's and Landon Carter's slaves, for example, frequently stole livestock and cloth to supplement their rations or to sell for liquor. Whites could not understand why their support of their slaves in a manner commonly thought appropriate to their condition did not produce respectful behavior and regularly applied the lash.[28]

The uneasy relations between whites and native-born blacks formed the basis for the social separation of the races. Whenever blacks and whites came together outside the work place, a ritual of black subservience ruled their intercourse. This deference covered great hostility. Both whites and blacks vented their aggression through a system of regular but highly ritualized conflict, in which slaves challenged individual whites without attacking the slave system itself. Despite all the conflict—and perhaps even because it gave slaves a limited outlet for aggression—whites began to give their slaves greater responsibilities and grant them freedom to form their own communities.

More and more planters saw little of their slaves away from work. As the holdings of planters grew in the 1750s and 1760s, masters did not subdivide their quarters, and as a result, the size of quarters increased, and a rising proportion of slaves lived on these large units. These quarters were little villages, often located in a gully several hundred yards from the plantation house, too far away to be seen. Masters had to make a special trip to the quarter if they wished to check up on their slaves' behavior. Apparently, masters visited slave quarters infrequently: when Ferdinand-M. Bayard visited a slave quarter in 1791, his hostess, he wrote, "could not imagine what

27. Fitzpatrick, ed., *Writings of Washington*, XXIX, 56, 83, 117; Lathan Algerna Windley, "A Profile of Runaway Slaves in Virginia and South Carolina from 1730 through 1787" (Ph.D. diss., University of Iowa, 1974), 133, shows that 19% (241 of 1,286) had one previous owner and 4% (45) had two or three previous owners.

28. Fitzpatrick, ed., *Writings of Washington*, XXII, 246, XXXIII, 11–12; Dissette, "Landon Carter," 8; Bacon, *Four Sermons, upon the Great Duty*, 89–90.

had detained me for such a long time in a Negro cabin."[29] Less wealthy planters probably saw their slaves more frequently, but their slave men sometimes left home in the evenings, preferring to go to larger quarters to talk, drink, or visit their families.

Whites probably welcomed these changes, for they helped separate the races. Wealthy planters feared alliance of poor whites and slaves and discouraged them from trading goods or planning crimes together. Even if some whites aided runaways, traded with slaves, or borrowed their music, others practiced social segregation. Washington insisted that his white workers not live with the slaves, but maintain a separate dwelling: "To mix them among the Negros," he wrote, "would be attended with many evils"; workers and their families "will get disgusted by living among the Negros."[30]

Interracial sexual relations and miscegenation, especially between slave men and white women, became even more disreputable, and their incidence may have declined after 1740. In Prince George's, for instance, only ten white women were charged with mulatto bastardy in the 1740s and 1750s, and they bore, in total, only thirteen mulatto infants, a rate less than half that of the 1720s and 1730s. Miscegenation demeaned a white woman and all her kinfolk and friends. When Mary Skinner, wife of a Calvert County gentleman, bore a black child in 1769, her husband was enraged. She had "after all the Love and Tenderness that could possibly be shown by Man to Woman polluted my Bed, by taking to her in my Stead, her own Negro Slave, by whom she hath a child, which hath occassioned so much Disgrace to me and my Family, that I have forbid her my Sight any more."[31]

White men probably continued to visit slave quarters to rape or conduct casual affairs with slave women with some unknowable frequency, but a man's reputation could be ruined by fathering a mulatto child; he "would be scorned, dishonored; every house would be closed to him." Although white women apparently tolerated casual liaisons between their sons or husbands and slave women, they drew the line at serious love affairs or cohabitation, for that would elevate black women to the status that only free white

---

29. Betts, ed., *Jefferson's Farm Book*, 6; Jesse Krasen, *Tuckahoe Plantation* (Richmond, Va., 1975), frontispiece, 111; plat of St. Inigoes Plantation, ca. 1810, drawn by Cary Carson; observation of three extant quarters in St. Mary's County; Ferdinand-M. Bayard, *Travels of a Frenchman in Maryland and Virginia* . . . , ed. and trans. Ben C. McCary (Williamsburg, Va., 1950), 14.
30. Fitzpatrick, ed., *Writings of Washington*, XXXIV, 13; Morgan, "Development of Slave Culture," 218–224, 227–235.
31. Prince George's Court Records, 1740–1759 (records of 1760s often omit race of defendant); *Md. Gaz.*, Oct. 12, 1769.

women should possess. During the early nineteenth century, a Virginia master who took a slave mistress could be sued for divorce by petition to the legislature, and, apparently, these petitions were often granted.[32]

Structure and Organization of Labor

Masters and their Afro-American slaves came together most often in the fields and workshops of the Chesapeake colonies. The growing dominance of native-born workers in the slave labor force after 1740 transformed both the structure and organization of work. As native slaves replaced African immigrants, blacks performed an ever-rising proportion of the agricultural and industrial labor of the region. In order to maintain control over production and ensure their own continued prosperity while slaves assumed more responsible positions, masters modified the organization of work. Native slaves recognized their changed position in the plantation hierarchy and used their increasing dominance of the plantation economy to control the pace of work.

The modest expansion of slave opportunity after 1740 can be explained by three related processes: a new willingness of whites to assign their native-born slaves every task needed to produce tobacco, an increase in the size of work units, and the desire of black workers to pass skills on to their children. At the same time that planters first trained slaves in crafts like carpentry and cooperage, the size of quarters was growing rapidly through natural increase. Masters found these larger units efficient, and the wealthiest gentlemen attempted to create self-sufficient plantations, complete with slave farmers, artisans, and domestic servants. Once trained, slaves often passed skills on to their sons, thus perpetuating occupational diversity.

White training of slaves, however, was limited to those jobs that did not require literacy. Slaves understood the power of literacy, and many probably wanted to read and write, but whites used their monopoly of reading and writing to help control black behavior, requiring written passes for slaves to travel alone. Although Samuel Davies, the Presbyterian revivalist, trained many slaves to read and write in the 1750s and although thirty slave children a year attended a school in Williamsburg between 1765 and 1770, nearly all slaves remained unlettered. Those who did learn to read and write proceeded to use that skill against their masters. About a twentieth of all Virginia runaways—probably mostly artisans and servants who had ac-

32. Bayard, *Travels of a Frenchman*, 20; James Hugo Johnston, *Race Relations in Virginia and Miscegenation in the South, 1776–1860* (Amherst, Mass., 1970), 237–250.

cess to books—knew enough to forge a pass, and more than half of them hoped to pass as free in towns, where their skill would be of great practical value.[33]

As natives replaced Africans, the number of artisans on larger plantations slowly rose. The Addisons, wealthy Prince George's planters, illustrate this process. The first two Addisons, who owned mostly immigrant slaves, trained few artisans. When John Addison, the immigrant, died in 1705, he owned five men, including a mulatto carpenter, one of the first slave artisans in Maryland. His son Thomas died in 1727, leaving two slave artisans among thirty-one male hands. John Addison of Thomas, who inherited the bulk of his father's slaves, owned twenty male hands, including two artisans when he died in 1764. His son Thomas inherited many slaves from his father and uncle. During the 1760s and 1770s, he trained at least four slaves in craft skills. When he died in 1775, he owned twenty-seven male hands, including four carpenters, a joiner, a shoemaker, and a tailor.[34]

As the proportion of slaves living on units of twenty or more slaves of all ages increased, the size of work units increased as well. Planters in Anne Arundel County, Maryland, for instance, operated increasingly larger work units. The proportion of slaves who toiled on quarters with only one or two other adults diminished from three-tenths between 1700 and 1744 to less than a sixth between 1745 and 1777. At the same time, the proportion who worked on units of ten or more rose from less than a fifth to more than a quarter.[35] Moreover, the wealthiest planters no longer divided their slaves among numerous small quarters, but operated fewer, consolidated plantations. More than half of Robert Carter's slaves worked on units of fewer than ten adult blacks in 1733, but only a fifth of the slaves owned by four wealthy gentlemen in the 1770s and 1780s labored on units that small. All four operated large home quarters, each with more than thirty workers, and more than half their slaves toiled on units with at least twenty workers (see table 43 and fig. 30).

As the size of plantations increased, more masters owned enough field hands to place men profitably in craft positions. Slave jobs were more di-

33. Samuel Davies, *Letters from the Rev. Samuel Davies, etc. Shewing the State of Religion in Virginia (Particularly among the Negroes)* . . . (London, 1757), 12–13, 6–7; Thad W. Tate, *The Negro in Eighteenth-Century Williamsburg*, 2d ed. (Williamsburg, Va., 1972), 76–85; Mullin, *Flight and Rebellion*, 76, 80–81, 93–94, 111, 114, 121, 130; Windley, "Profile of Runaway Slaves," 204, shows that 76 of 1,276 runaways forged passes and 45 of them attempted to pass as free.

34. Prince George's Inventories, box 2, folder 11, TB#1, 64–66, GS#1, 230–237, GS#2, 37–43, 334–336, box 21, folder 31; Prince George's Wills, box 10, folder 14, box 11, folder 15.

35. Walsh, "Changing Work Roles," table 3.

Fig. 30. *Size of Working Units of Large Planters*

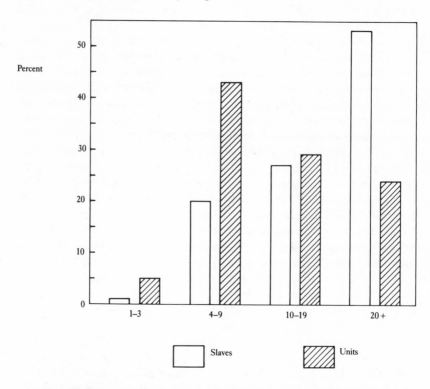

Sources: Edwin Morris Betts, ed., *Thomas Jefferson's Farm Book, with Commentary and Relevant Excerpts from Other Writings* (Princeton, N.J., 1953), 15–18 (Jefferson, 1774); Charles Carroll Account Book, Carroll Papers, MHS (Carroll, 1773–1774); Donald Jackson and Dorothy Twohig, eds., *The Diaries of George Washington*, IV, *1784–June 1786* (Charlottesville, Va., 1978), 277–283 (Washington, 1786); Robert Carter Deed of Manumission, Carter Papers, Duke University (film at CW)(Carter, 1791).

versified in Prince George's in 1776 than in 1733. The proportion of male slaves who toiled as agricultural laborers declined, and plowmen and mowers, who possessed specialized skills, began appearing in the county in the 1750s and 1760s. The proportion of artisans and domestic servants nearly doubled. Slave skills multiplied: until 1760, nearly all slave artisans were carpenters or coopers who repaired farm structures and made tobacco hogsheads, but by the 1770s, two-fifths of the county's tradesmen were shoemakers, blacksmiths, shipwrights, masons, and tailors. None of these artisans could be fully employed on a single plantation. Masters either had to solicit work for them or allow them to find work for themselves (see table 44).[36]

The number of slave craftsmen and domestic servants was directly related to plantation size. Artisans were rarely found on farms with fewer than five workers, but almost every plantation in Prince George's with more than ten laborers included an artisan or two. The wealthiest planters in the region owned a disproportionate number of artisans: more than a fifth of all men on four large Chesapeake plantations were craftsmen, four times the proportion in Prince George's. Nearly all the domestic servants—cooks, maids, waitingmen—lived on the largest plantations in the region. In fact, nearly a quarter of all slave artisans and a third of the personal servants in Virginia during the 1780s were trained on the plantations of only forty gentlemen, farms that housed but a twentieth of the state's slaves.[37]

Once slave artisans were trained, they could be readily sold or passed from parents to children. A wealthy heir did not have to train artisans, for they were bequeathed to him. In the early 1770s, Thomas Jefferson owned 41 slaves, including twenty-four workers and two or three artisans and four or five servants. The diversity of his slave force was greatly increased when he inherited 11 slaves from his mother and gained control of 135 slaves his wife inherited from her father in 1774. Among the Wayles slaves were four carpenters, four watermen, two smiths, and a shoemaker.[38]

Almost all women continued to work in the fields. Perhaps a twentieth of slave women in Prince George's were house servants, and a few more were spinners and weavers on large plantations. Only on the largest plantations, where masters had to clothe vast numbers of slaves, did slave women escape the drudgery of ordinary field work. Nine of the fifteen women who lived on Edmund Randolph's plantation in Charlotte County, Virginia, in

36. Gaius Marcus Brumbaugh, ed., *Maryland Records: Colonial, Revolutionary, County, and Church, from Original Sources,* I (Baltimore, 1915), 1–88 (Prince George's Census of 1776); Prince George's Inventories, 1760–1775; *Md. Gaz.,* 1760–1779; Betts, ed., *Jefferson's Farm Book,* 15–18; Charles Carroll Account Book, Carroll Papers, MHS; Donald Jackson and Dorothy Twohig, eds., *The Diaries of George Washington,* IV, *1784–June 1786* (Charlottesville, Va., 1978), 278–283; Robert Carter Deed of Manumission, 1791–1796, Carter Papers, Duke University (CW film).

37. Fig. 30. Jackson Turner Main, "The One Hundred," *WMQ,* 3d Ser., XI (1954), 367–384; "A Statement of the Inspector's Accounts from Oct 1786 to Oct 1787 . . . ," Auditor's Item #49, Virginia State Library, Richmond (VSL). Proportions calculated assuming that half the taxable slaves over 16 were men; a fifth of all taxed slaves were men; a fifth of all men of planters with 250 or more slaves (at least 100 in a single county) were artisans, and those with at least 120 in a county or 150 total were artisans; owners sold half their artisans; total artisans followed Prince George's proportions; and 7% of men on these plantations were servants and 1% in the Virginia population.

38. Betts, ed., *Jefferson's Farm Book,* 5–9 (facsimiles).

Table 44. *Occupations of Male Slaves, 1774–1791*

	Percentage in Group	
		Four Gentleman
	Prince George's[a]	Planters[b]
Occupation	(N=2,037)	(N=341)
Agricultural		
Field hands	82	50
Plowmen, mowers	4	9
Drivers	4	7
Family farmers	2	
Total	92	66
Semiskilled		
Servants	1	7
Carters	c	2
Watermen	c	2
Other	c	2
Total	2	13
Craftsmen		
Carpenters, coopers	3	12
Cloth trades	c	3
Blacksmiths	c	2
Shoemakers	c	2
Ironworkers	1	0
Other groups	c	2
Total	5	21
Grand total	99	100

Sources: Cited in n. 36.

Notes: [a]Estimated by weighting slave occupations found in inventories and newspapers by unit sizes on the census (adjusted for the entire county) and determining the number of drivers and family farmers from the size of units. [b]Jefferson, 1774 (52 slaves), Washington, 1786 (63 slaves), Carroll, 1773–1774 (99 slaves), and Carter of Nomini (127 slaves). Plowmen, mowers, and drivers (except drivers on Washington's quarters) estimated from size of quarter. [c]Less than .5%.

1784, worked as spinners, weavers, seamstresses, dairymaids, or nurses. Women on Randolph's plantations were fortunate: only one-sixth of the women owned by Washington, Jefferson, and Robert Carter of Nomini Hall in the 1770s and 1780s worked in the house. Carter's women, typical of these plantations, included ninety-seven field hands, six domestics, twelve spinners, seamstresses, and weavers, and two women who served the slaves as a nurse and a midwife. On rare occasions, women performed other skilled labor. One planter in southern Maryland advertised plow-women; women at Snowden's ironworks in Anne Arundel County may have been miners; one of Carter's women was a cooper.[39]

The home quarters of the largest planters—those who owned more than a hundred slaves of all ages—were diversified and self-sufficient agricultural villages. George Mason's father in the 1770s, for instance, "had among his slaves carpenters, coopers, sawyers, blacksmiths, tanners, curriers, shoemakers, spinners, weavers and knitters, and even a distiller." These men and women built and repaired the houses, made the tobacco hogsheads, tanned skins and made shoes, produced cloth and clothes, and finished all the iron tools needed on Mason's plantations. Since craft shops were located near the main house, a high proportion of adult slaves on their home quarters worked as craftsmen, and most of the nonagricultural workers lived near the large mansion. Two-thirds of the men living on the home quarters of four large planters worked as artisans, cartmen, or domestic servants, and they constituted seven-tenths of the nonagricultural male workers owned by these planters. Similarly high proportions of female domestics and cloth workers owned by three of these men lived near the big house.[40]

39. The estimate of house servants is an upwardly biased conjecture based upon ads in the *Md. Gaz.* and demographic data from Brumbaugh, ed., *Maryland Records*, I, 1–88, and assuming that there were no servants on plantations with fewer than 5 women, one servant on plantations with 5–9 women, two on quarters with 10–14 women, and three on larger plantations. See *Md. Gaz.*, Apr. 7, 1768 (1 of 12 slaves are female servants), Nov. 26, Dec. 3, 17, 1761 (3 of 20 slaves), Feb. 14, 1765 (1 of 15 slaves); Prince George's Inventories, GS#2, 334–336, 1775 (2 of 20 women). For spinners and weavers, see *Md. Gaz.*, Dec. 17, 1761, Oct. 27, 1763, Jan. 3, Feb. 14, 1765, Apr. 7, 1768. Randolph Papers, film at Colonial Williamsburg Research Department (CW); Eileen Starr, "Slaves Belonging to Peyton Randolph" (undergraduate paper, College of William and Mary, 1976); Betts, ed., *Jefferson's Farm Book*, 15–18 (Facsimiles); Jackson and Twohig, eds., *Diaries of Washington*, IV, 277–283; Robert Carter Deed of Manumission; *Md. Gaz.*, Feb. 14, 1765; Patuxent Iron Works Journal, Private Accounts Series, #1503, MHR.

40. Edmund S. Morgan, *Virginians at Home: Family Life in the Eighteenth Century* (Williamsburg, Va., 1952), 53; Carter Deed of Manumission; Jackson and Twohig, eds., *Diaries of Washington*, IV, 277–283; Betts, ed., *Jefferson's Farm Book*, 15–18 (facsimiles); Charles Carroll Papers, MHS (female occupations not indicated).

Masters faced new economic realities after 1750. Since they had turned more and more of the operations of their plantations over to slaves, they had to find new ways to organize work that would keep their workers content and improve productivity. Planters modified the age profile of slave work, the process of training slaves to labor in the fields and craft shops, and the way in which field hands worked in response to the increasing dominance of native-born workers.

Masters allowed slave children under age ten to play under the supervision of older children or an aged grandparent. Children between nine and thirteen or fourteen sometimes worked part-time in the fields and ran errands, watched younger children, or performed odd jobs on the plantation. Depending on strength and size, youths began working full time between the ages of eleven and fourteen: not a single child under eleven owned by Jefferson in 1774 and Washington in 1799 was listed as a hand, but half of those eleven and twelve and nearly all slaves over thirteen worked. Jefferson, who operated a nail-making shop, thought that slave "children till 10 years old [should] serve as nurses, from 10 to 16 the boys make nails, the girls spin; at age 16 go into the ground or learn trades." He followed his own advice, for only three of his eight workers under sixteen in 1774 labored in the fields.[41]

Competence in growing tobacco was acquired slowly, and field hands on large plantations were divided by age, sex, and strength. Boys became full hands in their late teens, and both men and women probably reached their greatest strength during their early twenties, when prices of field hands peaked. Women, counted as three-quarter hands, were less productive and worth less than men. Between the ages twenty and thirty-five, men continued to be very productive, but the prices for women began to fall, and the difference in the value between men and women continued to increase. Old men and women worked until they became habitually ill or lame. Elderly slaves were taken from the fields and given responsibilities in the house or slave quarters or set to tending livestock, but retirement was rare: every slave but one under sixty-five on Robert Carter's plantation in 1791 still worked, as did half the slaves between sixty-five and ninety.[42]

41. *Md. Gaz.*, Feb. 14, 1765, Feb. 7, 1760; Betts, ed., *Jefferson's Farm Book*, 77, 15–18 (facsimiles); Fitzpatrick, ed., *Writings of Washington*, XXXVII, 256–268.

42. William Tatham, *An Historical and Practical Essay on the Culture and Commerce of Tobacco* (London, 1800), repr. in G. Melvin Herndon, ed., *William Tatham and the Culture of Tobacco* (Coral Gables, Fla., 1969), 101–102; Allan Kulikoff, "Tobacco and Slaves: Population, Economy, and Society in Eighteenth-Century Prince George's County, Maryland" (Ph.D. diss., Brandeis University, 1976), 251–254; Testamentary Papers, box 25, folder 34, MHR; Carter Deed of Manumission; Charles Dabney Papers, Vols. IV, VII–IX, University of North Carolina, Chapel Hill (CW film) include ages of three men (two, age 19; one, age 17) and two women (both 17, one a half-share) at entry into the labor force.

Planters who desired to own artisans had to decide whether to apprentice young slaves to master craftsmen or to promote older slaves as a reward for faithful service. Before large home plantations developed, whites must have taught craft skills to almost all slave artisans. Extraordinary blacks were apprenticed as early as the 1680s. Mulatto Ned, born about 1685, became one of the first slave artisans in Maryland. In his late teens, he built a tobacco house for his master, but he was not fully trained as a carpenter and cooper until his mid-twenties. As many creole slaves matured, the number of apprenticeships probably rose. Robert "King" Carter urged his son George in 1730 to train "some young negroes of those I have given" him as "Trades men, Carpenters and Coopers for the use of his plantations." Slave apprenticeships began appearing in Maryland at the same time: Robert Bradley, a merchant-planter, apprenticed a slave to be a blacksmith in Prince George's in 1728; Joe, who belonged to John Skinner of Calvert County, was apprenticed to a Prince George's shipwright in 1745.[43]

A system of slave apprenticeship developed on larger plantations in the 1770s and 1780s. Charles Carroll of Carrollton and Robert Carter of Nomini Hall, for instance, chose to train youthful slaves: more than a tenth of their male slaves, age fifteen to nineteen, and nearly a third in their twenties, were artisans (see fig. 31). Carroll's slaves began training at even younger ages; a fifth of all his boys between fifteen and nineteen were already artisans, and several slaves began training even earlier. George Washington rarely rewarded older slaves for good performance. Between 1786 and 1799, six men became artisans on his plantations: four were trained in their teens or early twenties, a laborer became a bricklayer, and a carter became a carpenter. All four of Washington's new male domestic servants and three of his four distillers had learned their new tasks as youths.[44]

Once a large planter owned an artisan or two, these skilled slaves began to pass the mystery of their trades on to their sons. In 1728, Cooper George, one of Robert "King" Carter's slaves, apparently began teaching his twelve-year-old son to be a cooper. Apprenticeships to slaves probably did not become common until the 1770s, when large home quarters proliferated. Half of Charles Carroll's artisans under age twenty-five probably learned their trade from fathers or other kinfolk skilled in that occupation. Two of Washington's young ditchers in 1799 were sons of Boatswain, the head ditcher, and two of the four young artisans were the children of arti-

43. Chancery Records, VII, 2–12, 25–34, 50–52, MHR; "Carter Papers [Robert Carter will]," *VMHB*, V (1897–1898), 412, VI (1898–1899), 17; Prince George's Court Records, S, 10; *Md. Gaz.*, Mar. 12, 1752, Aug. 11, 1747.
44. Table 44; Carroll Papers; Jackson and Twohig, eds., *Diaries of Washington*, IV, 277–283, compared with Fitzpatrick, ed., *Writings of Washington*, XXXVII, 256–268.

Fig. 31. *Age of Slave Artisans.* In Prince George's County and on the
plantations of Charles Carroll and Robert Carter. Cohorts centered at
midpoint (15–19, 20–29, 30–39, 40–49, 50–59, 60 +).

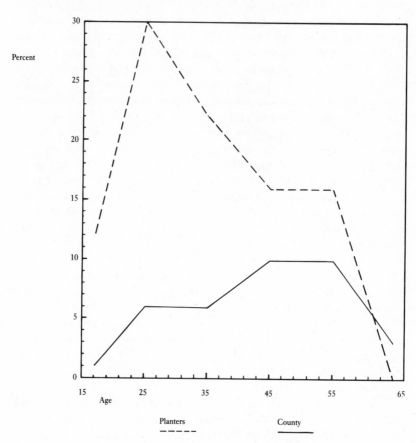

Sources: Prince George's Inventories, 1730–1769; Charles Carroll Account Book, Carroll
Papers, MHS; Robert Carter Deed of Manumission, Duke University (film at CW). An artisan
found in two different inventories is counted only once; percentages are computed from every
age above 14 listed in every inventory between 1730 and 1779.

sans. Both of Washington's postilions probably gained their positions because their mothers were housemaids.[45]

Only the wealthiest planters could afford to apprentice young slaves to white artisans or permit intergenerational slave training. Less wealthy planters either bought fully trained artisans from these gentlemen or waited to apprentice their slaves until their productivity as agricultural laborers began to decline, using the possibility of retirement to less strenuous and more prestigious labor as an incentive to their male workers. These two patterns are suggested by the high relative number of artisans over the age of thirty in Prince George's County, especially when compared with the youthful artisans employed by Carroll and Carter (fig. 31).

Women who became personal servants or cloth workers were trained in their early teens and became fully proficient by 16 or 17. Few women gained these positions later in life as a reward for service. The average age of fourteen servants advertised for sale in Maryland between 1748 and 1774 was 20.6, and eight were under 20. A girl of 16 advertised in 1751 was "fit for Plantation Work, or very capable of making a good House Wench, having for some Months served as such in a Small Family." The average age of seven spinners, seamstresses, and weavers on Randolph's Charlotte plantations in 1784 was 20.6: two spinners were 16, an assistant at the loom was 17, and the rest were between 20 and 25 years of age. Similarly, four seamstresses and spinners, all daughters of seamstresses or spinners, trained at Mount Vernon between 1786 and 1799 were in their late teens or early 20s.[46]

Though few slaves became artisans or domestics, slave hire for field labor became common for the first time in the 1750s because natural increase had created an oversupply of field labor on some plantations. Local planters in King George and Essex counties, Virginia, hired only twenty-seven slaves from administrators of estates in the 1740s, but planters in Middlesex County alone hired fifty-two slaves from estates between 1755 and 1763. Similarly, the number of slaves hired in southern Maryland more than tripled between 1750 and the 1760s and 1770s.[47]

45. Carroll Papers; Jackson and Twohig, eds., *Diaries of Washington*, IV, 277–283; Fitzpatrick, ed., *Writings of Washington*, XXXVII, 256–268; Morgan, "Development of Slave Culture," 113–114.

46. Randolph Papers; Starr, "Slaves Belonging to Randolph"; Jackson and Twohig, eds., *Diaries of Washington*, IV, 277–283, compared with Fitzpatrick, ed., *Writings of Washington*, XXXVII, 256–268; and ads in *Md. Gaz.*, Apr. 27, Dec. 21, 1748, Dec. 20, 1749, May 29, 1751, May 28, 1752, Dec. 17, 1761, Oct. 24, 1765, Oct. 20, Nov. 10, 1763, Apr. 26, 1770, Dec. 29, 1774.

47. Morgan, "Development of Slave Culture," 141; fig. 31 and sources cited there document 10 slaves hired, 1747–1759, 45 hired, 1760–1769, and 34 hired, 1770–1779. Not a single slave hiring case came before the Prince George's court before 1742, and the next case was 1747.

More than two-thirds of the slaves hired in southern Maryland worked as agricultural laborers. Nearly all the hired slaves were adult men; only a tenth were children and only a fifth women (see table 45). About two-thirds of those hired worked for at least one year, usually beginning in December. A third of the contracts were renewed for another six months or a year, but the longest term lasted only three years, and an equal number labored for a few weeks or months.[48]

Large Maryland planters could rent out some of their slaves for short periods and still have sufficient labor to make an adequate crop. Blacks were probably most often hired for a few days or weeks during planting, transplanting, and harvesting seasons. For example, Ninian Edmonston, who owned just one adult slave, hired a number of hands from his neighbor and kinsman Andrew Beall, who owned twelve adults, for fifty-two days in 1770. In late March and early April he used three or four of Beall's hands for fourteen days, perhaps to prepare hills to receive tobacco plants. In mid-August, four hands worked four days each, weeding the crop. During the harvest in late August and early September, two of Beall's slaves worked twenty-four days each for Edmonston, and in late September, four of them worked ten days, probably hanging tobacco.[49]

Hiring out both enhanced and detracted from slave life. Young slaves gained freedom of movement, saw the neighborhood, and met eligible marriage partners where they worked. Furthermore, hiring out allowed master and slave to avoid personality clashes. George Washington's Tom, for example, was hired out to neighbors when he and Washington could not live peaceably on the same plantation. Slaves in post-Revolutionary Elizabeth City County found hiring out a much less pleasant prospect. Virtually every master in the county either hired or hired out slaves. Most residents operated grain farms and did not need to keep large numbers of slaves. As a result, they redistributed slaves through a hiring system, thereby separating many families.[50]

A slow mechanization of agriculture reduced the work of most native-born field hands. Planters did not trust Africans with any but the most rudimentary tools. During the 1730s, a time of heavy slave imports, slave-

48. Fig. 31 and sources there document length of service for 56 hired slaves: 18 for less than a year (32%), 26 for a year (46%), and 13 for more than a year (23%).

49. Prince George's Court Records, XXIV, 221–224.

50. Clement Hill, Jr., Account Book, Hill Papers, MHR; Fitzpatrick, ed., *Writings of Washington*, II, 437; Charles County Court Record, LIX, 81–83 (1766), LXIII, 225–227 (1773), LXVI, 746–748 (1778); Prince George's Court Records, XXV, 63–64 (1761), all at MHR; Mullin, *Flight and Rebellion*, 87–88; Sarah S. Hughes, "Slaves for Hire: The Allocation of Black Labor in Elizabeth City County, Virginia, 1782 to 1810," *WMQ*, 3d Ser., XXV (1978), 260–286.

Table 45. *Profile of Slaves Hired in Southern Maryland, 1747–1779*

Profile	Percentage (N=89)
Status	
Men	69
Women	20
Children	10
Total	99
Work Experience	
Field labor	69
Reaping	2
Carpentry	11
Ship carpentry	11
Cooperage	2
Other crafts[a]	5
Total	101
Sex and Skills	
Males, agricultural	46
Females, agricultural	25
Males, crafts	29
Total	100

Sources: Prince George's Court Records (1725–1785) and Charles County Court Records (1750–1780), MHR; Richard Boarman Account Book, 1755–1782, and Basil Waring Account Book, 1761–1766, both in Gift Collection, MHR; William Fitzhugh Account Books, 1761–1774, MHS. A more detailed breakdown by decade will be found in Allan Kulikoff, "Tobacco and Slaves: Population, Economy, and Society in Eighteenth-Century Prince George's County, Maryland" (Ph.D. diss., Brandeis University, 1976), 247–248.

Notes: Each individual hired is one observation, no matter what the length of service. All work is assumed to be field labor unless otherwise mentioned. [a]Two for smithing, one for mill work, one for masonry.

holders in Prince George's typically owned only axes and hoes. A third of them owned a plow or cart, and merely a tenth owned both. All the planting, replanting, weeding, harvesting, and marketing of tobacco was done by hand. By the mid-1750s, nearly all working hands were natives, and planters bought plows, carts, and cartwheels for them to use. Two-thirds of county slaveowners possessed plows or carts, and half owned both, by the 1760s (see fig. 32). Substantial planters replaced this farm equipment frequently: Francis Jerdone, perhaps typical, bought two hoes of various types for each hand and one plow per quarter for his Albemarle farms each year between 1761 and 1770.[51]

This new technology, combined with the rising size of work units, led to greater division of labor in tobacco fields. Slave drivers and foremen, as well as cartmen, plowmen, and mowers, appeared on larger quarters throughout tidewater after 1750. Drivers and foremen, who were responsible for directing other slaves in planting, protecting, and harvesting crops, were chosen from the best field hands. For example, George Washington's Tom was a "Rogue and a Runaway," but he had been a foreman because he was "exceedingly healthy, strong, and good at the Hoe." Drivers reached their position by their skills as well as their strength. A slave driver advertised in Maryland in 1777 was a shoemaker, mower, and sawyer and "perfectly understands the management of tobacco." Plowmen prepared fields for wheat and corn and kept rows of tobacco free from weeds with their plows, while mowers cut grains and cartmen transported tobacco to curing barns and hogsheads to market. These skills were prized by slaveowners. When Zachariah Lyles of Prince George's offered to sell a number of slaves in 1763, he specifically mentioned only three "valuable young Fellows, that have been brought up to Carting and Plowing, and understand Plantation business of all Sorts."[52] Common field hands—women, teenagers, and the remaining men—planted, weeded, and harvested tobacco and other crops.

A similar work hierarchy could not develop on small farms, where masters and slaves worked together in every aspect of tobacco and grain cultivation. Although in the 1760s nearly two-thirds of Prince George's planters who owned one or two slaves possessed plows or carts and a quarter owned both, each of their slaves had to plant, weed, hoe, and harvest crops. Even those slaves who learned to use these new implements still had to work as ordinary field hands.

51. "'Itinerant Observations' of Kimber," *MHM*, LI (1956), 327–328; Tatham, *Essay on Culture of Tobacco*, in Herndon, ed., *William Tatham*, 17–18, 54–66; Morgan, "Development of Slave Culture," 455.

52. Fitzpatrick, ed., *Writings of Washington*, II, 437; *Maryland Journal, and the Baltimore Advertiser*, Dec. 2, 1777; *Md. Gaz.*, Dec. 29, 1763; Chancery Records, XXVI, 68–69, MHR.

Work Relations on the Tobacco Coast

Masters imposed the new occupational structure, the increase in hiring, and the mechanization of agriculture on their slaves. On larger plantations, a new social hierarchy based upon race, age, sex, and skills replaced the formerly undifferentiated system, and masters thereby lost some authority. Whites directed blacks; but far outnumbered in the fields, they faced not only individual slaves but collective black actions. Afro-Americans, who knew that masters could not make a profit without their skilled labor, used plows and carts to establish control over the rhythm and pace of work.

Slaves became particularly adept at playing masters against overseers on large plantations. Between a third and a half of the slaves in tidewater lived on plantations with overseers by the 1770s. Ownership and management of slaves were separated on these units. The master acted as business manager: he supervised his overseers, punished unruly slaves, visited his fields to observe the work, tried to increase productivity, and marketed the

Fig. 32. *Ownership of Plows and Carts in Prince George's County, 1730–1769.* For decedents with two or more taxable slaves. Data centered on five-year cohorts.

Source: Prince George's Inventories, 1730–1769, MHR.

crop, but did not work alongside his slaves. The master's son or other kinsman or a white overseer supervised the work of slaves; in return, he usually received a share of the crop.[53]

Overseers were caught in the middle between masters and slaves. Despite their responsibilities, they had little authority over slaves. Usually single men in their twenties, overseers rarely held the same position for more than a year.[54] Slaves knew that overseers were neither permanent nor vested by the master with great authority. Slaveowners expected overseers to work continually with the slaves to maintain high levels of productivity, but masters often superseded their orders, took the side of slaves in their disputes with overseers, and interfered in the daily management of workers. Overseers reacted either by allowing slaves to control their own work pace (hoping that they would produce more because they were satisfied) or by driving their charges very hard, forcing them to work when ill, and using the whip frequently to increase production and the size of their share. When overseers directed with a light hand, masters complained of low productivity; when they drove the slaves hard, masters thought overseers were vicious.[55]

The complex relations among native slaves, overseers, and masters can be seen in the 1769 conflict between Daniel Jenifer, a large slaveowner in Charles County, Maryland, and his overseer Richard Nelson. Jenifer promised to supply Nelson with seven hands, four horses, a share of the corn and tobacco crops, a tenth of the livestock raised that year, and three hundred pounds of pork. Nelson complained that Jenifer often took hands away from the crop and borrowed the horses, and Jenifer charged Nelson with frequent absences, with staying up all night and sleeping past ten, and with stealing livestock and crops.[56]

---

53. Estimate of proportion of slaves directed by overseers assumes that two-thirds of slaves residing on plantations of more than 20 blacks worked with overseers; Worthington C. Ford, ed., *Washington as an Employer and Importer of Labor* (New York, 1889), 28–35; Fitzpatrick, ed., *Writings of Washington*, XXXII, 267, XXXIII, 10–12, 97–100.

54. There were 334 nonhouseholding men, ages 20–58, in the 1776 Prince George's census (Brumbaugh, ed., *Maryland Records*, I, 1–88); 71% of these men (sons of householders or overseers) were between 20 and 28. Jefferson hired 10 overseers for one or two years between 1786 and 1800 (Betts, ed., *Jefferson's Farm Book*, 149–150, excludes stewards); Maryland records show 4 overseers who served a year, 1 for two years, 1 for four years, and 2 for less than a year. See Basil Waring Account Book, Gift Collection; Prince George's Court Records, R, 240–242 (1731), Z, 436–438 (1741), XXV, 194 (1762); Frederick County Court Records, IX, 488–489 (1768); Chancery Records, XIV, 311–312 (1785); Hill Account Book, Hill Papers (1770s), all at MHR.

55. Mullin, *Flight and Rebellion*, 29–31; Farish, ed., *Journal of Fithian*, 38–39, 129; "'Itinerant Observations' of Kimber," *MHM*, LI (1956), 50; Fitzpatrick, ed., *Writings of Washington*, XXXII, 184–185, 246, 281, XXXIII, 191–194.

56. Chancery Records, XIV, 311–322 (1785), MHR.

Although Jenifer showed his slaves that Nelson was not the boss by taking people from him at will, he did not enforce discipline himself, but visited Nelson only eleven times in the spring and summer of 1769. Lacking authority over the slaves, Nelson still had to direct them. He reacted to his lack of authority and his isolation from other whites in two ways. First, he sometimes left his slaves to seek white companionship; Jenifer discovered that Nelson was "not at home" on eight of his trips to the quarter. Second, he allowed the slaves entrusted to him to work with little supervision. For example, he left his hands with a seine at a stream "without any Controul or Direction" to catch herring. Several of the hands did not catch any fish, but one caught three thousand herring and gave them to Jenifer. Another time, Nelson became friendly with blacks, and during "the Holidays" he played "at Cards with Negroes who had come to the . . . plantation."[57]

Small planters, who worked daily with their slaves, had greater authority over their charges than had overseers. The master, rather than his workers, controlled the work rhythm. Nonetheless, Afro-Americans who lived on small plantations possessed some leverage. Each slave was more important to the master than a single hand on a large quarter. If a slave on a small farm was mistreated, he could reduce the size of his master's crop by running away for a few days during planting or harvesting. When a small slaveowner or a nonslaveowner hired slaves, he faced the same problems of divided ownership and management as overseers, and a person who hired a gang to help with planting or harvesting had to accept the work rhythms the group had previously developed.

Afro-American slaves manipulated the division of white ownership and authority and took advantage of lax white direction. "Blacks are capable of much labour," George Washington complained to Arthur Young, "but having . . . no ambition to establish a *good* name, they are too regardless of a *bad* one; and of course, require more of the master's eye." Thomas Bacon, in several sermons preached to slaves on Maryland's Eastern Shore in the late 1740s, warned slaves to be productive. Afro-Americans, Bacon asserted, often "work hard and seem mighty diligent, while they think anybody is taking notice of them, but when their masters and mistresses backs are turned, they are idle and neglect their business."[58]

Slaves structured their work around the changing seasons. Sometimes they worked hard; at other times, they labored at a slow, methodical pace and tried to avoid work. Overseers and masters drove slaves hard during the long summer of replanting, weeding, and harvesting tobacco, but after the

---

57. *Ibid.*, esp. 318–319, 322.
58. Fitzpatrick, ed., *Writings of Washington*, XXXII, 66, 204–205, 256–257; Bacon, *Four Sermons at St. Peter*, 35, 37–39.

crop was hung in the tobacco house, masters had to manufacture new work for their slaves if they expected them to continue to labor. George Washington, for instance, feared his slaves would have little to keep them occupied during the winter, so he told his overseers to force them to clear fields, repair plantation structures, and prepare the ground for a new crop.[59]

Afro-Americans who labored together developed their own work rhythms. Each member of the group had his own responsibility, his own place in the daily routine. When one member was ill or could not work, the group's work rhythms were disrupted, and work slowed down or halted. "If any one person, the most trifling hand, is ill but a day or a piece of a day," Landon Carter complained, "it generally excuses the loss of a whole day's work of the gang."[60]

The arrival of carts and plows on tobacco plantations accented the task-oriented work discipline of native slaves. Even during busy seasons, they could relax and work slowly for days and then use the new mechanical implements to complete their work. Landon Carter, for one, regretted introducing plows and carts on his quarters: "Carts and plows only serve to make Overseers and people extremely lazy," he wrote in 1770, and "wherever they are in great abundance there is the least plantation work done there for both Overseers and Negroes imagine this or that work will be quickly done with the plows and Carts and . . . are very little solicitous to do their proper parts of the business . . . till in the end every thing is to do and . . . must be slubbered and harried over."[61]

Afro-Americans were adept at pretending to be ill in order to avoid work for a day or two. Because there was such a high level of morbidity among blacks in the Chesapeake, masters could not afford to ignore their slaves' complaints and tried instead to tend to their illnesses. Masters tried to distinguish between legitimate complaints and malingering by looking for fevers, lameness, sores, or ulcers. If a slave was found to be feigning an illness, the whip could be used as punishment.[62]

Masters and overseers possessed few resources with which to demand completely efficient labor. If they paid constant attention to their charges, they might ensure productivity but risk being closely identified with an inferior caste; if they whipped their slaves into submission, they might injure them or create sullen workers. Incentives and relatively lax management might produce results: the slaves Nelson managed for Jenifer pro-

59. Fitzpatrick, ed., *Writings of Washington*, XXXII, 179, 202–203, 215.

60. Greene, ed., *Diary of Carter*, II, 588–589 (1771).

61. *Ibid.*, I, 386–387 (1770).

62. Mullin, *Flight and Rebellion*, 55; Fitzpatrick, ed., *Writings of Washington*, XXXII, 184–185, 197, 266, 319, 494, XXXIII, 242, 499–500.

duced a large crop of fifteen hundred pounds of tobacco per hand despite the overseer's many absences.[63] Most masters probably became resigned to the slaves' strategies and used a combination of the lash and incentives to increase productivity.

The working conditions of slave artisans differed significantly from those of field hands. In the first place, they avoided working in the ground, practiced new skills, and took pride in their craftsmanship. Some even learned a second or third trade. Harry was a "tolerable good shoemaker, clapboard carpenter, cooper, and indeed handy at anything he is put about, particularly waiting in the house, gardening, mowing, driving a carriage, and the management of horses." Stephen Butler, a mulatto born about 1730, ran off from his master in 1771; he played "on a fiddle, and is a wheelwright, Sawyer, tight Cooper, and House Carpenter by trade." When Luice, a mulatto woman, ran away in 1779 at age twenty-three, she was described as "an exceeding good cook and spinner but slo."[64]

Until the 1750s, slave artisans were carpenters and coopers who labored almost exclusively on their master's plantations making hogsheads, barrels, and tobacco houses. After 1750, slave artisans sometimes worked without direct white supervision, changed masters frequently, and were more likely than field hands to run away. By the 1760s and 1770s, many slave craftsmen were hired out or even managed to hire out themselves. These men had a great deal more freedom than field hands but were often caught in the middle between a plantation world they had left and a white world they could not join.[65]

Head artisans and self-hired tradesmen were the most independent slave workers. Tony, a cooper and sawyer who belonged to John Burle of Anne Arundel County, was an early example of a head artisan. He was the "Top Man" among Vachel Denton's coopers when Denton hired him in the late 1740s. In the late 1760s, Abraham and Bill helped manage the Snowden iron furnace in Anne Arundel. A white overseer directed them, but they managed several other slave founders. George Washington's Isaac, Mount Vernon's head carpenter in the 1790s, could make plantation implements and build simple structures and directed other carpenters under the supervision of a white overseer.[66]

63. Chancery Records, XIV, 311–322.

64. *Md. Gaz.*, Mar. 13, 1777, Feb. 14, 1771; *Md. Jour.*, Sept. 28, 1779.

65. Fig. 31; Mullin, *Flight and Rebellion*, 91–103, 121–123; Morgan, "Development of Slave Culture," 187–189. Mulatto Ned, a carpenter and cooper who belonged to Gabriel Parker of Calvert County, worked exclusively for him between 1713 and 1718. Chancery Records, VII, 25–34 (1738).

66. Testamentary Proceedings, XXXIII, 59–63 (1749); Patuxent Iron Works Journal, Private Accounts #1503, pt. 1, 52–53, 73 (I have inferred head artisanship of Abraham and Bill from

A small but increasing number of slave artisans hired out their own time in the 1760s, 1770s, and 1780s. The practice was so widespread to residents of Henrico County, adjacent to Richmond town, that they complained to the legislature in 1782 that "many persons have suffer'd their slaves to go about to hire themselves and pay their masters for their hire and others under pretence of puting them free set them out to live for themselves and allow their Masters such hire as they can agree on." The practice may have been limited to towns and surrounding areas: two of three examples of self-hire recorded in the *Maryland Gazette* in the 1750s and 1760s concerned town artisans. In 1756, Alexander Hamilton, an Annapolis doctor, complained that Ben, his cooper, "for some Years past, has, through my Indulgence, been permitted to increase his Trade for his own Benefit," and he continued this practice even though Hamilton now forbade it. Joe, born about 1739, was owned by Christopher Lowndes, a wealthy Bladensburg merchant. In 1764 he ran away, and Lowndes feared he would try to hire himself out, since "when he lived with some former Masters, he was allowed to look for Work in different Rivers." Finally, "a very good Negro Miller" worked at a gristmill on Rock Creek, Frederick County, Maryland, in 1764 when the mill was sold. The three owners lived miles away and did not list any other labor at the mill.[67]

Unlike field hands, artisans often worked in groups that included numerous whites. Black stevedores, water men, and ironworkers were most likely to labor with whites. Between six and twenty-four slaves and six white men worked for three weeks in 1762 at the same wages to unload the ship *Fishburn* in Norfolk. In 1761, Thomas Fleming built a schooner for Richard Barrett, a Prince George's merchant. Seven white and five black men worked two months each on the ship, and another white man labored a month. Barrett provided food and supplies; Fleming hired the men. The monthly wages Fleming charged Barrett indicate the relative position of whites and blacks in the ship carpentry trade: the director of the project received £7 10s., the other whites were paid £3 to £5, and the labor of slaves was valued between £2 and £3. Though whites directed the work and received higher wages, whites and slaves worked side by side with relatively equal work conditions.[68]

---

their value per month, double that of any other slave at the furnace); Fitzpatrick, ed., *Writings of Washington*, XXXII, 263, XXXIII, 244; Frank E. Morse, Notes on families at Mount Vernon, MS, Mount Vernon.

67. Morgan, "Development of Slave Culture," 186 (Henrico quote); *Md. Gaz.*, Jan. 1, 1756, Sept. 13, 1764, July 12, 1764; Mullin, *Flight and Rebellion*, 117, 156–157.

68. Morgan, "Development of Slave Culture," 131; Patuxent Iron Works Journal, Private Accounts; Account of the Ship *Fishburn*, Norfolk Borough Register, 1756–1762, Norfolk City Records, Virginia State Library, Richmond; Prince George's Court Records, XXV, 545–546

Slaves worked with whites at many of the iron forges and furnaces in the Chesapeake region. Few blacks labored there in the 1720s and 1730s, when nearly all skilled workers were white, but by the 1750s, blacks performed most skilled and manual labor. Between thirty and fifty slaves worked at most forges and furnaces by the 1770s, making these enterprises larger than all but a few tobacco farms. The ironworkers, about 1 percent of the adult slaves in the region, were the most privileged black laborers. They were paid for work done on their own time and purchased rum and other goods at company stores with the money they earned. Since forges and furnaces required waterpower, they had to be closed during droughts and freezes. At Snowden's ironworks, in Anne Arundel County, slave artisans worked an average of only 250–275 days a year, or 5 days a week.[69]

The Snowden's operations were probably typical of ironworks. Free whites, white servants, and slaves worked at the furnace and forge. Overseers were white, and free white men drove the teams of horses and repaired the works. In 1768, more than three-quarters of the seventy-four employees were slaves, and thirty-four of forty black men were artisans. (Another fifteen workers were black women.) They dominated every craft at the furnace: black colliers made charcoal to keep the furnace burning, and founders molded metal as it left the furnace. Two slave founders helped oversee furnace operations. The sixteen men at the forge may have included finders who heated the pigs, hammermen who pounded the metal into blooms, and chafers who reheated the pigs and drew them into bars. Women worked as domestics and mined coal. From 1768 to 1775, several skilled black workers died or were sold. The Snowdens replaced them with white servants, and by 1775 only forty-five slaves (and twenty-three whites) labored at the ironworks. Despite this attrition, three-quarters of the slave men were still artisans, and these skilled workers had long tenures: twenty-two of the twenty-nine craftsmen at the forge and furnace in 1768 were still on the job in 1775, and eleven in 1783.[70]

(1763); William Fitzhugh Account Book, I, 106, MHS (seven white men, one slave build a sloop).

69. Ronald L. Lewis, "Slavery in the Chesapeake Iron Industry, 1716–1865" (Ph.D. diss., University of Akron, 1974), 8–9, 47–73, 100–102, 137–138, 143–147, 167–172, 195–205; Patuxent Iron Works Journal, Part A, 52–53, 72–73, 91–92, 108–109, 121–123, 135–136, 145–146, 162, 172, 180–181, 188, 196–197, 206–207, 215, Part B, 5, Private Accounts. For estimate of ironworkers, see table 44. A similar result (for the entire region) can be found if one assumes that there were 40 workers in half of the forges and furnaces in the two colonies in the 1770s.

70. Kulikoff, "Tobacco and Slaves," 266–267; Prince George's Inventories, GS#2, 203–204; Michael W. Robbins, "The Principio Company: Iron-Making in Colonial Maryland, 1720–1781" (Ph.D. diss., George Washington University, 1972), 91, 111–120; Patuxent Iron Works Journal, Part A; Lewis, "Slavery in the Chesapeake Iron Industry," 192–196.

Thus the work experience of self-hired artisans and industrial workers contrasted greatly with the labor of the vast majority of slaves. These men could move from place to place far more freely than typical field hands. While they worked closely with whites, plantation slaves usually saw only master or overseer during the day's work. Artisans had to defer to whites always, and some of them stuttered and stammered in the presence of whites, fearing retribution if they did not behave properly. Field hands vastly outnumbered whites and could manipulate them to gain a few advantages. Though there were few distinctions (other than pay) between white and black industrial workers, agricultural tasks were racially divided between black field workers and white managers.

Female servants and cloth workers probably did not share the relative independence of male artisans. These slave women, mostly owned by great planters, labored "under the Eye of the Mistress." The importance of planters' wives in the work of slave spinners and weavers is suggested by a census of cloth production in twenty households taken in King William County in 1791. Five large plantations, where thirty-seven slave women lived, produced three-fifths of the cloth made by these families. Each of these planters was married, and seven white women (daughters or servants) lived in two of the households. Two slaveholders were widowed and employed no white female help. One of them (who owned two slave women) was the only household of the twenty surveyed that made no cloth; the other man (who owned four slave women) produced just seventy yards of cloth, only a third as much as all the planters in the survey, who owned three or four slave women.[71]

Masters, Slaves, and Revolution

A relatively coherent set of class relations between slaves and masters developed during the mid-eighteenth century. Masters held a monopoly of power over slaves; the insistence of the master that slaves be subservient and productive was guaranteed by the power of the state. Afro-American slaves recognized the power of masters but tried to work within it to gain what privileges they could. Rough compromises between masters and their slaves generally upheld the authority of masters but at the same time provided slaves with some ability to develop a semiautonomous life on their quarters.

71. Edward Carrington to Alexander Hamilton, Oct. 4, 1791, and enclosures, in Harold C. Syrett *et al.*, eds., *The Papers of Alexander Hamilton*, IX (New York, 1965), 275–276, 280–282.

Masters and slaves understood these working agreements rather differently. Wealthy gentlemen, who owned perhaps half the slaves living in the Chesapeake region, ministered to their slaves' health, tried to keep black families together, and permitted slaves to form their own communities. On occasion, they even considered slaves to be inferior members of their own families. In return, they expected obedience, as might any parent, and punished their children when they transgressed. When slaves tried to turn these privileges, granted by masters, into social rights, masters reacted with a vigorous and sometimes violent defense of their own prerogatives.[72]

The concern of masters for their slaves was severely limited. The vast majority of slaveholders owned too few slaves to permit extended slave families to develop, or to hire doctors to minister to their illnesses. They worked with their slaves and worried mostly about their tobacco crops. Even gentlemen hardly considered all their slaves members of the master's extended family; gentlemen knew their servants well, but their field hands only by name and reputation. Furthermore, they developed a great interest in rational management and tried to emulate British gentlemen in maximizing their production, a goal that conflicted with the familial model of slavery they sometimes espoused. These masters wanted their slaves to work systematically every day, "the presumption being," George Washington wrote, "that every labourer (male or female) does as much in the 24 hours as their strength without endangering the health, or constitution will allow of."[73]

At the same time that masters managed slaves in the tobacco fields, they sought to minimize the time they spent with them. Of course, they considered black slaves to be members of an inferior race, consigned to slavery in perpetuity and unworthy of equal social (and especially sexual) contact with whites. Most gentlemen therefore allowed slaves who remained productive during the day to run their own lives on the quarters during the evenings.

The Revolution challenged this system of class relations and racial control. Planters lost the monopoly of state power that had sustained their authority over their slaves. The British offered freedom to any slave who would fight the rebels, and many slaves risked disease and death to reach

72. Eugene D. Genovese, *Roll, Jordan, Roll,* 91–93, 144–147; and *In Red and Black: Marxian Explorations in Southern and Afro-American History* (New York, 1971), 134, define this familial ideology. For examples, see Mullin, *Flight and Rebellion,* 19–22, 70–72; Greene, ed., *Diary of Carter,* and Washington's letters to his stewards in Fitzpatrick, ed., *Writings of Washington,* Vols. XXXII–XXXIV.

73. Gerald W. Mullin, "Rethinking American Negro Slavery from the Vantage Point of the Colonial Era," *Louisiana Studies,* XII (1973), 412–413; Fitzpatrick, ed., *Writings of Washington,* XXX, 175–176.

the English lines. Some whig gentlemen and Quaker and evangelical planters took whig ideology literally and manumitted their slaves, thereby adding
to the problems of the majority of slaveholders.

From the beginnings of the Revolution, whigs feared the disloyalty of
their slaves. Rumors of a slave uprising began after Governor Dunmore of
Virginia removed some powder from a magazine in Williamsburg in April
1775. When patriots demanded its return, Dunmore threatened to free the
slaves of rebels, and citizens throughout the Chesapeake responded with
fear and anger. In November 1775, when Dunmore declared "all indented
Servants, Negroes, or others (appertaining to Rebels) free, that are able and
willing to bear Arms, they joining his Majesty's Troops," slaveholders in
both Maryland and Virginia reacted with rage.[74]

Though slaves did not rise up against their masters, three to five thousand of them, about 2 or 3 percent of the adult blacks in the region, ran to
the British. About eight hundred black men joined Dunmore's army, but
most of them quickly died of disease. Slaves continued to run away in large
numbers whenever British troops were nearby, and they left counties on the
James River, which the British often invaded, with particular frequency.
The disorders of the war provided a unique opportunity for slave families to
reach freedom together. Since many blacks never had an opportunity to join
the English and since runaways had to leave behind their extended families
for an unknown but possibly deadly fate, the number of runaways was remarkably high.[75]

Slaves ran away most frequently from gentlemen. Thomas Jefferson
lost thirty slaves, and eighty-two slaves left John Bannister's forge. These
owners were often absent fighting the war or lived on another plantation.

74. Jeannie Ford Dissette, "Slavery and the Coming of the Revolution in Virginia, 1774–1776"
(seminar paper, University of Pennsylvania, 1972), 19–51; Ronald Hoffman, *A Spirit of Dissension: Economics, Politics, and the Revolution in Maryland* (Baltimore, 1973), 147–149; Francis
Berkeley, *Dunmore's Proclamation of Emancipation* (Charlottesville, Va., 1941), frontispiece.
75. Sylvia R. Frey, "Between Slavery and Freedom: Virginia Blacks in the American Revolution," *Journal of Southern History*, XLIX (1983), 374–398; Benjamin Quarles, *The Negro in the
American Revolution* (Chapel Hill, N.C., 1961), chaps. 7–9; Mary Beth Norton, "'What an
Alarming Crisis Is This': Southern Women and the American Revolution," in Jeffrey J. Crow
and Larry E. Tise, eds., *The Southern Experience in the American Revolution* (Chapel Hill, N.C.,
1978), 211–215; Mullin, *Flight and Rebellion*, 72, 125–126; Dissette, "Slavery and the Coming
of the Revolution," 36–39; Betts, ed., *Jefferson's Farm Book*, 29 (facsimiles), 504–505; Herbert
G. Gutman, *The Black Family in Slavery and Freedom, 1750–1925* (New York, 1976), 242–244,
588. The estimate of runaways (lower than previous estimates) comes from two sources: one is
the number of slaves who left New York in 1783 with the British (multiplied by 3.0, assuming
that a third died and a third were recaptured), and the other uses all known estimates for
1775–1779 (multiplied by 1.5) and adds in runaways from individual planters, 1780–1781
(multiplied by 10).

Their slaves left despite warnings from their masters that a terrible fate awaited them. In 1776, Robert Carter warned some of his slaves that a British victory would lead Dunmore to "sell them to white people living in the west Islands, who are now friends and subjects of G.B." His rule was far more benevolent than theirs. "Do any of ye . . . wish to enter into Ld. D's service, and trust to the Consequences?" Though Carter's slaves remained at home in 1776, thirty-two of them ran away in 1781.[76]

Patriots fought the Revolution to remove the yoke of British slavery and institute a free government, but gentry leaders hoped to limit the consequences of their actions. While both Virginia and Maryland permitted free Negroes to enlist, they prohibited slaves from entering the army. Slaves were needed at home to support their masters and, furthermore, might demand freedom as the price for military service. As a result, fewer than a hundred slaves served in the armed forces of Virginia, even during the campaign of 1780 and 1781, when the patriots badly needed men. Most of the slaves served as substitutes for whites or illegally enlisted by claiming to be free.[77]

Gentlemen, however, could not prevent some bold thinkers in the Chesapeake region from connecting the political enslavement of whites with the physical bondage of blacks. Deistic gentlemen, along with Quakers and some evangelicals, persuaded both the Virginia and Maryland legislators to ease restrictions on private manumissions in the 1780s. A flood of manumissions by enlightened republicans and by religious Quakers and Baptists ensued. These manumissions created a substantial class of free black people in the region for the first time, thereby partially severing the connection between race and servitude and creating new problems for slaveowners.[78]

The disloyalty of many slaves during the Revolution and the stream of manumissions in the 1780s unleashed a torrent of racist thought. Dunmore's black troops were called "black bandetti" and the "Speckled regiment," and their fighting was ridiculed. "To comply with their *native* warlike genius," one writer insisted, they "will be gratified with the use of the sprightly and enlivening *barrafoo* an instrument peculiarly adapted to the martial tune of '*Hungry Niger, parch'd Corn!*' and which from henceforward

76. *Ibid.*; for Carter's speech, see Louis Morton, *Robert Carter of Nomini Hall: A Virginia Tobacco Planter of the Eighteenth Century*, 2d ed. (Williamsburg, Va., 1945), 55–56.
77. Luther P. Jackson, "Virginia Negro Soldiers and Seamen in the American Revolution," *Journal of Negro History*, XXVII (1942), 247–287, esp. 257 (I applied the ratio of slaves among 125 known black soldiers to his estimate of 500 total black military men); Quarles, *Negro in American Revolution*, chap. 5.
78. Jordan, *White over Black*, chaps. 9–11; Ira Berlin, *Slaves without Masters: The Free Negro in the Antebellum South* (New York, 1974), chaps. 1–2.

is to be styled, by way of eminence, the BLACKBIRD MARCH." Antimanumission petitioners from the southside added their voices, justifying slavery with Biblical incantations and expressing fears of pillage, rape, and rapine if more slaves were freed.[79]

This new racism was not based on the behavior of blacks and ignored the many skills of native-born slaves. The dark color of slaves proved their innate inferiority, and strict separation of the races by legal conditions and social rule seemed essential to maintain order in a good society. Black people, inferior by definition, could legitimately be made to accept the discipline and work conditions imposed by masters. The existence of slave families and communities, disciplined by white authority, seemed a small price to pay for the racial harmony and market production that the whites sought.[80]

79. Mullin, *Flight and Rebellion*, 134–135; Fredrika Teute Schmidt and Barbara Ripel Wilhelm, "Early Proslavery Petitions in Virginia," *WMQ*, 3d Ser., XXX (1973), 122–146; Jordan, *White over Black*, 308–311, 349–356, chap. 11.
80. Mullin, "Rethinking American Negro Slavery," *Louisiana Studies*, XII (1973), 410–418, comes to a similar conclusion.

Afterword
The Birth of the Old South

During the early eighteenth century, after slaves replaced servants in the Chesapeake labor force and the white population began to grow by natural increase, tidewater gentlemen and their yeoman allies constructed a stable, conservative social order, characterized by interlocking class, racial, and gender relations. The events of the Revolution and the economic and demographic disruptions that followed the war threatened to undermine these social relations, but gentleman and yeoman planters found ways to maintain racial superiority, reciprocal exchanges between gentlemen and yeomen, and patriarchal families. The creation of this slave society and its persistence despite social crises represent signal events in the birth of the old slave South of the antebellum period.

The development of slavery, especially with the growth of the native-born slave population, was the most crucial element in these social relations. Afro-American slaves produced most of the crops and performed much of the craft labor on tobacco plantations. Their labor not only freed rich gentlemen from working in the ground and added to their wealth but also permitted even small slaveholders to eliminate the field work of their wives and daughters. Slavery was so widespread that a large majority of white men were either slaveholders or might expect to own slaves sometime in their life. This spread of slavery created a common interest between gentlemen who owned many slaves and the rest of the white population and thereby consolidated the economic and political control of the gentry class.

Mid-eighteenth-century gentlemen had solidified their authority by acting as, simultaneously, taskmasters over their many slaves, patriarchal husbands of obedient wives, patrons of middling yeomen, and magistrates for the entire populace. White racism, legislative fiat, and plantation custom ensured the power of masters over their slaves; common male perceptions of female inferiority enhanced male authority in the family; and white yeomen accepted gentry rule in return for protection of their slave property and loans in times of distress. Only gentlemen commanded enough respect to deserve appointment to the bench. Acting as justices of the peace, gentlemen administered local government and decided cases civil and criminal.

Ordinary planters shared authority over slaves and women with their wealthier gentry neighbors and thereby gained a stake in the preservation of the prevailing social order. Although only a tiny number of planters became gentlemen, an ever-increasing number of men enjoyed direct authority over socially inferior white women and racially inferior slaves. Nearly all white men married. Most aspired to running a patriarchal household, and most owned enough property to take advantage of laws (such as the husband's ownership of his wife's property) that supported patriarchy. By the 1770s, more than half of tidewater's planters owned slaves, and many others inherited or bought slaves sometime in their life. Even a single adult slave added to farm income and to the comfort and status of the owner.

White women usually acquiesced in patriarchal family government because of the rights and privileges they enjoyed as planters' wives. Husbands made a home for their wives, shared familial responsibilities with them, and gave them the necessities of life. If husbands failed to keep their part of these reciprocal agreements with their wives, women complained and rebelled. Wives, moreover, reared their children, organized their own domestic activities in the household, made clothing, and formed their own social circles with women on nearby plantations. The wives of slaveholders benefited from the work of their slaves: white women did not work in the ground, and wives of large planters could direct the labor of slave women to perform much household drudgery, make clothes, and work in the garden.

In contrast, slaves could not escape from the overbearing power of their masters, who told them what to do, disciplined them for disobedience, and separated husbands from wives and children from parents at will. Nonetheless, masters often tolerated some shirking on the job and absences from the field in order to maintain a productive labor force. Moreover, they encouraged slave women to bear and rear children and permitted slaves to create their own plantation communities and kinship networks. Slaves came to expect to organize their own social life away from work and resisted attempts to disrupt their communities by running away or feigning illness.

Class, gender, and race relations in the Chesapeake, then, rested upon gentry rule, patriarchy, and racism. The Revolution, however, unleashed three crises that threatened these social relations. A new ideology attacked the basis of gentry political power by granting all white men a voice in making policy; economic and demographic decline seemed ready to change the social relations of production; and a growing class of freedmen, emancipated by their masters for ideological or economic reasons, presented slaveholders with grave problems of social control of slaves and free blacks. Planters grappled with each of these crises after the Revolution. Gentlemen permitted the yeomanry a role in policy-making in order to maintain power and used republican symbols to legitimate their continued authority. When planters in eastern Virginia abandoned tobacco production and took up herding and wheat culture, they retained their slaves and devised ways to maintain the old social relations of production. Slave masters, both large and small, fought to limit manumissions and reduce the rights of free blacks. They survived a period of rapid change and created a society even more racist, patriarchal, and gentry-dominated than that of the 1760s.

The Crisis of Legitimacy

As long as distinguished gentlemen served in local office and yeoman planters deferred to them as representatives of the hierarchical order headed by king and bishop, the gentry class maintained its prestige and power. Only when men of little stature served as magistrates at the same time that citizens rejected the primacy of gentry culture did the authority of gentlemen diminish. During the 1760s, Baptist dissenters living in piedmont Virginia, where newly wealthy men of humble origins served as justices, challenged the culture and authority of the gentry. Chesapeake gentlemen suffered more serious erosion of their authority in the 1770s and 1780s. Not only did the symbols of king and established church disintegrate, but the social stature of men serving in higher office declined, as some gentlemen turned loyalist and others served in state or federal offices. New political groups, unified by ideology, mobilized the electorate and thereby threatened to undermine the gentry's brand of personal politics and replace it with democratic anarchy. Yet the gentry class in Virginia (and parts of Maryland) weathered these political changes by welcoming yeoman participation in politics while hedging republican liberties with aristocratic forms of governmental administration.

By the end of the Revolution, popular sovereignty had replaced political hierarchy as a justification for authority, and the Episcopal church was the only remaining symbol of hierarchical government. The growth of radical, egalitarian Baptist congregations and of the Methodist splinter group, however, seemed ready to split Christians into warring factions. These sectarians found ready converts in piedmont Virginia in the early 1770s and gained adherents rapidly in every corner of piedmont and tidewater in the 1780s, increasing their members from about four thousand in 1775 to thirty-seven thousand in 1790, or about one-quarter of the families of the state.[1]

1. Number of Methodists is found in Arthur B. Moss, "Methodism in Colonial America," in Emery Stevens Bucke, ed., *The History of American Methodism*, I (New York, 1964), 131; and Richard M. Cameron, "The New Church Takes Root," *ibid.*, 288. Data on Baptists is drawn from Robert B. Semple, *A History of the Rise and Progress of the Baptists in Virginia* (Richmond, Va., 1894), 70–79; and William Taylor Thom, *The Struggle for Religious Freedom in Virginia: The Baptists*, Johns Hopkins University Studies in Historical and Political Science, 18th Ser., Nos. 10–12 (Baltimore, 1900), 40–41.

Tidewater gentlemen believed that Baptists and Methodists were dangerous sectarians who attacked the basis of society by granting spiritual equality to women and slaves, and insisted that the Episcopal establishment be retained or, at least, that religion be supported by taxes. But the Baptists and their sometime allies among Methodists, Presbyterians, and deists succeeded in a twenty-three-year campaign beginning in 1776 to sever the ties that had bound church and state before the Revolution. Not only were members of all religions granted freedom to practice their faith as they saw fit, but the assembly defeated proposals to tax the people to support their own minister and confiscated the glebes that had supported Episcopal clergy.[2]

The fight to end the religious establishment vividly illustrates the transformation of politics from the preserve of gentlemen to a popular movement, involving thousands of ordinary planters who took popular sovereignty seriously. Baptists and their supporters sent hundreds of petitions on religious matters to the assembly between the late 1770s and 1800. Twice, in 1776 and 1785, they inundated the legislature with so many petitions that they constituted a popular referendum on religious matters. Nearly a fifth of Virginia's freeholders signed petitions in both these campaigns for religious liberty.[3]

Buffeted by great pressures from their constituents, Virginia's legislators ended all state support for religion. Though they hardly could have retained the support of their evangelical neighbors if they had voted any other way, many came to favor separation of church and state because they saw the threat posed by dissenting groups recede. Although Baptists still attracted the poorest families, numerous yeomen and some wealthy planters joined their ranks during the 1780s and succeeded in civilizing the more unruly members. Gentleman legislators in piedmont, where Baptists had lived quietly since the early 1770s and had supported the Revolution, helped lead the fight against religious taxes in 1784, and they were joined by numerous tidewater colleagues in affirming religious freedom for all groups the next year.[4]

Only sustained organization, and not just occasional plebiscites on

2. This paragraph owes a good deal to Rhys Isaac, *The Transformation of Virginia, 1740–1790* (Chapel Hill, N.C., 1982), chap. 13, as does the rest of the Afterword, even though the arguments here take issue with his vision of transformation. See, as well, Thomas E. Buckley, *Church and State in Revolutionary Virginia* (Charlottesville, Va., 1977), for a detailed description of the debate over the establishment.

3. Richard R. Beeman and Rhys Isaac, "Cultural Conflict and Social Change in the Revolutionary South: Lunenburg County, Virginia," *Journal of Southern History,* XLVI (1980), 538–550; Buckley, *Church and State,* 25–26, 143–153.

4. *Ibid.*

moral issues, would support a successful democratic polity. Political parties emerged in the 1780s and 1790s in the assemblies of both Virginia and Maryland. Whereas colonial legislators had frequently voted in personal cliques, regional and ideological parties abounded after the Revolution: creditors and debtors, nationalists and localists, and Federalists and Republicans vied for support in both legislatures during the early decades of the Republic.[5]

Gentlemen either rejected organized political parties or sought to incorporate deferential political behavior into them. Until the 1830s, parties in rural areas maintained the old system of self-nomination by gentlemen and voice voting before candidates. Gentlemen, moreover, supported property requirements for suffrage in order to reduce the number of poor voters. In Virginia, respectable tenants had to wait until 1830 to gain the franchise, but an ever-growing electorate forced Maryland's assembly to extend the right to vote to all white men and to institute the secret ballot in 1802.[6]

Maryland's gentry class faced an increasingly large electorate during the early decades of the Republic. Economically and ethnically diverse groups, especially in western Maryland and Baltimore, competed for local, state, and federal office and formed effective political parties. The constitution of 1776 mandated the election of sheriffs, and citizens voted in ever greater numbers, with turnout reaching half to two-thirds by the late 1780s.[7] Although only a third of white men voted in federal elections in the 1790s, turnout increased to three-fifths in the 1803 congressional races (the first held after universal white male suffrage began), and high turnouts of two-thirds continued in years of intense political conflict, like those of

5. Jackson Turner Main, *Political Parties before the Constitution* (Chapel Hill, N.C., 1973), chaps. 8, 9; Norman K. Risjord, *Chesapeake Politics, 1781–1800* (New York, 1978); David Curtis Skaggs, "Origins of the Maryland Party System: The Constitutional Convention of 1776," *Maryland Historical Magazine*, LXXV (1980), 95–117.

6. Richard R. Beeman, *The Old Dominion and the New Nation, 1788–1801* (Lexington, Ky., 1972), 28–55, esp. 34–40; Charles S. Sydnor, *Gentlemen Freeholders: Political Practices in Washington's Virginia* (Chapel Hill, N.C., 1952), 121–124; Lucille Griffith, *The Virginia House of Burgesses, 1750–1774*, rev. ed. (University, Ala., 1970), 157–168; Chilton Williamson, *American Suffrage: From Property to Democracy, 1760–1860* (Princeton, N.J., 1960), 223–233, 138–151.

7. The relationship between diversity and homogeneity in Maryland is finely detailed in Whitman H. Ridgway, *Community Leadership in Maryland, 1790–1840: A Comparative Analysis of Power in Society* (Chapel Hill, N.C., 1979), esp. chaps. 1–4. Returns from sheriffs' elections are found in the Register of Civil Officers, 1777–1800, Maryland Hall of Records, Annapolis (MHR), which I compared with the number of adult white men in 1782, 1783, and 1790 (see Allan Kulikoff, "Tobacco and Slaves: Population, Economy, and Society in Eighteenth-Century Prince George's County, Maryland" [Ph.D. diss., Brandeis University, 1976], 428–433; and Evarts B. Greene and Virginia D. Harrington, *American Population before the Federal Census of 1790* [New York, 1932], 133–134, 154–155), to arrive at turnout figures.

1806 and 1812, when issues of war and peace dominated political discourse.[8]

Virginia's gentlemen, unlike some Maryland gentry, saw little need to mobilize the electorate. As a result, *fewer* men voted in Virginia elections between 1780 and 1830 than before the Revolution. Since Virginians overwhelmingly supported Republican candidates, only one in six white men bothered to vote in presidential elections between 1800 and 1832. Even local races, where candidates often disagreed ideologically, attracted few voters. Turnout in legislative elections in the 1780s ranged from less than a quarter to less than a third of the electorate, and party conflict between Federalists and Republicans after 1790 failed to increase voter participation. Five hotly contested congressional elections between 1803 and 1821 in the tidewater district that included the Federalist Eastern Shore and the Republican counties between the James and York rivers attracted only three-tenths of the white men on the Eastern Shore and about four-tenths of those living across the bay.[9]

Few Virginians voted during the early Republic, because gentlemen enforced property requirements for the franchise. Election judges prevented nearly all unmarried youths living at home from voting, no matter how wealthy their fathers were, and sometimes challenged poor householders, who often voted against the interests of the gentry when permitted to vote. In eight elections in Westmoreland, Buckingham, Amherst, and Greensville counties during the late 1780s and early 1790s, fewer than two householders in ten who owned no slaves voted, but four-tenths of those who held one to four slaves and half of those who possessed five or more slaves came to the polls.[10]

However well gentlemen succeeded in limiting suffrage, their continued authority rested upon maintaining their political base in their own counties. Neither eruptions of popular sentiment nor widespread voting necessarily reduced their power. Gentlemen pursued two strategies to preserve their local oligarchies: they continued to stand for office, often dominating elected positions, and they sought to retain control of the appointed judiciary. The result, according to a New England critic in 1804, was a

8. J. R. Pole, *Political Representation in England and the Origins of the American Republic* (Berkeley, Calif., 1966), 554–562.

9. Pole, *Political Representation*, 562; Norman K. Risjord, "How the 'Common Man' Voted in Jefferson's Virginia," in John B. Boles, ed., *America: The Middle Period: Essays in Honor of Bernard Mayo* (Charlottesville, Va., 1973), 41–62; Sydnor, *Gentlemen Freeholders*, 125–127; Daniel Porter Jordan, Jr., "Virginia Congressmen, 1801–1825" (Ph.D. diss., University of Virginia, 1970), 377–400.

10. Risjord, "How the 'Common Man' Voted," in Boles, ed., *America: The Middle Period*, 41–61, each county counting as one case.

society that "approaches nearer to a pure aristocracy than any other state" despite "*incantations* of *republicanism, liberty,* and *equality*" because "*public affairs* are in an absolute monopoly by the rich," who give the poor only "the liberty to quarrel about the support of a patron in an election."[11]

Although the social and economic status of legislators declined in the 1780s, after wealthy loyalists fled, the status of assemblymen and congressmen returned to its high pre-Revolutionary level by the 1790s. Maryland and Virginia legislators from older districts possessed somewhat less wealth in the mid-1780s than in the mid-1760s. Senators, in contrast, were nearly as wealthy as pre-Revolutionary councillors. Prominent men from the wealthiest families in Maryland, many intricately tied to each other by blood or marriage, served together in the state's federal ratifying convention in 1788. Wealthy men dominated Maryland's legislative offices in the 1790s and 1800s in rural, homogeneous counties such as St. Mary's and Talbot, and more than two-fifths of Virginia's assemblymen during the 1800s and 1810s belonged to the hundred most prominent families in the state.[12]

Virginia gentlemen fought to maintain the county courts as self-perpetuating oligarchies with full judicial and administrative powers, and despite conflicts with reform-minded lawyers who managed to create circuit courts with some original jurisdiction in 1788, they generally succeeded. The governor appointed justices, with the consent of the sitting bench, who insisted that other wealthy gentlemen be chosen. Justices, moreover, continued to serve for life during good behavior. When reformers urged changes in the court system at the constitutional convention of 1829–1830, conservatives beat back all challenges.[13]

Since the powers of justices were undiminished, wealthy men still sought seats on local benches after the Revolution, but the extent of their

11. William Eaton to Col. Alexander Sessions, June 24, 1804, in Louis B. Wright, ed., "William Eaton Takes a Dim View of Virginia," *William and Mary Quarterly*, 3d Ser., V (1948), 106.
12. Jackson Turner Main, *The Upper House in Revolutionary America, 1763–1788* (Madison, Wis., 1967), 101–114, 124–132, 269; and "Government by the People: The American Revolution and the Democratization of the Legislatures," *WMQ*, 3d Ser., XXIII (1966), 395–406; Jordan, "Virginia Congressmen," 345–347; Robert P. Sutton, "The Virginia Constitutional Convention of 1829–1830: A Profile Analysis of Late Jeffersonian Virginia" (Ph.D. diss., University of Virginia, 1967), 243–244; Philip A. Crowl, *Maryland during and after the Revolution: A Political and Economic Study,* Johns Hopkins University Studies in Historical and Political Science, 11th Ser., No. 1 (Baltimore, 1943), 136–141.
13. A. G. Roeber, *Faithful Magistrates and Republican Lawyers: Creators of Virginia Legal Culture, 1680–1810* (Chapel Hill, N.C., 1981), chaps. 5, 6; Albert Ogden Porter, *County Government in Virginia: A Legislative History, 1607–1904* (New York, 1947), 159–166; William Waller Hening, *The Statutes at Large: Being a Collection of All the Laws of Virginia . . . ,* 13 vols. (Richmond, Philadelphia, 1809–1823), IX, 117, XII, 730–760, XIII, 449–467; Sutton, "Virginia Constitutional Convention," 98.

dominance varied. In Albemarle County, where citizens lambasted the court for its aristocratic tendencies in the 1780s, many wealthy men sought state or federal office, and the wealth of justices declined. The average number of slaves owned by justices decreased from twenty-one in the 1770s to about fifteen in the 1810s. In Lunenburg County, where the holdings of prosperous planters grew rapidly during the second half of the eighteenth century, slaves held by county justices nearly doubled from sixteen in 1770 to thirty in 1815.[14]

Conservative Maryland gentlemen failed to maintain the integrity of the county court system, and the reduced responsibilities and prestige of justices eventually made the office seem less attractive to gentlemen. In 1794 and 1797, the Maryland assembly divided local courts into three panels: a district court which took over judicial functions, an orphans' court, and a levy court to handle administrative matters. The consequences of the breakup of the unified county court can be seen in St. Mary's County. The average slaveholding of justices there declined from thirty-one to nineteen, and acres of land owned from 1,064 to 496 between the 1790s and the 1820s.[15]

Virginia gentlemen succeeded much more fully than those in Maryland in keeping local authority in their own hands because most of Virginia's people, and a bare majority of whites, continued to live in the slave societies of tidewater and piedmont, while an ever-diminishing proportion of Marylanders lived in southern Maryland, the only part of the state unaffected by Baltimore's growth, the Philadelphia market, or antislavery sentiment. The Virginia gentry maintained their local power base by keeping a majority of the seats in the assembly and using this control to defeat attempts to reform the courts or slavery. Their ability to protect slave property gained them the support of the yeomanry, and their control of the legislature prevented reduction of their local autonomy.

The Social Crisis: Land Scarcity and the Social Relations of Production

During the pre-Revolutionary decades, at the very time when the gentry class enjoyed its greatest prestige and yeoman planters their highest profits,

14. Richard R. Beeman, *The Evolution of the Southern Backcountry: A Case Study of Lunenburg County, Virginia, 1746–1832* (Philadelphia, 1984), 231–236; Daniel B. Smith, "Changing Patterns of Local Leadership: Justices of the Peace in Albemarle County, Virginia, 1760–1820" (master's thesis, University of Virginia, 1972), 8–13, appendixes 1, 2.

15. William Kilty, *The Laws of Maryland . . .* (Annapolis, 1799), 1777, chap. 8; 1794, chap. 53; 1796, chap. 43; 1798, chaps. 34 and 91; Ridgway, *Community Leadership in Maryland*, 307–320.

a social crisis of substantial magnitude crept up on yeoman and gentleman alike. Chesapeake planters were running out of tobacco land east of the Blue Ridge Mountains. By 1800 nearly all piedmont land had been planted at least once with tobacco, and bulky tobacco hogsheads could not be profitably transported across the mountains. The old fields and upland acres many farmers had to cultivate were less fertile than bottomland, and they could not compete with planters who farmed acreage in southside Virginia. At the same time, the Revolution and Napoleonic Wars severely disrupted tobacco markets in Britain and Europe, forcing planters to shift to grain, and many of them did not return their lands to tobacco even after markets improved.[16]

Every possible solution to this relative land scarcity upset the relations between master and slave. When new frontier areas opened in the Southwest between 1790 and 1820, a quarter of a million whites migrated, taking 175,000 slaves with them and leaving the worn-out land to those who stayed. Whites who remained postponed marriage (thereby reducing the size of their families) and limited the growth of their labor force by selling excess slaves to slavetraders. Because so many people left, those who stayed could cultivate tobacco in the same ways as their fathers, but forced migration disrupted black families and made persisting slaves both fearful of being sold and less willing to be productive. When tobacco markets declined, farmers shifted from tobacco to grains. This small-scale agriculture often required planters to hire out slaves unneeded on their farms, further disrupting black life, or encouraged them to manumit some slaves and thereby anger their neighbors.[17]

Despite heavy out-migration and poor tobacco markets, planters in eastern Virginia and parts of Maryland strengthened their control over slaves during the early nineteenth century by maintaining rigid social and cultural homogeneity. They pursued three strategies to retain racial superiority. First, they discouraged northerners and immigrants from coming to the region, where they might have polluted the atmosphere with a free-labor ideology. Second, planters practiced old forms of slave management by continuing to produce tobacco, by adapting slave labor to grain farming, and by increasing slave production of cloth. And, third, they maintained discipline on their slave quarters by threatening slaves with sale and by keeping the number of disruptive free blacks low.

Since Chesapeake planters and merchants refused to invest in either rural industries or intensive family agriculture, little land and few job opportunities enticed migrants to the rural Chesapeake. In 1850 only eight of

16. See chap. 4, above, for details of these developments.
17. Migration estimates reported in chap. 2, n. 56.

every hundred free Virginians had been born outside the state, and similarly small numbers of migrants reached Maryland's Eastern Shore and Western Shore tobacco areas, but a third of the people of Baltimore and a sixth of the farm families of northern and western Maryland had been born outside the state.[18]

The white folk who stayed in the rural Chesapeake were, overwhelmingly, born in the region, and most of them were descended from a long line of slaveholding freeholders, men and women who had a great stake in the perpetuation of the slave system. They lived comfortably off the labor of their slaves, sometimes acting like benevolent lords over their people; and even if they owned no slaves, they knew that they were superior people in every way to lowly black folk. Some nonslaveholders had aspirations of owning slaves, but most householders without land and slaves left the region. Two-thirds of the landless residents of St. Mary's County emigrated during the 1790s, but only a twelfth of the men with land left the county.[19]

Slaves who lived on Chesapeake quarters continued to enjoy a full social life surrounded by kin and friends. When they wandered off the plantation to visit, they could establish thick social networks because slaves still constituted half the population. Since relatively more whites than blacks migrated between 1790 and 1810, the proportion of slaves in the population of piedmont Virginia rose from 46 to 52 percent, and half the people of tidewater remained enslaved despite the presence of some manumitted blacks.[20]

The human consequences of forced migration on slaves, however, were very great: migrants left loved ones at home, departed familiar surroundings, often changed masters, lost privileges they had enjoyed, and were forced to live among strangers when they reached their destination. Even the slaves carried to the Southwest by masters left family members behind in the Chesapeake region, because husbands, wives, and siblings often lived on different plantations. Slaves feared family separation so much that masters attempted to control their chattels' behavior with the mere threat of selling them to a slave trader.[21]

18. J.D.B. DeBow, *Statistical View of the United States . . . Being a Compendium of the Seventh Census . . .* (Washington, D.C., 1854), 116–120, 399.

19. For St. Mary's, see Bayly Ellen Marks, "Economics and Society in a Staple Plantation System: St. Mary's County, Maryland, 1790–1840" (Ph.D. diss., University of Maryland, 1979), 303–310.

20. *Ibid.*, 320, 326; Greene and Harrington, *American Population*, 131–134, 154–155; U.S., Treasury Department, *Aggregate Amount of Each Description of Persons within the United States . . . in the Year 1810* (Washington, D.C., 1811), 53–55a.

21. Allan Kulikoff, "Uprooted Peoples: Black Migrants in the Age of the American Revolution, 1790–1820," in Ira Berlin and Ronald Hoffman, eds., *Slavery and Freedom in the Age of the American Revolution* (Charlottesville, Va., 1983), 143–171.

Before the Revolution Chesapeake planters had perfected systems of slave management based on the production of tobacco for the market and the cultivation of grains and the raising of livestock for subsistence. In eastern Virginia, where grains replaced tobacco in the 1780s and 1790s, planters soon learned how to use slaves efficiently. Nearly all whites were still farmers, even as late as 1850. These men sold some slaves south but manumitted very few of them. Instead, planters hired out surplus workers to their neighbors, separating mother and children and husbands and wives in the process. As early as the mid-1780s, nine-tenths of a sample of farmers in Elizabeth City County, one of the first places to cease growing tobacco, either hired slaves from neighbors or sent their slaves to work elsewhere in the county. These slaves became extra family hands and participated in all the physical tasks of the farm, from dairying to chopping wood and from planting to harvesting grain. Poorer farmers and, especially, tenants eagerly sought to rent slaves, despite their high relative cost, because the labor of slaves increased their ability to consume. To meet this demand, large slaveholders in the county rented out much of their labor force.[22]

Planters who wished to keep all their slaves at home purchased spinning wheels, looms, and sheep, cultivated small quantities of cotton and flax, and asked their wives to direct their slave women in making cloth and clothes. As early as 1791, grain and livestock farmers in tidewater took female slaves from crop cultivation and had them "apply their hands to Manufacturing so far as to supply, not only the cloathing of the Whites, but of the Blacks also." In King William County in 1791, for instance, twenty possibly representative families made 1,907 yards of fine cloth for their own use and 1,007 yards of coarse cloth for their slaves, enough to clothe all the slaves they owned, provide underwear and shifts for white family members, and produce a small surplus of coarse cloth (perhaps 100 yards) and a large surplus of fine cloth (over 1,200 yards). All the families except one headed by a widower produced some cloth, but nearly three-quarters of the surplus of fine cloth was made on just five large plantations. These planters were married and owned, among them, thirty-seven slave women (but only thirty-one slave men).[23]

Despite the loss of population throughout the Chesapeake and the end of tobacco production in much of tidewater, planters and farmers managed to sustain their conservative social system. Families who owned no slaves left the region, and those who stayed owned or rented slaves. Rebellious

22. Sarah S. Hughes, "Slaves for Hire: The Allocation of Black Labor in Elizabeth City County, Virginia, 1782 to 1810," *WMQ*, 3d Ser., XXXV (1978), 260–286, esp. 264, 271.
23. Edward Carrington to Alexander Hamilton, Oct. 4, 1791, with enclosures, in Harold C. Syrett *et al.*, eds., *The Papers of Alexander Hamilton*, IX (New York, 1965), 275–282.

slaves could be sent south, and every slave who lived in the region knew that if the master were pushed hard enough, he would send disruptive slaves into exile. Social change in the 1780s and 1790s, in sum, was involutionary: it reinforced prevailing social ideals and strengthened prevailing social institutions.

From Slavery to Freedom

The greatest fear of whites during the 1780s and 1790s was that a class of freed blacks would grow in their midst, thereby tearing asunder the social contract between gentlemen and yeomen that protected the human property of all slaveholders in perpetuity. Maryland and Virginia legislators ignored these fears and sought to apply republican ideology to the vexing problem of slavery, and they were joined by evangelical ministers and Friends who insisted that manumission was the way of God. Enlightened men in the two assemblies quickly responded to these sentiments: Virginia's legislators freed slave men who had served in the army, and liberalized the state's laws on freeing slaves in 1782 by permitting private manumissions by both deed and will; and Maryland's assembly passed a similar act eight years later.[24]

Almost as soon as these laws passed, owners began to set their slaves free. In four towns and sixteen counties of Virginia, manumission activity surged in 1782 and 1783, diminished between 1784 and 1786, and then fluctuated around a hundred a year from 1787 to 1806, when private acts of manumission were forbidden. Families living in areas touched by evangelical religious fervor, Quaker sentiment, or declining economic fortunes freed slaves far more frequently than those in the rest of the region. Free black population increased rapidly in the towns, where slaves had already achieved some economic independence; on the Eastern Shore and in tidewater counties south of the James River, general farming areas with many Quakers; and in piedmont counties with active Quaker meetings. The large number of manumissions, combined with rapid natural increase among newly freed slaves, caused the number of free blacks living in the Chesapeake states to multiply more than six times between 1780 and 1800, when the free black population reached forty thousand.[25]

24. The best analyses of manumission, the development of a free black class, and antiemancipation thought and racism in Virginia and Maryland are found in Ira Berlin, *Slaves without Masters: The Free Negro in the Antebellum South* (New York, 1974); and especially in Peter J. Albert, "The Protean Institution: The Geography, Economy, and Ideology of Slavery in Post–Revolutionary Virginia" (Ph.D. diss., University of Maryland, 1976), a first-rate piece of scholarship.

25. Berlin, *Slaves without Masters*, 46; Albert, "Protean Institution," chap. 7.

Whites freed their slaves because the republican social contract enshrined by the Revolution encompassed both races and because the dictates of God and nature demanded manumission. Charles Copland of Richmond City, for instance, freed his slaves "from natural reason, that God created all men free; and that all Laws made to subjugate one part of the human race to the absolute dominion of another are totally repugnant to the clearest dictates of natural justice." Similarly, one manumitter in York County freed his slaves because "no Law moral or divine can or could give me a just right in the persons of My fellow creatures . . . and desirous to approbate the equitable Injunctions of our divine master Christ the Glorious Lord in doing unto others as I would be done unto."[26]

Most manumitters gave little thought to the role freed slaves would play in a slave society, perhaps assuming that they would occupy a place between slaves and the poorest whites. Few men denied the inherent inferiority of black people, and even most manumitters probably disagreed with Robert Pleasants, a Virginia Quaker who freed his many slaves and who contended that emancipated blacks should be given "suitable privileges, as an excitement to become useful Citizens." Robert Carter of Nomini Hall, a wealthy Baptist who freed hundreds of slaves in 1791, tried to put Pleasants's ideas into practice by turning his ex-slaves into a dependent peasantry. He succeeded for a few years by renting his people parcels of land and permitting them to hire blacks still held in bondage and by urging his neighbors to hire his former bondspeople.[27]

The vast majority of Virginia planters vigorously fought manumission. Fearing that a class of free blacks would destroy social order, they attacked religious leaders who preached black freedom, petitioned state legislatures to prohibit private manumissions, and railed against free blacks. Although Maryland planters failed to restrict manumissions legally, the Virginia assembly prohibited most private emancipations and required all freed slaves to leave the state in 1806. The free black community soon felt the impact of new legal restrictions in Virginia and diminished social acceptance in Maryland. Although the free black population grew rapidly between 1790 and 1810 in the Chesapeake states, few people freed their slaves, and many ex-slaves left the region for more favorable conditions in the North after 1810.[28]

As early as 1784 and 1785, when 1,224 Virginians signed antimanumission petitions, sentiments against freeing slaves appeared. These peti-

---

26. Manumission records, quoted in Albert, "Protean Institution," 272, 274.
27. *Ibid.*, chap. 5 (quote 178); Louis Morton, *Robert Carter of Nomini Hall: A Virginia Tobacco Planter of the Eighteenth Century*, 2d ed., (Williamsburg, Va., 1945), chap. 11.
28. Albert, "Protean Institution," chap. 6; DeBow, *Statistical View*, 63.

tioners shared the evangelical and republican ideals of those who freed their slaves but denied that their slave property was fully human. They had fought a war against England to protect all their property, including their slaves. "We have seald with our Blood, a Title to the full, free, and absolute Enjoyment of every species of our Property, whensoever, or howsoever legally acquired." Far from preaching the abolition of slavery, Christ permitted the system to thrive. Slavery was ordained by God who "Commanded his People, to buy of other Nations and to keep them for Slaves: And that Christ and his Apostles . . . hath not forbid it: But left that matter as they found it, giving exhortations to Masters and Servants how to conduct themselves to each other."[29]

Fear of social revolution lurked just below the surface of antimanumission sentiment. Many Virginians were too racist and fearful to permit blacks to become degraded, but free, rural peons. The petitioners of 1784 and 1785 thought that every conceivable evil would follow emancipation, from "Want, Poverty, Distress, and Ruin to the Free Citizen" and "Neglect, Famine, and Death to the helpless black Infant and superannuated Parent" to "Rapes, Murders, and Outrages" by the freed blacks. Robert Carter's neighbors shared these racist assumptions and refused to hire or rent land to his ex-slaves because "it gave considerable dissatisfaction to others, and neighbours around" and because the "People themselves . . . were quite unprepared with Team and Tools for its cultivation." When these freedmen did not find work, they sometimes lived by "the plunder of grain and of the stocks in their neighborhood" while subverting the loyalty of those still in bondage.[30]

Though Virginia courts failed to enforce the law requiring ex-slaves to leave, masters of other slaves made them feel so uncomfortable that most of them left rural areas. Between 1804/1805 and 1810, three-fifths of the free blacks of four tidewater and four piedmont counties migrated from the region. Free blacks who stayed faced a double bind. If there were few free blacks in the population, they had to associate with and marry slaves, thereby disrupting the operation of plantations and alarming masters. If the number of free blacks grew until they could form their own community, independent of the slave quarters, whites perceived them as a bad example for slaves and a potential fifth column against the slave system. Slaveholders therefore severely circumscribed the lives of free blacks: they refused to rent them land or hire them and sometimes forced them to live in white households.[31]

29. Frederika Teute Schmidt and Barbara Ripel Wilhelm, eds., "Early Proslavery Petitions in Virginia," *WMQ*, 3d Ser., XXX (1973), 133–146, quotes on 141, 144.
30. *Ibid.*, 146; Morton, *Robert Carter of Nomini Hall*, 265–267.
31. Albert, "Protean Institution," 81, 83; Michael L. Nicholls, "Passing through This Trouble-

Two societies, one free and racist and the other slave, slowly developed in Maryland and Virginia during the first half of the nineteenth century. On the Eastern Shore and in much of Maryland, slaves became free blacks and sank to the bottom of the white class structure, becoming agricultural laborers or sharecroppers. Black people who lived in Baltimore joined the urban proletariat, often performing the backbreaking tasks the growing city required. The white ruling classes in these areas, who held a diminishing stake in the slave system, kept Maryland in the Union. In contrast, southern Maryland and nearly all of tidewater and piedmont Virginia were slave societies on the eve of the Civil War, filled with men willing to give their lives to protect their peculiar institution, their way of life, and the social relations of production devised by their great-great-great-grandfathers.

---

some World: Free Blacks in the Early Southside," *Virginia Magazine of History and Biography*, XCII (1984), 50–70, esp. 63–69.

Index